Have Not Been The Same

Have Not Been The Same

The CanRock Renaissance 1985-95

MICHAEL BARCLAY • IAN A.D. JACK • JASON SCHNEIDER

NATIONAL LIBRARY OF CANADA CATALOGUING IN PUBLICATION DATA

Barclay, Michael, 1971
Have not been the same: the CanRock renaissance, 1985–1995

ISBN 1-55022-475-1

1. Rock Music — Canada — 1981–1990 — History and criticism. 2. Rock music —
Canada — 1991–2000 — History and criticism. I. Jack, Ian Andrew Dylan, 1973–
II. Schneider, Jason, 1971–   III. Title.

ML3534.B368 2001   781.66´0971   C2001-900812-0

Edited by Jennifer Hale and Michael Holmes
Cover and text design by Guylaine Régimbald–SOLO DESIGN
Cover and author photos by Catherine Stockhausen, www.pogofoto.com
Back cover photos clockwise from top, by: Richard Beland, David Blais,
Chris Black, Chris Black
Layout by Mary Bowness

Printed by Transcontinental

Distributed in Canada by
General Distribution Services,
325 Humber College Blvd.,
Toronto, ON M9W 7C3

Published by ECW PRESS
2120 Queen Street East, Suite 200
Toronto, ON M4E 1E2
ecwpress.com

This book is set in Utopia and Schmutz Corroded

PRINTED AND BOUND IN CANADA

The publication of *Have Not Been The Same* has been generously
supported by the Canada Council, the Ontario Arts Council and the
Government of Canada through the Book Publishing Industry
Development Program. **Canadä**

Copyright page continued on page 759

Disclaimer

When we first started this project, an older music writer told us, "It sounds interesting, but are you sure you can fill a whole book? Maybe you want to widen your scope a bit." Of course, our problem was never a lack of material, but deciding what and who to leave out. Every person who reads this book is bound to ask, "Yeah, but what about . . .?"

There may very well be a valid case made for the numerous artists we've omitted or merely skimmed over. But we weren't writing an encyclopedia, we were writing a story. Admittedly, some of the people you won't be reading about here are missing because they didn't move us the way our subjects did. Maybe they didn't win our entirely subjective battle of cool (a battle that the three of us waged amongst ourselves, as well). Maybe they got pinched for space. Most likely, they probably didn't fit into the thematic constructs of each chapter and would have distracted from the narrative on the whole. Some of those missing in action are discussed in the discographies. Some are just missing.

You'll also notice that most of the people interviewed are artists. There is a whole other book to be written about the Canadian music industry itself, and because this is the first book about this time that we're aware of, we felt it was important to let the artists speak first.

Our intention is not to make some flag-waving, faux-nationalist claim about the superiority of Canadian music. This book is meant to celebrate what happened here and to argue that it's as valid as any other nation's music — music that may have spawned dozens of books which focus on this time period. Great art accidentally produced here is just as important as great art accidentally produced by some schlep in a cultural behemoth like the U.S., the U.K., or even a small, insular community like Iceland or New Zealand. The first wave of CanRock (Young, Mitchell, The Band, Cohen,

The Guess Who, etc.) has been well documented, while the great changes wrought by the Renaissance are already in danger of being forgotten or taken for granted.

This book is dedicated to all the musicians, fans, technicians, engineers, promoters, clubs, journalists, indie labels, campus radio geeks and industry weasels who set these events in motion, put their lives and careers on the line, and gave this book a reason to be. It is also for the next generations.

Missing.
(Photo by David Leyes)

Thank Yous

Collective:

Jennifer Hale, Michael Holmes and ECW for believing in the magnitude of the project; Michael McLarnon and the staff of *Id* magazine for letting us hone our craft; the insane and devout fans who post old articles devoted to great Canadian musicians on the World Wide Web; all the photographers who helped this project leap off the page; Gord Downie; Judy & Walter Barclay for the retreats; everyone who took the time to speak with us; all the publicists, managers and artists who made our research easier, including John Borra, Angie Fenwick, Jake Gold, Don Kerr, Colin MacKenzie, Waye Mason, Patti Schmidt, Shelley Stertz, Chip Sutherland, Barry Walsh, and Woody Whalen. For allowing their personal archives, lyrics and/or photos to be ransacked and/or exploited: Chuck Angus, Tom Anselmi, Eric Baumgartner, Dan Bejar, Moe Berg, Chris Brown, Dave Clark, Judith Coombe, Jim Cuddy, Marc Demouy, Stefan Doroschuk, Bernie Finkelstein, Richard Flohil, Ben Gunning, Cathy Hendrix & Ron Sexsmith, Chris Hooper, Tracy Howe, Kevin Kane, Bob Lanois, James MacLean, Mike McDonald, Jeff Maize, William New, James Rocchi, John K. Samson, Skinny Puppy & Michael D. Ryan, Sloan, Alastair Sutherland, William Tenn, Ross Taylor, Tom Tremuth, Tim Vesely, Jonathan Wenk, Bob Wiseman, and Michael Phillip Wojewoda. A big collective thanks to those who went above and beyond the call of duty, and without whom this project would not have been possible: Mary Dickie, Howard Druckman, Jay Ferguson, Kevin Komoda, Chris Murphy, Don Rooke, Catherine Stockhausen.

Michael Barclay thanks:

The members of Black Cabbage: Nick Craine, Sheila Gruner, Michael O'Connell, Tristan O'Malley, Dave Withers, Kate Richmond, Mark Agnew and Sam Cino for teaching me invaluable lessons about creating Canadian music. Also, for pivotal and personal musical inspiration: Lewis Melville, Jeff Bird, Aaron Riches, Dave Clark, Chris Brown, Paul Mora, John Anderson, George Brasovan, and the Neutron Stars. Judy & Walter & Patrick Barclay; Lisa Moran; Victor Wolters & Jon Halliwell; Anicka Quin; CFRU-FM 93.3 at the University of Guelph; Ian Danzig, James Keast, Atsuko Kobasigawa, Chris Gramlich and the staff of *Exclaim!*; Mary Dickie, Stuart Berman and *eye* Weekly; Grant Lawrence and *Radio Escapade*; JPII 1985–1990 in Scarborough and UoG 1990–1993; The Ontarion; Dave Bidini for telling me this wasn't nuts; Three Gut Records for keeping my faith; the staff of *Brave New Waves* and *Night Lines* for saving my life.

Ian Andrew Dylan Jack thanks:

Cara for supporting the marathon and keeping my heart beating; The Kawartha Pine Ridge Board of Education for granting me a leave of absence; Andrew Peters, William Wallace, Scott McKeown, and James Cottrell (and their respective partners: Dina, Priya, Cathy and Lisa) for surrogate family, and going beyond the call of duty reading, editing, and keeping me from drowning; Shirley & Earl Mitchell for love and support; Rachel & Geoff for sibling ways; Doreen Lemmon and the late Malcolm Lemmon; Candace Minifie & Nathan Smith for friendship and Rock Hotel, Toronto; Kevin Komoda, a true kindred spirit, historical guide and for the Rock Hotel, Montreal; Aaron & Claire Ferguson; Dr. Bob Henderson for keeping me on this project; Mentors: D.G. Young, Kathryn Hayward (*The Silhouette*), Wendy Swain & Family, Wayne McCurdy & Family, Joan Arnott and Gus Mihailovich & Family; Musical Families: Bipolar and Headpets; Barbara McDonald @ McMaster University for reference checks; Michelle Mansey (Rock Hotel, Vancouver); Robert Driscoll (Rock Hotel, Toronto); The Newcastle Public School staff and community; Paula Witty; Beth and Marc Beranger; Don Smith; John & Erin Goheen; Carol Little & Family; Debbie & Susan; Dark Hall; Dawn Johnson for keeping my head in check; CDCI East '89 –'92; McMaster University *Silhouette* '93–'96; Queens '98; My extended family: The Downeys, The Nicholas & Oliver Clans; All other friends and family: past/present/future; Chris Murphy and Jay Ferguson for giving me stamina; The artists who inspired me to spend five years of my life writing about them; My co-authors for sharing this odyssey with me; In loving memory of Janice Anita Oliver.

Jason Schneider thanks:

All those across Canada who graciously shared their stories and answered my nagging questions; my family for allowing me to fulfill this dream; Shannon Lyon & Jeff Cowell for their boundless friendship and musical brilliance; Philip Bast & Lynn Haddrall at the *Kitchener-Waterloo Record*; James Keast and the staff of *Exclaim!*; all my friends in the Tri-City music scene (I cannot possibly list you all!); Kenton Augerman, Jen Brown, Terry Walters & Eva Rucki at CKMS, 100.3 University of Waterloo; Mark Logan & Kristine Wendell at Encore, the best record store in the world; the Hamilton bunch, especially Fran Porter for your unquestioning enthusiasm; Geoff Hill for the inspiration when it was sorely needed; the Fat Cats family; Marshall & Sylvia Ward, Scott & Christine Gillies, Greg & Christine Hutchings, Geoff Stubgen, Dylan Roberts, Mike Arnott, Kim Robinson, Leanne Shantz, Simone Wilson, Jeff Whittle, Bic Calavong, Keith Kowalski, Stephen Maltais, and everyone else who shared experiences that are behind my writing in this book; John Wright, Eric McCormack and Stan Fogel for giving me courage to write; Leah Bertrand for always believing; and Greil Marcus for the stamp of approval.

Foreword

It's officially unfair. The road.
It's the badly lit dream
where inanimate objects go to be lost . . . and found.
where cigarettes take up all your time
where "you mustn't escape and you mustn't get caught"*
where . . . obsessed with fresh . . . with relevant,
things can get all in a blur in a hurry
and a personal conviction fierce been in the family for years
is whittled to the music until
sitting amid Everything sugar
friends can become companions acquaintances strangers
until you're as lonely as a buoy,
discipline coming in waves and
all you wanna do is sleep

Sensitivity happens anyway
at the gig
on the marquee
where what's written's what's inside.
Tonight Only!
Everyone's Way More Interesting On Stage!!
The Guilty . . . the Released . . . Everyone!
Sensitivity happens
and the idea is
the more it happens the more it happens more.
Inside under the silent arch
lost in the innocence of our showmanship
in the dancing and footfall of our happiness
describing diminishing and re-describing itself
we get to be
contrary to popular belief
not as high as giants
but the size of a pellet
small
imperceptively
barely
rocking
in place
yeah.

(*Truffault's *The 400 Blows*)

— Gordon Downie, July 2001

Have Not Been The Same

"If I could describe 'cool' to you, it wouldn't be cool. So you'll have to take my word for it — these are cool bands. They're not all famous, they don't all play the same style of music. Some of them probably don't even like each other. What these bands all have in common is the ability to take a style of music, whether it's punk, country, blues, western, psychedelia, garage-rock, whatever, and warp that style until it becomes their own. Sounds cool to me."
— Del Picasso (aka Deja Voodoo's Gerard Van Herk), from the liner notes to Og Records'
It Came From Canada Vol. 1, 1985

"At some point during the decisive decade 1985–1995, the country and its people changed. If the Renaissance was the green conclusion to civilization's hardest winter, the Revolution that rocked Canada was the greening of our discontent. There occurred a sudden bursting, like buds in the springtime, of those barriers between thought and feeling that had kept Canadians from asserting their individual sovereignties and had left them indentured to authority far beyond its worth."
— Peter C. Newman, *The Canadian Revolution 1985–1995: From Deference to Defiance,* 1995

"Bring on the brand new renaissance, because I think I'm ready. I've been shaking all night long, but my hands are steady."
— Gord Downie, "Three Pistols," 1991

Overture:
Everybody Knows
This Is Nowhere

"All my cousins live here fat off the land. I hear them lowing but I can't understand. And in the line-up where their souls can be sold, they've never heard of this Canadian band. But the dinosaurs are dying each day. They're going to wish I never got up to play."
— Rheostatics, "Rock Death America," 1992

"If you read only the work of dead foreigners you will certainly reinforce the notion that literature can be written only by dead foreigners. . . . If, as has long been the case in this country, the viewer is given a mirror that reflects not him but someone else, and told at the same time that the reflection he sees is himself, he will get a very distorted idea of what he is really like."
— Margaret Atwood, *Survival*, 1972

In 1985, the landscape of Canadian music was changing. The promise made by maple music from the late '60s and early '70s had degenerated into a messy morass of imitative and embarrassing cultural icons, either espousing "hoser rock" or trying to be something they weren't. In 1985, a newer generation looked inside their own country and started to create art for themselves, for the right reasons. They opened a 10-year window in which a new canon of CanRock was created, a new legacy for future generations to expand upon and derive inspiration from. In 1985, audiences began to embrace this movement and decided that as a musical nation, we were no longer going to be the same.

Between 1995 and 2000, it became obvious that the golden era was over. Audiences were declining, indie labels were folding and major labels were dropping quality acts and signing derivative ones sure to make a quick buck. Although there was no shortage of great music, it became harder to hear, and the polarized mainstream musical climate began to look a lot like 1985. So many things had regressed that we could only look back at the 10 years between '85–'95 as a golden age, a defining moment, and indeed, since then, we have not been the same.

This book is not about the Juno Awards. This book is not about record sales. It's not about major labels. Or rock radio. Those elements might come into play, but first and foremost this is a book about music and the glorious, intelligent, beautiful, ridiculous, talented and fucked-up people who make it. This book is about a time and a place that deserves to be celebrated, even more so because the music in question was created in a climate of cultural bulimia, in a country with a nasty habit of eating its young and its old and leaving them for dead, where the people believe nothing of any great historical importance ever happens here.

There once was a great book written about the American underground in the '80s, which the post-babyboom author began by stating, "I grew up thinking everything had already happened." If the author had been raised in Canada, surely she would have added, "I grew up thinking everything had already happened . . . *somewhere else.*" After the people in this book hit the road and started to unleash now-classic albums, future generations wouldn't have to ponder such issues.

I Wanna Go to New York City

The year is 1985. Canadian music is right up there with Canadian television and Canadian film: the term "Canadian" is used as a derogative, or as a patronizing, medicinal adjective. Admitting you like Canadian music as an umbrella genre is like revealing an affinity for turnips. Some would argue that the youth of the early '80s had no opinion of their country's culture, but they most certainly did. They thought it sucked.

Impressions outside Canadian borders were no better, and as a result any interesting music that did come out of Canada tended to be dismissed as guilty by association. Peter Rowan, an east coast manager who helped launch the careers of Sloan and Eric's Trip, says, "Really, most music that comes out has been embarrassing Canadian music lovers for years and years, and has done nothing but have an ill effect on us trying to sell outside of Canada."

There's little question that the late '60s produced a series of artists who laid the template for CanRock as we know it today, although practically all of them had to find recognition in the U.S. first: Neil Young, Joni Mitchell, Leonard Cohen, The Band, Gordon Lightfoot, Steppenwolf and others. But for a new generation of Canadian artists beginning to forge their own sounds and identities, Canada was perhaps the last place they would look to for inspiration. Discussing his band's formative influences, Gord Downie of The Tragically Hip recalls, "There were certain Canadian groups that you sort of had to relegate to a different file; it was never considered on the same level as the other stuff you listened to, somehow not as exotic. Not as — or more — ambitious, hence making it less exotic." Speaking for himself, he continues, "There was a wish that [Canadian music] could be the same, that there would be no differentiation."

In 1985, the few heroes of Canadian rock were either extinct (The Band), in stages of irrelevance (Neil Young), in cultural exile (Stompin' Tom) or rather embarrassing in the first place (Loverboy). There were few people in the younger generation creating exciting new music that didn't sound like it came from somewhere else. Even the Canadian punk pioneers were more or less aping records made in New York City, Los Angeles or London, England.

In London, Ontario, The Demics recorded a single called "(I Wanna Go To) New York City," which in 1979 summed up the aspirations of most Canadian musicians prior to 1985. "I'm getting pretty tired / and I want to get out / I'm getting pretty angry, man / and it's no good to shout." Shouting was about all you could do to retain your sanity above the din of "Snowbird" and "Sometimes When We Touch," both considered proud touchstones of our national culture at the time.

Former *Maclean's* editor Peter C. Newman reflected in 1995, "Back in 1985, Canadians seemed so diffident about themselves that they behaved like strangers in their own land, while not feeling at home anywhere else. They neither proclaimed themselves nor the potential of their country and were happy in their ignorance. They had long before given up asserting their identities or challenging the righteous claw of authority. They remained deferential and blindly obedient to the powers-that-be. They fantasized about being Clark Kent instead of Superman. Treading water became a national sport."

"What's Going On Around Here?" the Rheostatics would ask years later, and before 1985 the answer was negligible. New York City was the place to be, and as the Max Webster song goes, "You can only drive down Main Street so many times."

Michael Timmins and Alan Anton knew this to be true. Their art-rock band, Hunger Project, played around Toronto in 1979 until they realized that nothing was happening. The adventurous and seminal Toronto club The Edge had closed down, and the Horseshoe Tavern had reverted to being an old-time country bar after a two-year flirtation with punk and new wave. "The scene here had dried up for a bit," says Timmins, "and we felt the lure of getting out of the city. We'd always take road trips down to New York to see a band or something, and it was just *the place*, like The Demics' song. We were 19, and thought, 'let's just go.' We rented a place in the East Village at Avenue B and 12th, and all four of us lived there. We hung out, got illegal immigrant jobs to support ourselves. It was fun, an exciting time being in New York and playing in a band. We'd do a monthly gig at CBGB's on a Wednesday night."

"Playing CBGB's seemed like the thing to do," says Greg Keelor, who moved down there around the same time with his musical partner Jim Cuddy. "It seemed pretty evident that Toronto was going down. We had gone down on one road trip just to hang out in New York, and it was pretty exciting in the late '70s. It was lawless and scary. Plus a lot of our heroes — everybody from Holden Caulfield to Dylan Thomas — walked those streets. It was very romantic and poetic, like all those Leonard Cohen songs."

Joe "Shithead" Keithley lived in Vancouver and moved to Toronto with his band The Skulls, thinking he was moving to the big time. He soon realized that Toronto wasn't big enough, and moved the band to London, England. Within a year he returned to Vancouver to start DOA, which quickly became renowned as one of the premier punk bands in North America. They had gained recognition by making connections along the west coast down to the

L.A. and San Francisco scenes, not by kowtowing to the Toronto industry.

John Borra, who played with many '80s Toronto bands who didn't get much farther than the Ontario border, says, "It is quite a phenomenon touring Canada in the sense that you drive so far for so little. You drive two days to get to Thunder Bay [from Toronto]. You can almost get to New Orleans in two days. You can go to New York City and back *twice* in the amount of time it takes to get to Thunder Bay. What's better for your career, getting to Thunder Bay or getting to New York City?"

(Photo by Chris Black)

Kurt Swinghammer, an artist and musician who started his career in the Niagara region of Ontario, recalls, "We would play basement parties, because there was nowhere else to play. I played once in a club that would book Max Webster or whatever, and the owner of the club actually punched me after the set! He couldn't deal with anything that wasn't rock."

Basement or rec-room shows were a natural extension of punk's DIY aesthetic, itself part of a continuum descending from '60s garage rock and homespun folk and country music. This music was being performed — quite literally — underground. Producer Michael Phillip Wojewoda has fond memories of concerts held in suburban rec rooms. "It would be all word of mouth and set up in someone's basement, and there would be 35 to 40 people, sitting cross-legged, up the sides of the wall and around the perimeter of the room. At that time it was all ska and mod."

During the '70s, the era of the term "blockbuster," the music industry became obsessed with large-scale profits. This attitude marginalized original or progressive music to the point where an artist like Elvis Costello was considered fringe and dangerous, although he did have a major label contract. For most bands in 1985, the major label system was the only form of validation available. The live scene was devoted to cover bands.

Kevin Kane of The Grapes of Wrath says, "I remember the whole naïveté of everything back then, when we were doing our early tours. Half our shows were in peeler bars, because they're the only ones that would let a band who dared play original songs get up on stage. Back then it was all cover bands, which now seems like a ridiculous concept to everybody. At the time [powerful west coast booking agency] Feldman's only had three original acts: Images in Vogue, 54·40 and The Grapes of Wrath. Everything else was Top 40 cover bands. Canadian bands were seen as being watered down versions of what was happening in England and the U.S."

Gord Sinclair of The Tragically Hip recalls, "When we first started, there was no one playing original music in the clubs. It was totally frowned upon. There was this one club we used to play in Sarnia where the guy made you write out your set list and the original artists who had done the songs, just to prevent people from playing original tunes. Original music was Trooper and Prism — those were the groups that would come to town. That was your perspective on what it was to be an original recording act, and the gap between what they were and what you were was so huge. You never thought you'd be a legitimate recording artist until you got the mega-light show and the tight pants and stuff like that. You never thought you'd get a kick at the can wearing work boots and blue jeans on stage."

John Critchley, whose band 13 Engines first toured the country in 1987, says, "It was a time before the music industry paid attention to things like how many people showed up. It wasn't about the numbers and how much did we make; it was all irrelevant because no booking agency in Canada would have touched us. The Agency was booking big-hair metal bands in northern Ontario bars for a week. That was how they were making their money, and Honeymoon Suite ruled the airwaves, so this was completely below the radar of that industry. We just had a lot of fun."

Bands touring the country for the first time were discovering all its complexities. John Mann of Vancouver's Spirit of the West says, "I really feel now that there's so many distinct societies in Canada and any of them can exist separately. Like the first time we played Newfoundland, we were introduced as, 'Ladies and gentlemen, please welcome *all the way from Canada*, Spirit of the West!' — and it felt like it. It's that different."

Maybe It's Just Not Good Enough to Go On Like Nothing's Changed

Michael Timmins eventually returned to Toronto after forays in NYC and London, and formed the Cowboy Junkies in 1985. Although his band would go on to sell millions of records worldwide on major labels, in the beginning they had no illusions of success. "In the mid to late '80s there was a lot of interesting music coming out of Canada, and there was no real industry here; it was very hard to make a living playing music," says Timmins. "People did it because they *had* to do it; it was a real labour of love. To think that anyone was going to be signed to a major label was just insane back then. It just didn't happen, outside of Loverboy world. It had been five to eight years since the punk explosion, which brought a lot of people into the music scene at a very young age. A lot of those people had matured, gained more musicianship and absorbed a lot more influences, and the music from those players was beginning to blossom."

The Cowboy Junkies recorded their first album in their garage, put it out and distributed it themselves and hit the road all across North America. They gained one fan at a time, often sleeping on that fan's floor after the gig. It was an attitude culled from years of working in a DIY scene where people were beginning to benefit from each other's accumulated wisdom. People in the underground scene "had been doing it by themselves for years, and they didn't need a major label or anyone else," says Timmins. "They knew how to run a studio, how to tour and how to promote their own records. There were enough independent distributors around, and enough independent record stores, that you could make your way across Canada by contacting enough of those people. Even campus radio, although it wasn't very powerful, was more cohesive than it is now. There was a weird patchwork of independent scenes going on across the country. There was never even a thought of trying to find someone else to help you beyond those in the community."

John Borra recalls, "It wasn't just about music: you got into underground books, underground movies and art. It wasn't just an underground music scene, but a general counter-culture scene. It was truly alternative. It wasn't mainstream. Everything on the radio was Honeymoon Suite and Glass Tiger and that sort of stuff, so there were very few bands around actually getting played on the radio. Therefore, it wasn't just all these [generic] alternative bands. They were all alternative in their own way and the one thing they shared in common was that they didn't sound like Glass Tiger, which left it open; it didn't define it as one type of sound."

In Vancouver, there was a very distinct division in the industry between corporate rock and the underground. Powerful Vancouver manager Bruce Allen and his business manager, booking agent Sam Feldman, brought BTO, Trooper and Bryan Adams to stardom. As a result, the Vancouver punk scene created its own set of rules. "They found their own gigs, and they rented halls," says Vancouver journalist Tom Harrison. "It gave [Vancouver punk] a real sense of purpose and direction. The politics were two-pronged. One is the general 'society is fucked,' and the other is 'we've got to show the Bruce Allens and Sam Feldmans that we mean business.' Everyone was helping each other because they were all in the same boat."

Vancouver also had an 'us vs. them' attitude with Toronto. So did most of the country, but Vancouver had enough talented bands to maintain a bit of snobbery about it, as well as access to a different market by travelling down to L.A. instead of trekking across the Prairies. Tom Harrison says, "In a typical B.C. way, a lot of the bands went down the coast rather than go east. They strengthened their ties with the L.A. and the San Francisco punk scenes. There was this antipathy toward Toronto, because it was the centre of the Canadian music industry. The universal feeling among the punk and new wave bands was that the Toronto industry was lame. They didn't like the Toronto bands by and large, and didn't trust or have any respect for the industry there. As far as they could tell there was no way that anyone would sign a Vancouver punk or new wave band. For them there was nothing to be gained by going to Toronto — that came later. So it made more sense to go down the coast."

Bill Baker of Vancouver's Mint Records says, "I found the Toronto music scene to be very industry-driven. The punk bands there all had this thing like, 'Hey, do you know who was at our show?' In Vancouver, I remember going to gigs where you wouldn't even see an *adult* at the show, let alone someone saying, 'Hey, is that the guy from BMG?' It just didn't happen."

Tom Harrison continues, "The difference between a lot of the Toronto bands and the Vancouver bands was that the Toronto bands had clubs to play and they could tour. They also had independent and major labels in their own backyard. There were people there to manage them. Because of that they didn't have the strength of who they were. A lot of it sounded derivative: 'If we sound like this, we can get deals.' The West Coast bands tended to be more original and self-contained. If you're doing everything yourself, who are you going to sell out to?"

Vancouver also had distinctive bands that had an influence beyond Canadian borders. DOA are credited with establishing the term "hardcore" as it applies to punk, and their sound can be heard in several generations of California punk. NoMeansNo were, and are, a very distinctive band. In some cases, both in Vancouver and beyond, artists were pioneering sounds that would later become commercially lucrative for everyone but themselves. In the mid-'80s, Toronto's Fifth Column was an all-female, political punk band, something unheard of until the riot grrrl movement in Olympia, Washington, five years later — a movement that would also acknowledge Jean Smith of Vancouver's Mecca Normal as a godmother. Fifth Column's friends in Shadowy Men On A Shadowy Planet were playing surf-influenced twangy rock-'n'-roll a decade before it was revitalized on the *Pulp Fiction* soundtrack and through numerous new underground American bands. Edmonton's Jr. Gone Wild were combining hardcore country, punk rock and '60s paisley pop five years before Uncle Tupelo would be hailed in America as pioneers of the "alt-country" movement.

In 1985, Vancouver's Slow — the band whose signature song provides this book's title — epitomized many of the elements that would comprise the "grunge" movement of the early '90s. Neil Osborne of 54·40 recalls, "I saw Jane's Addiction after Warner signed them [in 1987], and [a Warner rep] came up to me and said, 'What do you think?' I said, 'These guys aren't the real thing. There's a band in Vancouver called Slow: they're the real thing. This is just an act.' I actually became a really big fan of Jane's Addiction. But after seeing Slow, you couldn't convince me that Jane's Addiction was the real thing."

In 1980, Peter Rowan moved from Fredericton, New Brunswick, to Alberta, where he was amazed at the quality of the local bands, particularly Edmonton's Modern Minds, an early project of The Pursuit of Happiness's Moe Berg. "There was a great music scene out there," says Rowan. "I remember seeing the Modern Minds and realizing that there was awesome Canadian punk rock happening, and thinking that these guys are just as good as The Damned or whatever the flavour was at the time. It made me realize that the music that was happening here independently was on a level with anywhere in the world."

However, because these bands were largely unknown outside their regional scenes, the impression that most Canadian bands were merely mimics still prevailed. Martin Tielli of the Rheostatics suggests that part of the problem is the perception that Canadian bands should be beating the Americans at their own game, instead of being equally as good with a different aesthetic. "People are looking in the wrong place," muses Tielli. "They're looking for something that they don't realize already exists here. There's something that's equally as intense as the Velvet Underground, except it's not going to be that same thing. It's going to have a completely different face and a completely different expression in almost every way. It's not going to have the same kind of coolness as it would being from [the U.S.], so don't look for that.

"I was always looking for music that was trying different things," Tielli continues. "Like Jane Siberry. She's a folk singer who utilized technology, laboured over those songs on those second two records, and took conceptual things that Laurie Anderson did and made them more palpable to my ears. She put it into a song that you could sing and remember. Laurie Anderson doesn't particularly do songs. Siberry took all the great ideas from that stuff and put it in a different package."

I Can't Stop Writing Punk Rock coz I'm Stuck in a Ghetto of Folkies

Following the folk-rock explosion of the '60s — which included pop crossovers like Bruce Cockburn, Ian & Sylvia and Gordon Lightfoot — Canada's folk tradition retreated into its own insular world, interacting very little with the development of CanRock. Likewise, having an acoustic guitar on stage at a rock club would have you pegged as a hokey folkie. Kurt Swinghammer recalls playing Toronto gigs in the mid-'80s with an acoustic guitar. "People would say, 'Oh, he's a folk artist,' even if I had it running though my Big Muff [distortion pedal]. There was such a stigma about folk music at that time, it was so unfashionable. In Toronto, the perception was that you were doing music that was not relevant. It was short-sighted and frustrating."

By the mid-'80s, maturing punks began to realize the similarities between the folk community and the idealistic side of punk, starting with the DIY and anti-elitist aesthetics inherent in both. Some, like DOA's Joe "Shithead" Keithley, would suggest a direct lineage between his own bluntly political songwriting and that of folk icons such as Woody Guthrie. "I became aware of Woody Guthrie when I was about 18," says Keithley, "and I was a Bob Dylan fan in high school. One year Gary Cristal, who used to run the Vancouver Folk Festival, gave me a tape of some songs and said, 'These songs would really suit you DOA guys.' This was around 1988, when we were doing an acoustic act called Drunks On Acoustic — ridiculous songs like 'I've Been Working On The Railroad'; just the worst tripe that we could torture people with. Gary said, why not do something serious? He gave me a tape with Wobbly [International Workers of the World] songs and Utah Phillips." DOA played punk rock at the Vancouver Folk Festival, and Keithley would later develop his acoustic tendencies in his solo career.

Folk music's lack of pretension was refreshing after years of the belief that only abrasion could effectively subvert the glossy, bombastic mainstream music scene. It also lent a sense of history and context to the music, as opposed to the flash-in-the-pan pop that dominated the '80s. And though rootsier sounds initially seemed out of vogue, some of those bands have lasted the longest. Jim Cuddy, whose band Blue Rodeo played its first gig in February 1985, muses, "I think we were smart when we started, in choosing a form of music that wasn't youth-oriented or specific. It wasn't about radio trends or subject matter; it was not about the thoughts and feelings of a young person. I don't feel alien from the kind of music I'm doing now, and I'm very different than I was when we started."

Divisions between the folk and rock worlds started collapsing on the folk festival scene, which opened up to different styles during the '80s. Neo-traditionalists like Spirit of the West and Andrew Cash were demonstrating that acoustic music was no longer singularly dismissed by rock audiences. Folk festivals in Winnipeg, Edmonton, Calgary and Vancouver began establishing themselves as the pre-eminent festivals in North America, known for juggling musical genres and attracting large audiences of all ages. "There are lots of festivals in the States," says veteran folk promoter Richard Flohil, "but the kind of festivals you have here cross genres happily, and they know that the audience is not that old folkie stereotype. It's not a baby boomer, yuppie thing. There are tons of kids and teenagers, and they go because it's an event. They don't go because Elvis Costello or Joni Mitchell is playing. They just go."

At a folk festival workshop in 1985 you were most likely to find Willie P. Bennett jamming with other harmonica players. By 1995, you would be just as likely to find Bennett performing after a ska-punk band, or rock band Change of Heart in an ambient dub workshop, or Bob Snider crowd-surfing. At the 25th anniversary of Toronto's Mariposa Folk Festival in 1988, the backstage area was abuzz with the after-hours jam session with Stompin' Tom Connors, the Violent Femmes and the Hard Rock Miners.

Folk's egalitarian nature was another factor that aligned it with punk idealism, setting both camps apart from the competitive spirit of commer-

Don Kerr
(Photo by Graham Kennedy)

cial music. Don Kerr, a Toronto drummer and recording engineer who was ubiquitous on local recordings in the late '80s and early '90s, recalls, "With the songwriters on the scene in Toronto — whether it was Dinner is Ruined or Ron Sexsmith or Kyp Harness — there was never anybody causing any shit. There were no dictators. There was never any kind of fighting between bands or even within bands. It was the best thing about it: people being musical. Most of the songwriters are the least talented [band member] technically, but they end up setting the pace. I got a lot of gigs not because I was some kind of hotshot, but because I play along with whatever the songwriter is doing. And a lot of bass players in that scene were not great technically, not overly melodic or innovative, but their energy was there. That's what you want: someone who's really happy to be on stage and is giving each song their best. That's way better than some cat who thinks he's hot shit. There were none of those guys around."

You *Can* Come from Here

One of the most revolutionary changes wrought by the CanRock Renaissance also stems from folk — something so obvious that it seems incredible that it should even be an issue. But before 1985, Canadian rock acts rarely ever sang specifically about their own country, avoiding place names or other signifiers like the plague.

There are plenty of theories as to why this was. Perhaps bands didn't want to appear "far too Canadian," to borrow a phrase from Spirit of the West, because Canadianisms were the epitome of uncool in a scene that still pined to be anywhere else but here. For more commercially minded bands, perhaps they made a decision, conscious or not, to make their songs more "universal" and not limit them to Canada. When The Tragically Hip became superstars in Canada and nowhere else, some crippling culture commentators on both sides of the border suggested that the band's fate was doomed to their own country because of Gord Downie's choice of subject matter. "When American fans started coming to our shows," says Downie, "only at that time did it become an issue: 'When you sing about Canada, does that help or does that hurt? You're big in Canada but you're small down here, does that help or does that hurt?' After a while it's like the advice I used to give bands opening for us [in front of often hostile audiences]: 'It's got nothing to do with you and nothing to do with me.'"

Of all the prominent rock Canadian musicians to come of age in the '60s — if you relegate Gordon Lightfoot, Ian & Sylvia and Leonard Cohen to the folk world — only The Guess Who made a point of "Runnin' Back To Saskatoon," although their biggest hit, "American Woman," was Canadian only as reflected through a negative, by defining Americans as an "other." Otherwise, Joni Mitchell ("River") and Neil Young ("Helpless") only slipped into Canadian specifics when they were homesick; Robbie Robertson was too wrapped up in American mythology to bother with his native land. British writer Barney Hoskyns notes that the first lyrical manifestation of Robertson's roots was "Acadian Driftwood," written at The Band's twilight. "It took Robbie Robertson almost a decade of living in America to write a song about Canada," Hoskyns writes in *Across the Great Divide*. "Sitting in his Malibu beach house in the summer of 1975, he was writing about his homeland with the same empathy and compassion that had infused 'The Night They Drove Old Dixie Down.' Canada had finally become as distant and romantic to Robertson as the American South had seemed to him back in 1960." With this evidence forming Canada's musical canon, it's no wonder it took years to overcome this cultural insecurity in song.

"In the early '80s there weren't a lot of Canadian references being dropped into songs," says Kurt Swinghammer. "People didn't do it, and it always bugged my ass that people would change the names, just like changing the flags to make Toronto look like an American city [in film]. You don't expect painters to pull the wool over your eyes and paint something that they don't know, and if they do, they're called on it. Like with Rousseau, he never went to Africa and just painted from postcards. In Canadian music, there's always this tendency to mask things if you want it to work. There's always a sense that if you want to be successful, you gotta hide the fact that you're from Canada, which is so stupid. It's way cooler and more accepted now. Maybe that's just part of the evolution of a culture that's still young and growing and shaking off some insecurities about where it's from."

But slowly and surely, changes were afoot. "I think Andrew Cash is important, because he did it first around '82 or so," says Lewis Melville, who spent two decades playing in everything from acid rock and soul revues to bluegrass and country bands. In the '80s, he started to move into the rock world via the Rheostatics and the Skydiggers. Because of his folk background, the fact that rock singers began singing about Canada was nothing new to him. "It's not something that emerged from that time for me," he says. "It's something that a lot of people around me had been doing, and [Cash et al.] were just the new guys. During this time period, people like that started to emerge to the public. And that was exciting to me, because I'd known many people who were banging their heads against the wall."

Tom Wilson of Junkhouse and Blackie & the Rodeo Kings welcomed the change. "People like Blue Rodeo and Gord Downie have been embraced in such a huge way," says Wilson, "that suddenly you didn't have to be singing about the Mississippi River or have a poncey British accent to get your point across. You could sing about Lake Ontario or wheat kings or do what the Rheostatics do so fabulously well. That became really important to a generation of listeners. In the early '90s, it was a rediscovery. All through school we've been asked what we think the Canadian identity is, and after all our English teachers have finally dried up and been buried, and all those questions have drizzled to the back of our brains, the answer came out in the music we'd been listening to. It contained all those missing links that our education system was always trying to get us to think about: 'Where's our Canadian identity?'

"Well, our Canadian identity is music that's singing about this country," Wilson continues. "It's Gord Downie and it's the Rheostatics, and if they look back a little bit further they'll see that it's also Murray McLauchlan and Gordon Lightfoot. It's all there: we should stop being so British and asking what our identity is, stop worrying about how many books or records or movies we sell in the States, and be happy with who we are."

John Critchley adds, "We were proud to be from Canada and we definitely had Canadian influences in our music, as well as others from around the world. I'm proud of where I'm from and I've written songs about where I'm from. But I don't think music and politics should be confused. You should be proud of where you're from and write about what you know, but just to make a point of it because that is the case, then jingoism creeps in."

From the Neil/Joni generation, however, there was one artist who saw the state of Canadian song to be in such dire straits that an accusation of jingoism would never have occurred to him in his quest to mythologize his native land. He became a role model for travelling bands and independent recording artists across the land, yet he is usually deemed too hokey and uncool to be written into histories of Canadian music. He is Stompin' Tom Connors.

The Singer Is the Voice of the People

By 1978, Stompin' Tom Connors had been recording for over 10 years, and performing for about 20. He had sold thousands of his records off the stage and through stores, released on his own Boot Records label. He had played practically every hamlet in Canada and filled arenas coast to coast. He had won six Juno awards and was celebrated as a national treasure by the CBC and print media. But he couldn't seem to win any respect from the music industry, and country radio in particular. Frustrated by what he saw as a bleak situation for himself — and by extension any Canadian artist who chose to remain in Canada and openly challenge the industry's dismissive attitude towards homegrown acts — Stompin' Tom packed his Junos in a box, sent them back and retired from the industry.

"Tom is despised by the country industry, and he despises them; it's quite mutual," says Richard Flohil. "I wish it didn't happen, but it does. Tom started in the very late '60s, and his impact was incredible. He was doing something that was relatively rare, but radio wouldn't touch it. Especially now, a Stompin' Tom song sticks out of a music mix like a chainsaw on a manicured lawn."

Connors's recordings are indeed relatively lo-fi, and his voice descends from Hank Williams's nasal twang. These traits, combined with a blunt earnestness that isn't necessarily an asset in the music industry, distanced Connors from the country establishment. During Connors' prime period, country was shifting away from its rural roots and into "countrypolitan" (string-drenched country-pop) and later the "urban cowboy" trend. Stompin' Tom reminded the new school country folk what the music used to be like, and they didn't want to hear it. For Canadians who wanted to be seen as hip and worldly, he reminded them of what Canada was, rather than what they hoped it to be.

But although rooted in the past, Stompin' Tom did have a vision for Canada's future. He was mystified by this country's cultural denial of its own heritage, past and present, and dreamed of a day when Canadian artists were warmly embraced by their own people and their domestic music industry. He also felt it was imperative that Canadians have songs they could call their own, songs that celebrated the people, places and legends he had encountered while touring the country extensively. That's why his first album, 1967's *The Northland's Own*, included the titles "Sudbury Saturday Night," "The Flying C.P.R.," and "Streets of Toronto" — and why every album he's released since is dominated by songs about Canada. For the most part, Connors writes whimsical and comical portraits of characters like "Bud the Spud," "Big Joe Mufferaw" and the rag-tag crew of Maritimers in "To It and At It." He's also been guilty of writing ridiculously simple songs like "CA-NA-DA" and "Name the Capitals" which function much more effectively as children's music than they do as country songs. But at the core of all his work is the heart of a historian who wants to put Canadians in touch with their past and with each other, and on songs like "No Canadian Dream" and "The Singer (The Voice of the People)" he articulates his mission with an eloquence worthy of any poet laureate.

The ballad of Stompin' Tom Connors is a fascinating one, not to mention a long one: his autobiography spans two volumes and over 1,100 pages. In it, he cites an essay he submitted to newspaper editorial boards across the country on the occasion of his 1978 retirement: "What an impossible situation we leave our young Canadian talent to face. We ask him to be proud of his country and give him no reason to be. When he writes or sings songs about Canada he's considered 'hokey' and laughed at. When he sings songs like the Americans do, he's considered a copycat. And who wants to buy or hear songs that are sung by a copycat when the real thing can be obtained directly from the Americans themselves? That's why our talent goes nowhere — except maybe south."

In 1985, a young Etobicoke, Ontario, student rock journalist named Dave Bidini — who in his spare time played with his high school friends in the Rheostatics — travelled to Ireland to study literature at Trinity College in Dublin. Shortly before his trip, he had stumbled across an old Stompin' Tom album on vinyl, and put it on a tape with excerpts from Bob Dylan and The Band's *The Basement Tapes*. "I remember listening to it like crazy while I was abroad," recalls Bidini, "because I didn't know how to articulate and understand the place I came from to others, but I understood that by listening to his music. I learned that the people in Ireland loved Irish music. And not only did they love it, but they would tell anyone who would listen that it was the best fucking music in the world — which was not the case here, because people in Canada didn't like Canadian music, particularly. When I was over there and people would ask me about Canada, I didn't really know stuff so I played them Stompin' Tom."

In his memoir *On a Cold Road*, Bidini writes: "Tom's voice drew me back across the ocean, and the songs about bobcats and Wilf Carter that I'd once been embarrassed to listen to anchored my identity in a culture where nationhood was everything. They taught me who I was and where I came from . . . *My Stompin' Grounds* had conjured up a panoramic winter-land of railways and folk music and taverns and hockey rinks that was as unlike suburban Etobicoke as Europe had been."

When he returned, Bidini embarked on a search to find Stompin' Tom. Boot Records was still functioning, and the receptionist fielded several calls a day from people asking where Tom was and if they could book him into their community hall or arena. Bidini wasn't the only one on the hunt for Stompin' Tom. Peter Gzowski, host of the immensely popular CBC radio show *Morningside*, had been broadcasting annual pleas to bring Tom out of hiding. But Bidini was persistent, and one day in 1986 the receptionist let it slip that Tom was celebrating his 50th birthday party in Ballinafad, the town between Guelph and Toronto where he lived. Bidini and his Rheostatic bandmate Tim Vesely went out to crash the party and present a petition begging him to return.

Connors recalls in his autobiography: "At one point in the evening, someone came up to me with a message saying that there was some kind of newspaper reporter outside who wanted to see me. As I went outside with the intention of telling him to get lost, I found that he was very cordial and down to earth, so I told him that he and a couple of his friends were welcome to come in and have a couple of beers, as long as he left his camera in the car. Once I saw they had taken a seat and weren't bothering anybody, I went over and sat down and gave the guy an interview. He asked a lot of the kinds of questions that told me he was not just trying to get a story, but was also somewhat of a fan. He had also been trying to contact me for some time. I'm not sure how long he stayed or when he left the party, but I later became a fan of his and took [my wife] Lena to see his band a couple of times in future years. This was Dave Bidini, leader of the great band called the Rheostatics."

Bidini penned a full-page article in the Toronto monthly underground music magazine *Nerve*, describing Tom's rebellious history, Bidini's search for the lost legend, and why Canadians will be listening to Stompin' Tom for much longer than they will Cats Can Fly. The whole adventure inspired Bidini's band to be more consciously Canadian in their songwriting and presentation, which put the Rheostatics at the vanguard of many of the profound changes of the CanRock Renaissance. "Obviously that experience had a huge, profound impact on us playing the kind of music that we played," says Bidini. "That imbued the nationalism, had a huge impact on us being a Canadian band, and made us want to carry the torch."

Shortly after the *Nerve* article ran, Bidini received a call from Deane Cameron, who worked at Capitol-EMI. "He said, 'Can you tell me where he is?'" Bidini recalls. "I said 'I can't.' He said, 'Well, I respect that, but if I ever find Tom I'm going to sign him to Capitol Records.' And a few years later, he did." In 1988, Connors emerged to record his first new album in 12 years, *Fiddle and Song*, and through a series of events eventually was convinced to sign to EMI Canada by Cameron, who by this point was president of the company. A compilation of Connors's greatest hits, *A Proud Canadian*, was released in 1990 and went gold that November and platinum four years later, proving that Connors wasn't an irrelevant relic.

"But I still didn't know if Tom ever read my article or knew who I was, necessarily," says Bidini. "Tim [Vesely] and I went to see him at Massey Hall on his comeback tour, and there was a party at the [ritzy jazz club] Top O' the Senator later. Tom was there, and all these record-industry-type people, and I thought, 'It's gone all wrong, it wasn't supposed to be this way.' We were at one end of the bar, and then everybody cleared out except Tim and I, really drunk, and Tom and his entourage. And then as we were leaving, I went to Tom just to say thanks for the party, or whatever. He looked me straight in the eye and he said" — Bidini adopts a gruff Maritime accent for emphasis — "'Bidini! I've had to take a lot of shit from you over the years!' Then he got up and called me a true blue Canadian patriot and gave me a big hug, and it was a really beautiful thing. As it turns out, Deane had shown him the article and said that's what made [Deane] want to go and get [Tom] back in the music business. Tom read it and was deeply moved, and thought, 'You know, if the kids are okay, there's somebody out there for me to play to.'"

By the time Stompin' Tom performed his comeback tour, the Rheostatics had made their *Melville* album, which is rife with references to Saskatchewan, Alberta, northern wishes, Canadian winters, and The Guess Who, as well as a cover of Gordon Lightfoot's "Wreck of the Edmund Fitzgerald." And the poet laureate of the next generation, Gord Downie, had begun to sing songs about Group of Seven painter Tom Thomson and Canadian places and politics.

Downie admits, however, that he did so tentatively. "That feeling was in the infancy of its articulation," he says. "I didn't think I had total permission yet. I started realizing you *could* sing about Canada and about where you're from. I'd always wanted to do it, but never could figure out how. It's really weird, because it seems like it should be so easy. But back then it wasn't for me. And it was the Rheostatics that made me think I could, specifically the song 'Saskatchewan,' which is pretty darn beautiful. I wasn't really into them at the time, but that's how I started."

Just as the Rheostatics took Stompin' Tom as inspiration and not a direct model, many writers began incorporating Canada into their writing in their own unique way — whether it was Bob Wiseman's political songs ("Gabriel Dumont Blues") or Daniel Lanois celebrating "Wasaga Beach on the first of July" ("Lotta Love To Give").

In 1992, at the height of the CanRock Renaissance, Chris Brown of the Toronto soul band the Bourbon Tabernacle Choir penned a lyric that encapsulated the new generation's confidence, in a song called "You Can Come From Here": "So as they find you, and you know they're gonna come / Ask you for your papers, and you can't give them none / Now before the envy, before the greed / Before you lose track of yourself in confusion or need / And so not to worry, and so not to fear / If somebody asks you, you can come from here / Displaced or abandoned, in need of a past / You can come from here now if somebody asks." Stompin' Tom's message had finally sunk in, and without accusations of knee-jerk nationalism. The kids were alright.

Canadian imagery was also embraced, such as Shadowy Men On a Shadowy Planet using a postcard of Toronto's Nathan Phillips Square on their debut album cover, or Circle C re-interpreting the Canadian flag as their logo. In most cases, the artist wasn't consciously tackling Canadian subjects or trying to write a nationalist song, but simply doing what came naturally and with a new sense of confidence. "It's a pretty individual thing," says Geoffrey Kelly of the folk-rock band Spirit of the West. "It's hard to speak for what Gord Downie's sense of Canada is, or Dave Bidini's. It's affected our writing because we've seen a lot of Canada; we've seen those places, so at least we have a better mental idea of what Canada is. Because of that I'm able to write about it more honestly, but I don't think we're flag-waving guys."

"I don't know whether it's patriotism," says Toronto filmmaker Bruce McDonald, who made three smart and funny movies about Canadian rock-'n'-roll, beginning with 1989's *Roadkill*. "It's just where we live. It's unusual to see our own country in movies. [Making distinctively Canadian films] doesn't necessarily make you patriotic; it's just holding up a little window or mirror to where you live. I feel lucky that there's this place — that there's a frontier, a wilderness, a mystery to the land, that there are open spaces.

Most places in the world don't have that. I like that element to the land-scape — that it's not all fenced and blocked and built up, and you can still escape. It still allows you room to become a freak or an eccentric and hopefully to become an individual rather than one of the teeming masses of people in suits taking a subway to work."

Behind the Garage

For the "teeming masses," there was another significant shift in perception for Canadian music in 1985. Before that, Canada didn't boast many young superstars, let alone sexy ones. Charismatic figures like Carole Pope may have been overtly sexual, but she wasn't a pin-up idol; and nor, for that matter, were multi-platinum artists like Loverboy and April Wine. "Canada used to have a stigma over producing a lot of really ugly bands," says Moe Berg of The Pursuit of Happiness. "There weren't a lot of Canadian heart-throbs until probably Corey Hart and that was pretty late in the game. Now we've got people like Moist and Our Lady Peace and Edwin who have very attractive images, and a lot of the female artists in Canada are very attrac-tive. That wasn't the case back in the days of BTO."

That all changed when Bryan Adams and Corey Hart became teen sen-sations in 1984; within a year, Adams's *Reckless* album would become the first Canadian album to be certified diamond (one million copies), with Hart's *Boy in the Box* close behind. Ten years later, Alanis Morissette would be the first Canadian to go double diamond. As any cursory glance at the history of rock music will show, the teen market often dictates the course of the music industry. And while Adams and Hart didn't leave any worthy musical legacy, they had a definite impact on the cult of Canadian celebrity — previously a bit of an oxymoron — and created a genuine excitement for Canadian music. After that, for every Platinum Blonde or Mitsou there were also teenage screams for The Grapes of Wrath or Sloan. Youth no longer felt like they were watching a Heritage Minute when they went to Sam the Record Man and bought an album by a Canadian artist.

The dismal status of Canadian celebrity circa 1985 was clearly evident when the supergroup known as Northern Lights was unveiled. When Ethiopian famine captured the world's attention in 1984, British rock singer Bob Geldof rallied his country's leading musical lights to record "Do They Know It's Christmas?" a benefit single for famine relief. In Canada, manager Bruce Allen helped coordinate the Canadian equivalent, which became a best-selling single. "Tears Are Not Enough" featured much of the old guard like Neil Young, Joni Mitchell, Bruce Cockburn and Gordon Lightfoot, as well as newer pop stars such as The Spoons, Platinum Blonde and Luba. There were a few glimpses of the future, like Jane Siberry, but to pad the celebrity quotient, the all-star choir also featured musicians not noted for their singing ability, like Liona Boyd and Paul Shaffer. Even worse, representatives were added from Canada's primary cultural export — comedy — such as John Candy, Alan Thicke and Robin Duke. One can't argue with the earnest song, the spirit of intergenerational and cross-Canada camaraderie and charity. But artistically, was this song really what Canadian music was all about?

The Northern Lights single was produced by David Foster, a Vancouver keyboardist who cut his teeth playing barrooms with Ronnie Hawkins, but who came to epitomize glossy yuppie easy-listening schlock in the '80s through his work with Chicago and Céline Dion. There is an infamous scene in the CBC documentary of the Northern Lights session where Foster tries to tell Neil Young that his performance was good but that his voice was a bit flat. "That's my style, man," replies a sardonic Young.

Foster's production work, like that of fellow Vancouverites Bruce Fairbairn (Trooper, Aerosmith) and the later work of Bob Rock (Mötley Crüe, Metallica), was tailor-made for the digital era of the '80s, glossing over any imperfections that might exist in a natural performance. While Foster became a radio darling by following in the footsteps of polite Canadian easy-listening icons like Frank Mills and Hagood Hardy, the Neil Young production ethic was becoming prevalent in the underground. The thriving garage rock scene, led by Montreal's Og Records, helped lower any hi-fidelity expectations for new fans of underground music. By the early '90s, bands like Eric's Trip and The Inbreds were recording classic works in their basements (*Love Tara* and *Hilario*, respectively). With their single "Wake Me" and subsequent album *Fluke*, the Toronto band Rusty made a major breakthrough on rock radio with a demo recording so far removed from standard sonic quality that it would have given David Foster nightmares.

For those who wanted to record a step up from the basement, higher fidelity technology also became much more accessible for independent (read: cheaper) artists to make quality recordings on par with major label fare. As a result, many more Canadian bands were able to break through in the always competitive music industry during this particular time period. It will never be known how many earlier, mind-blowing, unrecorded Canadian bands could have instigated the events detailed in this book if they had had cheaper access to recording technology.

"There was always a lot of great music going on," says Lewis Melville, "but there wasn't the means to capture it or make it affordable. So people who didn't have money or the record industry [behind them] couldn't afford to take a chance on it because it wasn't popular, so it didn't achieve an audience." Melville argues that many of the perceived shifts that took place during the CanRock Renaissance happened merely because technology was there to capture them. "The music was always there, but this [renaissance] emerged from that period in technology, more so than from any changes in Canadian music. There's the recorded music of a lot of bands that you heard through the '60s and '70s, and then there was what they did at their live shows. What you put on your record is a sample of what you do live — a lot of bands would contrive a little pop song for their record, and their live shows were completely over the top. There was always a lot of music that was experimental and Canadian that was going on, but it didn't make it onto radio. The only place you ever heard it was live. Nobody was there with a tape recorder. You had to be there."

One of the most important Canadian exports from this time was Hamilton producer Daniel Lanois, whose approach to recording not only influenced his major international clients like U2 and Bob Dylan, but trickled down to upcoming Canadian artists who would work with his protégés, like The Tragically Hip and Blue Rodeo. Blue Rodeo's Greg Keelor recalls meeting Lanois on a drive back to Toronto from Hamilton, where Keelor's side project Crash Vegas was working with Lanois understudy Malcolm Burn. Keelor had just finished recording Blue Rodeo's first album with Rush's producer, and Lanois opened his eyes to alternative methods of recording; Keelor would take his advice to create Blue Rodeo's most beloved albums, *Diamond Mine* and *Five Days in July*.

"It was a very enlightening conversation, just asking him about his philosophy on making records," says Keelor. "He very coherently and succinctly debunked the whole record company/studio thing. He said, 'You could put a studio in your living room!' I was pretty naïve about recording, and didn't know the first thing about engineering. I always accepted whatever the engineer said in any studio I was in, and especially producers. They were the principals and the teachers. When I first started working at [Burn's studio], I thought, 'This is a joke! What, this little board and that little machine? Where's all the stuff?' Dan said, 'You don't need any of that stuff.'"

Some bands required even less. Vancouver's "cuddle-core" band Cub became an indie success story, selling 50,000 copies of their three albums through the then-fledgling Mint Records. Their 1993 lo-fi debut album *Betti-Cola* was recorded shortly after the three women in the band learned their instruments. "*Betti-Cola* was done in several different shifts," explains Mint's

Bill Baker. "Most of it was recorded in a guy's basement, with a DAT machine and a couple of microphones. Some stuff was done in Olympia, [Washington] for free, and some stuff was done for the CBC. The entire first album, technically, cost us $75 to record. But it's not like you listen to it and say, 'I can't believe it!' Instead, you listen and say, 'Oh yeah, I *can* believe it.'" The album's artwork, designed by original *Archie* comic artist Don DeCarlo, cost $500 — over six times as much as the recording.

What Cub lacked in high fidelity and instrumental skill, they made up for with charm and an affinity for catchy bubblegum melodies. Their endearingly primitive approach gained them legions of loyal fans, including Jello Biafra, Lou Barlow and Kurt Cobain. It also rubbed classic-rock audiences the wrong way. Baker remembers a vocal backlash against Cub from a fringe contingent of frustrated musicians.

"We'd get letters from people who had spent ten years learning to play awesome guitar and never got a break, because they didn't have that intangible X-factor that makes you talented, rather than just skilled," says Baker. "Then when you get people like Cub with talent but no skill making it, these guys would be saying, 'This is fucking shit. This shouldn't be on the radio.' They were very resentful, and it was probably salt in their wounds when our press release would read: 'And they just picked up their instruments! They don't even know how to play!' Cub were the very essence of what punk was, which was people who can't really play just doing it, and not doing it the same way other people do it. Cub didn't sound like Rancid, but in terms of the ideas behind it and the way it happened, it was very punk."

Up and Running

Although it's painful to admit, there's little doubt that the success of many of the artists in this book was due in part to Canadian content, or CanCon, regulations imposed on Canadian radio by the CRTC [Canadian Radio and Television Commission]. On January 18, 1971, federal legislation was passed that mandated that all radio stations must play a minimum of 30 per cent Canadian content. To a foreigner, particularly Americans, this still seems like a ludicrous notion. Yet one must understand the level of cultural denial that existed in Canada at the time, and to some degree, still does today. The legislation was lampooned by the business community, which saw Canadian culture as shabby, sloppy crap that could only survive with such "extreme" measures of support.

Radio executives thought that allowing more Canadian music on the air would crush the commercial aspirations of broadcasters across the nation.

Testifying before the CRTC hearings on the matter in 1970, one executive had this to say: "It is our belief that the implementation of the new proposals will raise the cost of broadcasting to the advertiser, lower the attractiveness of the stations to the listeners and thereby, for both these reasons, raise the cost per listener to the point where many stations will cease to be competitive in the advertising market and their incomes will drop significantly."

At the same hearings, Toronto rock critic Ritchie Yorke took the stand in defense of the cultural nationalists. "Any broadcaster who played 'Yummy Yummy Yummy (I've Got Love in My Tummy),' that memorable hit by the Ohio Express, should never get himself involved in a discussion on quality," Yorke fumed. "Radio management is just too damn lazy to audition new records. It is easier just to play the Top 40 off the lists sent out by the American music magazines. Create the demand and the supply will be there."

When the legislation became law, CRTC chair Pierre Juneau — for whom the Junos are named — made a prophetic statement that sums up many of the events encapsulated in this book: "The prophets of doom, the messengers of mediocrity will be overwhelmed by the new generation of competent, creative, confident artisans and by all those of the preceding generations who have already demonstrated their freshness of mind, their talent and their capacity for inspired leadership."

"I'm so into CanCon," says Bill Baker. "There are different ways it works. Some people look at it as a shield to keep out other stuff. There's lots of stuff that maybe gets elevated to levels it doesn't deserve to be at. But if it wasn't happening, it would just be the same stuff coming in from outside. People say, 'Oh, of course you love CanCon, because how else would that shit that you put out get played?' I've had that comment more than once. But we do live next door to an incredibly powerful country that controls every kind of media there is. Some people think we can take CanCon regulations away because we're up to speed, but I don't think so."

Corporate rocker Bryan Adams thought differently, and came out swinging in a 1994 interview. "I think it's a hugely mediocre system, and should be abolished," raged Adams. "Taxpayers should wake up and realize how much money they're wasting. It's up to artists and songwriters and producers to come up with the best they can. I don't think they should be under the wing of any government protection agency. You either have good product or you don't, and you should be in the open market like everybody else. I think it's good that Quebec has some sort of regulations so they can protect their culture, but I don't see why the rest of Canada needs it. People should be on their own. No one has ever played me just because I was Canadian."

"When I think about it from a dispassionate viewpoint, I think we shouldn't have to have it," says Scott McCullough, of Rusty and the Doughboys. "It's culturally biased, and if you have to protect your culture, maybe it should disappear. But then again, you can say the same thing about Native people in Canada, and I don't think *their* culture should disappear. CanCon, when you talk about it theoretically, doesn't sound like a good thing, but in practice it is. We wouldn't have the industry we have today without it."

"A lot of people hate CanCon, but it certainly helped," admits John Critchley. "The weirdest misconception people have of CanCon is they always think a radio station has to play a minimum [30 per cent] of Canadian music. What they don't realize is that even in the year 2000, that's a maximum — [the programmers] fill that and then they shut the door. They've done their duty, and even if there are 10 more great Canadian records, they won't play them until they turf one of the ones they have in their CanCon folder. It's important for people to understand that, because if that went away, radio stations just wouldn't play Canadian music, unless it came from America or England."

The decade between 1985 and 1995 was when Canadian acts could be themselves, discover their own voices and have a chance at reaching a wide audience in doing so. John Borra recalls the shock of seeing his peers rise to the top in the late '80s. "The Cowboy Junkies, to me, were such a weird band," he says. "It was like there were no rules, anything can go. They made one or two thousand copies of their second record [*The Trinity Session*] then got signed to BMG and sold a million. They couldn't have finished that record and thought, 'This one's gonna sell a million copies.' They were playing at The Cameron with all sorts of bands that were totally counterculture. I remember walking into a Second Cup, hearing it on the radio and thinking, 'Fuck, this is one of the weirdest bands that I've ever heard on some easy listening station.' How do you go from one of the wackiest bands in the underground to sliding right into the mainstream?"

Scott McCullough started off as a guitarist in the Doughboys, but found North American radio success in 1995 with the band Rusty, which also featured members of a long-suffering band called One Free Fall. "God knows, we'd all spent a lot of unsuccessful years in the music business, and although

(Photo by David Leyes)

we thought it was really good work, it still requires a lot of luck to have people notice it," says McCullough. "I don't even like the radio and the Top 40, so it was even weirder having it accepted. I'd been working under the assumption that good stuff doesn't get accepted. I was amazed that other people liked it as much as we did. Up to that point in my life I'd always hated the charts. I remember actually thinking, if we're on the radio, does that mean we suck? I've still got a double-edged feeling about it. I wasn't impressed by the new branch of rock radio. I thought it was just as boring and repetitive as old rock radio was. I was glad they were playing us, but I wasn't blown away by the competition."

John Critchley argues that the bland mainstream culture of the '80s directly inspired an active underground. "In the '80s, a lot of music came out of people wanting to hear *good music*," says Critchley. "It wasn't coming from anywhere else, so people just started making it. The end result being that I hope you can now be a successful band in Canada, and maybe never have to go anywhere else. That's a possibility now, whereas before it wasn't."

"You can be hugely successful in Canada, but people still want to know what's going on in America," says Kim Deschamps, a multi-instrumentalist who travelled the world with the Cowboy Junkies and Blue Rodeo. "Historically, in the era of Neil and Joni, there was no industry here. There was no possibility of making a living, and they all followed the Lightfoot example: release in the U.S., become a force down there, and then the Canadian public will take you seriously. That's less the case now, but it's still a factor. For some reason, Canadian listeners — and especially the industry people — want that validation, that approval from abroad, and especially from the south. Younger people I talk to in audiences and kids who are starting bands are less concerned about that. They're really encouraged by the fact that bands like Blue Rodeo can have a career in Canada and don't need an American career to make a living to produce work that they're happy with, and to keep going year after year. That is a really big deal to a lot of young players."

"Nobody really ever asked me too much about what it means, being Canadian," said Sarah McLachlan in 1999, after she became an international success. "Nobody knew I was [Canadian] and when I told them it was just like a footnote anyway. But nobody knew Joni Mitchell was [Canadian] either. If it matters at all, it's because we know who we are. I'd never want to leave Canada — this is my home and I got to be everything I am right here."

By 1995, the Canadian music industry had matured to the point at which interesting, innovative works were constantly being released by emerging artists from every region of the country. Some, if not most, even got played on mainstream radio. And whereas 10 years prior a major label deal would have been the only way for them to be heard, there was now a variety of outlets to help an artist find an audience. Dozens of Canadian albums were certified platinum or better every year. No longer did all-Canadian festival line-ups appear to be patronizing nationalist boosterism. Uniquely Canadian songwriting was not subject to mockery or ghettoized to the folk scene.

"In the '80s some people emerged that really did have their own voice," says Kevin Kane, who recalls buying the 1986 debut album by the Cowboy Junkies "practically the day it came out" on the recommendation of a friend working at Zulu Records. "I was really floored. I was so excited. They were Canadian, and it actually gave me pride. It was a special record, it was unique. So was Mary Margaret O'Hara. There were a number of people in the late '80s who had an identity. They had nothing to do with [the mentality of]: 'Well, we're just going to sell in Canada.' Most didn't physically leave the country to get signed, which is what everyone else had always done, except for The Guess Who."

Most importantly, Canadians no longer sought external approval to realize that what we were creating was truly exciting and inspiring. There's an urban myth involving Sloan, the sly band that launched the Halifax pop explosion of the early '90s, about how they once berated a disinterested audience in Washington, D.C.: "Fuck you, we're huge in Canada."

"[Campus radio] didn't advocate obscurity and anarchy and noise because it was trendy or elitist; it did so from a purity of intention almost impossible to recapture now: because it loved and understood the music and— in the unselfish, sacrificial nature of true love — expected exactly nothing in return."

— Gina Arnold

Did You Get My Message on the People's Radio?

When Lisa Marr of Cub started touring, she found out how far news can travel about a young underground band with no exposure from mainstream media outlets. "When I was a teenager, there were no shows where I lived in the interior of B.C.," she said in a 1996 interview, shortly before the band's demise. "Billy Idol and Corey Hart came, and I saw both of them. I had no idea about bands like the Clash until I started going to university. But it's really different now. We played a show about half an hour from where I used to live when I was a teenager, and there were tons of kids there and they know about all kinds of music. That just shows how things have changed in 10 years. There was no outlet then."

In 1984, three broadcasting institutions transformed the way Canadians saw and heard their own music. *Brave New Waves* and *Night Lines* were overnight radio programs on the CBC that harnessed the best qualities of alternative campus radio and made it accessible to enraptured listeners, music geeks and insomniacs across the nation. On television was MuchMusic, Canada's first music video network. It made up the rules as it went along, and, in the infancy of the music video medium, pretty much any Canadian artist with a half-decent visual idea suddenly had a national

Robynn Iwata of Cub, 1993
(Photo by Paul Clarke)

audience, even if — like Jane Siberry's "Mimi on the Beach" — the music would have been deemed uncommercial by radio playlist standards.

Meanwhile, campus radio began to take a firm foothold in university and college communities. By the end of the decade, there was a loosely affiliated network that helped make touring such a large country a bit easier for independent bands, who knew they could often count on at least one media outlet being aware of their music. Commercial radio, which had protested CanCon regulations since they were legislated in 1971, finally had a plethora of quality acts added to their playlist with which programmers couldn't argue. Toronto's CFNY was heralded as one of the most innovative commercial stations on the continent.

With this kind of support, Canadian music had a new environment in which to thrive. After years of floundering, there was finally a real Canadian rock music industry it could be proud of, almost in spite of itself.

It didn't matter where you lived across Canada. If you ever stayed up late at night exploring the boundaries of your FM radio dial, you were likely to stumble across the signal from CBC Radio Two (then called CBC Stereo), and suddenly find yourself part of a world you didn't know existed: a world of creativity and eclecticism, of intelligent discussion and unbridled enthusiasm. It was a place where John Cage and the Dead Kennedys co-existed, where a 7" single by a Fredericton garage band fit into a set with an electro-acoustic composer from Montreal. A world where Canadiana art rock and New York City hip-hop were accorded equal importance and respect. A world where the DJs were as smart as you always wanted to be yourself, and yet they never acted cooler than you. By according new Canadian music the same importance as groundbreaking music from around the world, these late-night shows gave Canadian music greater legitimacy. Simultaneously, it inspired new generations of Canadian musicians to look beyond their own borders for inspiration and to discard unconscious, parochial self-imposed limitations to their own creativity.

Prior to 1984, CBC Radio's only foray into so-called "youth programming" was based in Vancouver, starting with a show hosted by future MuchMusic host Terry David Mulligan called *The Great Canadian Gold Rush*. *Night Lines* host David Wisdom recalls, "Mulligan refused to play the Buzzcocks as examples of good music in the '70s, and I went up against him on that one. I think the CBC saw things were changing." Mulligan's show was eventually replaced by a program called *Neon*, hosted by J.D. Shane. "They were more interested in new stuff," says Wisdom, "and I was allowed to go on his show and do items on various things — mostly English music, which was my all-consuming interest for many years."

Neon was also receptive to the fertile west coast punk scene, giving the music unlikely national exposure on the public broadcaster. Kevin Lynn, who formed King Cobb Steelie in 1991, recalls, "When I was growing up in Fort McMurray, Alberta, around 1980, I used to listen to *Neon* religiously. It was great, because it was really isolated in Fort McMurray, but *Neon* was where I heard 'Holiday in Cambodia' by the Dead Kennedys for the first time, as well as all the Vancouver punk stuff like the Subhumans."

In 1984, the CBC decided to fill the dead air space in the overnight FM slot with similar programming. This decision spawned two programs: the weeknight *Brave New Waves*, based in Montreal, and the weekend *Night Lines*, originally based in Winnipeg. Initially, both were aired between 11 p.m. and 5 a.m., broadcast live to the Maritimes and then staggered across the country; through various stages of CBC budget cuts, they were eventually whittled down to four pre-recorded ("live to tape") hours between midnight and 4 a.m. The defining hosts of both programs reigned for over a decade: *Brave New Waves'* Brent Bambury hosted the show from 1985 to 1996, and *Night Lines'* David Wisdom hosted for 10 years beginning in 1987, when the show had relocated to Vancouver.

Patti Schmidt, who inherited *Brave New Waves* upon Bambury's departure, says the program regularly gets fan letters thanking them for opening their ears to new music and expressing shock that such a program exists. "I think it's the same kind of life-altering thing that happened when I discovered the show living in the crappy suburbs outside of Ottawa," says Schmidt. "It strikes a chord with a lot of people. It's the idea of a borderless beyond. Most of the tone of the letters we get are about that: 'Oh my god, there's more!'"

Brave New Waves was the brainchild of producer Alan Conter and Augusta LaPaix, the latter serving as the show's first host. LaPaix was working on the national call-in show *Cross-Country Checkup* in 1984, when one night in Toronto she found herself drinking scotch with the head of Radio Two, unaware of who he was. She told him about a long-standing dream she had had about doing a crazy all-night program on the CBC. At the time, the CBC was soliciting proposals for the overnight slot, and a 1983 internal report had warned of a "major audience crisis" unless the network reached out to younger listeners. "Let's face it," she says. "They were broke and desperate and knew that people like us weren't a dime a dozen: people who would work for nothing, work long hours, and be dedicated to it. No technician who had any seniority wanted to work on it."

In December 1983, LaPaix and Conter were given the green light, along with six weeks and three additional staff members to put the show together. The show went on the air on February 4, 1984 — a year that was briefly considered as the title of the program until LaPaix settled on *Brave New Waves*. The first song was Simple Minds' "Promised You a Miracle." "We were very much flying by the seat of our pants," says LaPaix.

Kevin Komoda was hired as an assistant music programmer shortly after the show began, as producers David Ryan and Sophia Hadzipetros were swamped with scripting and researching the six-hour show. "I remember going to the job thinking that no one cared, that the CBC just wanted something on the air in those dead hours," Komoda says. "I don't think they've ever acknowledged any of the show's success. Most producers watch ratings, and they don't even bother to calculate ratings at that hour. The only way you can actually substantiate what you're doing is by the volume of mail."

"We started getting huge amounts of mail right away," says LaPaix. "The mail would come from guards at Queen's Park in Toronto, guys on the oil rigs in the Atlantic, post mistresses in B.C., 13-year-olds listening under the covers late at night. We had such a range of people who were listening."

LaPaix claims that she wasn't basing the show on John Peel's legendary BBC show or anything else. "It was simply the desire to do something different, creative and fun," she explains. "The tone came through because of the personalities involved, and a sense that the music should be as cutting edge as possible. I had a real sense of the space of the place, a place that people came to every night: bring the people in and let us sit around and let's not be too serious. In fact, let's not be serious at all. It was live. If you had seen our preliminary notes — if I can call them that — we were talking about finding series from the archives and other broadcasters from around the world and running them on the show. All of that dissolved after a week. We found the format we could afford, which involved technicians who were as crazy as everybody else, and a live studio where anything can happen."

Every night there would be an interview, which could occupy the entire show if the guest wasn't bored. "We'd bring people in at 1:00 in the morning and feed them cheap wine, which we disguised as a taxi budget," recalls LaPaix. "Sometimes they'd stay until 3:00 or 4:00 in the morning."

When Bambury succeeded LaPaix as host in 1985, one of the show's signature strengths was his interviewing skills. While the producers of the show programmed the music and wrote the scripts, Bambury's main non-hosting function was researching his interviews. His informative, objective and thoughtful questioning either brought the best out of a mildly interesting subject, or matched wits with some of the greatest cultural minds of our time. Two of his personal favourite interviews were composer John Cage and avant-garde singer/pianist Diamanda Galas, who wrote a harrowing opera trilogy about AIDS called *The Masque of the Red Death*, which drew parallels between puritanical beliefs in the Middle Ages and the '80s conservative climate.

Bambury says, "John Cage represents *Brave New Waves* in some ways because he was somebody who could talk about philosophy and then relate the philosophy in a non-language way, in a musical way. Diamanda Galas was talking about culture as it existed and culture as it exists, and yet it was all still relating to music. Both of those interviews defined how the program presented culture not just in a musical way, but in a way that went beyond music. My own theory of the show was that if you can get your mind around this track of music we're going to play, regardless of where it comes from, then you can get your mind around any other idea that we bring into the show — or any other person, no matter how bizarre or opaque they seem. I always thought the eclecticism of the music was our way of saying: 'Don't expect us to be consistent with anything; we promise to try not to bore you.'"

It wasn't easy to program a captivating guest five nights a week, which led to some interesting experiments. Recalls Bambury, "In the early days, we'd have these almost experimental evenings where we'd bring in an academic, a dancer and a punk rock musician, put them together and hopefully they would talk. There were incidents where people clearly didn't know where they were, which made for really interesting radio."

Sometimes, the only thing interesting about it was Bambury's ability to get verbal blood from a stone. "We had punk rock bands whose mother tongue was apparently English, but couldn't speak a word. I found myself interviewing them several times and I called it a 'bowl of fruit' interview.

My argument was that you could put a bowl of fruit in front of the microphone, and I would get an interview out of it that we'd end up using. Then we could say, 'Well, it's not the worst thing we've had on!'"

During its first season, the staff of *Brave New Waves* knew the show had really arrived when it was criticized in the House of Commons. An Edmonton journalist wrote a piece complaining that the show hosted too many "radical feminist authors," which led to a police investigation on obscenity charges that were eventually dropped. It was later revealed that the complaint originated with an anti-*Brave New Waves* CBC employee. The segment in question was an interview with confrontational performance artist Karen Finley. Bambury, who was still a researcher at the time, says, "We interviewed her and she sounded rational and well-thought out. Then we played a dance single of hers where she was talking about stuffing yams up her anus." In the conservative '80s, Finley was undoubtedly a controversial voice, but as Bambury points out, "You can read about Karen Finley in *Time* magazine now. If she's safe enough for Time-Warner, she's probably safe enough for the CBC."

"We got into hot water a lot," he said in 1995. "In some ways I think we're not doing our job if we don't do that. We have to put things out there and then we have to be prepared to defend them. I think if we're not defining the extremes, then we'd be getting no letters, but the fact that we are means that we get them all the time."

In 1985, after 18 months, LaPaix abandoned her brainchild and moved to CBC's avant-garde 20th century music show *Two New Hours*, and the mantle was passed to Bambury. Bambury had started his radio career at the age of 18 as a sportscaster at a CBC affiliate in New Brunswick. "When this show was created, I happened to be working with one of the original producers before she moved on to this show," he says. "I heard about it and thought, 'That's exactly what I want to do.' At the time I was a university student, 23 years old. They brought me in a few months later to work part-time doing odd jobs, basically things like answering mail and setting up contest prizes." Shortly after the show's first anniversary, Bambury started filling in for LaPaix when she was ill, and it was the first time he had hosted any radio. "In some ways, it was a bit of a cliché, but I did graduate from the mail room and I did have an ambitious streak in me when I showed up here," he says, adding that he got the job "because they knew that I loved the show and I loved the format. It was my culture."

The culture consisted not just of music, but film, comic books, novels, poetry, performance art and fanzines. *Brave New Waves* was a guided tour through alternative culture, a wide-ranging definition that in the mid-'80s could include k.d. lang and Skinny Puppy, Laurie Anderson and The Grapes of Wrath, Public Enemy and Rational Youth. "Our philosophy was that music is music, and there shouldn't be any boundaries," says Kevin Komoda. "In a perfect world, you should be able to hear John Cage, Madonna and the Sex Pistols right next to each other. Often you don't, but if you're given the opportunity to do so, it's more fun."

The show often toyed with punk perceptions of cool. "My favourite moments were when guests picked certain things," laughs Komoda. "[Critic] Robert Christgau of the *Village Voice* picked Foreigner's 'I Want To Know What Love Is' as the definitive song of the '80s."

"I'd get harangued about stuff not being appropriate," Komoda continues. "Augusta didn't care, but some people were very political. Some listeners would write in and say, 'Nirvana's already popular; you shouldn't keep playing them.' I thought, well, we get a lot of hate mail anyway. Nobody wanted me to play [world-renowned Windsor, Ontario, minimalist techno artist] Richie Hawtin and Plus 8 stuff [Hawtin's label], either. We're always going to get hate mail about playing stuff that people don't like. That was always a constant fight. Even with a band like Pavement. I thought, what, just because campus radio is playing them all the time, we shouldn't? Should we not play anything campus radio is playing? That eventually burned me out, because you just start to hate music. But that was all internal. I don't think anyone else at the CBC cared. There were so many other shows that were more of a priority."

When alternative culture hit the mainstream and became "Lollapaloozi-fied" in the early '90s, the show's mandate was forced to change slightly, to dig even deeper underground. Bambury recalls, "What happened with the assimilation of alternative culture, I find, is two things. One thing is that the compact disc created a mini-rebellion. It didn't kill vinyl, it brought it back. Small independent units started producing their own vinyl 7" singles and making them available and putting stuff on them that's so outrageous that there's just no way it could be assimilated into corporate alternative culture. The second thing is that it encouraged people to do things themselves. Nirvana is a punk band, basically, and what they did is make people believe that they could do it themselves. There's a do-it-yourself ethic in music making, not just in music merchandising."

On the show's tenth anniversary program, Bambury touted *Brave New Waves* as "explaining fringe culture to a comfortable mainstream audience." In a later interview, he clarified, "I don't think our audience is mainstream.

I think it's out there, or at least adventurous. I think [the show's mandate is] about making fringe culture more available, rather than explaining it. And what is fringe-y to people in a small town might be more familiar to those who live in urban areas. But for a lot of people who listen to us, we're the only contact with things that go beyond whatever's on the alternative hour on MuchMusic. A lot of places don't have campus stations; a lot of places have bad campus stations. A lot of places have really good campus stations, though, and they give us a run for our money, and that's fine. I learn a lot from listening to the local one here [in Montreal], CKUT. A lot of campus radio folk hate our guts, and I don't blame them. I would too if I was in their place, because we get paid to do what we do. We're professionals and a lot of them are volunteers who work really hard at being volunteers. Sometimes they do shows that are better than ours. But I think we represent a standard for campus radio: the best campus programs can exceed that standard, and other ones can reach for it. Basically, we're paid to know what we know, and we had better be good at it."

In 1991, future host Patti Schmidt moved up from the ranks of campus radio to join the staff of *Brave New Waves*; when most of the show's original staff was hired, there was little campus radio to speak of in Canada. It was her dream job. "Part of the reason I decided to go to McGill was because it was in Montreal, which is where *Brave New Waves* was and is," says Schmidt. "I thought it would be a really cool city. The first thing I did after registration was march myself straight to CKUT. I wrote stuff for them, did overnight shows, and then got my own show. [The *Brave New Waves* staff] were looking for fill-ins for Brent, and the CKUT station manager at the time couldn't do it because of a funding drive. So she gave the producer of *Brave New Waves* five names of people at the station. We all marched our scared little hyperventilating butts down there and did some auditions, and I got a week. This was in February 1991. Then I did a week in June. Then the producer left and they needed a fill-in writer for a week, and I got that."

By that point in the history of both *Brave New Waves* and *Night Lines*, there was a generation of musicians who had grown up with the programs and knew of their ability to connect with listeners. For artists with little to no commercial appeal, it could also mean a difference in sales. Kevin Komoda recalls his friends at Cargo Records telling him, "'You must have played such and such last week, because we just sold a shitload of them in Edmonton,'" he recalls. "Bands started listening, and some people started to realize the effect the show could have. As it grew older, the loyalty was there between the entity of *Brave New Waves* and artists."

When bands were interviewed on *Brave New Waves*, they would give out their mailing address and receive widespread response. Says Jaymz Bee of the Look People, "*Brave New Waves* was unbelievable for the musicians and artists across the country. We got tons of letters from people across the country looking for us because of that. I don't know if it helped much in terms of record sales, but I know that musicians listened." Tony Dewald, whose band Deja Voodoo was a frequent guest, recalls, "*Brave New Waves* and *Night Lines* were incredibly good to us, with Canada being so big, and there was never any national press to speak of before *Exclaim!* magazine came around [in 1992]. But we'd get a lot of kids saying, 'Hey, I heard you on *Brave New Waves*, and you gave out your address so I'm writing to you. I know I'll never see you because I live in Yellowknife.'"

Kevan Byrne of King Cobb Steelie recalls that *Brave New Waves* was one of the first media outlets to notice the band's debut single. "If *Brave New Waves* hadn't played that first single and the first album, our first tour would have been a disaster," says Byrne. "People literally came up to me after the show and said, 'I'm here because I heard you on *Brave New Waves*.' That would be the only connection for people, other than campus radio."

Dave Clark of the Rheostatics says, "Those CBC shows were a huge thing for us. They were and are a great window for bands. Brent was fantastic; he really supported us. And we really dug in with Dave Wisdom and made

King Cobb Steelie, 1993: Kevan Byrne, Al Okada,
Steve Clarkson, Kevin Lynn, Gary Dutch
(Courtesy of Raw Energy/A&M)

friends with him, and he kept plugging us and said the most pleasant things about us which was a real honour."

Brave New Waves decided to start recording sessions in 1988, à la the BBC's John Peel, which provided a lot of bands with a sense of validation amidst a generally oblivious mainstream climate. The Rheostatics were pegged to be the first one. Dave Clark recalls, "We went to Montreal, and they said, 'Meet us at the studio.' We were used to going into little booths, and they took us into the room where they recorded the symphony. It was like walking into the Holodeck or something, and we just burst out laughing. We thought, 'This is it!' We set up our gear and cut the tracks one after another. It felt like an apex in time, like complete magic; I was in tears. It felt like four people having the absolute best time in their lives without any worry about who they are or what they were doing. It was really from the heart."

Kevin Komoda was in charge of the sessions. "Most were recorded in one day, and then I mixed six or seven songs the next day," he says. Komoda had memorable sessions with the Nils, Crash Vegas, Jale, Skinny Puppy, Cub and Phleg Camp, and recalls wanting to record a young Sarah McLachlan with a string section and meeting opposition from CBC Vancouver. "We were looking for funding to help out with the session recordings, so if other shows were interested in it, they could kick in a couple of grand and I could spend a couple more days in the studio with them rather than whipping it together," he says. "A producer in Vancouver said, 'I just saw Sarah McLachlan at the Railway Club. She's talentless and will never amount to anything.' I hear now he's claiming that CBC was on to her first, but *Brave New Waves* was on to her first. There was no support from any other show."

In 1995, when the CBC was hit with another in a series of brutal budget cuts, *Brave New Waves* was no longer considered so far underneath managerial radar that it couldn't escape the axe. The full time staff of five, plus one part-timer, was slashed to the bare bones: host, producer and a part-time researcher. Bambury, feeling a 10-year itch and also seeing the writing on the wall, left the show to become a host of CBC-TV's *Midday* program, where he used his formidable interview skills on considerably more mainstream social and political subjects. *Midday* was cancelled in 2000, and it seems exceedingly strange that it was outlasted by *Brave New Waves*, which has flirted with death since the beginning; Augusta LaPaix once held a celebration for their first four months on the air.

"I left the show with extraordinarily mixed feelings," says Bambury. "I left at a time that I felt was probably too long if I wanted to have a career beyond it. That's part of the reason I left; it wasn't because I was tired of it.

When I left the program, it was at its strongest. Everything was in tune. I was constantly surprised by the elements we brought together and put on the program. That was very hard to walk away from. I miss it a great deal."

Patti Schmidt was Bambury's heir apparent for several reasons, primarily because she had occupied the host's chair in his absence on numerous occasions in the past. More importantly, she was able to multi-task under the new skeletal staff, juggling hosting duties with producing, researching and scripting. The nightly interviews were scrapped, replaced with one a week, and in the wake of the staff cuts, the quality of the writing also took a hit. Because of the new restraints, Schmidt faced a steep uphill climb: not only was she shouldering responsibility, but she had to stand up to audience expectations after the departure of a beloved host, with a show that was literally half of what it used to be.

"I had to face a lot of people who would come up to me personally and say, 'I stopped listening to the show when you took over,'" she admits. "It's so hard to carry on in the spectre of a show that I thought was so tight and brilliant the last couple of years that [Bambury] was there: well-curated profiles and interviews every day, because there was a separate booker for them. I don't have those resources at my disposal. It's basically a music show now, not a wider-reaching cultural show."

Another reason for the major shift in the show was generational. Schmidt approaches her playlist with a firm resolution to find new material that even other alternative media haven't discovered — especially electronic music and the avant-garde programming that comprises the latter half of the show. Three-chord punk and major label sponsored "alternative" music is easily dismissed, as is anything that could conceivably slip onto mainstream radio. You won't hear the next Sarah McLachlan or Rheostatics, but you will hear the next Kid Koala or Dinner is Ruined. Definitions of "cutting edge" music have changed considerably since 1984; what may have been marginal then is entirely commonplace now. Fans of the early *Brave New Waves* — if their tastes naturally became more conservative with age — might be hard pressed to recognize it as the same show. New material from venerable Canadian bands who once defined the program could easily be deemed too commercial or "normal" to fit into the show's present format — NoMeansNo being a noteworthy exception.

Yet in many ways, the show is fulfilling its original mandate. Schmidt says, "I was surprised when we went back over the footage from the first program, when Augusta set up exactly what she wanted to do with the show. She was saying things about underground music and doing stuff that no one else was doing. That hasn't changed, but the content underneath it has."

Today, there is a new generation of *Brave New Waves* fans who may never have heard the show during the years that boasted Bambury, a budget and a full staff. After a steep drop in ratings following the cuts, Schmidt's show has regained a sizeable audience that's as faithful as the first generation, and plays as vital a role in a corporate-dominated media. Still, the show could be even stronger if it was properly staffed, but a restoration of its original structure is highly unlikely.

Kevin Komoda laments the fact that the teamwork behind the original show was often overlooked. "There was an article around the time of the 10th anniversary that made everyone seem like a hero except the people who did all the work," he says. "The CBC also showed incredible neglect when it came to the people who really supported the show rather than just the host. Patti's an exception because she researches, she picks the music and she's the host. You need really talented people. Before, you basically had an actor. A lot of listeners never realized that there were two or three other people writing it, researching it and programming it. Wisdom was basically a one-man show, though, whereas *Brave New Waves* was intricate and political."

Despite adversity in the post-Bambury period, *Brave New Waves* has survived due largely to the diligence and faith of Patti Schmidt, who is a firm believer in the show's importance. Says Schmidt, "I think it's the most brilliant privilege in the world to play the kind of music we do and talk to the people we talk to, because I don't think enough people know about it or care."

If *Brave New Waves* had a team of people responsible for its success, *Night Lines* was the sole domain of David Wisdom. The show had originated in Winnipeg with producer Ross Porter and a short stint with first host Ron Robinson, followed by two years with Ralph Benmergui. Benmergui left in 1987 to become — like Bambury eight years later — the host of CBC-TV's *Midday*. When it was decided that the show would move to Vancouver, the choice of host seemed to fly in the face of conventional radio protocol. "When they wanted someone to do *Night Lines*," David Wisdom admits, "I was hired because I had the software more than the skills. I had a huge record collection. I've never done campus radio and I've never taken training in radio."

At the time, Wisdom was working as a producer on the Vicki Gabereau show. He had started his CBC career on the day Elvis died in 1977, working in the record library. "They didn't want to put stuff like the Sex Pistols in [the record library]," says Wisdom. "I remember at one point them saying, 'What's the point in putting this Devo record in? Nobody will be listening to it in two years' time.'"

When Wisdom assumed the hosting duties for *Night Lines*, he was suddenly responsible for programming up to seven hours of radio — Saturday's broadcast would air live between 10 p.m. and 5 a.m. — and realized that he had to broaden his horizons. "I wasn't sure what to do at the beginning. I tried to please everyone, and then I figured to hell with them — I'm just going to play the music I really like. I had a couple of campus radio guys telling me what I should be playing, pushing me in this direction of industrial and really hardcore goth bands that I really never liked, like Skinny Puppy and Front Line Assembly. They were saying that this was all the rage; bands from the United States such as Ministry were really big time. But I could never warm up to that. It took me a year and a half to settle in and really feel that the show was my own, and really feel that people did appreciate what I was playing, and that there was an audience for the kind of ideas I had: non-elitist, and a wide-ranging variety of music.

"I also knew I had to play a lot of Canadian music, and I didn't know a whole lot about Canadian music, so I went out and started listening to anything Canadian I could find. I was very Vancouver-centric. We always had an idea that Vancouver music was cooler than Toronto music. Toronto music had a certain kind of feeling that we thought was much more show biz, like Carole Pope. In the beginning of the early days of punk, when there were people like the Viletones, we thought, 'Oh, Toronto people have it wrong. We have DOA, Los Popularos and a much better music scene going on in Vancouver.'"

In his search for new Canadian artists, Wisdom discovered that a Montreal indie label held the answers to his quest. "I got into Og Records' *It Came From Canada* series. I can't tell you how important that series was," he gushes. "They had early cuts from the likes of Ray Condo and Cowboy Junkies, to the weird bands like the Supreme Bagg Team and Chris Houston's band. I became aware of a much wider range of music, and started to realize that everything was different from each other, but there was a similar sensibility to it. There was actually something of a Canadian sound, which had a sense of humour to it, like the Dik Van Dykes, who were loose and didn't take themselves too seriously. It wove around the record store people, too. Record stores are always really important in music scenes, and there were two here in Vancouver: Track Records and Quintessence, which later became Zulu. The guys who worked there were musicians and turned me on to a whole lot of stuff. I remember going into Track Records, and the guy behind the counter said, 'Hey, we just got onto this Og compilation.' He was in the Zamboni Drivers, and this was just a guy down the street. I thought, 'This is great, the guy down the street just got on this fabulous *It Came From Canada.*'"

One of the most integral elements of *Night Lines'* appeal was its ability to make the listener feel like a part of a community. *Brave New Waves* was much more professional and occasionally professorial, whereas *Night Lines* simply sounded like a bunch of nerdy record geeks hanging out at home on the weekend. Wisdom relied on his audience to help create the atmosphere of the show, with the help of an answering machine. "What really opened my eyes to the regions across Canada was when I opened the phone lines up and took calls," he says. "I would ask the listeners to not just request something, but they had to answer a skill-testing question as well: recite a poem they just made up, tell a joke or answer a tough question or something. It was amusing, but I'd also learn a whole lot about what was going on in different cities by what they'd request. Then I'd go out and try to find it. For the most part, it was pretty good, and then I'd fill out my playlists to that kind of stuff."

The response was overwhelming, and Wisdom's limited technology of the day couldn't keep up. "It was so big that I had to shut it down after a few years because I just couldn't keep up with it," he says. "I would put in a 90-minute tape, because this was done before any digital equipment, and it was just an answering machine with a cassette running around. I'd have to come down in the middle of the night to turn the tape over. It was always filled. It broke a lot. And sometimes it 'broke' just because I couldn't face listening to hours of phone calls! But it was great, and it was part of what made the show really interesting." Some of the repeat callers, like Vicki from Surrey and Gilbert from Transcona, would be as integral to the show as Wisdom's regular weekly feature, "10 Singles in Alphabetical Order," taken from his collection of thousands of 45s.

Wisdom also invited the audience to write theme songs for the program, inspiring four-track weirdos from across the country to submit their work, such as Norm from Richmond. The most prolific *Night Lines* composers were the Ween-ish Maurice Pooby from Cortez Island and a woman named Eve Rice, from Winnipeg, who also fronted a band called Vav Jungle. More well-known bands also recorded material exclusively for *Night Lines*, when

the show picked up on *Brave New Waves'* lead and started recording sessions at the CBC Vancouver studio in 1991. Between then and the show's
demise in 1997, over 60 bands were captured; the last session was with the
Rheostatics, which aired on the show's final broadcast on August 30, 1997,
and was later released on DROG records. They became the band that started
the *Brave New Waves* sessions, and closed the *Night Lines* sessions. "I loved
that," enthuses Wisdom, who had been one of the Rheostatics' biggest champions since their debut album. "They were the first ones I wanted to do a
session with [in 1991]. Basically, they were in Toronto; it was and still is
very hard to get technicians at the CBC to record bands there. It's almost
impossible. But the Rheos one couldn't have been better. They even had a
song called 'The Pooby Song' and everything. The session made me think
that [*Night Lines*] had a purpose to it and had been worthwhile and was a
part of something going on in Canadian music."

In the spring of 1997, CBC brass decided that *Night Lines* had become
static and stuffy and had run its course. It was a time when the corporation was once again becoming paranoid about not capturing a younger
audience, which had led to the creation of an innovative program called
RealTime in 1995. *RealTime* was broadcast live across the country before
Night Lines every Friday and Saturday evening, dropping out of time zones
as the night went on for a grand total of eight hours a night. Hosted by
Leora Kornfeld and the seat of her pants, the show was truly pan-Canadian,
extremely eclectic, very pro-indie, light-hearted and ahead of its time for
its incorporation of internet technology. But in a short-sighted decision, the
CBC canned both it and *Night Lines* at the same time to create *Radio Sonic*,
hosted by the oil-and-water mixture of the young, perky Kornfeld and the
older, quirky Wisdom. Kornfeld left after two years, and the show soon
became a modified version of *Night Lines*, with a bit of a magazine format,
more concessions made to trends, and less personality. The former *Night
Lines* slot was succeeded by *Radio Escapade*, an open-format underground
music show with rotating hosts.

At such a self-conscious institution as the CBC, perhaps it's surprising that
Night Lines lasted as long as it did. "*Brave New Waves* and to a lesser degree
Night Lines were considered just way, way out there," says Wisdom. "*Brave
New Waves* got away with it earlier because it had a certain academic cachet.
They played what was considered art music. It had a more serious tone to
it. I sort of slipped through the cracks for ten years. They knew I was there;
they knew I was getting good response. Basically, nobody said a word to me
for ten years. They just let me do it. It was the best job I ever had.

"There was — and still is — resistance to the fact that there is such a thing as what they consider pop music on the CBC," he continues. "There are still producers here who think it's killing the CBC and don't understand why it's on."

Augusta LaPaix argues that outside of the rebel chic of subverting the public broadcaster, the late-night shows were also very much a part of the CBC's raison d'être. "Yes, we liked the idea of being rebels in the CBC. But it wasn't rebellious for its own sake or to be cool. It was to do something exciting and in touch with our times. Which — last time I read the CBC mandate — is what we're supposed to do: present stuff that doesn't get presented by others. It's very much a part of our role in an institution that has survived through the years."

For a generation of listeners, Wisdom and Bambury were the two most trusted broadcasters in Canada — not just for their playlists, but because of the unique combination of the late-night time slot, the national scope and the intimacy of radio. "Because [*Brave New Waves* is] on at such an odd hour, we strive to be eclectic to the point of being absurd," said Bambury in 1995. "It does mean that the people who listen to it are a really special breed. When people tell me that they're a really big fan and I find out they're talking about radio and not television, I always feel so much kinder towards them, so much better about it."

David Wisdom sighs, "Whenever I'm somewhere where people talk to me and say, 'Oh, I really like you on the radio,' they never talk to me about *RadioSonic*. They always go back to *Night Lines*. And I appreciate that; I think it was a real show and it had a real personality. When you're broadcasting in the middle of the night, you get people who really do listen and really do care about music, other than casual listeners who might just have it on in the car. The time of the night is really important for that. I do think we played the best music available and found new stuff that other radio stations would never, never broadcast."

Of course, the CBC was not the only game in town, merely the most professional. In the late '70s, radio stations had begun to pop up on university and college campuses, mostly closed-circuit or cable affairs that sometimes didn't broadcast beyond the campus cafeterias. But as they came into their own in the mid-'80s, suddenly a network for underground and alternative music was in place for any band touring the country. Powered by dedicated volunteers and funded by small levies on student bodies, campus radio stations offered their programmers and listeners exposure to a wide world of music, making it accessible to the local community and providing an alternative to corporate rock radio.

Much of the demand for campus radio was created in the wake of punk, when a flurry of new music was being released that didn't fit into the homogenized mainstream culture of the day. Some stations tried to adapt to the new alternative culture, like Montreal's CHOM-FM. "They were jumping on the next big thing, punk," says Kevin Komoda. "CHOM later retracted, said the whole punk explosion was a mistake and headed down a corporate programming lane. They refused to play the new popular U.K. groups and stuck to Pink Floyd and Kate Bush." CHOM's retraction caused a stir and led to several "I Hate CHOM" protest gigs. They were the last station in town to add hometown heroes Men Without Hats to their playlist — deeming them too new wave — and a decade later would also be the last to embrace Nirvana.

The history of campus radio in Canada dates back to 1950, when the University of British Columbia's Radio Club started broadcasting on a closed-circuit system to the campus residences. There wasn't much progression for the next twenty-five years, at which point the CRTC modified its FM radio policy to license campus and community radio onto the FM band. CKCU at Carleton University in Ottawa was the first to obtain such a license and started broadcasting on the FM band on November 14, 1975; their first song was Joni Mitchell's "You Turn Me On I'm a Radio." Slowly, a crop of other 50-watt stations started popping up in Southern Ontario, including Waterloo's CKMS (1977), Hamilton's CFMU (1977), Guelph's CFRU (1979), and London's CHRW (1981). In 1981, the first meeting of the National Campus/Community Radio Association was held in Ottawa. One of the items on the agenda was the Toronto Campus FM Project, which proposed a license for a station jointly run by the University of Toronto, Ryerson, and York. Ryerson's CKLN had been on cable since 1980, and would eventually get the license and move to FM in July 1984 with a whopping 14 watts. Obviously, campus radio was not being driven by universities in the larger urban centres.

Toronto was a bit of a different scenario, however. In the late '70s, CFNY started broadcasting from a suburban strip mall in Brampton, Ontario, with a format that founder Dave Marsden dubbed "The Spirit of Radio" and a playlist that whole-heartedly endorsed punk and new wave. More specifically, CFNY supported practically anything British. In an attempt to fill their CanCon quotas, they opened the airwaves to a lot of independent music, daring to put adventurous indie cassettes into rotation and giving major breaks to worthy acts like Jane Siberry, the Diodes, Scott Merritt and The Spoons, making them the only corporate station in Canada willing to do so. In North America, only KROQ in Los Angeles was considered as progressive. CFNY also boasted speciality shows dedicated to blues and reggae.

Daniel Richler, a Toronto television journalist, says, "During David Marsden's tenure, CFNY had been a heavy driver of alternative music, particularly in the club and dance vein. That was pretty avant-garde. I know that people in Vancouver didn't enjoy the same privilege, and CHOM in Montreal had abandoned that. After Marsden left, CFNY went through some fallow years. But I think they still need to be credited for fuelling an alternative consciousness among Toronto music lovers. That being said, I wouldn't give full credit for that to anybody except for CKLN and [the University of Toronto's] CIUT."

As the '80s marched on, such was CFNY's Anglophilia that most of the local or Canadian acts they played were merely aping British forms. Until The Cult released their comedic cock rock *Electric* album in 1987, the synth-obsessed CFNY seemed to have a pathological fear of guitar-driven rock, outside of early corporate-approved punk like The Clash and obvious U.K. candidates like U2, The Smiths and The Cure. Much of the Canadian music they chose to celebrate in the early days had more to do with fashion than quality. This would change near the end of the '80s, when the station hosted Canada Day concerts at Molson Park in Barrie. The shows featured consistently strong all-Canadian line-ups and an affordable ticket price. During the Lollapaloozification of alternative music in the early '90s, CFNY conveniently atoned for past sins by championing a diverse array of new music in its regular programming, but particularly during Dave Bookman's *Indie Hour*, and Kim Hughes's *Live In Toronto*.

But before the advent of campus radio and the CBC's foray into alternative programming, CFNY was the only source when it came to anti-dinosaur new music in Toronto. James Booth was a local musician and one-time manager of pioneering DIY Toronto band L'Etranger, who found himself employed as assistant music director at CFNY between 1983 and 1985. He was excited by the station's support of independent music, especially the program *Streets of Ontario*, which held an annual talent contest and pressed an album of the winners. "At first I thought, this is incredible, this is the place where I've always wanted to be," says Booth. "But it didn't take long after working there full time for me to realize how screwed up this place was. There were a lot of decisions being made about the programming that went against my image of CFNY as a fan. There was still Liz Janik and Peter

Goodwin doing *Streets Of Ontario*, and they were the two people who every week put their asses on the line and really went out and totally supported the local music community, but they were the only two people that were interested in that.

"I went in there as someone who was involved in that music community. You always think when you go somewhere that you're going to make things even better because you're so into it. I was also into all these other kinds of music that weren't being reflected on CFNY anymore; it was becoming this British disco/pop kind of station, with all these novelty hits from England. I thought I was someone who was really into the kinds of things that CFNY should be doing, and it was this constant battle. Never mind the Canadian stuff, I was looking at all these other bands like Rank & File and The Blasters and X, and they were just not interested in playing them at all."

On April Fool's Day, 1982, campus radio made its first venture into one of Canada's major urban centres when UBC's CITR moved from cable to a 49-watt mono FM frequency; their first song was Martha and the Vandellas' "Dancing in the Streets." At that time, they also launched their *Discorder* magazine, which would become a widely acclaimed and crucial source for information about underground music in Vancouver. Halifax's CKDU took to the airwaves in 1985, and Montreal's CKUT in 1987; Winnipeg would have an astonishingly long wait, until 1999. When CITR got a power boost to 1800 watts in February 1989, making it available to greater Vancouver, the first song they played was Slow's "Have Not Been The Same."

Some of the core staff and volunteers in the late '80s at CITR included Bill Baker, Randy Iwata, his sister Robynn Iwata and Lisa Marr. The two men would later start Mint Records; the two women would form Mint's flagship band Cub. Baker went to UBC for a degree in English literature, but it was his time at CITR that shaped his life and became his defining education. "Today, the university experience has been homogenized to the point where you go to school, learn the school part and get the fuck out of there and get a job," says Baker. "Randy and I could have cared less about what we learned in school, but what we did learn was all about music and the business of music from working at the radio station. The time we spent at the radio station is what benefited us, not what we did at school. There were so many times that I'd go to school for an 8:30 class, zip into the radio station for half an hour and spend the whole day there. At the time I'd think, 'Oh god, I'm blowing it by skipping classes.'" The ever-modest Canadian indie label mogul pauses, laughs, and says, "Then again, you could look at me now and say, 'Yeah, look what happened — you should have gone to classes, you bum! You'd have a real job!'"

Robynn Iwata, who today is an occasional host on CBC's *Radio Escapade*, started volunteering at CITR when she was 16, tagging along while her brother hosted a show. Throughout the next eight years she held several positions, including station manager, music director and *Discorder* art director, as well as coordinating the influential CITR-sponsored local talent competition, Shindig. "It exposed me to so much music in general," says Iwata, who says her musical pursuits in Cub and I Am Spoonbender can be attributed to her campus radio exposure to the Fastbacks, Beat Happening, Images in Vogue and Brian Eno. "It was quite shocking at first, just how much music would come in daily to CITR. A lot of the time, because campus radio usually has such low power compared to other commercial stations on the dial, it's hard to know if anyone's listening. But the coolest, best thing that campus radio can do is actively seek out new obscure music and information to share with the listeners, and not just rely on what promos show up in the mailbox."

Tom Metuzals, who later became a CBC producer and publicist for Perimeter Records in Halifax, grew up in Ottawa listening to CKCU, and would work at Canada's first bilingual campus station, CHUO at the University of Ottawa. "It was informative and informal," says Metuzals. "Suddenly I was finding out about music from peers and freaks: obsessive collectors who knew considerably more than I did. That was invigorating. I also listened to Top 40 radio, and CBC always played in our house, but there was something adventurous and exciting about the campus radio in Ottawa, something I could call mine. I discovered music from Africa, Australia, France — stuff I would have never heard elsewhere. CHUO was a breeding ground for kids looking for stuff to define themselves. A portion of my identity came from these bands, and by having a community around it, the station provided me with a social circle and structure. That place was not only my vocabulary, it was my daily bread."

King Cobb Steelie's Kevin Lynn lived in Edmonton between 1985 and 1987, where he attended numerous shows presented by the University of Alberta station, CJSR, including a NoMeansNo concert that changed his own approach to bass playing. When he moved to Guelph, Ontario, in 1988, Lynn started volunteering at CFRU and hosted a show there for the next seven years, as well as serving on staff as music coordinator. Comparing the two stations, Lynn says, "Guelph is a smaller community, and all the progressive stuff is centred on the university, so CFRU had a more central role than CJSR. CJSR would serve the U of A students, but not a lot of other people. You could get it all over the city, but it was pretty university-based. The difference with CFRU was that there were a lot of volunteers who weren't necessarily students, so there was a wider base of DJS, volunteers and listeners. It wasn't just a campus station; CFRU was totally central to what was going on. Lots of different bands played in Guelph as a result of CFRU, like Dinosaur Jr., fIREHOSE and lots of hardcore."

"It was and is very important, but when you're working at a campus radio station, it can be a bit insular," says Iwata. "It is its own little world." Campus radio's strongest effect was often on the local music community, which suddenly had a forum where their cassettes and 7" singles could be played. It would also be instrumental in promoting shows by local and travelling bands; often the station's staff would be booking the shows. "A large part of the Ottawa music community wouldn't have existed without community radio," says Metuzals. "The Ottawa club scene — the Roxy, the Rotters, the Underground — survived in part due to the support of the DJS on CKCU and CHUO. It was an important cycle: the clubs brought in the bands, which stimulated the radio stations to play the music, which in turn exposed more people to new music, which manifested itself in great local bands."

Lynn credits his time at campus radio with shaping the electronic and dub-influenced brand of rock he makes in King Cobb Steelie, one of the first Canadian bands to utilize a turntable on stage — although John Oswald claims to have been doing so in 1964. "There's a complete diversity of music [at campus radio] that people can play and listen to," says Lynn. "I was totally into Black Flag and the Minutemen and the pre-grunge years, but at CFRU people were also playing underground hip-hop and the dub stuff. The crossover of genres there definitely affected the music I started making. There would still be *Brave New Waves*, but you could never have access to [that kind of music] the way you can at a community radio station. You don't even have to be a DJ; you could work in the music library and listen to records all day and help to sort them. I found so many records that I would otherwise never in a million years be able to touch, let alone listen to. Without community radio, my whole world would be completely different. I'd probably be playing heavy metal!"

At Ryerson's CKLN in Toronto, there were shows by plenty of local personalities sharing their formative obsessions on air: Handsome Ned would spin traditional and neo-traditional country, Jaymz Bee would play vinyl recordings of '60s celebrities attempting to sing, Jeff Healey would play vintage jazz 78s and Grammy-winning musicologist Rob Bowman and drummer Andy Stochansky also had shows. "It was really awesome," says musician Kurt Swinghammer, who designed the station's logos and graphics in the late '80s. "There were a lot of really powerful people affiliated with the station at that period, and adventurous people who had amazing shows. It didn't have a political agenda that seems to dominate now. Maybe because it was new, people didn't realize that they could use it for their personal agenda, and they just played all this crazy music that no one was touching."

The best campus programming gave exposure to obscure new material, as well as providing history lessons about music that was in danger of being forgotten. In his autobiography, industry pariah Stompin' Tom Connors cites the support of campus radio in the '80s as one of the reasons he was enticed out of self-imposed exile. Dave Bidini tells a story about a 1998 incident at CJSW in Calgary during a fundraising drive. "A guy was on the radio one night playing electronica music mixed in with a Charlie Brown record, when the phone rang in the DJ booth," relays Bidini. "The caller asked, 'Can you play some Stompin' Tom?' The guy said, 'Yeah, I'm doing this thing right now, but I'll get to it in about 20 minutes.' So he finished his set, and then he played a bunch of Stompin' Tom songs. The phone rang again, and the guy said, 'Thanks a lot man, it was great hearing that Stompin' Tom. I got someone here who wants to talk to you.' It was Tom. He and his road manager were sitting in their Calgary hotel room; they got the numbers of every radio station in town, and CJSW was the only radio station that would play Stompin' Tom."

There's no question that campus radio is an acquired taste, and one that requires tolerant and attentive listeners. Because of its erratic programming — where a Mandarin-language program is followed by a blues program, followed by a hardcore punk show and then hip-hop — many potential listeners get turned off. Seeking out favourite campus shows is no more of a crap shoot than seeking quality television. People don't watch one television station exclusively every day expecting to see their favourite drama; they check the TV guide. Yet most music fans aren't willing to learn about schedules in radio, and give up on a campus station if all they ever hear at a random moment is an hour of speed metal, dancehall reggae or spoken-word programming.

Even among sympathetic listeners, there is also a frustration with the inherently amateur nature of campus/community radio, which by definition is a training ground with a high turnover. Richard Flohil laments, "There's no question it had a big impact and continues to do so. However, I have to say that I find most campus radio appalling. Most of their DJs are lame, they can't talk. What a shame. They're disorganized, their record library has been stolen, nobody's out selling what limited advertising they can sell to keep some money coming in, the equipment doesn't work, and so the audience diminishes and doesn't become as supportive as they ought to — mainly because the quality of it is so shit.

"It obviously had a positive impact, because it was a place where you could promote a degree of musical diversity," continues Flohil. "The programming did allow people to come to different kinds of music. Unfortunately, most of it got mixed up with left-wing politics, which affects the programming. I understand why in corporate culture we should have a voice of dissent, but it certainly does distract from the music. It did make a difference, though. There are committed programmers who care about it, just sometimes they're not very good at explaining why."

Kevin Lynn says, "The downfall for me is always the casual radio voice, the slacker attitude and apparent lack of enthusiasm. And politics certainly got in the way of how the staff was getting along, but I don't know if it affected what went on the air. I remember staff meetings where everybody was sitting around and 'visioning' — someone would break out the crayons and we'd all have to draw how we were feeling that morning. That's the kind of stuff that would happen at campus radio, because Guelph traditionally has a hippie hangover mentality that's in many of the community-based organizations. A lot of it is healthy, but it does get pretty funny sometimes."

Tom Metuzals is also disappointed with its current state, where the all-important open format shows have ceded airspace to specialty shows with a narrow genre focus. "In some ways — maybe just for me or people my age — campus radio is becoming rapidly less relevant and more juvenile," he says. "It's disappointing to go back to Ottawa and listen to campus radio. Even here in Halifax the general music programs are not very informative, the DJs spout clichés and song titles, giving me nothing to learn. And they sound juvenile — I don't remember it that way. It was fun, but we tried to inform as well. I used to love listening to the general music shows; it broadened my musical horizons. Now, little resonates with me, and I have to search out the specialty music shows in order to be satiated. I guess I'm getting older."

Regardless of whether or not stations have improved or declined — and one's opinion on the matter is often dictated by one's age and distance from post-secondary education life — campus radio remains vital for music fans and musicians. "It's of crucial importance," says Mint Records' Bill Baker. "Without CBC or campus stations, I don't think we'd ever get any airplay, let alone the incredible support that we did, beginning with *Night Lines.*

I'd say campus radio, as it relates to Mint, represents 90 per cent of our total airplay."

Seeking out CBC specialty shows and campus stations is the obsession of a select few. Most young Canadians either don't know those outlets exist, or they might not have access to them depending on their communities. For the large group of music fans who won't stray from their television sets for new information, the dawn of MuchMusic permanently altered the land-scape of mainstream Canadian music, with a few temporary gains for the underground as well.

Before MuchMusic, there was a national CBC after-school program called *Video Hits*, and in the Toronto market, CITY-TV had *Toronto Rocks*, which featured any local indie band with a video alongside Duran Duran. Toronto critic Howard Druckman recalls, "It was open enough that I once saw a video of a band on *Toronto Rocks*, I can't even remember their name, and it was these three puds from [Toronto suburb] Don Mills. The song went: 'Don Mills is dead! Don Mills is dead!' The video was just this grainy, super-8 colour thing of this band standing in front of various malls and gas stations and stuff in Don Mills. I was flabbergasted, I thought this was great. If that can get through on television, even locally, that's fantastic. It was sub-Ramones crud, but it was great sub-Ramones crud, you know? That was very encouraging."

Moses Znaimer is the media mogul who started CITY-TV in Toronto in the early '70s with the slogan "News, Movies, Music," and a mission to fully reflect the city's diversity, creativity and absurdity — many *SCTV* sketches parodied CITY-TV's early programming. Znaimer created MuchMusic in 1984 when the cable universe had just begun to expand. Because of protectionist Canadian content regulations, the wildly successful U.S. music station MTV was not available in Canada except with a satellite dish; a situation that continues to this day. And because MuchMusic was allowed to grow in a vacuum, it developed its own innovative style that today MTV is trying to emulate. In 1984, no one in Canada had any idea what a 24-hour music network would be like.

"It was more of a rec room than a TV station," says Daniel Richler, who co-hosted and produced the groundbreaking CITY-TV/MuchMusic show *The New Music* with Laurie Brown between 1983 and 1986. "I've seen a lot of American music shows, and they're all so synthetic they make me want to puke. Under Moses, the emphasis was always on a real personality. At that time, Americans on television mistrusted that. At MuchMusic, there was much more respect for a knee-jerk anti-establishment [mentality]. If we were in direct competition [with MTV], we would have jacked that up further. I think the instinct here would have been: 'How can we make this more personal and more unruly? How can we play our weaknesses as our strengths?' The weaknesses being that we didn't have the production values. Granted, MuchMusic soon started doing *Big Ticket* [concert presentations] and awards shows, but we never had the same kind of cash that MTV did. So we would have had to rely on imagination."

However, some rules were imposed by their broadcast license. In its first year of operation, because of the fledgling nature of the music video medium, MuchMusic was obliged to play only 10 per cent Canadian content, increasing to 30 per cent in their third and subsequent years. It was also to donate 2.4 per cent of overall profits, or a minimum of $100,000 annually to VideoFact, a grant program for Canadian music videos. A 1984 article in *Graffiti* magazine noted: "MuchMusic is obliged to play only ten per cent Canadian content in its first year, and although Znaimer has promised more well-rounded fare than the tunnel-visioned MTV presents, the fact is there just isn't that much decent, innovative video programming yet. MuchMusic will, of course, provide quite a stimulus for Canadian performers. MuchMusic will be crying, indeed *begging*, for Canadian content."

Daniel Richler recalls, "MuchMusic had to come up with a certain amount of CanCon, and that forced them to play less commercial bands at the time because there was still such a paucity of Canadian material on video." *The New Music* helped rectify that situation. "I quickly saw that there were new and alternative bands in Canada that did not have major record company support and could not afford to make their own videos, and therefore needed us to come to their concerts and make our own video," he continues. "A lot of that video concert footage that *The New Music* had been recording for years formed much of the ballast and substance of the music library that MuchMusic dipped into. We never thought we had to deliberately support the alternative scene on some kind of principle; it was simply a matter of inclination, and necessity."

On MuchMusic's fifth anniversary in 1989, original station manager John Martin told an interviewer, "It drives people crazy, but we like to play 30 per cent CanCon. There aren't any radio stations in the country that can afford to play that much. They are in a market with 20 other stations and they have to be real good at what they do in order to succeed. Fortunately, we're not in the same situation, so we can afford to do the massive philosophical things, like playing more Canadian music, without worrying about the guy down the block and what he's up to."

James Booth was hired at MuchMusic in 1985, shortly after his discouraging stint at CFNY, and found the freedom he had longed for in radio. "It was still a fairly new place," he says. "They were scrambling for programming and there was the opportunity for independent acts to get their videos played. A lot of what Much was going to be about was still being defined at that point. I pretty much got the opportunity to create my own job. I initially went in doing their music information stuff, since I was a person who knew a hell of a lot about music. But along with that I got to be a producer, and I went in thinking there should really be a show like [CFNY's] *Streets Of Ontario* that highlights all the independent bands from across the country. Some of them aren't getting played just because people in Toronto don't know who they are. I suggested the idea, and they said, sure, do it."

The show was called *Indie Street*, and after a brief stint for Booth in front of the camera, it was hosted by the more telegenic Erica Ehm. "The weird thing is that I went into CFNY with certain ideas and they basically got shot down before you even got started," says Booth. "At Much, where I thought I'd have to jump through hoops just to get anything to happen, I suggested an idea and they said, 'Great, let's see what it looks like.' I sat down with another producer, and basically the show as I envisioned it went on the air. The place where you'd it expect it to be the most restrictive was the most free."

Independent artists on MuchMusic weren't just ghettoized to *Indie Street*, but often slipped into regular programming. Suddenly there was a popular national medium available to artists who wouldn't make it past the lobby of a corporate radio station, and making a bigger impact because of the nature of video. Says Booth, who worked at MuchMusic until 1994, "After working at Much and talking to a lot of bands, the difference between radio and video is [that with video] you don't need a lot of plays to make an impact. With radio you need to have a record played over and over again, for people to remember it in the same sort of way. People can see a video once or twice and say, 'Yeah, I remember how the song goes.' Remembering the visuals helps you remember the song as well.

"Deja Voodoo did a couple of small videos that didn't cost them a lot of money, and being the person who would have programmed them, I remember that I wouldn't have played them more than two or three times. Around then Deja Voodoo did a cross-Canada tour and I was talking to [singer/guitarist] Gerard [Van Herk] after they came back. He said, 'It was amazing. You guys must have played the video a lot because everywhere we went there were all these people who came out to the show and that was the song they were shouting for.' He knew it wasn't from getting played on the radio; it was from a very limited amount of airtime on MuchMusic. I don't even know if I admitted to him how few times it actually got played. There were a lot of bands who were in the same place and discovered that when they went to do a cross-Canada tour, [MuchMusic exposure] would have been one of the things that actually helped bring people out. But it also tells you that in all those little towns, there isn't radio that's playing those kinds of things. It makes you think of how many people there are across Canada who are looking for a different kind of music, something that's uniquely theirs that isn't getting played on the radio."

MuchMusic would become a factor in breaking indie or uncategorizable acts onto radio, such as k.d. lang, Jane Siberry, Blue Rodeo and in the '90s, Moist. In the latter's case, a solid visual could launch a career more easily than a good song. If both elements aligned, the result was inevitable. "Easily the biggest indie breakthrough, and it's probably still true now, is The Pursuit of Happiness video for 'I'm An Adult Now,'" says Booth.

The song hadn't even been pressed to vinyl or cassette when the video became a hit across the country. TPOH's Moe Berg recalls the humble beginnings of their breakthrough: "We had this friend, Lou Guira, who's a film director now, and when he heard about the band, he immediately offered to do a video. I played him the demos and asked him which song would be the best to use and he picked 'I'm An Adult Now.' When it was done we took it over to MuchMusic, really clueless, and handed it to them thinking they might play it on [the late-night alternative show] *CityLimits*. We were really lucky, because this was a time when MuchMusic's programming policy was kind of loose."

When the band went on their first Canadian tour, they received a phone call in Winnipeg telling them the video had gone into rotation. "Whenever we got to a bar, we'd put on MuchMusic right away hoping we'd see it, but I think we only saw it once that whole tour," says Berg. "When we got back to Toronto, we had a show at the Rivoli that I'd worked really hard to set up — the bar was giving me a real hard time. We got to the show that night, and the bar was jam-packed, and it was clear that they were all there to see us. That's when we realized this video really meant something. I went to a Smiths concert right after that, and people said, 'Hey, you're that guy in the video,' and they kept asking where they could get the record. That's when we made the single. There was so little planning that went into it. We borrowed money from our parents, and friends of ours designed the jacket. It was totally by the seat of our pants."

"It was shot for very little money," says Booth, "but it was a great song and the video itself is just a cool little storyline that really works for it. You can be cynical and think to do something like that you need to have a marketing team pushing it but that was one that was just a total grassroots thing. People liked the video and it went into rotation, then got bumped up and played all the time, and probably still gets played every so often as sort of a golden oldie. It pretty much made their career in a sense; it helped them get signed and helped them become a big Canadian band at that point in time."

MuchMusic allowed Canadian youth to see reflections of themselves in their compatriot musicians, which did a lot to increase the importance of Canadian celebrity. Videos made Canadian musicians look much more interesting than they were previously perceived to be. "When I was a kid, I had an uneasy feeling that a lot of Canadian bands were cheezy," says Daniel Richler. "I never thought that April Wine were hard rockin'. Overall, there was a parochial self-consciousness that I suffered from, which told me that if someone was from down the street, they were uncool. It's how I felt about CITY-TV's early years, as well. When you see yourself reflected and you're that badly dressed and that stupid, you can't believe that's real life — let alone cool! So you rail against it, instead of trying to fix yourself up. I felt that way about a lot of local Canadian rock-'n'-roll.

"But when videos came out, the impression that they made on the next generation was that Canadian bands could be as mythical as any other. It increased the distance between us and the kids down the block. It allowed them to step into a cinematic dimension. Bruce Cockburn could play guitar like nobody else, but he was a very ordinary guy. But when you saw videos of him in Nicaragua and globetrotting, doing the things he did, that gave him this mythic aura. That also happened for a great many artists that people had never heard of before.

"Videos on television gave an almost hysterical visibility to Canadian pop," Richler continues. "*I* was chased down the street on numerous occasions, just because I was the nearest thing to a real celebrity! They couldn't get somebody from Duran Duran, but they'd yell, 'There's Daniel Richler!' I could see in their eyes the look of mad animals, these teenage girls were frothing. I would sign autographs when I'd be cornered in the alley behind Maple Leaf Gardens. I'd go home and think that when the hysteria dies down and this girl goes to her suburban bedroom and looks at the bus transfer where I scrawled my autograph, she was going to say, 'What the fuck is this? What came over me?' But that's what the video medium did.

It turned everybody into gods. It really gave a new desirable and juicy visibility to the music scene, so even dolts like me were recognized."

At some point in the early '90s, MuchMusic started to realize the enormous effect it was having on the youth market specifically, and began capitalizing on it and catering to it exclusively. Richler argues that this had less to do with shifts in musical taste than it did a corporate concern over children being exposed to alternative or less comfortable viewpoints. "The pressures began not so much with music as morality," says Richler. "Over the years, as MuchMusic aimed itself more specifically towards young people, they found themselves under tremendous pressure to sanitize and corporatize. At the same time, the music industry was growing more corporate and suddenly everybody had a concern. That meant the wild experiments of yore weren't as acceptable. It all comes with corporate desire. The moment that MuchMusic started doing contests with Hostess potato chips, there was a responsibility to children that went with it. Year by year, what was eroded at MuchMusic was the sense that rock-'n'-roll is for grown-ups. Alternative music in particular requires more sophistication; it requires having gone *through* teeny-bop pop. You don't become alternative until you've gone through something that it's alternative to, so it is by definition an older music style.

"The corporate process happened so fast that I don't think anybody knew what hit them. Suddenly a dinky little video put together by a Canadian down the street couldn't compete in its appearance, and television lost its affection for that stuff. Charming amateurism didn't cut it."

On MuchMusic, most strains of indie rock have been cast by the wayside, although the station's original independent spirit still holds true for burgeoning hip-hop and R&B acts on independent labels, true to the dominant trends of the day. Most indie rock bands have given up making videos that cost as much as their album did. "To spend $10–15,000 on something that gets one play on MuchMusic on their indie spotlight, that's tough to justify," says Kurt Swinghammer, who directed award-winning videos for Maestro Fresh Wes and indie act the Shuffle Demons in the late '80s. "There is life outside of Much. I'm surprised there hasn't been more of a grassroots approach to that. There's a Rogers Cable channel in every community in Canada, and often you do see some weird video that they're using to fill time. Certainly there should be the same incentive that drew people to CKLN: let's create a slot every day for an hour of independent video. Because it's irrelevant what station people are watching; they're constantly flipping, so it doesn't matter if you're on MuchMusic or Rogers."

Innovative programming remains on Sook-Yin Lee's *The Wedge*, although her show was cut from once a day to once a week. Nonetheless, indie labels like Mint are still thankful for MuchMusic's current support, however minimal. "I'm down with MuchMusic," says Mint's Bill Baker, "because I've never encountered a media outlet of that size that is as accessible and hands-on as they are. When we call MTV, we can't get our calls returned. Even [American punk label and Mint business partner] Lookout can't get calls back from MTV. But at MuchMusic, we'll send a video to them and I'll have someone's direct phone line and I can say, 'What did you think of the Maow video?' And they know what it is and they'll tell you. They do a great job. I wish they'd play our videos more, but the way they choose not to is a way I respect."

Today, MuchMusic has become as homogenous as any other mainstream outlet, with a predominant focus on teen pop. Kevin Komoda argues, "Like anything, whether it was mainstream radio like CHOM-FM or MuchMusic, when you first start out, it's an anything-goes policy. If it succeeds, it becomes an institution and becomes regulated. Eventually it becomes subjected to playlists and/or a formula. Even *Brave New Waves* is subject to that."

"Capitalism is killing music," read a slogan on the cover of a 1988 Billy Bragg album. Bragg may have been playing the role of the smug socialist. But one only has to look at the bland carbon copy "modern rock" station that CFNY became in the mid-'90s, and compare it to the flurry of creative music fostered by the CBC and campus radio; furthermore, one can look at what happened when MuchMusic, fostered by protectionist legislation, stopped pushing boundaries and started focusing on the best way to make the most money instead. Witnessing the creative effects of the commercial alternative to interventionist practices — practices that remain the scourge of capitalist libertarianism — Bragg had a point.

> "The world woke up one day to proclaim/ thou
> shalt not take part in or make bad art/ in
> these tough, tough times/ friends like mine
> would rather dash than dine/ on the bones of
> what's thrown to them."
> – Destroyer, "The Bad Arts," 2001

Glittering Prizes and Endless Compromises

The primary capitalist catalyst in the music industry, during this and any other period, is the record labels. The CanRock Renaissance was a time when major labels were far more receptive to signing non-commercial or unknown artists, sometimes even granting them their own label imprint. It was also a time when independent labels exposed many of the period's most creatively fertile artists. These changes in the music business have their roots in earlier chapters of Canadian rock, but in the '90s, they flourished.

Jeff Rogers, who managed The Pursuit of Happiness and started Handsome Boy Records, says, "Look at The Guess Who and [their manager] Jack Richardson — he mortgaged his house to put out their first record. If you look back through Canadian history at all those records, they're all on indie labels — or lots of them are. Because nobody would sign Canadian acts. They were all born out of the same thing as Handsome Boy or [Sloan's] Murder. I remember when Nettwerk first started, looking at their first sampler and being amazed at the artwork, thinking that it looked better than any major label album cover."

In 1985, there were three significant national independent labels: Fringe, Cargo and Og. Fringe, based out of a Toronto store called The Record Peddler, dealt mostly with local acts and became renowned for releasing a contro-versial album by the Dayglo Abortions from Victoria. Mostly, though, it was a distributor, as was Montreal's Cargo. Og Records, also based in Montreal, instigated a national network of bands through the *It Came From Canada* compilations, and created a DIY business model for the flood of indie labels that would flourish in the early '90s. Og was operated by the sludgeabilly duo Deja Voodoo, comprised of guitarist Gerard Van Herk and drummer Tony Dewald. Whether through intuitive know-how or sheer accident, Deja Voodoo and Og Records were at the centre of the Canadian independent scene.

Gerard Van Herk (left) and Tony Dewald (right) of Deja Voodoo
(Photo by Derek Sheplaw)

In 1982, the burgeoning National Campus/Community Radio Association held its national conference in Montreal, which coincided with a release gig at Foufounes Électriques for Deja Voodoo's 7" "Monsters in My Garage." "We didn't even know they were in town; we weren't the most intelligent promoters in the world," says Van Herk. Most of the conference delegates attended the gig, and brought singles, tapes and buttons back to their radio stations, giving the enterprising duo a framework to set up tours. After their first Canadian tour in 1983, Van Herk and Dewald assembled a full-length album and prepared to launch the Og label.

Og was named after two literary sources: the series of five children's books from the 1930s by Irving Crump, beginning with *Og Son Of Fire*; and Pierre Berton's 1961 book *The Secret World of Og*, about an underground fantasy world. According to the company's press release, the '30s Og character "invented or discovered trapping, net fishing, cooked food, agrarian farm management, animal husbandry and dogs." The record label's name "was chosen to honour his blend of ingenuity and primitivism."

Ever since their first cassette *Gumbo*, Deja Voodoo realized that there was strength in numbers. Dewald says, "We found out that in order to get a good price on cassettes you needed to make a crapload of them, and we figured we could never sell that many cassettes ourselves, so we signed another band, which was Condition." Montreal's Condition were an "urban primitive swing combo" led by the full-throated, campy and vampy vocalist/organist Julia Gilmore, who played lounge-inflected beatnik bop with an over-the-top attitude, eerie melodies and minimalist arrangements. Original saxophonist Eddy Strawiak and his later replacement John Sobol both squawked repetitive and hypnotic melody lines, while drummer Vinnie Vezina — like Tony Dewald — used a bare minimum of equipment.

Og's third release was the *From Montreal* 7" EP, featuring Condition, Deja Voodoo, Terminal Sunglasses and the American Devices. In 1985, Van Herk and Dewald made the prescient move of compiling some of their favourite bands on a compilation they named *It Came From Canada*, with artwork and clever liner notes penned by Van Herk under the pseudonym Del Picasso. Five of the 11 bands featured were from Montreal: Deja Voodoo, Ray Condo & His Hardrock Goners, The Gruesomes, Terminal Sunglasses — whose debut full-length was Og's third release — and My Dog Popper. Jerry Jerry was still in Edmonton at that point — he would later move to Montreal — as was his guitarist's side project The Dusty Chaps. Chris Houston and UIC were from Toronto, the Enigmas were from Vancouver, and the Calamity Janes were from Ottawa. *It Came From Canada* would be the first in an influential series of five; Dewald and Van Herk affectionately abbreviated the title to an acronym they pronounced "ickfuck."

"At the time, no one could have guessed how important it was," says James Booth, who under the name James Lord, fronted Toronto garage band The Ten Commandments, featured on Volumes Two and Three. "First off, it was the only thing like that that was coming out. All of them were great, but the first one especially was this solid compilation of really interesting bands, made even better by the fact that they were from all over the place. Every other compilation from around then had been specific to one area, like the *Vancouver Complication* album, and a couple of not-great Toronto compilations like *The Last Pogo* and *No Pedestrians*. *It Came From Canada* was the first one to really represent the entire underground scene."

Dewald recalls, "The first *ICFC* sold so well that immediately we said,

'Wow, we've got to do more of these!' We sold out the first pressing in a week and a half, just from shipping orders." Og immediately followed up with a Volume Two, featuring identical cover artwork and a roster representing a greater cross-section of Canada. "The compilations were comprised from a lot of the bands we saw that opened for us across the country," says Dewald, who admits there was a bottom-line financial reason for the compilation format. "We usually liked a song or two and yet knew that there was no hope in hell of these people selling even a few hundred albums. By putting a track on a compilation, we thought we could move a couple of records here and there in each band's hometown."

James Booth recalls, "It made all the bands feel like we were part of this community, and that we were all on the same level — even though some of the bands were a bit better known, like Shadowy Men and The Gruesomes. It created a focus and a profile for a lot of the bands that got on there. Being on that record gave you a certain amount of credibility, so they were incredible things."

Other than the obvious major centres such as Edmonton, Vancouver, Calgary, Victoria and Toronto, the series highlighted acts from Fredericton, Guelph and small towns in Ontario like Shedden. "We tried to get a balance," says Van Herk. "They were always heavily weighted towards Montreal and Toronto, but we tried to get away from that. If we had a choice between two bands we liked equally and one was from Montreal and one was from somewhere else, we leaned towards the 'somewhere-else' band."

The popularity of the ICFCs resulted in Og being deluged with proposals. "If you start a record company and have a mail box number, within a year's time you'll start getting more tapes than you could ever listen to," says Van Herk. "We found very few bands through the mail; it was usually a friend of a friend thing. But we listened to every damn one, even though they'd build up in a big pile. We'd write back to everyone who sent us a tape, because it was the right thing to do."

"We never signed a band based on one of those cassettes," says Dewald. "A few got onto the compilations, but we never signed a band for a full-length record that way. We were about to, with a band called Gordie Gordo and the G-Men from Waterloo, Ontario," shortly before the label's demise in 1990.

Og's biggest success story was their hometown heroes The Gruesomes, but there were other notable artists who brought attention to the label. Hamilton's Dik Van Dykes endeared themselves to Van Herk and Dewald enough that they appeared on ICFC Volumes Three through Five, and had two full-length albums released on Og, with song titles such as "Curling," "I Was a Teenage Gumby" and "Chain Letter Massacre." Fellow Hamiltonian Chris Houston, the early Forgotten Rebels' bassist who penned "Surfin' on Heroin," was another ICFC staple (Volumes One through Three), but was too weird even for Og. "He was a songwriting genius," says Dewald. "I really loved his songs. We wanted to put out an album of his, but he was way too weird to deal with."

Jerry Jerry and the Sons of Rhythm Orchestra moved on first to Pipeline Records and then to Aquarius Records, home of Corey Hart, but much of Jerry's career often got tangled up in legalities. "When I think of the recording contract Gerard gave me compared to the one I got from Aquarius, it was hilarious," says Jerry. "Gerard gave me this one-page thing typed on his old manual typewriter, and the one from Aquarius took six months to do."

The most successful Og associate was the Cowboy Junkies, who contributed an outtake from *The Trinity Session* to ICFC *Volume Four*. When included on their album's major label re-release, "Blue Moon Revisited" would become a mainstream hit in the wake of "Sweet Jane." "They weren't an especially Oggy band," admits Van Herk, "but we played a lot of shows with them, mostly out west. It was an incredibly odd bill. Their audience would go to the front of the room when they played, and our audience would buy beer. Then the room would shift when we went on." Dewald adds, "It worked out well because they'd go on and do extremely slow stuff, and by the time we hit the stage, the audience was dying to bop."

Michael Timmins of the Cowboy Junkies says that "Blue Moon Revisited" was left off *The Trinity Session* because their producer insisted that the vinyl album not have more than the standard 23 minutes a side — longer than that it starts to dilute the sound quality of the vinyl — and the album already included several covers. "The one track we gave to Og has become one of our biggest songs," says Timmins. "I have no idea why we left that one off." Dewald muses, "They felt they owed us something, I guess. I don't think we sold many more records as a result of it, but it was nice of them to come through."

Toronto's instrumental trio Shadowy Men On A Shadowy Planet, who appeared on ICFC Volumes Two through Four, took Og's DIY spirit to heart and carved out a wildly successful indie career on their own Jetpac label. Formed in 1985, they became one of Canada's most beloved bands for their musicianship, eventful live shows, absurdist wit and innovative visuals. They are best known around the world for providing music on *The Kids In the Hall* TV show, including its theme, "Having An Average Weekend." Featuring

Brian Connelly on guitar, Reid Diamond on bass and Don Pyle on drums, the surf-influenced Shadowy sound was decidedly retro, but considerably more advanced than their peers. The Shadowy Men were extremely talented musicians, and boasted underrated compositional skills as well, set to creative and extremely danceable grooves. They also attracted attention via their series of 7" singles between 1985 and 1988, featuring gimmicky packaging such as a board game or a Jiffy-Pop container.

The Shadowy Men's unique music and marketing skills were signals to other independent bands that they could be themselves and control their destiny. Kevan Byrne played in a band called Heimlich Maneuver between 1986 and 1989, and formed King Cobb Steelie in 1991. The Shadowy Men were strong supporters of King Cobb Steelie — Don Pyle produced their debut and would eventually join the band — and Byrne credits them with teaching him everything. "Shadowy Men were putting out 7" singles and making T-shirts and booking their own shows — the whole operation, from beginning to end — themselves," says Byrne. "And because they invited us to play with them, it gave us the confidence to do it ourselves, and they encouraged us. They made us think it was possible. Shadowy Men filled bars and sold tons of merch, and toured the country. People like John Peel in the U.K. liked them, and so did cool bands in the States like the Pixies. The first time I saw them was opening for Hüsker Dü on the *New Day Rising* tour, and it was a revelation to see a band like that. I'd never seen anybody do instrumental music and really hold an audience, but also because up until that point, I had the idea that music was about bands on labels doing things that were inaccessible and not part of my reality at all."

In 1991, Shadowy Men on a Shadowy Planet released their seminal album *Dim The Lights, Chill the Ham*. That same year, an unassuming four-song independent cassette by a new suburban band called the Barenaked Ladies would alter the rules of the music business. Toronto producer Don Kerr says, "There's no doubt in my mind — that flipped the music industry in Canada upside down. That was the largest thing." Based on the band's entertaining live shows and spontaneous sense of humour, the Ladies quickly became one of the largest acts in Toronto — thanks to support from indie-friendly station CFNY — and eventually the country. And yet their only available recording at the time was their indie cassette, which eventually beat out Michael Jackson to take over the #1 position on the HMV sales chart in downtown Toronto. The band's goals remained modest. In a 1991 cover story in Toronto's *Now* magazine, singer Steven Page said, "I don't expect or want to play Skydome or Madison Square Garden. But I would

Shadowy Men on a Shadowy Planet: Brian Connelly,
Don Pyle, Reid Diamond
(Courtesy of Cargo Records)

like to have a sizeable fan base across North America and Europe. That's where my daydreams are. For me, what validates us is selling out a night at the Bathurst St. Theatre." The tape would go on to sell 80,000 copies. Their first major label album, 1992's *Gordon*, would sell over a million in Canada alone.

Prior to the Barenaked Ladies, independent cassettes by local bands were rarely — if ever — stocked in chain stores, remaining the speciality of alternative-minded record stores or friendly mom-and-pop retail outlets. Vinyl was a bit of a different issue, although success stories there were still few and far between. The Shuffle Demons, a wildly dressed and musically-skilled saxophone-driven jazz band with comedic raps like "Spadina Bus" and "Get Out of My House Roach," sold 20,000 copies of their first two albums via distribution with Stony Plain. In the wake of the Barenaked Ladies' success, the *a cappella* musical comedy group Moxy Fruvous also became an indie sensation with their own cassette. The evidence shows that the always comedy-conscious Canadians were more than willing to embrace an independent act if it provided a few laughs along with the music. It says something about Canadians' conservative musical taste that a band like Nirvana started an indie craze in America, while the same trend here was jumpstarted by the Barenaked Ladies.

In 1992, Steven Page said, "I don't like to blow my own horn, but one thing I'm really pleased about is that we kind of laid the groundwork in terms of opening up retailers to sell independent records. It's really nice to go into a big record store and see all these independent tapes, and not just one copy of them, either."

At Toronto's Kumbaya Festival at the height of the Barenaked Ladies' indie success, Change of Heart's Ian Blurton took the stage wearing a scrappy, homemade T-shirt that read, "Barenaked Ladies suck." It was a snarky move that poked fun at the current love-in for the band, who were sharing the bill that day, but there were no hard feelings; Steven Page later wore a Change of Heart T-shirt in the video for "Brian Wilson." As someone who had released indie records since the early '80s, Blurton had genuine respect for how the Barenaked Ladies changed perceptions of independent music.

"The problem with Toronto is the business end of things," says Blurton. "There are the real industry-oriented bands and then there are the bands that just make records on their own. Those bands always get treated as second-class citizens, which is unfortunate because it's meant a lot of great bands have fallen through the cracks. It ultimately took a Cowboy Junkies or a Barenaked Ladies to change that whole philosophy. I remember thinking, 'What the hell is going on?' when that Barenaked Ladies cassette went gold. Their music was more accessible than anything [Change of Heart] had done to that point. But the fact that it was a cassette was a real change, because in Toronto there was a whole section of the industry that thought if you put out a record on your own, you were just stupid or something."

Although the Barenaked Ladies sought a more mainstream approach to their career by signing a worldwide deal with Sire Records in 1992, Page's father and brother continued to run a distribution company for independent product — a business they had to learn quickly when the Barenaked Ladies cassette began flying off the shelves. The band also became an insistent supporter of their peers, bringing bands like the Rheostatics, the Waltons and the Bourbon Tabernacle Choir on the road with them.

Page's co-frontman Ed Robertson muses, "It's hard to explain, because the way people see the indie scene right now, they wouldn't imagine that we had anything to do with it. Everybody sees us as this big mainstream thing, when really, we had exploded out of the indie scene. Back then, you couldn't get independent music into record chains. We were the first independent tape to be stocked, and it opened the door for a lot of stuff. It's nice to get recognition for that, and occasionally we do. Once a guy in a hip-hop band told me, 'You guys were always supporting hip-hop music in Canada, in every interview, and it meant a lot to us.' We were conscious of wanting to build things and make it viable, whether it be us, or the Rheostatics, or hip-hop in Canada. We thought, 'This can happen *here*.'

"There have been times when the music scene has been very competitive, and that kind of comes and goes," he continues. "But that time period of '91–'92 was one-for-all-and-all-for-one. It was very cool. Everybody was playing with everybody else and supporting each other at gigs."

The Barenaked Ladies' success story was a victory for independent music, but in some ways it was still a victory for just one band, a shamelessly entertaining and inoffensive band with wide cross-generational appeal. And while the band was able to stand up to the media spotlight and eventually carve out a long-term career, it helped them immensely to have a savvy manager when they were starting out. The U.K.-born Nigel Best, who worked at Warner Canada as a publicist, guided the Barenaked Ladies through their early stages, applying his British know-how for hype to make sure everyone knew who they were. But most indie bands didn't have that resource.

Lewis Melville, who played pedal steel on the band's signature song "If I Had a Million Dollars," says, "I don't think their success would have been possible without Nigel Best, because he totally understood the concept of making a band big, and what you had to do to do it. He had a pretty solid understanding of the standard professional tools to make that happen: visibility, promotional stunts, stirring up the media. He also knew

Ed Robertson of the Barenaked Ladies
with Dave Clark, at Rheostatics'
Christmas Party,
The Cabana Room 1991
(Photo by Lewis Melville)

that they could deliver the goods. He saw that and believed it, and he was willing to quit his job and do everything in his power to make it happen. And it did happen."

Best managed the Barenaked Ladies until 1995, when they had an acrimonious split, and Best retired from the business. This coincided with a serious slump in the band's popularity, caused by a backlash over the shelf life of their earlier jokes, weaker material and a natural Canadian inclination to resent massive success. The band managed themselves for a short period, before they were picked up by Terry McBride and Nettwerk Management, fresh off his huge success breaking Sarah McLachlan on a worldwide scale. Through McBride's aggressive management — which he honed while running the pioneering indie label Nettwerk — and the band's tireless work ethic, the Barenaked Ladies became one of the biggest bands in the world with the 1998 single "One Week."

Some observers felt that the Barenaked Ladies were merely one of many that opened the floodgate to small, independent bands in the early '90s. "I don't know that the Barenaked Ladies opened any doors for anyone," Melville continues. "I don't think they made anything happen or did anything that other people weren't already working on. They proved that if you follow a certain marketing approach that you can become successful. What was important with them, which they didn't really tap into, was that you can be successful as an independent. They didn't remain independent, and they decided to go mainstream in terms of the market. the Barenaked Ladies were one of many bands who demonstrated that the Canadian public was ready to buy music they liked independently of the mainstream industry."

One of those other bands was the Lowest of the Low, who struggled with issues of independence during their brief career. In the spring of 1992, they released their debut album *Shakespeare My Butt* independently, and over the course of the summer their live shows started to attract a fervent loyalty among fans. Primary singer/songwriter Ron Hawkins penned lyrics that perfectly encapsulated the existence of most twentysomething university students: hopelessly romantic, Marxist ideals, over-analysing heartache and drinking Guinness while discussing poetry, politics and philosophy. He also had a way with a melody, and the band's straightforward meat-and-potatoes arrangements were bolstered by perfect two-part harmony between Hawkins and lead guitarist and fellow songwriter Stephen Stanley.

Their booze-fuelled live shows and the strong support of Toronto's CFNY pushed the album's sales to near-gold status, which, needless to say, caught the attention of the industry. But the band members weren't sure they wanted to play the industry's game, which led to an infamous incident at an afternoon industry function at Toronto's Ultrasound club. Recalls Hawkins, "We were on tour, and we had lots of time to kill during the day, before soundcheck. We were browsing in a record store, where we found these SST T-shirts." SST was the California punk label that released seminal

'80s records by Hüsker Dü, Black Flag and the Meat Puppets. "We knew we had an industry showcase coming up, and I saw these T-shirts that said 'Don't suck corporate cock' and 'Corporate rock still sucks.' I said, 'We should buy four of these T-shirts and wear them at our industry party!' Some guys were understandably a bit queasy, and others were like, 'Fuck yeah, let's do it.' And others said, 'Are you sure this is a good idea?' I said, 'Wearing this is one of those things where anybody who would take offense to it, or anybody in the industry that doesn't laugh at it, we probably wouldn't want to work with anyway. And anyone who sees it and thinks it's funny and cheeky, probably knows us well enough to know that we do have an interest in our careers and are serious. But if they can't take a joke, fuck 'em.'"

The audience that afternoon didn't laugh. Yvonne Matsell, who booked Ultrasound, recalls, "The band were so in-your-face with it. It was almost like they'd punched the A&R guys out," she laughs. "I really believe that created an urban story that's haunted Ron ever since, because I think he's a wonderful songwriter and a great performer. It was certainly a punk thing to do, but the A&R guys didn't see the funny side of it at all. I was just like, 'Oh god!'"

In their wish to remain independent, the Lowest of the Low were alone among the major indie successes of the early '90s. A major label deal was still seen as a trophy, a reward for all the hard work an artist did while independent. "We never wanted that," says Hawkins. "We never wanted to be in board meetings talking to people about demographics and bean counting in general. I know some of that has to go on, but we wanted to keep that to a minimum."

For their second album, 1994's *Hallucigenia*, the band decided to step into the game a bit by licensing the album to A&M. "We formed our own record label, basically," explains Hawkins, "which was a holding company so we could issue ourselves cheques for the things that we did. A&M at that time did a production and distribution deal so that we would make a record and they would buy it off us and distribute it and mass produce it, and they would get a cut from that. And even that involved an awful lot of meetings in boardrooms with people who wanted to talk about making the video next week. I probably didn't handle it well at the time, but it frustrated me, this idea of selling records like you would shoes."

Over time, the Lowest of the Low model has proven to be venerable, particularly for a band like Sloan, who control everything they do until the album is finished, at which point they take advantage of major label distribution and clout. "It makes so much more sense," says Hawkins. "You get to tap into the things that majors do well: they know how to distribute, they have a high profile and they have money. If you hand them a finished product, then you ensure that they don't bully or drag out the process of creating songs or the artwork or anything. It's your statement, you're done with it, you hand it to them and they either say 'pass' or 'let's go.'"

Sometimes even that model isn't the best route for an artist, particularly if they lie so far outside the mainstream to begin with. Dale Morningstar of the decidedly strange Dinner is Ruined was signed to Raw Energy, a label that was distributed by A&M. Raw Energy put out Dinner is Ruined's second album, *Love Songs from the Lubritorium*, and gave Morningstar complete creative control. They also released the first King Cobb Steelie album and a definitive compilation of early '90s Canadian punk acts called *On the Road*; the latter two were discovered and compiled by Amy Hersenhoren. "She has an incredible drive and instinct," says Morningstar. "Then she left the label, and a lot of the insight and energy left as well." As Morningstar was about to deliver his next record, *Worm Pickers Brawl*, he decided at the last minute to do it himself.

"If someone's going to fuck up, it might as well be me," says Morningstar. "I thought they were trying to bite off too much, and it didn't make much sense to me. They wanted to put out five records in one month, by five different artists, including me. You should put out one record a year if you're lucky; it should be a special thing. Sub Pop could have done that, maybe Sonic Unyon might do that over six months or something, because they have a great reputation and they can do that. Raw Energy was putting out a lot of bad records. I thought, who's signing these bands? What insight does this label have in terms of what bands they want on their label? I had the album mastered, and I went to their offices to drop it off one day. We sat down, and I said, 'Well, I've decided I'm going to put it out myself.' They were very gracious, but I'll never forget their faces."

Ron Hawkins says that the Lowest of the Low's major label dealings added more tension to a band that was already feeling plenty of strife. "That was messy and weird and put a lot of strain on us," he says. "It wasn't why we broke up, but it was one of the reasons. It certainly added to it. We were going along like a freight train and then slammed into a wall and stopped. Lots of good things were about to happen, like we were supposed to go to Australia and we were getting ready for a third record. A million things happened and pulled us in different directions. It was awful, and we didn't talk for a long time."

Shortly after the release of *Hallucigenia*, the band abruptly announced their break-up in the middle of a tour. For many reasons — including the band's lyrical connection to their audience and their fiercely independent stance — Lowest of the Low fans were intensely loyal, and the split caused bitter reactions that haunted Hawkins's solo career. "Because I left Lowest of the Low at its pinnacle, when it could have gone farther than it had, I think people feel estranged," muses Hawkins. "Obviously the industry takes a dim view of that, like 'who does this kid think he is to walk away from that?' Because we're supposed to want that. I also think that audiences are very protective about what it is they love. They feel — and rightfully so — that they've given a lot of themselves to coming to shows and analyzing the music and everything else, and when you walk away from it there's a sense of betrayal in the audience. I paid for that for a while; I didn't think enough about that. It doesn't mean I should have continued to do something that was played out for me, but still, I can understand the sense of betrayal on their part." Such was the band's enduring appeal that, when they re-formed for two Toronto shows in November 2000 at the Warehouse — seven years after the split — they immediately sold out both shows at the 2,200-capacity venue.

Former indie artists who did sign to major labels often left their new bosses a bit confounded. The politically active Celtic folk-rock band Spirit of the West had garnered a strong fan base while an indie band and later on folk label Stony Plain, which had distribution from Warner; they were signed directly to Warner for the 1990 album *Save This House*. "We were a difficult band to market," says Spirit of the West's Geoffrey Kelly. "There was no track record to go by. Looking back through the files, there was nothing that was similar. It was sort of unique, and to [Warner's] credit they left us alone a lot because they just didn't know what to suggest when we were recording. They would come into the studio and listen to the stuff, but they didn't really know enough about that kind of music to make a suggestion. They left us to produce ourselves and let us get on with it, which I think was pretty admirable."

Other bands were not only left to produce themselves, but were granted their own vanity labels by their corporate parents, who were hoping to ride the success of indie music. The labels figured they could do this by granting "street-level" bands the resources to sign bands that befuddled the confused corporate industry, still reeling from the unexpected success of Nirvana and the Barenaked Ladies.

After the Cowboy Junkies stumbled onto international success with an album originally pressed on their own indie, Latent Records, guitarist/songwriter Michael Timmins was allowed to resurrect Latent with BMG backing. He used it to release records by his friends the Corndogs, Pat Temple and John Bottomley. The experiment was short-lived, however. "From my point of view it was too much work, and BMG was never really into it," says Timmins. "It was sort of a pat on the head for me, like, 'Okay, go off and play record company president.' It was frustrating because one day I'd be in there fighting for Latent stuff, and the next day I'd come back and fight for Cowboy Junkies stuff, and there was too much fighting going on. It became frustrating for the bands as well. Their first record would be fun because there would be money to make the record and they weren't really expecting anything, and for the second record there was no money there and they were hoping it would sell a bit more. I didn't have any control over that, it was totally BMG, and they weren't doing anything to promote them. It was nice to put some records out, but the shortcomings of it became evident after a couple of years."

In 1994, when indie fever was at a fever pitch, King Cobb Steelie had garnered rave reviews for their 1993 debut self-titled album, which fused the progressive aggression of Fugazi with a sample-heavy love of Jamaican dub. The respect they were accorded by critics and fellow musicians meant that King Cobb Steelie was considered part of the new creative vanguard of CanRock. The King Cobb Steelie aesthetic was one that the corporate industry didn't pretend to understand — like the band's decision to work with legendary sound scientist and dubwise American producer Bill Laswell, whose work was widely unknown to the Canadian industry and public — but if the band ended up being the next big thing, the majors wanted on board. After recording their second album with their own money, the Laswell-helmed *Project Twinkle*, King Cobb Steelie was signed to EMI at the same time their friends in Change of Heart were being signed to the EMI affiliate Virgin. EMI gave KCS and Amy Hersenhoren, who managed both bands, start-up money for their own "indie" imprint, Lunamoth.

"It was an interesting prospect, and I was surprised that any label would offer us anything like that," says King Cobb Steelie's singer/guitarist Kevan Byrne. "And I'm still confused as to why they did. Maybe they thought we could create some kind of farm team for them. The Canadian music industry in particular was really caught off guard by this swell of independent music, whereas in the States, labels like SST and Touch And Go had been around for quite a long time and been successful. In Canada, for that kind of music, there wasn't anything like that except for Cargo."

In its two-year history, Lunamoth released decidedly non-commercial records by the avant-garde Ottawa rock band Wooden Stars, the New York City post-rock dub band Ui, and a 7" single by Hayden. It soon proved dysfunctional, both internally between the band and Hersenhoren, and externally with EMI. "It could have worked if the personalities were able to accommodate each other, but they weren't able to," Byrne confesses. "There was too much ego all around and not enough business sense. At the same time, Lunamoth had a lot of potential because we were all very passionate about music. The idea was to give a wide profile to bands like the Wooden Stars who would never have that opportunity before.

"EMI doled out a couple of hundred thousand dollars on the label," Byrne continues. "The first two records were Change of Heart [*Tummysuckle*] and King Cobb Steelie [*Project Twinkle*], so some of it went to the production and promotion of those records. It wasn't EMI calling up stores, it was the Lunamoth office. The promotion and marketing was at least half a Lunamoth effort. The smaller bands would be exclusively Lunamoth, and EMI would have nothing to do with it. This was their way of not 'contaminating' Lunamoth with the stigma of a major label so that we would still look hip or cool. Then if those bands ever got big, EMI would have the right to make the first offer to them, or pluck them from the farm, if you will."

Cashing in on "indie cool" became a corporate mission, and major labels were eager to co-opt indie success into farm teams for their profit margins. Mark Milne, who co-founded the Sonic Unyon label in 1993, recalls greeting most of the major labels' advances with bemusement. "At that time the majors were looking for something to sell," Milne says. "They saw a band like Nirvana selling as many records as they were, and they thought, 'How do we find bands like that? We have to find independent bands with credibility. We have to find these labels — who are they and what are they doing?' All those labels called us and said, 'Maybe we can talk and do some kind of deal.' We met with most of them for the sheer fun of it, because it was always way more entertaining than something we'd ever consider.

"They were discussing all kinds of configurations of totally ridiculous things," Milne continues. "Once we went to Sony, and the guy said, 'Maybe we could take your bands when they get to a certain level, and in the meantime you can help us develop some of our artists. Like, maybe the next time there's an Our Lady Peace, you guys could release that for us first.' We thought, 'What, so we're your farm team?' All the labels that *did* do deals like that — like the kind they were hinting they would offer us — where are those [indie] labels now? They're either not around, or they got out of their deal, if they could, because it turned into a nightmare."

Sonic Unyon started in Hamilton, Ontario, with a few friends pressing independent cassettes and promoting shows together. Tristan Psionic was the central band, featuring Milne on guitar, and his fellow Sonic Unyon co-founders Tim Potocic on drums and Sandy McIntosh on guitar and vocals. Cooperation and a sense of community, as well as basic marketing skills, quickly turned the basement operation into an all-ages local phenomenon. "We'd have a show and 10 of us would go out and poster, and we'd all call radio and press to get interviews," says Milne. "For any band on the bill, the main things we expected of them was a) to show up and play and b) to get out and poster. We'd make handbills and try and set up press. If one of the bands tried to put a show together, then it wouldn't have worked nearly as well. It was about helping each other out.

"At Tristan Psionic's first show, we had 200 people there, but those were all our friends and people who hadn't seen us before," Milne continues. "We were pretty aware that it would usually wear off pretty quickly. But then things started to pick up. We'd put shows on with bands we knew would do well together, and after a year it started getting ridiculous; we'd get 500 people out. That's a result of a couple of things: we were putting together smart shows, and it was also becoming cooler to like indie bands then."

Greig Nori of Treble Charger with Sandy McIntosh of Tristan Psionic and Sonic Unyon, at X Club in Hamilton, 1994
(Photo by James Rocchi)

What made Sonic Unyon different than many localised independent labels was that they hit the road and got their albums in stores across the country. A fortuitous association with Eric's Trip led to a national tour and the beginning of Sonic Unyon's indie empire, which today includes a national distribution company and an entire building in downtown Hamilton that houses a retail store, offices and rehearsal space.

"We had played with Eric's Trip a bunch of times, something like 40 shows," Milne recalls. "We booked a show for them in Burlington, and got to know them. They started asking us to play more shows with them, and then asked us to be the opener on this Canadian tour. During that tour, that meant we could drop off the records we were selling — which at that time were a couple of cassettes, a compilation CD and our own CD — at any record store we could. We'd leave them there on consignment and follow up on it afterwards. At that time, retail was really receptive to that kind of thing. And those who were skeptical became receptive when they noticed the records were selling, and the compilation was charting well on campus radio. The CBC played it, and all the campus stations, and we were making a bit of a name for ourselves because we were playing all the time. I wouldn't say we were relentless, but aggressive."

The height of Sonic Unyon's early hometown success came when they organized an all-day festival named WoolSock in 1994, named after their bassist at the time, known to the outside world only as Wool. "It was held out in a field in north Burlington," says Milne. "This kid who lived on a farm let us do it there. Change of Heart played, 13 Engines, and about 10 other bands. It poured rain. I think 600 people came, and it was a $10 ticket. We built the stage ourselves, and got someone to bring a P.A. It was illegal; we didn't have permits for anything. We thought we'd see what happens, and we got away with it. The cops came and saw there was no trouble."

When they tried to pull off a similar event the following year, their own success and visibility created trouble. "In the year that had passed, we had more experience and more of a name for ourselves," says Milne. "So when we said we were doing it, it was well-publicized and people in the mainstream found out about it. People in the township heard about it, and started saying, 'This is not happening here!' There were no permits, but it was private property and the guy who owned it said he was allowed to do it, and that he had similar events there before and no one complained. But [those events] weren't publicized, and ours was going well — we were going to sell a lot of tickets. We had a lot of good bands, people were calling us well in advance and were driving in from Buffalo, from everywhere.

"But it got cancelled the night before. Bands were showing up, the stage was being set up, and we went to court on the phone — Tim was representing us on the speaker phone with the lawyer for the region and the judge. The judge placed an injunction on the event, at five minutes to six in the evening. As soon as we got off the phone, I called [CFNY's] Kim Hughes in Toronto to get her to announce that it wasn't happening, because people were coming in from everywhere. Then Darrin from the X Club [in Hamilton] heard that on the radio, called us and said, 'If you want to salvage it and put it on in the club, that's fine with me.' We called Kim back and said, 'Okay, we're moving it here, but not everyone will be able to get in.' There was a limited number of tickets." Every band played a 20-minute set, and WoolSock '95 was somewhat salvaged.

At that time, Sonic Unyon's clout was huge, due largely to the success they had with Treble Charger and Hayden. Treble Charger's *NC-17* album had been moving similar numbers to Tristan Psionic's debut, until Treble Charger's video for "Red" went into heavy rotation at MuchMusic, which caused *NC-17* to sell exponentially more copies. The major labels watched with great interest.

"The indie thing was really hot," says Milne. "The majors couldn't understand why a label like ours could sell so many records on consignment out of the HMV store on Yonge St. We used to pick up money there in cash, and I remember going there and cleaning out all the registers. I walked out of there with $6,000 cash once. The security guard was staring at me saying, 'What the hell is going on? Who's this guy?' They'd be watching me the whole time, and the manager told me they were checking to make sure I didn't have a gun in my pocket as we went to each register."

Vancouver's Mint Records started in 1992, and became a prominent national label with primarily Western Canadian artists. "Our mandate at the time, if we even had one, was to document what was going on in Vancouver," says Mint's Bill Baker. "There's never been a decision to put out a style, it's always been down to whether we like it. Unfortunately, there's also the reality of, 'Will enough other people like it so that we can make our money back?' Which is unfortunate, because a lot of record labels do it even though they know that it won't sell, just because they feel it deserves to be out there. I love the idea of being able to do that, but at the same time I don't have that luxury. One total dud could sink us forever. A lot of labels have a flagship act that is the breadwinner, and that allows you to put out more risky stuff. Part of our problem is that our main breadwinner [Cub] is a) defunct and b) not that much of a breadwinner to begin with. It's a very ominous thing to have looming over you when you're trying to decide on a band. You think, 'These people are really nice, they're really good, we really enjoy them, they work hard and are willing to tour, but I don't think we can make any money.' And if that's the only reason you're not putting out the record, it really sucks."

"I admire Sonic Unyon and Murder and Nettwerk and everyone who has an independent spirit on every level," says Jeff Rogers. "I think there's a kinship between independently minded people. It's a Canadian thing to say, 'Oh, we're in Canada — how do we get people to pay attention to us? We'll just do it ourselves.' It's easier to do it yourself than it is to beg some British or American person to do it for you. Because of that situation, I think some of the major labels in Canada have adopted an independently-minded spirit, and those labels are the ones that are having success."

Yvonne Matsell, whose Ultrasound club made her the most influential club booker in Toronto in the early '90s, says, "The music industry was much more open at that time. After the Barenaked Ladies, the labels realized that they [the labels] could have been selling those records if they had gotten in on the ground floor. I'd get A&R guys calling me, asking about certain acts. They would be following the indie charts that Sam's and HMV would send out to everybody; that's what was tipping them off. They would say, 'tell me about this band.' It's like anything else. You struggle with bands in the beginning because you believe in what you see and hear, and then you try and help them get an agent, and the agents don't get it — but they get it when the room is full. That would always be a bone of contention with me: when an artist really needs help, they're not given the opportunity, until they've actually done all the groundwork themselves."

By the early 1990s, a smart, unique band who recorded in basements outside major urban centres could ascend from getting their indie cassette played on CBC's *Brave New Waves* and enduring mockery from the Canadian corporate industry, to launching an American bidding war, touring Europe and opening for the biggest band in Canada. Such is the story of The Inbreds, from Kingston, Ontario.

Bassist Mike O'Neill and drummer Dave Ullrich started making four-track recordings in Oshawa, Ontario, in 1989. They both moved to Kingston to attend Queen's University, where they began performing and releasing cassettes and 7" singles. The band was driven by O'Neill's clever pop songwriting and his unique playing style, which involved playing the bass like a rhythm guitar. His intricate skill never sounded overbearing or prog — thanks to Ullrich's tasteful Ringo-ish drumming, and a distortion pedal that often sounded punk.

They started their own indie label in 1992, PF (Proboscis Funkstone), to release home recordings by themselves and other Kingston bands. The first Inbreds cassette, *Darn Foul Dog*, caught the attention of a writer at the new Canadian alternative music monthly *Exclaim!*, Jim English, who gave it a glowing review and invited the band to play their first Toronto show at the Cameron House. "I think we were seen as, 'Let's check out this band from

Kingston,'" muses O'Neill. "I think if we were from Toronto, it would have been hard to make it. But we were kind of exotic or something."

Darn Foul Dog also caught the attention of CBC's seminal late night radio program *Brave New Waves*, albeit for an odd reason. "I was talking to Patti Schmidt, who was a researcher there then, and she said, 'We get a garbage bag full of tapes every week.' I thought, yeah, I know what you mean by *that* — a *garbage* bag," says O'Neill. "She said, 'It was

The Inbreds: Mike O'Neill, Dave Ullrich
(photos by Catherine Stockhausen)

really the minimalist artwork on the cover of the tape that caught our eye, and then we listened to it and liked it.' You know what the minimalist artwork was? Dave's dad was trying to explain a dirty joke that was on the inside of a bathroom stall at the GM plant in Oshawa. It was a drawing of a dog taking a poop and the caption was a guy saying, 'You darn foul dog! I said *sit!*' That got us on *Brave New Waves*, and all of the sudden we were getting letters because we said our address on the air."

An extremely lo-fi video for the song "Prince" encountered a low level of rotation on MuchMusic, but it was befriending the Rheostatics that made things start to happen for the band. Drummer Dave Clark became a big champion of The Inbreds, and with the help of Clark and Rheo associate Lewis Melville, the band compiled their early recordings with some new material on the 1993 release *Hilario*, co-released by PF and the DROG label, co-owned by Melville and Dave Teichroeb. The album became a campus radio hit, at a time when such a feat attracted the attention of major labels.

The Inbreds found that they had a helpful fan in the assistant to the BMG executive who had signed the Cowboy Junkies. On her recommendation, the executive scheduled a listening session with the band. "He threw *Hilario* on and said, 'You tell me what song you want me to listen to,'" recalls O'Neill. "His assistant was right there. We said, 'Okay, "Matterhorn," the first song.' He listened to about 15 seconds of it, and he skipped it and started listening to the next song. He turned to us and said, '*Not very tight,* is it? I'm going to pick one here.'" He picked the song "Farmboy," the last song on the album which is also the very first and goofiest song the band had ever recorded. "He put it on and listened to it and said, 'You know what it reminds me of?'" continues O'Neill, adopting the executive's condescending tone. "'The show *Hee-Haw.*' It was so humiliating, and I think he was trying to humiliate his assistant too, by saying, 'You don't know what you're fucking

talking about.' It was terrible. That was the only label interest we'd ever had in Canada right there."

Through a fluke event, they did get the attention of the more sympathetic Sub Pop label, Nirvana's original home who was using their new success to sign Canadian bands such as Jale, Hardship Post and Eric's Trip. While on tour across Canada with the Rheostatics, The Inbreds made a big impression on one young fan in Saskatoon. "This guy made a top 10 list of his favourite Canadian bands and posted it on his Web site,"

says O'Neill. "Joyce Linehan was an A&R person for Sub Pop, and she was an Internet freak. She fired off money to all the top 10 bands he listed, just to check them out. We got this letter in the mail with a cheque for 10

dollars from Sub Pop. We thought, is this for real?" During long drives back to Kingston from Toronto or London, O'Neill and Ullrich would often have dream-on discussions about what American indie label they would ideally sign to: Touch And Go, Dischord or Sub Pop. In the meantime, they recorded their second album, *Kombinator*, with Clark, Melville and Dale Morningstar, for $1500.

Linehan brought *Hilario* to Sub Pop head Jonathan Poneman, who held a party where he played several bands Sub Pop was interested in signing. One woman at the party worked for Tag Records, a faux-indie subsidiary of Atlantic Records, and went back to New York to tell her boss, Leila Turkin, about The Inbreds.

"Suddenly we had two labels bidding for us, and that's all you need," says O'Neill. "When we first met the people from Tag, they were gross. They were like, 'Have you heard of a guy named Michael Stipe?' We said, 'Uh, yeah.' 'Would you like to talk to him?' Dave and I were laughing to ourselves, they were trying so hard to impress us. Leila Turkin was saying, 'Yeah, I used to work for Def Jam. Do you guys like Def Jam? I know the Beastie Boys.' We thought, 'Well, that's impressive, but you're not being very cool right now.'

"Then it all started," he continues, still sounding like a modest Kingston student incredulous at the series of events. "Joyce would fly all the way up to Kingston and take us out to a used CD store and buy me the Byrds' *Sweetheart of the Rodeo*. I thought, this is what it's all about. Then Tag would say, 'Come down to New York, we'll fly you down.' We thought, why are they throwing money around like this? It's so ridiculous. Leila said, 'Do you guys want to talk to Mike D of the Beastie Boys? I got him on the line here.' So we talked to Mike D, and it was cool, but it was so weird. Then [Sub Pop's] Jonathan Poneman was the most charismatic person I've ever met. We flew to L.A., and he showed us the place where John Belushi died and told us stories about Led Zeppelin. We couldn't believe it. We'd be walking away saying, 'Jonathan, it might be early to say this, but we're going with you.' He'd say, 'It's okay, boys, but I'm glad to hear that. It was nice hanging out with you boys again.' We thought he was so cool."

However, The Inbreds eventually signed to Tag, knowing that their Canadian peers Jale and Hardship Post were beginning to find their relationship with Sub Pop souring. Tag picked up *Kombinator*, which had been released in Canada through PF/DROG, and re-released it in North America and the U.K. with Warner's clout. The band toured Europe with Teenage Fanclub and Buffalo Tom, and in the meantime Tag signed Rusty and The Inbreds' Kingston neighbours Weeping Tile. The Inbreds started recording their third album, *It's Sydney or the Bush*, which featured more elaborate instrumentation, including string sections.

Before they were even finished recording, there was a serious turn of events in 1995. "We were half way through recording, and something happened at Warner where heads rolled all the way down, and Leila Turkin was gone," says O'Neill. "Suddenly, there was no one at our label that gave a shit. But for a while there it looked good. We got a review in *Billboard*. They reviewed a bunch of singles, and they picked [*Kombinator*'s] 'Any Sense of Time' over 'Rock-'n'-Roll is Dead' by Lenny Kravitz. But it was over in no time."

The American experience brought them some Canadian respect from the industry, although it proved to be fairweather in nature. "As soon as the word got out that Sub Pop was interested and there was a bidding war, suddenly people were interested in us," says O'Neill. "Then we were offered a very large publishing deal; this guy was really interested in signing us for publishing, and at the time he was thinking that we were in it for the long haul — we were on an American label, there was going to be a payoff. One day we were at a Juno party, because *Kombinator* was nominated for a Juno. He comes up and says, 'Hey guys, did you hear about Leila?' We hadn't yet. He said, 'Well, Leila got *fired*. Good thing I didn't sign you, eh?' It was really harsh. We thought, 'Great, I'm glad you believed in the songs, asshole!' Then years later, I read this story where he was interviewed and he was talking about sticking by Len, that he knew that Len would do it and when everyone else was giving up on them, he stuck by them. I thought, this doesn't sound like the same guy!"

It's Sydney or the Bush was still released in Canada through Warner in 1996, and by this time they had moved to Halifax for personal reasons as well as to be close to their many friends in that city's exploding music scene. That summer the band accepted an invitation from The Tragically Hip to join their Another Roadside Attraction tour, alongside the Rheostatics, Eric's Trip, Matthew Sweet and Spirit of the West. It didn't help the fate of their new album much, although the Hip's benevolence did have a small trickle-down effect. "We played Montreal after the tour, and not that many people came out. Every other city, the audience always grew, except Montreal, which was always the same — it never got worse, it was always a different 30 people," laughs O'Neill. "But at this one show, there were five guys there who were all wearing ball caps and looking around. They were all crowded in together as if they were in a huge audience, but they weren't — the place was empty, and they were kind of grooving along. They were definitely guys we brought from the Hip audience, like an alien ship brought these five people."

For their final album, *Winning Hearts*, the band returned to their indie roots and released it through Sloan's Murderecords label. Although it was their finest work since *Hilario*, it was also their swan song. Dave Ullrich became a computer programmer and Mike O'Neill embarked on a solo career, releasing his debut album in 2000 on Halifax's Perimeter Records, an adventurous indie with distribution through Universal Canada. Appropriate to the state of mind of most of his peers in the aftermath of the CanRock Renaissance, it was titled *What Happens Now?*

Under the Volcano:
The Fallout of
Vancouver Punk

It is spring, 1997, and Art Bergmann arrives at a dingy Hamilton, Ontario club to play a show. For the past several months, he has been living in Toronto and playing places like these by himself, with just an acoustic guitar, to crowds mostly comprised of old punks who recall the legends of his self-destructive behaviour, or the few who want to hear the large number of memorable songs that have actually been the backbone of his reputation. Bergmann knows they also expect to see the part-Lou Reed, part-Keith Richards persona he has cultivated over the past 20 years, and he is more than willing to indulge whoever is in the audience. However, it is never clear just how much of it is really an act.

This night he is accompanied by his new Toronto manager, as well as his attractive blonde wife, who dotes upon him like a nurse and is as protective as a mother grizzly guarding her cub. Both she and Bergmann begin drinking heavily well before he takes the stage. The opening band, a group of young locals, play to a small gathering of their friends, but the few people in that camp beat a hasty exit immediately after the set. Bergmann begins playing, unconcerned that the room is empty. After finishing the first song, he calmly gulps his drink and heaves the glass against the nearest wall where it shatters, clearly without the dramatic effect that was intended. His wife automatically brings another drink, and a regular pattern is established — after every two or three songs, another glass lies in shards on the stage, much to the chagrin of the bartender. The scene becomes an uncanny metaphor for Bergmann's career; despite building an impressive body of work, his momentum has been shattered, for various reasons, after nearly every record.

In 1997, there aren't many pieces left to pick up.

Arthur Frank Bergmann was born in Langley, British Columbia on February 8, 1953 and raised in the Mennonite faith. He says with characteristic cheekiness, "I didn't speak until the age of three. Then I heard Elvis singing 'How Great Thou Art,' and the clouds opened and I was turned on to rock and roll." More specifically, it was hearing his older brother's record collection as an infant that laid the foundation. The elder Bergmann was already into rock and roll and constantly spun classic rockabilly by Eddie Cochran, Warren Smith, Elvis and Buddy Holly. By the time Art reached adolescence and heard The Beatles and The Rolling Stones, he was well versed in where they were coming from. Bergmann was soon devouring every new one-hit wonder he heard on AM radio.

When he was 13, Bergmann also became interested in his older brother's guitar. He took the traditional route of learning three chords from a book, after attending one fruitless lesson. He was determined, though, and after a summer of working odd jobs, his brother allowed Art to buy his '61 Stratocaster from him. Figuring out Beatles and Stones songs led to the forming of a band upon entering high school. They played the hits, then-current favourites like Led Zeppelin, which Bergmann scoffs at now. "I always wanted to just be the back-up guitar player and maybe screaming the odd back-up vocal like Keith [Richards]. No one ever did it right so I had to take over," he says.

Despite trying to stay true to the music that originally inspired him, Bergmann found that simply playing stuff people wanted to hear in order to have a good time was nearly as satisfying. At least it gave him an excuse to indulge in excessive behaviour at shows as well. This was the attitude that fuelled The Shmorgs, Bergmann's post-high school band that tore up the B.C. interior between 1972 and 1976. "We started out playing at parties when we only knew six songs that we'd play over and over for hours. We'd go into extended jams, everybody would be pissed off," he says. "Eventually, we played anywhere and everywhere. People loved us, we had a huge following in the valley. Thousands of people would come out just for the party, it didn't matter who was playing. We thought we could continue that vibe, but wisely the singer gave up and went to college and is now a politician."

British Columbia's longstanding hippie idealism was at a peak during the early 1970s, and no band worth its salt would stoop to rehashing worn-out rock and roll songs in order to win over an audience. The laid-back California sound was in vogue, and Bergmann took a back seat in The Shmorgs during this period to what future bandmate John Armstrong (a.k.a. Buck Cherry) described as, "'lead' guitarists; the types who never sully themselves with actual chords and only ever have to change the skinny strings."

Bergmann's tastes were making him more and more an outcast. "The Shmorgs put out an album, but it was very misdirected the way it was produced," he says. "The mid-'70s was an awful time and I hated all the bands. In '76, a friend of mine started turning me on to The New York Dolls, Iggy Pop, Bowie, Lou Reed. I couldn't believe it when I heard Lou Reed. I'd heard 'Heroin' when I was 16 but I didn't understand it. It sort of laid there in my subconscious until somebody brought it around again in the mid-'70s." Presumably this same friend unwittingly finalized Bergmann's break from The Shmorgs when he passed on a cassette he'd picked up in England by a band called the Sex Pistols.

Punk had already found a foothold in Vancouver with the city's large Anglophile population, which kept tabs on the British music scene, as well as in an underground art scene that found inspiration in New York's anti-hippie stance. In the summer of 1977, Bergmann was living in White Rock, just outside of Vancouver, with a new group of like-minded friends and what would be the final Shmorgs line-up, now featuring Buck Cherry on lead guitar. Their performances were getting more raucous as a result of Bergmann's regular trips to see The Furies, The Dishrags and The Skulls (later DOA) at Vancouver's Japanese Hall. It was just a matter of time before Bergmann jumped headfirst into the action. In the spring of 1978, Bergmann told the rest of The Shmorgs he was quitting for good. "They said, 'Nah, you go and have fun with your weird new friends.' So I did."

Bergmann says now that it felt more natural playing in front of a roomful of kids on speed than in front a few hundred stoned hippies. "There were all these voices in the dark going, 'You can scream as loud as you want, you can say anything you want, you can do whatever you feel like.' I'd been fired from so many bars for playing my own music. In those days you'd get seven nights at a bar. We'd drive 500 miles for a week-long gig and get fired after Monday night, and have no money to get back home.

I had hours of original material, so I started going insane in Vancouver, and people really liked it."

After moving to Vancouver to live among the core players in the city's punk scene, Bergmann came to be lionized after The K-Tels debuted in February, 1979. Their sound was minimalist, in order to ensure Bergmann's songs got across without any interference, but also to recapture the spirit of Bergmann's favourite '60s garage bands. Among their covers were *Nuggets* favourites "A Question Of Temperature" and "I Had Too Much To Dream Last Night," which provided the young punks with a small history lesson. Drummer Barry Taylor and bassist Jim Bescott were a perfect fit; hardly amateurs, but without any pretensions that they were the focus of attention. In retrospect, it might seem like a route similar to the one followed by Elvis Costello — making the transition from "pub rock" to punk — but Bergmann's songs at the time were coming from a much darker place. A younger band which would soon become a major inspiration for Bergmann, The Replacements, would also write a song called "I Hate Music" (the first K-Tels recording, appearing initially on the *Vancouver Complication* compilation album), but Bergmann's experiences made its sentiments more believable by comparison.

The K-Tels quickly built a following with regular gigs through the spring of '79, including opening the soon-to-be legendary Smilin' Buddha Cabaret, but it was this first recording that truly established them. Shortly after the appearance of "I Hate Music," the band received a threat of litigation from the K-Tel label, famous for cheap hits compilations and other mail-order products of questionable quality. Bergmann rode the wave of publicity as far as he could, before agreeing to change the band's name. Upon settling on The Young Canadians, they continued writing and performing at an intense pace. While others in the scene were concerned with getting their mohawks looking right, Bergmann poured out his frustrations in simple anthems like "Automan" and "Fuck Your Society."

In September, they entered Little Mountain Sound to record the *Hawaii* EP with aspiring producer Bob Rock. Rock had landed a job as an apprentice engineer at the city's premier studio and, along with cohort Ron Obvious, became instantly in demand as a route for the young punks to make quality recordings. "Where I was from, Victoria, there was nothing happening, so I went over to Vancouver and got a job at the studio," Rock says. "Basically, I resigned myself to the fact that nothing was going to happen for me musically. But when I started at Little Mountain in about '76, everything was starting to bust open because of punk in England." Rock had been behind the board for The Pointed Sticks, the first VanPunk band to break out of the city, going as far as signing with Stiff Records in England. The Young Canadians did not have their sights set quite so high. Both the *Hawaii* and *This Is Your Life* EPs came out in 1980 on Quintessence Records, an arm of the shop of the same name run by Kitsilano punk fan Ted Thomas, and the source for much sought-after imported product.

Rock says the sessions were enlightening in many ways: "Back then everybody in the audience spit at you as a way of showing affection, so when [The Young Canadians] came in the first time to do *Hawaii* we were all in the huge main studio at Little Mountain. Art came in with his hair dyed blue and we started setting up. He opened his guitar case to get out his '61 Strat that was the envy of everybody, and that Strat stunk so bad from the spit and everything that had been thrown at him that it cleared the room. Of course, Art was used to the smell, but everybody at the studio couldn't even be in the same room as the guitar.

"But I'm so proud of those records I did with them. I just loved The Young Canadians. I've played those records for everybody, and a lot of them go, 'Uh, Bob, what are you on?' I just say, 'You don't get it.' They had so much abandon about them. They were tremendous."

The Young Canadians would go on that year to open for Bob Geldof's

Art Bergmann in Vancouver
(Photo by Kevin Statham)

Boomtown Rats and follow their peers DOA to California. "At that time each band was a huge inspiration," Bergmann says. "We used to go up and down the west coast a couple times a year and play with the Dead Kennedys and The Germs in L.A. I also loved Alejandro Escovedo's band Horrid Nuns, he was a part of that scene too. There were lots of people who were just there at the moment. Too bad it was too frenetic."

By this time, Bergmann's tendencies toward punk's overindulgence were tearing the band apart. "That whole time's a fucking blur," he says. "I remember one time rolling in broken glass at a Subhumans gig. That was fun. I think I was snorting amyl nitrate — that rush stuff kids do in the locker room. You go into a blackout when you do that. I don't think it was an epiphanous moment, but the Subhumans warranted it." Bergmann did stop short at including a picture of himself, lying naked and bound on a beach, for the inside sleeve of *Hawaii*.

The Young Canadians disbanded in December, 1980, but Bergmann wasn't about to quit. "I didn't really hang out with those guys. We were just three mismatched personalities that played really well together but didn't hang out together. I wanted a band to be a band that I hung out with — like, if you don't show up for rehearsal with beer, or any other substance that would do as a substitute, then you're out of the band. That was my credo."

By 1982, Bergmann had convinced old friends who were having similar fall-outs with their respective bands to join him in a supergroup that would at least ensure a communal good time. Buck Cherry was lured away from The Modernettes, Gord Nicholl and Tony Bardach from The Pointed Sticks, Bill Shirt from Active Dog, and Zippy Pinhead from The Stiffs. The hype around the soon-to-be christened Los Popularos caused them to be self-conscious early on, but eventually they became focused enough to work their way to Toronto after quickly recording four tracks at Vancouver's Ocean Sound, which would surface on the *Born Free* EP. "We would play for pitchers of margaritas. What a cheap band we were," Bergmann recalls. "We were aggressively anti-social, but [vocalist] Bill [Shirt] was the opposite. Zippy Pinhead on drums was this enfant terrible, just a fucking party machine. Bucky didn't last long in that band, one tour maybe."

It was during this period that the inspiration came for Bergmann's most infamous song "Guns and Heroin." As the legend goes, Bergmann was acquainted with a high-profile Vancouver drug dealer, who agreed to finance a recording for the new band as part of a money laundering scheme. "He gave us the money on the assumption that he'd make a million bucks back, like, a month later," Bergmann says. "We used some of it to get this Oldsmobile Vistacruiser, the kind with the little skylights along the back. It was the coolest thing on wheels. One time we were at The Smilin' Buddha, we had 13 people in the car, all our equipment and six cases of beer; that was a record. So we took the thing to Toronto and when we got there the cops told us to get off the road because we were blowing blue. We parked at Sherbourne and Wellesley and we drew straws every night to see who would stay in the car and watch our meagre possessions while the rest of us tried to find places to sleep. After two weeks we had girlfriends, places to stay, and people coming to hear us."

Bergmann was beginning to feel comfortable in Toronto, but the rest of the band was feeling homesick for the west coast. Dates were subsequently set up to get them back home. "For some reason we left. What a dumb idea," Bergmann says. "We went back through northern Ontario to play Winnipeg, Saskatoon and Regina, where we had quite a few fans actually. We ended up in Calgary, broke. Zippy quit, he wouldn't get back in the car because it had no headlights. We were using flashlights to get to Calgary. I got a job the next day doing seismic surveys way up north, mile 175 of the Alaskan highway, and that was it for a couple of months. I got back to town with a big paycheque, and that's when we put out [*Born Free*]. It all went for shit after that because I had all these songs and I wasn't happy with Bill the singer. I thought I could sing better, more aggressively."

One of the new songs he had was "Guns & Heroin," written after the investor in the Los Popularos album finally cornered Bergmann and attempted to find out what happened to his money. The dealer waved a gun in Bergmann's face, but eventually let the matter drop after being convinced that the Canadian music business wasn't as lucrative as he had imagined. The man would ultimately be sentenced to a life term for murder a few years later. Bergmann is able to look objectively at the situation now and is still pleased with the results it produced on record. "It didn't really scare me at all. I just thought, guns and heroin and music is a nice analogy. They're all about the same thing, selling product."

The song would become the centrepiece of Bergmann's next incarnation, once again a bandleader, but this time with much more control. He called upon other stalwarts of VanPunk — bassist Ray Fulber of The Scissors and drummer Taylor Nelson Little of The Shades, along with old friend Gord Nicholl — to make a four-song demo. Bergmann dubbed the new outfit Poisoned, and the resulting cassette met with such an overwhelming response upon its release in 1983 that Bergmann quickly went back in the studio with Bob Rock to record an EP with the band, assuming quite rightly, that the rest of the country was now ready to accept him on his own terms.

By the time he did the Poisoned record, Bob Rock was already a small part of the music business establishment Bergmann had always railed against, yet his success was always tempered with a loyalty to his peers. Rock's formative years in Victoria were spent immersed in the guitar heroics and extravagance of early '70s rock and roll. While he recognized that the music was rapidly falling out of favour with others of his generation, Rock nevertheless became fascinated by the sound of those records and the recording process itself. While in high school he befriended a son of two of the many

British expats who gravitated to B.C.'s familiar dampness. Paul Hyde was also a fan of the glam scene, which had revitalized the spirit of rock and roll for so many young Brits, and was an aspiring songwriter. During the first wave of VanPunk, Hyde was in the unique position of having instant credibility simply because of his accent. Rock says, "I recognized right away that punk was just a cross-over of the stuff Paul and I were into at school, like Iggy and the New York Dolls, along with Bowie and Mott The Hoople. After I started working at the studio, Paul and I decided to put a band together. We had been to England together, but things never really developed while we were young. Paul had lived in Toronto for a while too, and when he came back he had things like Rough Trade's first album, and that whole attitude that melded into the new wave thing."

Of course, Vancouver did have an established community of rock bands by the time punk arrived. At the turn of the '80s, anyone looking to break into the business inevitably had to pass through Bruce Allen's office. A hard-nosed manager in the style of Albert Grossman and Peter Grant who established his reputation with the multi-million selling Bachman-Turner Overdrive, Allen was then on the cusp of breaking his two newest acts, a ragamuffin rocker named Bryan Adams — who had hounded Allen for two years to take him on — and a made-to-order arena rock combo called Loverboy. Rock's work on the pivotal Pointed Sticks sessions in 1979 not only set the standard for other VanPunk bands, it brought him under the wing of Little Mountain's principal house producer Bruce Fairbairn, known mostly for his work with B.C. prog-rock band Prism, and the man Allen tapped most often to create a radio-friendly sound for his clients. This unlikely relationship — the classic rocker and the punk — would bear its first fruit when Loverboy's first two albums became huge hits on both sides of the border. "It was my job," Rock recalls now. "I got my training doing technical stuff with jingles during the day and then trying to copy my favourite records with bands. But my attitude has always been, if the band has a clear idea of what they want, then it's up to me to provide it."

Longtime Vancouver music journalist Tom Harrison explained the division in the city's rock scene that Rock was managing to bring together: "By the time punk rock came along there was a definite business establishment here. Bruce Allen and Sam Feldman ran Bruce Allen Talent Promotions which managed BTO and Bryan Adams and Prism. Some very successful bands, like them or hate them. Those bands became a symbol as well of the music establishment — the whole mainstream thing. Bruce became the major figure of opposition. Sam Feldman, his partner, branched off into the booking agency and between them they had a lock on all the clubs in Vancouver and the radio stations — two AM stations that played Top 30, CKLG and CFUN, and the FM stations CFOX and CFMI. When the punk thing started happening there was no way they were going to let that stuff on the air or in the clubs."

As radios all over North America blasted out songs by Adams and Loverboy, Rock's newfound job stability allowed him to concentrate on the output of the band he had formed with Hyde. The Payolas were nurtured in the same musical soil as the other VanPunk bands, but they embraced a wider musical scope, particularly ska and reggae. Of their first two singles, released on separate tiny labels, the infectious "China Boys" set them apart from their peers. Although its slightly condescending tone could be misconstrued as a punk snub of the city's large Asian population, it tapped into the same spirit as The Vapors' equally dumb-but-catchy "Turning Japanese" and put the Payolas firmly at the pop end of the punk spectrum. This attracted the immediate attention of A&M Records, but unlike in other global punk scenes, Rock maintains their signing received more praise than backlash. "Most of the bands in Vancouver wanted to succeed, they wanted to get out and see the world. We were on the fringe of the scene but I don't think anyone was upset because I'd worked with so many people at Little Mountain. The difference between us and a lot of the other bands was that I had a job."

By giving the Payolas the first major-label deal of the original VanPunks, A&M recognized their hit potential and the band didn't disappoint. Hyde in particular took advantage of the artistic opportunity and began establishing himself as one of the most distinctive Canadian voices of the era. Although their self-titled debut in 1980 didn't cause many commercial ripples, the label still allowed them to indulge in a little hero worship by seeking out former Bowie guitarist Mick Ronson to produce the follow-up, *No Stranger To Danger*. Ronson agreed, much to everyone's surprise since he'd had little production experience outside of his co-credit on Lou Reed's *Transformer*. When *No Stranger To Danger* was released in 1982, it was clear the Payolas could no longer be called a punk band. The sound followed on the heels of The Police in incorporating a heavy reggae influence, which got the first single, "Eyes Of A Stranger," heavy airplay.

The Payolas became the toast of the country that year, picking up four Juno awards in early 1983 — including Single Of The Year for "Eyes." Rock felt satisfied with the route they had taken: "I'd produced the first album, and I shouldn't have because I didn't know what I was doing. I didn't trust anybody in Canada that the record company was throwing at me, but I just didn't have the perspective or the experience," he says. "Working with Mick Ronson changed my life. First of all, the man was my idol for playing with Bowie and all those people. We even had Ian Hunter from Mott The Hoople there working on a song with us. Mick was just the consummate sideman/ producer guy, which is what I've always strived to be."

Ronson would go on to produce their modestly successful follow-up *Hammer On A Drum*, notable for the duet between Hyde and Rough Trade's Carole Pope on "Never Said I Love You," and even toured with the band on keyboards during their stint opening for New Zealand's Split Enz. Rock recalls fondly, "The funniest thing was that after we played the first date, all the guys in Split Enz were on stage going, 'Is that Mick Ronson? Who's this band?'"

Despite this recognition and other highly successful appearances, such as the massive Police Picnic show outside of Toronto (where the band shared the stage with Elvis Costello, The B-52s and Sting and company), by 1984 A&M was losing its patience waiting for the Payolas to reach their full commercial potential. Rock points to many factors, but the most publicized was the label's distaste for the band's name. The term "payola" epitomized the ugly side of the music business since the beginning of rock and roll, when it was common practice for record company promoters to pay disc jockeys to play their product. After several scandalous incidents, not the least of which being the public humiliation of pioneering DJ Alan Freed, the recording industry went to great lengths to put a cap on the practice, although Rock's own experience proved it was mostly lip service. "We were working with a promo guy, and he said to us, 'I will never, ever break you guys because your name's like a slap in the face to me. It's how I make my living.' It was just stupid, and meanwhile 'Eyes Of A Stranger' was number one on KROQ in Los Angeles. If you do that nowadays you're pretty much guaranteed a hit everywhere, but back then it only mattered in L.A."

With frustration building on both sides, A&M threw down the gauntlet by insisting the band modify its name to Paul Hyde & the Payolas and record its next album with Canadian pop prince David Foster. The resulting album, *Here's The World For Ya*, was a vain attempt to get the band onto mainstream radio. "The fact is, none of the new bands at that time sold a lot of records," Rock says. "We got as far as we could and it ended up that music took a turn again where it wasn't possible for us to break big in the States. We were forced into making an attempt at a commercial album with David Foster and it really broke the band up."

All parties could see the change coming. A&M dropped them in 1986 and the cursed Payolas name was put to rest. Soon after, Bruce Fairbairn had Rock engineer a new Prism album, an unassuming start for their renewed partnership at Little Mountain Sound.

Like Bob Rock, brothers Rob and John Wright of NoMeansNo came from Victoria; the pair, however, felt frozen-out of the Vancouver punk scene. Rob, born in 1944, and John, born eight years later, embraced music as a means of escape from the relatively safe confines of what is commonly observed to be the most affluent city in Canada. And like many of the young American bands also beginning to form in suburbs, they turned their aggression inward, examining the isolation and boredom of their lives. Even though punk was still making inroads across North America during the first half of the 1980s, its spirit was already being transformed by this new energy from the suburbs, and also by a reaction to negative media representation. The caricature of the punk died pathetically along with Sid Vicious, although news reports of punk concerts still took aim at the mohawk-and-leather-jacket image. While the London and New York punks clung to their art-consciousness, creating new wave, no wave and other genres, much of the new generation was instead hooked on the pure adrenaline rush of the music. They also built upon the do-it-yourself approach of the original punks, boldly putting on their own shows and making records specifically for the growing number of kids searching for the punk experience. On top of it all, as if wishing to inflict additional injuries on heroes who suppos-edly sold out, new bands across America began playing extra fast and with an aggression closer to Iggy Pop's confrontational stance than Malcolm McLaren's prefab revolutionary dogma as voiced through Johnny Rotten.

Unlike in Britain, where stars like Rotten and Joe Strummer were per-ceived as having a modicum of political clout, choosing the punk lifestyle in North America in the early 1980s was often simply deemed a cry for help by the middle class. As Art Bergmann still says, echoing William S. Burroughs, "How can I be a punk? That's someone who gets fucked in jail as far as I'm concerned." There may have been some truth to the general-ization that the North American hardcore scene (like every musical movement) was populated by social misfits, but smashing this stereotype hinged upon how successfully they voiced outrage toward the societal boundaries drawn in the early 1980s. Those at the forefront were Henry Rollins, who led Black Flag around America, and most significantly, a band from Minneapolis called Hüsker Dü, whose brutal honesty, steamrolling wall of sound, and unwavering determination would make them instant legends. While The Ramones revelled in the fact that "Sheena Is A Punk Rocker" in the mid-'70s, musicians were now understanding there was a lot more to the lifestyle than the fashion. It was a confusing time to be young, as hardcore critic Joe Carducci pointedly observed: "Despite the general hostility to things hippie and sixties, these 'punks' in most instances were hoping to redo the social drama of that decade but in more realistic terms. But the fact that Reagan never precipitated a war seemed to send the rad corps into the realms of the fantastic. Bands with their feet on the ground concentrated on their music and, as far as lyrics went, with things internal."

Rob Wright says, "I think what really makes us different is we've always wanted to be ourselves, to the extent that if you're going to be yourself, you're going to be different from everyone else. Most bands, unfortunately, are always trying to be the band they really like and, unfortunately, they usually succeed.

"I'm allergic to cool," he continues. "We've always been nerdy guys from Victoria. One of the reasons we never got into this style thing is because in Victoria there was never a competitive scene. There just weren't enough people — you couldn't divide the audience, or no one would have anything. Everyone went out to everything that started out, at the beginning anyway, whether you played really dumb new wave or really strange stuff like we did as a two-piece. Everyone knew everyone else, so if you put on any airs, people would just smirk. Not to say that people didn't have the hair and the leather jackets. I think I looked like a punk rocker for about two weeks a long time ago and then I thought, 'This is way too much trouble.'"

John Wright puts it in simpler terms: "People were interested in hearing anything. A lot of bands didn't come to Victoria because it's on the island and it's expensive to come over on the ferry."

Part of the Wright brothers' approach was picked up from a new focus on the potential of pushing their abilities in different directions as a compliment to the primal-scream-like thrust of the songs. "We were different because we started a lot earlier than the actual hardcore/Minor Threat/California scene," Rob Wright says. "The bands we listened to when we started playing music were The Ramones, The Stranglers, The Sex Pistols and then PiL and the 'second wave' in England. It was a little more avant-garde, where the attitude was to try new things — reggae rhythms, funk — just to try to shake things up."

John adds, "We've always considered ourselves a hardcore band in the sense that we played with a lot of intensity and a lot of emotion. You don't

NoMeansNo in Halifax: Andy Kerr, Rob Wright, John Wright
(Photo by Eric B. Brown)

have to play really fast music and scream lyrics to be hardcore. You just
have to put your whole self into the music."

The Wright brothers began NoMeansNo in the late 1970s as a duo,
recording in their home; John on drums, Rob on bass and guitar. The name
was inspired from anti-rape graffiti commonly seen around Vancouver at
the turn of the decade. The brothers felt it connected with their own philosophy — then as now, not exactly part of the strict punk party line. "We've
always tried to put forth a little respect for the female part of the planet,
and tried to emphasize our opinions about male and female relationships,"
John says. "NoMeansNo seemed like a very appropriate name for what we
were singing about at the time."

While NoMeansNo remained strictly a recording experiment, the brothers
honed their chops in other bands. According to Rob, "We were doing four-
track recordings and we figured we'd have to get some live experience, so
we joined up with a guy who owned a music store and started doing these
bar gigs. We were called Castle because the guy's name was Rob Castle —
and because he owned the store, we had all this equipment. We played
'China Grove,' and 'My Sharona' — four sets, 40 minutes each, and that
was the first we played live." John was also part of a band called Infamous
Scientists, first on keyboards, then moving to drums when the need arose.
The guitarist was Andy Kerr, and the two immediately connected.

By the early 1980s, NoMeansNo had released a single, an EP, and their debut album, *Mama*. The brothers' obvious closeness as a rhythm section established the band's trademark hectic time-changes and, combined with their age and an irreverence born in the suburbs, put their music on a seemingly higher plane than the average punk band. They knew they needed a guitar to fill out the sound for live shows, however, and Andy Kerr was offered the position. "Andy didn't really want to join right away because he told us he liked NoMeansNo as a two-piece, but we finally convinced him because he was a great guitarist and singer," John says.

In Rob's view, "He had a much better idea of stage presence and performance. We'd always been a studio thing and he loosened us up quite a bit. A lot of the tension in the early music came from the fact that he was completely off the wall and we were very disciplined and structured."

As a traditional power trio, NoMeansNo got its first attention within the wider Vancouver music scene in 1985 after UBC radio station CITR began playing a demo of "Self-Pity," recorded for the *Undergrowth* compilation cassette. A year later the song reappeared in a new version on the *Sex Mad* album, marking the early high point of Canadian hardcore.

From the opening crash of the title track, *Sex Mad* roared out of the speakers like no other Canadian album before. Following in the wake of Hüsker Dü's *Zen Arcade*, *Sex Mad*'s 10 tracks play out like a psychiatrist's notebook detailing the growing hostility lying just below the shiny surface of mid-'80's North American society. Still, Rob Wright is quick to explain that his best songs have never had specific messages. Today, *Sex Mad* sounds like the product of the turmoil within a youth movement still searching for an outlet of expression. And like the best hardcore albums of the era, it is a patchwork of sound and rhetoric; only a glimpse of what lay just over the musical horizon.

"The purpose of music is not to make you rich and famous, nor is it a platform for whatever political axe you've got to grind, which I find even more oppressive sometimes," Rob Wright says. "It's about making a connection with people and sharing what you have in common with someone. I get to say 'Fuck you' to everyone in the world. All those simmering things that most people carry around as ulcers 24 hours a day, I get to spit them out on stage to people with some applause at the end and a few dollars. The more you move towards music as a means of earning a living or getting a political message across, the more you're moving away from the central part of what music is, bringing people together. That's the feeling you get when you're at a great concert; in that moment, you don't have to further the progress of mankind."

NoMeansNo began spreading that feeling as they toured *Sex Mad*. The shows were put on by the small pockets of hardcore fans across the country, but the size of the venue or the numbers in attendance rarely mattered. Jonathan Cummins, later of The Doughboys and Bionic, summed up a typical show at this time in his tribute to *Sex Mad* in *Chart* magazine's first Top 50 Canadian Albums poll: "Around 1985, there was a 'punk' club on Toronto's Bloor Street called Ildiko's (later The Bridge), where most of the punk bands around played — including mine, supporting NoMeansNo. We were sitting on our borrowed Peavey amps, watching the band members set up their equipment for soundcheck, thinking, 'These guys are going to suck.' They definitely didn't look very 'punk': the drummer looked like a dork, and the bassist looked like my dad. Then they launched into 'Sex Mad.' After we finished picking our collective jaws up off the floor, I ran to the phone and told my friends to come down as soon as possible, because this was going to be a show not to be missed. Of course, only nine people showed up; but those nine people walked out of Ildiko's changed forever."

Another telling incident occurred during the band's first tour of the U.S. where a gig in a Mississippi pizza parlour was cancelled due to a brawl between the other bands on the bill and the promoter, ultimately ending with the building burning to the ground. The Wrights later discovered it was all planned out by the owner as an act of insurance fraud, hoping to blame the arson on the punks.

Rob Wright may avoid overt political messages in his songs, but the emotional intensity and often prog-rock structures of NoMeansNo material went over many heads at the time. The teenage malaise of the mid-'80s still had its roots in the eternal struggles of sex, drugs and rock and roll. As older musicians around the world took up political causes, the natural reaction for young musicians was to avoid politics altogether and get back to the basic needs of the North American adolescent.

Tom Anselmi was another child of the B.C. suburbs who embraced rock and roll at an early age. Born in the late '60s, he was younger than the punks. The Vancouver bands were the closest connection he could make to his favourite records, and these musicians subsequently became Anselmi's role models. He says, "The Modernettes' 'Teen City' was a great record and the first four DOA records are all incredible. Those were my idols. When I was a kid and I met Mary Jo from The Modernettes on the bus, I couldn't believe she was there. I thought she was a rock star. I guess I never really wanted to play music. My father was a musician, and he had a really hard life. But when I was about 12, I started creating these fake bands and 'promoting' them with graffiti."

It was at this age that Anselmi met aspiring guitarist Christian Thorvaldson, and the two began hatching plots for bands, one envisioning Anselmi on stage playing a typewriter, à la legendary rock critic Lester Bangs. The next year Anselmi was sent to private school where he finally took the plunge and joined a punk band with fellow student and drummer Pete Bourne. Upon one of Thorvaldson's visits, the three met up with bassist Eric Marxsen whom they knew from another band. "We all took acid and decided that night to form a band while walking to Chris's parents' place," Anselmi says. "We started jamming together, but in three years we only played one gig. Pete decided that he wanted to move to Toronto and Eric decided that he wanted to be a singer, so Chris and I started looking for alternatives and that's when Terry and Hamm came into the picture."

Drummer Terry Russell, and bassist Stephen Hamm, along with guitarist Ziggy Sigmund, formed a new band with Anselmi and Thorvaldson in 1985. The biggest influence on the rhythm section was flashy '70s hard rock: Alice Cooper, KISS and T-Rex — music that Anselmi had never paid much attention to. Nevertheless, he recognized the music's link to the Velvet Underground and Stooges records he loved and ultimately threw himself into the role of a rock and roll frontman. "With Terry and Hamm it was great, but in a way it felt like a step backward," Anselmi says. "[Chris and I] didn't have the same kind of chemistry with them. Where they were coming from influenced us and where we were coming from influenced them. It was a very impure band. It had its moment, but it was too much of a mixture of many things to be a truly great band."

They called themselves Slow, and from the outset their mission was to destroy everything around them — or self-destruct in trying. Anselmi chalks it up to teenage stupidity, but in a few performances Slow went beyond any of their peers in terms of sheer audacity and impact. "Every time we'd play, we'd usually get shut down," he says. "That was sort of the intent. We'd get booked into places where we knew it was going to be a problem, and then we'd just break everything.

"There was a gig at this horrible rock bar that was doing 'alternative Tuesdays' or whatever. We had Cretin from the Dayglo Abortions doing sound for us; I don't even know if he did sound but he certainly was awful. We started telling him, 'Turn it up!' and we could see the bar manager going, 'No, no, no!' So I started saying to the crowd, 'The management doesn't want us to turn it up, what do you think of that?' Then Terry started doing these drum rolls and I started *sieg heiling*. Of course they shut us down immediately, dragged me offstage by my hair into the back room and confined me. We got a lot of press from that, and that was sort of the beginning of it."

Among those instantly converted by Slow's early shows was Grant McDonagh, who had taken over Quintessence Records after the shop's closure in 1981. He reopened it as Zulu Records, and also continued running a label of the same name as an extension of the store. McDonagh got Slow into Vancouver's ancient Aragon Sound in August, 1985 to first record a single, "I Broke The Circle," then a six-song EP, *Against The Glass*. The results remain staggering to this day, although Anselmi recalls little of the experience. "We were just so stoned and drunk at that point that I don't remember much," he says. "I never realized how good it could sound. A lot of that has to do with Chris. Right away, Chris understood something about being in the studio; overdubbing and other basic things that we didn't know about. The records we were listening to at the time were Bob Ezrin-produced things like KISS's *Destroyer* and Alice Cooper's *Love It To Death*, that whole layered sound."

With their recordings, Slow brought a unique swagger to the punk scene by revisiting the music most original punks were taught to abhor. But the energy of "Have Not Been The Same," the single extracted from *Against The Glass*, is undeniable. Built around a stinging, disjointed riff from Thorvaldson, the song rumbles up to speed until Anselmi's entrance. Just as a teenage Alex Chilton miraculously found soul while recording The Box Tops' "The Letter," Anselmi's voice explodes as if he's been waiting all his life for this moment to unburden himself: "I've been drinkin' but drinkin' doesn't make me feeeeel allllright. . . . " The band steps on it for a Ramones-like chorus, and the rest of the song continues on a roller coaster of time changes before Anselmi reels them in, just as it seems the train will completely run off the rails.

While those harbouring a secret devotion to hard rock ate it up, the hardline new music crowd wasn't sure. "The scene at that point, as it always is — indie rock, college radio — is all based around what happened two years ago, in my opinion," Anselmi says. "When our first single came out, CITR said, 'We're not playing this, it sounds like Goddo.' We said, 'Yeah, you're right, it does.' We were insulted actually, but we realized that these people don't have a fucking clue. They were just thinking, it's not new wave, but we knew we were way cooler than all those college radio geeks. They didn't know that '70s hard rock was cool and that it was one of the main influences of punk rock; from Iggy to Alice to the Sex Pistols. We started doing covers by those bands — we did 'I'm Eighteen' and we did 'Gimme Shelter'

Slow, at home in Vancouver: Terry Russell, Stephen Hamm,
Tom Anselmi, Christian Thorvaldson, Ziggy Sigmund
(Photo by Bruce Lam)

by the Stones a lot."

Slow were not the first VanPunk band to revisit hard rock — even DOA was playing Led Zeppelin's "Communication Breakdown" at the time — but the real surprise came when they played out of town and discovered other bands attempting the same punk/metal hybrid. "When we went to Seattle about a year or so later, it was, 'Oh they're doing it here too,'" Anselmi says. "Actually, it was only us and Green River at first, and then later there was another band called Malfunkshun. When we met them, we said, 'So, you're into Aerosmith too?'" In a few years, members of these Seattle outfits would merge or splinter off into bands such as Mudhoney and Mother Love Bone, the latter eventually becoming Pearl Jam.

For someone like Bob Rock who was already straddling both sides of the punk/hard-rock fence with his production work, the melding seemed natural. "As we all know about punk music, there was a certain part of it that was a scam," Rock says. "There were some people that took it for real and took it too far, like Gerry Useless of The Subhumans who became part of the Squamish Seven and ended up going to jail for blowing up a B.C. Hydro substation. But for most people the wind fell out of it when there was no money to be made."

However, these musicians who would eventually make up the core of the "Seattle sound" still had to pick up some fashion tips from their northern neighbours to complete the full effect. Anselmi says, "The one thing I always noticed about Green River was that there were always girls around, really hot young girls. They had this sexy thing going for them; they were all cute to some degree and they had this real glammy rock and roll vibe, whereas we never had that. We were way more degenerate. We thought they were nancies actually. They started wearing what we used to wear — plaid shirts, big boots, messy hair — after they put away their lipstick."

With a cheap video for "Have Not Been The Same" getting a surprising amount of airplay on MuchMusic, showing Anselmi in all his demento glory, the task was to get across the country. They found other contemporaries like Soul Asylum after shows in the American midwest, but the main objective according to Anselmi was, "to get wasted on two dollars a day, every day. It was just a marathon binge.

"We got our first taste of actual fame in Toronto. [Promoter] Elliott Lefko took us to this party which we were supposed to play at. It was on the lake and there were all these models there. We drove up in our van without a muffler — dirty, wasted teenagers — and people were like, 'You're Slow?' Then Hamm and Christian went upstairs and turned on the hot tub and it overflowed into the whole mansion. We ended up not playing, but there was this model who was saying, 'Come home with me.' I was like, oh my God, what is going on?"

"I brought them to Toronto because I'd seen their video and it was really amazing," Lefko says. "Their first show was with Soul Asylum, then the next night they did their own gig. They were so good, so incredible, but so fucked up. It didn't seem like it was because of drugs; they were just the kind of guys who could walk down the street and get into an accident by making one wrong move. To get to Toronto they spent all their money, so they had none to get back home. So they slept in their van, parked in front of my apartment on St. George Street for three weeks. While Tom was sleeping, he was inhaling the inner lining of the van and he had to go to the hospital because he was swallowing fibreglass. Ziggy got into a fight at a club in Hamilton and broke his arm. Chris got into a fight with Bunchofuckingoofs and hurt himself. They were that type of band, everything would happen to them, but once they got on stage, they were so good."

Most of the publicity that fuelled the tour came from the band's appearance at the Expo '86 New Music Pavilion. Aside from their recordings, this incident turned out to be Slow's crowning achievement. The whole sordid tale has been subject to many revisions by eyewitnesses over the years, and it shows that a revolution of some kind had begun. Anselmi remembers, "There were a lot of bands, like DOA, who were saying they wouldn't play for political reasons. Then there were the bands that didn't really give a fuck, like 54·40, Bolero Lava, Art Bergmann. We were asked to play and we figured, if they're stupid enough to ask us then we're gonna play. The original idea was to take off all our clothes and run through the crowd to a boat that would be waiting — we lived directly across False Creek from there — and we'd just disappear. But we were too useless to actually make that happen, so we just got really drunk and put on a fairly typical Slow performance. I'm really amazed that no one used to get hurt, because I was very irresponsible. I'd be drunk and I wouldn't really care.

"Expo had come up with this idea, which they told us about at the show, that there were these two-by-fours holding these sheets of translucent paper. They said, 'We're going to open the curtains and you're going to be hidden behind these sheets of paper, and you're going to bust through them.' We were like, okay, sounds good. So I go on stage, pick up these two-by-fours and start hurling them into the audience. The audience starts surging backwards and all I see are strollers getting pushed out the door and all the tourists escaping. We were left with whoever was into staying. I don't remember much of it, but I remember that; it was a good moment. It was my 18th birthday too."

As the band played, Anselmi ultimately followed through with the plan to take his clothes off and organizers instantly pulled the plug. But by then the audience was already wrapped up in the spirit of the performance and turned their energy to other targets once the music stopped. "The kids rioted; they were shaking the BCTV pavilion where they were broadcasting the news. The feature movie that night was *Rock 'N Roll High School* and they had to put it on 20 minutes early. The next day we left on tour. It was a very serendipitous event for us."

By 1986, Art Bergmann was on the verge of a breakthrough. The success of Poisoned led to a deal with prominent Toronto independent label Duke Street which offered a plan to give Bergmann's songs the respectful treatment they deserved. But the plan was also to present Bergmann as a solo artist along the lines of Lou Reed, especially since the name Poisoned was causing some confusion with the L.A. glam-metal band Poison, fronted by one Bret Michaels. "We wanted no part of that, no confusion whatsoever," Bergmann says. "We played in Kamloops and we got all these fucking blonde bimbos in leather showing up going, 'Where's Bret?' Then after they'd heard us they said, 'Your band's pretty good but get rid of your singer.'"

While Bergmann was reluctant to release an album under his own name, preferring to remain a member of the band, the label's marketing hopes fell into place when frequent Lou Reed collaborator John Cale was convinced to produce the sessions. It seemed a perfect match since Cale was also behind the board for such genre-defining albums as The Stooges' debut and Patti Smith's *Horses*, but Bergmann holds few pleasant memories of the experience. "[Cale] was working in Vancouver with a band called The Scramblers and a guy put us together," Bergmann said. "Cale heard the tape and we talked. I should have known by his aloofness that he was the wrong choice, but the guy's one of my all-time idols. The guy's done amazing work, but he was on Antibuse and playing squash at six o'clock every day while I was trying to do the album. I gave up in disgust and that's why that album has no guitar on it."

Nevertheless, *Crawl With Me* gave Bergmann his first mainstream exposure. The backing band was still basically Poisoned, and the album kicks off nicely with their live staple "My Empty House" — a terrifying scene from a broken relationship that would become a Bergmann trademark throughout his subsequent body of work. It is followed by "Our Little Secret," a surprise single, considering its gritty descriptions of incest. Hearing the song now, it's even more surprising that this was most of Canada's first exposure to Bergmann. The music is very much of its time; jangly guitars, synthesizers substituting for a string section, and sugary backup vocals. The power of Bergmann's words still dominates, but like the album overall, it stands as one of Bergmann's biggest losses in his many battles with record companies over creative control. Ten years later, he still felt the disappointment. "People love that album, and it brought the songs out, but so what? All this tinkily keyboard shit all over it." Bergmann says, "We had to nip that in the bud," in reference to Cale's well-known keyboard style, first popularized through his work with The Velvet Underground.

In retrospect, a glossier sheen was probably needed to establish Bergmann in the late-'80s pop world. The message of "Our Little Secret" is still there for those who want to hear it, but for most others it's simply a catchy song. Similarly, for the casual listener, the jovial backing on "Final Cliche" removes all the power from that song's tale of suicide.

Despite this blatant attempt to capture a rapidly fading new wave vibe, Bergmann was never branded a sell-out. He was now writing about heroin — and doing it better than anyone since Lou Reed. In the early '80s, Chris Houston had written the infamous "Surfin' On Heroin" as a member of

The Forgotten Rebels, but in general there were still years before the drug made its comeback through the publicity surrounding the Seattle scene. It had never gone away in the VanPunk community or in the city as a whole. Vancouver's ports remain the gateway for much of the heroin trade in North America, and the city's drug subculture suffers several overdose deaths every day. Bergmann has always been reluctant to go into specifics regarding his habit, instead allowing the experiences to manifest themselves in the songs. He insists that any sordid details have been released solely for the press to exploit.

"All this stuff about me being in rehab all the time is a load of bull-shit," he says. "Someone came up with that just to get writers to write about my dope habit. They latched onto that like a bone when it came out. 'April '93, Art went into detox. . . .' I've kicked so many habits. According to them I've gone maybe five times since then. What's new? It's part of the process.

"I pride myself on functioning," Bergmann continues, citing an earlier example. "The Popularos were all on acid leaving on tour and the car broke down leaving Vancouver. I called up the guy who sold us the fucking thing and told him to fix it. We were all peaking on acid, the guys were laying in a ga-ga mess and I was dealing with the mechanics of the situation."

After touring in support of *Crawl With Me*, Bergmann was adamant that the next album should capture a raw, live sound akin to The Young Canadians' recordings. Part of his stand was also based on his newfound

Art Bergmann with cop
at Junos, 1996
(Photo by Richard Beland)

fondness for The Replacements. The young Minneapolis band had started as a typical American teenage punk combo in the early '80s, but by the end of the decade their creative force, Paul Westerberg, had developed into one of the most clever and sensitive rock songwriters around. What Bergmann saw in Westerberg was the familiar anti-establishment fire, but also a way with words that could make a listener laugh and cry within the same song. The Replacements' mid-'80s hat trick of albums — *Let*

It Be, Tim and *Pleased To Meet Me* — were the perfect mix of excess and sentimentality that Bergmann had always sought and he readily admits these records were in the front of his mind when he set out to record *Sexual Roulette*. "I thought, 'That's it, that's the sound' — stuff falling apart, but with a lot of happy accidents," he says. "*Sexual Roulette* was the album I'd always wanted to do. [Producer] Chris Wardman had heard the John Cale record, but after he saw us live he said, 'Ah, now I get it.' A more visceral experience was required. We approached it as how the songs on *Crawl With Me* should have sounded."

Wardman, a former member of Toronto new wave band Blue Peter, struck up an instant working relationship with Bergmann which lasted through his next two albums. *Sexual Roulette* finally showed all of what Bergmann was capable of doing. A further exploration into the lives of Bukowski-esque characters dealing with addictions, psychoses and AIDS hysteria (the title track), the album's unbridled energy finally made a lot of young bands and critics realize what all the fuss over Bergmann had been about. Any doubts were erased by the opening track "Bound For Vegas," a scathing indictment of ageing rock stars. Bergmann's own age drove the point home even harder, and the song's refrain coincidentally became a well-timed response to Pete Townshend's "Hope I die before I get old," as the latter embarked on yet another "farewell" tour with The Who in 1989.

Bergmann's own tour in 1990 was marred only by opening slots for The Tragically Hip at Toronto's Concert Hall where he baited the hostile audience with sarcastic comments like, "Your heroes will be on soon." However, at the tour's end, Bergmann received a major setback when Duke Street Records closed down, thus leaving *Sexual Roulette* in stores without any promotion. It was an undeserved fate for the album, but the bright side was that Bergmann's recent acclaim had many in the industry interested in helping him out. A deal was soon made with Polygram and work began on the *Art Bergmann* album. Upon its release in 1992, it showed an unusual return to the dense, post-punk sound hinted at on the *Poisoned* EP. On the other hand, fans who had been invigorated by the stripped-down sound of *Sexual Roulette* were put off by the pop sheen given to songs like "Faithlessly Yours," "If She Could Sing," and his unabashed tribute to Westerberg, "Message From Paul," which were also part of a series of videos showing Bergmann and friends cavorting on his honeymoon in Spain. The timing seemed wrong for a well-crafted collection of dark pop songs when hard rock was finally filtering into the North American mainstream. Outside of that context, *Art Bergmann* is the overlooked gem in his catalogue.

"I don't know what a hit single is. I don't write hit singles," Bergmann says. "Each song to me is more important than anything else I've ever done. As far as I'm concerned, *Sexual Roulette* is radio friendly. Most of the songs I keep playing I hope are still apropos today. The '80s to me was one amorphous mess. I can't tell one event from the next or one defining moment. Music to me is like the Sex Pistols' early stuff when they didn't know what they were doing but they were playing rock and roll. It was defined, then The Pistols came out and redefined it. Until Nirvana I don't think it got redefined again."

Bergmann ran into difficulties securing funding to tour with his band, which forced him to promote the new album solo as part of an unusual cross-Canada package tour in 1992. Called the Big, Bad & Groovy tour, it featured Montreal funk band Bootsauce, and young Vancouver bands Pure and Sons Of Freedom. While SOF seemed the heirs to Bergmann's VanPunk legacy with their hard-hitting and influential eponymous debut on the Los Angeles label Slash, Pure were a shallow attempt at the nascent Brit-pop sound, and Bootsauce were widely derided as Canada's unflattering version of the Red Hot Chili Peppers. The tour set out unpromisingly in the dead of winter, with Bergmann immediately realizing he didn't fit in. "It was pretty nasty," he says. "I was butt-boy — blame it on Art. Anything that went wrong, it must be Art. Bootsauce had way too many managers and I had Greyhound tickets to get from gig to gig because no one would allow me on the buses; I would supposedly be a bad influence. These were adults who drank far more than I could ever hope to drink because I don't like to drink a lot of beer. I like rocket fuel, that's my weakness."

Polygram passed on another album and it seemed Bergmann's career was rapidly reaching its nadir. "In the old days I got so sick of writing songs that it made me write more songs. I was throwing away so much stuff. What's the fucking point? Around then I decided to wait until there's a gun to my head and some money on the line before I said something into a microphone. It's became the old 'confess under torture.'"

In 1993 he was asked to contribute to Sony's Neil Young tribute album *Borrowed Tunes*. The label was sufficiently interested to fund a further four-song demo, which eventually turned into a full-blown album. The sessions, once again with Wardman's dense production dominating, brought out the most painful flashes of Bergmann's fascination with sin and salvation up to that point. *What Fresh Hell Is This* was the appropriate title, and unlike *Art Bergmann*, there were no obvious singles that the label could pin their hopes on. The best they could do was "Contract," a rant in the style of

"Bound For Vegas," which instead made Bergmann sound simply old and bitter. It's not that *Fresh Hell* doesn't have its moments — the best come when the old combination of wit and sentimentality returns, such as on "Buried Alive" and "Beatles In Hollywood" — but the overall feel is of someone deliberately trying to infuriate his bosses. For that reason alone, the album is perhaps Bergmann's most powerful punk statement. And not surprisingly, it was his last experience with a major record label to date.

"To me, that record sounds a bit older," he said. "The style's all over the map. I didn't think people would take to it, and of course people didn't. It was just a case of, 'Oh, here's another record deal. I'm stuck in the middle of Sony Corporation recording more songs — I think I'll shoot up in the washroom.' It's nice to be with a record company, it's like a security blanket. 'I need a cab ride, I gotta pick up my lyrics somewhere.' They get you a cab and fifty bucks later you're across town at some weirdo's house buying dope."

Fresh Hell included a new version of "Guns And Heroin" as a message that Bergmann's situation really hadn't changed since he'd first recorded the song, and it seemed obvious he had no future at Sony shortly after the album's release. With typical Canadian music industry hindsight, he was awarded a Juno for Best Alternative Album shortly before being dropped in early 1996.

As younger bands began dominating the mid-'90s, Bergmann dropped out of sight for a time. There were more rumours of rehab, and when he resurfaced in Toronto playing solo acoustic shows, the starkness of his performances was both compelling and tragic. Songs that were bogged down on record now contained a new clarity, but somehow the shift to troubadour was too drastic for such a legendary confrontational performer. Nevertheless, Bergmann was once again amidst the people and things that inspired him. He was always a firm believer in suffering in order to create, and the new songs would slowly begin coming again. Whether anyone cared to hear them anymore hardly seemed to matter. "I always try to stay down and dirty, that's the task to get the real shit," he says. "It's hard to do without getting buried."

With the demise of the Payolas in 1986, Bob Rock and Paul Hyde were faced with the choice of whether or not to continue on with their songwriting partnership. They took a working vacation in England at that time to rekindle the magic, although soon Rock's presence was needed back at Little Mountain Sound, where Bruce Fairbairn was churning out sessions for the increasingly commercial hard rock bands seeking the magic formula of Bruce Allen's clientele. That year, Jon Bon Jovi brought his band to town.

The chiselled New Jersey rocker was riding a wave of success as his mix of contemporary heavy metal clichés and textbook Springsteen-isms was striking a chord with middle-American kids who couldn't connect with Michael Jackson or Madonna. Bon Jovi's next album would be a sure-fire hit, but how much of a hit would depend on the right production. Fairbairn's knack for capturing big sounds, coupled with the relative isolation of Vancouver, became the obvious choice to get the job done.

In almost a coldly calculated way, *Slippery When Wet* — named in honour of the strippers Bon Jovi frequently went to see following recording sessions — was all over the radio as soon as it was released. It quickly went on to become one of the biggest-selling albums in a decade noted for *Thriller* and *Born In The USA*, and brought heavy metal to the mainstream, albeit in a highly diluted form. "We did that whole album in six weeks," Rock says. "They had the songs and it sold three million in about a month. It was unstoppable. With albums like that, everything lines up and it's almost like falling out of bed. After that everybody wanted to work with Bruce and me, and that was tremendous. But Bruce made the money, which is why I ultimately decided to become a producer. When an album sells 14 million and I end up with $10,000 Canadian, it made me go, hmm, I'm not going to get far this way."

For Bob Rock it also meant a further step away from his adopted punk community, but one that was at least easy to reconcile within himself. "I was never a huge heavy metal fan," he says. "I think the heaviest thing I liked was Slade or Thin Lizzy, so to me it was never this situation where I felt uncomfortable imposing my opinions on people. The musicians I admired were just a different breed, and I think that really helps the situation."

Some wondered if it was all at the expense of his partnership with Hyde, but in 1986 the pair landed a deal with Capitol. As in Bergmann's case with Poisoned, all parties wanted no confusion over a name so the project was given the rather awkward moniker, Rock 'N Hyde, although it was basically a retooling of the Payolas' formula. The album was titled *Under The Volcano* after the novel by Malcolm Lowry which details one man's descent into alcoholism — a book published while the author was living on Vancouver Island. Just as the main character, The Consul, sought redemption for his sins, so too was Hyde exploring how the world might possibly recover from the damage the human race was inflicting upon it. The first single, "Dirty Water," expressed this sentiment most directly and restored a lot of their credibility lost in their previous work with David Foster. The new band did a successful cross-country tour playing a set heavily stacked with Payolas hits, but at its conclusion, Rock was immediately back at Little Mountain

Sound where the feeding frenzy over Fairbairn's skills was in full swing.

Little Mountain Sound's international reputation was solidified in 1987 when Aerosmith's *Permanent Vacation* unexpectedly put that band at the forefront of American music again after nearly a decade. The sheer demand for Fairbairn's services after this success forced some work Rock's way, and the apprentice proved to have just as much of a golden touch. In quick succession came Mötley Crüe's massive seller *Dr. Feelgood*, and The Cult's *Sonic Temple*.

In 1990 came perhaps Rock's biggest challenge. From 1983 on, Metallica had risen steadily from the American speed metal underground, building a legion of devoted fans and legitimizing a genre largely known for its cast of cartoonish, Satan-worshipping characters. Metallica played hard and fast music with lyrics detailing traditional teen angst, but also wider social themes. They were the band that refused to sell out in the image-conscious '80s, but by the '90s they were poised to headline stadiums and needed an album that would ensure every seat would be sold. When it was announced that Rock would be producing, die-hard fans feared the worst.

"I had bought their previous album, . . . *And Justice For All*, and it was almost unlistenable to me, to be quite honest," Rock says. "I bought it just because I'd seen so many kids wearing Metallica T-shirts and I figured this was a band I should hear. I wasn't interested until they played Vancouver on the *Justice* tour with The Cult opening. I'd just done The Cult's record so I was there to see them, and I decided to stay and see Metallica. When I heard them then, they didn't sound anything like the record; they had all this power and everything else that was missing in the studio."

Coincidentally, Metallica had Rock's name at the top of their list to mix their new album, but when Rock got the call, he told them adamantly that he wanted to produce it instead. "After they heard that, I think they thought, hmm, he's gutsy. I know they thought about it for a while before they got back to me. They came up

Bob Rock in metal mode
(Photo by Kevin Statham)

to see me in Vancouver — which is very rare for them to go anywhere to see anybody — but they came up and we had dinner. The waiter came up and said, 'Excuse me guys,' and Lars [Ulrich] and James [Hetfield] were expecting him to ask for their autographs, but he turned to me and asked, 'Are you Bob Rock?' I said yeah, and he asked for my autograph. I signed something for him and James and Lars were going, wait a minute here!"

Despite this promising start, the sessions in L.A. were difficult as the band adjusted to the new process of overdubbing, and Rock's generally unorthodox approach to metal. When finally released in 1991, *Metallica* (or *The Black Album*) created an immediate revolution in metal's perception. Much to the naysayers' chagrin, the band did not lose its old fanbase because of a different sound, it instead gained thousands more through radio's acceptance of the record. Moreover, with their integrity still intact, Metallica was virtually handed a place in rock's pantheon, with some critics going as far as proclaiming them the heirs to Led Zeppelin's heavy metal throne. The band would go on to consolidate its power with subsequent albums and a controversial headlining slot on the Lollapalooza tour.

The album also stood as the high point of Rock's career as a producer, as his classic rock fantasies played out before his eyes. Any trace of the punk who once screamed out guitar solos for the Payolas was gone, and no one seemed surprised by his next career move. In 1993 he formed Rockhead, an appropriately named quartet whose only purpose seemed to be to illustrate how Rock's musical sensibilities had been permanently altered by his recent production work. Neither the eponymous album or live performances approached any of the work of Rock's production clients, and the band suffered an embarrassing fate at the height of grunge. If Rock was successful in turning the clock back to the '70s for a brief time in the studio, that time was now up.

Eventually, he realized it too. "The thing about working with Mötley Crüe and The Cult and all those people, those guys believed that their stuff was the best and they strived to be the best at what they do. They really thought they were doing something with it, and that's the same emotion that Lars and James and Metallica have. As long as that's there, that's always been the main thing with me. That's where I differed with the Bon Jovi people. I produced one album, *Keep The Faith*, and after that I realized where they were coming from. That's definitely music for finance, not music for art, and that's where I draw the line."

By 1999, based at a studio on Maui, Rock had restored his strong track record of mainstream production successes with artists like Tal Bachman.

But he also resumed working with Paul Hyde. A sign, perhaps, that the worlds of art and commerce could be bridged again.

For their part, Rob and John Wright simply refused to change. By 1987, North American hardcore had become a separate world, with an intricate network of live venues, record labels, fanzines and campus radio stations connecting the continent with little assistance from the music industry establishment. Its strict code of conduct imposed by the fans caused any artist raised in its environment to be branded an outcast at any hint that they might defect to the big leagues. Much of this attitude stemmed from the success of labels like SST in southern California, started by Black Flag's Greg Ginn, and Dischord in Washington, DC started by Fugazi's Ian MacKaye, which proved that bands didn't need to be on a major label to reach a national audience. Another of these influential ventures was Alternative Tentacles, started by Jello Biafra, singer for the San Francisco punk band the Dead Kennedys. By the mid-'80s Biafra was already a legend, not only for his riot-inducing performances, but also by his surprising showing in the 1979 San Francisco mayoral campaign, in which he placed fourth out of ten. Biafra created Alternative Tentacles as a means to get the band's music directly to the fans in its purest form after conservative groups across North America called for censorship of their albums. As the VanPunk bands ventured south, they inevitably hooked up with the DKS at venues like Mabuhay Gardens, the I-Beam or Berkeley Square. When NoMeansNo came to town on their first American tour in 1986 with DOA, Biafra immediately felt a kinship and offered to release their records in the U.S. This meant American punks being introduced to NoMeansNo through *Sex Mad*. Although it didn't have the impact of albums by similar American bands, just as in Canada, most who heard it became lifelong fans.

With a firm base now established in the U.S., 1988 proved to be the band's most productive year. First came *The Day Everything Became Nothing*, then *Small Parts Isolated And Destroyed*, and finally *Wrong*, considered their finest work, and the album that opened the eyes of those who had chosen to ignore *Sex Mad*. The power of *Wrong* probably had more to do with its timing than anything. The end of the 1980s was being hailed as also the end of an era of greed and tyranny. Yet, Rob and John Wright knew better and *Wrong* dug even deeper into the dark side of the developing global village than their previous releases. "I don't have much faith in the rational," he explains. "I was raised a Methodist, United Church of Canada, which means Protestants that are Christians who don't believe in anything. It's the most empty, vacuous religion you can imagine. But ironically my philosophical readings, people like Sartre, Heidegger, Aristotle, and some extremely objective thinking, reversed me. I have no logical, or rational, or literal affinity with any religion. But on illogical faith, emotional hope — the things that religions do that bind people together and get them through their lives — I can relate to that completely.

"All the imagery that I use, I feel completely comfortable with. I'll use the word God in songs and I don't feel any hypocrisy or necessity to believe in that word or that symbol. Like most people, I'm concerned with the spiritual side of life. Everyone thinks about, 'What does it all mean?' as much as they think, 'What am I going to eat tonight?' and I decided a long time ago that's what I should sing about. I should do it in a way that people can relate to — that I can relate to — and not censor myself or rationalize everything."

Musically, the sound was honed to a razor-sharp edge, with the brothers' bond giving the rhythm section the force of a single instrument. *Wrong* was rightly praised throughout the hardcore nation, and the band consequently found a new audience in Europe. The repression of rock and roll in eastern bloc countries was cited by some overzealous critics as one of the prime motivating factors for the downfall of Communism, but it was clear that punk and hardcore philosophies had been adopted as pseudo-religions by many European youth disillusioned with their societies. Bands there braved severe punishment by simply forming, much less releasing records or playing in public. So when acts were freed to perform in both eastern and western Europe, North American hardcore bands often found crowds of ardent supporters who had never even heard them before. "DOA did their first tour of Europe in 1985, so we had this really romantic notion of playing there after hearing about their experiences," John Wright says. "Our old manager

NoMeansNo's Rob Wright at
the Commodore in Vancouver,
December 1993
(Photo by Paul Clarke)

at Alternative Tentacles was over in 1988 and played *Sex Mad* for this Dutch band called BGK. They liked it and said they'd try to get us in this big festival put on by the Dutch government. We got accepted and managed to get four shows in Holland that paid something like a thousand guilders each. That covered the plane tickets so we figured a few more shows would pay for the van and everything else. We ended up losing about $2,000, but Alternative Tentacles in England was able to pay the bills by taking our royalties over the next year or so."

NoMeansNo eventually made enough connections to return to Europe several times, albeit on a much smaller scale. They played shows at squats in places like Poland and Yugoslavia, making lasting impressions everywhere they went. More albums came, followed by more six-month excursions around the world, to the point that the brothers had to concede that the band was generating enough revenue to make it a full-time job. "Suddenly there was a lot of money being made," Rob says. "There was also a lot of attention being paid in the press in Europe and a lot of people coming out to the shows. At that time in Europe, in a priority list of bands, there were Fugazi, Bad Religion and us. It was a good and bad position to be in because pressures began to build at that point."

Rob quit working as a dish washer and roofer and John gave up his odd jobs bartending and waiting. Andy Kerr, however, was looking for more. In 1993, while on tour in Europe, he decided to remain in Amsterdam with his fiancée, the woman who booked most of the band's European shows, and start a new life. "He just got sick of touring. It had got quite big," Rob admits. "He wasn't really comfortable with that, especially in Europe. He turned 30 and decided he had to take a left turn and do something different. He was a huge part of the band, obviously, but the essential beginnings of most of the songs was a huge rhythm section emphasis with me and John. That's why we carried on. When John and I write songs together, they are NoMeansNo songs, and as long as we're playing together, it'll be NoMeansNo."

That philosophy carried the brothers through the next few years, as they experimented with new approaches. A new guitarist, Tom Holliston, came on board, and a second drummer, Ken Kempster, briefly added to an already rhythm-heavy sound. Rob began playing solo as Mr. Wrong and recorded with Jello Biafra, but the Wrights found their biggest success through their spoof project The Hanson Brothers. Conceived as a marriage between The Ramones and the brawling hockey-playing trio from the film *Slap Shot*, it built upon the success DOA also found marrying punk and hockey in their

DOA's Joey "Shithead" Keithley at Town Pump
in Vancouver, 1995
(Photo by Paul Clarke)

video for "Takin' Care Of Business." The 1996 Hanson Brothers album *Gross Misconduct* received plenty of attention for its punked-up cover of Stompin' Tom Connors's "The Hockey Song," as much as for a campaign initiated by the Wrights to have legendary goon Tiger Williams inducted into the Hockey Hall of Fame.

It all may have been a pleasant diversion from the Wrights' usually jaded world view, but it did allow them to reach a new audience without fully compromising their principles. They truly did love both The Ramones and hockey. Rob Wright, by then in his mid-forties, continued to travel the underground circuit playing night after night to the faithful with the same passion as when NoMeansNo started. Most of his contemporaries had given up the cause long ago, but somehow the brothers had survived, integrity intact, to see punk rock finally break into the mainstream. Although most of the Canadian kids scooping up Green Day and Offspring CDs still had not heard of NoMeansNo, the magic was there to be discovered, and the band remained content to spread the message, one kid at a time.

"NoMeansNo has taken on its own life," Rob says. "When you do a band, you control how it happens. After you start doing it, and the audience grasps onto it and you do it for a while, it takes on a life of its own. We couldn't get up there and do a 1930s jazz ballad and call it NoMeansNo — although maybe we could, because the parameters are wide enough for it. But ultimately it's a hardcore, aggressive, personal, intense music. That to me is what the whole movement was about; it was never about a style of playing music or what you looked like. All those things were what eventually killed it."

The hardcore scene was not for everyone. It was a world where the original punk ethic of do-it-yourself was taken to the extreme. While some interpreted this as staying true to punk's anarchic philosophy as well, others saw it as the Wright brothers did, as simply an opportunity to produce the kind of music they wanted to make. When Slow returned from its cross-Canada tour facing a decision of whether to ultimately continue on as they were, the independent music revolution just south of Vancouver was underway. In Seattle, Washington, and surrounding small towns, the combination of KISS and Iggy Pop that Tom Anselmi had spearheaded when joining Slow was taking hold. Green River singer Mark Arm put away his make-up, put on a flannel shirt, and formed Mudhoney with no expectations beyond writing songs as good as the MC5's. They recorded a single, "Touch Me I'm Sick" and asked their friend Jonathan Poneman to release it on his tiny label Sub Pop, little more than a mail order service of unusual music for friends spread out across the country. The response to Mudhoney from campus radio and the underground press suddenly made Sub Pop a viable label, consequently forcing the major labels to reassess their attitude toward such ventures.

The shotgun marriage between hard rock and punk was already passé for Tom Anselmi by this point, yet that didn't stop the impact of Slow from being felt. The band broke up after returning to Vancouver from the tour, with bassist Hamm and drummer Russell resurfacing in the more Seattle-ish outfit Tankhog and guitarist Ziggy Sigmund eventually ending up in Econoline Crush. For Anselmi and guitarist Thorvaldson, the first instinct was to regroup with their former rhythm section Eric Marxsen and Pete Bourne. The latter pair were still interested as well, and all four were soon living together and playing every day. "We had this house on Homer Street and we started jamming all the time," Anselmi says. "We didn't play gigs at all; we just kept at it until we got what we considered to be a good sound. Then we heard that this girl from Geffen was interested in Slow, so I called her up and she asked if she could have a tape. I said, 'No, but if you come over to the house you can hear us.' She came over and said, 'How much do you need to make a demo?' We said, 'Five thousand bucks,' thinking Canadian, and it came American."

The quartet's new sound was far removed from Slow's fury. Their experience had given them a new, wider perspective and the intention became to create something more intellectual, more intense, more adult. "We wanted to be successful with this band, but there was always this pull," Anselmi says. "It's so hard at that age to let yourself be successful, you really have to have your act together. Our whole career was constantly sabotaging itself. With Slow it was, play a nightclub and break everything. You think we'll ever play there again? Then the same kind of thing happened on a much larger scale at Geffen."

Geffen's openness toward the band came at the cusp of the Seattle feeding frenzy, in which labels that had amassed fortunes throughout the decade on the strength of multi-million-selling albums and the CD back catalogue boom were now in a position to allow a new generation of A&R reps mine the regional scenes and college radio playlist they had been weaned on. They convinced their bosses that these bands were true stars and more often than not they in return received carte blanche, at least until deadlines had to be met. For the new quartet, their honeymoon with Geffen was filled with temptations that were often too hard to resist, and often too outrageous to take seriously. When discussing potential producers with the label, Albhy Galuten, the mastermind behind the Bee Gees and the *Saturday Night Fever* soundtrack, was mentioned by someone, and to the band's shock the request was taken seriously. "He was one of the people that approached us. He heard our tape and loved it. We talked to him and we liked the guy. We loved *Saturday Night Fever* too, but it all seemed way too out there," Anselmi says. "Another person we turned down was [Led Zeppelin's] John Paul Jones, which in hindsight was probably a mistake. But we were so full of ourselves — 'John Paul Jones? Whatever.'"

The new band also signed on with Lookout Management, headed by longtime Neil Young and David Geffen associate Elliott Roberts, who set the band up in L.A. to work out their material. While there, the excesses of their individual lifestyles became magnified and fuelled their increasing arrogance toward their situation. Trying to settle on a name, they fervently stuck by the idea of simply using the copyright symbol. The decision was a first step in the quick souring of their relationship with the label. "They hated it, but we thought it was all part of the game," Anselmi says. "David Geffen said, 'Everyone hates this name, Tommy. I hate it, the marketing people hate it, the lawyers hate it, your manager hates it — but if you want to use it, then go ahead and use it.' I said, 'Okay, thanks, I appreciate it.' I didn't have a clue, I didn't get what he was trying to tell me. He was saying, change your name, fool, or I'm going to bury you."

The band eventually settled on British producer John Porter and set off to Rockfield Studios in Wales to record, where the sessions revealed the band's new musical diversity. The songs had a more high-brow feel, with Anselmi now singing more poetic lyrics, and the music ranging from the hard-edged orchestrations on "The Climb" and "Mission," to the delicate, acoustic touches on "R.S.V.P." Overall, the record resembled a dark, distant cousin to R.E.M.'s *Out Of Time*, but, once again, it was hardly what Geffen was expecting. For its release, the band allowed their name to be modified to Circle C on the spine, but retained the cover art, a simple black and white photo of a Canadian flag unfurled over a west coast beach, but with the Maple Leaf replaced by the copyright symbol. "There certainly was a lot of pressure," Anselmi says. "We were all 21, signed to Geffen, signed to the biggest manager in the world, the biggest lawyer, we're going off to Europe to make a record, and just three years ago was Expo. It was heavy. I couldn't even admit how much pressure it was, but most of the pressure was coming from ourselves. We didn't want them to tamper with us. We were coming from a music community where you had U-J3RK5 [you-jerks] who later went on to become the three most famous conceptual artists in Canada — Rodney Graham, Jeff Wall, and Ian Wallace. To buy a Jeff Wall now is $400,000 or something, when then U-J3RK5 were opening for DOA. For us, it was just anything goes."

The album was released in September 1991, the same week as Nirvana's *Nevermind*, and the label soon realized — if it hadn't already — which record would generate a bigger response. The band's attempt to make unique videos were all rejected by the label as unwatchable. Yet those who had been following the band's progress immediately embraced the album. "That was a great record," says Blue Rodeo's Greg Keelor. "I thought that was going to be huge, I couldn't understand why it wasn't. In my own mind, I thought it was better than Nirvana. It definitely had an influence on us."

With most of the songs being rejected by radio as being too abstract, the band's only options were to remain in L.A. and squander what remained of their money, or to go on tour. The first option was too good to resist. "There was a lot of darkness in our lives at that time," Anselmi explains. "Our business dealings were filled with this incredible waste and that translated to what we were doing personally, as far as embracing a lot of excess." Anselmi started writing new songs in order to break the cycle, and that time in L.A. was best captured on "Radio," which eventually appeared on their second album, *Love Story*: "Like a deer caught in the light, I can't help but look ahead / Like a hummingbird in flight, I'm going nowhere as I beat with all my might."

Breaking the cycle finally rested on the possibilities of a cross-Canada tour. Still, the legacy of Slow's touring experience nearly proved to be the new band's undoing. Problems translating the album live caused already present tensions to rise, and audiences hoping to see a newer, better Slow, often saw a band openly fighting themselves on stage. It almost came to an end during a show at the University of Waterloo when a stunned crowd watched the band ostensibly dissolve right before their eyes. "That was a notoriously bad gig. In our own mythology, that was our Waterloo," Anselmi says. "That whole tour sucked. It was just a disheartening experience. Morale and morality were at an all-time low."

"I got to work with them a little bit when I first started working with MCA Concerts," says Elliott Lefko. "Tom had sent me all these T-shirts with just their Copyright logo on them, and it was one of those Spinal Tap things — they got all the dimensions wrong and the logo was too small. We couldn't do anything with them. But I loved their record, it was grandiose and beautiful.

"I recently saw Tom Anselmi and if there's a real rock star in Canada, it's that kid. It's a shame that band never achieved the success that was due, because he was a prima donna. It's only now that he's able to act halfway normal and be nice to people. He was such an asshole to people for so long that they wanted to bury him. When I see him now, I think, that guy's a star."

Upon the expiration of their Geffen contract, the band found themselves back at square one, with those who still cared wondering what had happened. Anselmi took off to Europe to rejuvenate, and all four members worked to clean up their personal lives. In 1994, they regrouped and spent the last of their money to set up shop in a derelict building in Vancouver's drug-infested east end. The idea was modelled after artist co-ops Anselmi had seen in Europe, with bands, visual artists and others sharing the space. There, they set up a recording studio and worked on new material with a renewed spirit of independence. "It was a good move on our part, but it much delayed things because we had to build the place first. It was like constructing an opera house in the jungle," Anselmi says.

Eventually the new songs did come, and the band hooked up with manager Allen Moy, who secured them a deal with BMG. Now older, wiser, and simply named Copyright, the band finally received a full-fledged Canadian release with 1997's *Love Story*. Although deliberately more accessible than their debut, the album showed the band's growing confidence, especially Anselmi's writing ability. Most critics touched on the many unexpected

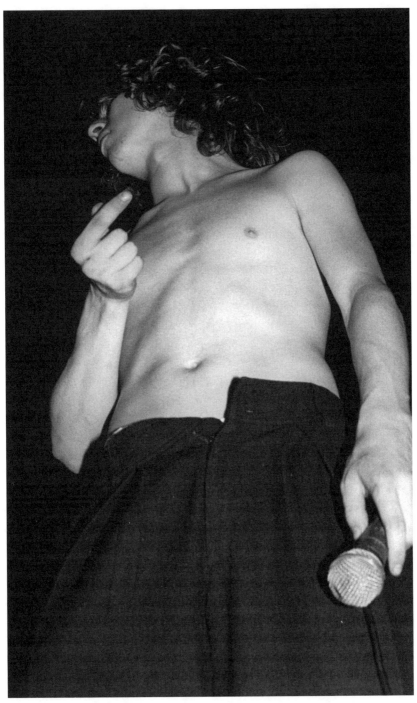

Slow's Tom Anselmi at RPM in Toronto, 1986
(Photo by Bruce Lam)

positive themes in the songs, but *Love Story*'s epic opener "Transfiguration" told the real story. Buried within its many mood shifts was the result of the band's 11-year journey to find themselves: "Through all transfiguration / An essence must remain . . . Come out / The winter's over." Anselmi admits that remaining in Canada has ultimately allowed he and his bandmates to develop the beautiful and compelling music they continue to produce.

"One of the great Canadian attributes is overview, and I think that's part of what makes us such a critical band," Anselmi says. "We're afforded that position in terms of the rest of the world living here, but even growing up in Vancouver is removed from everything else. It's its own world."

> "Montreal is definitely different. Montreal has this aura. I've lived everywhere. I've been around, and nothing compares to the feeling in Montreal. It's art."
> — Mack MacKenzie

Folk of the Eighties: Montreal

It's a summer night in 1990 and Les Foufounes Électriques is a sauna, packed full of sweaty bodies. The Ste. Catherine Street establishment lives a double life as a punk club and a late night discotheque, and it has been that way since it opened in 1985. The club has a history riddled with temporary closures, management shuffles, varied formats and legendary drug problems, and whether the city's residents realize it or not, Les Foufounes says a great deal about the musical culture in Montreal.

Tonight's show is also very telling. Though the audience has filled the house to witness a rebirth of local favourites Men Without Hats, the party will be shut down before midnight to make way for the dance crowd. "Montreal has never been a live band city," explains local musician Kevin Komoda. "Disco remains rampant based on certain cultural behaviours, meaning socializing is more important than seeing a band. You could never pick up a girl if you were seeing a band. Girls love to dance, and you go where the dancing is."

Interestingly, the band playing tonight rose to fame in the '80s through their own brand of electronic dance music. It is therefore quite a surprise when Men Without Hats leader Ivan Doroschuk takes the stage with a guitar slung around his shoulder. Aside from some incidental keyboards from Ivan's brother, Colin Doroschuk, Men Without Hats have ditched their synthesized past for this evening's full-on guitar attack. Flanking the lead singer are two notable guitarists from the city's underground scene: John Kastner, Anglophone working-class hero and leader of the Doughboys; and Felix Matte, lead guitarist of Francophone alternative darlings Idées Noires. Behind the front line is Ivan's youngest brother, and staple Hat member Stefan Doroschuk on bass, and prog-metal demigod Michel "Away" Langevin of Voivod on drums. Throughout the humid evening they run through some new material, as well as revamped versions from their keyboard past including "The Safety Dance," "Pop Goes The World" and "On Tuesday." Even Montreal's Madonna-esque pop tart, Mitsou, makes a cameo in her go-go attire to romp through a revved up version of her dance hit, "Bye Bye Mon Cowboy." Here on the same stage is the spectrum of Montreal's musical extremes: symbols of punk, metal, pop, electronic, dance, rock and country co-exist on one stage. Then again, this is Montreal.

The significance of *Sideways*, the 1991 album that resulted from this community experiment, lay in Ivan's desire to capture a special period in Montreal's musical history. As the signs of a punk resurgence brewed throughout North America, Ivan brought his assortment of musician friends from their St. Laurent Street watering hole, The Bifteck, into the studio. Together, the Doroschuk brothers — along with Michel Langevin, John Kastner and Felix Matte — liberated themselves from the various avenues that had brought them notoriety and re-explored the joys of playing straight-ahead rock and roll. For the first time in years, Men Without Hats put their blinders up to record company expectations and stopped worrying about writing a hit album. With *Sideways*, Ivan rediscovered the primal urge that had inspired the self-admitted "total hippie guy listening to Genesis" to quit law school in France in the '70s, and find his place in the Montreal underground.

"I came back to Montreal with the wave that brought punk rock to America," he explains. "Everything was brand new. It was like the new hippie movement where the clothes, the posters, the music and the drugs were all our own. That was exciting. The same thing [happened] when we did the *Sideways* record. It was that kind of feeling. It was the early '90s and you had a feeling that something was going to happen. John Kastner was telling me over and over for years that this band Nirvana was going to be the biggest thing in the world. He played *Bleach* every time he could. Getting together with him and writing all these songs and putting that record together —

[grunge] hadn't happened yet, but we felt that something was going to happen. There was more of a community spirit back then because there were a lot of people who knew what you were trying to do. It was kind of a movement."

As much as Montreal has reflected the influence of major musical movements, there is more to this city than simply mirroring popular trends. Montreal could be regarded as the most paradoxical of all the Canadian music centres. Despite its size, the city offers very little in terms of a music industry infrastructure, yet its European aesthetics and cultural tone have long been attractive to transient artists. Montreal has a well-developed Francophone scene with an audience primarily contained in Quebec, yet it boasts a small Anglophone musical community that in some cases is known internationally. The city is renowned for its loyalty to progressive rock and has long been crowned the "dance capital of Canada," but it is also a sanctuary for musical risk takers. It is this chemistry that helps explain why Montreal has fostered some of Canada's most thriving movements, from the primitive garage music of Deja Voodoo and Og Records in the '80s to the experimental post-rock scene revolving around Godspeed You Black Emperor! in the late '90s.

One-time Foufounes manager Dan Webster remembers the attractiveness of the city when he moved from Edmonton in the early '80s: "It was a wide-open city. It was just after the PQ (Parti Québécois) came into power, and it was a very socialist state. Apartments were near squatter's rates; you could rent a place for $100–$200 a month. At that time it was as liberated as any culture that existed, and probably still does, in Canada. There wasn't a lot going on in terms of an organized music scene, but the chaos and the unbridled-ness was very attractive. Everything was accepted. It was a punk utopia."

Gerard Van Herk and Tony Dewald of Og Records toured the country extensively in Deja Voodoo, and would spread the gospel of Montreal's appeal. "Gerard and I are huge Montreal-boosters," says Dewald, "so we'd go around talking about how great it was, and people bought into it. Montreal is welcoming to artists because it's very cheap to live here, you can get a lot done, and it's close to central Ontario — a place where you can make a lot of money — without having to pay the exorbitant rent to live there. Montreal has always had a weird scene for live music, and it has to do with the winter and the isolation. You're allowed to develop on your own, you play your own brand of weirdness and because there's not a lot of clubs that you could play at, there was no homogenous sound like what was coming out of Toronto at that time."

"It's kind of like New York," remarks Ivan Doroschuk. "It's very close-knit and it's a weird place. It has the French side, which is well-developed, and they have their own star system. The English side has nothing. It is made up of expatriates from other provinces who come to Montreal to hang out. I've seen so many people come through Montreal. That's why it reminds me of New York. You don't meet a lot of New Yorkers, you meet a lot of people from out of town."

Though it was the Anglophone scene that first garnered a national profile in the early '80s, the Francophone culture in Montreal has been the dominant force over the history of the scene's development. Doughboys' leader John Kastner says, "For an English rock band in Montreal there is no business for you at all. There have always been amazing bands, but there's no industry. If you can get the French kids to like you, it's a super amazing place. For us, coming from Montreal, the reason we did so much [outside of the city] was that there was so little for us to do there."

He continues, "We're only really known in the English circles and that makes Montreal, for us, about as big as Kingston. They fucking resent anybody who ever got out of there."

Born October 9, 1957, Ivan Doroschuk was the eldest of three. Like both his younger brothers, Colin and Stefan, Ivan came into the world on the campus of the University of Illinois while his father Eugene attained his Master's and Ph.D. When the University of Montreal offered his father a position, the family relocated to the posh Montreal suburb of Outremont. According to Ivan, the Doroschuk brothers grew up in an environment that fostered music and socialist beliefs. Their mother Betty taught singing at McGill University, which along with their father's accordion playing, kept music omnipresent throughout the home. All three boys took music lessons from a young age; Ivan and Colin received keyboard instruction, while Stefan studied the violin. As teens, the brothers picked up the guitar and fell in love with various genres of popular music. In Ivan's case it was the Peter Gabriel-era of Genesis and Roxy Music, while Stefan jammed on the weekends to Lou Reed, David Bowie and The Stones. "Our family is music," admits Colin who would later study opera and composition at university. "We have a real knowledge of musical form. From the age of five and six we were already hearing the Bach cantatas. My father was planning to be a musician and he got sidetracked. He married my mom, who was a musician, and he wanted his sons to be musicians."

All three boys were educated in French at Stanislas, a private boys' school in Outremont. Here, Ivan befriended Jeremie Arrobas, and with the other Doroschuk brothers they formed Wave 21, a short-lived high-school band in which Arrobas read his poetry over the Doroschuks' music. After high school, Ivan studied law in Nice, France; he dropped out after a year and returned to Montreal. He enrolled in a Film and Communications program at McGill University, but this too would be sacrificed in a few years time as Ivan's passion for music took a hold of his life.

Picking up a part-time job as an orderly at the Montreal General Hospital, Doroschuk met two ex-Torontonians: bassist Dave Hill, and drummer John Gurin. Together with guitarist Pete Seabrooke, they formed a noise guitar band in 1978 that was named Men Without Hats. For the band's first couple of years, they remained a guitar/bass/drums combo, creating their own originals and covering The Cramps and Chris Spedding. Men Without Hats evolved through various personnel changes, eventually including all three Doroschuk brothers for the band's initial live performances at the infamous Hotel Nelson in Old Montreal.

The Hotel Nelson, described by former *RearGarde* writer Warren Campbell as "the scene of many a punk rock riot," provided a venue for gigs by Lou Reed, Teenage Head and The Mods. "Back in the late '70s, you couldn't do punk shows," explains Ivan. "Punk had a bad name, and that was one of the only places in town that would book them. We'd been playing parties in people's houses, but that was our first professional gig."

In 1979, Marc Durand, a journalist from *Quebec Rocks* and an aspiring manager, approached Ivan to join a Montreal band he was managing named Heaven Seventeen. Not to be confused with the U.K. new-wave group Heaven 17, this Montreal quintet was an amalgam of popular musicians Tracy Howe and Scott Cameron from the Normals, Roman Martyn of the Young

Heaven Seventeen, 1979: Tracy Howe, Ivan Doroschuk, Denis Duran, Kim Duran, Roman Martyn
(Courtesy of Tracy Howe)

Adults, Kim Duran and Lysanne Thibodeau. When Thibodeau and Cameron left the band, Kim enlisted her brother Denis Duran and Ivan agreed to join on keyboards and vocals. Says Tracy Howe, "Heaven Seventeen was meant to be Montreal's first post-punk band, along the lines of John Foxx-era Ultravox and Howard Devoto's Magazine. We were the first new-wave band in Montreal to add synthesizers and we were quite self-consciously arty, doing songs with poetry by Nietzsche in German for lyrics."

After a six-month stint with the band, which included an opening slot for XTC at the St. Denis Theatre, Ivan departed and reactivated Men Without Hats in 1980. Inspired by a new love of Kraftwerk, Ivan left the guitars in their cases and Men Without Hats was reborn as an electronic act. He enlisted the services of manager Marc Durand, and with his Stanislas school mate, Jeremie Arrobas, began creating the first synthesized MWH songs — sometimes while trying out equipment at local music stores.

Though local underground bands like the 222's, the American Devices, Ulterior Motive, the Chromosomes and the Blanks all continued to explore guitar music, the new wave of the late '70s and early '80s brought a keyboard vogue to Montreal. Kevin Komoda, who later joined Rational Youth, explains, "Historically, keyboard-dominated music has always been popular in Quebec. Quebec even has its own Depeche Mode cover band. Many of these keyboards were inexpensive and available, and that had a lot to do with how people approached forming a band. It could also be local trends. New wave was becoming more fashionable than guitar-driven punk. Joy Division started using the string machine and other electronic gadgets, plus the Stranglers were also very popular locally. Men Without Hats and Rational Youth had that punk DIY ethic, but used keyboards instead."

"Kraftwerk was always really big in Montreal — a lot of the spacey keyboard [music]," says Ivan. "Quebec really does seem like a different country. I don't know what the rest of Canada was even listening to. I talk to people my own age and they were listening to Bruce Cockburn while I was listening to Kraftwerk."

Interestingly, this contrast of electronic and folk music made its way into the band's mentality. Their first EP, a four-song, 10" vinyl record released independently in 1980 was entitled *Folk of the '80s*. Like much of the band's early music, the title appears minimalist, yet is a multi-layered concept. It was Ivan's way of describing the era's keyboard-driven movement. "The synthesizer is the folk instrument of the '80s," he said at the time. "Technology has made it possible for a non-musician to make music. Brian Eno was the first person who made it legit for a non-musician to take a synthesizer and say, 'Hey, notes aren't the only thing. Sounds are something too.' Guitarists can tell if you're good or bad. They can pin down how many years you've been playing just by looking at you. But with a keyboard player, imagination is more than enough. If you have any amount of vision you can create virtually anything your little heart desires."

There are the obvious double meanings of the title *Folk of the '80s*. The term "folk," in its meaning as either "people" or "protest music," manifested itself both ways in Ivan's writing. The first EP started the trilogy of releases centred on these concepts, and was followed by 1982's *Rhythm of Youth* — unofficially known as *Folk of the '80s Part II* — and completed by 1984's *Folk of the '80s Part III*. These recordings are self-reflective and deal with the excitement and fears of a decade: "Antarctica" and "I Got The Message" were inspired by the budding new-wave movement; "The Safety Dance" and "Living in China" were tongue-in-cheek peace anthems in the age of nuclear threat and political unrest; while songs such as "I Like" exposed Ivan's sentiments on indulgence and egocentricism.

Around the time of the EP, various musicians entered and left the fold, including former Heaven Seventeen members Tracy Howe, Roman Martyn and Lysanne Thibodeau, as well as another Stanislas acquaintance, Jean-Marc Pisapia, Mike Gabriel and the other Doroschuk brothers. In 1982, Men Without Hats solidified its line-up as the three Doroschuk brothers with Allan McCarthy (Spoons and Forks).

"The people that would be brought in from time to time all wanted to be chiefs, not Indians," remarks Stefan Doroschuk. "Three separate bands came from MWH before we recorded our first record. Two of them became known: Rational Youth and The Box. The third band, Isinglass, formed by Jerry [Arrobas] and a friend of mine, Mike Gabriel, were tricked into leaving Men Without Hats only a few months before we recorded *Rhythm of Youth*. Unbeknownst to me — and maybe Ivan also — Marc [Durand] had convinced them that he was willing to kick Ivan and I out of the band and go into the studio with Jerry and Mike as Men Without Hats. He brought us into his office and told us that we'll be kicked out of our own band if we don't start toeing the line a bit more. Ivan and I burst out laughing. Marc caved in a few weeks later, I think after having listened to Jerry and Mike's demo of their forthcoming 'Men Without Hats' record. They were pathetic as musicians, and that's why you've never heard of Isinglass. That's how we got Allan [McCarthy] into the band at the time."

Jean-Marc Pisapia only lasted a few months in Men Without Hats. He went on to start the short-lived Checkpoint Charlie with Arrobas and Gabriel, and then the more popular outfit The Box — once again under Durand's management. The Box were a Francophone band known for their polished live performances and, because most of their songs were sung in English, became one of the few Québécois bands to make a dent on the national charts in the '80s. Early singles like "Must I Always Remember," "My Dreams of You," and "L'Affaire Dumoutier" established an Anglophone fan base, and garnered respectable sales for their 1984 debut *The Box* and 1985's *All the Time, All The Time, All The Time.* With 1987's platinum-plus selling *Closer Together* The Box confirmed a national presence with three hit singles — "Closer Together," "Ordinary People" and "Crying Out Loud For Love." The album also spawned the career of backing vocalist Sass Jordan (formerly Sass Turner of The Pinups), who would rise to commercial heights with her own work later in the decade.

Like Men Without Hats, there was a subtle bilingual element that surfaced in The Box's music. Press reports frequently referred to these bands singing in both English and French as being "Pierre Trudeau's dream come true." Though Pisapia admits the choice to sing the majority of their work in English was intentional, it was for a different reason than Men Without Hats. "In Quebec there was a huge musical scene in French in the '70s. If you were to pick up a guitar and just strike it, you would be an instant star. At the end of the '70s, the identity crisis started to fade away. In the '80s, people started to get a little bit fed up with the independence thing, and this love story about Quebec with itself was kind of fading out. The music scene literally vanished. In 1981 you could count on one hand the acts that were around Quebec. We were absolutely alone with Men Without Hats, Corey Hart, and Luba. Even then it was unthinkable in those days to be able to speak English and not use it in this business. It's a difficult enough business as it is. If you are not going to use all the tools to make it, you are stupid. In those years the political thing was not very strong. It was in a slump, so we used it. If you were to do the same thing today, you'd be dead."

Ivan looks at his choice to include both of Canada's official languages in his music as being more instinctual than commercially driven. "I was more on the English side, although I consider myself more of a Francophone. I didn't connect at all with the French music scene there. I used French because it was just how my brain worked. The images I was writing — sometimes the translations were in French images. I wrote in French because it was part of me. The language thing [in Quebec] comes and goes. At the beginning the media was calling me a sell-out. They didn't realize that both my parents were English and that I was born in the States and basically came to their country and learned their language. The French press was leading everybody to believe I was a real Francophone that had chosen to sing in English to make money."

Tracy Howe also found a new life after his brief stint in Men Without Hats. Howe lasted long enough to gain a credit on *Folk of the '80s*, even though he did not actually play on the recording. "I didn't feel comfortable in Men Without Hats at all," Howe admits. "Ivan, now that he was the leader of the band, treated everybody else like domestic help. You were just there to execute his vision exactly the way he wanted it. Plus, he and the rest of the band were all from the same private school in Outremont, and I wasn't part of the clique. Jeremie Arrobas's father had, prior to my arrival, bought the band thousands and thousands of dollars worth of equipment and bankrolled the recording and manufacturing of the first EP. We used to practise at Jeremie's father's house in Outremont. One Saturday I went there for a rehearsal and found Jeremie there alone. He was livid. Ivan had taken most of the equipment out of the rehearsal room the night before and sold it at La Tosca Music, because he didn't like it anymore and wanted something else instead. Jeremie said to me, 'That's it. He's out. Let's you and me do a

band together.' I said okay and we told Marc Durand what had happened. He started making plans to try and get Martha Ladly from Martha and the Muffins to join Jeremie and myself. But within days the Outremont boys had all closed ranks, kissed and made up, and Ivan wanted me out. Jeremie didn't last much longer after that, either."

After Howe's departure, he met Bill Vorn and started Rational Youth with the intention of being a "pure electronic band." In the summer of 1981, Howe and Vorn released the first Rational Youth single "I

Rational Youth, 1983.
Kevin Komoda, Angel Calvo,
Denis Duran and Tracy Howe
(Courtesy of Tracy Howe)

Want To See The Light/Coboloid Race," an apocalyptic William Gibson-like vision of the future on the YUL independent label, co-operated by manager Marc Demouy. After their well-received second show opening for Orchestral Manouevres in the Dark at Le Plateau Auditorium, Rational Youth established a solid name in Montreal's electronic scene and began work on a full-length album for YUL. Halfway through recording their debut, they enlisted keyboardist Kevin Komoda. Komoda had traded the completion of his secondary education for an early start in the Montreal scene, and already had played with Mack MacKenzie, The Blueprints and Action Man on Assignment. Since the original duo of Rational Youth had used programming technology like the MC-4 and 808 drum machine to compensate for their limited keyboard abilities, they needed someone who could actually play. "He was a great musician," Howe says of Komoda. "He had a lot of style and added a lot to the visual aspect of the band on stage."

The resulting 1982 album, *Cold War Night Life* was, like Men Without Hats' music, also heavily rooted in Kraftwerk, but there were enough idiosyncrasies to differentiate between the two bands. Besides Rational Youth being a completely electronic band, their lyrics conveyed a stronger political undercurrent. "Close to Nature" begins the minor-key collection with an admitted apprehension about technological development and the realistic possibility of nuclear threat. There is also a Cold War thematic parallel to early '80s dance culture that carries through much of the album, which is evident on "Ring the Bells" and "Dancing on the Berlin Wall." The debut record found its niche in the college market and the dance clubs of North America and Europe, propelled by the singles "Saturdays in Silesia" and "City of Night." This spawned a world tour which lasted for most of 1982. According to Howe, *Cold War Night Life* earned the distinction of being one of the best selling independent albums of the '80s.

Vorn would part ways with the band after *Cold War* to focus on studies while Howe, Komoda, and new recruits Angel Calvo and Denis Duran carried on to release their major label debut, 1983's *Rational Youth* mini-LP, on Capitol Records. Despite a successful promotional campaign and tour of Canada, inner politics and personality clashes led Rational Youth to bitterly part ways.

In the aftermath of this dissolution, Tracy Howe recorded 1985's *Heredity* with some hired guns. Though released under the Rational Youth banner, it's essentially a Tracy Howe solo album. The album enjoyed respectable sales in Canada — buoyed by the single "No More and No Less," which received some mainstream radio play — but the U.S. campaign bombed and Rational Youth was subsequently dropped from Capitol's roster. While touring *Heredity* with members of the Toronto bands Boys Brigade and Blue Peter, Howe came to a career crossroads. "I moved to Toronto in an attempt to escape YUL management, who were starving us to death," he says. "In the summer of 1985 we had been booked for well over $100,000 worth of gigs, but I don't think any of us saw more than $200 of it. By this time I was fed up with the whole business. I put together one more tour by myself — a series of dates at universities in the Maritimes — and all the guys in the band and I split a nice bit of money when it was over.

After a final gig at Dalhousie University in Halifax, in January 1986, Howe completely removed himself from the music business, and took a position working for the Ontario New Democratic Party in Toronto until 1997, when a huge cult following in Sweden brought him out of retirement. Along with former Digital Poodle member Jean-Claude Cutz, Rational Youth released *To The Goddess Electricity* on Sweden's October label in 1999.

After the 1980 independent release of *Folk of the '80s*, Men Without Hats started attracting attention in a typically Canadian manner. No one in Canada was interested in signing the band, but they caught the interest of a couple of international labels. One was the U.S. affiliate of the U.K. punk label, Stiff Records (The Damned, Elvis Costello) who offered to re-release the EP. Subsequently, Men Without Hats became one of the few acts to score a U.K. deal prior to a Canadian deal, when Statik Records (The Chameleons U.K.) offered to release the group's first proper album. The band would soon sign a U.S. deal with Sire.

The full-length debut, 1982's *Rhythm of Youth*, was recorded in Old Montreal's Listen Audio Studios with manager Marc Durand, and is the quintessential Men Without Hats album. It's the finest example of early electro-pop music recorded in Canada, as every song's distinctive melody is coupled with the raw energy of a young punk band. Buoyed by Ivan's charismatic vocal delivery and the instrumental prowess of the four musicians, half of the songs on *Rhythm of Youth* were released as singles: "The Safety Dance," "I Like," "I Got The Message," "Living in China" and on the U.S. release, a remix of "Antarctica" from the first EP.

What is truly impressive is how much the band was able to accomplish, musically, given the limited technology available for electronic bands at the time. Stefan Doroschuk notes, "We had started doing pulse bass before sequencers were made, so we had a Prophet 5 keyboard modified to take a click track through a Doctor Click, triggered by a LinnDrum.

Men Without Hats, early '80s: Ivan Doroschuk,
Colin Doroschuk, Stefan Doroschuk
(Courtesy of Stefan Doroschuk)

When we started to use the first Macintosh computers for sequencing, it cost us $3300 for a Mac Plus!"

It would not be until radio picked up on the "The Safety Dance," a year after *Rhythm of Youth* was released, that the album's popularity gained momentum. Along with Ivan's instantly recognizable baritone, the dance pop song became readily identifiable with its memorable synth riff and a staccato chorus chant. It topped the charts in many countries, making MWH one of the year's major buzz bands. To many it would seem strange that a pop hit would be regarded with such importance, yet over time, the success of "The Safety Dance" shone a global spotlight on the relatively unknown band from Montreal, illuminating other developing Montreal artists in the process.

"I remember when Ivan received his first royalty check for 'The Safety Dance,'" Montreal country rocker Mack MacKenzie recollects. "He was working as an orderly at Montreal General Hospital. It was a very happy time for them. It was healthy for such a small scene to see that success."

"I didn't think Montreal reacted the same as the rest of the world," notes Kevin Komoda, who was touring with Rational Youth. "Radio took a while to start playing it, and at the time I was on the other side of the world watching 'The Safety Dance' on MTV every 30 minutes. Meanwhile, nothing was happening in Montreal. Not that it mattered, but I think some of the more envious locals secretly ignored how popular Men Without Hats were in the rest of the world."

The song's video introduced Ivan as the figurehead for a band that up until this point had been visually represented by the simple logo of a faceless man wearing a hat with a red slash over his visage. It features Ivan as a pied-piper type character, jigging through a medieval setting and leading the townsfolk through the dance accompanied by a dwarf jester and a blonde maiden. The clip is also evidence of the ways Ivan was using his growing profile to support others in the local scene: his video character conspicuously sports a button that reads "Deja Voodoo."

It's hard to imagine two more diametrically opposed bands than Men Without Hats and Deja Voodoo. The former was obsessed with modern technology and enjoyed major label support, while the latter went out of their way to sound as primitive as possible and ran their own indie empire, Og Records, on the side. Montreal being the close community that it is, however, even these two bands eventually crossed paths.

"I thought they were fucking great," enthuses Ivan. "I saw a lot of their gigs, hung out with them and went to the [Deja Voodoo] BBQs and everything. I tried to get them hooked up with Marc Durand. He wanted to turn them into an Adam and the Ants-type thing with huge disco drums behind them. They were looking for management and better distribution at that time, but they didn't go for it."

"Once people started to talk, we realized how far apart we actually were," says Deja Voodoo's Gerard Van Herk. "They had marketing people who knew what to do, and of course no one knew what to do with us, because neither did we."

Through some dumb luck and a determined business sense, Deja Voodoo helped focus the nation's eyes on Montreal's garage-rock scene, linking it to likeminded artists across the country on Og's *It Came From Canada* compilations. Gerard Van Herk and Tony Dewald began Deja Voodoo in 1981, after a brief stint as the Halftones. Over the next eight and a half years, they hardly altered their sound: Van Herk played an overdriven, swampy guitar; and DeWald's drum kit contained no cymbals or hi-hat. Together, they pounded out primitive blues with incomprehensible or goofy lyrics inspired by trashy horror films, '50s bubblegum pop, and cemeteries. Their most apt album title was *Big Pile of Mud*, and typical song titles would include: "Surfing on Mars," "Duh Papa Duh," "Wall of Paisley," "Red Garlic Shoes" and "I Wanna Come Back From the World of LSD." They described themselves as "sludgeabilly" and, although inspired by The Cramps, had a signature sound that didn't sound like much else. "We realized that every song sounded the same, but that's what rock-'n'-roll is about," says Van Herk. "It didn't really matter, like the Ramones. We'd always play not as fast as possible, but as hard as possible, and if we had room for jokes that was [all the better]."

In 1981 Deja Voodoo was very much alone in Montreal; the number of similarly minded bands was "somewhere between zero and none," says Van Herk. "When we started, there was very much a synthesizer, clubby dance kind of thing going on, and we were very different. Which was nice in a way, because bands could sound like whatever they wanted to outside of that; there was no tradition. There was no big established live music scene of any kind. You could do whatever you wanted, because no more than 13 people were going to like you anyway."

In their first year of existence, Deja Voodoo didn't stray beyond Montreal, Ottawa and Quebec City. But they soon learned that there was an entire country waiting for them, with fans that were longing for something primal, fun and the antithesis of every other musical trend of the day, including the hardcore scene that was manifesting itself in Montreal. "I didn't like that kind of music," says Dewald, "We were both completely into discovering old stuff; our tastes kept getting older and older, like cave people making rock records. Nothing else mattered. Hardcore? Whatever. One of the things that qualified people to be on Og was that they listened to or knew about stuff from the past, and they would fuck with it to make it their own."

While on their first Canadian tour in 1983, Van Herk and Dewald discovered kindred spirits nationwide, particularly a rowdy bunch of Edmontonians who called themselves Jerry Jerry and the Sons of Rhythm Orchestra. Jerry Jerry and his friends — guitarist Reverend Rockin' Roland, guitarist Ace Picks, bassist Blake Cheetah (later of the Asexuals) and drummer Sparky the Happy Troll — were fixtures on the early '80s Edmonton punk scene as jokers and rounders. "We had a little band we put together called Them Essentials," says Jerry. "We decided the most radical thing we could do in alternative music would be to have facial hair. And maybe it was — big moustaches, sideburns, beards, which nobody had at that time. It was as uncool as you could possibly be. Jerry Jerry wasn't a serious band at the time it started, either. It was what we called a 'fuck band.' It took four or five years before I considered myself a performer. It was a drinking club.

"We were a seven-piece at that time, playing a kind of music that nobody else was playing," Jerry continues. "There was no way to define it. The one I always liked was: 'Canadian city boy thinks he's a hillbilly preacher singing late '60s Texas acid rock.' When you're playing outside of labels it's good because it makes your music somewhat timeless, but it's negative because it makes it harder to sell yourself as a product, because you can't say what you are. That's the story of my life."

The first Sons of Rhythm Orchestra recording was a cassette with the archetypal Albertan title *Fighting Socialism*, recorded and released by local luminary Barry Peters. Van Herk recalls, "People kept telling us, '*You will love this band.*' Then eventually someone got around to sending us a tape, and we said, 'Yes! We will love this band!'" The two bands soon shared a gig at the Edmonton Ski Club.

"We drank six cases of beer during sound check, we had two bottles of Jim Beam on stage, and altogether we drank 14 cases of beer," relishes Jerry. "I smoked two packs of cigarettes during our set. We were pretty wailed, and spending our youth fairly quickly. They liked our energy."

Tony Dewald concurs, "They were completely wild. Jerry Jerry was one of the few bands ever that completely blew us off the stage. We were a pretty good live band, but they completely wiped the stage with us. They were completely amazing. The amount of liquor they consumed was just stunning."

In 1985, Jerry Jerry and the Sons of Rhythm Orchestra recorded *Road Gore: The Band That Drank Too Much*. When it became a favourite on *Brave New Waves*, *Night Lines* and campus radio, Jerry started to get itchy to leave both the western touring circuit and his hometown. "We were sharing rehearsal space with SNFU and hanging out with Moe Berg and k.d. lang, so we had a good thing here for a while," says Jerry. "But the town started driving me crazy and I had to get out. Montreal offered so many contrasts: a nice city, a lot of people in a small space, lots of history, lots of nightlife, ease of lifestyle. And there's decadence that only comes with decay as well, which is nice. There's something part and parcel about this whole business that can really only flourish in decadence, on a societal downward spin."

Jerry packed up the members of the SRO who wanted out as well, and relocated to Montreal twice: "I moved there in '86, and then again in '87. The first one didn't take," he laughs. He wasn't the only artist to make the move. "A lot of Westerners were moving to Montreal at that time," says Van Herk. "There was a bit of an expatriate community. There were bars that sold beers you could only get in Saskatchewan, just because there were so many Westerners living around St. Henri. It was some hipster version of Americans going to Paris in the '20s, where you could go to this cool city where you can have a good time and have cheap rent."

Another key émigré was Vancouverite Ray Tremblay, who had played in

The Secret V's. Upon his move to Quebec, Tremblay adopted the stage name Ray Condo and rallied a skilled backing band called the Hardrock Goners to play old-time Western swing. Although extremely traditional and capable of tapping into the long-standing Québécois love for country music, Ray Condo and His Hard Rock Goners appealed to the underground alternative crowd for the same reason Deja Voodoo's proto-blues did. Although considerably less punk, Ray Condo injected a traditional form with newfound energy and a zippy fashion sense.

"Even though we were playing different music," says Van Herk, "it's still Montreal — where at that time you wouldn't get on stage wearing yesterday's T-shirt and jeans. That's just the way people are in Montreal; you put on make-up to go to the corner store — women, too! What happened with a lot of Og stuff was that there was that rockabilly revival, which of course appealed to Montrealers because it meant dressing up and doing your hair. The actual musicians who listened to that stuff would take rockabilly back to its roots and listen to R&B and blues. There were tendrils of interest going back to all of that stuff, and there was a record store in Montreal called Cheap Thrills where you could get a lot of it on reissue. There was also a campus radio show we'd listen to that would play all that."

By far, the most successful Og band was comprised of four snotty teenagers who ate too much junk food, watched too much cheezy television and horror movies and told really bad jokes. Taking their name from the Flintstones' creepy neighbours, they were The Gruesomes. And their fashion sense — a combination of the Ramones and early Beatles — made them hard to miss, even before they started playing music.

"They were the sharply attired guys that would come to our shows," says Dewald. "You couldn't miss them, because they were so cool-looking. They dressed like that all the time; they were king mods at their high school. One day they invited us to come to a party at their house, in their garage. They were in a band and could barely play, but it was a lot of fun. They started playing gigs and by their fourth show they were playing in front of 1,000 people."

Bobby Beaton was The Gruesomes' singer, guitarist and primary songwriter, and he and his bandmates had been sneaking into Montreal clubs with fake IDs since the age of fourteen. "We thought Deja Voodoo were really cool and really outta site," says Beaton, in his typical parlance. "The thing about the Montreal bands that we all really liked and appreciated was that they were funny, treating things halfway as a joke — trashy, fun rock and roll. There was always a lot of humour with bands like Deja Voodoo and Terminal Sunglasses. We'd go to see those guys and by watching what they were like, their stage patter and such, it really influenced us."

The Gruesomes formed when most of the members were 16, and Beaton doesn't mince words about his band's early talents, or lack thereof. "We were so bad that we had to practise every single day for nine hours at a time in our parents' basement, plugging away, trying to learn how to strum these three-chord songs. People would come to see us knowing that the band sucked and would watch in amazement as these four kids who couldn't play at all hammered out these cheezy, primitive tunes, screaming and yelling about putting down girls."

Whether it was The Gruesomes' look, their youth, or their reverent approach to ramshackle '60s garage rock, they found an audience immediately in their hometown, where fashion has always been known to play a part in a band's appeal. "Montreal is not a hardcore rock and roll city, it's a showboating, show-off city," says Beaton. "It's not the gritty rock and roll you'd get in Toronto or Vancouver. Montreal bands often come from a conceptual point of view, and that includes dressing up and such." According to Van Herk, "They had a broader appeal than a lot of other bands, which helped. Anyone who decided they didn't like them just went away, and other people just liked them. They'd get people from the ska scene. They had the correct number of instruments — and good hair."

Within their first year, saturation soon wore out a bit of their initial welcome. "We played every single weekend for a year and a half in Montreal," says Beaton. "We were slowly getting bigger and bigger, but people were getting pretty sick of us. It went from: 'The fabulous Gruesomes, oh they're great!' to 'How many times have we seen these overrated guys?' By that time we could actually play our guitars and we were going on tour."

They soon found a receptive audience in the rest of the country, with Toronto being a particular stronghold. "The Gruesomes had a look and an easily sell-able schtick that people buy into right away," says Beaton. "Toronto always understood where we were coming from: the look, the joke, the angle of the songs. And they appreciated the music, too. Our first show in Toronto was at Larry's Hideaway. We were very young kids when we came down, barely out of our parents' house. We said, 'Hi, we're The Gruesomes from Montreal!' and went into our first song, which was 'Bikers From Hell,' and a wicked fistfight broke out. This guy was smashing another guy's head into the monitor right in front of us. This was the *first song*!"

When there wasn't drama in the audience, The Gruesomes gained a reputation for ridiculous stage scenarios, particularly on their annual Hallowe'en shows in Toronto and Montreal. "We would do Vincent Price horror schlock stuff," says Beaton. "We would get plywood and build a coffin, and I would come out of it in a Dracula cape and run around the stage. These props

John Davis of The Gruesomes
in Halifax
(Photo by Eric B. Brown)

were cheap, do-it-yourself props, none of this laser light show stuff. I'm talking about phony-looking hieroglyphics on a sheet that we'd hang up, then two guys would come out and piss on us, and I'd come out as the mummy. We did the werewolf once, where I was the werewolf and had to be shot by [guitarist] Gerry [Alvarez] with a silver bullet from a cap gun. But of course, we used a starter pistol and it wouldn't go off, so I had to lunge at him three times until finally he could shoot me. This is the level we're working with here. The props would fall apart and the themes would not work, but the audiences liked it even more. They just laughed harder."

Between 1986 and 1988, The Gruesomes released three full-length albums and toured the country constantly, becoming minor superstars. In 1987, they set an attendance record at Toronto's Lee's Palace. "We were playing the biggest clubs in each city," says Beaton. "We used to tear up the prairie provinces, especially Saskatchewan, where we played at a Holiday Inn ballroom for hundreds of people in Saskatoon. It was like Beatlemania or something. We'd try to talk to the audience and crack jokes, but we couldn't because they were screaming so loud. The local radio station sponsored a 'meet The Gruesomes' contest where the lucky winners got to shake our hands and we signed autographs for them. I'll never forget walking into this big room carrying my guitar, and people noticing us as we were walking in and just starting to *scream*. Around the late '80s, Gruesomania hit Saskatchewan."

They were also having a noticeable effect on younger bands, most of whom can be heard on the 1996 compilation *Time Machine: The History of Canadian '60s Garage Punk and Surf 1985–95*. One such band was Vancouver's The Smugglers. In 1988, the biggest thrill of The Smugglers' teenage lives was their second gig, playing with The Gruesomes at St. David's United Church at a show promoted by Nardwuar The Human Serviette. "It was a total disaster," recalls Smugglers' frontman Grant Lawrence. "Much like Altamont, Nardwuar hired the wrong force to do security — skinheads. They stole the door money and one of them was found having sex in the pews upstairs. The next morning — The Gruesomes stayed at my house — John Knoll, the drummer, was on the phone with the church secretary taking notes, completely deadpan. I looked down at the notes and it said, 'Washroom: blood, vomit, diarrhoea smeared on walls.' The church was hysterical because Nardwuar told them we were having a community talent show with jugglers. Even the altar got damaged — people ran amok through God's house!"

The Gruesomes also made forays into the States, where a similar scene was thriving, but without the sense of humour and fun. "Bands like the Fuzztones or the Chesterfield Kings took what they did very seriously," says Gruesomes bassist John Davis. "It might have frustrated them that we did so well playing with them — we were a bunch of talentless punk losers. We made fun of everything and everybody all the time. Our sense of humour was totally negative and evil. We were just asses."

"We played in New York and Washington a few times," recalls Beaton. "It was harder, because as soon as we crossed the border, where our records were not available, we couldn't get the money or the fans we could in Canada. But we'd get these crazy hardcore fans. In Canada, normal people and everyone would go see The Gruesomes, and there'd be a select minority who would be totally into the '60s trip, who looked like Austin Powers. They'd come to see The Gruesomes because that's the type of music we play.

"In the States, we would *only* get those people: Beatle-booted, super mushroom bowl haircuts, paisley shirts, girlfriends with vinyl miniskirts and go-go boots. One time in Washington, D.C. we were totally broke, so we said, 'Folks, we're The Gruesomes from Montreal, and we're going to take up a collection to maybe get us some gas to get to the next city. Thanks a million.' This guy came up to me with the boots, the haircut, the Lennon glasses — whole works. He said, 'Man, you guys are great. You play just like it was 1966.' I said, 'Thanks!' He said, 'Here you go buddy, here's some change for you,' and gave me a handful of coins. Before he left, he turned to me and said, 'Hey, by the way man, check the dates on those coins.' I swear to God, in that handful of change, *every coin was from 1966.* That was the level of his devotion to '60s music."

In 1983, Men Without Hats were very much of their own time, when "The Safety Dance" became a massive techno-pop hit, selling two million copies worldwide and firmly establishing the band's international profile. They spent most of 1983 on the road promoting *Rhythm of Youth* and discovered that with their newfound popularity came the expected trappings of fame. As much as the band attempted to focus on their music, the pressures of the industry soon took their toll. None of the Hats were thrilled about playing the music business game, and their attempts to distance themselves from the pop-star life gained the band a bad reputation; they were "enfants terribles," difficult in interviews and refusing to appear on standard industry platforms such as the Grammy Awards or *Solid Gold*.

Colin Doroschuk recollects, "We were in the studio recording the second album [*Folk of the '80s Part III*] when 'Safety Dance' took off. It went all over the planet. It was a year and a half before we got back to the album. We actually refused a lot of stuff. But we're musicians; we're mostly into making music, exploring music and mixing exploration with music and commercial success. We refused [to appear at] the Grammys. We had just come off tour and we were in the studio and we didn't realize that we were offending everyone in the business. At that point the Grammy show seemed very tacky. We got a wicked backlash. Obviously, we didn't mean to offend anybody."

Ivan admits, "In those days I wasn't into it. It's a more accepted thing in the business now. At that point, I wasn't prepared to do anything. I wasn't into being famous. I was more into making music and doing whatever I was supposed to be doing well."

"I should have listened to Arlo Guthrie," continues Ivan. "He came to a show and gave me a good piece of advice. He said, 'Dude, space out your fights,' because he could see that I was going to get into some serious traffic jams. I was going at it like I was out to save the world and that was it."

Though *Folk of the '80s Part III* had an infectious follow-up single to "The Safety Dance" in "Where Do The Boys Go?", the album failed to have the same impact as its predecessor. Part of this was due to MCA's token promotion of the album — a reaction to the band's antics during the *Rhythm of Youth* campaign. Part of this was also due to the material itself. The songs continue to display Ivan's uncanny melodic gifts, but the record mirrors the unrest felt by the band at the time. There is a melancholic tone that carries from the tongue-in-cheek "No Dancing" — a slow music box-based number that is the antithesis of "The Safety Dance" — to the sombre reflection of "I Sing Last/Not For Tears." Ivan best expresses his reservations toward the band's fame on the angular and self-explanatory "Messiahs Die Young."

A great deal of the tension was between band members and/or with manager Marc Durand. Stefan Doroschuk notes, "I didn't participate very much in the making of that record, so the album suffered from a lack of direction; it was rather crudely produced. On the song 'Mother's Opinion' I got into the studio to do my guitar track and do a warm-up take. About two-thirds of the way through the song I stopped and said, 'Okay, let's take it for real.' But Marc said, 'No that's good, we're keeping it.' After protesting for a while, I told him, okay, at least let me finish the track. But no, they wouldn't hear about it. The unravelling of that album was largely due to the massive egos generated by our early success."

Ivan describes Durand's approach to management as "punching people on the way up." According to all Doroschuk brothers, Durand soured a working relationship with the president of MCA America and angered so many individuals in the music industry that they ended up sitting out their MCA contract, and would not land another deal until 1986 when the band signed with Polygram. To further fuel the flames of acrimony, Durand would later release a compilation CD, *Greatest Hats*, in 1996, without the band's consent. "I don't have much to say about him, and all of it negative," states Stefan. "He had a chance to be a big Montreal manager, but he was so thoroughly obnoxious, ignorant and disgusting as a human being that he always lost his artists after a short while."

"He was good at what he did," says Colin. "He was pretty tireless. He [also] had a knack for not answering the doorbell and peeking out the curtains when the bill collectors came. He's just really a crooked character, and at some point if you're not honest, people won't deal with you anymore. That's happened to him now. Nobody wants to deal with him."

Stefan continues, "After *Part III*, Ivan and I couldn't go on the way we were, so we kicked out Colin and Allan — although Colin made some guest appearances on later albums. Before [1987's] *Pop Goes the World*, we also dumped Marc to complete the purge."

In 1985, Sire would release a collection of the band's early-1980s recordings under the title *Freeways* and the band did a brief tour before disappearing from the public eye for two years. It officially capped an era, as electropop's popularity began to wane in the face of a resurgence of guitar-driven music. All the Doroschuk brothers pursued different avenues: Ivan reacquainted himself with the city's underground community; Stefan played with local country rockers Three O'Clock Train under the alias Billy Joe Parker to escape record company contractual hassles; and all brothers made cameos on Three O'Clock Train's first EP, 1986's *Wig Wam Beach*.

Formed in 1984, and led by Mack MacKenzie, Three O'Clock Train were Montreal's foremost purveyors of country rock. Contemporaries of Blue Rodeo, both bands found themselves used as points of comparison in the mid-'80s. Says MacKenzie, "They've told me when they first started touring everyone told them, 'You guys sound like just like Three O'Clock Train,' and about two years later, everybody was telling me, 'You guys sound just like Blue Rodeo.' We would be playing at the Cameron House [in Toronto] and they were playing at the Horseshoe. We would time it so we could take our breaks to go and watch each other's bands. Neither of us had records back then."

"If Mack grew up in Toronto, he would be known across the country the way Jim Cuddy and Greg Keelor are," claims one-time roommate Warren Campbell. "He had a core of fans but success eluded him."

Born in Lincoln, Maine, Mack MacKenzie lived a transient life; his childhood spent in various states, his teens in Montreal, and his first adult years in Alberta and British Columbia. In the late 1970s, still in his early twenties, MacKenzie returned to Montreal with the will to start a band. Inspired after seeing Rick Trembles's band the American Devices, he formed Sid Serious and the Pseuds in 1979. When the Pseuds disbanded in 1982, MacKenzie decided to move into country music. "I always played country music as a kid, a lot of Buck Owens and Johnny Cash. I came to Montreal and there wasn't any country music in Montreal," explains MacKenzie. "We were still punk rockers, but we were just playing country. We wanted to be a country band because there were too many punk bands."

The first incarnation of Three O'Clock Train coincidentally featured two young punks, Alex and Carlos Soria, who were already dabbling in their own high school punk band called the Nils. However, the brothers chickened out before Mack MacKenzie's first gig at La Steppe, and the singer was left to perform solo. In time, Three O'Clock Train found its rhythm section when another popular trio named Ulterior Motive disbanded. Bassist Dave Hill and drummer Pierre Perron were assimilated into MacKenzie's project. Mackenzie would later thank Ulterior Motive singer Keith Rawlings for providing him with a rhythm section by covering his song "The Devil Likes Me" on Three O'Clock Train's first EP. By the band's third gig they were opening for Men Without Hats. In its early years, Stefan Doroschuk often played lead guitar for Three O'Clock Train, but MacKenzie eventually found a full-time lead guitarist and backing vocalist in his brother Stuart.

In the mid-'80s the band built an audience playing local venues like Station 10, La Steppe and Tatou, and released two recordings on Bill Varvaris's

Pipeline Records: 1986's *Wig Wam Beach*, and 1987's *Muscle In*. MacKenzie's songwriting and distinctive upper-range tenor, teamed with Hill and Perron's driving rhythms, produced an appealing country-rock hybrid — whether with shit-kickers like "Train of Dreams" and "Fingers," or with sad-eyed laments such as "Fire I Can't Put Out" and the Phil Spector-inspired "Be My Baby."

The band's following was growing and work had already begun on their second full-length album, *It Takes A Lot to Laugh, It Takes a Train To Cry*, when things came to a dead stop during a western tour in 1988. The band's final gig unexpectedly took place in Edmonton when MacKenzie left his band after the first set of the night and proceeded to make his way back to Montreal. MacKenzie says, "I was tired of playing with the musicians I was playing with, and I wasn't happy. I never wanted to be on the road and playing bars. I never liked it. So I left. I gave the band everything: the money, the van, everything. That was it — I was fed up. I still like music, but I did not want to do that anymore even though we had success. I'd rather be a writer more than anything else."

In the winter of 1985, Ivan Doroschuk walked into The Rising Sun — a reggae bar turned punk-rock haven — on Ste. Catherine Street. After the club Cargo closed in 1984, The Rising Sun was one of the few places in Montreal that would house punk shows. When the pop star descended upon the underground establishment, on this particular night, L.A.'s Black Flag had just performed. John Kastner, then-singer for the Asexuals, was DJing that evening, and remembers that Ivan's presence turned a few heads. "The first time I ever met Ivan he gave 60 or 70 people free acid and gave every-body in the bar free drinks," says Kastner. "He was kind of this gay pop rock star whose music we all hated, but we thought, 'Wow, this guy's out there. He's got the attitude.' That was the beginning of Ivan coming on to the hardcore scene. He was really in the same headspace as all of us were."

Ivan remarks, "I always thought of Men Without Hats as an electronic hardcore band with a hit single."

Ivan also became a familiar presence at various live venues such as Station 10 and La Steppe. He became a good contact for people needing soundmen, stagehands and equipment. In the case of the Nils, the pop star helped the band release a long-overdue proper recording. Ivan had seen the young ramshackle punk band play live a few times and the Nils' songwriting talent impressed him. During the sound check for the Nils' opening gig for Joan Jett at the Spectrum in 1985, Ivan offered to produce the young band.

"That's Ivan. That's the way he was," Alex Soria admits. "He was always hanging out in bars and always out for a jam and working with other people. That's a great attitude. That's something that's lacking in this city as far as the music scene. There's no more of that. It's a little more dog eat dog now."

Ivan financed the recording of the Nils' debut EP, *Sell Out Young!*, and designed the primitive cartoon cover. Stefan also assisted with his brother's pet project, and agreed to waive his fees to produce the four-song recording, though he had never heard the band. Stefan knew his brother would need his studio expertise, and after seeing the Nils play live, understood the challenge ahead of him. "When Alex came into the studio, the first thing I told him is that I'm going to want to clearly hear every word he sings," says Stefan. "We finished mixing that album at 5 a.m. before I had to grab my bags and go meet our tour bus."

Alex Soria was born in December 1965, and grew up in the south shore across from Montreal. In 1978, at the age of 12, Soria formed the Nils with bassist Guy "Chico" Caron and drummer Terry Toner. The band played their first gig in 1980 at Hotel La Salle opening for The Dischords, and soon after this, Alex's older brother Carlos joined the band for bass and guitar duties. Between learning their instruments and membership shuffles, it took the band an extended period of time to get off the ground. As Carlos Soria often noted in interviews, "We started when we were kids. We couldn't play, but we had heart."

"I first saw the Nils at a Concordia University Arts gathering," recounts Kevin Komoda. "Terry Toner had his mom drive them in one of those fake wood station wagons. He had so many drums, and he was so short that you could only see the sticks race across the kit when he did a drum fill. The sound was really bad, but I thought the songs were good — what I could make of them. I thought the shows were always a bit of a disaster, mainly because of the sound and the laidback quality of Alex's voice."

After the release of the Nils' *Now* demo in 1982, Alex defied his tag as "the shyest frontman in rock and roll" and the band caught the attention of California's BYO Records. Impressed with the demo, they asked the band to re-record "Scratches and Needles" for their 1983 compilation *Something to Believe In*. A year later, while Alex was still in his teens, the Nils contributed "Call of the Wild" to the Montreal underground compilation *Primitive Air Raid*. As well, two EPs — 1985's *Sell Out Young!* on Psyche Industry, and 1986's *Paisley* on Seigfried Records — gradually moved the Nils profile beyond their city limits.

It was the *Sell Out Young!* EP that attracted the attention of other artists and labels, mostly via word-of-mouth. Though the recording was not highly championed by either the band or their label, the songs on *Sell Out Young!* are pop punk treasures and confirm Soria's reputation as one of Montreal's best songwriters. The Nils remain the classic case of a "band's band." They were never commercially successful, but became a favourite of many artists including Superchunk, The Goo Goo Dolls and Hüsker Dü's Bob Mould, whose mother once sent them postcards, and thanked the *Brave New Waves* staff with cookies and fudge when the radio show played Hüsker Dü and the Nils. The influence of songs like "Daylight," "Fountains" and "Freedom," could also be heard on recorded work that Foo Fighters released nearly a decade later. At the time, the Nils' influence was most obvious in their own community.

"I think the Nils very much influenced the Doughboys and the Asexuals," says Dan Webster. "They had a really good energy and Alex had a great songwriting style, but Alex was really reliant on his brother and people around him. He would go where people led him, including people like Ivan.

Alex Soria of the Nils at El Mocambo in Toronto, 1988
(Photo by Eric Kearns)

He was just a guy writing songs. It's music that's as important as any of the bands that came out after Nirvana. It's just as strong, but it just didn't focus itself. That's the way it is, in terms of being at the right place at the right time."

On a smaller, but still significant scale, Dan Webster carved a well-timed niche in the city's punk scene. Along with partner Randy Boyd, and later

John McKenna, Webster formed Psyche Industry, one of the city's first independent labels dedicated to promoting underground music. Over a two-year existence, the label released 14 albums including local artists such as the Nils, the Asexuals and Condition, as well as Toronto's Groovy Religion and Victoria's NoMeansNo. Set in a uninsulated loft in Old Montreal, Psyche Industry brought some organization to the city's ungoverned punk scene.

When Webster moved to Montreal in 1983, the 22-year-old Edmontonian became one of the city's group of dedicated punks, hanging out at the Cargo club on St. Denis Street and organizing gigs. Webster hatched the idea of a Montreal punk compilation as a means of documenting a period of development in the city's alternative scene.

In order to produce the compilation, Webster and company organized a fundraising event called Freedom 84. The multi-band punk show was held in the basement of a church on the corner of Cherry and Barry Street, and featured Toronto's Direct Action, Ottawa's Porcelain Forehead, Montreal's No Policy and the Asexuals. Attended by the city's few hundred punk rockers, the fundraiser managed to raise two-thirds of the costs to produce the compilation.

Released in 1984, the 15-song *Primitive Air Raid* featured recordings — some cruder than others — from a variety of local bands, including the Nils, Red Shift, the American Devices, Vomit and the Zits, Genetic Control, No Policy, Fair Warning and the Asexuals. In Kastner's eyes, it was an appropriate time to document the activity in Montreal's underground. "Freedom 84 was really when the whole scene around the Cargo Club was at its peak. We only got 300 people to the shows, but it was the same 300 people all the time and 100 of those people played in bands. It was a really close scene." For most of the bands on *Primitive Air Raid*, it was the first and only time they were committed to a tape. For John Kastner's Asexuals, however, it was only the beginning.

The Asexuals stood out from most of the bands on the compilation due to their young age and the fact they were from the Beaconsfield suburb, not Montreal's downtown. "We were just a bunch of kids from the West Island, and we were the only punk rock band from the West Island," explains vocalist Kastner, who formed the band in high school with guitarist Sean Friesen, bassist T.J. "Plenty" Collins and drummer Paul Remington. "Everyone else played bad metal. We had one competing band; they were called Rogue. That was Brock's [Pytel, later of the Doughboys] band. We hated them and they hated us. We did one of our first shows with them at Memorial Beach and we were called Johnny Jew and The Holocaust. But everyone was too offended by our name so we called ourselves Dead Dog for that show."

Remembers one-time Doughboys guitarist Scott McCulloch, "They were a few years younger than me, so they were at an age when punk rock was all they'd heard. They were the first people I knew who were raised solely on it. They were the first true hardcore kids. I didn't like a lot of hardcore. I'd drive around in the car with John and eventually get so pissed off I'd throw his tapes out the window and say, 'Fuck hardcore! Play something else.'"

The historical relevance of the Asexuals didn't stem from their music, which was typical teenage hardcore fare with sloganeering political lyrics like "Contra Rebels." Instead, they were notable for what they were able to accomplish from sheer will and limited talent. Propelled by Kastner's strong work ethic, the Asexuals became the first Montreal hardcore band to make records and tour extensively outside of the city. "John was always a go-getter," explains Dan Webster. "He went out and found studios and recorded and had the drive to do it. He kicked all the downtown bands' asses."

Born August 12, 1966 in Montreal, John Kastner, like many children of the 1970s, was drawn to rock music through the massively popular KISS. In junior high, Kastner first played in rock and metal bands, but soon became a dedicated listener of punk and hardcore music. As a 12-year-old, he often bussed downtown to watch musicians like Chris Barry and his band, The 222's through the windows of various city clubs. Although Barry would go on to join The 39 Steps, who would release an album on RCA and make an appearance in Woody Allen's *Hannah and Her Sisters* — the greater percentage of Kastner's role models in Montreal's punk scene never went as far as leaving the city, or releasing a 7" single.

The Asexuals' frontman realized early on that if his band was to do anything, they had to make it happen themselves. The band members, barely 17 years of age, began work on producing a single. Through his factory warehouse job in the summer of 1983, Kastner earned enough money to finance the $700 cost for Morris Appelbaum to record and press a 7". Kastner then phoned Og Records' Gerard Van Herk about releasing the *Featuring: the Asexuals* EP. Van Herk didn't know the band, but agreed to help, simply informing Kastner to write the label's address on the back of the single; it was the only time the new indie became involved with a hardcore band.

In 1984, the young band worked with Applebomb again and recorded their first full-length album for Psyche Industry, *Be What You Want*. Around this time, the Asexuals started to make valuable contacts with some of the bands from the U.K. and the U.S. they were meeting at the Cargo — especially L.A.'s Youth Brigade. Formed by brothers Adam, Mark and Shawn

Stern, Youth Brigade were DIY pioneers in the early '80s hardcore scene. Through the formation of their own label, BYO (Better Youth Organization), the release of their own recordings and compilation records and the band's infinite touring, Youth Brigade became a huge influence for the Asexuals.

"When we met those Youth Brigade guys, that changed everything for the Asexuals," says Kastner. "They gave us a few numbers and I started phoning people and getting more and more phone numbers. I booked this tour on the east coast all the way to Florida and back from my parents' phone. Our record had just come out in January 1984. We had to drive to Toronto in a snowstorm to pick it up and sleep in the van on the side of the highway on the way back — in January! No other Montreal band had a record and they all thought we were these rich kids who managed to get money to make a record."

Kastner's support for his musical endeavours came from his parents' liberal-mindedness about their teenage son's rock and roll exploits; they also provided a basement and backyard for band practices and punk shows. "They knew I wanted to play music," he says. "I started buying KISS records and was going to see KISS shows when I was eight. By the time I was 14, they figured 'this is what he wants to do.' They were pretty lenient about it, but they'd get pissed off because I used to run up the phone bill so bad."

Prior to the Asexuals' first U.S. tour to Florida, bassist T.J. Collins announced that he had broken his finger, and the band was forced to recruit a quick replacement. Kastner says, "T.J. thought it was too sketchy that we were going to take off to America when we didn't know anybody. He got really scared and he made up a story that he had broken his finger. We knew he hadn't. So we got Carlos from the Nils to play bass on the first Asexuals tour."

T.J. would join the band on their second U.S. tour after the release of 1985's *Contemporary World*. But the 40-date, summer coast-to-coast trek across North America exposed larger concerns than a faked injury. The ties between the band and their singer began to weaken. After completing a second support tour in the winter of 1986, Kastner either quit, or was booted out of the band — depending on who you ask. Kastner confesses, "On that tour we didn't get along because I was the guy who was doing everything and it used to piss me off that those guys did nothing. We got in a big fight when we got back. It was a 'them against me' sort of thing. I said, 'Fuck you guys. I do everything, so if you're not going to be cool about it then I'm going to leave.' They said, 'Fuck you, so leave.' That really divided the Psyche gang. It divided a lot of people in the Montreal scene at that point."

Dan Webster says, "When Kastner was breaking up with the Asexuals, the guys wanted to get rid of him because they thought he couldn't sing. They wanted to be the Replacements and he didn't have a voice that was going that way. I talked to him about it and I thought he deserved better. But he went out the next day and formed the Doughboys. He went at it and released a record in a couple of months. He wasn't going to sit and wait around."

After severing ties with Kastner, smoker-voiced T.J. Collins moved from bass to rhythm guitar and lead vocals, and took over most of the song-writing duties. With 1988's *Dish* and 1991's *Exile in Floontown*, the Asexuals completely abandoned their hardcore roots and indulged an overdriven rock sound. Both albums contain some decent melodic moments, but most of the time they come across as little more than a popular bar band. The Asexuals maintained a loyal cult following in scattered pockets around the world, but ultimately parted ways after the long delayed follow-up to *Exile*, 1996's *Fitzjoy*.

Aside from the typical artistic and political differences that brought an end to groups like the Asexuals, many attribute the fragmentation of Montreal's early '80s punk bands to drug abuse. Drugs took their toll on numerous groups, including No Policy and Genetic Control, and earlier bands like the Chromosomes. Dan Webster says, "Around the time I came here [1983–1984], I was seeing a lot of all those people in those early bands and a lot of them had problems. Later on the drug of choice became cocaine, although there were still a few of the old heroin problems that stayed with some of the bands."

One of the more notable bands wrestling with significant drug demons was the Nils; the fact that they had the most potential to reach a wider audience made this all the more tragic. Notes *Sell Out Young!* producer Stefan Doroschuk, "Basically they couldn't keep their shit together long enough to make something happen. They were too busy shooting heroin. That's the real reason why the Nils never made it, no matter what anyone else says."

It did not seem that the Nils' self-destruction was inevitable at the time. When Profile Records — the home of rappers Run-DMC and Vancouver punks DOA — contacted the Nils in 1986, it appeared there was a bright future ahead. The Sorias had initially thought the label interest was a joke, that is, until they received a 42-page contract for a seven-year recording deal in the mail. "I'm sure there aren't too many musicians that actually read those things," says frontman Alex Soria of the band's quick acceptance of the deal. "We just signed it. We had nothing to lose."

It seemed like a good move. Along with generation-spanning guitar hero Chris Spedding in the producer's chair, the Nils committed their most realized batch of songs to their 1987 eponymous debut. Songs like "Bandito Callin'," "River of Sadness" and "Wicked Politician" added another layer of timeless melodies to the Soria catalogue even though the re-recordings of "Daylight" and "In Betweens" lacked the initial fervour they had on the EP. The album sold 10,000 copies — a respectable number for a Canadian punk band. Unfortunately, in the U.S. market, this was far from a success. When the hip-hop-oriented label started paring its roster, Profile not only dumped the band, but forcibly seized some of the Nils' signing incentives.

"I used to buy weed off their drummer," recalls Scott McCulloch. "One day I was over and saw they got all this brand new gear [from Profile Records] sitting at their house. Then another day I came and everything was gone. I asked what happened and they said, 'Profile Records came and took all the gear back.' The [label] came to Montreal with a truck and took all their gear! I felt so bad for them."

Record company hassles aside, this was a band that was not a textbook definition of stability. Drugs had always been a problem, but the extent of their effect on the band escalated during this period. Days before the U.S. tour in support of *Nils*, the band's drummer had a breakdown and had to be rescued in a Montreal park by paramedics. After a round of Ontario shows supporting *Nils*, Carlos came up with his own way of dealing with his issues: he told his roommate that he was going to the store for a carton of milk, then phoned his brother Alex a few days later from California. "He emptied the Nils' bank account and fled to California for four years," says McCulloch. "He thought everybody hated him, but they all just wanted him to come back."

Mag Wheel Records head Woody Whalen elaborates, "He stayed with other bands, and sometimes his dad. When he wore out his welcome, he came back a few years later. That's when Alex briefly formed Los Patos in the late '80s. He also recorded under the name Black Sox on a Nettwerk tribute to Donovan. Carlos still does odd things, and has stolen lots from family, band and friends. Alex is better off without him."

Carlos eventually returned in the early '90s, and after the brothers made amends, they attempted to reform the Nils. James MacLean, a long-time fan of the Nils and manager of the Doughboys, tried to assist the band he felt had never received its due. It didn't work. "They were a band I always loved," explains MacLean. "They were influential for everyone, but unfortunately drugs and lack of motivation [ended the band]. We put them back together and I brought in Lonnie James [The Super Friendz, The Lawn] to play drums. I said, 'Lonnie, don't hate me for this. This could be really amazing, or this could be a nightmare.' Unfortunately, it turned into a nightmare. They did one tour across Canada and the interest wasn't there. They were a hollow shell of what they used to be. You knew they'd been there. They'd been written up in *Rolling Stone*, *Spin*, and *Billboard*. They'd been really close in the '80s, and they just didn't have the heart to make the comeback."

"It wasn't about music anymore," admits Alex. "That's what did it for me. After that tour I didn't really want to [continue]. The band wasn't fun anymore." Alex completely removed himself from music for three years while he recovered from his experiences with the Nils. He worked in a deli in Montreal, but was eventually pulled out of retirement by the enduring interest in his old band. Mag Wheel Records released a 1996 compilation album entitled *Green Fields in Daylight* that culled all of the Nils' recordings except the Profile LP. The Nils were also celebrated with a Mag Wheel tribute album, *Scratches and Needles: A Tribute To The Nils*, which featured a variety of bands including Rusty, Punchbuggy and Down By Law. In 1999, Alex Soria started anew with a quintet named Chino. As their 1999 EP *Mala Leche* suggests, Soria had not lost his ability to write amazing power pop songs that too few people get a chance to hear.

After a couple of years out of the public eye, 1987 saw the long-awaited return of Men Without Hats. With new management, and a new deal with Polygram U.S.A., Ivan and Stefan Doroschuk went to England to record their third album, *Pop Goes the World* with Zeus B. Held. As the infant on the album cover suggests, *Pop Goes the World* is a concept album that focuses on universal hopes, experiences and fears, through the rites of passage of two young protagonists, Johnny and Jenny. It is too pop to be prog rock, but too arty to be simply dismissed as bubblegum. The album is very much an indulgence in layering, and its symphony of keyboards occasionally brands the work with 1980s production values, but it is a brave record that begs to be played in its entirety. It is very much a consolidation of Ivan's electronic folk as the album echoes '70s prog greats with its various guest vocalists and ambient effects, and subtle salutes to the genre: the Pink Floyd twist in "Bright Side of the Sun" and the use of Jethro Tull's flute maestro Ian Anderson throughout "On Tuesday." *Pop Goes the World* still showcases Ivan's ability to be current with strong synth-pop singles such as the title track and "Moonbeam."

Despite this successful return for the Doroschuk brothers, Men Without

Hats soon became entangled in the complicated world of major-label music again. As a single, "Pop Goes The World" went number one, and the album went platinum in Canada. But conflicts with the band's U.K.-based management resulted in the band not playing a single gig in Canada. Having signed to an American branch of Polygram, Stefan Doroschuk notes that, "Polygram Canada was a fairly dead label at the time. The Canadian branch released what the U.S. told them to, and they didn't have their own A&R department until we did [1989's] *21st Century.*" Instead, the band played 60 dates over four months in the United States and never capitalized on their success in their home country. The title track eventually hit the *Billboard* Top 20, but by then it wasn't a point of pride.

"If you want a background on what went on during that period, you should read *Hit Men,*" confesses Ivan, in reference to Fredric Dannen's controversial tell-all of the American music industry payola scandal. "You can basically apply that book to Men Without Hats. He could be talking about me. It's the payola scandal of the late '80s, the story of the fight between MCA and Polygram. I was leaving MCA and going to Polygram at that time. There was this huge payola thing that was pretty hush hush."

Ivan says that payola involved not only the amount of money, but how fast it was paid out. "These guys were taking it from anybody," he continues. Not everybody can be Number One. It becomes who pays the most, who pays the fastest. They had a track record that you'd be paying them further on down the line, too. I guess for any business dealing with that coin, you'd have to get up in the morning and be a mean kind of guy to attack it. I wasn't into the warrior aspect of it anymore. It was fun at the beginning. Punk and new wave was all brand new, but by the time *Pop Goes the World* came around there was no scene left. That was it."

Although the band's 1989 follow-up, the verbosely titled *The Adventures of Men and Women Without Hate In The 21st Century,* had its moments, it is ultimately a less charming affair. Like Ivan's songwriting for Francophone pop diva Mitsou on her 1990 *Terre des Hommes* album, *In the 21st Century* has a few great hooks, but seemed to be a transparent attempt to further elevate Men Without Hats' place in the pop pantheon. A year after this release Ivan began to find his musical feet again while his brother was knocked off his. When Stefan was left bedridden for six months after being hit by a car in 1989, Ivan began to jam with his friends from the Bifteck club. This eventually resulted in the band's final album *Sideways,* a guitar-rock project inspired by his developing friendships with some of the local guitar bands — and individuals like the Doughboys' John Kastner and

Ivan Doroschuk and Mitsou in Toronto, June 1990
(Photo by Rick McGinnis)

Voivod's Michel Langevin, both of whom had provided a new reason for the media to focus on Montreal.

The genesis of the Doughboys was sparked by a chance meeting between John Kastner and his childhood nemesis Brock Pytel, formerly of the teen metal band Rogue. While postering on St. Laurent Street for a Tupelo Chain Sex gig, Kastner casually asked Pytel if he was playing drums. Pytel informed the ex-Asexual that he was singing for another band and he didn't have a kit. When Kastner promised to find drums for Pytel, he joined on the spot. Eventually, Montreal staple John "Bondhead" Ascencio was enlisted on bass, and Kastner drew Montreal-native Scott McCulloch back from Toronto to play lead guitar. A few years Kastner's senior, McCulloch was also raised in Beaconsfield and had known Kastner since he was nine years old. McCulloch had even held a summer stint with the Asexuals, thus making him one of the first logical choices for Kastner to enlist in his new band.

Officially born at the end of 1986, the Doughboys were another vehicle driven by Kastner's tireless work ethic. Unlike the singer's situation in the Asexuals, the Doughboys allowed him to hone his songcraft. The Doughboys left hardcore behind, and found inspiration in the mid-'80s Minneapolis underground, principally Soul Asylum and Hüsker Dü. "When we formed Doughboys, all we really wanted to sound like was *Made to Be Broken*-era Soul Asylum — two screaming harmonies, and some weird time signatures," says McCulloch. "That was our model at that point."

Whatever was recorded at Studio Victor, a RCA orchestral studio in Old Montreal with fifty-foot ceilings, massive windows and a mahogany interior — not a typical punk rock studio. Steve Kravac — drummer for My Dog Popper and a live engineer who would often dress up in a Bonhomme de Carnival suit at Men Without Hats shows — produced the album and managed to capture the band's youthful energy. Written primarily by Kastner, but with three songs by Pytel, the 10-song album showcases what would become traditional Doughboys devices: building guitar riffs, gang vocals and anthemic songwriting such as that found on "Tradition" and the excellent "The Forecast."

Later member Jonathan Cummins says, "The Doughboys sound is probably more Kastner's songs, but a lot of the early Doughboys fan-favourite songs are Brock's." Pytel's songs are reminiscent of Hüsker Dü's Grant Hart, and the album's melodic sense is the most indicative on his songs. One of his tracks, "You're Related," was made into the band's first video; it introduced the Doughboys to MuchMusic viewers across the country with a montage of the band's energetic performance and accompanying stage diving. Pytel cringes at the memory of having some of his drum sounds replaced by triggered Neil Peart samples, but he still holds fond memories of the album. "I think it reflects the zeal of youth, and innocence broken, but not truly lost," he says. "It's also a pretty good collage of the sounds of the day. It adds Canadian flavour to the movement of punk to pop."

Before *Whatever* was released, the band embarked on a U.S. tour billing themselves as "The Doughboys featuring the ex-singer of the Asexuals." McCulloch claims the tour was loosely booked, but the band still lucked out by linking up with the Descendants and the first solo tour for ex-Black Flag singer Henry Rollins. This quickly brought the fledgling group to some larger venues and introduced them to audiences over three and a half months. "We were promoting this non-existent record in a country it wasn't even out in, but we had the greatest fucking time doing it," McCulloch says. "It was the greatest tour I've ever done in my life."

Scott McCulloch's enthusiasm would not be sustained, however, and he parted ways with the band shortly after the release of *Whatever*. "I had trouble getting along with John on the road," McCulloch confesses. "I was way less responsible in those days and way more willing to just say, 'fuck it.' My girlfriend had left Montreal and moved to Kingston, so I was all bummed out. I went to Kingston to visit her and by not coming back to Montreal they basically kicked me out. I wasn't planning on coming back, so John replaced me while I was gone. I ended up getting really pissed because we had our stuff in storage in Montreal and when they got all their stuff out, they left the door unlocked. When I got back, all my good shit had been stolen and all my other stuff was lying in a huge heap in the middle of the floor. All my memorabilia, and all the stuff I had saved in my life to that point was wrecked. Then I ended up losing all my equipment because I'd fallen behind on my payments after giving John money during the tour to pay his rent. My equipment got seized and all my shit was destroyed, so I got this serious hate-on for those guys. I ended up not playing for a while because I was so soured on music."

McCulloch was quickly replaced by Jonathan Cummins, a guitar wiz who had grown up in Toronto and was kicked out of a variety of schools until he dropped out in ninth grade after his final attempt at the alternative school SEED. He had honed his chops in a variety of bands, but it was after Kastner witnessed a live set of Cummins's band Circus Lupus — that also included NoMind drummer Paul Newman and future I Mother Earth bassist Bruce Gordon — that Kastner asked Cummins to become a Doughboy. "I said yeah without even hearing them," Cummins remembers. "I moved out there without a guitar. They thought I owned my own equipment, but I actually didn't. I showed up and the next step was they had to buy me equipment. I just showed up with a skateboard and a bag of clothes. I never owned a guitar until I joined the Doughboys."

Doughboys, circa *Crush*, 1993: Peter Arsenault, Jonathan Cummins, Paul Newman, John Kastner
(Courtesy William New)

During these personnel changes, *Whatever* was finally released through Bill Varvaris's local Pipeline Records. Along with Psyche Industry and Og Records, Pipeline was a noteworthy force that found a temporary home for a few of Montreal's musical outsiders, and it was funded from profits from Varvaris's importing business, Bonaparte Records. Bonaparte had initially been created as a means for Varvaris to access import records at cheaper prices. It gradually grew to be the nation's second largest importer, next to Toronto's Record Peddler.

Varvaris was a man whose life orbited around his musical passion. Not only did he possess a wealth of musical knowledge and an enviable record collection, but he was also well-regarded by many in the Montreal music scene. He had documented the late '70s Montreal underground with a three-issue run of his fanzine, *Surfin' Bird*, that preserved Montreal's early underground: the Chromosomes, the Blanks, Lorne Ranger, Electric Vomit — and its later incarnation as the American Devices — and the 222's. Pipeline Records became Varvaris's next means of validating the local underground, releasing albums by Three O'Clock Train, the Doughboys, Jerry Jerry and the Sons of Rhythm Orchestra and Ray Condo and his Hard Rock Goners. Kevin Komoda reflects, "Maybe it's me being idealistic, but Bill loved music more than the idea that he could make money from an artist's music."

Komoda continues, "Bill was a key figure, if only as a catalyst and as someone who was around from the very beginning. Personally speaking, I owe much to Bill because he was very supportive and guided me through some tough times after Rational Youth split. His friendship spread throughout the Montreal scene. Bill's local fame started escalating as Bonaparte grew. He helped support the local misfits and band members by employing them at Bonaparte.

When Psyche Industry faded in late '86, Bonaparte absorbed its key staff — Dan Webster, Randy Boyd and John Kastner — and for a short while, both the label and the import business became one of the biggest deals in town. Unfortunately, Varvaris lacked substantial business management skills and problems accumulated. Mack Mackenzie, who worked for Bonaparte remembers, "He was bringing in a lot of product and a lot of product was left on the shelf. Phil Hill and Randy Boyd started working for Bonaparte. They talked Bill into bringing in an efficiency expert [Eric Goodis]. He came in and ended up buying the place. [Goodis], Randy and Phil sort of pushed Bill out, but Bill was sort of losing it because he hadn't written anything down and he was stuck with a lot of stock."

When Bonaparte collapsed, Goodis formed Cargo Records with Randy

Boyd and Phil Hill as partners, and he hired most of the Bonaparte staff. For many years Cargo operated as Canada's largest distributor. Varvaris, unfortunately, did not recover well from the loss of his business and his label. According to Kastner, "[The situation] ruined Bill so much that it drove him into his parents' basement in LaSalle. First it drove him into his little apartment and he wouldn't leave. Bill just didn't deal with anything. After it closed he went into his apartment and never came out. Eventually the tax people showed up at his house and took his whole record collection. No one ever saw him after that."

Pipeline disintegrated two months after the release of *Whatever*, and left the Doughboys without a label. This situation did not last long as the band's persistent touring and a CMJ showcase gig in New York eventually attracted American punk label Restless Records. Restless released the Doughboys' second album, 1989's *Home Again*, which had been recorded on tour in California, and funded by Pytel through a loan and some inheritance money. This would be the last time Pytel contributed to a Doughboys record.

Between mounting political battles, personal issues and "punchings in the face," Brock Pytel found his reason for leaving the band. Pytel confesses, "We were starting to go in different directions, particularly John Kastner and I. I had started a daily meditation practise and was not drinking or smoking dope anymore. John Bondhead and I were also vegetarian, myself trying to eat macrobiotic. For the last two tours I coped by literally not speaking for days at a time and travelling with cooking supplies and a small stove. It got really difficult to be at the centre of the party all the time. John resented my being different and I think he was embarrassed by it, and I ended up taking a lot of crap in order to keep the band together. I eventually started doubting the value of what kids were getting from us as an example. Musically, I was also feeling an urge to expand while John was pretty committed to the sound we had already established."

Ironically, the Doughboys' next album was an exploration of many musical avenues. With former NoMind drummer Paul Newman filling the vacancy created by Pytel's departure, the band began work with Michael Phillip Wojewoda on 1990's *Happy Accidents*. The album title was apt, and was far from a victim of Kastner's musical tunnel vision as the band displays a richer melodic bloodstream, and a more eclectic approach than their previous works. In addition to Kastner and Cummins's punk/metal fusion, the band experiments with acoustic songs, jangle pop, and an assortment of mixing effects and instrumentation. In the case of Bondhead's "Sunflower Honey" and "The Apprenticeship of Lenny Kravitz," one would be excused for thinking the record-pressing plant had put the wrong band onto the album.

Cummins says of working with Wojewoda, "He had a good sense of melody, and he had worked with Change of Heart who were one of our favourite bands. He had a really keen sense of harmonies, which in hindsight we went a little bit overboard on. A lot of songs on *Happy Accidents* ended up sounding like 'Bohemian Rhapsody.' I even wrote acoustic ballads that weren't even supposed to be on the record. Listening to that record — a lot of it is just embarrassing. It's just so far removed from what I listen to now. It's like looking at a scrapbook where you are wearing goofy shirts."

Like Men Without Hats' *Sideways* album, the guest list on *Happy Accidents* was drawn from musicians frequently seen at Les Foufounes and The Bifteck, and featured contributions from two especially noteworthy figures. Ivan Doroschuk added his keyboard talents to a couple of tracks, while Voivod drummer Michel Langevin contributed both the accordion to "Tupperware Party" and the CD artwork. Kastner had first met Langevin through ex-SNFU manager Gubby, who worked with Kastner at Cargo. Langevin and Kastner became close friends despite the fact Voivod's music came from a radically different universe than the Doughboys.

The Voivod history is as extraordinary as the concepts and artwork that Langevin extracted from his hyper-creative mind for each album. It is strangely coincidental that one of the most influential and celebrated North American metal bands originated in a Northern Quebec town that is home to North America's largest aluminum factory. The influence of growing up in the shadow of this environmental monstrosity was reflected through the themes on their 1989 album, *Nothingface*, perhaps Voivod's creative and career apex. This album also embodies the two main influences on Voivod and Quebec hard rock audiences in general: progressive rock and metal.

Langevin says, "All those underground progressive bands — Van der Graaf Generator, King Crimson, Gentle Giant, and even German bands like Nektar and all those Krautrock bands — they were huge in Quebec and also in France. But if you go around Canada and in the U.S.A., people don't know much about them. They're all very much cult bands. Here in Quebec we all grew up listening to Black Sabbath and progressive rock. Our roots really lie in progressive rock mixed with the heavy stuff from the '70s."

The members of Voivod, each with their own nickname — drummer/conceptualist "Away" (Michel Langevin), guitarist/songwriter "Piggy" (Denis D'Amour), bassist/songwriter "Blacky (Jean-Yves Theriault), and singer/lyricist "Snake" (Denis Belanger) — formed in 1982 through various connections at the local college in Jonquière, Quebec. The band's big break came when independent music journalist and acquaintance Wayne Archibald forwarded a very rough demo to Metal Blade Records in Los Angeles. The label was impressed enough to ask the band to re-record a song for the label's compilation *Metal Massacre #5*. Shortly after, Metal Blade offered to release the band's 1984 debut, *War and Pain*.

Like their compilation track, *War and Pain* was recorded in a jingle studio in Jonquière. Voivod's early mission was to be the loudest band on the planet and the horror-struck studio engineer requested they use an effects box called a "Rockman" that allowed them to record at low volume but still get a heavy sound. They would comply for the compilation track session, but the band refused to use the device for the *War and Pain* sessions and subjected the studio staff to aural torture. Influential U.K. metal magazine *Kerrangg* was similarly unimpressed in their first assessment of the band. "*Kerrangg* said we should be called 'Void Vod,' and we 'were the worst band on earth,'" says Langevin. "It's pretty funny considering how they regard us now. We were really influenced by the new wave of British heavy metal. [We were influenced] riff-wise by Motorhead, but lyric-wise, it was from listening to Discharge, Conflict and the Dead Kennedys — the music that made us aware of nuclear weapons in Europe and the political downside of the U.S.A. The result was hardcore metal and very harsh."

Blacky says of the band's early days, "We played maybe three times in Jonquière before we moved to Montreal. We recorded the album before we had even done a show. It's amazing in the sense that we didn't have much experience, but that was the only way we could have done it. We had a small following in Jonquière. Our first show had maybe 200 people. Generally people were pissed off because we had managed to get a contract, and Deaf Dealer, the local 'white metal' band, was a lot more popular. When we arrived in Montreal the club bands didn't like us either; we hadn't played the game. We didn't come up the way everyone else had."

After completing the recording of their first album, Away quit his studies in nuclear physics at l'Université du Québec á Chicoutimi, and both he and Blacky were kicked out of their parents' homes. The band relocated to Montreal to a shared apartment, and adapted to life as artists. Away remembers, "We only had 153 bucks each from welfare every month. With peanut butter, we would take the seal off carefully, eat the inside, leave one centimetre of peanut butter, fill it up with water, put the seal back on and take it back to the grocery store and say, 'Well, we wanted crunchy.'

Voivod, original line-up: Michel "Away" Langevin,
Jean-Yves "Blacky" Theriault, Denis "Piggy" D'Amour,
Denis "Snake" Belanger
(Courtesy of James MacLean)

We did that for a year. We found ourselves in many shameful situations like stealing clothes off outside hangers. In '87, royalties started to come in, and we were able to live off our music."

In 1985, Voivod found a creative means for a publicity-blitz when then-manager Maurice Richard acquired a grant from the Quebec government for the band to embark on a school tour for "educational purposes." Blacky remembers, "It was supposed to be a lecture demonstration with a performance, but it was actually just an autograph signing and a rock show. We had smoke machines and pyro, the whole kit. I think it was one of the best things we did in terms of people getting to know us."

In the same year, the band turned misfortune into another means of exposure. After their gear was stolen from the practice space they shared with hardcore bands SCUM and Fair Warning, Voivod organized and headlined a benefit show that drew an impressive audience of 3000 to a Montreal roller rink. Dubbed *World War Three*, the festival also included Celtic Frost, Destruction and Possessed, and raised enough money for Voivod to replace their losses and finish the recording of their second album *RRRÖÖÖAAARRR*. The show also led to a label deal. Voivod handed a tape of a rough mix demo to Swiss band Celtic Frost who were already on Noise Records. Upon Celtic

Frost's return to Europe, they gave the demo to the label in Berlin and Voivod was signed for a three-album deal. Voivod would travel to their label's hometown to record 1986's *Killing Technology* and 1988's *Dimension Haltröss*.

Berlin proved to be an influential turning point for the band both thematically and musically. "Back then The Wall was still there and there was a really oppressive feeling in the city; I think you can hear that on the album," explains Away. "We had also discovered industrial music because Harris Jones, who recorded the *Killing Technology* album, was also recording the Einstürzende Neubauten guys."

In true prog rock form, Voivod had always made concept albums based around its namesake. As an adolescent hooked on comic books, horror, sci-fi and Tolkien, Langevin created his own "post-nuclear vampire" named Voivod. "I mixed it up with a little bit of sci-fi because I was living by a factory and the industrial aspect was always in my drawings," says Langevin. "I was falling asleep with all those factory sounds, and I was trying to imagine monsters that could make those sounds. I would dream about them and then I would wake up and draw them. It was only later when we formed the band, that I asked the guys if we could put it into music and lyrics. They agreed and it's always been the same. I always wrote the concept and Piggy always wrote the music. He writes the best soundtracks for my stories. I couldn't really deal with anybody else. He's the musical genius of the band."

Throughout Voivod's first four albums, the band traced the development of the Voivod character. As Blacky details, "After a man-machine (*War & Pain*), a machine (RRRÖÖÖAAARRR), and a space ship (*Killing Technology*), Away decided that the next album — *Dimension Haltröss* — should be Voivod's mind exploring the limits of the three previous dimensions." The band's next album marked the end of this conceptual chain, and began a series of changes in many of the band's ideas.

In 1988, Voivod signed a deal with Mechanix, a subsidiary metal label of MCA, along with a new management deal with Pierre Paradis of the Donald K. Donald empire. Creatively, Blacky remembers 1988–1989 as a "volatile but productive" period in which he assisted primary songwriter Piggy to reach new heights. *Nothingface* was the result of this peak period in the group's history as a new musical path began to diverge from the band's previous travels. With producer Glen Robinson, the Jonquière quartet created a psychedelic masterpiece that melded the band's metal sensibilities with progressive, alternative and classical music. "We had had it with thrash," Blacky admits. "We wanted to go in another direction. We were all evolving, listening to different kinds of music. It made sense for us to adapt our music to what we were listening to. I was listening to a lot of classical music: Ligeti, Penderecki, Bartók, as well as contemporary stuff like Chrome, Dead Can Dance, Psychic TV, Scratch Acid."

Nothingface greatly benefited from the perks of major label funding. Prior to this album, Voivod had lowered production costs by recording live in the studio and releasing videos that Away had created on a Commodore Amiga computer. *Nothingface* was the band's first serious multi-tracking experience, and along with the release of their first big-budget video for the band's stunning cover of Pink Floyd's "Astronomy Domine," it was the hope of everyone involved that this would be the band's passport to a wider audience. "It worked," Away says. "The video was playing on MTV. We sold a quarter of a million copies of *Nothingface*. My management asked me what band I wanted to tour with. At this time I was really into Faith No More and Soundgarden. We ended up touring with those guys for three months all over the U.S.A. It was great. Then we toured with Rush. It was a very good year for Voivod."

Both experiences left their mark on the band, motivating them to further explore the realm of mass acceptance. After the experience of the Faith No More/Soundgarden tour and Away's involvement in Men Without Hats' *Sideways* album, the drummer admits Voivod felt the powerful currents of the imminent grunge movement. "We knew we were up against something big when we toured with Soundgarden and we hit Seattle and we heard about all those bands," says Away. "The buzz was already starting around Nirvana and we thought, 'Okay, this is the '90s.' One of our goals was to be a part of rock and roll history. We knew we were a part of rock and roll history in the '80s, and now it's a new crowd. It was really exciting to hear Soundgarden. They were a tough act to follow."

Inspired by these influences, 1991's *Angel Rat*, is unsurprisingly the most accessible of all the Voivod releases, with shorter songs, focused ideas and slower grooves. The album travelled further down the psychedelic stream, but *Angel Rat* possessed its share of melodic choruses and traditional rock rhythms. Lyrically, Away moved from the persistent sci-fi/technology under-pinnings of his previous work, instead drawing upon classic mythology and fairy tales ("Golem," "Clouds In My House"). The album echoes '70s-era Rush classics like "By-Tor and the Snow Dog," and the presence of Rush producer Terry Brown only reinforces the comparison. Though all members stood behind the material as some of their strongest work, the studio experience was less than ideal.

"The label wanted a hit, the producer wanted a hit, and of course we did as well," says Blacky. "It's too bad that we couldn't really control the album, because there was a lot of potential in the material. I think the pre-production demos sound 10 times better than the album. I hate the final mix. It's all a waste, really, about $250,000 of pure waste. Terry Brown wanted us to take every song and edit them in order to produce a hit album. That pissed me off, and I know Piggy wasn't very happy either, but in the end he resigned himself to the situation."

After Blacky had finished recording his bass tracks, he expressed his concerns to the band before leaving for a week-long break from the studio. According to the bassist, his return to the studio became a three-against-one situation, something that became clearer when he tried to give input in the control room. Blacky says, "When Terry let me know in the control room that my job was done and I didn't have to be involved any further — which I thought was absurd — I left for Montreal and asked for the recording sessions to be suspended so I could have a meeting with the band, or else I would not attend the final mix. At the time I was considering pursuing a new career, without getting in the way of the band. I was seriously interested in electronics and production/recording. But a lot of things had happened along the way to cause dissension between us and the breaking point was the fact that I felt we were heading for a catastrophe with Terry Brown. We had two meetings after I left the *Angel Rat* recording sessions that never amounted to anything solid. Voivod was no longer a democracy."

Even Away, whom Blacky cites as his biggest opponent in band power struggles, admits the rest of the band was unhappy with the end result of their sixth album. "It was a bit of a mistake. Even though we wanted the album to be really psychedelic, we still wanted it to be heavy. The parts we wanted big are not big. At the end everyone was a little disappointed with production. It was just a little too soft for Voivod."

Angel Rat sold a respectable 150,000 copies, and Voivod carried on with a session bassist after Blacky's departure. The dissolution of Mechanix coincidentally occurred during this unrest within the band, but Voivod was saved from the hassles of finding a new label when they were quickly assimilated into the MCA roster. According to Away, 1993's *The Outer Limits* was another peak period for the band as the direct signing to the major brought a larger recording budget, and Voivod would later embark on an extensive tour of the United States. As the title implies, the album continued the band's journey through psychedelic metal territory. In an attempt to replicate the success of "Astronomy Domine," *The Outer Limits* contained another fine cover of a Pink Floyd song, a walloping version of the obscure "The Nile Song." The Québécois group had become a musical inspiration for some of the day's leading metal and alternative acts, including Metallica, Soundgarden, Sonic Youth, Foo Fighters and Sepultura. But the band would remain in the commercial shadow of their peers — something that became an issue within the band.

After the band returned to Montreal from playing its final tour date in Alaska, Snake announced he had enough of the grind and resigned.

Away says, "It's hard for me to figure out after all that hard work why somebody would quit. Everyone had their own personal reasons and I had to respect that. I think Snake was disillusioned because at this point we were obviously a band of the '80s and something else was going on in the '90s. I think he wanted more and to be a bigger rock star. He was seeing the glass half empty, and he was totally disgusted with the industry and went into the woods for a year and cleaned his mind up."

A month after the singer's departure, the band found a bassist/lead vocalist in Torontonian Eric Forrest and Voivod reinvented itself as a power trio. Much to MCA's chagrin, the band revisited its early history and unearthed Voivod's harder roots. This led the label to release the band from their contract and Voivod returned to operating as an independent. Since then, Voivod has remained a trio, releasing on the independent imprint Hypnotic Records. They still earn more respect internationally than they ever have in Canada.

During the late '80s, Deja Voodoo was acquiring an international audience as well — only most of them lived in rural Finland. "We toured extensively in Finland and played a lot of small towns. We made tons of money going there," says drummer Tony Dewald. In 1990, Deja Voodoo released *Live at the Backstage Club, Helsinki Finland*, which firmly endeared them to the Scandinavian audience. "We recorded a song in Finnish, a cover of 'Rockaway Beach' by the Ramones," Dewald explains. "There was a Finnish Ramones clone band and we basically stole their translation. Once that came out, a lot of the Finnish people went nuts for us; 'A Canadian band playing songs in Finnish? My god!'"

Their other European hotspot was Greece, where impressions of Canadian music were minimal. "One guy told me the only musicians he knew of from Montreal were Deja Voodoo and Corey Hart," says Gerard Van Herk. "We had to admit to him that we never hang out together."

Deja Voodoo and Og Records had been a full-time concern for Dewald and Van Herk since 1987, when they quit their jobs as sandwich makers in

Montreal and became full-time musicians and label impresarios. "By 1989, we were touring five or six months of the year, maybe more, and we had enough money to pay for new releases," says Dewald. "That's where all the touring money went to." Their tour overhead became considerably cheaper once they sold their 1959 Edsel. Van Herk says, "Once we started touring by bus and train, the advantages of being a two-piece band kicked in. On the last European tour, we had seven shows in six days in four countries. We'd just hop on the train and not have to worry about staying awake. All our equipment fit into four big packages; we'd take two each."

Although Deja Voodoo had managed a healthy existence on an extremely primitive musical premise for eight years, both members knew that it had run its course before the turn of the decade. "It was still growing," says Van Herk. "I guess from the minions of geeks' point of view we could have kept it going, but I was married at that point and wanted to be home more. Even years before, we'd tell people how much we disliked seeing really old guys playing in bands that didn't know when to die." Dewald adds, "We did our last show on December 19, 1989. When we started [as the Halftones] in 1980, we had said that when we turned 30 it was all over. Gerard turned first; he's a year older than me."

Although nowhere near the age of 30, the members of The Gruesomes were also running out of steam after five years of hard living. "We were all 21 or 22 and had been doing this for so long," says Bobby Beaton. "We were always on tour, and we couldn't stop otherwise we'd stagnate. We basically got sick of the lifestyle, of having to live inside a van all the time. We had been playing every single weekend of our lives, non-stop." The final decision was made in 1990, when the mother of guitarist Gerry Alvarez forced him to quit the band, because she was concerned for his health.

With post-mortems being written for Og's flagship act and its most commercial band — as well as the marginalizing effect the CD revolution had on vinyl — Og's time was up. "We considered continuing, and we had obligations; we promised a couple of bands that we'd put stuff out," says Van Herk. In its last year, Og released records by the Ripcordz, UIC, Supreme Bagg Team, Captain Crunch & Let's Do Lunch, and the Vindicators. "I felt bad," says Dewald, "because Voodoo was subsidizing Og a fair bit, and once we stopped being a band — and especially once we stopped doing all these gigs — we weren't in contact with everyone all the time. It trickled out at the end. And when The Gruesomes decided to call it quits at the same time, that kind of sealed it."

Although independent music would flourish in the early '90s, very seldom did a single label contain the national scope that Og boasted. Fellow Montreal label Cargo would distribute many of the new indies, but it didn't have the same sense of identity and fun that Gerard Van Herk and Tony Dewald brought to the table. The death of Og was one of several symptoms marking the end of an era in the Montreal scene, where there was one band left ready to take it to a whole other level.

In 1990, John Kastner brought an old punk from Montreal's "Cargo scene" named James MacLean back from Toronto to manage the Doughboys. MacLean's first job was to get the band out of the unsatisfying Restless contract, which failed to keep their records in stores around the world. With Ten Commandments' bassist John DesLauriers replacing the departed John Bondhead, the Doughboys released a farewell EP for Restless, *When Up Turns To Down*, and MacLean began hunting a new deal. "We were tired of each record coming out on Restless only selling 10–15,000 records when we believed we could be doing a lot better," says MacLean. "We were making records on $5–10,000 budgets. All we were being told was that 'you're on recoup.' In Canada, distribution kept changing for Restless. It was Capitol, then someone else. It was always available, not available, then it would be an import price. In our own country we didn't have good distribution or a good price code. We were better known in the U.S. and Europe. We were getting front covers on the *NME*, but in Canada, CFNY didn't even know we existed. We always felt it was this boundary with the 401 [highway]. There was always this boundary between Montreal and Toronto bands.

The Doughboys watched their American friends in the Lemonheads, the Goo Goo Dolls and Big Drill Car make the transition from independent labels to major labels. MacLean and the band took the cue and the Doughboys, now with ex-Jellyfishbabies Peter Arsenault replacing Deslauriers on bass, eventually signed with A&M. *Crush* was released in 1993 and was a commendable major label debut. Produced by Daniel Rey (Ramones, Iggy Pop) and mixed by Dave "Rave" Ogilvie (Skinny Puppy, Sloan), the band released their finest melodic work to date, a glorious marriage of power pop, punk rock and heavy metal from start to finish. The album's appeal was evident through its three singles — "Shine," "Fix Me" and "Neighbourhood Villain" — that were all heavily rotated on MuchMusic and modern rock radio. "Shine" became the theme music to MuchMusic's alternative music show *The Wedge* for several years.

Not only was *Crush* the first time a Doughboys album was consistently

available in stores, A&M went as far as re-releasing the band's entire catalogue — except for *Whatever*, which would be remastered and re-released
by the band and sold at shows. Never prone to laziness, the Doughboys
promoted the album through an endless series of tours across North America
and parts of Europe. *Crush* eventually sold 75,000 copies in Canada, but
the band would only reach a cult-sized audience in the U.S. The album
was released a year before Green Day's *Dookie* and the Offspring's *Smash*
would explode and boost sales for many pop-punk bands. Jonathan
Cummins says, "The *Crush* tour was the most we ever toured. People had
this illusion that we were these huge-ass mega stars or whatever, but when
we crossed the border it was the same old thing that we always did. We
almost broke-up throughout that whole tour; it was way too fucking long.
That was pretty much a year straight, and that sucks, I'm not into that and
I would never do that again."

In order to build on the momentum the Doughboys had created with
Crush, the band immediately entered the studio after the tour. However,
some band members fell prey to the label pressure to reproduce the last
album's success, and conflicts arose. Cummins explains, "We did a whole
record and the record company said there was nothing we could take to
radio. What I thought was a fucking great record, John was eager to go back
into the studio and do some more songs because he thought it wasn't as
strong as *Crush*. I said, fine, we'll do more songs. That was obviously part
of my decision of 'I've had it with this.' The album started to get more of
a pop leaning. I love pop music, but it seemed like it didn't have any character to it. Basically, I can play punk rock and that's about it. Writing nice
little pop songs, I'm not good at. That's what the Doughboys were doing."

"Making that record was really hard for [Cummins]," Kastner says,
"because the producer came down on him hard and Jonathan didn't deal
with it really well. A lot of it came down to the fact that he wanted more
songs on the record and he wasn't going to get it. Every producer we worked
with would cut Jonathan's songs out and he would freak out every time.
We would spend so much energy just trying to make sure Jonathan wouldn't
freak out so bad. It wasn't our idea. These producers — when you go work
with these fucking guys — they just take over and it's kind of out of your
hands and it sucks. I don't want to do that again."

"It was just a band," says Cummins, who went on to front his own
power rock outfit named Bionic. "I got out of it for a reason. I'm glad I got
out of it. I'm not going to sit there and be like Chris Houston and talk
about my past glories forever. I hate people like that. Toward the end I had

nothing in common with the typical Doughboys fan. We were playing music that I wouldn't be buying."

After the guitarist's departure, the Doughboys drafted former Mega City Four guitarist Wiz, who had co-penned "Shine" and "Fix Me" on *Crush*. The Doughboys released *Turn Me On* in 1996, which failed to achieve the commercial or critical heights of its predecessor. The album had its moments, with some catchy pop songs like Kastner's "Diamond Idiot" and Peter Arsenault's "Everything and After." But between inconsistent material and the industry's decreasing interest in power pop the result was poor sales; A&M soon dropped the band. Kastner admits to being disappointed with *Turn Me On's* promotion and the concessions his band made to label demands. "I always felt more comfortable in the DOA/SNFU/NoMeansNo world than the 54·40 world. We never really wanted to do it." The Doughboys accepted an offer to open for the Offspring's 1997 tour and then unofficially parted ways.

The death of the Doughboys and the downsizing of Voivod marked the end of another era for Montreal. Throughout the '90s there were a few sparks that drew brief attention to city, but there would not be a full-blown movement to bring the scene together. The early part of that decade saw varied successes: dancefloor genre-mixers Bran Van 3000; the ska of Me, Mom & Morgantaler and later the Stomp Records label; rockers Tricky Woo and Bionic; as well as Francophone heroes Grim Skunk, to name a few. The end of the decade brought further hopes of a possible growth in the city scene when U.K. electronica label Ninja Tune opened its North American office in Montreal and signed local turntablist Kid Koala and other musical trailblazers. Avant-garde collective Godspeed You Black Emperor! released several critically lauded albums, two of which found spots on the 2000 poll of *Chart's* Top 50 Canadian Albums of All Time.

Though not as important as some of the other progress in the city, the biggest headlines to come out of the mid-'90s Montreal music community surrounded the bassist of the relatively unknown Tinker — Melissa Auf der Maur. The daughter of the late, famed Montreal journalist Nick Auf der Maur was assimilated into Courtney Love's popular grunge quartet Hole when the original Tinker line-up splintered in the wake of bassist Jordan Zadorozny's preoccupation with his side-project, Blinker the Star. Auf der Maur was introduced to Love by The Smashing Pumpkins' leader Billy Corgan, and filled the bassist/backing vocalist vacancy after Kristen Pfaff died of a heroin overdose in 1994. She would play with the band throughout 1995's Lollapalooza tour and would join in recording *Celebrity Skin*. In 2000

Auf der Maur left Hole to join The Smashing Pumpkins on their farewell tour. Upon the Pumpkins' demise she would focus on her solo career.

Some veterans of the scene resurfaced throughout the decade in new configurations. Kevin Komoda was charmed out of musical retirement by *Brave New Waves* host Patti Schmidt and their new band Pest 5000. The two formed their own Derivative Records label — which along with the Pest 5000 catalogue released recordings by fellow Canadians Jale and Moon Socket, as well as international bands like The Grifters and Ladybug Transistor. The quintet that also included former Doughboy John Ascencio, violinist Geneviève Heistek and former Nils/Tinker/Bionic drummer Alex McSween created intriguing art-rock, akin to that of Boston's Dambuilders or L.A.'s that dog, on numerous 7" records and two CDs, 1996's *Interabang (?!)*, and 1997's *Palimpsest*.

Stefan Doroschuk teamed up with Three O'Clock Train's Mack Mackenzie again for their Mackenzie-Parker Gang country rock project, which also enlisted Michel Langevin on drums. Since the *Sideways* album, Men Without Hats attempted to record new material a few times — and Ivan recorded a solo French jazz record and a techno project — but lack of interest and Ivan's perfectionist streak has kept the recordings in the vaults. The same is true of recording sessions he conducted with Me, Mom & Morgantaler's Kim Bingham and Kevin Komoda. Ivan and John Kastner worked together on the musical score for a mid-'90s TV movie named *Platinum*, about a Montreal label and an all-girl alternative band. It was a project that rock and road director Bruce McDonald was hired to save — but unfortunately could not.

In 1997, Ivan finally followed up *Sideways* with *The Spell*, an independent solo dance record produced by Roxy Music producer John Punter. The record made a modest dent on the Canadian dance charts, but failed to recapture the attention enjoyed in the '80s by Men Without Hats. In truth, the material paled in comparison to his early songwriting. Even with more recent Men Without Hats projects, Ivan continues to insist that he is not interested in the possibilities of success, but in continuing to make music. "I'm just not from that kind of school," he says. "I don't really care about being famous. I guess it's because I had it so early on that I didn't have to be like bands that stay together for 20 years before they get the hit. I was just lucky, but you can only stay in so many hotels."

In 2000, Ivan left his home of many years to support his wife's acting career in Toronto. It was strangely coincidental for one of the godfathers of Montreal's music scene to leave, just as a new generation of artists started to garner attention. The past five years had witnessed a number of changes in the city's scene. John Kastner and former Asexual Sean Friesen also left Montreal, both relocating to Hollywood to start new projects. Kastner created All Systems Go! with former members of Big Drill Car, and later drafted his old Doughboys' mate Peter Arsenault into the fold. Cargo Records, the one-time largest independent distributor in Canada, folded in 1997 as a result of overestimating its expansion in the early '90s. Cargo continues to hold satellite offices in the U.S. and the U.K., but there are no plans to return to Montreal. Finally, in 2000 Woody Whalen moved his Mag Wheel label from Montreal to Toronto. The operation boasted a variety of strong under-ground bands including Alex Soria's Chino project, and carried the spirit of Psyche Industry — something that was evident by its 2001 compilation release, *Space Age Air Raid*.

Kevin Komoda surmises, "It's always a constant change. It has grown, but it's also more fragmented with different scenes: ska, punk, emocore. . . . The funny thing about working at Cargo Records was that all these people who liked and breathed different kinds of music worked under one roof and argued all the time. I do not think much has changed. There will always be a lack of places to play, and the language imposes certain restrictions — much more now than in the '80s."

"I'm a little worried now," Michel Langevin admits. "In the '90s, all the labels and business left town. We were left with a bunch of bands and no place to showcase them. It's pretty dead. There's a French scene that's pretty healthy, and there is a Godspeed You Black Emperor! scene and Ninja Tune scene that's a huge deal in town. Montreal's a great town, but I had two best friends, John [Kastner] and Ivan, and they left. It's been hard for me to deal with that. Over the years, I've always thought they were the two most talented people I knew in Montreal."

"We were lucky enough to come up through a movement," says Ivan. "The problem with a lot of bands now is that there is no movement. There is no birth of [something like] rock and roll or heavy metal in the '70s. Since punk, there's been rap that's been pretty steady, but there's been nothing new to pull people together. That's where the sense of community has been lost. The pie is smaller and there are more people at the table. With all the technology changing, it's a hard time to do these things."

"I believe the sound of Side Two of this record
has a lot ot do with touring Canada in absurd
vehicles, staying on floors of people you don't
even like, reaching the perfect age to make
decent rock music."
— Dave Rave (McIntosh), review of Change of
Heart's *Slowdance*, *Nerve*, June 1987

Yeah, It Matters:
Change of Heart
and Post-Punk
Toronto

One of the first unusual things you see upon entering Ian Blurton's apartment just off Toronto's Queen Street West, is a certified gold record originally presented to Max Webster. That Toronto band, the launch pad for singer/guitarist Kim Mitchell and lyricist Pye Dubois, defied all global trends in the mid-1970s by hooking much of Canada on its abstract prog-punk stew via a few subversive party anthems. Seeing such a piece of memorabilia in Blurton's dwelling at first seems a typical slice of '90s kitsch; that is, until one realizes that Ian Blurton is serious about all the music he listens to.

The fact is, the parallel between Max Webster and Blurton's band Change of Heart is not far off. Both were led by adventurous guitar players who sang lyrics mostly written by someone else in the band. Both also snubbed their noses at popular conventions, preferring instead to produce intense, genre-blurring albums. Perhaps most importantly, both bands never received the public attention they deserved, often playing second fiddle to their more commercially successful cousins — Rush, in Max Webster's case, and Blue Rodeo and The Tragically Hip in CoH's case.

By the time Ian Blurton decided to put Change of Heart to rest once and for all in January, 1998, it was with a reluctant admission that such a legacy, placed upon the band for the better part of its 15-year existence, was now more a burden than a benefit. Blurton's musical ambition had become so synonymous with the Canadian indie rock revolution that while most young musicians saw him as a god, the industry was wary about intruding on his distinct space, the "Kingdom Of Blurtonia," as his first solo project would proclaim. Simply put, Change of Heart made truly progressive music in an era when many musicians were heading in the opposite direction. As wave followed wave into the 1990s, the band failed to catch a ride on any of them, yet there was always something distinctly passionate about a Change of Heart song. The lyrics were often opaque and strange sounds consistently hovered above the fury of Blurton's guitar playing, but the overall effect produced a rush that no other Canadian band could match. It was dramatic, complicated and earthy all at once, not unlike Ian Blurton himself.

Born in Chicago in 1965, Blurton grew up in Toronto when his family moved there, via Ohio, in the mid 1970s. Playing music was part of his life from an early age, when he first took to his father's banjo. He eventually had it taken apart and in the process discovered most of the sound was generated through percussion. This prompted a move to the drum kit at the age of eight. Blurton's passion for music was further fuelled by his parents' decision to enrol him at SEED, one of the many alternative education facilities that Toronto enshrined in the wake of new liberal arts curricula developed in the 1960s. For Blurton, the environment was a natural extension of things he had already been exploring.

"You didn't even have to go to class if you didn't want to," he explains. "It was more a matter of setting your own goals. A lot of people went there, like Mike Armstrong, Bernard Maiezza, a lot of my closest friends still."

Although Blurton was taught the basics of most subjects, music took top priority. He developed as a drummer through listening to Robert Wyatt's parts on Brian Eno records, while at the same time absorbing most other mainstream pop he heard on the radio. By his mid-teens, a math teacher at SEED had encouraged Blurton to learn guitar.

Blurton's first public performance was on drums in the school band for a production of HMS *Pinafore*, but this soon led to more advanced territory. In Grade 10, the school allowed him to take a sound studies course at the Ontario College of Art which entailed listening to John Cage works for an entire year. Following this heady experience, Blurton was ready to form a band. "I tried out for a bunch of bands on drums when I was 13 and 14 and got turned down because I was so young," he says. "I found it really frustrating. Then Rob moved in down the street from where my mom and I lived and we started playing together."

Rob Taylor was a few years older than Blurton and already immersed in punk rock, yet he was drawn to Blurton's prematurely advanced musical knowledge. "Rob and I initially bonded over a lot of the soul music I knew from growing up in Chicago, but of course there was all the punk stuff too. We were more interested in the second-wave stuff like Gang Of Four. They were the band that we wanted to be." Taylor picked up the bass, and together with various guitar players, the pair began banging out a sound in the basement of Blurton's mother's house.

Most who saw punk as the future of rock and roll knew that the music's intensity could only be sustained if it were transferred to a more danceable form. The Clash had jumpstarted the movement by covering reggae songs and working with legendary Jamaican producer Lee "Scratch" Perry, but in the late 1970s, the quickest road to reaching a wide audience was through disco. While some bands like Blondie blatantly exploited the notion, others saw it as merely a subversive method to get anarchy on the dancefloor.

No band accomplished this better than Gang Of Four, the Leeds-based quartet whose minimalist funk was shot through with anti-fascist theory. Their best-known North American album, 1979's *entertainment!* was the next stage of the white riot that The Clash had originally ordered. Yet as the musical malaise of the 1980s grew, the experimental possibilities that dance music brought to punk made the old guard sound suddenly passé. In Britain there were now many musicians and fans alike who felt burned by the failure of the promise of revolution punk originally held. Those less politically inclined now had a wide-open field in which to explore more personal artistic ambitions. Siouxsie & The Banshees and Bauhaus earned the mantle of creating goth rock through deconstructing David Bowie's apocalyptic nightmares, while others like The Teardrop Explodes and Echo & The Bunnymen found inspiration via the un-punk-like ingestion of LSD, which led to new interpretations of The Doors' primal psychedelia, and remnants of obscure American avant-gardeists like Chrome and Suicide. It all grabbed the attention of Toronto's art school crowd which had been hip to Brian Eno and new wave from the beginning, in turn spawning a new vital scene in the city.

Blurton and Taylor found themselves in the midst of this scene mostly through Blurton's school connections, and in turn they discovered a receptive atmosphere for what they were attempting to do. "We couldn't play any other songs," Blurton says. "We could play 'Brand New Cadillac' or maybe

'The Kids Are Alright,' but that was about it. For our first show, we put effects on everything; distortion boxes and flangers on the vocals and stuff. It probably sounded more like Chrome than I would have known at the time."

With Blurton on drums, the band was serious right from the start. "Our first manager played guitar and it was just the three of us in the beginning. He quit pretty soon after and Rob and I started writing songs because Rob wrote a lot of lyrics and it seemed like the thing to do. We were typical bored kids in the suburbs with nothing to do at night — so we might as well jam."

They took the name Change of Heart, which didn't seem to signify anything at the time, yet it was also the title of an obscure 1940s movie that told the story of a young female songwriter who falls in love with the bandleader who has stolen her songs. The name would identify the band's first two releases, homemade cassettes *The Black March* and *Push*. Although each contains a predictably primitive sound, some elements of the band's future go-for-broke style are evident amid the collision of drum machines and synthesizers, as Blurton abandoned drums for the guitar. Most importantly, there is a definite melding of traditional punk and pop forms that would also become a Change of Heart trademark. "We did [those tapes] on a four-track Portastudio, just the worst possible way to record," Blurton says. "Not that it was a Portastudio, but we were doing everything wrong. But as a learning experience it was great, it was so hands-on. We were right into trying out drum machines and manipulating tempos."

This approach was difficult to translate live. Blurton and Taylor were even reluctant to do shows after 1983 when they added the solid foundation of drummer Ron Duffy and percussionist Mike Armstrong. "It was terrifying," Blurton admits. "We wouldn't face the audience at all for the first two years. We didn't do that many shows then, maybe 20 or 30, but as soon as I was finished singing a line I would turn around and walk to the back of the stage. Rob and I were fairly shy people so playing on stage wasn't the most normal thing."

As Change of Heart slowly made its way around the Toronto club circuit — The Beverley Tavern, The Cabana Room, 100 Bond Street, Larry's Hideaway and The Bamboo — Blurton began finding many reasons to engage the audience, mostly to keep up with other bands they played with. "There were some awesome bands at that point; The Rent Boys and The Young Lions were my favourite Toronto hardcore bands. The Young Lions' bass player lived up the street, so he was a god in the neighbourhood because he'd actually gone on tour with DOA in the States. L'Etranger was very important to

Change of Heart at Beverley Tavern, 1985: Ron Duffy,
Ian Blurton, Rob Taylor, Mike Armstrong
(Photo by Bruce Lam)

us at the time, as was Fifth Column. I have two sisters and the one who's just ahead of me turned me on to all sorts of music. She was really good friends with a lot of those people so I got introduced to them through her. It was awe-inspiring."

The connections often sprouted into collaborations as soon as Blurton revealed his drumming ability. In January, 1984, he was recruited by Steve Rhodes and Stew Black for Jolly Tambourine Man which produced the 7" single, "Apple Strudle Man/Sweater In Sri Lanka," a heavily processed, quintessential slice of post-punk Queen Street weirdness, notable for also featuring Fifth Column's Caroline Savage as the "hot chick on accordion." Later in the year, Blurton's drumming was also briefly enlisted by Michael Timmins for his new project Cowboy Junkies.

At the same time, Blurton joined a neo-psychedelic band called Slightly Damaged, which included mad keyboard scientist Bernard Maiezza. If all this musical output hadn't blurred his creativity already, things would get even stranger when Blurton took up with Neal Arbick and A Neon Rome.

Neal Arbick first gravitated toward punk while growing up in Mississauga, just outside of Toronto, but didn't join a serious band until befriending several musicians from around town. His first band was The Result, and soon after Arbick was fronting another called Jesus And His Mutants, based on the "second wave" that attempted to combine the fury of The Stooges with the artistic daring of Roxy Music. Bernard Maiezza described his first encounter with that band: "One night in 1984, I went down to the Ontario College of Art to catch a gig by a band called Jesus And His Mutants. I had heard a song they did on the radio — it sounded like Alien Sex Fiend, but back then the death cult thing was all the rage. As it happened, I was not impressed with the band much, and particularly found the lead singer to be kind of arrogant and oppressive, flailing his mic around while repeating a line that went something like, 'Jesus, motherfuck, Virgin Mary, uh huh,' over a cheezy bass, keyboard and drum machine groove. I remember leaving with a very bad vibe; a bit confused as to why I was feeling such a strong negative reaction to this guy, since I usually liked that sort of thing."

Jesus And His Mutants didn't last much longer after that gig, and Arbick moved permanently to Toronto. Once there, he connected with fellow Mississauga resident, drummer Ken Burchill, who in turn introduced him to bassist John Borra, who had recently split from The Generics. All of them cultivated their friendship by attending weekly gatherings of independent musicians called Elvis Mondays. "It was pretty much the way it's always been, five or six bands in one night," Borra says. "Most of them now are rock bands, whereas back then there would be poets — Meryn Cadell was one of the regulars — and things like the Minimalist Jug Band who was one guy who played a washtub bass and strung together lines from all kinds of different songs. It was really good. Then there was this taxi driver who was an Elvis impersonator, and of course the bands. At that time, some of them would host Elvis Mondays. Groovy Religion was the first and that's when we starting going."

Groovy Religion and Elvis Mondays were both brainchilds of William New, a Toronto punk from day one who spent the last 18 months of his teen years in jail for a botched robbery. "When I was 16 and 17, I was a little criminal guy with torn-up clothes that were safety-pinned together and a punk hairdo," he says. "It was fun, unabashedly so, but being in jail took the wind out of my punk-rock sails because when I got out I had to start doing something." For New, the easiest thing was forming a band. He and guitarist Steve Muhabir first appeared as Malibu Barbie, then as Handsome Dog. Like Jesus And His Mutants, Groovy Religion grew out of a compulsion to experiment with given styles. "We didn't have a drummer, so we were using a drum machine," New says. "You can't play punk rock with a drum machine, so we ended up playing this moody, ethereal, spooky type of music. When we finally added a drummer, we had this batch of songs already done with the machine, so all we needed him for was to keep a beat."

Elvis Mondays started as a Groovy Religion residency at The Beverley Tavern in 1984, and its success immediately gave New an opportunity to unite the Toronto independent scene under its banner. "The Beverly would book two bands a week; one from Monday to Wednesday and the other from Thursday to Saturday," he explains. "It made it really tough on the band playing at the beginning of the week, and those that couldn't get enough people to come out obviously had a hard time then convincing the club to let them play on a weekend. At some point the booker decided this was unfair, so he made Mondays a separate night and booked bands from Tuesday–Thursday and then the bigger bands just played Friday and Saturday."

New continues, "I was in the right place at the right time because I'd just put on this three-night multi-band extravaganza called 'The Elvis Presley Memorial Beatfest,' so I was approached to do pretty much the same thing every Monday. Groovy Religion hosted it for the first year."

Later, with Forgotten Rebels bassist Chris Houston hosting, Arbick, Borra and Burchill used the Elvis Mondays open stage to introduce their new band A Neon Rome, which also included keyboardist Russell Ardito and guitarist Kevin Nizel. After several more appearances in the ensuing weeks, they formed bonds with the other regular participants. "We met Change of Heart and Groovy Religion and started doing gigs with them," Borra says. "We just kept coming back, whether we were playing or not. It became a real social thing; everyone was about 18 or 19. The Bev became a chance for A Neon Rome to play on a weekly basis and get a following."

The band's sound would come to be defined through a chance occurrence. "One night we were at Kevin's place," Borra explains. "He was living with Mike Dent, the soundman at The Beverley, who had an enormous record collection. We found this Psychic TV record and started digging it. I guess it was an EP that was supposed to be played at 45 [rpm] and we had it at 33 [rpm] by mistake. We didn't realize it and we were going, 'Whoa, this is the best!' That night Neal and Kevin and I went back to Neal's place and wrote a bunch of songs that were all really slow and murky like that."

Borra continues, "Neal and Kevin decided that night too that they didn't want Kenny in the band and I was left with a choice of who to be loyal to. I stuck with the band, and we did some shows as a three-piece playing this slow, atmospheric stuff. That's when we met Bernard."

Bernard Maiezza says, "About a year after I saw Jesus And His Mutants, I saw A Neon Rome at an Elvis Monday at The Bev. They were way cool, playing epic songs that were usually built around a single repeating theme, growing in intensity while Neal delivered a much more passionate — almost spiritual — performance than the Mutants fiasco.

"Afterward, Neal approached Ian Blurton and me and said that this was Russ and Ken's last show and he was looking for replacements. At first Ian declined, saying he was too busy, but I told him to join after I saw them three nights in a row the next week as a three-piece. Even without drums they'd managed to put in a very intense performance, and even with Neal's acrobatics and Kevin's guitar-god posing, I think it was obvious to most people that something special was going on."

Maiezza debuted with A Neon Rome at the next Elvis Monday. The drummer from Jesus And His Mutants was supposed to do the gig, but when he failed to show, Blurton was persuaded to jump behind the kit. Blurton recalls, "They had a song where they wanted a drum roll like on 'In The Air Tonight' by Phil Collins, then they wanted to go into a Prince-like slow groove. I thought that was pretty strange. They were playing with a bunch of drummers, but I joined full time about three months later because it was really natural playing with Bernard."

"We were trying for something a little weirder," Borra says. "I was listening to hardcore, but we were more influenced by the British side of things — PiL, Bauhaus. By 1984 when A Neon Rome started, punk was considered dead. Even in 1982 when I was 16 and first heard the Sex Pistols, it felt like I'd missed the boat. Most of the great bands from Toronto doing that stuff, like Living Proof and The Young Lions, had broken up by the time we'd started."

A Neon Rome continued to raise many eyebrows over the next several months, both through their performances and in how they promoted themselves. The band took the phrase "a new heroin" to describe their sound, and posters called out to heroin addicts to come to the shows. According to Borra, "We had a pretty favourable reaction from the get-go. Well, mixed at least. There were definitely people who loved to hate us, but that was all part of it too. Our attitude was basically 'just go for it.'" Standout gigs at this time included opening for The Jesus And Mary Chain's first North American show at RPM. There were also several memorable nights with the Cowboy Junkies and three-band bills with Change of Heart and Groovy Religion. "Neal would sometimes make posters in the shape of a cross and paint them fluorescent orange and we would plaster downtown with them," Borra says. "We would always have black lights and stuff hanging behind us, different props. It always made the night an event.

"One time we made this wooden cross and painted it fluorescent orange and hung it in the middle of the stage, so when the show started it was just black lights and this glowing cross. In the end it would all get torn down because Neal would always be swinging the microphone and wrecking stuff. It was a pretty circus-like atmosphere and people would get out of control."

With the band's line-up now intact and performing regularly, Arbick had the opportunity to indulge in what Maiezza calls "the rock myth lifestyle." A Neon Rome became his life and Arbick began giving in to every creative urge he had, from regularly taking LSD to decorating his apartment in day-glo spirals and broken glass. "Some of his ideas were admittedly derivative of the Velvet Underground/Patti Smith thing," Maiezza says. "But it was Neal's dedication — almost verging on naïveté — and the way he'd get all wide-eyed and excited when talking about his ideas that made him convincing."

William New says, "Neal was the first person in my life that I've felt like a mentor to, just because he was so vulnerable and so fragile in some ways. He needed his friends to be supportive and helpful to him. Maybe 'mentor' is the wrong word because I really admired what he did and a little of it trickled into what I do."

Scott McCullough, who would later join the Doughboys and Rusty, was living with New and Nizel at the time on Euclid Street and recalls witnessing Arbick's transformation. "William and I tried to sell hash for a while to pay our rent," he says. "We'd buy lots but we wouldn't be able to turn it over, so we'd end up smoking it all and not be able to pay our rent. We had one customer, and it was Neal Arbick. I remember one day he came over and said, 'I heard this great band today, they're called The Velvet Underground and they've got this song called "Heroin,"'" and William and I just laughed at him. He was just discovering that stuff; he was sucking in all those influences and then putting them right back out again.

"But A Neon Rome influenced a lot of people in the scene, they were the most exciting band around for awhile," McCullough continues. "It reminded me of early Patti Smith, the way her songs were these big pieces that started quiet and built up. They were purposefully artsy, and Neal was one of those guys who could step over that line and really thrill people. There's that line where it's still a regular rock and roll show, but if you cross it for a while it makes for a really exciting performance."

Even Greg Keelor fell under A Neon Rome's sway during Blue Rodeo's early days on the Queen Street circuit. Keelor's love of the band led to his friendship with Blurton, although their first meeting didn't suggest it at the time. He explains, "The first time I met Ian Blurton was when he was playing with A Neon Rome at RPM and we got into a huge fight. There was this big switch in the dressing room on the wall and we were all looking at it in some form of inebriation. Finally, I went over and started to pull it down and he was like, 'Don't! Don't!' I pulled it down and everything on stage went out. It was A Neon Rome, so I thought they'd love it that everything went out and then went back on. But Ian freaked out — 'You prick! You asshole! Who the fuck do you think *you* are?' I go, 'Who the fuck do you think you are?' Then I found out he's playing with the Cowboy Junkies on the same bill, and I thought, whoops."

At first everything Neal Arbick tried seemed to work. A Neon Rome had a respectable following after their stint hosting Elvis Mondays, and they went on to play regularly at Lee's Palace and Larry's Hideaway. Yet cracks were beginning to show in Arbick's demeanour, at least for Blurton. "The first proper show I ever played with them was at Larry's Hideaway and Neal had brought this beautiful old lamp with a shade on it, and that was the only light on the stage," Blurton says. "He'd poured beer on himself and whenever he touched the lamp the thing would just be spitting out sparks so we all thought he was gonna fry. Then he started swinging it around and at the crescendo of one song he smashed it into the stage and dove into the shards. He got up with a big hole in his arm with all this blood coming out, and right then he looked at me and squeezed his arm so more blood started coming out. I just thought, 'Oh God, this is pretty serious.'"

Blurton continues, "I ended up quitting after Neal threw glasses into the audience one night and one exploded at a table and cut this girl around her eye. I thought that was obscene. If he wanted to cut himself, that was one thing, but intentionally hurting people in the audience is not necessarily a good idea. There were a lot of drugs being taken at that point."

That night turned out to be A Neon Rome's last Elvis Mondays performance as it ended in a melee with the audience. "At the end of the night there were these crazy guys who were all drunk and revved up and they started fighting with people," Borra recalls. "I remember 20 passive, skinny musicians all standing around with mic stands in their hands trying to figure out how to deal with these two large maniacs. It was a very heavy night."

According to Maiezza, the scene continued when people rushed into the club to say that someone was jumping up and down on the roof of a car parked outside. The musicians went out to see, brandishing whatever they could to potentially defend themselves. Maiezza ended up talking the man down, only to discover at that moment everyone else had retreated to the club, leaving him to fend for himself.

Chaos was the common rule in Arbick's approach, as a January, 1987

A Neon Rome at El Mocambo: Kevin Nizel, Neal
Arbick, Bernard Maiezza
(Photo by Bruce Lam)

Nerve review of an A Neon Rome/Change of Heart/Groovy Religion show at Lee's Palace testified: "Neon Rome is a comedy act, make no mistake. As another high-flying Black Label pathetically fails to shatter above the heads of the band, Neal warns us to 'pay no attention to my mother, who's here tonight.' The rest of his act is equally amusing, especially the Neon Rome seasonal U2 tribute which ended, as all Neon Rome songs end (at some point), with all the instruments making an epic rock noise while Neal twists--'n'-shouts on the floor with his belly-button kissing the sky."

Others in the scene, like booker Elliott Lefko, were also partially willing to ignore the antics for the sake of the music. "I believe they were dangerous to the audience to a certain extent, and they were also dangerous to themselves. From wherever they came from in Toronto, they knew that they were making sophisticated, universal music. I don't know from what place inside of them it came from, but it was amazing."

Just prior to Blurton's acrimonious departure following their final Elvis Mondays appearance, A Neon Rome's growing notoriety had attracted the interest of Keith Bates, a self-styled band manager without a track record, but with a bankroll earmarked for the band's first album. "We found out he had a very wealthy father," Maiezza says. "But he would never tell us where the money was coming from. And though he never really understood what the music was about, he was convinced we were the next big thing and drew up piles and piles of contracts officially turning the band into A Neon Rome Inc. in which we bought shares for $10 each. Keith had to lend us money for that because we were all broke. We also had this really cool corporate seal to notarize our documents. We argued over who got to use the thing."

Shortly thereafter, the band undertook its first recording sessions with Andrew St. George, who just previously had worked with pop-metal band Killer Dwarfs. It was the first time any member of A Neon Rome had been in a professional 24-track studio and they immediately felt a need to create the required ambience. "We had candles all over the studio, it must have been a hundred," Borra says. "I'm sure we drove the engineer crazy. Our songs at the time weren't even songs, they were just these loose jams. It wasn't until we started recording that things became defined. After they were on tape it was like, 'Well I guess that's how it goes.'"

Maiezza has similar memories: "Kevin was throwing his guitar around and Neal insisted on doing multiple vocal overdubs — mostly the word 'yeah' — creating a really cool psychedelic effect. One of my keyboard tracks got accidentally erased, or so they claimed."

Blurton recorded several drum tracks for the album, and his departure prompted a phone call to former drummer Ken Burchill to play the final two songs, "The Prayer" and "Cums A Wolf." With the final product, *New Heroin*, finished, all that remained was finding someone willing to put it out. Despite playing around southern Ontario and making the occasional trip to Montreal, A Neon Rome's following was still largely limited to Queen Street. Arbick's enthusiasm had him in charge of promoting the band, which usually consisted of distributing posters, fliers and causing scenes at other band's shows. Once Bates came into the picture, the view became more global.

"Keith sent the tape to New Rose in France. They liked it and put the record out," Borra says. "To us, that was a real success — 'Wow, we're released in Europe.' Then we had to parlay that into getting an American deal, so we sent records to Twin/Tone and sst and all those other labels. There wasn't any follow-up, so we didn't get any replies. We didn't really have the organization to get that happening."

It was indeed a triumph getting the album released on Europe's premier indie punk label, but the feat went virtually unnoticed outside the band's circle of friends until Elliott Lefko created his short-lived Rightside label solely to release *New Heroin* in Canada. "I loved that record," he says. "I thought, how can anybody not put out a record like this, with such a beautiful sound and beautiful cover? You wonder why a band like that never got signed or ever got anything happening for them, because they were incredible live, too."

Aside from positive mentions in U.K. music papers *Melody Maker* and *Sounds*, few in the mainstream cared at all. Bates determined that something was needed to capture the band's visual presence. By his reasoning, a single video could not do them justice, it had to be a full-scale movie in the tradition of *A Hard Day's Night* and *Don't Look Back*.

Change of Heart had always been Ian Blurton's main focus throughout his moonlighting stints with other bands, and his disillusion stemming from A Neon Rome reaffirmed his faith in the material he and Rob Taylor had been writing. Blurton says, "The idea was to gain as much experience as I possibly could and bring it back to the band. I ended up playing with a lot of people that way. But from '86 on, Change of Heart was definitely a constant thing. Not necessarily touring all the time, because we didn't have any money, but we wrote a lot of songs."

Beginning in the summer of 1984, the band worked hard playing the Queen Street circuit, taking any available gig. Eventually they saved enough money to record a proper album. When *50 Feet Up* was released in 1986, it contained the sound of a true live band, attributable mostly to a light-year improvement of Blurton's guitar playing and singing, not to mention Taylor's writing ability. "We all contributed to the sound," Blurton says. "You could sing something off the top of your head and Rob would adapt it into something that made sense. Ron Duffy was the arranger and he made sense of all the musical ideas that were flying around. The songs actually were less structured than before because the better we got as musicians, the more we felt we could just do whatever we wanted."

Blurton cites the song "Northwinds" as the turning point in the Change of Heart sound, where free-form jamming became a key ingredient. Unlike the goth-dada of A Neon Rome, Change of Heart took a more direct aim at reaching their audience, and while they had still not yet reached full cohesiveness as a band, the album showed a greater emphasis on instrumental prowess than most of their contemporaries had displayed up to that point.

50 Feet Up turned out to be their formal introduction to greater Toronto, and the band was soon faced with the task of promoting themselves in the local media. A Super 8 video was made for "Ten Miles" and Blurton found himself an unlikely guest on the regional video show *Toronto Rocks*. It was all part of a world that Blurton's creative training taught him to be wary of, and a decade later he still seemed amazed that anyone paid attention at all. "We were all fascinated by the circus element of rock and roll," he says. "When I was 11 I had a job at a head shop on Yonge Street. It was a really good eye-opening experience because they'd get contracts for shows at The Gardens or The Ex. For example, they made T-shirts for Van Halen's first show at The Gardens. They made the ones sold inside and they also made the bootleg ones sold outside. I learned a lot about how rock and roll works at that level.

"When it came time for us to do press, there was an element of that insidious nature to it. Even just not using a photo in the press at that time was pretty strange. People definitely thought it was weird."

Still, the band's main goal didn't differ from that of every other underground band they knew: getting out of Toronto. A western-Canadian tour was set up in the summer of 1986 through scrounging favours and making new friends with anyone who could help. With a tentative itinerary leading to Vancouver, Change of Heart set out in a four-seater Volvo pulling a U-Haul obtained from a friend who worked at the company. "The first night we played in London, Ontario where this woman was stealing my drinks from the stage," Blurton says. "I asked her to stop and she turned around and threw all the glasses at me. They were breaking off of my knees. In the end we got ripped off by the bar, and then discovered we'd locked the keys in the car. Then we had to drive to Winnipeg and play four nights. We got ripped off in Winnipeg, too."

Things didn't really pick up from there as shows were held in any available venue — this was the time before a national club circuit was established. In Saskatoon, they played what Blurton describes as a "schnitzel house," and then, after a triumphant Vancouver debut, the bar once again failed to pay them. Blurton doesn't harbour any regrets over the experience. "A band can be a band without touring, but a band really becomes something after the first tour. Either it becomes something or it breaks up. There's a certain bonding aspect and the opportunity to play every night changes everything. We came back a pretty different band, and our eyes were opened to a lot of different kinds of music that our circle of friends in Toronto weren't necessarily into."

That circle of friends recognized Change of Heart's evolution following the tour; most soon determined to gain similar experience. "Change of Heart always got themselves on the road," Borra says. "When they went on their very first tour I was very envious. They'd always gotten themselves across the country, which is not easy to do because it's such a huge place. It's expensive to take four guys to Vancouver and back; it's hard to make a tour pay for itself."

Elliott Lefko concurs, "They were the quintessential band travelling across Canada in a van for $100, back and forth. They did it so many times. Ian never had the attitude; or, he never had attitude, period. That was the good thing about him, he just wanted to play. You wonder how the guy ate for all those years, because there was never any money coming in. But he'd always be playing gigs."

The financial restrictions were never a consideration since the band found themselves caught up in the romance of touring their country in much the same way as R.E.M. and the Meat Puppets were re-drawing the map for bands in America. The pioneering spirit of Change of Heart and others began to rub off after a few trips across the country. Fans who wished to see them in "proper" venues inevitably had to create their own. "We could feel something building the whole time," Blurton says. "There was a guy in Saskatoon who was trying to get a university radio station, and other people getting into booking shows. By the next year there was more of a touring circuit for a band like us. The regular bar bands had their own circuit, but those weren't the kinds of places we wanted to play."

Following the first tour, Change of Heart plunged into making a new album. A deal with the new national distributor Fringe Product, operated through Toronto independent store The Record Peddler, seemed to legitimize what they had been working toward and subsequently no expense was spared in the studio. When *Slowdance* was released in 1987, it was a big step forward sonically, although the album hasn't aged well in Blurton's view. "There was a whole pile of money spent when we made that record," he says. "It was actually the first digital independent record in Canada. That means nothing now, but at the time we thought it was a good idea. It should have probably been a smaller record, sound-wise."

Blurton's reservations aside, *Slowdance* is distinguished by one of the finest high-energy jams the band managed to get on tape, "Stress Monkey," which closes side one and then comes roaring back to set the tone for side two. However, the overall cleaner sound turned off reviewers who appreciated the roughness of *50 Feet Up*, especially in the U.S. where several underground publications had praised them. It was a situation the band refused to find themselves in from that point on.

"Part of the revolution in Canada was the fact that people took more control over how their records were being made and how they sounded," Blurton says. "The guy who mastered records in Toronto at the time was very, very conservative in his approach. You'd put on *Metal Circus* by Hüsker Dü and it would come flying out of the speakers, then you'd put on a

Canadian record and it would be half the volume.

"Personally, I had this whole conspiracy thing going about how the major labels wouldn't let indies have records sound as good because mastering is super important in terms of how good a record sounds. Now, I just think Canada was really conservative and a lot of the major labels in Canada sent their records to the States. We got the last two Change of Heart records mastered in the States and the difference is astounding."

Blurton is careful not to include producer Michael Phillip Wojewoda in his dismissal of *Slowdance*, since by then he was just as integral to the Change of Heart sound as the band members. Wojewoda was another of the SEED alumni who had gravitated to the underground rock scene. "I went to SEED because my younger brother went there," he explains. "I was a Grade 10 dropout, and he had left public school in North York to go to SEED and really loved it. He'd tell me, 'It's great, you can smoke pot and everything!' I thought it would be a write-off but I decided to go for a year anyway and it was good on a number of levels."

One was meeting Blurton, who was a good friend of Wojewoda's brother. At the end of Wojewoda's first year, the trio contributed a song to SEED's audio yearbook, a cassette Wojewoda assembled of interviews with students, spoken-word pieces and music. Their song was recorded in the makeshift studio the Wojewoda brothers had set up in the basement of their mother's beauty salon. "Ian is playing drums and singing, my brother is on guitar and I'm on bass," Wojewoda says. "It's the lead-off track on the cassette, after a speech from the principal. I only ended up getting one credit the whole year, and that was only because I got a job at the Music Gallery. It was a job in the arts, so they figured I was making an effort."

Soon after Change of Heart came into being, Wojewoda began his close association with the band when he received an unexpected call prior to a show to do their live sound, normally handled by the frequently drug-hampered Mike Dent. It was new territory for Wojewoda since he was by now more at home in the studio. From *Slowdance* on, he became Change of Heart's choice of producer as well.

The expense of recording that album forced the band to do three gruelling cross-Canada tours to try to recoup some of the money; a fruitless proposition in the end, since most of their earnings went toward keeping themselves on the road. Percussionist Mike Armstrong left the band halfway through, later to resurface in King Cobb Steelie, while Blurton resorted to taking a job waiting tables at Just Desserts to help pay off the debts.

For A Neon Rome, a cross-Canada tour in the traditional manner was out of the question — at least in Keith Bates's mind. Perhaps recalling Malcolm McLaren's touring philosophy, "Always first go where you're least wanted," Bates envisioned a series of shows in northern Ontario — small lumber and mining towns — where the expected hostile receptions would be turned into a groundbreaking film. The idea of an A Neon Rome road movie was actually first initiated by Neal Arbick, but his original sketch proved, not surprisingly, unwieldy.

"We wanted an intro that showed sharks circling around an underwater camera," Bernard Maiezza explains. "Then the camera would break through the surface and the band would be on a floating stage. Opposite the stage and across the water, a horde of screaming fans are rioting out of control, some falling into the water and being eaten by sharks. Of course, we were joking at the time, but little did we know that Keith was taking the idea very seriously."

As Bates and the band continued to throw ideas around for the movie, untested filmmaker Bruce McDonald was approached for help. McDonald was a familiar face within the Queen Street scene, and was an admirer of the band. A Ryerson film school graduate originally from Kingston, he had just made a mark by editing Colin Brunton's *The Mysterious Moon Men Of Canada*, which won a Genie Award for Best Live Action Short Drama. The pair, armed with $70,000 in grants, were now looking for the right vehicle to turn into a full-length feature film, which McDonald would direct and Brunton would produce. The idea of documenting the drug-fuelled band on tour immediately appealed to McDonald's sensibilities, although he also saw it as an opportunity to incorporate some of his own ideas. Maiezza continues, "The story Bruce had still had the shark scene, but now featured rioting gangs of youths chasing Neal down alleys lit by fires, and a 16-year-old girl who murders her parents at the end."

The band went along with the concept in principle, leaving it in the hands of Bates, McDonald and Brunton. Instead, they turned their attention to recording a new album that would be released in conjunction with the movie. A Neon Rome entered the studio again with Andrew St. George, who by now had been won over by the band's sound, yet Arbick's behaviour was becoming increasingly caustic. "Frictions between Kevin and Neal had escalated to the point where Neal said he could no longer work with him," Maiezza says. "It was decided to unceremoniously dump Kevin and get a new guitar player. I never felt good about going along with this decision and thought that his stage presence and writing style were missed from the band."

Kevin Nizel was replaced by Crawford Teasdale, but it still didn't solve the problems that the rest of the band was having with Arbick. The singer was taking LSD on a more regular basis and consistently arriving hours late for rehearsal. When he did show up, he would usually just lie on the floor, being either too stoned or too burned out to contribute anything. Live shows were an even bigger problem, as Arbick often forgot to follow the rest of the band or would simply babble incoherently over the music. It became obvious that he was in no shape to make an album, much less go on tour in northern Ontario. Arbick evidently realized this himself soon after recording sessions got underway and decided to make some drastic changes in his life.

"I thought Neal was the perfect frontman," John Borra says. "He was real arrogant, always shooting his mouth off and going into these rants. But about a year before we broke up, Neal started to become more withdrawn. He was just falling apart. When that happened, everything else started falling apart too, because Neal was really the focus when it came to promoting ourselves. It took a lot out of all of us."

Despite this drama, A Neon Rome persevered in the studio. All the members, especially Maiezza, were keen on exploring new sonic territory, and the bulk of the sessions were taken up with programming drum samples and extensive overdubbing. It was during this 18-month period that the band's fate was sealed. First to go was Bates, who had fallen out of favour by funnelling most of the band's earnings into the film instead of paying for studio time. McDonald was having his own problems with the manager as well. "Bates was causing a lot of tension with everybody," the director says. "He came over with a baseball bat one day. Luckily my partner was there with me too, so he managed to deal with him. Bates was talking about setting up this stadium tour, and he was just out of his mind. I was like, 'No, you don't understand, this is just a couple of guys with a camera in a couple of hotel bars.' When it collapsed he just went insane."

However, McDonald was still committed to the project, which now shared the album's proposed title *All The Children Are In*. Plans were still in place to film a northern Ontario tour, now mostly as a way for McDonald to obtain further funding. Everything rested on Arbick's shoulders, but as recording sessions dragged on, he rapidly retreated within himself. "At the start of the sessions, Neal was still very much into the rock thing," Maiezza says. "But the change began when he stopped doing drugs, started talking more quietly and trying very hard to project a humble attitude. Soon after, he painted his psychedelic apartment white and started an almonds-and-raisins-only diet, to be followed by periods of total fasting, shaving his head, and taking a vow of silence."

Arbick's gradual acceptance of transcendentalism effectively marked the end of A Neon Rome. His spirituality was now at odds with the band's confrontational approach, while his vows of silence — the first lasting three months, and the second six months — made it impossible for anyone to communicate with him, let alone get him to sing. Borra and Maiezza tried to adapt, helping to write appropriate music for Arbick's new lyrics about God and Mother Earth, but it was all too much for drummer Ken Burchill who left again, this time replaced by Wild Things drummer Dogface. The last line-up also included percussionist Tootsie, described by Maiezza as "a 250-pound would-be transvestite, whose big dream was to go to Amsterdam to have a sex change operation. The first time I met him, he was wearing a ballet tutu with a strategically placed hole in the pubic region, and was spinning in a circle to the noise made by a radio tuned between two stations. The whole thing was turning into a freak show, which seemed cool to me since I did sometimes dream of running away and joining the circus."

At the same time, Maiezza was trying to be the new liaison with McDonald who had managed to get some financing without the benefit of tour footage. McDonald brought in his friend Don McKellar to write a screenplay that still revolved around the band but also included a female lead, to be played by Valerie Buhagiar. McKellar was to play a would-be serial killer. On the eve of filming, according to Maiezza, McDonald got into a vicious argument with the band's soundman over how the music would be used, which effectively detached A Neon Rome from the project they had inspired. McDonald would complete the film, retitled *Roadkill*, by inserting a fictional band called The Children Of Paradise, fronted by a singer who had taken a vow of silence. In the film's symbolic climax, the band is killed by their manager, a cutthroat Toronto businessman. There was a new soundtrack too, featuring everyone from The Ramones, to Cowboy Junkies, to Stompin' Tom Connors. "We had some money, so Don came up with this story about a girl sent out to find this band in northern Ontario," McDonald says. "I like to finish what I start, so even though A Neon Rome kind of imploded, I still wanted the movie to get made, and the end result is basically what we were left to work with."

Upon its release, *Roadkill* immediately launched McDonald into the front ranks of Canadian independent filmmakers, but it proved an ignoble epitaph for A Neon Rome. The band managed to play a final show at The Rivoli, where Arbick barely moved and barely sang above a whisper. *All The*

Children Are In was completed in early 1989, but by then Arbick's public presence was almost non-existent and the band agreed there was no point in releasing it.

"The day after the final sequencing of the album was done, I got a phone call from Neal saying that he could no longer stand behind the views presented on the record," Maiezza says. "He didn't want any of it to be released except the last song we recorded, 'Human Beings,' which he wanted as a single. I thought, great, a year-and-a-half in the studio and $15,000 for a single. He proceeded to say that he was leaving the music business to devote his time to developing himself spiritually. It was apparent to all of us that this was what he had to do, since his situation was clearly causing him a lot of pain."

As the members of A Neon Rome adjusted to life without the band, Neal Arbick continued his spiritual journey of self-discovery, and much to everyone's surprise, came out the other side with his faculties intact. Immediately after leaving the band, he barricaded himself in his apartment and fasted to the point where his doctor threatened to put him in a mental institution. It was at this point that Arbick met Baba Hare Dass, whom he credits with saving his life through a more balanced approach to meditation. Arbick admitted in a 1993 interview, around the time A Neon Rome reunited for a one-off show at the invitation of *Exclaim!*, "I went through so much pain with drugs and the whole rock and roll lifestyle, which I lived to such an extreme, that everything became so painful that I just didn't want to live in this world anymore. It wasn't that I wanted to kill myself, but through meditation I got glimpses of other planes of reality, and they were more real and more vivid than my drug experiences because there was nothing artificial about it. I realized I could do this by myself, so that's when I tried to run away from the world and become a hermit. I was no longer in the physical world.

"Then I met Baba Hare Dass, who basically said, 'What are you doing? You have to live your life, you have to eat and sleep and communicate with people.' He helped me realize that I could still live in the world and still pursue spiritual things."

By the mid-1990s, Arbick was teaching yoga to mentally-challenged adults. More amazingly, he was playing music again. His band Mahendra featured Teasdale and Dogface from the final A Neon Rome line-up, and played Arbick's new songs, a mix of rock, classical music and raga, with strong spiritual overtones; about as far away from *New Heroin* as you could get.

The confusion that eventually culminated with *Roadkill* seemed to mark a turning point among the Elvis Mondays crowd. Neal Arbick's transformation from an Iggy-like punk icon to a quiet student of meditation gave everyone a real example that the road of excess may in fact lead to the palace of wisdom, but it was a road few were equipped to follow. The mood in the late 1980s was much more communal, as musicians realized they were truly responsible for their own survival. Records could be recorded and released cheaply, campus radio stations would play them and touring could be accomplished with a little bit of effort. While roots rock had been a Queen Street staple since the early '80s, the genre's inherent camaraderie suddenly applied to the punk scene as well.

Groovy Religion had released its first album, *Thin Gypsy Thief*, in 1986 through Montreal's Psyche Records. The sound stayed true to the band's goth-psychedelic foundation and was strengthened by the work of drummer Glenn Milchem and bassist Scott Bradshaw. However, the impenetrability

Groovy Religion: Steve Muhabir, William New, Scott Bradshaw, Mike Poliwoda
(Photo by Jim Bell, courtesy of William New)

of most of the songs — aside from a tense version of The Animals' "We Gotta Get Out Of This Place" — didn't grab much attention. For William New, attention was never the main priority. "We had a really good band and it made for a really good show, even if we only played every few months," he says. "There may have been some mystique in that, but it's not for me to say. That first record deal found us; we'd never sent a demo to any label. The guys from Psyche were in Toronto from Montreal and happened to see us and signed us. I don't know how many copies the album actually sold, but I know we still owe them $300. There was really no one to pay when the label folded."

In reality, the laissez-faire structure of Groovy Religion ended up contributing more to the band's mystique than the actual music, as New's job booking Elvis Mondays made him a focal point of the scene and

Milchem's skills quickly made him an in-demand session player. By 1990, Bradshaw had also reinvented himself. Under the new banner, the Scott B. Sympathy, he put together a powerful collection of neo-folk songs, *Neil Yonge Street*, with help from Ian Blurton on guitar, John Borra on bass and a special appearance by folk icon Willie P. Bennett. The project turned out to be a rejuvenating experience for Blurton. "It was pretty hodgepodge, but really fun," he says. "We never rehearsed, so the band could just fall apart at any time or it could gel at any time. That was probably the downfall of the band because we had a lot of shitty nights, but there was a free thing there that allowed you to do stuff that you wouldn't think possible."

Working with Bradshaw seemed to firmly point Blurton in the more rootsy direction he and Rob Taylor had already been toying with as a result of their cross-Canada touring. "Once we got to know the country a little bit, we could write about it," Blurton says. "A lot of Canadians were weaned on Gordon Lightfoot and Anne Murray, Hank Snow and Stompin' Tom. We never tried to emulate those things, but they were definitely there. Punk rock was folk music to us. At one point the label we wanted to be signed to was Stony Plain, hands down, because we thought Holger Peterson would understand that punk and folk were what inspired us to play in the first place."

An almost entirely new Change of Heart catalogue was created in the three years after *Slowdance*, but the band instead opted to start with a clean slate when enough money was found to record a new album. With Michael Phillip Wojewoda — who by this time had worked with nearly every independent Toronto artist — again producing, the band released *Soapbox* in 1990 through Cargo Records. The album was warmly embraced by campus radio, and went into high rotation on CBC's *Brave New Waves*.

A further pleasant surprise came when MuchMusic inserted "Pat's Decline" into a semi-regular rotation, effectively giving Change of Heart their first mainstream national exposure. The song's appeal exemplified the new direction that Blurton and Taylor had taken in their writing; the lyrics remaining ambiguous, but held together by an irresistible chorus that evoked warmth and intimacy. The song's melody would coincidentally reappear a few years later in Pearl Jam's "Daughter."

The airplay provided more opportunities to play and the band jumped at the chance to discover the rapidly expanding alternative touring circuit. They ventured to the U.S. west coast, and also New York, but for Blurton it was more about nurturing the grass-roots spirit in Canada. "There was a lot of youthful, you-can-change-anything stuff, and that was definitely what we were trying to do — cheap ticket prices, all those things," he says.

"We'd see what bands like FIREHOSE and the Meat Puppets were doing in the States and be really inspired. They weren't punk; they were just playing what they wanted to play and being really honest, and people picked up on that." Highlights of their 1991 itinerary included a tour with The Doughboys in February, a 9th anniversary show at the Ultrasound Showbar in Toronto on March 16, and a European tour during August and September.

If anyone in the Elvis Mondays scene hadn't picked up on Change of Heart's mission yet, they began to once the inevitable retreat from nihilism spread in the early 1990s. After the dissolution of A Neon Rome, John Borra picked up his acoustic guitar and headed to Vienna to try life as a busker. He was inspired to go by his friend Frank Nevada, whom he had met during a brief stint with Nevada's band The Boneheads.

Borra eventually developed his own repertoire during his six months in Vienna with Nevada, and upon his return felt more in tune with both his own songwriting abilities and how to back up other songwriters. He was welcomed back into the Change of Heart circle, as was Maiezza, whose keyboards were now added to the mix. The only loose end was drummer Ron Duffy whose accident-prone nature was getting to the point where, at the end of 1991, all parties felt it was time for him to move on. "Ron had injured himself a bunch of times," Blurton explains. "Either he'd been hit by a car, or he'd clipped a car while riding his bike, or he'd fallen off the back of the truck doing his job unloading newspapers. It just kept happening, so he ended up quitting the band."

Duffy's departure became the catalyst Blurton and Taylor needed to reassess the band's direction. Despite the breakthroughs gained through *Soapbox*, the album was now nearly two years old and the pair once again had a backlog of new material. What they decided was simply to get it all out and make a clean break. What they probably didn't count on was that this collection of songs would become Change of Heart's definitive statement.

"We'd booked Reaction Studio for January 4–7 when Ron quit in November," Blurton says. "We had 12 songs and I remember Rob and myself looking at each other and wondering what we were going to do. We ended up clearing out — not in a negative way, but in the most positive way — all the songs that had accumulated over two years. We took those songs and wrote a bunch of extra songs in a really fast period of time; literally a month. We started rehearsing the band in December and played one show, then went into the studio. It was a super-intense creative period of time, where all the options had been completely taken away and everything was wide open. That's probably why that record is so sprawling."

A theme of community began to emerge through the songs as the weight of their undertaking became evident. The band was determined to record as much of the record as possible during the four days they had booked, and this required the help of everyone they could get. Glenn Milchem was immediately behind the drums upon Duffy's departure and many others were called upon to fill out the sound, including the return of Mike Armstrong on percussion, Anne Bourne on cello, a makeshift horn section, a chorus of voices that included John Borra, Don Kerr and Wojewoda, and even a brief cameo by Triumph's Gil Moore on gong.

Milchem recalls the whirlwind month that preceded the recording: "We rehearsed at Spartan Studios, and once the core of Ian, Rob, Bernard and I were comfortable with the material, additional musicians were brought in and Michael came to listen and offer suggestions on sounds and arrangements. The true test was the New Year's Eve gig at The Rivoli, which also featured the very cool Phleg Camp and a mind-blowing reunion set by NoMind. We managed to play most of the songs without any major disasters and reactions to the new sound were positive. After one more rehearsal for last minute fine tuning, we hit the studio at noon on Saturday, January 4."

The mammoth arrangements recalled the great 1960s pop records of Phil Spector and Brian Wilson, so it ultimately made perfect sense to title the project *Smile* in tribute to the great lost Beach Boys album. Once they had entered that '60s mindset, the themes of the album shone through in the tone of Taylor's lyrics. "We went in with a concept," Blurton says. "The downfall of western civilization and the industrial revolution were big on our minds. We were at that age when we were realizing what an impact industry was having on the world and how much damage it does. At the same time, we didn't want to preach about it, we just wanted to try to write about it. There are definitely preachy lyrics on that record that we would change at this point."

With everyone firmly behind the concept, the sessions were surprisingly smooth, although not a minute was wasted. "We'd always wanted to make a live record," Blurton says. "*Time Fades Away* by Neil Young is one of my all-time favourites and the attempt was to try to capture something like that, obviously without an audience. But finances ultimately determined it because Cargo could only give us three grand, and that's what the record cost. Michael was excellent on that record. He focused all 13 people and helped with last-minute arrangements, but everyone was throwing in ideas, so it became a little community over four days in the studio. The days were really long, 18 or 19 hours, and only one song didn't make the record."

What makes Wojewoda's work on *Smile* even more remarkable was how he managed to squeeze it in between two other huge sessions, the Rheostatics' *Whale Music* and Barenaked Ladies' *Gordon*. "They were all being recorded simultaneously," he says. "The way it always worked was, everyone wanted to work at the same time, and I was young and dumb enough to try to do it. *Smile* I could do because it was live to two-track, and we could edit it later. Plus, my wisdom teeth were coming in and I needed money for the dentist, so that helped me decide to do it too. I think it's the best record I ever did with them because it's the only one where I was stoned as well. I'm sort of straight-edged when I work, but I was really high on painkillers."

However, Wojewoda admits, "I botched the mastering job. I botched it like you wouldn't believe; I always feel like a lawyer defending myself over that. But everything else about it I'm really proud of. We spent a lot of time with rehearsals and pre-production, listening to different combinations of players. A lot of it was theoretical, and I knew it could be done logistically. I told them, 'This is the way it's going to work — it's not going to be about the energy of the first take — you're going to play each one of these tunes about eight times. The first four are going to be for me, to get it worked out, and the next four are going to be for you to nail it. If you keep a positive attitude and look forward to repeated attempts at it to sort out your business, then we're going to get a record that has that energy and that works. It's really incredible musicians who rise to that occasion."

Michael Phillip Wojewoda at Reaction Studios, 1993
(Photo by Graham Kennedy)

Milchem has similar positive memories of the recording process: "Michael arrived feeling fatigued after a sleepless night because of his wisdom teeth. Ian brought cognac and honey for his voice and a picture of Barry White for inspiration. Bernard proceeded to set up nine keyboards in a circle around himself, prompting several Rick Wakeman jokes. We were recording by the afternoon, and it was exhilarating to hear playbacks and know we were listening to the finished product. But it could be intimidating; at the end of one long day, Ian looked up with bleary eyes after hearing a finished take and said, 'unreleasable.'

"We finished the last song at six in the morning on January 8, exhausted, but pleased we'd managed to complete all 22 songs in only four days. We called a cab to take us home and as we drove toward the office towers on Bay Street, it reminded me of why we play music in the first place — to experience and preserve what little is left of our humanity."

Smile's 22 tracks — Blurton combined two when he laid out the cover, so only 21 were listed — were pieced together over the following weeks by Wojewoda and Dale Morningstar. The band once again met with critical raves upon the album's release, where most picked up on the ambition behind the production; some even drawing parallels between landmark hour-plus LPs like *London Calling* and *Zen Arcade*. But the biggest effects were seen in the independent music community, which took the two-month burst that created *Smile* as a rallying cry signalling that complex and emotionally charged records could be made on small budgets. Change of Heart, if they hadn't already, became the model for success in the indie world, and the tributes were plainly displayed in the amount of time the band's T-shirts (also designed by Blurton) turned up in other bands' videos. Sloan's Andrew Scott sported one in the original "Underwhelmed" clip, Steven Page of Barenaked Ladies wore one, appropriately, for "Brian Wilson," and Milchem reminded everyone where he came from by wearing one in Blue Rodeo's "Rain Down On Me."

The album's appeal spread to unexpected places as well. A program director at a commercial station in Swift Current, Saskatchewan was so taken that he inserted "There You Go" into rotation and the song eventually made it to number five on the station's chart. However, the now-common practice of other radio stations picking up on what makes one's playlist didn't happen in this case and Blurton blames Cargo for not building on the momentum. The band realized they would once again have to do the work themselves through touring, and set out with the core of *Smile*'s players to all parts of the country.

One of those asked to come along was John Borra, although the invitation was initially to drive the van. "I said I wanted to go on tour and they said they needed an extra driver," he says. "I didn't want to be away for two months and not play, so they agreed to have me open the shows and then I sang backups for their set." While the task of mounting the shows was at times daunting, the band was mesmerizing as it often ran through *Smile* in sequential order as if it were a rock opera like The Who's *Tommy*. The biggest breakthrough in the band's sound turned out to be Maiezza's keyboards and samples which allowed more room for the rest of the players to stretch out. Yet, in the punk resurgence of the early 1990s, having keyboards in a band was taken as a deliberate slap in the face against those attempting to exorcise the demons of new wave. Although Blurton's attitude toward keyboards was more akin with the extreme psychedelic sounds of Hawkwind and Can that Maiezza had turned him on to, few hardcore punks grasped that world until much later on.

"When Bernard joined the band, people in Toronto were aghast that we had a keyboard player. We lost a lot of fans in Toronto because of it, but luckily other people replaced them," Blurton says. "The classic story is when we played Gilman St. in Berkeley, California. It's the hardcore co-op run by *Maximum Rock 'N' Roll* and they're really serious about it. We were head-

Smile powwow session, January 1992, Reaction Studios:
(clockwise from left) Bernard Maiezza, Don Christensen,
John Borra, Michael Phillip Wojewoda, Ian Blurton, Ron Anicich,
Glenn Milchem, unidentified, Anne Bourne
(Photo by Bruce Lam)

lining over five super-fast hardcore bands and I have no idea why. We probably should have been on first before anyone got there. We weren't allowed
to load in until the band before us went on, so we had to carry our gear
through the mosh pit. I don't think they'd ever had a band with keyboards
there before so it was a real struggle to get to the stage. Then when we set
up, the place cleared, just from the keyboards. It was hilarious, people giving
us dirty looks and everything. Bernard is a lot more aggressive than guitar
players in some cases and the sound is a lot more than you can get out of
a guitar."

Back in Canada, they received a hero's welcome when the *Smile* tour
hit the Maritimes, just as what would become the Halifax Pop Explosion
was in full swing. As one of the few Toronto bands to make the effort to
go east, Change of Heart had already provided a small lifeline for some
Halifax bands like Jellyfishbabies to come to Toronto. In the fall of 1992,
they were supported by Sloan and Eric's Trip, both on the cusp of massive
national exposure through signing American record deals, but who nevertheless paid tribute by accepting second billing on their home turf. The
ever-modest Blurton simply took it as a genuine compliment that those
bands held Change of Heart in such high regard. "I thought it was great,"
he says. "It was the kind of thing a lot of bands from Toronto had been
wishing would happen to them. Around that time a lot of people had the
perception that Sloan and Eric's Trip and the other East Coast bands came
out of nowhere and were these overnight sensations. We knew that wasn't
the case, so it was an honour to play for their crowds."

After another cross-Canada trip supporting Crash Vegas, the strain of
touring was showing on Rob Taylor, who informed Blurton that this leg
would be his last with the band. Change of Heart had weathered threats
of break-up after nearly every album they put out due to financial constraints, but this was clearly a different situation. "That was the one where
we went, 'Fuck, this is Rob,'" Blurton says. "But I think we were going in a
way that, even if it was going to be a part-time thing, it was still great to
be in a band. We'd just gone through a big change, in that *Smile* was a
really deep record and we weren't really losing money on the road anymore.
MuchMusic was playing the 'Smile' video a bit, so people were starting to
know us as more than just the name. I don't think there was any question
about breaking up at that point."

There was also an immediate offer to join The Tragically Hip on a brief
southern U.S. tour that the band couldn't turn down. Singer Gord Downie
had become a huge admirer of Blurton after hearing *Smile*, and humbly

offered the dates. "Ian Blurton is the kind of guy I totally think is king," Downie says. "I had *Smile* and had listened to it a lot, and it really intimidated me just from the stereo. Then one night I heard him on this radio show, and someone asked him, 'What are you into lately?' and he said, 'I like The Tragically Hip; I like the way they do things.' I thought, fuck, no one's ever said that, especially a guy like him. He noticed that we were trying to work from within, trying to do things independently within the confines of a major label. After that I thought, okay, now I can meet him because I don't think he hates me."

A natural replacement for Taylor on bass was John Borra, who immediately locked in with 17-year-old drummer John Richardson who had joined in the wake of Milchem's defection to Blue Rodeo almost immediately after *Smile* was completed. Blurton recalls; "We had that Hip tour in literally four weeks and we were all freaking out wondering where to get a drummer, then John came along and he was just awesome. He lied about his age too; he said he was 18, as if that's any difference from 17."

Everyone understood it was a different band from then on, although in many ways it remained a natural progression, in keeping with Blurton's view that Change of Heart could go in any direction any member was willing to try. The organic collectivism displayed on *Smile* may have been the pinnacle of the Canadian indie rock vision, but the new line-up was equipped to do a lot more.

The short tour with The Hip in the fall of '93 was the new band's first test and Blurton instantly felt it was working. "America rocks a lot harder than Canada does," he says. "Possibly the best show I've ever been involved in was in Dallas opening for The Hip and it was just mayhem. It was completely insane. There was a guy in a wheelchair in the pit spinning around with the slamdancers. There was a pregnant woman laying on the stage holding her stomach. There were fights through the whole set, and people kept chanting, 'Hip! Hip! Hip!' I was in a particularly cranky mood so I walked up to the microphone and said, 'Fuck you, The Hip fucking suck!' Gord Downie was sitting right there and started laughing. We got totally energized and it was just a really great show."

The band also won a 40-date opening slot for Blue Rodeo — possibly some payback for stealing Milchem away — who had been fully embraced by mainstream audiences with their overtly laid-back *Five Days In July*. "We shouldn't have been opening for them," Blurton says of the country-rockers. "I have this memory of us playing in Brockville, Ontario and the aisles actually filling up and people exiting the theatre while we were on stage. I think

Change of Heart, post-*Smile*, 1992: Bernard Maiezza, Rob Taylor,
Glenn Milchem, Ian Blurton
(Photo by Graham Kennedy)

perhaps Blue Rodeo brought us on that tour for exactly that reason, to piss off their audience."

At the conclusion of that tour, the band set about recording the follow-up to *Smile*. With the fresh dynamic interplay among the new members, it was decided this time to make a "real" studio album. Even though some demos of songs that would eventually comprise the heart of the new album had been done prior to Taylor's departure, the bulk of the lyric writing now fell on Blurton's shoulders. He felt confident in following Taylor's lead. "He was my biggest writing influence for sure," Blurton says. "Rob was my hero for a long, long time and still is. We both came out of that Kerouac/Ginsberg/Burroughs school of cut-up, but ultimately songwriting is like channelling something. It's a matter of keeping a journal and scratching out what doesn't work. That's probably why our songs seem a little more disconnected because a lot of the lines get cut out and not replaced. They're just moved around, so what might have been a plain, straight-up story at one point is now all over the place."

Maiezza assumed a more predominant role in the sound as sessions for *Tummysuckle* began at Toronto's Chemical Sound with engineer Daryl Smith. The keyboardist was now collaborating on songs like "Trigger," "3 Word/4 Letter" and the epic soundscape "Mardi Gras Bringdown," creating the dub-like backdrop for Blurton's ever-more aggressive guitar figures. Blurton had also become interested in incorporating dub, especially after doing a cross-

Canada tour in early '94 with King Cobb Steelie, who carried on the tradition of politicized dance-punk pioneered by Gang Of Four, and had enlisted Mike Armstrong on percussion.

Shortly after completing *Tummysuckle*, Change of Heart took a further step into studio experimentation by producing a single with Plunderphonics inventor John Oswald. His technique of audio cut-up perfectly complimented the band's new direction, and the resulting "Tummysuckle Ruse" 7" remains in its own category within the CanRock pantheon.

In the summer of 1994, the band played selected large-scale events to launch the new album, including The Tragically Hip's Canada Day show at Molson Park, and Edgefest at the Ontario Place Forum. Blurton says their appearance at the Hillside Festival in Guelph convinced him that things were coming together. Apart from the band's memorable main stage set, the weekend was highlighted by an ambient dub workshop with King Cobb Steelie, who were then just finishing recording an album with renowned dub producer Bill Laswell. "That weekend was a real turning point for us," Blurton says. "We weren't headlining but we were pretty far up on the bill, and that was when we went, 'Wow, this could be really good.'"

Soon after, they took the unusual step of entering Toronto radio station CFNY's Discovery-To-Disc contest, in which the winning independent band took home $100,000. While most observers agreed that Change of Heart's reputation and longevity made the outcome a foregone conclusion, they faced stiff competition that year from Treble Charger and The Killjoys, among others, which Blurton says led to some uncomfortable situations. "The competition thing created a lot of bad feelings between the bands," he says. "Everyone was really paranoid, which is not necessarily a good thing. I do consider Treble Charger and The Killjoys my friends to a certain degree, but it was weird that one band was the winner and four others were losers. I mean, Treble Charger have said this too, but ultimately it would have been better if all five bands had gotten twenty grand. Of course, we spent all the money, but it would have been better for the scene."

Whether it was a "lifetime achievement award" or not, judges did declare Change of Heart the winner, which instantly brought renewed attention to the band. Although they received several major label offers, it was decided to stick to their recent arrangement with King Cobb Steelie's Lunamoth label, which in turn licensed *Tummysuckle* to Virgin. The album would reach a national audience at the end of 1994 in a much-improved remixed version. "We signed the deal because Virgin gave us what we wanted, ultimately," Blurton says. "It was kind of funny because it was basically the deal Rob

Taylor and I had wanted back in '86 and it just took that long for the industry to come around to us. We definitely got chased but we kept it to just a licensing deal so we still own all the masters to all our records, which has always been really important."

They also accepted an invitation, along with the Odds, to be a part of The Tragically Hip's first cross-Canada arena tour, going on first in the face of The Hip's increasingly dogmatic audience. The tour began on the East Coast in January, 1995 with Change of Heart trying to reconcile its newfound fortune with the fact that most people in the arenas barely acknowledged their presence. "Touring with The Hip was great just in the way that they handle themselves," Blurton says. "They're the band we've learned the most from in that way, and in the way they treat other bands. Everything down to the last detail is taken care of in a totally respectful way. It's hard to describe, but they make you feel that you don't have to conform to what they do at all, and they don't want you to. If you want to spit on the audience, you're allowed to — basically. Not that we'd spit on the audience."

Even with the conflict that accompanied the Canada Day '94 show, The Tragically Hip never wavered from their stance in hand-picking their opening acts from that point on. Gord Downie explains, "We don't want to be put into some 'benevolent uncle' role. We want to get pushed, and get pushed [musically] by someone who inspires us. If we're any good at all, I get a feeling it's because of some of these bands. That night in Dallas when Ian said, 'Fuck The Hip,' I thought, yeah, that's what I would have done.

For Borra, the tour was the first practical opportunity he'd had to be a working musician since his time busking in Vienna, but it was also the beginning of his detachment from Blurton. "All these things — winning the contest, signing the deal, and doing the big tour — all happened within three or four months," Borra says. "We were starting to draw a small salary and I was totally digging it. That had been everything I had been working toward. In the three years between A Neon Rome and Change of Heart, I was playing as a sideman and making a little cash playing as often as I could. I was anticipating something like Change of Heart coming along and when it did it was great, I was totally into it, but I had also started writing these songs which after a couple of years eventually took over. That was the weird thing; I was thinking, 'I can't wanna quit this band.' If you'd asked me five years before that what my dream situation was, it would have been that band, but Ian and I were writing songs separately and it was frustrating because I didn't feel I could bring my songs to the band. I was feeling like a sideman again."

As the tour plowed across the country in the dead of winter, cementing the fact that The Hip were unquestionably the most popular band in Canada, big budget videos for *Tummysuckle*'s "Trigger" and "Herstory" hit regular rotation on MuchMusic. Despite each song's infectiousness, the "arty" perception of the band remained the biggest barrier impeding the kind of sales Virgin was expecting. The only solution was a return to the club circuit, which gradually increased the rift between Blurton and Borra. Blurton characteristically chalks up the arena tour as a learning experience of living out the rock and roll fantasy without falling prey to it. "We became a little lazy at that point," he says. "The problem with doing that kind of tour and not being successful at that level is that you get accustomed to it even though

it's not necessarily yours to own. We did the arena tour and then came back across Canada with King Cobb Steelie and Hayden and we didn't tour that record again. That was it. That was probably a mistake; we should have been out on the road constantly that summer, but then John left the band."

Change of Heart in Halifax, 1998:
Ian Blurton, Rob Higgins
(Photo by Catherine Stockhausen)

Borra's acrimonious departure from Change of Heart in the summer of 1995 seemed on the surface to cut the final ties the band had to its Queen Street origins. Rightly or wrongly, *Tummysuckle* was deemed ground zero, and consequently, fewer older songs were performed live, aside from an occasional selection from *Smile*. The eventual fall of Cargo Records had put much of the band's pre-Virgin catalogue out of print anyway.

By contrast, Borra's new songs went deeper into Queen Street's country-rock roots, reviving the spirit of Handsome Ned. Borra began showcasing his material during shows with old friend Frank Nevada and eventually formed his own band, which included former Ned guitarist Steve Koch and original Blue Rodeo drummer Cleave Anderson. He also continued to play bass with Groovy Religion, which he had done since 1990 when they enlisted him for their second album, the ostentatious *Tom — A Rock Opera*. The album did little to perpetuate the myth of the band apart from showing that their original art-punk spirit wasn't quite dead.

By this time Groovy Religion guitarist Steve Muhabir was a successful accountant married to a doctor, while William New continued to book young bands at the El Mocambo and put on regular tribute shows to his main influences, The Velvet Underground, Love and The Stooges among others. And of course, he still booked Elvis Mondays.

"Right before I moved to the El Mo," New says, "there was a Monday at The Drake when One Free Fall — which was half the guys who became Rusty — played a showcase for a prospective label deal. I had it all set up and Elliott Lefko phoned me to ask if I could put this other band on. It ended up being The Tea Party, a band I'd never even heard of at the time. We had both those bands playing showcases for their respective labels and they both got signed partially on the basis of the performances they gave that night."

If the industry had finally caught up with the Elvis Mondays crowd, it did so only as a means of capitalizing on the new rock revolution coming from south of the border. Yet, as the perceived under-achievement of *Tummysuckle* showed, the Canadian labels remained extremely cautious in dealing with hardened underground veterans such as Change of Heart. As John Borra tried to explain, "Especially in the early days, it felt like we were doing something — not dangerous — but something more like making art, even though that's a pretentious thing to say. We were trying to shock in a certain way."

Even if Change of Heart had won the respect of the industry through 10 years of perseverance, by the mid-1990s, many other bands were surpassing them commercially with a more streamlined approach that just happened to be more palatable to the masses. William New tried to put it in perspective in 1998: "There's probably 5,000 bands in the Greater Toronto Area, of which I probably know the names of 500, and the average person would know 50 or less. And of those 50, maybe half are making a living as working musicians. That's how much of a crapshoot it is even if you've got the coolest combo around. It's a matter of the public's taste, as well as all sorts of other machinations and political things for the public to even hear you. Even with a band like Change of Heart being signed to Virgin, and trying to get the machinery in motion to play their records and videos, maybe they just didn't get enough of a hearing for people to figure it out."

In 1996, Change of Heart forged ahead with new bass player Rob Higgins and recorded the most overtly rock album of their career, *Steel Teeth*. After the usual rounds on the national club circuit, they joined The Tragically

Hip's Another Roadside Attraction tour in the summer of 1997, but once again it failed to boost record sales. Following a short club tour of Ontario in October, Ian Blurton quietly announced the dissolution of the band a few months later. The news hit most fans, and the underground musical community, like the news of the death of a friend.

Even though their effort to break into the mainstream was unsuccessful, it seemed impossible that a band with such unlimited creative resources couldn't continue. But the struggle was clearly too much for Ian Blurton. He would go on to make guest appearances with friends' bands, find a new career as a prolific producer and eventually make his own records again with his Blurtonia project. The music would live on through the many young artists who had been touched by the band, but, as more than one observer noted, the demise of Change of Heart effectively ended an era of Canadian independent music that might never be repeated.

"It's no small thing, experiencing another passage of Change of Heart. I'm starting to get anxiety attacks when this happens. What if Ian Blurton succumbs to burn-out? Sixteen years of bars, bands, broken vans and the low end of the road. Who's gonna come up with such musical intensity, such fiercely independent, blistering guitar noise? Not many bands out there even come close. Deep grooves, spacey experimentations, rampant riffing, slabs of electronica, twisted lyrics that seemed to matter and all this wrapped in a work ethic that made it happen so consistently, other bands felt intimidated getting on stage with them. They pasted another fat layer of R&R patina on the walls of The 'Shoe during as CMW gig with King Cobb Steelie. Flew in from Texas to an Edgefest at Molson Park and turned a 45-minute set into a major showpiece that should have and could have gone on for hours. The night John Borra quit, amidst all the mental turmoil that perpetrated, they still tore the roof off Lee's with The Smalls and Econoline Crush. (I even think the agitated pissed-offedness added to the punky "who gives a shit" full-throttle roar of the evening.) Blew us away introducing *Steel Teeth* in Peterborough with Weeping Tile at an Amnesty Intl. show. Filled a mostly empty room with torrents of sound that forced the unsuspecting small crowd into a huddle up against the wall in Kingston one night with Tristan Psionic, and were the absolutely roughhouse, rowdy boy centrepiece that gave Canadian hard rock credibility to the "Hip"'s latest Roadside Attraction. I credit CoH with pumping spirit back into my enthusiasm for hard R&R and giving me a shove into this CanRock thing. I've been having a wail of a time ever since. I just can't picture the whole thing without an adrenaline jolt from these guys every so often. What makes it even more puzzling is that prog rock is on the move again and CoH should have been in the thick of that. I just don't get it and I'm not alone. My family and I can't believe we've all let another version of this major Canadian band slip away."

— Noisy Boy, posted on the Internet 1/29/98

Northern Wishes & Visionary Flounders

Sitting in his basement on an insufferably humid Toronto afternoon, Rheostatics guitarist/vocalist Martin Tielli is contemplating his formative musical influences. "Bizarrely enough, I'd say it was 80 per cent Canadian bands. I don't know why," he says, fondling his trademark Steinberger guitar, surrounded by his paintings and Rheostatics memorabilia. "I'm not patriotic when it comes to music, but really, everything I liked was coming from Canada: Jane Siberry, Bruce Cockburn, Neil Young. Easygoing yet progressive. I'd like to figure out exactly what it is, the characteristic that I like about Canadian music."

Citing these influences, Tielli pauses, then continues, "It would be an understanding of the sublime, the beauty, fragility and a certain complexity combined with a certain eclecticism borrowing from all kinds of different things."

Unwittingly, he's summed up much of what has made the Rheostatics the "quintessential" Canadian band, a term they themselves tired of hearing long ago. But it's unavoidable, they truly don't sound like anyone else. Furthermore, their eclecticism doesn't sound like it could have come from anywhere else but here, and their collected body of work encapsulates what it meant to be a Canadian rock band between 1985 and 1995. On a Rheostatics album self-consciously Canadian lyrics accompany music that alternates between suburban psychedelic rock epics, acoustic folk anthems, pure pop, country hoedowns, Crazy Horse workouts, spoken word, children's music, punk, Euro cabaret, space rock and cinematic soundscapes. All of these genres are approached with a joyous sense of discovery, a flagrant disregard for what may or may not be considered cool, and a monstrously talented musical collective capable of the utmost subtlety and the most grandiose drama. It would be a stretch to say that it works every time — because of course it doesn't; it can't. Still, their ambition is admirable and their batting average is unusually high.

More than any other single band of the CanRock Renaissance, the Rheostatics' work, on stage and on albums, epitomizes the creativity and diversity of which Canadian bands were, and are, capable. Their odd career also embodies the trajectory of CanRock's musical maturation. They started off as derivative mimics of British and American forms — new wave and funk, respectively — before leaving their suburban basements to travel the country. Somewhere across the prairie spine, en route to an independent music festival in Vancouver, the four lads found their voice, and after a few bumps and a brief break-up, started unleashing classic albums into the canon. Two singles ("Claire," "Bad Time To Be Poor") cracked the consciousness of the mainstream media, but for the most part they won their fans over one at a time at gigs and over the people's radio. Several of their former opening bands went on to worldwide success, and as a result our heroes got a crack at the American market with a big-budget record that ultimately didn't expand their cult audience any more than their traditional word-of-mouth appeal.

Twenty years, several record labels and two drummers later, they found themselves with a devoted national fan base that's still pulling in young converts. Not to mention a secure place in the hearts of many of their peers — some of whom are the biggest bands in Canada and the world, some of whom are quietly practising their craft down the street — whom they've inspired to strive for greater artistic heights.

The musical bond between Dave Bidini and Tim Vesely began in 1979, when both budding musicians were 15 and attending Kipling Collegiate Institute, in Etobicoke, a western Toronto suburb. Bidini had just started playing guitar and Vesely played double bass in their high school orchestra. They enlisted high school friends Rod Weslake on drums and Dave Crosby on keyboards and started germinating their brand of "original new wave rock," finding the name Rheostatics in a physics textbook. Within the first year, Weslake was replaced with Graeme Kirkland, who would later become Toronto's most renowned professional busker and who can still be found playing a set of buckets outside of the Rivoli club.

In a neighbourhood not too far away, at Martingrove Collegiate, Dave Clark was already a professional drummer at the age of 14, playing Israeli and Italian weddings. Kirkland shared a drum teacher with Clark and the pair played hockey together. Clark hooked up with the fledgling band but was initially reluctant to dig his teeth into the Rheostatics' "really goofy music." Clark says, "I was a jazzbo. I played in big bands, and I thought all this stuff was stupid. But I was having fun — I soon realized that I was the stupid one, and that this was a really good time. I didn't have much connection to kids my age. I thought that going out on weekends and getting pissed up was a real waste of time, compared to playing music. These guys wanted to have fun and write music. It was a very positive way to grow up."

Like most teenage bands, the Rheostatics played their high school, where they did a reggae version of Talking Heads' "Heaven." But unlike other teenagers, they started playing downtown and out-of-town gigs almost immediately. Their first big show was at The Edge club in February 1980. The opening band that night was Popular Spies, featuring Graham Stairs, the man who would start Intrepid Records in the early '90s, and release *Melville* and *Whale Music*.

The band's first out-of-town gig was later that year at the Kent Hotel in Waterloo, where they opened for L'Etranger. "It was the first time we'd encountered a real band in a real dressing room in a real club," says Bidini. "They had just come from opening for the Dead Kennedys, and they were freaked out because they had been spat at. They were shaking, they were so nervous. But they had leather jackets on, and torn jeans — they were a real fucking band, and we just borrowed our parents' car to go to the gig. I thought at the time: 'I don't want to be like that. I don't ever want to have to do rock-'n'-roll, don't ever want to have to be opening for the Dead Kennedys.'"

The few gigs the band would play garnered more attention than the average high-school band, mostly because of the ambition of the young Dave Bidini. "We had a lot of support from students at Dave's school," says Clark. "Dave was a popular guy, for good reasons — he's very affable. We got a lot of press early on because Dave knew how to contact people, and that gave us an edge over others."

Dave Crosby left in 1981, after they recorded a 7" of "Satellite Dancing," backed with a Devo-esque take on The Who's "My Generation." James Gray, later of Blue Rodeo, was in the band briefly but "had too much talent," according to Bidini. To fill in the gaps, in 1983 they enlisted a three-piece horn section that Dave Clark met while enrolled in Humber College's music program for one semester. The horns were dubbed The Trans-Canada Soul Patrol and they came from a rather different school of music. "These guys were real rubes," says Bidini. "They had never heard 'Louie Louie' before. They only knew Brothers Johnson and all these lite jazz fusion-type cats." Most of the material, which sounded like that of the British neo-funk band Level 42, was written by Bidini and sung by Vesely. "Dave couldn't sing very well then, he was pretty off-key," says Vesely. "I could shout a little closer to key."

In the summer of 1985, Bidini left to study in Ireland, while Vesely took up an offer to play with Andrew Cash and L'Etranger, a year-long venture that would encourage him to pick up the guitar and begin to write his own songs on Cash's four-track. The horn section had been reduced to one occasional saxophonist by this time and Dave Clark thought the Rheostatics were "at a bit of a dead end," so he too started working outside of the band. He would soon meet the missing piece of the puzzle that would alter the course of the Rheostatics.

In 1984 Martin Tielli joined his first band, Water Tower. "We played live seven times, including one battle of the bands," he recalls. "Our bass player broke it up because he couldn't handle the clichés of being in a band. To him, he felt like an idiot when we 'counted in' a song; he said it felt too much like the Partridge Family: 'One! Two! Three! Four!' I figured that enduring clichés was worth the outcome."

Dave Clark joined Water Tower shortly before their demise, and was struck by Tielli's original material. Tielli had seen the Rheostatics play live, and he was intrigued by "the fact that they were so comfortable on stage, and I was so uncomfortable on stage. Musically," he says, "nothing really attracted me to them. I thought it was fun and good but it wasn't my kind of music at all. But they were famous as far as I was concerned — I was being asked to join the famous band. And the first thing I was doing was playing funk, which was not the kind of music I knew."

Bidini had seen Water Tower play, and wasn't as taken with Tielli as Clark was. "I saw this little kid and it freaked me out that he looked so much like Neil Young then. Martin dressed so much like him, had the fringe jacket and everything. It made an impression. And I hated Neil Young at the time. I felt sorry for him and thought this poor kid was locked in the '70s."

When Water Tower broke up in 1985 Clark invited Tielli to jam with the Rheos, over the objections of Bidini, who had just returned from Ireland. Bidini recalls, "When he showed up for practice it was like, *this* is the guy? He was way better than me the minute he started playing. I was intimidated and threatened. But it was my own fault, because I never considered myself to be any good anyway. I was a very limited guitar player. I thought that I had better a) practise really hard, or b) if you can't beat him, join him. I didn't practise any harder, though."

Tielli started playing gigs with the band, including one at the large lakeshore venue RPM where, according to Clark, he looked like he was going to die. "Martin did a few gigs with the horn section," says Bidini. "It wasn't even like he was going to be a serious part of the band, it was just to have another guy, trying to get some interesting new sounds involved. When the horn section left, we realized he could play the horn parts on his guitar. That became his job for a bit. That's when we started to write and find our own sound."

Although Bidini and Vesely were already getting into folk music via Stompin' Tom Connors, Tielli had been immersed in folk for as long as he could remember, mostly because of what he calls his "Neil Young disease." "Everything about [Young's] music represented everything I loved: dirt roads, fields, open space, and stuff that isn't clean and polished," says Tielli. "Everything sounds like it's breaking down. When I first got into music at the age of 14, I was a folk environmentalist fascist. I was not going to play *any* electrical instrument, *ever*. I wanted to experiment using natural sounds, natural reverb and building instruments, and perform in an acoustic trio, with acoustic bass, guitar and a snare. Until I got out of my Catholic school and went to a weirdo alternative school [School of Experiential Education] I knew zero musicians. By then I could afford an electric guitar. I can't tell you how fast that [acoustic philosophy] died once I got my hands on an electric guitar."

The material that would appear on their 1987 debut *Greatest Hits* was worlds away from the band's funk beginnings. As their tastes broadened they started discovering records by Camper Van Beethoven and Washboard Hank, as well as country and the Celtic music Bidini had heard in Ireland. They weren't trying to fit into any downtown scene. "We were still pretty Etobicoke-based in our whole approach," says Vesely. "The music scene was something to do on the weekend — come downtown to play a show, go home and hang out. We were in awe of a lot of things, Queen Street bands like the Vital Sines and the Rent Boys, all those funky, dark things. We saw all that stuff but it didn't really echo with us."

There was at least one person who decried the band's shift from funk to folk. But then again, Jaymz Bee — bandleader of the decidedly bizarre Look People — has strange taste in music. "At the time they were a three-piece funk band, they played a show with me and Al Waxman," says Bee. "The Rheostatics did a really hot set, without the horn section, and rocked the house down. This was way pre-Tielli. Bidini was the coolest, guitar-playing, dancing-around, being-weird guy, like a David Byrne character. I thought they were the coolest band ever."

Bee tried to recruit Bidini into the Look People for an extended European stay. "He played a couple of gigs with us, but he didn't go to Europe," says Bee. "He said that his band was really happening and that I should come out to see them. I went to see them, and I couldn't stand it! I said, 'You guys are *country*! What the *fuck* is this?' I'm sure I really offended him. I thought Martin was just in outer space; I didn't like him. But it wasn't that I didn't like him, it was that I walked in expecting this funk band and I got this weird thing. So I thought, 'Well, obviously Bidini's lost his mind. He's not coming to Europe to tour with our *amazing, best* band in the world — he's going to stay with this Canadian country act.'

"I saw them again when we came back. And because I had decided that I was a bit harsh and maybe I should give them a chance, they absolutely blew me away. Martin did the opposite: rather than me thinking he's a creepy guy with no talent, I thought he was a genius, like Mary Margaret O'Hara. He went into a special land all of his own."

In 1985, the teenaged Martin Tielli emptied his bank account, borrowed a Walkman from a friend, travelled downtown to Sam the Record Man on Yonge Street to buy Jane Siberry's album *The Speckless Sky*, and listened to it as soon as he got it. It would alter the way Tielli perceived folk music and its relationship to modern technology, particularly the song "One More Colour," which one day would become one of only three covers the Rheostatics would record; the others are by Gordon Lightfoot and Neil Young.

Siberry began performing in Guelph, Ontario, where she had moved to take microbiology at the university there. She had started writing songs as a teenager in suburban Toronto in the early '70s, but found her voice once she moved away from home. Although she would later foster a persona that her detractors would find unbearably arty, Siberry says that her academic pursuits in the sciences gave her an essential grounding, one that can also

Jane Siberry on the beach, 1984
(Photo by Bruce Lam)

be heard in the progressive nature of her music.

"If anything, I became more critical as a listener," she says of her science degree. "It taught me where you can go instead of just wishing you could be a good dancer, or wishing you could learn how to meditate. If you can knuckle down for four months and study eight hours a day, it showed me how far you can go if you systematically do it. The process of being totally inside something in order to make a huge leap in quality or learning, is something very familiar to me now. Until you're inside it, you can't trust your musicianship or your producing abilities. That's the same place I got to by being totally immersed in a science degree."

She formed a duo with Wendy Davis called Java Jive and performed frequently at a local Guelph restaurant that hosted folk music, the Carden St. Café. After adding bassist John Switzer the band was short-lived, but Switzer would go on to collaborate with Siberry for the remainder of the decade. Her debut album of acoustic folk was released in 1981 and caught the attention of the fledgling Duke Street Records, who released her follow-up, 1984's *No Borders Here*.

Siberry had since moved to Toronto and was performing with Switzer, Guelph guitarist Ken Myhr, and drummer Al Cross. Her music had evolved significantly, incorporating much more technology of the time, including a Fairlight computer, also heard on recordings by Kate Bush, Laurie Anderson and Peter Gabriel. Kurt Swinghammer recalls, "Jane Siberry was pretty remarkable for achieving this really state-of-the-art big band — she had a Fairlight guy, and any time you saw a TV screen on stage, that was pretty significant at that time; [a Fairlight] cost $60,000. That was a real achievement, but her records from that period sound really dated because of it: time-capsule type sounds. The drum sounds are very specific, Linn drums. But at the time it was very impressive."

The songs on *No Borders Here* carved out impressions of Siberry that haunted her for years — that of the eccentric waitress who writes opaque poetry that no one really understands, certainly not in a mainstream CanRock world. The album alternates between completely dismissible fluff like "I Muse Aloud," wordplay such as "Symmetry," and compelling narratives like the fluke hit single "Mimi on the Beach," a seven-minute track with a catchy chorus and a distinct Laurie Anderson influence.

No Borders Here sold 40,000 copies, capturing the attention of a lot of new fans. They were drawn to Siberry's personality, her uniqueness and — for other musicians, at least — the quality of her band, especially the innovative guitar work of Ken Myhr. Of her early records, Dave Clark says, "They were eclectic and very inspiring. She was playing with interesting sounds and odd time signatures and vocal textures that were really cool. She seemed like she really cared, doing what came naturally. Her early records were works of subtle beauty. She took a folk aspect of music and made it really interesting."

Also unbecoming of the imagined persona people developed for her, Siberry was a tireless worker. "Jane Siberry paved a lot of roads for non-commercial music that did really well," recalls Toronto promoter Elliott Lefko. "I first saw her when she was doing her folk stuff. I thought she was really beautiful and very talented and very poetic. I started to work with her when I was taking musicians and getting them to do poetry and spoken word and performances, and she fit into that well. She had a firm understanding of what it takes to be successful and all the hard work she had to put into it.

"She took a lot of chances, too, and sometimes she'd miss the mark," he continues. "But because she did that, she stayed ahead of the game and didn't get lost, whereas so many other people just got lost and became clichés afterwards. She never did become a cliché, even now. People like her have a very broad sense of what's going on in the world. You can see that the wheels are always moving in their head. They're always thinking about how they can change things, how to do something different from what everyone else is trying to do. She was never going to let anybody tie her down. It all came from within her."

By the time *The Speckless Sky* was released in 1985, Siberry had her first bona fide hit single with "One More Colour," her first gold record and her first American release. The new age label Windham Hill distributed the album, re-released *No Borders Here*, and Siberry began to develop an audience south of the border with a 50-date North American tour. She was also developing a more theatrical and choreographed performance, and her band now included Anne Bourne on keyboards and backup vocals, as well as two other back-up vocalists. And although her songwriting was still playful, *The Speckless Sky* was a much more focused album with better pop songs ("Map of the World Part II"), more adventurous experiments ("Vladimir Vladimir"), and the first of many haunting, heartbreaking ballads ("The Empty City," "The Taxi Ride").

After *The Speckless Sky*'s popular reception, Siberry's taste for ambition was channelled into her next album, *The Walking*. For the first time in her career, expectations were higher, partly because it was also her first release for Warner in the U.S., who bought out her contract from Windham Hill for $100,000. Warner's vice-president of A&R, Roberta Peterson, first became intrigued with Siberry after seeing the "Mimi on the Beach" video. Peterson flew to Vancouver to catch *The Speckless Sky* tour, along with Warner's senior VP Michael Ostin, who was going to see Honeymoon Suite. Peterson persuaded him to check out Siberry as well and the skeptical Ostin was completely won over.

But *The Walking* would prove to be Siberry's most abstract album, with several tracks hanging around the 10-minute mark and only the title song retaining her melodic gifts. "I was trying to encapsulate myself," says Siberry. "I was trying to get as close to what I heard in my head on to tape. It was draining in that I was breaking up with John Switzer at the time and a lot of the songs are about that, and there was a lot of tension there that was frustrating. Musically, the focus was long and intense, but overall it's a joy," she insists, adding that she shaved her head after the album was completed. "I love the way people instinctively do these things," she continues. "I believe that hair is a great channeller of energy and holder of energy and a symbol. And symbols come from very esoteric reasons, I think — very solid, physical reasons. When I shaved my head, I was shocked at how much energy I was sensitive to."

Reaction to the album ranged from polite to lukewarm to hostile. A particularly acerbic reviewer from *Graffiti* magazine wrote: "There was a play written about a man's obsession with a Canadian pop singer that had the working title of *I Love You, Anne Murray*. I am currently working on a somewhat similar piece entitled *I Hate Your Guts, Jane Siberry*. . . . [*The Walking*] is not a record at all. It's actually a frighteningly disturbing chunk of hell."

Reviews of the following tour were positive, though Siberry herself was itching for something new. "It was a different stage in my career, where I was examining certain boundaries — pushing them and seeing what they brought," she explains. "At a certain point I thought the buck was going into the wrong bang. At a certain point I cleared out all the clutter and didn't even bring my own lighting person. I also didn't wear jewellery for a long time in photos."

Siberry started playing more acoustic-oriented shows, sometimes as a duo with Myhr, and started appearing at folk festivals, previewing material that would form *Bound By the Beauty*. "*The Walking* had an odd sense of 'definitive Siberry' afterwards — when you work towards something and create something definitive for myself," she says. "When I did *Bound by the Beauty*, I deliberately changed the parameters, which is how I like to work sometimes, just to see what happens. Everything that reminded me of Jane Siberry, I didn't do. I ended up with a Jane Siberry record, but it eliminated something. Otherwise I would have felt like I was in a loop, repeating myself. I went for anything I heard in my head, which was pure in its own way. It ended up sounding more country."

The most straightforward Siberry album, *Bound by the Beauty* sounded totally refreshing compared to the synthesized sheen of her earlier work and also fit in perfectly alongside neo-roots albums like the Cowboy Junkies' *The Trinity Session*. It was recorded on an apple orchard north of Toronto and it sounds like both a physical and musical departure from the downtown art scene; "Something About Trains" is so country it could have been written by Ian Tyson. Siberry borrowed k.d. lang's keyboardist, Teddy Borowiecki, who adds honky-tonk piano and colourful accordion textures to the songs. "Bound by the Beauty" and the intentionally corny "Everything Reminds Me of My Dog" were radio hits, but it was the ballad "The Valley" that was the album's centrepiece, a song that many of her peers considered to be her finest composition to date; k.d. lang has consistently referred to it as one of her all-time favourite songs, although she has yet to record it herself.

In 1991, while she was preparing for the long process of creating her next album, Siberry was asked to contribute a track to a Bruce Cockburn tribute album, and called up a potential collaborator to see if he'd like to perform the song with her. "I was in my basement, waking up in the morning, or probably the afternoon," recalls Martin Tielli. "My mom said, 'Martin, phone!' I picked it up, and it was Jane Siberry. 'Hello, this is Jane Siberry calling from Vancouver. I wanted to say that I really like your voice and your songs.' I just started laughing, like who is this? She kept talking, and I went along with it because I thought it was a joke; I thought it was a girlfriend of mine. Then I started to realize it was her voice; it was too good [an imitation]."

Their collaboration on "A Long Time Love Song." was one of the highlights of Intrepid Records' *Kick At The Darkness*, which also featured the Barenaked Ladies' "Lovers in a Dangerous Time."

In 1987, the Rheostatics were finalizing their shift to roots music before recording *Greatest Hits*. "That's when we shucked where we had been and went to where we were at," says Dave Clark, citing The Band and Fairport Convention as new influences. "Dave was discovering acoustic guitar. He and Martin egged each other on, and everyone kept upping the ante."

This new productivity inspired them to traverse the country they'd already started to sing about in songs like "Canadian Dream," a Vesely composition about his eye-opening travels with L'Etranger. Vesely set up a Rheostatics tour with the help of Sandy Pandya, Andrew Cash's future wife and manager who was then based in Regina, and Jay Scott in Vancouver. Scott was organizing a festival of independent music for that summer, which featured Deja Voodoo, DOA, Oversoul Seven, Bob's Your Uncle, October Crisis, and a ragtag team from Toronto that included 13 Engines, UIC, Suffer Machine, Pigfarm and the Bookmen. "There was a massive traffic jam heading towards Vancouver," says Dave Clark. "The whole thing was a meeting of the minds, and we were so high on the idea of being away from home."

The band had tartan jackets [inspired by Washboard Hank] made for the occasion, and hit the road — for two and a half months. There were no more than three gigs a week and they spent most of the time camping and hanging out with new friends and acquaintances. "It was triumphant when we played in Vancouver, because all these bands were from all over and it was like a competition, even though it was a festival," recalls Bidini. "We won a lot of hearts when we went in there. Some people who had never heard our music before were singing our music."

Tielli, who is the youngest member of the band and was 19 at the time, remembers the experience with a considerably more mixed reaction. "The first tour across Canada was a mind rake," he says, "starting with Thunder Bay, which was a place of debauchery that I'd never seen or experienced

Rheostatics, 1991:
Dave Clark, Tim Vesely,
Dave Bidini, Martin Tielli
(Photo by Anne Zbitnew
courtesy of Dave Clark)

before, and I was right in the middle of it. The first tour was a socializing experience for me. It basically fucked me up for 10 years. Just hanging out with so many new people all the time, drinking with them and losing control, wonderful things like that. It's one thing to go to India or Italy or whatever, but to go across Canada is to meet a lot of people that you do actually understand. That was my first time meeting so many people my age, and hearing what they had to say, and being very impressed by them. Really nice people who had similar ideas as me, who had done amazing things. Also falling in love, and gross sexual encounters. But that was only in Thunder Bay, may I stress. And really hating other people, guys who thought they were cool, people who thought they were hipper than hip, everything I was against." Tielli was inspired by the Prairies and the scenery in general, which would creep into material he would pen for the *Melville* album, which was all written when the Rheostatics returned from the tour.

Dave Clark had started to recite some of his nonsensical poetry during sets, partly to fill time left void by technical difficulties. "Martin had the shittiest gear in town and he always had to tune it, after almost every song, sometimes after half a song," says Clark. "His gear wouldn't work, and he'd be backstage hammering these effects boxes back together that were just crap. While he was doing that, I would jump upstage and it would be this free improv thing. And that would stretch into our music; then we started forsaking set lists and segueing songs one after another."

There was one other important thing the band would discover — rock and roll. On the way home their vehicle had broken down and they hitched a ride back with 13 Engines. The two bands would also share gigs, combining the dates that they had booked separately before they left. Tielli began covering John Critchley's song "Indian Arrow" in the Rheos' set. "[13 Engines] were more straightforward with their sound and we were more eclectic, but it meshed well," says Clark. "It was inspiring to hear a band chunk it out on a couple of chords and really make it happen. We became the best of friends, and Tim was never the same after that."

Tim Vesely in particular was a huge 13 Engines fan, ever since their days as the Ikons. Dave Clark would later move into the 13 Engines communal house on Bathurst Street. "They lived like the Replacements, it was pretty wild," says Clark. "The one woman who lived in the house used to rake all our junk into the centre of the room every Saturday morning and scream at the top of her lungs. It was pretty evil."

When they returned to Toronto, *Greatest Hits* was released to a rather tepid reaction, with the exception of those from *Nerve* magazine and David Wisdom, the host of CBC's *Night Lines*. Wisdom had heard about a band who had a song about popular Toronto Maple Leaf Wendel Clark and asked a Vancouver record clerk who it was. "I found *Greatest Hits* on LP, it had just come out," says Wisdom. "I thought every song was really, really good. I liked the sound right away. There was something funny about it, but at the core it was something serious. It wasn't trivial. It sounded like people who really cared about what they were doing. It also sounded really Canadian to me, rather than aping any English or American sound. And despite the fact that the guys were pretty young, there was something a little older about them. They weren't posers at all. I read that through the music before I ever talked to them."

Bidini recalls, "He sent us a postcard back and said, 'You're the greatest band in Canada.' I was blown away, thinking, from *that* [album]? Wisdom was the first guy to come out and say 'these guys are special,' and that's a beautiful thing. It was pretty nice getting a postcard from a CBC DJ when nobody else would even take your calls."

The next step for the Rheostatics would be an eight-gig, 28-day tour of Ireland in October, 1988, set up on a handshake by an acquaintance from Bidini's Trinity days. Although there were highlights on the trip, the biggest lesson, says Vesely, was that the band "learned how much we hated each other. It came to a head over there. We were probably dreaming more than we should have been, in terms of going over there and doing anything. It was ambitious. It put a bit of stress on it. We always did it for fun and didn't really expect anything to come of it other than a good time. By then, we'd been doing it for a few years, and then we thought that was it for the band."

"I was still wrestling with the idealisms I had before I joined," says Tielli, who initiated the break-up. "I wasn't particularly into being a silly band, and things were really silly. I didn't like hosers."

"Martin didn't know what he wanted to do," says Bidini. "He was unsure about the whole rock-'n'-roll thing. The '87 tour took a bit of a toll on him, because he had only ever been in his basement, really. We were a little older, and we came into rock-'n'-roll knowing what was part of the package, but I don't think he did, really."

The band played one gig without Tielli, an invitation to play a *Brave New Waves* anniversary show in Montreal that they felt they couldn't refuse. Tielli tried to start another band, to no avail. "I realized that it would have to be good, and I would have to be totally in control, writing all the parts — and I wasn't ready for that," he says. "I couldn't find a situation that was as good [as the Rheos], great players and intuitive. We had already developed this way of working together that was really efficient and instant."

Instead, he went back to school and earned his high-school diploma. Vesely did some travelling, and Clark went on the road with Pigfarm. Bidini did some work as a fill-in host for *Brave New Waves*. After a year's break, Tim Vesely brought the band back together when he and Tielli had started hanging out again. Vesely had some fiction published in an Erindale College anthology of student writing, and his professor asked if the Rheostatics would play the launch party at the Rivoli.

"It totally made sense," says Tielli. "I don't think we ever even talked about it. We just played the gig, and it was a blast." Dave Clark recalls, "I told Dave that I would never get on stage with Martin again. But I did. We got together and jammed and it was way better, like we were never apart. We did need the breather. For Dave, Tim and I, we were basically each other's family since we were post-pubescent. I saw more of them than anybody I know, and vice-versa. It was very invigorating."

"People appreciated us playing," says Vesely. "People like [Toronto music critic] Howard Druckman saying, 'I'm really glad you guys got back together' made us feel really good. We recorded a demo in two days, which was *Melville*."

The *Melville* sessions were recorded and mixed in the space of two weeks in December 1989, buoyed by the band's newfound enthusiasm and a host of new material. Once again, it was a dramatic departure from the band's past. There were two distinctively new features. One was Tielli's use of the Steinberger guitar, which allowed him to become far more dramatic and evocative, giving the band new soundscape possibilities. The other was Clark's drumming style, which avoided obvious beat placements and, together with Vesely's bass, transformed what should have been simple three- or four-chord folk songs into complex grooves that were complementary rather than prog-sounding.

"I started looking at music and rhythm differently," says Clark. "I didn't feel that the drummer was responsible for holding down the groove for the whole band and the band agreed — it was everybody's responsibility. Shifting simple grooves around, coloration and modulating times was the way to go about doing things. It didn't come out as some sort of mathematical thing; it was going with my gut."

The band steered away from conventional arrangements and work-shopped songs until they found their natural surroundings. "We'd play them any way we felt we could until we hit on something," says Clark. "Sometimes it happened in a second, sometimes only after we played it a bunch of times. I read about the Beatles, how they would try a song in every different feel they could think of, and that's what we did. I like musicians who can take something simple, add one or two things to it that change the song completely."

The band called on Michael Phillip Wojewoda to produce the sessions. Wojewoda had started his career working at The Music Gallery, the hub of experimental music in Toronto. He was hired there through the recommendation of John Oswald, who had dated Wojewoda's sister. "It was a great place to have your first experiences, because the music wasn't just some blues band," says Wojewoda. "It was some guy stripping to his waist, rubbing his body with oil and setting his cello on fire. And the better part of it is, that if I don't record it well, no one's the wiser!"

When he was called to work on *Melville*, Wojewoda had honed his craft with the likes of Change of Heart, the Shuffle Demons, the Doughboys and the Plasterscene Replicas. But *Melville* was an album that didn't sound like any other. He says, "Every band has a critical mass, if they have it at all. It's a combination of people and players. I started getting connected to what they were all about dynamically when they did that cover of [Gordon Lightfoot's] 'The Wreck of the Edmund Fitzgerald,' which I absolutely insisted that they did for *Melville*," Wojewoda continues. "It had that improvising, soundscaping quality that they do so well. People were struck by the exotic combination of elements, especially the tracks that mixed the prog rock with folk, on tracks like 'It' and 'Christopher.' The understanding of dynamics is something I learned from them, and then applied to other projects. Especially Martin, and not just volume dynamics."

The mood in the studio was enthusiastic, which spread to anyone who happened to eavesdrop on the proceedings. "Gaggles of other people would drop by during a playback," recalls Wojewoda. "They'd stand there and listen, and just say 'wow.' Whether you think you're making 'Stairway to

Heaven' or not, and whether or not it's going to be critically accepted or have commercial value, you can tell if it's good."

David Wisdom was even more taken with *Melville* than he was with *Greatest Hits*. "It still moves me deeply, that record," he says. "*Melville* is one of the great Canadian albums. I put it up there with music by The Band and Neil Young, their very best work." Years later, when the band released an album of material they recorded for a *Night Lines* session, Wisdom would pen the liner notes, with this to say: "They've got that high, lonesome sound that makes me feel sad and joyous, a fleeting speck in the universe and part of something eternal, all at the same time. Since I've started listening to the Rheostatics I have become a Canadian citizen, and as I swore my allegiance to the Big Dominion that song of theirs, 'Northern Wish,' was running through my head."

The singing and songwriting balance was tipped in Tielli's favour on *Melville*: Vesely wrote and sang one track; Bidini wrote four songs, two of them sung and partially co-written by Tielli ("Northern Wish," "Saskatchewan"); and half of the songs were written solely by Tielli, who had composed furiously during the band's hiatus. In fact, most of his songs on both *Melville* and *Whale Music* were written while he was working an overnight job that would provide direct inspiration for one of his greatest narratives, "Self-Serve Gas Station." "I'd get maybe six or seven customers a night," recalls Tielli. "I set up a four-track, and I had no choice other than to sing. I would write about incredibly inane things, and eventually you go from the inane to the insane and everything in between. I wrote about 60 songs."

Tielli claims most of the songs that would become Rheostatics standards were conceived during one two-week period, when he let a homeless kid sleep in the gas station. "I got fired from that job because they thought I was gay," he laughs. One night, he went in for his shift and the girl working before him was having a birthday party at work. "There was a bunch of these little rocker chicks hanging around. I was sitting there looking at my itinerary. The following morning my friend was coming to photograph me for the [University of Toronto student paper] *Varsity*, playing my sitar in the gas station. I had written down '7 a.m. Dave's coming by.' And just above or below that I had written 'bring vaseline,'" which Tielli used to help lubricate his hands for the sitar he was still learning how to play. "The girls said, 'Let me see what you're writing!' They read this, and my face dropped. I said, 'No, I have dry hands!' I wasn't convincing enough and they fired me, supposedly because I didn't show up for a day."

The influence of the band's suburban upbringing would echo through many of their greatest songs. Along with the then-unusual practice of writing explicitly Canadian lyrics, the Rheostatics also stood out for unashamedly coming from Etobicoke, not Toronto. The suburbs were something you were supposed to leave behind when you moved downtown, but it informed the Rheos' approach and solidified their reputation as existing outside of "downtown cool."

"I never liked living in the suburbs," says Tielli, "and I would have hated it more living in the city. But it's not a matter of choosing what to write about; it was a matter of writing what I knew. A lot of it on my part would have been: 'What the fuck am I doing in this wasteland?' Which wasn't that bad of a wasteland; it's more of a wasteland now than when I was a kid. 'What am I doing here and how do I get out to the country?' was my concern for most of my youth. People would say, 'Why do you write about this stuff? Cut out this Canadian shit.'"

Shortly after recording *Melville* Bidini enlisted them in Save the Rails, a musical caravan weekend tour protesting cutbacks to Via rail service by the federal Tories. Bidini had a wedding in Columbus, Ohio, however, and had neglected to tell his bandmates about the tour. "The first thing I heard about it," Dave Clark says, "was when I read in the newspaper that we were playing." Also on the tour were the Skydiggers, Stephen Steve & Big Smoke, Pat Temple's High Lonesome Players, the Cajun Ramblers, Positively Stompin' and the Grievous Angels, with tour organizer Chuck Angus. "It was a whole bunch of folkies and I don't think we ever rocked as hard as we did," says Tielli, who would later compose the lyric: "I can't stop writing punk rock / because I'm stuck in a ghetto of folkies."

There were three dates in Cochrane, Timmins and Kapuskasing, and Dave Clark recalls the tour as being "a proud and ignoble moment." "We were pretty extreme," laughs Tielli. "Naked in the snow in Kapuskasing in February and things like that." The booze-fuelled Rheostatics were the bad boys of the tour who got into trouble with Angus, but it was there they met violinist Dave Allen and pedal steel guitarist Lewis Melville. Both were playing in Pat Temple's band, and both would shape the band's sound over the next two years.

Lewis Melville would have a particular impact on the band, which is why they eventually decided to name their recently-completed album after him. Melville had been playing rock, soul, country, bluegrass and experimental music around the province since the late '60s, and lived in Guelph, where he worked as a biology lab technician. In 1993, he and his friend Dave Teichroeb would start the indie label DROG (Dave's Records of Guelph), which launched with the re-release of *Greatest Hits* and would continue to have a long association with the Rheostatics. A quiet, unassuming man, Melville holds deep convictions about making music outside of the worlds of commerce and artifice. With little prompting, he's always more than willing to share these beliefs at length with younger musicians.

Dave Clark recalls, "When we started playing Guelph, it became a real bastion of support for what we did, because we could come out of town and have these special moments playing at the Albion Hotel. There was a certain team effort; everyone felt like they were going for it together. Our sets started getting longer and longer until we could just play for hours. The audiences were playful and great listeners. Then Lew started sitting in and that started stretching out our minds a bit more. Lew had great textural ideas and he'd say, 'Come record at my house!' We made all these great recordings, some of which we went on to re-record for albums, but some of them eclipse what was done on albums. Others never appeared but were great songs."

In Toronto, audiences were realizing that this was a new chapter for the band, full of infinite possibilities. Yvonne Matsell had just started booking a new Queen Street club called Ultrasound, where a few years later she would book the band for annual week-long stints dubbed Green Sprouts Music Week. The club's soundman was Gary Stokes, who would later tour with the band and record their *Double Live* album. Matsell recalls, "The first time I booked them, which was in 1990, Gary Stokes and I both kind of looked at each other oddly. The way the Rheostatics are to new people — nobody gets it, I think. Gary turned to me as if to say, 'What have you done?' The next time, the light bulb went on over both our heads. It just sunk in. But the first couple of times, it was like, "*What* is *this*?" Now I hardly ever miss a show in town. I just love them. They're magic, they really are."

Another band Matsell saw magic in were, like the Rheostatics, bred in the suburban experience. Scarborough's Barenaked Ladies were quickly moving from a novelty comedy duo to a real band with a very real audience. Matsell first encountered them just before Ultrasound opened, when she was booking for Albert's Hall, and gave them one of their first gigs. For three months in the fall of 1990, they played every Monday at Ultrasound. Matsell remembers, "I would advertise 'Barenaked Ladies No Cover' and I would get dirty old men calling up asking what time the girls went on. The first couple of shows I booked for them were frighteningly bad. Not from their point of view, but bar sales. My bartender used to hate me for these early week shows, because she wasn't making any money."

The Barenaked Ladies first encountered the Rheostatics at the South by Southwest festival in Austin, Texas. Recalls the Barenaked Ladies' Ed Robertson, "It was a defining moment for me, like, 'Oh my god, this band represents everything I believe in about rock music: they're adventurous, they're smart, they're amazing, and so identifiably Canadian.' I was watching them in southern America, thinking, 'Fuck, yeah! Fuck off, all you other shit bands! The Canadian contingent is down here kicking ass!'"

Robertson's co-frontman Steven Page was usually seen sporting a *Melville* T-shirt on stage, and sang the band's praises whenever possible. All the Barenaked Ladies made a cameo in the Rheostatics' video for "Aliens." When the Ladies' popularity began shooting through the roof, they invited the Rheostatics along to open several shows. "We were trying to spread the gospel," says Robertson.

The Barenaked Ladies shared a sense of humour with the Rheostatics, although for BNL the humour was front and centre with only the occasional sombre song, while the opposite was true for the Rheos. In the early '90s, there was a wave of bands who tapped into Canada's comedic tradition with mixed results. The most popular got record deals, and as a result there was an American perception that Canadian music was a big joke. In 1993, a story on CNN lumped the Rheostatics in with the Barenaked Ladies, Moxy Fruvous, and the Crash Test Dummies as examples of "Canadian comedy rock."

Jaymz Bee, who claims to have given BNL their first downtown weekend show at his Beehive club, had been more interested in a good joke than a good tune since his band the Look People started in 1985. In many ways, the Look People were the comedic id for every Toronto band with a sense of humour because nobody else came close to being as outrageous, daring and downright stupid.

Bee recalls, "Steve Leckie [of the Viletones] wrote a letter to *Now* magazine saying, 'If I hear any more about these Barenaked fucking Ladies, I'm going to puke. It's bands like Look People, Moxy Fruvous, Corky and the Juice Pigs, and The Pursuit of Happiness that make me sick, bla bla bla.' I sent a letter back the next week saying, 'In response to Mr. Leckie: I think you should lighten up and get a life. Thank you for including my band among all these best-selling bands, and by the way, when I moved to Toronto I saw the Viletones and loved it. So you're the reason I'm in this business, and if you don't like it, it's your own fault!'"

Jaymz Bee moved to Toronto from North Bay, Ontario in the early '80s hoping to be an actor. He landed work on the muppet show *Fraggle Rock*, but shortly after was trapped inside his house as it burned down, an experience which quickly sent him home to recover in the North Bay hospital. "It took a couple of months before I could wipe my own butt," Bee recalls. "When I came back, I was a freaky hippie guy, absolutely happy to be alive and it hasn't stopped since."

He soon found work as an X-rated musical puppeteer. "I used to play in between stripper acts," he says. "The most memorable was Caballero's in Pickering, the all-time low in my career. They wanted me on the middle stage *while* there was a stripper."

His first band was the Bee People, which he started with Clay Tyson, son of pioneering Canadian folk duo Ian and Sylvia Tyson. Like Bidini's Stompin' Tom obsession, Bee had a fixation on another '70s icon of Canadian culture. "We decided we'd be a band where we only dressed in black and yellow and we only sang songs about Al Waxman: about his dog, his movies, his life, anything we could think of. We ended up with an hour-long show, just about Al Waxman. We'd get him to come out to charity events and he'd MC. The fact that he showed up three or four times freaked us out, because we were a punk band, there was nothing melodic about it."

The gimmick worked, especially for the Toronto media, who wanted to know why these wacky punks were focusing on the star of CBC-TV's *King of Kensington*. "Whenever I had ever taken any kind of course where they start talking about the Canadian identity, everybody kept saying we didn't have one," explains Bee. "I kept saying, that's because we have no monarchy — we should have a king of Canada, like Al Waxman. When I looked through his bio and the things he'd done with his life, I realized that this wasn't even a joke. This guy is pretty cool; he does all this charity work that no one even knows about. We had a thousand card-carrying members of the Al Waxman Fan Club within a year. Daniel Lanois called us up, because we'd sent him a demo. He said, 'This stuff is great, you have to capture it now, because you'll break up any day.'" Which they did shortly after.

In 1985 Bee hooked up with a couple of stray Swiss musicians who had come to Toronto looking for fame and fortune. They soon realized their shortcomings and broke up. Bee heard they were looking for something new, and figured he would audition and convince the band to take him back to Switzerland with them. The scheme worked, and for the next three years Bee and his right-hand man, drummer Great Bob Scott, moved to Switzerland to focus on the Look People, returning to Toronto for brief

Kevin Hearn and Jaymz Bee of the Look People,
at Call the Office in London, Ontario, 1994
(Photo by Richard Gilmore)

periods of time. "A lot of bands here envied us," says Bee. "Because we were a weird band that shouldn't even be able to sell a record, and we were getting huge tours opening for Los Lobos or Bob Geldof or Wishbone Ash or Uriah Heep in stadiums. We'd always steal the show. Audiences in Europe love over-the-top stuff. Everyone said we were like the Tubes or Frank Zappa. They weren't afraid of Bob's magic ass."

The magic ass of Great Bob Scott was a consistent part of a Look People show. Scott would perform a strip routine as part of his drum solo, with his posterior as a particular focus. "There were many times when I begged him to find a new thing," admits Bee, unrepentantly. "Like at Lollapalooza, of all places, up in Molson Park [in Barrie, Ontario]. We never got into trouble in the U.S. for nudity, and we did Lollapalooza down there too. But in Barrie Bob did a drum solo, took off his clothes, and then had some drunk hippie take some peaches that were sitting in a bowl and smush them into his ass. It looked disgusting, it was all fleshy and stuff. The cops came over, pulled me off the stage and said, 'You get that guy back behind his drum kit. If he comes out front one more time, he's going to jail.' I said, 'Thank you officer, my friend's retarded. Thank you for giving us another chance.' There was also one time at Lee's Palace [in Toronto]. He was about to take his clothes off and we saw a couple of cops walk into the club, so he didn't. He danced around a little bit, and the second they left he took his clothes off and ran along the bar and did his Nadia Comanici routine and it made all the papers."

The Look People were favourites on the campus circuit across Canada and released several independent albums, with thrash-funk songs like "Trucker Butt," "Lousy Lover Lousy Lay," "Looking For a Job That Doesn't Suck" and a cover of War's "Low Rider." Their bizarre, colourful and creative videos were played on MuchMusic, especially the no-budget one for their song "Five," featuring the Bourbon Tabernacle Choir's Dave Wall. The closest they got to mainstream success was as the house band on an ill-fated CBC-TV late-night talk show starring former *Night Lines* host Ralph Benmergui.

After a gig in Hollywood where a band consisting of porn stars opened for them, the Look People split. The joie de vivre was gone, and for Bee that was inexcusable. "There was a lot of dissent, which is normal in any band," he says. "But we used to always laugh at how lame something is. Suddenly, we were watching MuchMusic in Winnipeg and I heard my bass player cutting something up, like it was hurting him. I always said that what separates us from other bands is that other bands act like losers by being mad at anyone who has any success. I say we live in an age of plenitude, there's enough for everybody. Lots of people have different shit, so who cares? Why are you getting upset about stuff you don't like? I could tell that the main thing about our band was changing. Our strength was always being happy for people's success and laughing if somebody sucks and makes it. I thought that if this band doesn't snap up and get happy, we might as well pull the plug."

The day after the Hollywood gig, Bee met with Great Bob Scott and put the band out of its misery. "I said, 'I know we have a few shows booked in Saskatoon to play on the way home, but I don't want to do them. If we were going to do a last gig, last night is a memory: playing with porn stars in Hollywood. Playing in Saskatoon — which we've done 10 times — is *not* a memory.'"

Though their music may not have been memorable, the Look People were theatrical masters to whom no idea was too absurd. "We were really popular among media, artists, musicians and actors," Bee boasts. "Anyone in the arts would say, 'This is the freakiest band ever.' We were so fearless. The problem is, when your audience is all musicians, they're either a) broke and have no money, or b) they're famous and they don't want to pay anyway, because you're lucky that they're coming to see you. You never make money if you're an art band!"

If the Look People united a community of freaks and the Rheostatics invited their audience to join "the family of rock," as they sang on "Beerbash," the collective known as the Bourbon Tabernacle Choir were a community unto themselves. For most of their career, they were a nine-piece soul orchestra, with four singers, three primary songwriters, two guitarists, a saxophonist and a keyboard wizard.

In December 1992, the Look People opened for the Bourbon Tabernacle Choir at Toronto's Concert Hall for their annual Christmas party. 13 Engines was also on the bill. The evening culminated with the Bourbons covering Sly and the Family Stone's "Thank You (Falettinme Be Mice Elf Again)" with members of the Look People, the Barenaked Ladies and the Rheostatics on stage with them — while Great Bob Scott jumped around in a garbage can wearing an undershirt with the inscription "Santa Blew Me."

Chris Brown was the Bourbon's keyboardist and mouthpiece: Michael Phillip Wojewoda affectionately describes him as "a sonic onslaught of emotional verbosity." Brown recalls first meeting the Rheostatics when the two bands shared a bill at the Diamond, and Bidini invited him to join them for a late-night session at a campus station. "I went down and played live on air with them for three hours and was blown away," says Brown. "It felt like The Band, it had that nature. They had really centred themselves around this music, which was so beautiful.

"They were a big part of my musical education," he continues. "Because the Bourbons had our own little cosmos happening, and because we were touring and keeping so busy, in one sense you're connecting with people, but in another it's very insular. Suddenly you become aware of this band that's operating down the street from you that blows your fucking mind: the subtleties within their music, and the amount their personalities came out in their singing. It's brave, nothing but brave."

The qualities that drew Brown to the Rheostatics apply to his own band as well. The Bourbon Tabernacle Choir held their first gig at their high school, Lawrence Park in North Toronto, in 1985. "The first gig was sort of ridiculous," Brown says. "You'd have a couple of stoners on the student council who'd persuade the principal that he should have these lunchtime concerts. There were about 14 people in the actual band, there were dancers, and there was someone with one of those huge hoop bubble blowers that makes those four-foot bubbles." Present for the first gig was the core band of Brown, vocalist Kate Fenner, guitarists Andrew Whiteman and Chris Miller, and bassist Jason Mercer, as well as another lead vocalist, Pete Mercier. Senior student and drummer Gregor Beresford joined shortly after, and vocalist Dave Wall hooked up with them within the first year. Saxophonist Gene Hardy was added in 1990.

In the mid-'80s, the sound of vintage soul music was hard to come by. Eighties soul was obsessed with synthesizers replicating the sounds of live horns and strings, and fashion substituted for emotion. Exploring the roots of this rich music wasn't in vogue, but it was this quest that united this group of misfits. "We were our own support group," says Brown. "We would always be the people coming to high school functions with a bag full of LPS and dominating the turntable. The first stuff I started copying was early James Brown and Sly Stone organ style. If you're playing music, sooner or later you're going to get into that music, because it's so deep. We just happened to hit on it really early. I would say that the scope and depth of that music is what sustained us and kept us together, especially back then. "

They hit the highway upon the release of their second cassette, *If Hell Had a House Band*, in 1989. In the ensuing years they would be an immensely popular live act: their circus-like atmosphere attracted anyone looking for a party, and their consummate musical skill attracted the musicologists. Brown's vintage Hammond B-3 organ was a sight in itself. "Back then it was actually an issue that I had a Hammond," says Brown. "Every magazine article would say: 'And they *actually move this thing around*. Because there's a thing called a DX7, and this guy is either an idiot, or he's poor!'"

The sheer size of the band was central to their appeal, as the singers often traded lines and different instrumentalists would vie for the spotlight. When it worked, it was a celebratory community on stage, while other times — mostly in the band's earlier days — it was too much. "When you're young and you're finding your feet, you can be all over the [musical] road," says Brown, "so someone else can very easily occupy some space that you've got your eye on. There were a lot of problems early on in the band with that, particularly with me. I would tend to railroad through things and not be very considerate. It took a while. But one of our skills was that we really made an investment in one another as friends, as people. That's what kept us together, as much as the audiences and perhaps even more so."

Elements of the Bourbons' community spirit are evident on their full-length debut CD, 1992's *Superior Cackling Hen*, although it was burdened with production that distracted from what made the band so appealing live. "We were neophytes to big production," says Brown, "and we allowed ourselves to go a little farther into that than we should have at the time. But I think there's enough simple, straightforward shit on that record, and the writing is strong."

The album's most enduring song was Brown's ballad "You Can Come From Here," which encapsulated the self-affirmation and sharing spirit that existed among this new generation of Toronto musicians and the like-minded compatriots they met on the Trans-Canada. Dave Clark recalls, "It was this huge explosion, a time when we met all these people, bands who encompassed a lot of what a lot of other bands were doing. It was really exciting to see, and it was a really friendly community." For their next record, 1995's *Shyfolk*, the Bourbons hooked up with *Melville* producer Michael Phillip Wojewoda.

In the early months of 1992, Wojewoda made three of the most important Canadian records of the decade: Change of Heart's *Smile*, the Rheostatics' *Whale Music* and the Barenaked Ladies' million-selling *Gordon*. More impressively, he made all three albums in three months.

Recalls Wojewoda, "I did *Smile*, which was [recorded and mixed live in] four days, then I did *Whale Music*, which was two weeks, then with a weekend to spare we went to Quebec with the Ladies for three weeks. I got back and started mixing *Whale Music*, then started overdubbing and starting to mix *Gordon*, mixed it up to a point, then finished remaining mixes of *Whale Music* and then remaining mixes of *Gordon*.

"And then I just died," he laughs. "The thing I thought was so ironic is that all three have heavy Brian Wilson references."

Wilson, of course, is The Beach Boys bandleader whose perfectionist streak first resulted in workaholicism, and then colossal sloth fuelled by creative paralysis. *Smile* is named after the legendary lost post-*Pet Sounds* album that apparently put Wilson's mental condition over the edge. *Whale Music* is named after a humorous and touching Governor-General's Award-winning novel by Paul Quarrington, about a thinly fictionalized Wilson character. And in what is perhaps his best lyrical achievement, BNL's Steven Page wrote a song called "Brian Wilson," in which the narrator parallels his own writer's block with that of the reclusive, anti-social title character.

Wilson battled to musically articulate the visions which haunted him, and was never the same after finishing *Pet Sounds*, the album most critics and fans hail as his strongest achievement. Down the street from the Rheostatics, it was becoming clear that a woman who created a towering masterpiece of her own was never going to follow it up. The mystique surrounding her would become one of the greatest enigmas of the CanRock Renaissance.

When Toronto singer Mary Margaret O'Hara released her *Miss America* album in 1988, the response was immediate and overwhelming — in Britain. She was signed to the U.K. branch of Virgin Records, and the British leapt all over the album with effusive praise. Although the British music press is well known for overstatement and descriptive diarrhoea, this time it was warranted. *Sounds* raved about "a voice baked in the kiln of heavenly delights." *Time Out* magazine went so far as to call her "the most cathartic female presence to emerge in white popular music during the Eighties."

Hyperbole aside, the music of Mary Margaret O'Hara is hard to pin down. There are elements of torch and twang, spacious art-rock and a reggae lilt, bound by creatively complex rhythms executed with ease by a band that makes the most difficult idea sound organic. But the key is O'Hara's voice. On the ballads, which hearken back to the jazz standards she grew up listening to, she caresses the melody with equal amounts of curiosity and confidence, weaving in and out of Don Rooke's ethereal slide guitar. On the more upbeat numbers she can skitter across the melody like a turntablist manipulating a vocal sample: spitting out half a line, retreating and stuttering certain syllables, and then releasing the lyric again with a different inflection that imbues it with a totally different meaning. She frequently slips into a spine-chilling, quavering vibrato that could easily be followed with a guttural yelp or laugh, challenging traditional notions of beauty by juxtaposing her tonal perfection with the unexpected or jarring.

"I'm in the church of Mary Margaret O'Hara," enthuses Toronto jazz/pop singer Holly Cole, who has worked with O'Hara, covered three of her songs and employs the talents of O'Hara's bassist David Piltch. "The first time I saw her in concert, I thought she was clairvoyant. She seemed like a medium for a higher being that was translating something really compelling and musical and groundbreaking to me, and to us in the audience. I was really blown away."

When R.E.M. stopped in Toronto on their 1998 tour Michael Stipe praised O'Hara from the stage. He would show up at a gig of hers in Brooklyn later that year, as did Robbie Robertson, who wanted to sign her to the Dreamworks label ten years after *Miss America*'s release.

When faced with such a work, two questions obviously emerge: where did it come from, and how can she follow it up? There's one elusive answer to both, and fans are still waiting for O'Hara to confirm it.

Mary Margaret O'Hara was one of seven children in an Irish Catholic family where her creativity was encouraged. She and her two sisters, Maureen and Catherine, would sing three-part harmony as children, while Mary Margaret would also dabble in writing and visual arts.

She graduated from the Ontario College of Art and performed briefly with a soul band called Dollars, although she didn't have any grand designs to be a singer. Sister Catherine O'Hara, who is well known to the world as an original cast member of *SCTV* and a film actress, was performing in Toronto's Second City troupe at the Old Firehall Theatre. Between shows, she and her friend Robin Duke (later of *Saturday Night Live*) would hop over to the nearby Jarvis House for dinner and sometimes catch a cover band called Songship playing there. "They got talking and the band members told them their singer was leaving," says Mary Margaret. "For some reason, Catherine told them, 'My sister's a singer,' even though I hadn't sung with a band in years." Robin Duke, Catherine and Mary Margaret would later appear together on *SCTV* as The Lemon Twins, backing vocalists for fictional polka kings the Schmenge Brothers, played by John Candy and Eugene Levy.

Songship had been around since 1973, formed by bassist Hendrik Riik and guitarist Rusty McCarthy, both refugees from Toronto's influential Yorkville scene of the '60s. "The first night I played with the band we sang covers but I couldn't sing them straight," says O'Hara. "I sang it as a parody and the band went along with it."

At Carleton University in Ottawa, a young Hugh Marsh, who would later be one of O'Hara's key collaborators, first saw her in Songship. "That was a very weird experience," says Marsh. "They used to do 'Born to Run' and really strange stuff, with Mary jumping around and doing her thing. All I remember is 'Born to Run,' really, and I thought, 'What the *hell* is that?'"

In 1980, shortly after Marsh was scooped to play in Bruce Cockburn's band, he was sitting in with Songship, becoming a regular fixture in 1981 when they changed their name to Go Deo Chorus and started performing all-original material. By that time, O'Hara was one of four vocalists — all vying for the spotlight with their original songs. They played mostly boozecan gigs, but the band could also be regularly found at the El Mocambo and the new Rivoli club on Queen Street; O'Hara designed the Rivoli logo that has lasted over 20 years. "By the time I joined Go Deo Chorus," recalls Marsh, "the nucleus for most of those (*Miss America*) songs was already in place."

Riik and McCarthy's original material eventually started taking a back seat to O'Hara's compositions, although she appreciated sharing the spotlight. In a *Now* cover story in March, 1983, O'Hara said, "Rusty and Hendrik's singing gives me a break and it also makes me feel I'm not too much for the audience." She was too much for one promoter in Montreal, who fired the band because of O'Hara's erratic stage movements, and told her that she "belonged in a padded cell."

In its initial stages, Go Deo Chorus had moved away from their soul roots and spent most of its set in a more exploratory mode. "Initially we didn't like setting up structures in our music and we did a lot of improvising," O'Hara told *Now*. "Now we realize that you go to a higher level of improvising if you work from a structure."

This applied to her lyrical delivery as well, a trait that would become part of her trademark. "Sometimes I can speak better of the feelings inside me through sound," she said. "Words sometimes lock me in. There was a time when I did a weird sound in every song I sang, but I knew I was going to an excess to bring something out."

Another trait of her later career was also evident in Go Deo Chorus: her reluctance to capture her muse on disc, never feeling that it was the right time to record. Responding to the *Now* writer's assertion that the band has taken a "somewhat unique long term approach to success," O'Hara responds, "Personally, I don't mind the time passing because I know it's time I can think and get more out of myself. People will say to me, 'You have waited too long, this is your time,' but I never believed in that. That might be foolish, but it always feels like things are moving towards something that is right.

"We've tried recording on some levels, but we have never been satisfied. We almost released an EP last year (1985) but it just wasn't right. I didn't want a record around to serve as a statement of what we are. As we start to get better known, people say, 'Don't change this and keep that.' People want to complete the picture for you. I have been afraid that if something were to click in the past we would have to push a certain future and not be able to change."

Go Deo Chorus broke up in 1983, the day after opening up a large gig for the Parachute Club. But the band's drummer, Bruce Moffett, believed that O'Hara's songs deserved attention, and he and manager Jody Colero started shopping a tape around. "He managed to get some money from EMI Canada," says Marsh. "They let us go into the studio, and we did three tunes, one of which is on the record, 'Body in Trouble.' That was from those sessions. Those were done in at least '82."

The demo caught the attention of Virgin U.K., who were impressed enough to sign O'Hara as a solo artist to a seven-record deal. And so began a prolonged, four-year struggle to get *Miss America* made, and a never-ending battle for O'Hara to balance her perfectionism and uncompromising vision with the demands of a commercial career.

"When Virgin came along, I said, 'Well, this [demo tape] isn't the way the music is going to be — I'm going to change this and this and this,'" said O'Hara in 1988. "And [Virgin] said, 'Do anything you want.' They asked me whom I'd like as a producer. From the beginning I said I'd like to do it myself, or co-produce if that was necessary. They said 'okay' but they kept trying to get me to work with somebody."

That somebody was Andy Partridge of seminal new-wave band XTC, another artist very particular about his studio work, and ironically, one that would battle with Virgin later that decade over his own artistic vision. XTC was inactive at the time, and Virgin insisted that Partridge take on some production gigs; Mary Margaret O'Hara was one such assignment.

The original recording began in Wales, with O'Hara, McCarthy, bassist Dave Piltch and drummer Mike Sloski, who was in Songship for a brief period and would also later play with Cockburn. Marsh was delayed a couple of days, and when he arrived was surprised to hear that Partridge had already left. "He lost it after two days," says Marsh. "I arrived in the evening; he had left that same morning. The story I heard was that they were sitting in the common room, and he had introduced them to a Linn drum machine. He had it in this old battered suitcase, and he opens it up [dramatically], like he'd figured we'd never seen technology like that before! He had some wild idea that he would program all this drum stuff and that the whole album should be based on military marches."

"He had very strong ideas about things," said O'Hara. "We tried to rehearse, but with everything he'd say 'Oh no, you can't put that bass against that drum.' I couldn't have someone between the musicians and myself. I produce myself, musically."

Folk producer Joe Boyd (Nick Drake, Kate and Anna McGarrigle, R.E.M.) was called in to supervise the remainder of the main tracks, and his hands-off approach was much more conducive to O'Hara's creative process. The recording took a month and a half, and then the band returned to Canada for Christmas, leaving the rough mixes with Virgin. Marsh recalls, "There was a lot of tension when they received the rough mixes for the first time, because it included a lot of the stranger stuff — a bunch of material that didn't make it on the record. It wasn't what they had in mind for the record at all. They were more interested in stuff like 'Body's in Trouble.' I don't know what they wanted, but they were definitely upset by the weirdness, they thought it was way too outside. And it *is* pretty out, but it's very cool."

Overdubs and re-recording took place at home in Toronto, with some new songs detracting from the "weirdness" that Virgin was suddenly uncomfortable with. "I don't think Virgin knew who they signed at first," says

O'Hara. "I do think, in the end, they got what they wanted. It just took a certain amount of time for them to accept certain things in me. They never had a problem with my voice. It was the way I write music, and that's what I don't intend to change."

To some ears, O'Hara's music might sound like a series of random accidents, assembled by an incredibly proficient band. In fact, says Marsh, her music is very meticulous, and O'Hara always has very specific ideas about the rhythmic tension that underplays all of her material. "Mary is very deceptive, rhythmically," explains Marsh. "It's not just choosing to play in two different time signatures at the same time, but she does really interesting things with the internal divisions of the beat, like where things start." Getting technical, he continues, "She'd have eighth-note triplets, and she'd have someone starting their counter-rhythm on the second beat of the eighth-note triplet. There was a lot of complex stuff. But when it was locking [together], if you were an outside listener, you wouldn't really notice it. There was this nice collision. She had a hard time translating that to us sometimes, because she didn't speak in musical terms."

It was Marsh's role to transcribe her musical vision onto paper for the other band members. "The amazing thing is, I'd say, 'No, she can't possibly be thinking that. There's no way she's hearing [the beat] *there*,'" he recalls. "But she'd be right, every time, bang on." Don Rooke, whose dreamy lap-steel playing is one of *Miss America*'s most intoxicating features, says, "It's a mathematical phenomena, but it's natural. It's not like she's sitting in front of a computer displacing rhythms."

"Mary would be interested in a part per se," continues Marsh, "but she would always say, 'Play it, but don't play it.' It was used as a jumping off point. She'd constantly want to feel this push and pull. To me, that played a larger part in her music than chord changes or melody." It also meant that much of the recording sessions in Wales was focused on Piltch and Sloski nailing down the rhythms.

What exactly happened over the course of the album's four-year gestation is hard to pin down. "There was at least a year when nothing happened," says Rooke. "She wanted to make it as good as she could, and that takes a while. She wanted to keep working on it until it was as good as what she was hearing."

"[Virgin] listened to it and thought it was strange, but then they said, 'Go ahead,'" O'Hara explained in 1988. "That happened twice. They didn't want the album, but they didn't drop the album, so we spent years just talking. They offered a few things and I kept saying no."

In the meantime, her band — McCarthy, Marsh, Rooke, Sloski and either Piltch or Riik on bass — were getting restless. "It was frustrating," says Rooke. "It was great to do gigs, but we were hungry enough that we always wanted to do more, and it never evolved into a heavy working scene." Whenever she played, however, she was making huge impressions. Recalls Toronto artist Kurt Swinghammer, "The first time I saw her it was just her and Hugh Marsh; maybe Don Rooke too. I was astounded, because I'd never seen a more vulnerable performance in my life. I'd never seen anybody who was that spooked yet still willing to perform. So often there's this artifice of someone who's in control, and in 1985 I didn't know of any other performers who were willing to be that exposed, like a raw nerve on stage. She was all flustered, but she was so compelling."

Another Toronto guitarist who was taken with her was Michael Brook, who saw her perform at the Music Gallery in early 1988. He heard about her long-delayed project, and convinced Virgin to let him help bring it to final fruition. He re-recorded four tracks, adding his "inifinite guitar" sound to three: "To Cry About," "Anew Day" and "When You Know Why You're Happy." The record was finished within a couple of months of Brook coming on board, and his participation in the project has been contentious ever since. In the early '90s, *Now* ran an interview with him where he talked briefly and modestly about his work on *Miss America*, and praised O'Hara's creative vision. The next week, O'Hara fired off a scathing missive to the letters section, saying that Brook was assuming far too much credit for a project he entered into at a very late stage, and assailed him with a variety of dictatorial adjectives.

"[Brook] brought organization to it and got it done," says Rooke. "I don't think perfectionists can ever be completely happy with something. I think it represented something she worked very hard on, and if she were to do another record it would sound very different."

In 1989, O'Hara described her firm belief in her singular vision to *Canadian Composer* magazine: "When I think of compromise, I think of the best meaning of the word, and I think the meaning of the word is 'the best of both worlds.' But sometimes compromise becomes accepting someone's bad judgement and that's a bad thing. Compromise in the way of saying: 'I'm going to do this because it'll help me get better up' — that kills me. To some it might look foolish, to some it might look courageous."

Miss America was released in October 1988 to an ecstatic reaction. Even O'Hara herself seemed pleased with the final product. "When I didn't get

Mary Margaret O'Hara
(Photo by Don Rooke)

this record out for four years, I felt kind of discouraged," she said. "But I'm happy with this album. I will, though, learn to respect deadlines. I was penalized four years for not realizing that. I know the business now."

Reflecting on the album's response three years later, she said, "Certain things are always alive for me on that record. Certain sounds are always relevant. They never go away. Then I look at other things and think, 'Gee I'd like to move on from there.' You're always growing and, in another way, you're left with what you've always had. But the music doesn't have that much to do with me; it's more a part of the listener. Maybe that's why I find it so hard to talk about. The record has its own life now. I'm through with it!"

No one expected *Miss America* to be a commercial hit, and it wasn't. Even the most listener-friendly songs — "Anew Day," "My Friends Have" and "Year in Song" — sounded miles away from a radio climate that was still resistant to anything outside the norm. But O'Hara believed that the purity of her music would break through to those who needed to hear it, even if they didn't know it. "You always think that if something flows, it's going to hit everybody — and they'll all know whether they like it or not," she told *Now*. "I hope I get the chance to eventually reach people. I hope not to have an initial burst and expect this to be *the* album. But I do hope this album accurately shows the direction I'm going to take."

Much of the initial press focused on O'Hara's character, and perhaps that was unavoidable. Most artists are relatively normal people, and there are very few whose train of thought naturally traverses a different set of rails. Listening to *Miss America*, it's apparent that O'Hara approaches obvious processes in an unconventional way, but many in the press were caught off guard by her disarming charm and candour, if not her scattershot thought processes as captured by the constraints of speech.

In a *Melody Maker* interview from November 1989, O'Hara is described as "slightly distracted by the possibilities of life," and comments on the notion that her distracted nature was linked to her mental state: "I think a lot of the people they say are mentally ill, it's just *ways of thinking*," she said. "Think of all the gifts slotted under the name 'diseases.' Because they don't know the workings of the brain, they label things as negative. It's what they've been *told*. But I think if I was really studied, they'd say I was sick or something, y'know? And too bad a lot of people have been told that. But people sure rise above things, don't they? You see it every day. There's a lot of weird things they get over."

In November of '88 O'Hara launched the album with a show at the Horseshoe Tavern in Toronto, her first local gig since a Go Deo Chorus reunion the previous Christmas. The single and video for "Body's In Trouble" wouldn't be released in Canada until the following February, when she played a highly-publicized show at the much-larger Diamond club.

In March, the band went to play a series of dates in the U.K., debuting at the Duke of York Theatre in London. Every music critic in town turned up for their first glimpse of the enigmatic talent, and the next day unleashed the usual arsenal of bewildered hyperboles. *Time Out* called it "one of the most important concert debuts of the year." *Sounds* praised "a voice that appears to be clinging white-knuckled to the bare face of life." The strangest review came from the *New Musical Express*: before admitting that O'Hara's performance brought him to tears, the reviewer described her as an "epileptic Edith Piaf. In Mary Margaret O'Hara, God has successfully crossbred the little sparrow and the tumble dryer."

There were a few jaunts to New York City and an opening gig for Blue Rodeo at Massey Hall in December of 1989, but that was it for North American appearances. There was a second U.K. tour which also brought the band to Denmark to play the Roskilde festival, alongside Metallica and Crowded House. They recorded a tense session for BBC DJ John Peel's show, which began with the band's power bars catching fire and melting due to an electrical conversion problem.

There was a scheduled television appearance in Ireland, on the popular Gay Byrne's *Late Late Show*, but O'Hara got the boot at the last minute when a producer decided he couldn't deal with her performance style. "I don't think it was my dancing," she explained in a 1991 interview. "I was singing 'Dear Darling,' so I was hardly moving my body. It was mainly my voice they had a problem with. I was doing the soundcheck, just working out where to stand, going through the song very loosely. I thought I was doing okay; I wasn't mangling it. This guy who was supervising the whole thing got really nervous. He must have had a horror of a day and I guess I was the last straw. I started doing my dance, not wild, just, uh, normal. He was looking at me very strangely, stuttering, like he didn't know what to do. Then he edged up to me and said, 'You don't move like that, do you?' I nodded. Then he said, 'Well, you don't sing like that, do you?' The next thing I knew I wasn't doing the show anymore." She would fare much better on the U.S. variety program *Night Music*. One of that week's other guests was Sting, who after witnessing her performance told her, "That song you just did fried my brains." She responded, "You've marinated mine with yours for years."

As audiences began discovering the magic O'Hara can create on stage, they also discovered a sense of humour that she shares with her sister

Catherine. Blue Rodeo's Greg Keelor, who recalls being "madly infatuated" with O'Hara during her Songship days, says, "She seems so fragile sometimes on stage, but when you're having a drink with her, she's *funny*, and rude, and a joy. It's still a huge treat, even if Mary's just in the bar. It doesn't matter if she's singing or not — if she's just there, it makes for a better party somehow." Of her stage persona, Keelor says, "There are a thousand voices inside her, and you never know which one is going to take the next line, or the next word, or the next syllable. She could be singing a song straight, then she'd go into Judy Garland land, and then into whatever list of female iconic singers. She goes all over the place. It's everything from heartbreaking to breathtaking to hilarious."

The last major show she performed in Toronto — of her own material, with the *Miss America* band — was at the Elgin Winter Garden, on February 13, 1991. The *Toronto Star* review read, "O'Hara is that rare talent, a singer who can make you believe, if only for a second, that she is being sung by the song, that the music is moving through her like a heartbeat or a breath, that all that magical noise is simply *happening* to her."

That winter she released the *Christmas* EP on Virgin, featuring "Blue Christmas," which she had been performing for years. There was one original, "Christmas Evermore," an ethereal excursion with a syncopated shuffle. All four songs — recorded with Rooke, Marsh, McCarthy, Sloski, Piltch and a string section — sound very traditional, closer to Patsy Cline than the Mary Margaret O'Hara everyone had fallen in love with. That said, her voice is still ripe with heartbreaking majesty, especially when combined with Rooke's slide playing on "Silent Night."

Around this time, there was an attempt to record new material, some of which she had been playing since *Miss America*'s release. Some of these songs would later be covered by Holly Cole, and some would resurface when she made guest appearances with Don Rooke's new band, The Henrys. In November, 1993, she joined Jane Siberry, Holly Cole, Rebecca Jenkins and Victoria Williams for a CBC taping of Christmas songs, broadcast on Christmas Day on the CBC and National Public Radio in the U.S. O'Hara contributed an original, "Never No," and assumes lead vocals on "White Christmas." The show was released in Canada in 1994 on an album titled *Count Your Blessings*.

Beyond that, her recording output has been limited to backing vocals and tribute albums. She's hardly a recluse, and can be spotted frequently on Toronto stages performing with others, including The Henrys and The Glass Orchestra. And when she puts her mind to it, she's capable of working very quickly. Don Rooke tells the story of a Henrys' song, "Goddess of Maya" from their 1998 album *Desert Cure*, that she transformed at the last minute.

"I phoned her a month or two before, to see if she wanted to sing on it," Rooke recalls. "She phoned me back, coincidentally, the afternoon before we were going wrap up and mix the next day. She said, 'Do you still want me to sing on it?' I took the tapes to her at 4 p.m., picked her up at seven, and she had listened to it, in her words, 'one and a half times.' She'd written lyrics and she came and recorded the song. There was a melody, and she wrote these words that fit in between the phrases of the melody perfectly, and it sounds like it was made to be that way. I thought she was going to sing some atmospheric stuff. It was mind-boggling. We were high-fiving each other in the other room!"

The more she retreated out of the spotlight back into Toronto's artistic community, the greater the mystique grew around the world. People like Michael Stipe, Kristin Hersh and Vic Chesnutt would continue to sing her praises in interviews throughout the '90s. In 2000, both Britain's *Mojo* and America's *Spin* magazines mentioned her when doing "where are they now?" stories on cult artists.

"People are still knocked out by her," says Toronto promoter Elliott Lefko. "With her, it's her beauty and her fault that she can't understand the mechanisms of commerciality. She won't go down that road. In a way it's really good artistically, because she's able to put out a record like she did, and play with the Glass Orchestra or do an evening of love songs, and then you won't see her again. That's the positive. The fault is that if she'd learn to take a step towards the centre of the road, she could be huge. But she won't, or she can't, or she doesn't know how, or whatever it is."

After the laborious process of recording *Miss America*, O'Hara is in no hurry to follow it up. That album was a chore to make because of her own expectations for herself. Today, compounded with the expectations of her rabid cult audience, it's much easier to take things one small project at a time. In a prophetic quote, she told *Now* in 1983: "I have to trust that it's better to do something small that feels good than do something bigger that's just confusing people."

In 1991, when her *Christmas* EP was released and the mystique was already growing, she gave a revealing interview to *Melody Maker* in which she discussed some reasons why she has never embarked on another large project and confronts the predictable, if not sad, accusations that her sanity may have something to do with it.

"When I look back, it's sad to think that it was sitting on a shelf ripening for four whole years, like it was going to rot," she told the magazine. "I didn't want to let so much time pass. But I've gone and done it again. Maybe there's something wrong with me. Maybe my thoughts move from the wrong side of my brain. I keep asking people what their brains are like. My own brain doesn't amuse me. It knocks me around. The whole 'Mad Margaret' thing is something that I learned to dismiss and even laugh about. Nuts, screws, washers and bolts. It's always seemed to me like an easy excuse for dismissing my music. They're nuts to say I'm nuts. If I'm nuts, well, it's my birthright to be myself. It's too easy to take someone who's got something to give and say, 'Ho ho, they're idiosyncratic, quirky, or plain nuts.' I read this stuff that's written about me and I think, 'Who is this person they're talking about? Is that me?' It's probably all my fault, though. I'll be doing these interviews and I'll be relaxing, thinking I'm yipyip, saying all these wise things. Meanwhile, I'm coming across like a nut. Well, that's what I get for trying to be wise.

"The biggest problem is narrowing down the possibilities. I don't have a problem deciding about breakfast. That part of it is easy. Getting out of bed in the morning involves a decision. Just lying there can be addictive. It's just that I can let time pass without feeling this need to get a million things done. I'm not into goals, really. Sometimes I think I should be. But you don't always know what's going to happen. I'm going to create goals for myself — work for the moment, live for the moment. Give myself a better reputation. Hmmm. Then again. . . ."

When it came time to follow up *Melville*, the Rheostatics almost found themselves in a sophomore slump. Wojewoda recalls, "Even though *Greatest Hits* was already out [before *Melville*], *Whale Music* had a sophomoric anxiety about it, which led to a lot of rap sessions and freaking out. I got into big fights with Dave Clark, because he kept saying, 'It's gotta be great. We have all this pressure, people have all these expectations.' Finally, everyone just went '*Fuck it!*' For two days I couldn't even get them into the studio, and we only had two weeks to make the record. What was amazing was that *Whale Music* is even better, and went even further than *Melville*."

To ease the tension, the Rheostatics drew on the musical community they'd immersed themselves in over the past two years: Lewis Melville, Dave Allen, Tannis Slimmon of The Bird Sisters, UIC's Joey Bechta, the Barenaked Ladies (dubbed "The Scarborough Naked Youth Choir"), and from the Bourbon Tabernacle Choir, Gene Hardy and Chris Brown. "Having a lot of guests on the record was like a buffer," says Wojewoda. "That helped them get past the fact that none of them wanted to play, because they were too freaked out to be there."

Chris Brown recalls, "They thought they were going too far in the studio. I sat with them and said, 'Don't think about anything else. Don't think about the live show or being able to recreate anything other than spirit.' I remember a really wonderful, really loose creative time, and letting stuff happen. They're all such individuals that it's amazing they could come together like that."

Whale Music opens with a lush string section — which is actually multiple overdubs of Dave Allen's violin — introducing the theme of "Self-Serve Gas Station." The song slowly evolves from a rich country ballad into a howling rock epic, set to lyrics detailing crippling suburban ennui: "To say that this is anything / is saying much too much." It establishes a tone of elegance that continues through the rest of the album.

Lyrically, there's a recurring theme of escape and coming to terms with both the past and present, and it's Bidini who scores most of the best stories. The narrator in "Queer" consoles his brother, who has been banished from the family home by a homophobic father after a violent confrontation: "I don't care about the damage / But I wish you were there to see it / When I scored a hat trick on the team that called you a fuckin' queer." The musician in "Rock Death America" wants desperately to shrug off the stigma of being a Canadian band always compared to foreign examples: "Someone said we sounded like the Replacements / but we'd never be the Beatles or Byrds / someone said we should've stayed in the basement / instead of littering our noise on the earth." The slacker in "Legal Age Life At Variety Store" is a curbside philosopher who muses, "I'm the king I am therefore what kind of a fool am I?"

Lewis Melville argues that one of the band's main strengths is Bidini's lyrics, including "his social awareness and his ability to put that across." He explains, "Bidini writes very straightforward and in-your-face lyrics that really capture the mood of what it is he's talking about. It is rare — capturing the mood, not just saying it, but getting the essence of it. He's very good at capturing the simple and expressing it in a very powerful way."

Whale Music's biggest strength, when compared to the rest of the band's catalogue, is that all three principal writers are in peak form. Vesely pens what is perhaps his best song, "King of the Past," and Tielli wrenches some of his most emotional and dramatic performances on "Shaved Head," "California Dreamline" and "Dope Fiends and Boozehounds." The latter closes the album and encapsulates much of its lyrical and musical ambition, making it *Whale Music*'s definitive song.

One of the biggest boosts the band received was from Neil Peart, the überdrummer for hometown heroes Rush. Bidini had interviewed him for an article; when he asked about Peart's favourite new Canadian bands, Peart cited the Rheostatics — completely unaware that Bidini was in the band. They invited Peart to play on a couple of *Whale Music* tracks, including "Guns," a piece by Clark which consisted of a poem and a drum solo. "I didn't even want to have him out," admits Clark. "I was too afraid of having a hero come out and play." But Clark and Peart got along famously. "The way he played drums, you could tell that he'd been playing stadiums all his life: the power, the conviction," says Clark. "It hurt my ears with the headphones on. The control room was full of people watching: the Barenaked Ladies, our band, and others. This was a big moment, because he was a CanRock god — well, an international god. The talkback button was on by mistake, and we heard [BNL drummer] Tyler Stewart say, 'Look at Dave, man, he's out there *shitting his pants!*' I said, 'No, I'm not! This is great!' When I was there this adrenaline took over me and I felt completely supercharged, like I could jump over walls."

Rheostatics recording overdubs for *Introducing Happiness* at Grant Ave. Studio in Hamilton, 1993: Martin Tielli, Dave Bidini, Tim Vesely, engineer Linda Duemo, producer Michael Phillip Wojewoda, Dave Clark
(Photo by Dave Clark)

"Almost everything [on *Whale Music*] was planned with half a day's notice," says Wojewoda. "So much of what they do is just chaos, then you edit it away to give it some order, and then the listener must follow suit to provide the rest of the order. Recording them is like wildlife photography; it's just noise most of the time."

Lewis Melville adds, "The texturing was done by Michael Phillip, but the band worked out of a lot of the ideas at shows. They had a pretty good idea of what they wanted to do, but didn't know exactly how to pull it off. Michael Phillip is as creative a producer as you can find. He's totally involved, he's very positive and supportive, and he's very sensitive to the mood of a recording. He's pretty good at steering around trouble spots, but he's not totally successful in the case of the Rheostatics, because they tend to have a mind of their own regardless of what anyone else thinks."

Immediately following *Whale Music*, Wojewoda went to work on the Barenaked Ladies' *Gordon* album. He got the job at the last minute. "They came in and sat on the couch for a day, ended up singing, and before they left they said, 'We'd love you to do it,'" says Wojewoda, who refuses to take much credit for *Gordon*'s success. "The machine was already in place," he argues. "When I [started recording], the artwork was already done: the photos, the layout, everything. They had pig latin wherever the lyrics were to go. It didn't matter. They just plugged me in, chose the songs, and were ready to go. In the hands of another capable producer, it probably would have done just as well. Their success has been largely based on their live shows, their tenacity and charisma. I knew I was a cog plugging into something, but I felt very comfortable with that idea. I thought, 'Great, if I don't fuck up, then all the better.' I almost liked it more, because so many indie records come and go, and I knew someone was going to play this when it was done."

Wojewoda wasn't a fan of the band at first, particularly their lightweight humour, which he thought overshadowed their real strengths. "I got the yellow cassette and I heard it and thought, 'Ehh, collegiate schtick.' Then I heard 'The Flag.' There's an insightful darkness to Steven [Page] that made me like it, and I realized that I could do something with that. I could be party to elevating that out of the collegiate stuff, and give it a serious twist."

The *Gordon* sessions were haunted by the spectre of the still-uncompleted *Whale Music* sessions, which both Wojewoda and the Barenaked Ladies knew were special. "We were laying down the beds for *Gordon*, and Michael Phillip would bring in rough mixes of *Whale Music*, and we'd say, 'Our record's *shit!*'" laughs the self-deprecating Ed Robertson. *Gordon* went on to sell a million copies in Canada, but Wojewoda didn't reap any immediate rewards — quite the contrary. "It was the brokest I've ever been," he laughs. "My phone stopped ringing. My whole indie base thought either I wasn't cool or that I was in L.A. being fabulous. I was dying for work, really bad."

In the meantime, a job Wojewoda had started in the summer of 1991 had taken on a new life and was on its way to being another milestone in the CanRock Renaissance: Jane Siberry's *When I Was a Boy*. Wojewoda was involved in the genesis of the album, what would become a small role in a much larger project. He got the job through John Switzer, Siberry's former partner, with whom he was collaborating on an album by London, Ontario band Suffer Machine. Recalls Wojewoda, "I told John that at the time I was going through a little impasse on a learning curve, where I needed to watch someone else work, just to learn stuff. Then Jane was about to make another record, the first one John wasn't going to be involved in. John and I were heading out to London to record more Suffer Machine stuff, and he says, 'Jane's going to be doing this thing, and she needs an engineer and I'd be really comfortable if you did it.'"

Wojewoda ended up being only one of many producers and engineers Siberry drew from to create her masterpiece. Like Mary Margaret O'Hara's *Miss America*, Siberry's *When I Was A Boy* drew upon the talents of many luminary talents, but ultimately encapsulated the essence of one woman's singular vision. Although Brian Eno and Michael Brook assumed the reins for some portions of the recording process, it was Siberry that steered the mammoth project to completion — remarkable not only because of the people involved, but because it was her first foray into being her own boss. "By the end," says Siberry, "there were a lot of people who had worked on it, and yet the end touch was most strongly myself, which felt very right."

Of her earlier work, she says, "I began hearing decisions being made by other people that I had thought were wrong but didn't trust myself enough. I demurred to someone else's decision and later realized that my decision was better. That's when I started trusting myself more, and that's been an ongoing process. A lot of producers have a levelling effect. I think the opposite is required, but that probably doesn't work as well in a commercial world. To me, the best producers reflect and exaggerate. With any producer who's coming in to direct things — including Brian Eno and Michael Brook, more high-profile producers — it's still collaborative."

The recording started in Vancouver, with just Siberry, her longtime guitarist Ken Myhr and Wojewoda workshopping the songs. Says Wojewoda, "One thing that was tough about working with Jane was not necessarily knowing what you wanted, but rather knowing what you *didn't* want — discovering through process of elimination what way the record would go. It led to a lot of cul-de-sacs and a lot of fatiguing."

One key track completed there was "Calling All Angels," which German director Wim Wenders had commissioned for his new movie, *Until the End of the World*; the stellar soundtrack also featured Patti Smith, Lou Reed, Talking Heads, and others. In an inspired move, Siberry asked k.d. lang to sing the song as a duet at a time when lang was just about to leave her country music beginnings behind her. The two weren't very well acquainted before the session, beyond an unusual meeting at lang's legendary first

Toronto appearance at Albert's Hall. "She wandered into the washroom with her microphone and started singing from there, and I happened to be there at the same time," Siberry recalls.

On a more serious note, Siberry cites the "Calling All Angels" track as a huge step forward in her own singing, thanks to lang. "k.d. lang has been someone I've always trusted as a musician and as an artist," says Siberry. "Working with her, I've been open to watching her and learning from her — what she presents and how she uses her energy. I think the word 'musician' is very close to the word 'magician' and it makes sense because you're juggling energy and you're creating something, working to create change in the air through sound. When I worked with her I thought she had an invisible but profound effect on my singing. It was only a four-hour session, but two weeks later my vibrato changed. Many years later I realized when I heard her again that the change had come from her; that she had taught me something without even saying anything."

Meanwhile, Siberry was discovering that she had a big fan in Brian Eno, who wrote her a letter via Warner raving about *Bound by the Beauty*, and expressed bewilderment over its lack of success. He soon struck up a correspondence with Siberry, in which he encouraged her to "follow the path of most feeling and least resistance." The letter read, "This sounds like weird advice, the opposite of what you might have expected from me. But so often we are frightened of our own ideas, either because they pop out so effortlessly, or because they seem too familiar to us."

Siberry flew to London to work with Eno, who produced two tracks: the ethereal "Sail Across the Water," which would be the album's first single; and the sensuous "Temple," which is the most muscular track Siberry has ever recorded. Although Eno's sonic influence can be heard all over the album, simply adding his name to the list of contributors helped as much as his presence. "Really, Brian's most important contribution to the record has been his name, in a funny way," says Siberry. "Even before people had heard it, they perked up their ears knowing that he had worked on it." In the album's liner notes, she coyly gives "a special thanks to Brian Eno for his left knee."

Returning from England, Siberry set out reworking everything she'd amassed up to that point. For the first time in her career, she was working outside of the writing/recording/touring loop that had seen her deliver four albums in five years. By the time *When I Was A Boy* was finally completed, it had been four years since *Bound by the Beauty*. "I was a different person," she says. "I hadn't been able to catch my breath for a long time, and when I made that record there were a number of long lulls. I was waiting for

Warner Brothers to assign a producer, and assign singles. Plus, I had time to do other things, so I did a lot of healing and growing and it reflects that."

Several songs from the initial sessions were discarded, and surfaced later on a trilogy of live albums Siberry recorded in 1997 (one, the double CD *Child*, was released in 1998; the other two didn't come out until 2000). Consequently, *When I Was a Boy* has a very distinct thematic link, which alternates between surrendering to the unpredictability of love and taking it by the reins. In what was a very conscious move to connect with audiences through both her lyrics and her music, Siberry focused on articulating her personal vision in a very universal way, tackling philosophical questions of life and love with mature wisdom, demanding answers from her god, her lover, and herself. There are also several references to caregiving, culminating on the nine-minute rumination "The Vigil (The Sea)," a gorgeous long poem about a journey into death. As a whole, Siberry draws the listener in with some of her most intriguing and accessible material, but isn't afraid to indulge in tracks like the improvisational ambient piece "Sweet Incarnadine." *When I Was A Boy* bears little resemblance to any other Jane Siberry album, although it's undoubtedly her crowning artistic achievement.

"Finally, when it was done, there was a very curious non-reaction from the record company," she says. "A couple of them didn't want 'The Vigil' to be on it; they didn't get it or understand it. It's very filmic, and they didn't know what to do with that. But on a pop record, you only need one or two singles, so who cares what the rest is? That album had a funny, quiet entry into the world, and now it has sold more than any other [Siberry album]."

A year after its release, she told *Rolling Stone*, "This record is more whole in a funny way. It is more accessible to the people who drive red Camaros. It is also more masculine. Before, my work has always had a sense of graciousness and hospitality, like the good mother. I don't think I could be called a female singer/songwriter with this record."

In November 1992, when the album was still a couple of months away from completion, Siberry landed the opening slot for the premiere of Mike Oldfield's *Tubular Bells II* in Edinburgh, Scotland. Appearing with keyboardist Bob Wiseman and performing her new material, Siberry was eaten alive by a rabid crowd, an experience that was at first devastating but ultimately liberating.

"It didn't go over well," she says, "and the record company freaked out. So I said fuck you, and felt free. It crystallized a side of me that went from hoping people liked me, to: 'Well, what do you really want to do if no one likes you?' It was a very powerful place to be."

She said in 1993, "I was dumbstruck. I came back to Canada and went up north and cried for two weeks. Then something snapped. I took all the power back that I had put outside myself trying to please [others]. The worst show of my life has become the best show because it's given me the ultimate freedom to care only about what I think is really good. How my career does is secondary.

"That was the key to freedom," she surmises, alluding to Kris Kristofferson, "having nothing to lose."

After the Edinburgh gig, Siberry knew then that it was all on herself. "It was a huge show and we bombed. Or, *I* bombed, because Bobby was just accompanying me," she says. At this point, she was determined to leave her longtime collaborators behind — Ken Myhr joined the Cowboy Junkies for several years — and seek new ways of presenting her material. About choosing her musical cohorts, she says, "Intuition is a parameter. If I'm meeting them out of the blue, I will audition with them and start improvising and see what happens. That's usually the most telling thing — how well they listen, and when they listen, what they hear."

Later in her career, Siberry would perform with a jazz-inflected band featuring pianist Tim Ray, and record her live trilogy with a large cast of characters, including a horn section. But when she went on tour for *When I Was a Boy*, she performed solo and billed the show "The 'It Ain't A Concert' Concert," balanced between songs, poems, stories, audience interaction, and videos. "Before that I was experimenting with big bands, and for *When I Was a Boy* I stripped it right down," she says. "It was such a big record, and I felt I could only go out alone." The tour received mixed response, with many reviewers wondering why there wasn't more music in the program. On the heels of her best album, it was an odd way to promote herself, perhaps ensuring that she was eventually destined to operate outside of any commercial expectations whatsoever. She would leave Warner in 1995 of her own volition and set up her own record company, Sheeba, which would focus primarily on selling her back catalogue and revisiting older material: releases included songs she wrote as a teenager, the live albums, and an album of spirituals.

A couple of months after the release of *When I Was A Boy*, Siberry was scheduled to play the Hillside Festival in her old university town of Guelph. To back her up, she called on the Rheostatics, who had begun adding their cover of Siberry's "One More Colour" to their live set. Says Dave Clark, "We did it because Martin and I were both big fans, Martin in particular. One day I was walking down Spadina, and ran into her and said, 'We should play together sometime.' Then she phoned us up."

The band was excited to do it, although warning bells started going off once rehearsals started at the Gas Station studio. "I was into it," says Tim Vesely, "maybe because I'd had experience backing other people up before. But she rubbed the two Daves completely the wrong way, so they were going in the opposite direction that Jane and me and maybe Martin were."

The show was to be the closing event of the weekend-long festival, with Siberry performing first and then the Rheostatics closing the night. After a long delay, they took to the stage, and although there were moments of magic, it was clear that the much-anticipated fusion was going to work like oil and water. "When we took the stage, she became a different person than in the rehearsals," says Vesely. "She was out of touch with us, and had a completely different way of thinking about us as people. I didn't pick up on it; the two Daves did for sure. I was concentrating on my parts. But I remember the experience pretty fondly, and musically, we did pretty good." Tielli says, "I've got a videotape of it, and I don't think there was a problem; she didn't think there was a problem. It was the Daves, they didn't dig it. And onstage, she was uncomfortable."

At several points in the performance, Siberry wryly poked fun at the lack of synergy, asking: "What is this, some kind of game show?" as well as, "What am I doing on stage with these clowns?" "My face went red when she said that," says Tielli. "But when I watch [the videotape of the performance], it was fine, other than that shit. I think she thought that Bidini jumping around didn't quite fit the ambience she was trying to create. He was like a boy, a bouncing rabbit of rock with these giant lead feet. There was a spotlight problem."

"We had gone from being very free to accommodating someone else's vision," says Dave Clark. "We tried to the best of our abilities to do that, and I still deeply respect her songwriting to this day. But it was an unpleasant experience, to put it lightly."

Afterwards, the Rheostatics were scheduled to back up Siberry for a taping of the MuchMusic show *Intimate and Interactive*, but retracted, partly at Clark's insistence. "I said, 'You guys can do what you want, but I'm not doing it,'" says Clark. "I called her up and told her. She's a great musician. Everybody has times in their life when they're not as on the ball as they are at other times."

Today, Siberry recalls, "It was just an interesting thing. Some kooky things happened, and I don't really know what to make of them still. They're a pretty emotional band. Musically, they're in a different world." She pauses, before adding, "It's a different degree of refinement."

The Rheostatics had a few shaky shows of their own around that time. Because of their adventurous nature onstage, they were capable of either the most transcendent moments or a meandering mess. On the heels of the accomplishment that was *Whale Music*, which had musicians across the land uttering the name Rheostatics in hushed and reverent tones, their live shows were burdened with high audience expectations. Although their carefree nature had initially attracted a lot of people to the band, suddenly there were new fans who were looking for the perfection found on the studio recordings.

Lewis Melville, who was often found on stage with the Rheostatics during that time, says, "The weakness of the band is that they don't have the strength to be consistently strong. They can collapse easily. Tim would be the guy who they'd fall back on. Tim is the foundation." Mike O'Neill of The Inbreds frequently toured with the Rheostatics. "I spent a lot of my time watching their shows and being jealous, because I thought they were incredible," says O'Neill. "They'd have really great shows and shows that weren't as great, and I thought that was a beautiful thing. We toured with bands later on in our career who would play the same show every night, and it didn't even make any difference."

In November 1992, the Rheostatics staged a show at the Bathurst St. Theatre in Toronto, their first venture outside of the bar circuit, and the same venue where the Barenaked Ladies held their first big show. They took to the stage in tuxedos, which they had rented to sing the national anthem at a Maple Leafs game the night before; it was also the week of Dave Bidini's wedding to childhood sweetheart Janet Morasutti, the co-writer of "Northern Wish" and "Dope Fiends and Boozehounds." "We put everything into that show," recalls Tielli, "and that might have been one of the best. That was a big step, musically and performance-wise." They were joined on keyboards by Kevin Hearn of the Look People, the first of many appearances he would make with the band; he would later join the Barenaked Ladies and become a key Rheostatics collaborator in the late '90s. The magical evening closed with Dave Bidini's "When Winter Comes." The coda of the song — normally sung by Tielli — was sung a cappella by Meryn Cadell, Tannis Slimmon and Michelle Rumball (Grievous Angels) as fake snow fell from above the stage.

While *Whale Music* made converts one by one, the Barenaked Ladies were taking over the world. They were managed by Nigel Best, an aggressive British expatriate who soon added the Rheostatics to his roster. When BNL signed to Sire records, Best convinced the label to take the Rheostatics as well. A remastered version of *Whale Music* was re-released on Sire in 1993, but didn't have a significant effect on the Rheostatics' visibility, or their schedule. "We never met the people from Sire records," says Vesely. "We've always chugged along at the same kind of pace. Even at that time, we'd take our two/three month hiatus, where we barely talk to each other or even think about being in the band. The best part of that whole experience was learning how [major labels are] not really a part of music, and that you don't need record labels or managers."

A major label deal did, however, mean the opportunity to use a major-label budget. Wojewoda insisted that they go to Compass Point studios in the Bahamas in March, 1994. "I had to convince Tim," recalls Wojewoda, "who wanted to spend it wisely and thought they should keep it. I said, 'When are you ever going to get a chance to do something fun?'" Tielli says, "We were in the Bahamas thinking, 'Are we going to pay for this for the rest of our lives?' But we have an amazing ability to put things like that out of our minds, so we had a blast. It was almost like we were getting along."

Dave Clark was beginning to question what he thought was the focus of the band at that time. "We had all these older songs that we were really enjoying, and newer stuff that Tim was writing, which was the direction the band ended up going in, straightforward pop stuff. Leading up to the recording, the band started closing in on itself. We didn't work with Lew anymore; we started using less people as guests on stage, unless it was Green Sprouts Music Week. There was less adventure in the music, and for me it felt like we were rewriting stuff we'd already done."

Wojewoda's initial excitement about the recording quickly dissipated as his notoriously weak constitution caved in at the worst possible time. "I landed a sinus attack and an ear infection: tinnitus, burning hot, and sick as a dog for the whole thing," he says. "I had no fun in the Bahamas; I just felt a burden of responsibility. There are nuggets on the album, but everyone had to be served on that one. The need for democracy overtook clarity of the album, and I was too sick to do anything about it. I was physically ill, and just thought, 'what the fuck.'"

With 18 songs, *Introducing Happiness* is incredibly eclectic and sprawling; if *Whale Music* was their *Sgt. Pepper's, Introducing Happiness* is certainly their *White Album*. Much of it sounds like solo material fleshed out by the band, as opposed to a true team effort, particularly four songs in the middle of the album: "Digital Beach" (Tielli), "Earth" (Bidini), "Row" (Vesely) and

"Full Moon Over Russia" (Clark). Much of the album's best writing belongs to Tielli, and Bidini's best song, "Jesus Was a Teenager Too," is sung by Tielli. It's a huge, head-spinning and confounding album, the sound of the Rheostatics blown up to a 70mm wide-screen and THX sound, magnifying the band's best and worst moments, wrapped in a sparkling package of pristine and innovative production. It's also the most comprehensive Rheostatics album, featuring their most conventional material (the title track) alongside their quirkiest and most fascinating ("Uncle Henry").

It doesn't sound like a major label debut, partially because their label didn't seem to care what they did. Vesely figures the song selection was a reactive measure. "In our limited dealings with managers and industry stuff, they always say 'Focus! It's too much crap in there,'" he says. "So naturally we're going to do even *more*; it's part of what we do. We thought, fuck that, let's throw it all in and take it even further."

Just before they started recording they were contacted by Richard Lewis, a film director who was adapting Paul Quarrington's novel *Whale Music*; Quarrington played the Rheostatics for Lewis, and the band was commissioned to work on the score. In the novel, the Brian Wilson-esque narrator, Desmond Howell, is living in seclusion, trying to create a symphony for the whales that surface outside his seaside mansion, because he feels only they truly understand him. His world is turned upside down when a young woman named Claire stumbles into his life and brings him closer to reality. Her presence inspires him to write a pop song about her, which leaks out to his former manager and becomes a comeback hit.

It's not surprising that it was Vesely, the most concise pop songsmith in the band and "the singles guy," who rose to the occasion. "We took the scripts home," he recalls, "and I was looking at this little part that had these lyrics, 'Purify me, purify me Claire / clarify me Claire.' I put some chords to it and brought it into the band sheepishly, because I have a hard time introducing new songs and I wasn't really sold on it, but it was part of the soundtrack job, so I thought, whatever. The song came easily, because I sat down and thought of simplicity and a catchy melody. We were all into playing a simple beat and a simple song."

It was the first single from *Introducing Happiness*, and became the band's first hit. The colourful video was directed by the Look People's Jaymz Bee. Tielli says, "Dave Clark hated it, but we were totally successful at what the assignment was. Nobody's picked up on how funny that is: the assignment was to write Desmond Howell's hit song, and we did it — and it's our only charting hit, except maybe for 'Bad Time to be Poor.' It's funny as hell that we can do it if we want to. I don't want to, particularly."

The band debuted the song at a noon-hour concert outside the National Gallery in Ottawa, and workshopped it at Toronto's Gas Station studios before heading to the Bahamas. Recording the demo session was Dale Morningstar. "I was never a huge Rheostatics fan," recalls Morningstar, "until they recorded demos for *Introducing Happiness* at the Gas Station. I was sitting at the board, and on the other side of the screen they were working on 'Claire.' I thought, 'Fuck, this is like the Beatles or something' — the whole communication between the four guys, arguing to make a better pie. That was very inspiring, and that's how I got to know Dave Clark."

Today, Dale Morningstar is known as the co-proprietor of Toronto's Gas Station studio, as well as the adventurous, unconventional bandleader of the avant-garde rock band Dinner is Ruined. But when he started his musical career in the Niagara region of southwestern Ontario — living in basements, recording in isolation on four-track recorders, and avoiding the practically non-existent live music scene in the area — he wasn't playing the wonderfully strange music he's known for.

"Dale Morningstar was so pop back then, I thought he sounded like Rick Springfield," says Kurt Swinghammer, another artist who started in the Niagara area in the early '80s. "He was really clean cut, had a really cute blonde girlfriend, they had a little house together. It was the purest pop. He even *looked* like Rick Springfield."

Morningstar's first tape was in 1984, a collaboration with his friend John Press, a keyboardist who would later be known as Dr. Pee. Morningstar had applied for and received a government grant for the project, which ended up costing him $7,000 for four songs. "It was synth pop," he recalls. "I had these lame tunes with no balls at all, watered down and slick. I sent it away, and record companies actually liked it. Majors were calling me and asking me, 'Hey, do you play live?' Because it was what was in at that time in Canadian commercial rock. It wasn't as bad as Glass Tiger, but it was sappy, slick, and catchy. Fortunately, I didn't have it in myself to get a band together. I had no experience. I had all the gelled hair then, too. I was 24 or 25. I was lucky that I didn't get it together, otherwise people would look at me now and go, 'Oh, *that* guy. He did something in '84.'"

Morningstar's approach began to change when he started reading Toronto's *Nerve* magazine, which also distributed to select locations around Ontario. "That inspired me," he says. "They had this stuff about the indie rock ethic and doing it yourself, and it made sense to me. *Nerve* turned

Dale Morningstar of Dinner
is Ruined at Gas Station
studio, 1994
(Photo by Richard Beland)

me on to scouting some records out." On *Nerve*'s recommendation, Morningstar sought out four specific records: R.E.M.'s *Fables of the Reconstruction*, Sonic Youth's *Sister*, Hüsker Dü's *New Day Rising* and The Jesus and Mary Chain's *Psychocandy*. "Those four records totally changed my world around," he raves. "I found them really difficult at first; I didn't know if it was good or bad or what. Those records would jar people. I'd play them for certain people in my house, and they'd have to leave. I knew there was something good there."

That influence bled onto his first full-length, self-titled album which he finished in 1986 but wasn't released until two years later. Recalls Morningstar, "There was one review of it I'll never forget, which said: 'it has all the impact of a small underwater fart.'"

The small scene that did exist in the Niagara region was splintering. Two other artists that Morningstar would cross paths with later were also operating there at that time: Kurt Swinghammer and Ron Sexsmith, and both were about to move to Toronto. In the early '90s, Swinghammer and Sexsmith would share gigs where they would cover each other's songs and cheekily bill the evening "Sexhammer."

When Morningstar moved to Toronto in 1988, he played a few gigs with St. Catharines musicians, and then called Swinghammer to see if he could recommend a drummer. "Kurt said, 'I know this guy Don Kerr. He's heard your record and I don't think he likes it, but here's his phone number anyway,'" says Morningstar. "I called Don and he had a gig at Lee's Palace that night with a band called Wipeout Beach. He had long straggly hair, one side of his head was shaved, and he looked like Jesus. We got together later in his basement to play. He was drinking goat milk, and I thought this was *freaky*."

Swinghammer had also recommended Kerr to Sexsmith, who as it turned out worked at the same courier company as Kerr. "I was a bike courier and he was a foot courier," says Kerr. "The next day at the end of work, I had to put the face to the name, because I'd only ever heard him over the [courier's] radio. There was this really shy and jerky, nerdy guy who looked about 14. He was the most nervous guy I'd ever seen, and I thought, 'This guy's a songwriter? This guy gets up on *stage*?' He couldn't open his eyes on stage until about five years after that, even though he'd been playing in bars since he was 17. He used to be a human jukebox, playing in these biker bars with his acoustic, and he'd get a whole room of people dancing."

Kerr and his high-school friend Steve Charles, a bassist, sat in with Sexsmith for a practice. "We played a couple of his songs," Kerr recalls, "which I thought were great, and then he wanted to try an old Stevie Wonder song, 'I Was Made To Love Her,' which was one of my favourite songs of all time. This was in the '80s, and this guy was as far out from the popular styles as we were." The trio clicked, and played their first gig at a Christmas party in 1987.

By 1990, Kerr and Morningstar were close friends, working at the same Vietnamese bakery and discussing their philosophies of music, which led them to pool their home recording equipment and record the first Dinner is Ruined release, *Burn Yer Dashiki* with bassist Al Kelso in 1991. One track from the album, "Stuck Pig," caught the attention of Amy Hersenhoren at Raw Energy Records, who used it to lead off the seminal 1993 indie rock compilation *On the Road*.

The basement apartment set-up was dubbed The Gas Station, and was used mainly to record projects Kerr was involved in, including a cassette by Sam Larkin. The first outside project they recorded was Lazy Grace, a Queen Street roots supergroup that included Andrew Cash, Andy Stochansky, Lynn Simmons and Kersti Mcleod. The track was for a compilation entitled *Moose*, which also featured Bob Snider, Anne Bourne, and much of the Save the Rails crew, including the Rheostatics and Grievous Angels.

Kerr and Morningstar would always work separately on Gas Station projects, the only exception being the studio's first "big" gig, which was Change of Heart recording a track for a Donovan tribute album on Nettwerk. "They were the first band we ever recorded on the 16-track," says Morningstar. "Glenn Milchem was playing drums. We were trying to figure out the gear, and we thought, 'These guys must think we're fucking morons! Glenn Milchem must think we're imbeciles! Where does this cord go?'"

Their live show was a little more together, and although experimental, much more focused than what they were about to become. "We were a tight band," says Morningstar. "We were noise rock, very influenced by Sonic Youth at that time. Al was into noise, playing his bass with a screwdriver.

Don, meanwhile, came from this whole XTC background, more traditional. And I was the Rolling Stones guy who was converted to Sonic Youth and detuned guitars, making it like an exorcism. A lot of times we didn't go over that well. We had a real bite and edge to us, and there weren't a lot of guitar bands around here who were that in-your-face."

Kerr was enjoying himself, but would soon start dedicating more time to other projects. "I thought *Burn Yer Dashiki* was really good," says Kerr. "It was really hard-hitting, alternative rock right before it was happening. [Dale] was writing these amazing songs like Ian Blurton. I'd go from harmonizing with Ron [Sexsmith] one night, to freaking out with Dale the next. But I got tired of Dinner is Ruined as it got less song-based, which it wasn't live. Dale's great in the studio making a song out of a sonic soundscape. But live, he'd always be freaking out and nervous. I got tired of that angsty stuff and started leaning towards songs."

Kelso had left the band before Kerr and Morningstar went to work on the next album in 1993, called *Love Songs From the Lubritorium*, their first for Raw Energy. The album moved away from experimental punk rock by using a much larger palette, including banjos, horns, mandolins, kalimbas, vibes and other folkie instruments colouring Morningstar's unusual vision. It would be the definitive Dinner is Ruined recording until 1999's *A Maggot in Their Heads*.

Although Kerr's influence can be heard all over *Love Songs*, he decided to leave upon its release for entirely musical reasons; he and Morningstar moved to a larger warehouse space in 1991 and continue to run The Gas Station together to this day. He started playing more frequently with Bob Wiseman, who Dinner is Ruined had backed up for a series of shows. Morningstar went on tour for the first time in his life, taking on Western Canada with an entirely new line-up in August, 1993.

The band started becoming weird for its own sake, often eschewing all *Love Songs* material for free-form improv. At one show in Guelph, Morningstar, after clearing the room, began screaming into a baritone horn, running off stage and outside of the club, where an angry bouncer chased him into the street and demanded he come back. The local weekly described the show as "flashbacks without the acid."

Morningstar recalls, "The wind went out of my sails when Don split the scene; the bottom just fell out. Everyone's replaceable, even me, but the rhythm-man is king. That threw back the Dinner is Ruined train for a couple of years."

In 1994, the Rheostatics were experiencing problems in their rhythm section as well. After the release of *Introducing Happiness*, Dave Clark became increasingly disenchanted with the band's state of affairs. "We ended up getting stuck in business, which is the worst place for any band to be," he says. "I'm the type of person who doesn't deal well with an overload of negativity. We would go out and have these incredibly ecstatic live shows, with everything from the deepest angst from the darkest pits of our being, to the brightest, happiest times. Certain people started to feel the pressure of commercial aspirations. We were working hard, had girlfriends and were trying to get a life. At the same time, spending that much time with the same four people locked us into a pattern of socializing, so everything was a little bigger than it could have been."

Things came to a head while the band was touring in the U.K. in the fall of 1994. "You could see that people were getting tired," says Clark. "We'd get to a gig and all people would do was complain about their gear. I thought, 'Fuck, a year ago we were playing on gear that we were hammering together.' For me it was becoming less about the music and more about everything around it. The joy of it just left me. I enjoyed the people — Dave, Tim and Martin were fun and really nice guys. Martin in particular is hilarious; no matter how much angst was going on between us, he was always very funny and is to this day. But I knew I had to quit and I couldn't bring myself to do it, because it would be quitting something that had been such a huge part of my life."

Looking back, Vesely says of Clark, "He thought we were more industry-oriented than we actually were. His interest had gone further and further away from keeping within the mainstream. It might have appeared that that's what we were doing, because people would latch onto the song 'Claire,' even though we were doing all this other stuff. He was reacting against that more than he should have. We definitely weren't as far apart as he thought we were — or we thought he was."

In October 1994, the Rheostatics played two fateful gigs at the Zaphod Beeblebrox club in Ottawa, with Dinner is Ruined opening the show. "They set up all this wacky gear," says Clark, "and I hung out with them because it was exciting to hang out with different people. They were really eccentric guys." With a hint of disdain, Clark continues, "This was just after that single 'Claire,' and we started to get more of a collegiate audience. It was different; we were getting more guys [in the audience], I don't know why. [Dinner is Ruined] played, and people felt threatened and wanted to beat them up. Of course, they weren't afraid at all. I was sitting there thinking,

'This is great!'"

"All hell broke loose," says Morningstar. "That was the phase of DIR where we just brought all sorts of shit on stage and tried to make as much racket as we could and keep it going. It was a college drinking crowd, and they were booing us. Dr. Pee ran out into the crowd along the stand-up bar with a microphone, looking for whoever was booing us. I found some movie poster and I hurled it into the crowd and it hit some gal in the head. This guy came up to me and tried to start a fist fight with me while I'm on stage, and I was like, 'Hey, fuck *you!*' It was pandemonium, fucking lunacy. Clark was just snapping pictures. The next night was all-ages, and these kids were totally into it."

Morningstar continues, "But after the first night, Pee and I went to a party somewhere in Ottawa and then left to go back to our hotel room. This was Ottawa, it was October and it was freezing out and Pee had the window rolled down. I told him, 'John, roll the window up.' He just said, 'Michael Stipe.' Because Michael Stipe always has to travel in his own van so he can have the window down, apparently. I said, 'Fuck off, Michael Stipe, you're not Michael Stipe, roll up the window.' I pulled the van over and said, 'Look man, it's fucking cold, have some decency and roll the window up! I'm giving you to 10, either roll the window up or get out!' He got out and said, 'All right, fuck it.' We were miles away from where we were supposed to be, and I said, 'John, 10 count. Here we go . . . bye!' I drove off to our buddy's house, and didn't hear from John. The next night at soundcheck, the Rheos were asking, 'Where's Dr. Pee?' 'I don't know, left him by the side of the road.' He showed up. He had slept in a parking lot garage. He ran into some prostitute and her john, who woke him up and turned him on to some hash. The Rheos were like, 'What? You guys did *what?*'

"Later that night, while we're playing on stage, halfway into our set, I heard this drum. I turned around and there's Dave Clark playing his drum kit on stage with us. Clark's been a part of every gig ever since. He told me he was hearing voices on stage that night telling him, 'This is your part. You belong in this. This is part of your future.'"

"After that I was a big fan," says Clark. "They had freedom and a real spirit. It wasn't cerebral. It wasn't from the head down; it started at the crotch. I started going out on gigs with them, and they didn't even ask me to learn any music."

Clark's last gig with the Rheostatics was playing "Claire" on Rita McNeil's CBC-TV variety show. After that, they held a band meeting. Says Vesely, "We sat down eventually when his days were up and he was ready to quit and we were ready to tell him to quit. He came up with this ultimatum list of all these points. At the time, we thought, wow, you can't bring an ultimatum to the band and say 'this is what we should be doing.' So we said, 'Yeah, maybe you should look for something else.'"

Clark says, "When I was leaving the band, I said, 'This is the way I'd stay in the band: if we had Kevin Hearn join the band; change our management; and start paying ourselves so we can live' — and a bunch of other things that subsequently happened, but I didn't have the patience to stick around." Vesely concurs: "A couple of years down the road we ended up being at all those points, which is a bit unfortunate. Maybe that's what it took."

Immediately after his departure, Clark booked a gig at Ultrasound with Lewis Melville, Kevin Hearn, Bourbon Tabernacle Choir guitarist Andrew Whiteman, and Rheostatics guitar tech Tim Mech. He dubbed it The Woodchoppers Association, and it was completely improvisational, free-form music, which continues today with an ever-revolving cast of characters. Clark and the other members of the Rheostatics had an acrimonious relationship for years, and they didn't bury the hatchet until the band's 20th anniversary shows in March 2000 at Ted's Wrecking Yard in Toronto. Dinner is Ruined opened two shows, and at the end of the second show, Clark sat in with the band for the song "People's Republic of Dave." "It was nice to see the guys," says Clark. "It tied a bowtie on something that will be looked at as a beautiful and wonderful time. I strongly reiterate: the time that stuff was going down, when I wasn't enjoying it, was very, very small compared to the other 99 percent of it that was fantastic. The band was magic. I've since had that magic with other bands and other people."

The last thing Dave Clark recorded with the Rheostatics was a version of Neil Young's "Everybody Knows This is Nowhere," a spirited collaboration with the Bourbon Tabernacle Choir recorded live at the Gas Station by Don Kerr that featured all eleven members of both bands, including six vocalists trading lyrics.

The Bourbons were inspired by the creatively conducive environment of The Gas Station, and booked it to record their next album, *Shyfolk*, with Kerr engineering and Wojewoda producing. They had now been together for almost 10 years, a time during which they had grown up together and defined their individual musical characters inside the context of the band. Founding guitarist Andrew Whiteman left in 1994 to embark on a multi-faceted musical journey. Singer Dave Wall made an acoustic solo album, *Lozenge*, that featured most of the Bourbons, tapping into gospel influences that sounded more convincing than most of *Superior Cackling Hen*. The band as a whole soldiered on and became more focused, not just because of Whiteman's departure, but because they looked deeper into themselves and created not just soul music or an imitation thereof, but music *from* the soul.

All of the band's cumulative experiences infused *Shyfolk* with the joy of their communal live show and the wisdom that they had gained as individually maturing artists. "I *really* like the Bourbon record," says Wojewoda. "It cemented me on the virtues of The Gas Station — that notion of a cult of energy that works really well. There's something about Don Kerr and the way he creates a space that allows that, or that people give over to it when they're there. It was another one of those critical mass things, and [the Bourbons] rose to it. Material-wise, it's just stronger."

The Bourbons' internal community was splintering, however, and before the album was finished, they had lost their drummer. Gregor Beresford left during recording to join Tom Cochrane's band, but not before they captured the album's defining moment. Chris Brown's father was dying of cancer at the time and the song "Simple" was about acceptance and departures. Kate Fenner handles the vocal, and most of the song is driven by bassist Jason Mercer playing sparse chords; Brown, Dave Wall and Gene Hardy comprise a sombre horn section, and Chris Miller delivers an emotional guitar solo. The song was cut live, with Fenner in the control room, the rhythm section and guitar in the main room, and the horns in the large Gas Station bathroom, which was often used for its acoustic properties. "Before it started," Wojewoda recalls, "Chris read a poem. There was an electric energy of that one take. I live in a studio, practically, so I look for those special moments. It was a culmination of so many things that I love."

For a period just before and after the album's release, the band cut down on their intense touring schedule at the suggestion of their new international management, which also handled Billy Bragg. The business strategy was to hold back and create a demand for the band, but for a band that thrived on live performance it was a retarding move. It also hurt sales; *Shyfolk* sold half as many copies as its predecessor.

"That's when I went crazy," says Brown, "because I realized that I was dependent on all these people, and I didn't want to take this break. It was about two months of downtime, which is extraordinary. We did a couple of gigs here and there. We should have been doing things we already knew how to do, instead of worrying about all these things we didn't know how to do."

At Brown's suggestion, the band relocated to New York City and began building an audience there. "At first audiences were small," says Brown. "But

Bourbon Tabernacle Choir, 1993: Gregor Beresford,
Chris Brown, Andrew Whiteman, Jason Mercer, Kate Fenner,
Gene Hardy, Chris Miller, Dave Wall
(Photo by Grant Martin, courtesy of Yonder Records)

within a month we were packing places. November '95 was the first month we spent in New York. By then, we were all getting a bit paranoid. I was so intent on breaking new ground that I stopped apologizing at some point. I kept saying, 'I know what's going to happen if I don't.' And it happened anyway."

By the next spring, the band broke up. Everyone moved back to Toronto, except Brown and Fenner, who stayed on and started performing as a duo. Of the band's disintegration, Brown says, "You always have to check your reasons for being a part of anything all the time, and if you're not totally there, then you probably shouldn't be there. Some people stuck it out longer than their heart did, so that when it came down to the very big questions, it wasn't: 'Should we go with Brown or not.' It was: 'Should we tell Brown to fuck off or should we slap him around.' It's not like I was right. I would have done anything. But people were down for the fight. And once you realize that, then you've got to kill it. You got to stop. It's gonna get ugly, and what is it going to prove? What are you doing, and why are you playing music, anyway? You've already cut yourself off from so much, and you didn't do that so that you could cut yourself off from yourself."

Their demise was mourned, but many of the members moved on. Brown and Fenner not only released powerful and moving records on their own, but they would also serve time on the road as part of the Barenaked Ladies and The Tragically Hip. Jason Mercer joined Ani DiFranco's band. Dave Wall joined the Flying Bulgar Klezmer Band and became a Jewish cantor; both he and Whiteman penned songs for their friend Gordie Johnson in Big Sugar.

"They were an incredibly important band," says Lewis Melville. "They were one of the most successful club bands to play anywhere in Canada, and a lot of people got to see them without realizing that they were witnessing something quite rare. They were incredible, creative, sincere musicians with a lot of talent and a lot of music that we're all going to be hearing in the next 20 to 30 years. They were a community, too; there was a social element to their existence that was very strong. It was all there, and if you look back you can see that, but it didn't really come into a strong focus. They had to deal with the fact that there was so much talent in that one band, and not necessarily enough room for all of it.

"Maybe [large success] wasn't their fate," he continues, "and their fate is to be successful in other areas. They're still young, in terms of musical contributions. They made a big one already, and I'm sure they'll go on to make even greater ones."

In 1994, Dale Morningstar was slowly piecing a band back together while he recorded the next Dinner is Ruined album, *Worm Pickers Brawl*. It was a much more claustrophobic work than *Love Songs*, and even further removed from conventional rock forms. After the album's release Dr. Pee took a leave of absence for the birth of his first child, and by this time Dave Clark had entered the fold. With a new European distribution deal under his arm, Morningstar enlisted Clark and set up a tour of Germany and five other countries as a duo. The next Dinner is Ruined album, *Ice Cream Drugs Rubber Goods*, featured the new core line-up of Pee, Clark and Morningstar, and featured some inspired moments with the sound of a band finding its feet.

The follow-up, *Elevator Music for Non-Claustrophobic People*, was a left-turn into experimental soundscapes, pieced together from live recordings, providing for very difficult listening. "I wanted to make a cinematic, instrumental record, very experimental," says Morningstar. "The idea is for us not to repeat ourselves. *Elevator Music* was really difficult for me to make. It involved a lot of cutting and pasting of tape, and living with that music was very draining. It wasn't like going in there and playing as a band. It was taking snippets of the band and twisting it into something. Partly because one of the guys was having a kid and didn't have much time, and it was the wintertime, and I wanted to get on with something."

But by 1999's *A Maggot in Their Heads*, the new unit had finally coalesced and started delivering consistently mind-blowing shows that balanced psyched-out improv madness and conventional song structure. Their stage presence became less alienating, inviting the audience to participate instead of pushing them away.

"We've learned something in the last couple of years: just let it go," says Morningstar. "Don't even think about it. We've gotten to some stage now as a band, where we can go into any club, anywhere, with any kind of crowd, and pull something out and make these people think, 'This might not completely be my cup of tea, but these guys know what they're doing. There's some humour there, but at the same time they're very serious about what they're doing.' That wasn't necessarily there a few years ago. There was a lot more indifference before, and now there's more respect or something. We're trying to bring people in. We never wanted to push people away, but before it was about being angry for the sake of it."

"Dale has a certain kind of charisma," says Dave Clark. "He doesn't let things get in the way of his vision. He has a way of really inspiring me to be myself. He's one of the people I really respect for that. He takes care and puts thought into everything he does."

After Dave Clark's departure, the Rheostatics were determined to continue. *Introducing Happiness* had only been out for four months, and "Claire" had just won a Genie award for best original song. After a month, they started to get antsy and decided to move on. Their first call was to Don Kerr. "I saw the name Rheostatics everywhere, all my life," says Kerr, "but I never saw them until two years before I joined the band, when they walked into the studio." Kerr had never heard *Whale Music* before, and the first time he saw them play was at a benefit gig at Sneaky Dee's, where Kerr was accompanying cellist Anne Bourne.

Kerr got the call to join in February, 1995, and the first song he played at his first Rheostatics practice was "A Midwinter's Night Dream," a Tielli song that would appear on *Blue Hysteria*. Their first gig together was an unannounced show opening for London, Ontario smart-rock band Adam West at the Horseshoe. The second was in Calgary, kicking off a western tour. The band took on much more of a rock edge right away, with a faster version of "Saskatchewan" and a more straightforward, riff-rock approach to "Fan Letter to Michael Jackson," from *Introducing Happiness*. The latter was released as a 7" single, marking Kerr's first recorded Rheostatics appearance.

Because Dave Clark was such an integral part of the band's sound, the difference was jarring at first. "I loved Dave Clark," gushes Yvonne Matsell. "I adore Don as a person, and he's wonderful as a musician. But that was really hard for me to deal with, hearing Don play the first couple of times. All their material is in my head, because sometimes they'd come in [to Ultrasound] and rehearse for hours at a time. I remember waiting to hear Dave's fills, and it was throwing me off. But now, he's been a great choice." Kerr knew that he had an uphill battle for the fans' acceptance. "At first there were some drummer fans who said, 'I could play those parts better than that guy,'" says Kerr. "But most fans knew that it was a different thing."

The band's next project was a commission, like the *Whale Music* sound-track. This time, the National Gallery in Ottawa wanted the band to compose music to celebrate a retrospective of paintings by the Group of Seven. The band would debut the music live at the gallery. To pull it off, they enlisted the help of Look People keyboardist Kevin Hearn to help them with the composition and performance.

"We just scraped it together," says Kerr about the initial performance. "We had never even run through the whole thing. We thought we'd have the day to rehearse it at the site, but we got there and the P.A. was still in the truck. The only time we did the whole thing was in front of the audience. It was amazing to turn around and look at the visuals." The multi-media show was accompanied by projections of film and slides thematically linked to Group of Seven work.

When it was over, they decided to work on the music a bit more and commit it to disc, which they did in the space of two weeks. They would perform it live on two other occasions, this time with Bob Wiseman filling in for Kevin Hearn, when the exhibition travelled to Toronto and Vancouver. "It made me think that the sky's the limit," says Bidini. "The fact that if that project became a reality, created its own momentum and had a life of its own, then anything's possible. I didn't think we'd be able to pull it together, that people would like it and that it would be an important part of our career, but it has."

The time had now come to focus on a new album of songs, *The Blue Hysteria*, which again marked a few changes for the band. They had been dropped by Sire in 1995 due to "corporate ennui," says Bidini. Not only was *The Blue Hysteria* the first "real" album with Kerr, but it was the first time since *Melville* that they had decided not to work with Wojewoda. The song-writing and arrangements were also quite a departure.

"When we went to The Gas Station and started recording," says Bidini, "we all thought we were going to record live and be a bit more rock. That's one of the reasons we didn't want to work with [Wojewoda], because we wanted it to sound more like four guys playing together. There were some things we wanted to try. I thought editing ourselves would be a problem on *Blue Hysteria*, but it wasn't really. To me, *Introducing Happiness* sounds more self-indulgent, but not in a bad way."

"When I joined the Rheos," says Kerr, "everyone was like: 'Yeah! We can play some straight-ahead rock now, and no one's going to turn the beat around on us!' I was having fun; I like to play more groove-oriented than Dave Clark sometimes. But everyone was unleashing these rock songs, and I don't like rock music at all. I like something to be straight ahead, but grooving and soulful, like the Bourbons. It was like everyone was getting their ya-yas out after Clark was gone. There are some dumb heavy metal approaches. 'Bad Time to Be Poor' is a good song. Everyone just wanted to plow, and I'm thinking, 'Hey, I like to do the weird shit too!' But that was just a phase."

There was some interest from other major labels for *The Blue Hysteria*, but the band decided that they were better off charting the waters themselves — especially with a raw, warts-and-all rock record. "[Major labels] never know what to do with *any* of our records," says Bidini. "There's no 'Claire' on [*The Blue Hysteria*], that's for sure. But then again, there *was* 'Claire' on the last one, and it didn't really matter."

Through some twist of fate the Rheostatics landed their second hit single with another Vesely composition, "Bad Time to Be Poor," a pointed swipe at the individualistic turn in Ontarian society following the election of an arch-conservative provincial government: "It is a bad time to be poor / 'cause we don't give a shit no more / if you want to go for help don't look next door / the line's been drawn and staked outside." That climate also seeps into Bidini's "Feed Yourself," a homicidal tale that details a girl's gruesome murder and the urban paranoiac witch hunt that follows.

Otherwise, *The Blue Hysteria* falls short at a time when they were poised to capitalize on increased awareness of the band. As a first impression for new fans, *The Blue Hysteria* does not suggest the rich history of the band nor their continuing potential. The two best songs — "Feed Yourself" and Tielli's "A Midwinter Night's Dream" — were bettered on the band's 1997 *Double Live* album. Oddly enough, the album's most enduring performance is a goofy ode to The Who's "A Quick One" entitled "Four Little Songs," a live favourite consisting of four linked vignettes sung by each band member.

Upon the album's release, the Rheos were chosen to open for The Tragically Hip on a 30-date cross-country arena tour in November, 1996. It was an experience Bidini would later detail in his 1998 book *On a Cold Road*, where it would take on mythological meaning, and rightfully so — it was a nod of approval from the country's biggest rock band, one that would expose the band to hundreds of thousands of new fans.

The Rheostatics had played with The Hip before, both on multi-band festivals: Canada Day 1994 at Molson Park in Barrie, and in 1995 on the Another Roadside Attraction tour. Both incidents had them on in the middle of the day, but this time they were *the* opening act. That tour undoubtedly brought them plenty of attention, new fans, and for Bidini, the opportunity to eloquently write his way into the CanRock pantheon. The members of The Hip would sing the band's praises in many interviews, and on stage Gord Downie would sing excerpts of *The Blue Hysteria* material in the middle of Hip songs. Not only did it give the band short-term publicity, but also a permanent place in Hip mythology. On their live album *Live Between Us*,

Martin Tielli, July 1, 1994,
Canada Day in Barrie
(Photo by Chris Black)

recorded at the tour's Detroit stop, Downie opens the show — and the album — by saying, over the beginning of "Grace Too," "This is for the Rheostatics — we are all richer for having seen them tonight." Says Tielli, "I was up in the rafters when he was saying that. I was up on the catwalk, 200 feet above the audience. I was shaking in my boots, mortified and grateful as hell."

Earlier that evening during The Hip's soundcheck, Bidini was interviewed and modestly downplayed the importance of the tour. "It's going as well as can be expected," he said. "We're all a little sick of doing short sets and the same kind of response night after night. It's a little hard to keep playing just for yourself, because that's all you can really take back from it, but it sounds really good. We played in Vancouver, and the best night was the second night of the tour. As soon as we came out on stage, a big 350-lb guy in a Team Canada sweater got out of his seat, stood at the top of the stage and started waving his fists in the air before we'd even played a note. He was our audience, and it was great."

Reflecting for a minute, Bidini continued, "I thought about what [this tour] would be like with Dave Clark. His whole thing was to really take things to the extreme, and he would have relished this scenario. We're playing it pretty straight. Then again, compared to The Hip, we probably sound like the Local Rabbits: we're moving around, going crazy, trying funny things, playing weird, goofy music. We feel like we won some kind of lottery."

Don Kerr recalls, "We were basically musical ushers as people were finding their seats. We just went for it. We wanted to be ourselves. There was none of that thing: 'We gotta scale it down, play the same songs every night and hit them with the most impact.' Although we felt that way a bit at Maple Leaf Gardens. It was Toronto, and we wanted to be tight and exciting. That was an unbelievable thrill, playing two nights at Maple Leaf Gardens. The second night I rode my bike there."

Those two gigs closed the tour, and ended a productive 18-month period that saw the Rheostatics redefine who they were, setting a template for the five years to follow. Kerr was now juggling commitments with Ron Sexsmith, his old friend who began touring the world in 1995 on the heels of an international recording contract. In 1998, he'd enlist Vesely into Sexsmith's band, which ensured that the Rheostatics became more of a part-time band that focused on specific projects and limited touring. They released the comprehensive *Double Live* album, a session recorded for the final night of David Wisdom's *Night Lines* program, and a kaleidoscopic children's album — *The Story of Harmelodia* — produced by Wojewoda that picked up where the sonic experiments of *Introducing Happiness* left off. In November 2000, they joined producer Ian Blurton to start recording their first "real," non-project album since *The Blue Hysteria*. In May 2001, Kerr announced that he was reluctantly retiring from the band, citing exhaustion and scheduling conflicts from juggling the Rheostatics with Ron Sexsmith and running The Gas Station.

On that night in 1997 at Cobo Arena in Detroit, Bidini mused about the band's future. "I was thinking about ways to take our music to another level," he said. "It all starts by sitting down with the guitar and a crazy idea and seeing how far you can take it. It's the same process whether you're writing your first song or your thousandth. We're trying to do something that hasn't been done before — by us, and by other band's standards, too."

The Outsiders:
Punk, Politics and Poetry

In 1989, the Berlin Wall came down and the world celebrated the culmination of democratic revolution in the former Eastern Bloc nations. As parties raged on that autumn weekend, the boisterous soundtrack of Western music illustrated for many how the tide had turned. Yet amidst the posturing and blatant nationalism inherent in the event, one Canadian stood briefly on stage in Berlin, his songs of social justice meeting the reality of capitalism's triumph head on.

Almost nobody there knew who Andrew Cash was. In the spirit of the occasion he was given the platform to sing the title track of his album, *Time And Place*, and even though few could understand the words, its message of hope at least resounded within him. "On one level it had nothing to do with anything other than people coming together to share a positive historical experience; one that was full of hopeful possibility because, just like the release of Nelson Mandela, nobody really expected the fall of the Berlin Wall in our lifetime," Cash says. "When you're a musician, you're definitely part of a universal citizenry because music spans nationalities and politics and any artificial boundaries."

How Cash came to be in Berlin on that weekend was pure chance. His record company at the time, Island, had him on tour opening for one of their bright new stars, Melissa Etheridge. The tour happened to be passing through when everything came down. "One of the more vivid images I have is being on the tour bus and going through a stretch of East Germany to get into West Berlin," he describes. "On the other side of the highway it was bumper to bumper for miles, as far as you could see, all these little cars heading out of East Germany for the first time in their lives."

During his free time, Cash spent hours in bars and on the streets trying to make sense of what he was seeing. Although he had built his career on writing socially conscious rock music, there were too many contradictions in Berlin to take in all at once. The opening of the Eastern Bloc was in essence little more than a victory for Western consumerism, as Cash witnessed in the hordes of window shoppers chomping at the bit to buy previously unavailable items. But seeing the first flashes of a society experiencing the freedom of movement was overwhelming. This was a moment of celebration and Cash gave himself over. "Someone had arranged a concert 24 hours beforehand at this arena like Maple Leaf Gardens, 10 or 15 thousand people," he says. "It was general mayhem. They got Melissa and me there just because we were in town and we each did a song. That was quite a buzz; it was one of those situations where you don't fully grasp it when you're right in it. I remember that the actual concert we were supposed to do was a little anti-climactic after that.

"The whole experience was unreal, but after I got home I heard a song on the radio that was directly about the Berlin Wall, and I knew it would be out of date in about two weeks. The fall of the Wall was a victory for freedom, but it also represented a victory for multinational corporations. It was an exciting place to be, but it didn't dramatically alter me. I came back feeling that if freedom means just being able to shop, then that's not real freedom."

Born in Scarborough, Ontario, in 1962, Andrew Cash grew up in a strict Catholic household. It was an upbringing he took to heart, and in his teens, his interest in music was first piqued when he heard his core beliefs of equality and justice articulated by songwriters. "My entry into music reads like a textbook of that time," he says. "All music was way too complex to really fathom as a teenager until we heard The Jam and The Pistols and The Clash. Then you could see a way into it. Those were the bands I got excited about, and also there was something really right to me about the mix of social commentary and rock and roll. It seemed like that was what rock and roll was all about, and here it was again."

Even though punk had found an audience in Toronto from its inception, hard rock dominated the airwaves, and consequently a lot of kids' styles and attitudes. It was even more the case in Toronto, where albums by hometown heroes Rush were mandatory accoutrements to adolescence, with their mixture of head-spinning riffs and sci-fi poetry. "Most everyone we knew was into Rush, which I hated and still do," Cash says. "It was all part of that fantasy world that you can easily get sucked into as a teenager if you need that as an escape. I never felt I fit in even though the first band I really liked was still one of the biggest in the world, The Rolling Stones."

Cash soon met another neighbourhood Stones fan named Chuck Angus. Their friendship strengthened through their shared Catholic upbringing and staunch opposition to the status quo. By the summer of 1977, their attitude was affirmed when British punk hit North America. "I bought the Sex Pistols album at a mall in Scarborough. It was a major event," Angus recalls. "I walked up to the counter and people got out of the way. The person at the counter had this look like I was holding a dead dog or something. She said, 'You're not actually going to buy that thing, are you?' and I said, 'Yeah, I am.' My parents never cared what I played, but my mother said, 'I don't ever want to hear that in my house.' I knew right away that I had something really powerful."

Cash was on board with punk right from the start as well, although he admits to being equally moved at the time by the breathless performances of Bruce Springsteen, whose music brimmed with the spirit of early rock and roll combined with overt Catholic angst and an urgency to break the shackles of the nine-to-five routine. Both worlds inevitably overlapped when Cash and Angus witnessed Elvis Costello's North American debut on *Saturday Night Live*. "We stayed up to watch because we heard the Sex Pistols were supposed to be on, but it turned out to be him," Angus says. "He did his whole thing of stopping in the middle of a song and doing a totally different one, and afterwards we all just looked at each other and said, 'What was that?' He looked really weird, and it didn't sound like we thought it should sound. Now I look back and it sounds like such wonderful pop music to me. It's amazing how different it was back then."

Cash and Angus immediately decided to form a band. After each learned the basics of guitar and bass, respectively, they enlisted Cash's high school friend Peter Duffin on drums and considered hiring a singer. Word of the new band got passed on to an acquaintance, James Booth, who tried out for the job. "At the audition, Andy Cash was showing me the parts and telling me what they wanted," he says. "I knew at that moment I wasn't the person who should have been singing the stuff, and I even said to him after, 'I don't understand why you're looking for a singer because *you* should be singing.' They still went through the process, but in the end I said to them, 'If you ever want a manager, I'd be totally interested in doing it,' because I thought the songs were so great."

Cash and Angus instinctively knew from the start that they needed to write songs that reflected the world around them, a world that few other bands they knew cared about. "We had zero role models," Angus says. "There were no Canadian bands that we could look up to. All the musicians we knew wanted to beat us up. When we were in high school all the kids wanted to be Rush — they had kimonos and an incredible amount of equipment, but they never played anywhere. The only gigs we could get when we started out were battle of the bands in our church basement in Scarborough. It would be us and four Rush clones. They'd all come in with 30-piece drum kits and expensive equipment, and we'd have the shittiest amps and guitars. Everything we did was geared toward going downtown and playing clubs. All these guys in the Rush clone bands would say to me, 'Well, we're going to skip the bar scene, it's a dead end,' as if they were going to go right to Maple Leaf Gardens."

The trio's distinctiveness prompted the choice of the name L'Etranger, from Albert Camus's novel, and they debuted at Booth's high school. "I threw together a lunch-time concert with them and the local heavy metal band," Booth explains. "Everyone took their lunches and threw it at them, the whole room was a total fucking mess. I got in so much trouble over that."

The experience only strengthened L'Etranger's resolve to establish their own identity. Their determination became even more crucial when they finally did break into the Toronto punk scene in early 1980 and discovered there were in fact other bands who shared their approach. Cash says, "The first club we played was The Turning Point, which was where every band played its first show. It was on Bloor Street and you got three nights if you brought your own PA. We got all our friends to come.

"There was already a scene there; bands like The Demics, the Mods — they were a phenomenal band — the Viletones, the Battered Wives. They were mostly 20 to 30-year-old guys playing at The Horseshoe or The Edge where under-agers couldn't get in. Our goal in life then was to open for the Mods at The Edge."

L'Etranger was arriving at the tail end of Toronto's first punk wave, an era that saw promoters Gary Topp and Gary Cormier almost single-handedly create the scene by providing venues for punk bands from all over southern

Ontario, while bringing bands like The Ramones to Canada for the first time. Booth has nothing but praise for the pair. "If anybody deserves credit for the stuff that happened in Toronto, it was The Garys," he says. "When I started managing L'Etranger, it seemed logical that they were the first guys I should talk to, and they didn't make it difficult. I was thinking, 'Oh, I'm just this kid in high school,' but the fact that I could phone them and they would take some time and lead me through some things, and maybe get behind you if they thought it was worthwhile, was amazing."

By the time the scene fell apart, bands like L'Etranger were already picking up the pieces and trying to follow the lead of The Clash into new sonic and philosophical territory. "L'Etranger was incredibly idealistic, almost nauseatingly so," Angus says. "I cringe when I think about it now, but at that age it did attract a lot of people to us. We really wanted to change the world, and we thought our band was going to play a part in changing the world. That was as much a part of making music as anything."

Cash adds, "Part of it was the naïveté you have at that age when you believe the world should be ordered in a different way. Of course, as you get older most people get to a point in their life when they expect that things can only be fucked up. Part of it was also a product of our upbringing, which for Chuck and me was the idea that you should be working toward a just world, that your private life should somehow be focused on that. As artists, that was part of our training, and in a strange way both of us still believe that you should be engaged in the culture that you're in.

"In any other artistic field — film, painting, literature — that's a given, but in pop music you sometimes have to apologize for it. Maybe for that reason, we were slightly fascistic about it. We had this code we all believed in."

After a major boost from the Turning Point gigs, Booth worked diligently at persuading The Garys to book L'Etranger at The Edge. They had better luck getting opening slots at The Cabana Room in the Spadina Hotel, which would most often be packed for L'Etranger's set and empty for the head-liner's. Eventually, the band did get a gig at The Edge, opening for a new-wave band called The Scenics on a Sunday night. Angus says they knew this would be a make-or-break show. "There was no fun in L'Etranger, it was work, work work. We practised 35 hours a week. We never liked being called a punk band, because to us the punk bands tended to be slackers. They were in it to get drunk on stage. We had strict rules about not drinking at gigs. In June 1980 we made a commitment to each other — everybody's out of school whether you had your diploma or not. All our jobs then had to be arranged for nights so we would be able to practise during the day when we wouldn't be burned out. We wanted that gig to be a knockout punch; we wanted so badly to go down well at The Edge."

Everything went off as planned, and L'Etranger was soon working its way through The Edge's weekly schedule doing headlining gigs until ultimately

Chuck Angus of L'Etranger,
Andrew Cash in background
(Courtesy of Chuck Angus)

achieving a weekend top billing. From there they set their sights on Larry's Hideaway, again enduring many nights opening for sub-par punk bands from the U.S. before getting an opportunity to headline. By this time the band's live reputation was widespread around town, with Cash being touted as a frontman with uncommon passion while the band as a whole was lauded for its energy and strong work ethic.

"My first club gig was with L'Etranger at The Edge," says producer Michael Phillip Wojewoda, who would go on to be the band's regular soundman and recording engineer. "They had that DIY thing early on. They wore their influences on their sleeve in a big way, but they played full-on and emerged into what they were naturally."

Angus says, "We played with so many bands in the early '80s, and so many who became bigger than us. We even tried getting into the reggae scene, which was a big influence on everybody at that time. We opened for Leroy Sibbles, which was really big time to us. I can't remember how we went down with the Jamaican audience. But most of the great bands then, like The Rent Boys and The Young Lions, they had great flash but they couldn't sustain it. The Mods were our favourite band and then one day they just broke up. It seemed in Toronto you could only go so far, so we figured if we kept working as hard as we could we wouldn't fall into that trap."

In 1982, Booth — still in school — helped release L'Etranger's first EP, the six-song *Innocent Hands*, under his own Sensible label. The EP was made with the simple goal of showing off the Cash/Angus songwriting partnership in contrast to their often frenetic live versions of the songs. On record, they ring with the sharpness of Elvis Costello's *My Aim Is True*, and Cash's vocals similarly spill out almost faster than he can keep on top of them. The seeds of the revolution they desired were apparent in "Goliath," a challenge to greedy corporations, and in "Taken Away," a Neil Young–style acoustic ballad that suggested a connection with something deeper than the fashion of punk. "We thought The Clash and The Jam and The Pistols were just great songwriters, that's what we were into," Cash says. "The rest of that scene didn't interest us much, and it would have been a lie for us to play any involvement in that scene, whether it was American hardcore or British punk. Toronto was definitely an intersection for those two cultures. We got to see The Jam all the time even though they were never big in America, but the curse was it was difficult to get an audience interested if you didn't fit into either of those scenes."

The solution, as always, was to test their appeal outside of Toronto. This began in earnest on the strength of a second EP, *Running Out of Funtown*, and their evolving live show. "We didn't even bother sending the EPS to record companies," Angus says. "Maybe we figured that would be selling out, but I don't think they would have paid attention anyway. Once we started playing regularly between Windsor and Ottawa we were fairly busy all the time. It made us forget about trying to go to the States or England, but I think that made us less hungry after a while too, especially when we realized there were lots of kids outside Toronto who were into what we were doing. Ottawa had the best live scene and the best audiences at the time. It was obviously a lot smaller than Toronto's and it made us realize we couldn't rest on our laurels just because we had lots of gigs back home. The people in Ottawa knew that if they didn't love the music and go to every gig, it would fold up. We sold out two nights at The Roxy there one time because people knew the record. We couldn't get over that."

Wojewoda says, "We would roll into Halifax or Moncton and there would be a gaggle of people who knew about them already and had spread the word. I'm sure there were curious stragglers. At Dalhousie, they had us down in this rec room, which was a nightmare gig because they didn't provide any monitors. This was because Jane Siberry was playing upstairs and she had rented all the gear in town, but we ended up getting monitors from somewhere. I was impressed that word of mouth had created this kind of buzz, as modest as it was."

However, by this point L'Etranger's relationship with Booth had become strained, as his increasing knowledge of the music business conflicted with the band's overriding ideals. "They refused to be promoted in certain ways, but we weren't in any position to negotiate," Booth says. "After the first record had been out for six months, we had a battle because Andy couldn't understand why it still couldn't be front-racked at some of the record stores on Yonge Street. I'd worked in record stores and I understood that they felt it wasn't selling enough to be on the front racks. Andy wanted me to go in and scream at these people to put it back and I tried to tell him that they'll remember that when you put out the next one. Even with The Garys I realized that if you tried to force them to do things, all you ended up with was a guarantee you'd never get booked by them again. The band wanted somebody who was going to be a rebel and shake things up, and if nothing was happening, they'd get even more pissed off with me. What it all boiled down to was most people in the music business had more power than them, and yet for L'Etranger, all they saw was where they were going to be down the road, and they expected everyone else should see it too."

From 1984 on, L'Etranger continued making lasting impressions throughout southern Ontario's university circuit. Along the way they would give other Toronto bands like the Rheostatics their first gigs outside of town, as well as forging lasting friendships with local musicians. One of the more significant came after a gig in Hamilton when a local band called Direktive 17 opened. It was fronted by a spritely, bespectacled McMaster student named Andy Maize who also happened to be a huge L'Etranger fan. "They were a really good, aggressive, politically conscious pop band. That was really exciting to play with them," Maize says now. "I had seen them for the first time at The Turning Point. It was one of the first times I'd ever gone to a club and they were playing with a group called Disband that had Michael Phillip Wojewoda, Paul Myers [brother of Mike], and a guy named Bruce P.M. who was in a later version of L'Etranger, so it was a memorable night."

Maize grew up in Toronto and was a few grades behind Jim Cuddy and Greg Keelor at North Toronto Collegiate. After falling under the sway of punk, as well as The Rolling Stones' *Some Girls* album, Maize's time at McMaster was largely spent getting a band together. However, with only a knowledge of the trumpet, he concentrated on his voice and his role as a frontman. In 1982 he joined new-wave trio Direktive 17 and immediately injected a brash new attitude into the band's obvious British touchstones.

After honing a new batch of original songs with gigs around Hamilton, the band recorded its sole EP at Rainbow Sound in Niagara Falls. For most of its six tracks, Maize does a pretty good impression of The Cure's Robert Smith, but his unique persona is evident behind the chiming, sub-U2 guitars. The overall sound was enough to win CFNY's Great Ontario Talent Search in 1985 and bring the band more gigs, some better than others.

"We played at a Junior Farmers' convention in Creemore, Ontario," Maize says. "Everything was so late getting started that everyone was a little bit tense anyway. We went on and played on a stage that was two hay wagons tied together inside the arena. If we moved at all everything would start swaying. We were playing with a mod band called The Purple Hearts, very British Invasion. We went on wearing our jackets and skinny-legged pants and after about a song and a half, the five or six hundred fairly drunk junior farmers start chanting, 'Play rock and roll! Punk rock sucks!' So we played 'Substitute' by The Who and The Jam's version of 'Heatwave.' We lasted about another four songs before we were pulled off the stage."

Winning the CFNY talent search also gave Direktive 17 a chance to make a full album. After emerging from the studio with a finished product produced by Wojewoda, the band found their promised distribution deal gone. "It was with Quality Records, which at that point was a real label. But right when our album was supposed to come out, they became the new K-Tel, just doing TV sales, and they bought us out of our deal," Maize says. "I told the other guys we should go ahead and press up a couple of thousand copies to sell at the shows and worry about getting another deal later. They wanted to wait and by then I couldn't see any point in going on if we weren't going to move forward."

Maize had heard that his old high-school friend Josh Finlayson had recently returned from a period of living in England, and Maize was curious to hear what had come of the excursion. Finlayson had been raised on Woody Guthrie and folk music but embraced British punk's energy as well. After playing in several semi-serious bands, he took the brave step of trying to break into the British scene after finishing high school in 1982. The band that made the move was called The Ramblers, with Finlayson on bass. After finding living spaces in London's predominantly black Brixton section, the band made enough connections to meet Clash manager Bernard Rhodes and briefly became another of his clients. "We ended up meeting all the guys in The Clash and we realized they were big rock stars. After that we thought we were going to be the next big thing," Finlayson says. "That's what we wanted, but I ran out of money after about four days. I had gone down to King's Road and spent it all on some silly boots."

The Ramblers tried unsuccessfully for two years to crack the London scene. All the while Finlayson was living above a reggae record store called Desmond's Hip City and waking up every day to the pounding bass of the shop's sound system. Upon turning 20, he ultimately gave up on becoming a rock star and returned to Toronto in hopes of renewed prospects. "I had a friend who told me about this guy he knew named Wayne Stokes who was trying to set up a home studio and eventually his own label," Finlayson says. "I didn't know Wayne, but I was really interested in writing songs and putting a new band together. Home studios weren't as common as they are now, so I saw it as a great opportunity. I ended up meeting him and he liked my ideas, so I moved into his place and helped him get things set up in the basement. We actually didn't do that much recording, we spent more time smoking pot."

When Andy Maize heard that Finlayson was back in town, the two quickly reconnected over their shared love of folk music. "We understood that folk and punk shared the attitude that the music wasn't about technical proficiency," Maize explains. "It could be done over three chords or whatever it took to get the message across, that was what was important.

Andy Maize of the Skydiggers, September 1995, at Alumni Hall in London, Ontario
(Photo by Richard Gilmore)

Direktive 17 was obviously really influenced by English music of the time, which didn't have a lot of singing. Toward the end I heard R.E.M. and things changed. They had great harmonies, even though you couldn't understand the words, but that's what I've always loved, groups with a lot of singing." Maize's vocals were soon an integral part of Finlayson and Stokes's regular jam sessions, which revolved around traditional songs, Neil Young songs and new material that was slowly emerging. All the while Stokes was trying to get it on tape, leading to some frustration from the rapidly gelling writing duo.

"Wayne got pretty involved in the recording process, he was learning as he went along," Finlayson says. "I've always felt that a band has to go out and play if you want to move ahead. You can't feel like you're sitting there waiting, which is what a lot of recording is. As Wayne kept up with that, Andy and I ended up going out as a duo."

Calling themselves West Montrose, after a tiny southern Ontario town, Maize and Finlayson set out to see the country in the classic troubadour tradition, taking any gig that came along and honing a set of traditionally-based songs. "My dad had a pretty extensive record collection, and when I started playing guitar I was learning stuff by Doc Watson, Jimmie Rodgers and Hank Williams," Finlayson says. "Around '85 or '86 I read this great biography of Woody Guthrie called *A Life*, by Joe Klein, and after that it got passed around to a lot of people I knew. I know Andy read it and Andrew Cash read it too.

"His most famous song, 'This Land Is Your Land,' has become an American national anthem when he wrote it during the Depression as a rebuttal to 'God Bless America.' It's an unfortunate irony, but it made Andy and me realize when we started that the songs had to be really direct, we couldn't hide behind any gimmicks. Just having two voices and one acoustic guitar made us do that pretty effectively."

As West Montrose was out exploring the nation, L'Etranger was hitting a roadblock. After cutting ties with manager James Booth, the band made a big mistake in hiring someone new, simply on the basis of his involvement with Rock Against Racism. Booth explains, "I'd heard through the grapevine that they were so happy to have this guy as their manager because he had the same political ideology as they did, but after about a year he ripped them off for an incredibly large sum of money from all these shows he had booked for them and took off. Many years later I ran into Andy and he kind of admitted at that point that many of the things I'd told them about the music business were true, even though they never wanted to believe it."

L'Etranger continued to attract a healthy live following between Ontario and the east coast, but the pressure of keeping up an intense performing schedule in order to survive was beginning to show. Although the band still refused to solicit record companies, Capitol was sufficiently interested to offer them an audition in 1985. Chuck Angus recalls that the executives spent most of the session trying to get the band to sound like U2. "The Canadian industry wanted it to sound like America or England so that in the eyes of their parent companies it wouldn't look like they were wasting their money," he says. Shortly after, Angus realized that L'Etranger had reached the fate that had claimed so many of their mentors. "We couldn't get any more press, we'd gone as far as a band like us could go. I still really believed in the band, but I wanted to do something more. I was starting to get influenced by the Catholic Worker Movement, and working with the poor. I always thought I'd stay with the band, but once I started really working in the inner city, my wife and I got married and started taking in homeless people. That's why I left; I wanted to stay on good terms with everybody."

Despite Angus's departure in 1985, Cash continued on with L'Etranger, enlisting Rheostatics bassist Tim Vesely and adding Bruce P.M. on keyboards. The new line-up recorded a four-song EP, *Sticks And Stones*, but shortly after its initial pressing, Cash heeded Angus's advice that the L'Etranger name was now excess baggage in this new phase of his career. "I didn't want to pretend it was still L'Etranger but I didn't want to see this really good EP die, so I released it again," Cash says. "L'Etranger was really me, Chuck and Peter, but you learn these things in hindsight. We really should have stopped then, but the basic human instinct is to carry on. We made some really interesting music when Tim joined, but it wasn't as much fun at that point. Everything had changed, so it was time to move on." The EP was quickly re-pressed under the guise of an Andrew Cash solo release, and suddenly the Toronto press, as well as the industry, took notice of his new direction.

Cash retreated to work on more songs and come to grips with his new status as a solo artist. To help with this transition, Cash set up a residency every Monday night in late 1986 at the Spadina Hotel. The weekly gathering became known as Acoustic Meltdown and soon turned into a showcase for other songwriters working in the new folk style. "That was the best thing I'd done in my musical career to that point," Cash says. "This was years before the unplugged concept, but that's what we were doing. People would come every week and you'd feel like you had to be better each time."

Two of those who were there every week were Maize and Finlayson. Their sound fit perfectly with the setting and they became part of the attraction themselves. "We'd all play for two or three hours; it was Monday so we'd be done by about 11," Finlayson says. "It was really quiet; people really appreciated that as well, going to a club where they wouldn't be assaulted by volume. I had spent a lot of years playing electric guitar at ridiculous volumes."

Many new alliances were formed as a result of the gigs, eventually leading to bands such as Lazy Grace, Bird and Wind May Do Damage. One of the weekly regulars also looking to get something started was Andrew Cash's brother Peter, who often roadied for L'Etranger and now was usually found working the door at the Acoustic Meltdowns. One night, Andrew mentioned to Andy Maize that his brother had songs that Maize should hear. "Andrew came up to me and said, 'I've got a tape of some stuff that Pete's done,' and I thought, jeez, Pete was just the roadie. I never knew he played guitar or sang. Andrew said he thought Pete's songs would fit in with what Josh and I were doing, but I couldn't for the life of me picture what those songs would sound like. Shortly after that we were all at a friend's house on Isabella Street and Andrew put the tape on and it was like, wow."

With Peter Cash now involved, Maize and Finlayson saw they had a full-fledged band shaping up. They reconciled with Stokes, who agreed to be the drummer, and the rest fell into place after Maize saw an ad in a musicians' classified that read: "Adequate bass player looking for individuals to form a band with like-minded influences — country, R&B, rock and roll." The ad was placed by Ron Macey, a Vancouver native whose last experience playing in a band had been in 1966. In the early 1970s, he moved to London, England, eventually running his own pub and being at ground zero for the punk revolution. However, with the scene fading by the early '80s, a friend from Toronto convinced him to move back to Canada and get involved with music again. "I was coming out of a job and a marriage, and when all that falls apart at the same time, the only way to really deal with it is to go inside and take care of yourself," Macey says. "I rented a bass and started playing with some friends in a basement. They all had lives and I didn't, so one of them suggested I form my own band, which I'd never done before. I put the ad in *Now* magazine — the only time I've ever done that either — and I started getting calls from guys saying, 'I'm in the studio tomorrow, can you learn the charts and dash off some funk tunes?' It felt pretty cartoonish. Then Andy and Josh called and told me about the acoustic Mondays thing. The minute I walked in there and heard them, it felt like home. They were playing all the stuff I grew up listening to."

As soon as Maize and Finlayson saw the lanky bassist with the Elvis-style sideburns, they knew he was the man for the job. "I remember Josh saying, 'Even if he can only play one note on bass, he's the right guy,' because Ron just looked so fantastic," Maize admits. "We'd get together in my living room and learn tunes, and the only thing about him that worried us was that he drank too much."

"I just needed something to soothe my nerves," Macey laughs.

With Andrew Cash's stock rising once again as a result of the Acoustic Meltdown nights, the question of signing a record deal cropped up. With little money and a few copies of *Sticks And Stones* left, he sent one to each of the major labels in Toronto on a longshot, hoping that they would be interested although several were still not signing many Canadian artists in 1986. Upon running out of stamps, Cash went to Island Records to deliver a copy in person to their A&R representative, and was met with a quizzical look from the receptionist. "They said, 'A&R person? Well, we don't really . . . oh, okay, we'll take it.' That was it, I didn't really think about it. I was still really naïve and not really hopeful of my chances," he says. Yet shortly afterward, he got a call from the label saying they were interested in working with him.

William "Skinny" Tenn had been put in charge of signing the first Canadian artist to Island, which soon led to his long involvement in Cash's career and management duties with other artists. "I had a box of tapes and albums to go through and a lot of it was really good," Tenn explains. "Ron Sexsmith was one of those under consideration, but once I heard Andrew I knew right away he was the perfect fit with what the label was doing. We had a lot of fun during that time travelling around the world."

When word got out that Cash had signed with Island, he was suddenly thrust into the media spotlight, although much of the attention focused on the deal itself. "For a lot of people it was a big deal because they'd known me from L'Etranger for so long, and now wasn't it great that I was getting something going for myself? But I hated all this focus on the fact that it was this big record company signing a Canadian. The whole spin made me really uncomfortable. I kept thinking, 'What does it matter?' But it did matter because Island had a respectable reputation with Bob Marley and U2, who were *the* band at the time. It was interesting."

For the recording of his first Island album, Cash was intent on replicating the feel of the Acoustic Meltdown atmosphere and called upon many of the participants to form a new band. Peter Duffin remained on drums and was joined by guitarist Graydon Nichols, bassist Peter MacGibbon, fiddler Jim Ediger and Andy Maize on backing vocals. Playing predominantly acoustic music still was not wholly accepted in the pop world, but Cash had felt the change coming both in himself and in musicians he knew. "We went through our own sort of acoustic, folkie phase in L'Etranger which was frustrating in a way because it was hard to pull off live," he says. "The invention of the Takamine acoustic/electric guitar really changed a lot of things because it allowed rock bands to play an acoustic guitar on stage, which we weren't really able to do prior to that. The other thing was that I'd spent eight years in a band that was really loud."

The track list for the album was compiled largely from songs Cash had been playing regularly at the Acoustic Meltdowns, as well as remakes of

Murray McLauchlan and Andrew Cash, recording on CBC Radio's
Swinging On a Star, 1988
(Courtesy of William Tenn)

two songs from *Sticks And Stones*: "Trail Of Tears" and "Time And Place," which would become the title track. With its release in 1988, *Time And Place* presented Cash as a ragamuffin folk-rocker. His social conscience was still predominant, but the attempt to convey it in the first video for "Smile Me Down" was weighed down by overt images of suffering. More successful was the clip for "Time And Place," which showed the band in rehearsal mode; the interplay between Cash and Maize gloriously shining through. All in all, it was a challenging period of adjustment for Cash, who was suddenly vaulted onto the national stage.

"It was really difficult because the mainstream Canadian music industry at the time didn't have a clue about street culture," he says. "I gave Island a list of campus stations that I used to get tons of airplay on and they were like, 'What are these?' It was a typical Canadian company in that all they worried about was getting played on Q107 and CHUM.

"As far as videos went, that was also really difficult because the kinds of things I wanted to do were just non-starters. The whole scene was dominated by commercial production companies. It was Island's first venture into A&R in Canada so they were also really cautious. The bands on the other labels were Loverboy, Glass Tiger, Honeymoon Suite, people I had nothing in common with, so I had to really work to convince them that what I was doing was all right. I like to think that those of us who got signed around that time made it easier for bands who came after."

In reality, by 1988 many Canadian music fans were already acclimatized to hearing about contemporary issues in pop songs, largely through the music of Bruce Cockburn. The Ottawa-born singer/songwriter began his career in the late 1960s as a folkie whose intricate guitar style often wove spells around his ruminations on spirituality and nature. Through a successful partnership with manager Bernie Finkelstein and his label True North Records, Cockburn quietly released a stream of consistently-selling albums in the 1970s that established him as a truly unique Canadian voice, someone who purposely avoided venturing south of the border in search of success, which nevertheless came with his 1979 hit, "Wondering Where The Lions Are."

Sometime in the early 1980s, his approach changed. Cockburn's Christian values had begun to slip into his songwriting by his fourth album, but his worldview dramatically altered when, around the turn of the decade, he started experiencing conditions in Third World nations. The first impressions of these trips turned up on albums like *Humans*, *Inner City Front* and *The Trouble With Normal*, but the real breakthrough came with 1984's *Stealing Fire*. While Cockburn had long before dropped the public image of the rustic troubadour, he now appeared as an electric guitar–toting revolutionary, no longer willing to be a passive observer. His main target on the album was the U.S. government's secret war in Central America. Cockburn had accepted an invitation from the relief agency OXFAM to visit the region extensively early in 1983, immediately after finishing *The Trouble With Normal*. The previous year the agency had invited Canadian politicians to tour the various regions, and now they hoped artists would be more effective in spreading the message that help was needed. For three weeks, Cockburn and the others stayed in refugee camps, often playing for the children gathered there, and he returned with a cache of songs that no longer stood as metaphors for suffering and injustice, but as genuine reports from the front lines.

"My baby boomer background made me uncomfortable and suspicious of political movements," Cockburn said shortly after the release of *Stealing Fire*. "I went to a few demonstrations but that was more out of curiosity than any kind of commitment. Although I agreed with the sentiments being expressed, the demonstrations didn't seem like they would have much to do with anything. Of course, time proved they did change things.

"I saw that especially after going to Central America. I didn't get interested in politics until I started looking at what it meant to love my neighbour. I had always been a loner, and the concept of loving the people around me was a novel one. In Nicaragua I witnessed a whole nation of people working together to better their situation. In contrast, the Guatemalan refugees are the terrible but obvious outcome of a society where people don't have a voice. Seeing this made me realize why we had politics at all — and why this is really worth working at."

Stealing Fire opens with Cockburn's signature post-'70s track, "Lovers In A Dangerous Time," a stunning encapsulation of the kind of resistance amid the most repressive conditions that he had witnessed. Not surprisingly, the song's power translated to other parts of the world experiencing the same revolutions. Even Bono, the most self-righteous lyricist of the era, bowed to Cockburn's poetry when he paraphrased the song's key line, "Nothing worth having comes without some kind of fight / Got to kick at the darkness till it bleeds daylight," for U2's otherwise overblown "God, Part II." If "Lovers" jolted some longtime fans into Cockburn's new philosophy, their jaws were left agape by the militancy of "Nicaragua," with its description of adolescent rebel soldiers that states, "In the flash of this moment, you're the best of what we are / Don't let them stop you now." Immediately following is perhaps the most provocative song ever to make it onto North American radio in the 1980s.

"If I Had A Rocket Launcher" is a song of its time, but its unprecedented outrage echoes the reaction to every crime against humanity that has come since. Somehow Cockburn made the subject matter palatable, probably through his world-weary vocal that resounded with the first-hand accounts that comprised the verses. It was perfect blues for the global village; as the leading economic nations revelled in prosperity, the focus could no longer merely be on individual segments of society that were being ignored, but entire nations that for one reason or another were mired in cycles of poverty and oppression.

Cockburn himself admitted to being shocked when his new American label, Gold Mountain/A&M, wanted to release "Rocket Launcher" as the album's first single. Although the song once again helped bring Cockburn critical acclaim south of the border, it was hardly the sort of fare one expected to hear on Top 40 radio. In Canada, where it followed on the heels of "Lovers," the song arguably marked the pinnacle of Cockburn's artistic impact in his homeland. Yet Cockburn was not through. On 1985's

Bruce Cockburn live at MuchMusic, 1996
(Photo by Richard Beland)

World of Wonders he shifted his aim directly at politicians and world leaders. The mission statement is set out in the opening track, "Call It Democracy," which showed American listeners that the rage of "Rocket Launcher" wasn't an isolated incident. In fact, the lyric sheet of the American pressing was nearly censored over lines like, "North, south, east, west / Kill the best and buy the rest / It's just spend a buck to make a buck / You don't really give a flying fuck / About the people in misery." The song was also undoubtedly the first to criticize the International Monetary Fund, known for saddling Third World nations with unrepayable loans that left most at the mercy of American corporate interests.

Cockburn knew precisely what effect the song would have in the U.S. and took the backlash in stride. "Canadians love to flirt with anti-Americanism in a humorous way because it makes us feel independent, but that's about as far as most of us take it," he said in 1985. "My audience didn't — until relatively recently — tend to see things in political terms. I could talk about political things but they weren't taken that way. For instance, one of my older songs, 'Burn,' is overtly anti-American but it's trying to make the point that Canada has very much the same client-state relationship that your average Latin American country has with the United States. We're better off so there's no resistance to the relationship, but if we were ever to swing too far to the left, it would be Prague '68 revisited."

World of Wonders was another welcome shot of truth in an otherwise bland mainstream Canadian rock scene. True North capitalized on Cockburn's new popularity by releasing the compilation *Waiting for a Miracle* in 1987, featuring the new, hopeful title track. By the time of Cockburn's next all-original album, 1989's *Big Circumstance*, the rest of the global pop world had begun supporting social causes, which took away much of the album's impact. On the first single, "If a Tree Falls," Cockburn had to resort to reciting the song's warning of rainforest depletion, a subject that had suddenly taken the place of African famine relief as the cause célèbre. However, as always, Cockburn's perspective markedly stood apart through the song's fatalistic vision, summed up in the line, "Busy monster eats dark hole in the spirit world."

By the early 1990s, the pressure of being identified as a radical and a symbol of the newly fashioned political correctness movement was beginning to show. Cockburn's albums following *Big Circumstance* showed a noticeable return to spiritual matters. He explained it in 1997 by saying, "I don't see the idea that I'm politically correct. It just doesn't fit who I am. I smoke cigarettes; I'm involved in recreational firearms. Is that political correctness? It has hit me, though. I remember seeing a headline that read, 'Bruce Cockburn: Canada's Cultural Conscience' and it made me cringe. Talk about baggage — no thank you."

These contradictions had dogged Cockburn through his most politicized era, but more often than not his music silenced the critics. By the mid-1990s — when he was in his fifties — he had settled into a familiar groove of recording, touring and international acclaim as both a songwriter and musician. If there were issues to be dealt with, Cockburn was no longer forcing himself to be the instigator. "I realized that as soon as it's an image, it's not human anymore, and I wanted a human relationship with people, I resisted any attempt to hype me into something that wasn't realistic.

As an extension of this, Cockburn eventually threw his energy behind causes that on the surface transcended political ideologies, such as the drive to ban landmines. A cross-Canada speaking tour he undertook preceded the historic Ottawa treaty on December 3, 1997 banning landmines worldwide, which the United States pointedly refused to sign. For this reason, Cockburn, along with other artists such as Emmylou Harris, Steve Earle and John Prine continued to raise the issue at their concerts together and separately.

"Every artist has the responsibility not necessarily to educate, but at least to tell their audience how they see things. Whatever an audience gets out of my music comes down to a matter of trust. The church that I went to when I lived in Ottawa was a very alive Anglican church. They used to have regular healing services, which was unusual for a mainstream church, and also unusual because the services worked most of the time. Once I asked the priest what it felt like, what was that energy like when he laid his hands on people. He answered that the people who got healed were often-times not the ones he laid his hands on, it was the ones in the back rows, the ones that came in just to get out of the rain. I feel that was the lesson for me. I take it on faith that something good is coming out of my music."

As punk rockers continued to discover the possibilities of acoustic music through the 1980s, that journey not only inevitably touched upon the folk songs of Woody Guthrie and his followers, but often went further back to the rebel music of the British Isles. The first British folk-rock wave developed in the shadows of psychedelia when guitar virtuosos like Bert Jansch and singers like Anne Briggs inspired Fairport Convention and Nick Drake to create modern twists on traditional themes. That music was pushed aside by punk, but in the confusion that spawned the rebirth of the scene in the early '80s, songwriters like Billy Bragg and Shane MacGowan discovered in traditional music the same desperation they now faced in their adult lives amid the Thatcher regime. MacGowan's band, The Pogues, was a loose conglomeration of Irish exiles and London punks who played in the traditional Irish style. But with the poetically gifted — and painfully alcoholic — MacGowan front and centre, the band cultivated a broad-based following that transcended its punk roots.

For many Canadian musicians of British descent, the arrival of Bragg and the Pogues in the mid-'80s was nearly as important as the previous British Invasions. For Geoffrey Kelly, already a casual participant in the west coast folk scene, these new artists only confirmed the similar ideas he had been having in updating his approach to the music. Kelly, born in Scotland, moved to Vancouver with his family when he was nine. Although the traditional music of his native land was always in his subconscious while growing up, it wasn't until Kelly made a year-long pilgrimage back to Europe around 1980 that he fully connected with the sounds.

"By a fluke I was dragged to a folk club one night in Austria, and I met this Scottish guy named Dougie McLean who was a young guy and was playing traditional Scottish music in a real contemporary way," Kelly describes. "That was the start of making me realize how this music could be quite contemporary. When I got back from that trip, I started collecting music that was similar to that and discovered stuff like The Bothy Band. Eventually those bands started coming over to Canada in good numbers in the early '80s. They were playing the Vancouver Folk Festival, and every time I saw them play, I always noticed how the crowds just went crazy. It always got the best response when one of those bands got up and started pounding out the jigs and reels. Everybody would start dancing, and I got more interested in that."

Kelly began supplementing his guitar playing with other instruments like the penny whistle and the bodhran, becoming immersed in studying the music on his own and through skilled players in the city. He eventually persuaded his high school friend J. Knutson, who had more experience in rock bands, to pick up the music and they began performing around Vancouver as a duo. In 1983, Kelly's fiancée Alison was in theatre school where she had befriended fellow student John Mann. Mann was a folk fan with punk leanings, but hardly as serious a musician as Kelly. At the Kellys' wedding, Mann hit it off with Knutson as well, and was finally asked if he played music. Mann lied when he said yes, but the trio found enough common ground to keep rehearsing after their initial jam session. "The stuff we all brought into the band was really different," Kelly says. "J. was a rocker, John knew some Stan Rogers songs, and I played some Irish tunes. It was, 'Here's what we have, let's start messing around with it.' We didn't have many of our own songs off the top; we did Bruce Cockburn, Eric Bogle, Richard Thompson, Billy Bragg, people like that, and from there we realized that any long-term thing was going to involve writing our own songs. We slowly started doing that."

The trio called themselves Eavesdropper and began appearing on the Vancouver pub circuit where Kelly and Knutson had first appeared. It wasn't easy work; the pubs were cramped and noisy and the audiences mostly indifferent, but the belief that they were making exciting music only furthered their conviction to win over listeners. In fact, the music they were doing was unusual on the west coast at the time. Their only legitimate contemporaries in Canada hailed from the east coast, where British folk obviously had a greater foothold and had been modernized by bands like Newfoundland's Figgy Duff and Toronto's Rare Air. Kelly, Mann and Knutson felt separated even from those bands.

"We weren't very good, but we had tons of energy," Kelly says. "That was very new to the folk scene in Canada and people got off on that — 'Wow, these guys are jumping around.' It was really unheard of in the folk scene, and we realized early on that it was working for us."

Mann adds, "What made us different when we started was we were opening for Art Bergmann at The Savoy in Vancouver and Barney Bentall and all these other rock bands, so we were competing with them in a sense. You're the opening band, so you don't want to come on and be some kind of hairy-legged folk act. Those gigs were really good for us, and that's what we took to the folk world. We always simultaneously straddled those two environments."

The band's major turning point came early on when increasing confusion over their name finally prompted a change. At a gig on Vancouver Island, they arrived to find themselves billed as Eavesdroppings, a joke that was now going too far. They were already in the midst of recording their first album, and the title Kelly had suggested, Spirit of the West, summed up the album's predominant themes of B.C. life. It was thus an easy leap to use it as an all-encompassing moniker for everything they represented, and the now-eponymous album was released in a small pressing in early 1985. It immediately got them noticed by the wider western folk music establishment; first came an appearance at Seattle's Northwest Folklife Festival, then a prestigious spot at the 1985 Edmonton Folk Festival. "We sold more albums there that year than anyone else," Kelly says. "No one there had heard one note of our music before we played, and the spot we had on the main stage was Friday night. It was pouring rain, so maybe a third of the whole audience was there, and we still managed to create enough of a buzz. Our workshops over the next two days were packed and it turned out to be one of the greatest weekends ever for me. Suddenly we realized that we could do this."

The excitement of their Edmonton appearance resulted in most other major Canadian folk festivals booking Spirit of the West the following year with one exception: "Vancouver was the only one that didn't carry us for some reason," Kelly says. "It was a bit of an issue in the local papers, because they were behind us and they ended up really turning on the festival's artistic director at the time."

The band released their second album, *Tripping Up The Stairs*, on the respected Canadian roots label Stony Plain, founded by Edmonton Folk Festival director Holger Peterson, which found their still stripped-down sound expanding as Kelly and Mann especially became more confident on stage. After meeting Hugh MacMillan at that year's Calgary Folk Festival, things took a giant step forward. Mann says of their initial encounter, "The woman I was seeing at the time had previously gone out with Hugh when she was living in Alberta, and she would always tell me what an amazing musician he was. He was playing with the Great Western Orchestra, doing country swing. When he came off stage I started talking to him, and he figured out who I was. I told him we were thinking of expanding the band, because right then Geoff and I were each trying to play a little bass and we were absolutely terrible, and we really wanted someone else who could do it. We ended up on the same bill at an Expo gig later on; he came up and played with us a little bit, and that was that."

The arrival of MacMillan only increased Knutson's ambivalent feelings toward the band and he left Spirit of the West shortly after the Expo '86 gig. The remaining trio then went to work on the next album. When finished in late 1987, *Labour Day* became arguably the first Canadian Celtic-rock album to reach a pop audience, especially when Toronto radio station CFNY picked up on it. The album's influence would eventually spread further as producer Danny Greenspoon would go on to work with other major Celtic-rock artists, including Great Big Sea. "We'd known Danny first as a musician, he played in a band called The Romaniacs that were on the folk circuit doing klezmer-y stuff," Kelly says. "We started making *Labour Day* on our own and really botched things up. We recorded things without a click track, so when we went to do percussion overdubs, everything was out of time. We made a lot of elementary mistakes like that. Danny salvaged that record."

The sound showcased MacMillan's prowess on a variety of stringed instruments, and more importantly, Mann and Kelly's increasingly acute observational writing. Several of the songs, such as "Profiteers," chastised the city of Vancouver for promoting Expo at the expense of the poor, while "The Hounds That Wait Outside Your Door," a scathing impression of their first trip to Britain the previous spring, stands alongside Billy Bragg's most powerful anti-Thatcher diatribes.

However, the song that brought the band its first national exposure carried the loaded title, "Political." The song is actually an apology from the singer to his former lover for allowing their differing ideologies to break up the relationship. Mann admits the song is largely autobiographical, since the relatively few political songs the band had written up to that point had nevertheless caused local activists to rally around them under the false impression that Spirit of the West was putting forth similar agendas.

Mann says "Political" directly reflects his relationship with Jean Smith who, after their break-up, joined guitarist David Lester to form Mecca Normal, the minimalist punk duo whose string of early releases on Olympia, Washington's K Records foreshadowed that area's politically charged Riot Grrrl movement of the early '90s. "We had a great time together," Mann says. "I learned so much during our time together, and I think the whole band was affected by my relationship, just because her ideas were so strong. Through her we were opened up to issues that we may not have really thought about; feminist issues especially."

Kelly adds, "She really walked the walk, as opposed to us who were on the fringe — observers more than participants in a lot of things. That's valid to stand back and see the whole thing and write about it, but Jean was the kind of person who was right in it. She still lives it. We eventually realized we weren't in it and maybe sometimes it wasn't our place. We felt less committed to writing about it."

Spirit of the West put their energies into touring following the release of *Labour Day*, which turned into a gruelling month-and-a-half trek across Canada and a further three months in the U.K. The trip turned out to be too much for Hugh MacMillan, who left the band upon their return home. Undaunted, Mann and Kelly decided that two people were now required to fill the void and enlisted bassist Linda McRae and fiddler Daniel Lapp.

The move turned out to be essential, as the band's previous road work was paying off. They had built a large university audience with a crowning achievement coming in the form of three straight sold-out nights at Vancouver's Commodore Ballroom. Yet the time spent in Britain was just as satisfying. "That was a really fun time with Linda and Daniel, even though that line-up never recorded," Kelly says. "We did another six-week tour of

Spirit of the West, 1993: John Mann, Geoffrey Kelly, Linda McRae,
Hugh MacMillan, Vince Ditrich
(Photo by Raeanne Holoboff, courtesy of Warner Canada)

Britain where we just kept going up and down the country, even going to the Shetland Islands. The first two weeks of the tour we decided not to book hotels and just wing it at gigs, trying to find people to stay with. John would be on the mic, 'We have nowhere to stay, can anybody help out?' It was this big adventure and we kept upping the ante. Eventually we had to bail on the plan."

When Lapp informed the band he was leaving after that tour, Mann and Kelly begged MacMillan to return and it was this line-up that would record 1990's *Save This House*, their first to receive major-label distribution. The label interest essentially came from their growing live reputation, but the reps who did come out to the shows were more often there as fans. Most labels were still figuring ways to market the latest wave of rock bands, and were hardly prepared for a contemporary Celtic group without a drummer. "A lot of Warner reps from different cities were coming to see us and reporting back to [A&R head] Bob Roper, 'You've got to see these guys,'" Mann says. "He came and saw us at The Diamond in Toronto, and it was a really raging show. He got the impression that night that he should sign us just based on the fact that we could draw large crowds without really having any radio play."

Once again produced by Danny Greenspoon, *Save This House* exceeded most expectations the label might have had. The album caught the imagination of a young audience that was discovering acoustic music for the first time through artists like Tracy Chapman and the rejuvenated Paul Simon, but Spirit of the West's energy was altogether different. Songs like the title track put forth a strong message in favour of environmental protection, but there was enough wild abandon in the music to make it a great party album as well. The song that would become their signature was a tailor-made drinking rant, tossed off and nearly forgotten after the band's last British tour. "It seems 'Home For A Rest' appealed to people of a certain age in university and it's become this sort of university anthem," Mann says. "I found out from a friend of mine who's a travel agent that one tour group uses it to rev people up, and that's great."

"It's all Danny Greenspoon's doing, because that wasn't one of the songs we originally had slated for the record," Kelly adds. "We'd gone through every song we had and he said, 'Is there anything else you have that might fit?' We said, 'Well, we've started this one song,' and we played a couple of verses of what we had. We didn't feel it was ready, but he forced us to get it together. It was a diary of touring in Great Britain, and initially more of a poem than a song."

Even though the band was increasingly doing benefit shows in support of environmental causes, Mann admits the song "Save This House" appeared just as spontaneously. "The idea is pretty simple, treating the planet as where we live, but the whole song came about very quickly too," he says. "We were doing a songwriting segment on CBC Radio where we were supposed to come in with something half-completed and work on it over the radio. We were really busy and became very laissez-faire about the whole thing, so we came in with nothing. We realized when we got there that we needed something, so Geoff had this one part and I pulled out my guitar and started noodling around and the song was written in about 10 minutes."

With the backing of a major label giving them a newfound exposure at home, Spirit of the West now concentrated on reaching the next level in Britain. Their boost came from an unlikely source when they encountered British band The Wonder Stuff in Vancouver, a friendship that ultimately would also trigger a drastic change in both bands. Spirit of the West was doing another multi-night stand at the Commodore, which was to host The Wonder Stuff later in the week. Wonder Stuff frontman Miles Hunt had arrived early to scope out the venue and was immediately enthralled with SOTW. While The Wonder Stuff were primarily practitioners of the nascent Brit-pop revival, their sound occasionally included traditional instrumentation. Above all, Hunt's sharp wit set his band apart from their peers, a facet that had already made Kelly and Mann fans. When the pair found out that Hunt had enjoyed the shows, they mailed a package of CDs and T-shirts to Hunt's management company and the two bands hooked up soon after when SOTW returned to England.

"We were at a pub in London called The Cricketers' and Miles and a couple of the guys in the band came," Kelly says. "Then they came to another gig we did at a folk club in Hampstead, and after that they invited us into the studio with them. They were working on some b-sides or something, and we recorded 'Will The Circle Be Unbroken?' with them. The two days in the studio with them were unbelievably exciting; our heads were spinning because they were such a huge band and we'd never met anyone like that before."

Mann adds, "They were fighting it out with The Stone Roses to see who would get the cover of *Melody Maker* and the NME each week. Miles would walk down the street and people would have these amazed reactions. It was really fun and exciting. If they had come later, they would have been huge everywhere, but North America wasn't really embracing British bands at that time."

The Wonder Stuff invited SOTW back to be part of the bill for their next large-scale British tour, which included two shows at Brixton Academy that saw Jane's Addiction wedged in between the two bands. The experience only proved to Mann that it was time for Spirit of the West to become more rock-oriented, and at the very least, add a drummer. Upon returning to Vancouver, they began a search that quickly turned up Vince Ditrich, then coming off a stint in Paul Hyde's band. On the surface, Ditrich admittedly didn't fit the vegetarian/activist image that most people had of the other members, but his incredible versatility and presence made him a natural fit. "Vince came out to a show and saw there was an opportunity for him to slip into a band and be really involved, not just be a side guy," Mann says. "We quickly realized he could do anything we asked him to, musically or otherwise; he's extremely charismatic on stage. And having different political views from ours was very healthy for all of us. He had a real levelling effect on the way we thought."

Despite the enthusiasm the band now felt at their greatly expanded sound, long-time fans were a little more wary. The 1991 folk festival rounds seemed to draw the dividing line among their audience. In Winnipeg, Mann appeared with a red flying V guitar as the band debuted the first fruits of its new direction. They intended to carry this momentum straight into recording their next album, which this time took place in Los Angeles with producer Joe Chiccarelli. While he understood that SOTW was trying something new, he encouraged them not to stray too far from their trademark sound. "We were so enamoured with electric guitars, Geoff and I were both playing them," Mann says. "Our producer at the time was saying, 'This sounds like album six and you haven't made album five yet. Don't give up everything.' It's probably good that we didn't, but we lost a lot of fans with that record."

Not surprisingly, that record, *Go Figure*, remains an enigma for both the band and fans, despite a few rousing anthems like "D for Democracy," which displayed the full potential of adding electricity to the traditional instrumentation. Adjusting to having a drummer in the studio for the first time proved the biggest obstacle, leading to frequent conflicts with Chiccarelli. All in all, the band agrees it is their least satisfying effort. "That record was a real bastard to me," Kelly says. "It was too soon; we'd only played with Vince for a few months and we were still sussing things out with him as we were making the record. It turned into a real struggle and even though I think the results are good for the most part, it was the least happy record to make."

Instead, Spirit of the West found solace on the road, embarking on their most intensive touring schedule yet, and for the first time all the band members committed to travelling. The schedule turned into a two-year layoff from the studio, and when they finally moved into Vancouver's Mushroom Studios with producer Michael Phillip Wojewoda in 1993, most of the bugs had been worked out of their sound. Wojewoda seemed to be the perfect choice to guide the recording, as their initial collaboration on a track for the Joni Mitchell tribute album, *Back To The Garden*, had gone well. Kelly admits that SOTW had never been more prepared to make a record, since many of the songs that would comprise *Faithlift* directly reflected their time on tour and had quickly found a place in their live show. The most overt was the album's lead-off track, "5 Free Minutes," a manifestation of Mann's homesickness. "That song's about being in Germany and being away too long," he says. "I was sick of living in a small van and then having people come up to me going, 'I've got a friend in Saskatoon, do you know him?' That song's just about not having any personal space."

Faithlift also yielded two more successful singles — "And If Venice Is Sinking" and "Sadness Grows" — gaining many new fans they had lost with the previous album and erasing any misconceptions that they couldn't cut it as a full-fledged rock band. Kelly cites the strength of the songs and the right choice of producer for the about-face. Wojewoda remembers, "They were [Rheostatics'] *Melville* fans. When we did the Joni Mitchell track, I played them an unmastered mix of 'California Dreamline' and when the time came, they approached me to do *Faithlift*. They really wanted to make a good record, which makes things easy for me."

As Spirit of the West celebrated its first decade together at the height of its popularity, the inevitable maturity was beginning to isolate them from their long-standing university pub-crawling audience. The sophisticated folk-rock of *Faithlift* now sounded miles beyond the simple jigs and reels they had started with. It was evident that the overall growth of Celtic music in the early '90s had pushed SOTW to diversify, but it was also clear that following the *Faithlift* tour in 1995 they had reached a crossroads. Unlike the previous tour, which had fully prepared them for the studio, the band cut *Two-Headed* under a tight schedule in March due to more pressing matters.

The compelling idea of recording a live album with the Vancouver Symphony Orchestra was quickly realized literally days after work on *Two-Headed* had wrapped. Subsequently, that album was overshadowed by the *Open Heart Symphony* album and TV special when both were released in spring 1996. This was preceded by SOTW's slot on Another Roadside Attraction in the summer of '95, an extension of their friendship with The Tragically Hip. Their experience opening for The Hip in the U.S. had resulted in the song "Our Ambassador," about flag-waving expatriate Hip fans, but the Roadside shows always ended with the two bands on equal terms, playing Gordon Lightfoot's "Sunny Side Of Life."

At the conclusion of this high-profile period, harsh reality finally set in. The band's longtime manager Janet Forsyth retired from the music business, and Linda McRae tendered her resignation to resume a solo career she had put on hold for eight years. Even though Spirit of the West continued on, doing a national symphony tour in 1996 and recording the more traditionally-based *Weights & Measures* in England the following year, it was more than a little unjust that their place as Canada's Celtic-rock leaders had been usurped by Great Big Sea, Natalie McMaster and Ashley MacIssac. While these newer artists had undeniable mass appeal, their songs hardly contained the same sense of rebellion and wit. After bringing traditional music to a new generation, that music now belonged to the pop machinery. As Wojewoda said of *Weights & Measures*, "Warner deep-sixed that record: no video, no promotion, no nothing. Their only excuse that I kept hearing was, 'Spirit of the West is a tough sell in 1998.' I agree with that, but it's not impossible."

No longer under contract with Warner following that album and a shabby hits package, Spirit of the West has come full circle and will continue to make music, at least as long as Kelly and Mann choose to work together. But like the artists who originally inspired them, the band now has a body of work that will stand in the coming decades.

While young artists speaking out against the contemporary ills in the larger world kept the spirit of traditional folk music alive in the 1980s, those with less lofty ambitions found it easier to cast a new light on the personal politics that increasingly dominated North American society. In summer 1986, video-show viewers were shown a clip by a sparse power trio fronted by a lanky guitarist sporting large, painfully uncool prescription glasses. The music was a simple variation of a three-chord blues riff, but as the video moved the singer through different seedy locales in downtown Toronto, his mostly spoken lyrics immediately revealed a unique reversal of the entire sex-drugs-and-rock-and-roll cliché. After only a few airings, this video for "I'm An Adult Now" made The Pursuit Of Happiness a national attraction, striking a chord among a growing segment of music fans who realized that if they weren't the person singing the song already, they soon would be.

The voice singing the song belonged to Moe Berg, a 27-year-old Edmonton native who had toiled around his hometown for a decade in post-punk bands like The News, Modern Minds, Troc 59 and Facecrime. "Punk rock was totally new to Edmonton and the Modern Minds are credited as being the first punk rock band there," says Jr. Gone Wild's Mike McDonald. "I was 16 when I first saw them and it was one of those moments. They were fierce high energy, with clever lyrics that seemed to address issues that concerned me personally. I saw every show of theirs I could. I knew all their songs. I pestered them at gigs and dropped their name to friends to seem important. Moe Berg was my hero, and I wanted to do what he was doing. I knew all this the first time I saw them play."

A songwriter since he learned guitar at a young age, Berg says that by the time he formed the Modern Minds with Bob Drysdale and Kim Upright, punk had made him realize his own life could provide compelling material. "We weren't a political band per se, we were writing about teenage alienation," he says. "That's probably what appealed to people like Mike at the time; we were all just nerdy kids trying to work things out. There was always a pop element to it too, and that influenced the themes."

Despite a strong local reputation, Berg realized that his only shot at making a living at music lay in Toronto. "I moved to Toronto in 1985 and started looking for a band out here, which was totally miserable," Berg says. "What I ended up doing instead of getting a bunch of Toronto musicians was meeting up with a bunch of people I knew from out west."

After enlisting drummer Dave Gilby, an old bandmate from Edmonton, and bassist Johnny Sinclair, originally from Saskatchewan, Berg quickly began developing a new bag of songs which stressed his two main obsessions: metallic '70s power pop and sexual politics. To help with both, the original Pursuit Of Happiness also featured the female back-up vocals of Tam and Tash Amabile, friends of Gilby's from Winnipeg. Within their first two months together, the band had recorded several demos, including "I'm An Adult Now," first heard in video form and only later pressed when demand for a single became outrageous.

The song was among several eventual TPOH standards that Berg had written before he left Edmonton, although he didn't place it above the others. "It was a real stream-of-consciousness thing," he explains. "I developed this technique where I'd put myself in a situation where I'd be ruminating, then I'd put down whatever came into my head. It was one of those songs where I got this idea and bang, everything just came out. I'd written down tons and tons of words and then I put the best parts in a certain order.

"I look at it as kind of a whimsical thing; the words were things I'd been thinking about, but now I'd say it was almost Howard Stern-esque. I was pushing these ideas to be a little more provocative. Just before I left Edmonton I played a couple of solo shows and people kind of laughed at it, which made me think it had potential."

Upon releasing a second single, the equally stinging "Killed By Love," TPOH signed on with manager Jeff Rogers and label interest from both Canada and the U.S. ensued. After several deals fell through, during which they kept up a busy Canadian touring schedule, the band finally signed with Chrysalis Records out of New York in late 1987.

The need to put on a good live show had by then also prompted Berg to make changes in the band. Gone were Tam and Tash, replaced by Leslie Stanwyck and Kris Abbott, the latter also beefing up the sound with rhythm guitar. "I really, really liked them and got to meet them at a party one night," Abbott says. "Then Moe and I kept bumping into each other on the Queen streetcar, so one day I gave him my number and told him that I sing and play guitar, and to give me a call if he ever wanted to jam. We did get together, but I could see that he wasn't that into writing for a second guitar player. It took a while for that sound to evolve. When people ask me who my guitar influences are, in a way it was Moe — because for a long time after I joined the band I was basically double tracking everything he did."

Abbott and Stanwyck's presence added to the sexual dynamics within TPOH, which would spill over both in Berg's songs and the band's own personal lives. At the time there was no other band even remotely like them: a rhythm section that could have been moonlighting from an AC/DC tribute act, one statuesque female and one tomboy and a frontman seemingly experiencing all manner of identity crises during the course of a show.

Only Berg's idol Todd Rundgren could possibly make sense of all this, and to everyone's amazement, he agreed to give it a shot. "Chrysalis asked us who we'd want to produce the record, and I said Todd Rundgren, not even thinking that it would be possible," says Berg. "The next time we played Winnipeg after we signed, we were doing our soundcheck when a guy comes up and goes, 'Is there a Moe here? Phone call.' I picked up the phone and it was Todd Rundgren. He had gotten the tape and phoned right away to start critiquing the songs — telling me what a crappy guitar player I was!"

In typical Rundgren fashion, the sessions at his upstate New York studio were not easy, although as a longtime admirer, Berg came prepared for the producer's idiosyncrasies. "When I hear about people not getting along with Todd in the studio, it's totally understandable to me," Berg says. "Fortunately, I got off on all his antics. He made me take songwriting more seriously because a lot of those early songs were very intuitive. During my first con-

The Pursuit of Happiness backstage, 1991: Brad Barker, Dave
Gilby, Moe Berg, Kris Abbott, Michelle Rundgren, Todd Rundgren
(Courtesy of Moe Berg)

versations with him he'd ask, 'What's that song about?' and I'd be stammering, 'Um, uh,' and he'd say, 'You'd better figure out what these songs are about before *Rolling Stone* asks you. You're going to look like an idiot.'"

Rundgren's stamp is all over *Love Junk*, partially smothering the raw innocence of the indie versions, even though the new "I'm An Adult Now" also became the band's calling card in the U.S. courtesy of a big-budget video for MTV. The real pleasures were in Berg's new songs, especially "Hard To Laugh," a brutal warning to any guy longing for the girl of his dreams, and "Consciousness Raising As A Social Tool," an equally pointed jab at the new "enlightened" generation.

Overall, Berg's work was marked by a keen sense that, from a male perspective, definite societal changes were taking place, and not everyone was ready for them. The biggest of these changes was apparently the fruitlessness of traditional sexual views in the era of safe sex and political correctness. The unprecedented sense of guilt and/or jealousy that reared its head in "I'm An Adult Now," stretched to "She's So Young," which further chided innocence in the face of the singer's own jadedness. And just when it seemed Berg was pushing the boundaries of male chauvinism, he delivered a punchline like the tongue-in-cheek "Looking For Girls," which exposed the ugly side of the male psyche with obvious disdain, much like Vancouver's Odds would later do with "Heterosexual Man."

While Berg often played devil's advocate to feminists, it was at times hard to tell where exactly Berg did stand in terms of sexual politics. "There were times when I was confronted," he says. "There was one club owner who would never, ever have anything to do with us. She said she'd never book us because we were so incorrect. We were also the only band to get a bad review in [Canadian songwriter's association] SOCAN's magazine. It was another one of these things where the guy thought we were sexist or something." The debate carried on with TPOH's second album, 1990's *One-Sided Story*, once again produced by Rundgren. It contained the scathing "Two Girls In One" and the timely "New Language," which openly took a shot at the PC movement.

Problems also stemmed from the band itself fracturing into two separate camps. Sinclair and Stanwyck had begun a relationship that had also sprouted a new songwriting partnership to challenge Berg's authority. Shortly before the release of *One-Sided Story*, the pair left abruptly to form Universal Honey. "I always refer to *One-Sided Story* as our paranoid record," Berg says. "I can hear it now in other band's second records; how they sound a bit freaked out by what's been going on. Once we became successful, the second record really reflected the paranoia we felt."

The departure seemed the perfect soap opera subplot to accompany TPOH's music, and Kris Abbott agrees that the band's unique structure only heightened the drama. "When TPOH started, it wasn't common to be a co-ed band," she says. "I think we're more realistic because we're in mixed company. People always assume that guys are difficult to work with, but my problems haven't come from the guys in the band."

Berg adds, "Being co-ed helped the PC forces not take us too seriously, but also I wasn't a macho, menacing kind of guy. I wouldn't come off as Andrew Dice Clay or whatever. The irony is, that kind of stuff and that kind of attitude became really popular later on with all these pop-punk bands. Someone said to me, 'Green Day writes about the same things you used to write about — masturbating and feeling weird about girls.'"

With a full year of touring looming, Berg enlisted his friend Brad Barker on bass and Susan Murray-Vincent on vocals, later replaced by Rachel Oldfield. Following the tour of 1990–91, TPOH found themselves without a record deal. Their A&R rep at Chrysalis had taken a new job at Mercury Records, leaving the label to ponder whether this quirky little band from Canada was worth keeping anymore. After they were unceremoniously dropped, prolonged negotiations eventually led to a one-album deal with Mercury.

Released in 1993, *The Downward Road* displayed a harder-edged sound overseen by producer Ed Stasium, known for his previous work with The Ramones and The Smithereens. Although the album was another successful demonstration of the now well-established TPOH aesthetic, it seemed that even fewer people were now prepared to accept Berg's complicated worldview. A few bands, most notably the Odds, had followed suit with a string of similarly clever and well-crafted power pop albums throughout the '90s, but by 1995, TPOH had ultimately given up on cracking the U.S. market, instead signing on with Canadian independent Iron Music. This arrangement produced *Where's The Bone*, named in honour of their former A&R rep Mike Bone, and featuring the minor novelty hit "Gretzky Rocks." This was followed by *The Wonderful World Of The Pursuit Of Happiness* in 1996.

Despite the downsizing of the band's commercial scope, Berg's inventiveness as a lyricist never diminished. He would go on to record a solo album in 1998, *Summer's Over*, and begin a new career as an author, without officially stating that TPOH was over. However, it seemed that with such a dense body of work already behind them, the band would be hard-pressed to capture their audience's attention as they did with their groundbreaking early material. Berg admits as much himself: "As I became older and started to understand what it meant to be a songwriter, I got a lot better in my opinion. I wrote better lyrics and I thought the musical structures were more sound, but at the same time, they were never as popular as the early songs I wrote. Maybe the craftsmanship of songwriting isn't necessarily so desirable. It's possible that just being intuitive is the way to speak to a young person, and the more you think about it and the smarter you get, you end up losing your audience."

If Moe Berg's songs seemed to voice the frustrations of the average guy in the modern world of gender politics, the subject of traditional politics still weighed heavily on the minds of many other Toronto songwriters. The neoconservative tide established by Thatcher and Reagan had bolstered Brian Mulroney and the Progressive Conservatives to unprecedented popularity in the late 1980s, bringing along such divisive policies as the Goods & Services Tax, the North American Free Trade Agreement, the failed Meech Lake Accord to incorporate Quebec into the constitution and Native uprisings. Each day, news of massive layoffs, interest rate hikes and Quebec separatist actions touched everyone's lives to one degree or another, placing an even heavier burden on those merely struggling with a day-to-day existence. Suddenly the realities of politicized pop for the global village were brought home and songwriters found the act of communicating these ideas far easier.

To coincide with his 1989 European tour with Melissa Etheridge, Andrew Cash had released his second solo album, *Boomtown*. Whereas his debut held out hope for the suffering, its follow-up exposed the new Canada as he saw it: endless job losses destroying the fabric of both small town and big city life, and those out of work wondering — as one song decried — "What am I gonna do with these hands?" Produced by Don Dixon, best known for his work on early R.E.M. albums, *Boomtown*'s bleak messages were offset by a more pronounced middle-American blue-collar sound. The aim was to build on the progress *Time And Place* had made on radio and video, but soon Cash would find himself challenged by his more acoustic contemporaries.

"I was really happy that Andrew hadn't let all the work we did with L'Etranger go down the drain," Chuck Angus says. "I was working construction to help pay bills and one hot summer day I was digging a ditch when 'Time And Place' came on the radio. At the time I remember thinking it was a hilarious situation, but I was never into taking that route." By then Angus had already formed the Grievous Angels, a loose street busking group with vocalist Michelle Rumball and fiddler Peter Jellard. The band's original intention was to play the traditional Irish and country songs in which Angus had recently immersed himself, but by 1990 they had released *One Job Town*, a moving country-rock collection that delved deep into the rural Canadian experience. Angus's main preoccupations as a writer were the struggles of life in northern Ontario, from the simple pleasures of a weekend hockey game to the dangers of working in the mines. "By the time I left L'Etranger I was pretty tired of the scene, I was pretty tired of the music," he says. "My background was The Clancy Brothers and Hank Williams, and it seemed a lot of people were turning back to that stuff around then. And Stompin' Tom; I realized then that he was writing songs about places where my grandfathers had worked. The Angels were never intended to be a serious band. We happened to get a gig one night at The Cabana Room opening for Andrew and it worked. The next thing we knew, we were touring the country. It all seemed to fall into place."

With Rumball's departure after the release of *One Job Town*, Angus began regularly taking the band to the small towns he had been writing about, eventually relocating to Cobalt, Ontario, where he continued to tour and record on a part-time basis while becoming increasingly involved as an advocate for northern issues through his magazine *High Grader*, and as a presenter on TVOntario.

In Andrew Cash's absence, his Acoustic Meltdown nights were taken over by the band his brother Peter was now a part of. The name Skydiggers had been batted around for Andrew's backing band but instead he opted for The Ambassadors. The other name stuck with Andy Maize and with this new identity the band quickly expanded on their Monday night following. Unlike many of the other emerging Queen Street roots-rockers, the Skydiggers stuck with an almost exclusively acoustic sound, powered by the Ron Macey–Wayne Stokes rhythm section. Another crucial feature was the three-part harmony of Maize, Cash and Finlayson, which recalled the original Byrds and Buffalo Springfield line-ups. On top of it all was the unpretentious vigour of Maize's stage presence; his flailing arms often recalled a flightless bird, and his between-song ad libs never failed to charm a crowd. "My thing for the show has always been to make the audience feel welcome," Maize says. "Rather than creating a separation between us and the audience, we've always tried to do the opposite, to try to make everyone feel included. Obviously, some nights it's easier to do than others, but what we've always done hasn't been that technically difficult. We've always wanted the people in the audience to feel that they could be up there doing what we're doing."

Macey adds, "Spontaneity was a big part of it early on. We were a brand new band just getting to know each other, so there was a lot of innocence to it. It was common to hear Andy introduce a song, 'Bear with us, we just learned this song this afternoon.' Our mandate was to learn a couple of new songs a week so we'd have something new every Monday. In a sense they were live rehearsals and it was really neat how the audience would roll with us."

With their expanding set of Peter Cash originals, combined with a few Maize/Finlayson compositions, the Skydiggers virtually stumbled into a record deal after only five months. Their champion was Derrick Ross, former drummer with The Spoons, who was now working in the Canadian office of L.A.-based independent label Enigma. With ambitions to make his own signing, Ross approached the Skydiggers, who immediately recognized an opportunity. "We really wanted to record our first album live because that's where the magic was happening," Maize says. "The people at Enigma said up front that we couldn't do that; since they had the money we agreed. We tried to make a live record in the studio even though we were missing the key ingredient of the audience. It took 10 days, plus six days of mixing, for 14 songs. There was tension, but it was a creative tension in knowing we were trying to achieve something in a form that we weren't used to."

When *Skydiggers* was released in early 1990, it presented those outside of the Queen Street crowd with probably the most accurate audio representation of the Acoustic Meltdown vibe. The songs were mostly intimate

Skydiggers, 1992: Josh Finlayson, Peter Cash, Andy Maize, Ron (Ronny Von Johnny) Macey
(Courtesy of Fre Records)

snapshots of unrequited love and quiet desperation that clearly reflected the band's own intimate relationship with its audience. The simplicity was almost unnerving; "I Will Give You Everything" could not have been a more honest expression of devotion, while "Monday Morning" and "At 24" voiced the growing depression among the post-baby boom generation.

Visually, the band boldly stood out as well. Each member's penchant for different facial hair and work clothes established an anti-image more effectively than many of the other Canadian musicians similarly unconcerned with their looks. It all may have seemed to be a conscious decision to keep one foot in the past, but the whole package still took many by surprise. "I never put much thought into how we looked," Finlayson says. "Being in a band is a pretty insular existence, and it was funny how people would react differently to how we looked in different parts of the country. After our first gig in Edmonton, the review said, 'The Skydiggers looked like they had a 6 a.m. appointment with a jackhammer,' and we thought that was hilarious. That was who we were at the time, and it was all part of being genuine."

The band spent most of 1990 on the road, occasionally backing Andrew Cash, including a set at his wedding in Saskatoon to his now-manager Sandy Pandya. The year culminated with a six-week jaunt opening for Blue Rodeo, yet their momentum was nearly derailed shortly after when word came that Enigma was drastically scaling down its operation, leaving its Canadian employees out of work, and the Skydiggers' album in limbo. "We were on the verge of our American release and there were 15,000 copies of the CD sitting in the warehouse that we couldn't get our hands on at that point," Macey explains. "We spent the next 18 months floundering, playing gigs, which was all we knew how to do."

While the band waited for its contract to expire, Derrick Ross worked at setting up his own label to release the Skydiggers' next album. They already had a wealth of new songs, many of which stemmed directly from their recent experiences. When *Restless* finally emerged in 1992, it was heralded by the grinding first single, "A Penny More," on the surface a swipe at those seeking to abandon the disadvantaged. However, Maize says the song was not originally intended to carry such a strong message. "I came up with the idea for the song when I was watching TV one night and these two women were singing Scottish folk songs *a cappella*. The way their voices combined, it was a drone almost like Scottish bagpipes and that's where the song came from. The words are trying to come up with some traditional folk sort of thing. It's two songs put together; the 'take me where I want to go' thing counterbalances the other part of the song. Maybe it's about how money can't buy me love, but it's really not as harsh as other songs on that album."

Maize alludes specifically to the opening track, "Accusations," a direct byproduct of the Enigma situation: "One night my wife and I were relaxing when the phone rang and it was one of these guys from California. They were trying to convince us to stay with them even though they had nothing to offer, and they owed us money. I said, 'Let's end this,' and hung up. Ten minutes later the phone rang again and it was another guy from California. I had the same conversation with him and hung up. Ten minutes later, a third guy calls. I got this picture of all of them sitting in the same room and after one of them got turned down, they'd get together and go, 'Okay, you call him now and try this.' It was a very confusing evening, and that whole song comes out of that night's conversation. That's why it's got that telephone vocal effect on it, too."

Restless was quickly followed up by *Just Over This Mountain*, featuring, like its predecessor, many of their well-tested live staples such as Peter Cash's cross-country travelogue "80 Odd Hours," and the modern folk ballad "Joanne." The album contained many more effortless examples of the band's songwriting poignancy, placing a greater emphasis on its quieter side. "Early on we were lucky to tap into the college and university circuit and some of our quieter material was sacrificed because of that," Maize says. "There's always been an imbalance between our live shows and our recordings because we've always tried to capture the live energy but still do justice to the quiet songs. That's where *Just Over This Mountain* comes from; we wanted to take that album out and play in theatres and more listening-type situations. Unfortunately, we didn't have the opportunity to do that."

Instead, the band returned to toiling on the national bar and university pub circuit until the frustration with their independent status came to a head. Ross's label, Fre, had done a sufficient job given its limited finances, but as one of the top live club draws in Canada by 1995, the Skydiggers agreed that a wider audience was now within their grasp. That year, the band found a deal with Warner and set about recording all-new material, including the first Cash brothers' collaborations to make it on record. *Road Radio* turned out to be the fresh start the band had needed to revive much of the energy that had been lost over years of touring. "It was definitely a new beginning for us, and we went into making that record much like we wanted to make our first record, which was basically live," Maize says. "At least 75 per cent of that album is all of us playing together in a room and that was our goal; when you come to see the Skydiggers now, this is what we sound like."

Despite the album's first two powerful singles, "What Do You See," and "You've Got A Lot Of Nerve," the band's hope of finding a new audience did not occur, and they resigned themselves to the fact that selling 50,000 copies in Canada was nothing to be ashamed of. "I know that in a lot of ways we're like a lot of bands in this country," Finlayson says. "We're on a different scale, because we don't sell huge amounts of records but we've been able to go out and play live and make a living doing it. We played so many places that we've been able to go back and do smaller cities. A lot of bands won't do that, or can't do that, or wouldn't be asked, and that feels good."

Upon signing a new licensing deal with MCA in 1992, Andrew Cash likewise feeling a need for a fresh start. His frustration at playing the major-label record company game had turned his rage inward, prompting him to form a powerful four-piece electric band, dubbed The Little Ones. As a further indication of his renewed iconoclastic stance, he chose former Blue Rodeo keyboardist Bob Wiseman to co-produce his new album, entitled *Hi*. Wiseman's recent production work with several Toronto singer-songwriters suggested it would be a good match, especially since his largely hands-off approach would allow Cash to do what he felt served the songs best. "I was happy with my first two records, but there was a five-year gap between *Boomtown* and *Hi* and a lot had changed," Cash says. "There was a whole

Andrew Cash and the Little Ones,
1993: Randy Curnew, Kevin Fox,
Andrew Cash, Paul Taylor
(Photo by Ivan Otis,
courtesy of MCA Records)

album recorded between those two that never came out, which might have explained *Hi* better for some people. If there was one big difference, it was that I remembered I could play electric guitar. I'm not quite sure how it happened but I wasn't interested in playing it for a while and suddenly I realized that's what I'd started out doing. Also, times had totally changed by then; it was easier for me to do that within a mainstream record deal than maybe it was in '88."

Hi partially showed those who had never witnessed Cash's L'Etranger days what they had missed. However, his maturity added an even harder edge to songs like "Hey Maria," a harrowing tale of domestic violence. This song would be a standout on an album in which the music finally complemented the simmering rage beneath Cash's lyrics.

Between the lines, Cash was also taking aim at how artists were now being commodified in the new music business climate through product endorsement and tour sponsorship. It was by then virtually impossible for an established band to do a full-scale tour without sponsorship, or for even a small band to avoid playing gigs sponsored by a major brewery or tobacco company. Following *Hi*'s release, Cash drew the line by refusing to play industry showcase events financed whole or in part by cigarette and alcohol corporations, and urging other Canadian artists to do the same. While this proved to be a tough sell, Cash went further by testifying before a 1997 Senate committee examining the effects of cigarette advertising. He brought to its attention a national club tour in which a major tobacco company paid several bands $500 a night in exchange for hanging its logo over the stage and advertising the tour on radio and in newspapers. "In rock and roll, there is a direct relationship [with tobacco]," Cash told the committee.

"What you have here is young people at a very vulnerable time in their lives, the exact age that most people start smoking."

Cash's vocal opposition to these issues made it seem inevitable that at the end of his MCA contract he would return to releasing his records independently. With a small change to The Little Ones' line-up — old Acoustic Meltdown friend Jason Collett replacing Paul Taylor on bass — Cash assimilated himself into the band, reemerging in 1995 under the moniker Ursula. The band's album, *Happy To Be Outraged*, continued the hard-hitting sounds and themes of *Hi* but reached a far smaller audience. Once again, Cash was at a crossroads, and for the next few years he set music aside to concentrate on writing penetrating socio-political exposes for Toronto urban weekly *Now*. "I'm not one of these romantic Canadians. I don't find tons of romance in barren tundra," he says. "I think Canada is those things, but my reality is very different from that reality. I love Toronto, even though its the place that everyone else in Canada loves to hate."

The Skydiggers failed to have their major-label contract picked up as well, and Peter Cash informed the others that he was leaving following their summer 1996 touring schedule. As the band's main songwriter, his departure left many fans feeling that the Skydiggers could not continue on without him. However, they pressed on with singer/songwriter Paul MacLeod filling in and Finlayson and Maize taking over the bulk of songwriting duties. When they returned in 1997 with the independently released *Desmond's Hip City* — inspired by the record store Finlayson lived above in London — it was with an entirely new approach. The title track featured sampling and drum loops while Finlayson-penned tracks like "November in Ontario" and "The Shape of Things To Come" raged with a fury the band had never shown before. While aesthetically the band had never sounded more vital, the business side once again dogged them. Still unable to get the rights to their first three albums, which had been unavailable for years, the band resorted to releasing *Still Restless*, a collection of the demos they had made for their second album, which sounded remarkably similar to the final product. On its heels came the long-delayed live album they had always wanted to do, accompanied by more of the usual touring.

As a band that had been forced to find its niche in bridging country, rock and folk audiences in the shadow of Blue Rodeo and others before them, the Skydiggers' legacy had emerged remarkably intact. Fans still danced to "Monday Morning" and swooned to "I Will Give You Everything," but the task of building on that legacy as an independent band proved daunting. Musically, *Desmond's Hip City* showed that their best days still lay ahead and the hope of releasing more new material was now the biggest motivating factor. "We knew at the start that our method of working would serve us in the long run, especially in a country with the population of Canada," Finlayson says. "We've been happy with everything that's happened, but if the band is going to carry on, the future ultimately lies outside the country."

Music didn't seem to be in the future for either Andrew or Peter Cash, but in 1997 they each realized that they had been avoiding the obvious potential of performing together for too long. Quietly, they began writing songs and putting them to tape over the course of the next two years. When they finally released *Raceway* in 1999, it lived up to most expectations, combining Peter's deep country soul with Andrew's impetuousness, all tied together with harmonies that could only come from brothers. After two decades of work, it was a fitting tribute to each other's talent and perseverance. And for perhaps the first time, the craft of songwriting took precedence over Andrew's political views. "I've come to accept that I'm not looking for a tranquil life," he says. "That's probably a myth anyway in this country — everyone has to work hard. Music has to start celebrating that fact, not romanticizing it. But to do that you have to live that life and I don't know anything about how most other people live their lives. The greatest lie you can do is write about something you don't know about."

"When it comes to making music, if I could
invent a way to get it from my heart into yours,
without doing all that hard work, I would be
very happy. But until that day, we have to go
into the studio and just do it."

— Brian Wilson

Acadian Driftwood: The Creation of the Daniel Lanois Sound

It's just like every other house on the street, so much so that if you don't know its number you'll miss it completely. Only when you step onto the porch and see the small sign near the door will you know you've arrived at Grant Avenue Studios in Hamilton, Ontario. At first, the building's anonymity is disarming, until you realize that anonymity has probably been its biggest asset over the years. The only shred of exhibitionism is a wall of gold and platinum records; everything from Raffi's *Singable Songs For The Very Young* to U2's *The Unforgettable Fire*.

In fact, there's not much about the interior that would suggest it is any different from the other houses on the street either. A staircase just inside the front door leads up to a modest kitchen and offices that were formerly bedrooms. A flight of stairs on this second floor leads to the attic, which has been converted into a makeshift den, with TV, stereo and an enviable handful of vintage guitars and percussion pieces for those moments when new inspiration is needed. To the left of the front door is the control room and the studios themselves. An immaculate baby grand piano takes up most of the space in the big room.

A first-time visitor with any knowledge of those who have worked here is immediately overwhelmed by visions of Johnny Cash and Emmylou Harris, or maybe The Edge and Brian Eno sitting closely together in the main studio, and later huddled around the board listening to a playback. Then come thoughts of these legends at the end of a session, stepping out into the tough streets of downtown Hamilton, going unnoticed among the common street characters and unrecognized by the shop owners who still faithfully blast the local AM oldies station from behind the counter.

This was the proving ground of Daniel Lanois, now acknowledged as Canada's greatest record producer and arguably the most influential producer of the post-punk era. Hamilton itself hasn't changed much from the time Lanois and his older brother Bob became interested in recording music. Yet their career in the city marks them as instigators or accomplices in nearly every musical phase it has gone through since the late '60s. By the 1980s their groundwork — and especially Daniel's insatiable drive to create new sounds — completely revolutionized popular music once it was given an opportunity to reach a wide audience. Although thoroughly committed to harnessing the latest recording technology, Lanois never allowed his experimentation to overshadow the essence of whatever artist he was working with, including himself. His roots in folk and gospel music revealed themselves in every project he participated in, and his collaborative abilities added a new dimension to the traditional role of the producer. Above all, his work helped renew awareness of rock and roll as an art form and of a song's ability to convey deep messages of faith and hope.

This intoxicating dichotomy between traditional song form and the cutting edge inevitably drew in the rest of the Hamilton music scene as well. Now that Daniel Lanois has spread this sound he created in Hamilton all around the world, the cult he left behind in his adopted home town continues to carry on his methods and struggles to maintain its status as one of Canada's most vital musical communities.

There's a phrase Daniel Lanois once used to describe his main musical influence: "the tobacco-belt sound." He was referring to the music created in the early part of the century as a result of migrant workers — many from Quebec — coming to the rich tobacco fields of southwestern Ontario for seasonal jobs. One might dare to draw a comparison with the Okies celebrated in Woody Guthrie's songs, or the descendants of black slaves who still picked the cotton fields of the American south well into the twentieth century. However, that would be downplaying what Lanois obviously feels is a large part of the Canadian songwriting heritage. The music heard in those fields during the long, hot, late summers and early autumns inevitably spread into a surrounding community already steeped in English folk and country music. One only has to listen to the plaintive singing of Rick Danko to hear it.

A native of Simcoe, Ontario, Danko grew up in that environment with little more than a radio beaming in the powerful American rock and roll stations as an outside stimulus. The rest of his entertainment came from music he and his family made together on Saturday nights, with young Rick taking the fiddle and trying to sing the high lonesome harmonies that were required. Nearly a lifetime later, after playing rock and roll with Ronnie Hawkins and Bob Dylan, Danko returned to those roots when the time finally came to make his own music as a member of The Band. His high tenor seems always on the verge of cracking, but its purity is a direct product of its origins. Whenever Danko takes the lead, especially on "Unfaithful Servant," his verse in "The Weight," or "It Makes No Difference," the voice pulls the listener into the song and the entire performance as it unfolds. It's the way music should be made — the natural communication between musicians gathered in the same room — and that theory has been the cornerstone of Daniel Lanois's career.

It's not surprising that Lanois related to the Québecois migrant workers; he was one himself in some ways. Born September 19, 1951, in Hull, Quebec, Lanois grew up in a Francophone household that was a meeting place most weekends for his extended family. After a large meal, they would gather to sing along to the accomplished fiddle playing of Daniel's father and grandfather. This was the music of Lanois's youth, traditional French and Irish jigs and reels, a music rooted in the lives of common people and played simply out of joy. Lanois did not fully come into contact with rock and roll until 1963 when his parents separated and he moved with his mother to Hamilton, the place where Canada had been formally introduced to rock when Ronnie Hawkins set up shop at The Golden Rail five years earlier.

As he entered his teens and picked up on the British Invasion, Lanois also picked up the guitar. The family had settled in Ancaster, just outside of Hamilton, and as young Daniel became proficient on the instrument he quickly earned a reputation as the local guitar hero. Hearing Jimi Hendrix only pushed him harder. He would play endlessly, to the point where, at the age of 16, he earned recognition in the local newspaper through a lengthy display of Hendrixian technique at a talent show. Not surprisingly, he was in demand by everyone looking to form a band at Ancaster High. "He was definitely the hot shot guitar player," says Bob Doidge, who first met Daniel when he auditioned for a Motown-style band Lanois was in.

"Dan had the biggest amp around — he built it himself and it was huge. I was just picking up the bass, but I was actually a trumpet player so they got me in the band. My heart wasn't in it though, and eventually we got together a psychedelic band doing stuff by Cream, The Doors and Hendrix."

At the same time, Doidge and Lanois became part of a folk group organized by teacher Gary Muir as an extracurricular activity. The group would learn traditional songs, but also contemporary work by Bob Dylan, Gordon Lightfoot and others. Lanois was enamoured not only of the music, but with the lifestyle of the troubadour. That meant getting an education that school couldn't offer. "We all quit school and those guys went to Florida on their motorcycles," Doidge says referring to Daniel and his brother Bob. "I went to play with a band Ian Thomas had formed called Tranquillity Base — very light acoustic rock with an electric harpsichord. He got a contract with RCA so we were recording an album. Dan and I would write back and forth when he was in Florida and mostly talk about recording. He got intrigued by it, came home on his bike, sold it, and bought two Traynor mixers, a little Sony home tape recorder and a homemade speaker cabinet."

Lanois set up the gear in his bedroom back at his mother's house in Ancaster and started making tapes with friends. His brother had continued journeying on through Europe, and when Bob returned to discover Dan's new interest, the elder Lanois's innate fondness for technology took over. The gear was moved to the laundry room and more was added to approach the quality of a professional studio, even though neither had ever been in one. "That was at a time when there was no such thing as four-track boards or home studio gear. There were only six studios in all of Toronto, so it was before its time as a place to record," Doidge says.

The studio was legitimized with a name, MSR (Master Sound Recordings), and the brothers found themselves running a small business after putting up posters around town advertising their $60 flat rate. While Bob Lanois managed the equipment and the finances — boosted through producing radio jingles for local businesses, including one for African Lion Safari that required recording an authentic roar — Dan continued to work regular gigs with area musicians, many of whom were now calling upon the brothers for affordable demos.

Among them was a proto-punk guitarist named Edgar Breau who, after his own pilgrimage across the country upon dropping out of high school, returned with a reaffirmed disdain for all mainstream popular culture. He was determined to form a band in the spirit of the free-form expression that had spawned the Syd Barrett–era Pink Floyd, The Velvet Underground and The Soft Machine. Breau cultivated potential members through avant-garde record collecting circles and by 1973 he had a full-time unit consisting of bassist Kevin Christoff, drummer Neil DeMerchant and Ping Romany (a.k.a. John LaPlante), who provided most of the chaos through a collection of oscillators, tone generators and other sonic hardware. Called Simply Saucer in tribute to the Floyd album *A Saucerful Of Secrets*, the band began terrorizing the high-school circuit with its deliberately grating sounds. They were following a similar path to the one that Roxy Music and German bands like Can had already carved, yet Canada had never experienced the likes of Simply Saucer before, which led to hostile reactions wherever they played. Like that of their heroes, the band's music relied heavily on atmospheric sounds, evoking a nightmarish sci-fi vision instead of the more commonplace complement to natural and chemical stimulants.

With audiences baffled by their live shows, Simply Saucer decided to record in July 1974 in an attempt to focus the chaos. Their emphasis on technology immediately caught Bob Lanois's imagination and he agreed to work with the band, albeit only after Breau had schooled him on the finer points of what John Cale had brought to the VU and The Stooges. The

Daniel and Bob Lanois at Kingsway Studio in New Orleans,
May 1990
(Photo by Margot Peters, courtesy of Bob Lanois)

resulting one-day session sounds predictably ragged in this context, with the band pushing themselves as Bob Lanois clearly struggles to maintain some level of sonic consistency. While songs like "Here Come The Cyborgs" and "Electro-Rock" aged well enough to earn admiration in the late-'80s post-punk world, apathy toward Simply Saucer plagued them continually. No money was available to release a full album, causing the sessions to be shelved until the eventual 1989 retrospective album *Cyborgs Revisited*, which also included a 1975 live recording produced by Bob Lanois. Although interesting from the perspective that it is perhaps the definitive document of Canadian anti-rock in a live setting — from the roof of Hamilton's Jackson Square mall — the sound shows the obvious disadvantage Canadian musicians had in terms of cutting-edge technology, and the audience's overall wariness toward anything they hadn't heard on the radio. When punk came in 1977, Simply Saucer did try to accommodate it; Ping Romany was replaced by a second guitarist and they managed to record a 45 ("She's A Dog/Can't Change My Mind") which received the by-then expected lukewarm response. The band folded by the end of the decade, with Breau's distaste for the mainstream grown even more intense.

The bold attempt by Simply Saucer to create a uniquely Canadian avant-garde sound — as opposed to the stagnant imitations of overblown British prog-rock — was not lost on Bob Lanois. Soon he and Daniel had their studio filled with the latest sound manipulation gadgets they could afford or build themselves. "Bob made this huge thing — and people still talk about it today — that when you were all finished your mix, you'd put it through this thing called the 'Bob-ometer,'" Doidge explains. "It had two big dials and it was all welded shut so you couldn't get inside to find out what was in there. Bob knew what it did, and we sort of had an idea, but people would call up asking to use it before they went to Toronto to get their records mastered. There could have been nothing inside of it — I know for a fact there was something — but the dials were big enough that when you turned them and asked people to listen for the change, they'd hear a change. That's what we learned about gizmos; if you think a certain piece of gear is going to save the day, it can't help but inspire the project."

By the mid-1970s, Daniel's guitar-playing skills were in demand by many Hamilton artists. One of the most successful of the period was Ray Materick, who enlisted Lanois on lead guitar and pedal steel in his band, as well as hiring Doidge on bass. A Brantford, Ontario, native, Materick learned his craft at the tail end of the Yorkville coffeehouse scene and was caught up in the singer/songwriter boom of the early 1970s. He signed to David Geffen's

Asylum label (home of California country-rock) and found national fame with his 1974 album *Neon Rain* and the single "Linda Put The Coffee On." Daniel Lanois joined the band in the wake of this success and was part of the 1975 follow-up, *Best Friend Overnight.* The experience brought Lanois in closer contact with the Canadian folk-rock community, now a shadow of its former self in the encroaching corporate atmosphere. With their business still growing, Lanois encouraged all he met to believe that his facility could provide not only reasonable rates, but also an open environment where he and Bob could contribute arrangements and instrumentation as well.

With the limitations of their basement studio starting to show — not to mention that it was still their mother's house — the time had come to find a new facility. The problem remained in somehow replicating the homey atmosphere that most of the clientele had grown to appreciate. In 1975, while Dan was working with Ray Materick, often opening for big acts like Santana, Bob Lanois began looking for a new space. His technical instincts and knowledge of his brother's experiences in other studios led to a strict rationale. "Dan and I were recording with different people who would do things in Toronto at the bigger studios," Doidge says. "Most of them are the size of a gymnasium. We'd be recording our tracks and you could barely see the control room. We didn't want to go with that kind of image, so we decided to build around the concept of having five or six people together in one room. There was discussion of whether to move to Toronto or not, and we decided we wanted to stay around here and make it work."

The choice eventually came down to either a space in an industrial mall on the outskirts of town or an old house in downtown Hamilton. Although they understood the house on Grant Ave. would initially be far more trouble, the intangibles made it impossible to turn down. "It had a big parking lot, a pizza place and a variety store close by," Doidge says. "That's one thing most people don't think is important, but at three o'clock in the morning when you're 20 miles out of town and somebody needs a pack of cigarettes, it's a big deal." During the next year, Bob Lanois and a few assistants rebuilt the house in the image of what they felt a studio should be. Often it defied accepted logic in acoustic design, but they slowly discovered that what initially might have seemed to be limitations were actually advantages. With the casual atmosphere intact and a new 16-track board installed, Grant Ave. Studio officially opened in 1976 and became the focus of the brothers' lives for the next decade.

They found unexpected success immediately with children's artist Raffi, whom they had previously recorded at MSR, which gave the studio a much-needed financial foundation. Bob and Daniel followed it up with a string of albums by artists like trailblazing blues band Downchild (Dan Aykroyd's inspiration for The Blues Brothers), and folk legend Stan Rogers. The brothers also worked with songwriter Willie P. Bennett on his second and third albums, 1977's *Hobo's Taunt* and 1978's *Blackie & The Rodeo King*. While Bennett never had as high a profile as his contemporaries due to sporadic recording, the experience was a breakthrough for Daniel in terms of firmly grasping his folk roots. He and other Canadian songwriters would go on to sing Bennett's praises in the coming decade. Bennett, who later gained new exposure through playing with Fred J. Eaglesmith, says of the recording today, "I didn't know Daniel well, he was a passing acquaintance. But *Hobo's Taunt*, there's something about it that's timeless. I don't know why. Whenever I put that record on and listen to what contemporary folk singers are doing, it sounds every bit as much in the mainstream."

In 1977, Bob and Daniel also began an association with eccentric Toronto songwriter Joe Hall. During a residency at the Black Bull Tavern on Queen Street, Hall acquired a reputation as a challenging and often humorous performer, although firmly rooted in the folk tradition like his sometime collaborator Mendelson Joe. The brothers first recorded Hall on the 1977 album *HJ Boenke*, then *On The Avenue* the following year, featuring Hall's new band, The Continental Drift. That unit included Tony and Paul Quarrington who, while fitting in with Hall's unusual style, grew to enjoy working with Bob and Daniel more. In late 1978, Tony pulled together his own project, The Anthony B. Quarrington Limitation, for the album *Top Ten Written All Over It*. The recording featured Daniel on guitar and keyboards, but unfortunately failed to live up to its title. Consequently, Paul Quarrington hooked up with his old songwriting partner Martin Worthy, and found greater success with their *Quarrington Worthy* album, again engineered by Bob and Daniel, and featuring Daniel on guitars. However, with punk and new-wave taking over, Paul wisely gave up music to become one of the country's best-loved novelists.

In 1979, the brothers worked with folk legend Sylvia Tyson on *Sugar For Sugar, Salt For Salt*, and reunited with Ray Materick — long since dropped from Asylum — on *Fever In Rio*. Although Daniel again contributes songs and guitars to both records, there is little to indicate what was shortly to come, especially in light of the pervading musical trends. It seems plausible that a generic, radio-friendly sound was what the artists were looking to achieve, but after 1980 Lanois would never again be accused of making an ordinary record.

As the Canadian music industry struggled to understand punk in the late 1970s, the avant-garde made a play to take over. Sparked by a similar spirit of rebellion displayed in Vancouver and Montreal, young southern Ontario rockers latched onto the raw power brought to town by The Ramones and formed their own versions; Hamilton's Teenage Head being the most commercially successful with their rockist approach. However, many more went deeper into punk's spirit of artistic freedom. These were the kids already in post-secondary arts programs or attending the Ontario College of Art, seeking anything besides post-hippie dogma. They took as their musical heroes shapeshifters like David Bowie and, perhaps the most unlikely hero of all, Brian Eno.

It was regularly argued in the 1970s, often by the man himself, that Eno wasn't a musician at all. As a founding member of Roxy Music, Eno helped usher British rock into the electronic age through his primitive synthesizer and tape loop experiments. Upon discovering the restrictions of being a "pop star," and finding a distaste for live performance, he retreated to the safety of other musicians who shared his desire for pure musical risk. Against all logical conventions, he succeeded — at least critically — with his first batch of solo recordings, several in collaboration with King Crimson guitarist Robert Fripp. One night during this period, Eno had a record on and began drifting in and out of sleep as it played. The experience fascinated him so much that he set out to recreate the feeling for a fully conscious listener through new compositions. These lengthy suites of electronic sounds, eventually dubbed "ambient" music, were labelled inconsequential aural wallpaper by their detractors, but more often hailed as densely packed emotional responses to the excesses of traditional rock and roll. The subsequent mystery surrounding Eno's talents and his general ego-less attitude toward writing and recording furthered his stature among the growing anti-establishment communities in England and North America. This position solidified in the mid-'70s through his collaboration with Bowie on the still-controversial Berlin triumvirate *Low*, *Heroes* and *Lodger*.

By the end of the decade Eno appeared tired of British rock's posturing and ventured to his spiritual home, New York City. It was here that he discovered the primitivism that never truly existed in British punk, and began what he called "doing research." The results were heard on the ground-breaking *No New York* compilation featuring art-school bands such as The Contortions, Teenage Jesus and the Jerks, Mars and DNA. Some of it remains unlistenable, but the music clearly points the way toward the innovations

Sonic Youth would make a few years later. As critic Joe Carducci observed, "[These groups] used traditional line-ups but effectively turned each instrument in on itself as if each player had to analyse each act of hitting, picking and singing rather than merely attempting to reach a groove with the others and swing it. It was like staring down at a bicycle's mechanisms while you ride so as to better experience the act of riding."

The period also brought Eno in contact with David Byrne — a Hamilton resident, briefly — which led to his work on several Talking Heads albums, notably their breakthrough *Remain In Light*, featuring the novel incorporation of traditional African rhythms. Meanwhile, Eno continued to develop his own ambient music, finding unexpected success with 1979's *Music For Airports*, his first official ambient album, which was admittedly designed to "get people prepared for death."

Yet, as Eno's cult grew, he constantly searched out more adventurous musicians with whom to collaborate, preferably in places where he could work in anonymity. "I see myself maneuvering to maintain mobility," he said in a 1979 interview. "I often work by avoidance rather than by having a sense of where I want to go. What's often happened is that I've been faced with an option that careerwise looked tempting, and yet for some reason I didn't want to do it, so I'd just avoid it. By avoiding it I'd find that I'd gone somewhere else which can suddenly become interesting. I really like the behind-the-scenes role, because all my freedom is there."

It was during Eno's stay in the New York underground that he began hearing rumblings from Toronto, where minimalist composer and trumpet player Jon Hassell was a visiting lecturer in York University's music department. Through Hassell, Eno was introduced to one of his students, an adventurous guitarist named Michael Brook, then in a new-wave band called The Everglades. Brook had done his time in several typical Toronto bar bands throughout the early 1970s, but always seemed on a higher plane. After enrolling at York and studying with Hassell, he built his own studio, The Crypt, and developed his "infinite guitar," a technical modification providing endless sustain, intended to capture some of the essence of classical Indian music, which both he and Hassell went on to study through vocalist Pandit Pran Nath. Hassell was so impressed by Brook's approach that he asked the young guitarist to engineer his *Vernal Equinox* album, recorded at York in 1976, and the piece that ultimately won Eno's lasting friendship. "Jon Hassell had a very specific agenda," Eno says. "It was to make what he called 'future primitive,' or 'Fourth World' music; his other description of it was 'a coffee-coloured classical music.' His idea was that the musical cultures of the world were a huge resource that the snobbery of western classical music had obscured and not taken seriously enough."

For his part, Michael Brook had already gained a reputation with The Everglades for continuously playing between songs while the rest of the band paused, and that spirit of virtuosity set The Everglades apart as they rose through the Toronto club scene, opening for Talking Heads, The B-52s and others. When a demo for Warner Bros. was rejected, Brook left the band to become part of Eno and Hassell's new collaboration, as well as aiding Eno in creating video installations for various art galleries. The piece they assembled for the Computer Arts exhibition at the Ontario College of Art in 1981 turned out to be one of the galvanizing events within the Toronto avant-garde community. The highlight was the trio's performance of the ambient piece "Mistaken Memories" with Eno and his instruments hidden from the audience in the auditorium's balcony.

Despite Lanois's existence on the fringe of Toronto's avant-garde scene, the first encounter between Eno and Lanois actually came as a result of the Englishman seeking out the producer of a single that had landed in his lap by a Hamilton duo known as the Time Twins. The recording was one of Daniel's increasing experiments done after his paying clients had gone home for the day. "When Dan found out that Eno was interested in what he was doing, it confirmed his already existing tendencies," says longtime Hamilton music journalist Bruce Mowat. "The things Dan was doing after-hours around 1980–81 were going along the lines of what Eno was doing. When they started working together, it just honed Dan's technical skills."

While many deemed it a great coup when Eno came to Hamilton, not all saw it that way initially. Legend has it that Bob Lanois, not recognizing the name when Eno first called the studio to book time, asked for money up front. Eno arrived with tapes of his latest production project, Harold Budd's *The Plateaux Of Mirror*, which took Daniel by surprise. "I was a little disappointed with the tapes he brought," Daniel says. "They had a lot of hiss on them. He had lost the good copy, but we made it work." Once that album was completed, Eno became a regular presence in Hamilton into 1981, with Daniel often driving him to the surrounding countryside to record natural sounds which would later be dubbed onto sessions they had produced at the studio. At Grant Ave., Eno found the perfect setting for ambient recording, mostly because of Lanois's own sense of adventure. "If Brian asked him to put a microphone at the other end of the parking lot to record a cymbal set up two rooms away, Dan was game to try it," Doidge says. "Most people wouldn't do that because it goes against the rules, but as long as I've known Dan, he's been a great rule breaker. Brian Eno's cut from the same cloth when it comes to that."

Lanois himself states that Eno's biggest influence was in pushing him to abandon traditional recording methods altogether. "With Brian, we would start with a piece of music and 18 hours later we'd still be working on it," he says. "It would be transformed from this little piano number into a complex textural piece. It came at a really good time for me. I was ready to begin something whereby I could apply a lot of attention. I appreciated his ability to focus. He knew the approach he was taking; he knew what he wanted."

If Grant Ave. can't be considered the birthplace of ambient music, it certainly has a claim to being the place where some of the best was recorded. The studio's close confines often led to every inch of the building being used for microphone placement. It was situations like these that produced the true ambient sound as, sometimes by accident, leakage from all over the house was put down on tape. "[Ambient recording] was a retaliation against what was going on with recorded music at that point in time," Doidge explains. "You've got to remember that in 1980 people were really only about five or six years into 24-track recording. Before that, 16-track came about around 1970, so it's not like we had a 50-year run on a style of recording. Therefore, multi-track recording got to a point where every tom drum had its own track and got this huge defining sound. Ambient recording throws that feeling out the window." A new world had suddenly opened up for Lanois and the studio's focus immediately shifted from folk and country artists to young bands trying to master the sounds that Eno had pioneered. The first to come along happened to be the band that Lanois's sister Jocelyne had just joined.

Martha and The Muffins had formed around 1977 in the Toronto suburb of Thornhill. The core of the band — Mark Gane, his brother Tim, Martha Johnson, Martha Ladly and Andy Haas — were musically illiterate art students energized by new-wave. After a year of honing their first attempts at songs into danceable tunes that still retained an edgy tension, they found themselves meeting with Virgin Records at the behest of King Crimson's Robert Fripp, who happened to be in the audience at their first New York gig. The Muffins signed in the summer of 1979 and soon after recorded their first album, *Metro Music*, at the Manor studio in Oxford, England. The album made a surprising impact both in Canada and Europe, largely on the strength of "Echo Beach," which accomplished the unthinkable by tying Anne Murray's "Could I Have This Dance?" for Song Of The Year at the 1981 Juno Awards.

However, the instantaneous success led to friction within the band, and the follow-up album, *Trance And Dance*, suffered greatly as a result. By 1981, they had lost bassist Carl Finkle and keyboardist Martha Ladly and were seeking a fresh start. Upon recruiting bassist Jocelyne Lanois, the band had the further luck of gaining a new producer when she disclosed that her brother was working closely with Eno. "Eno was a definite influence on our music," says Martha Johnson. "When we met Dan, we realized that, like us, he was interested in using the studio as a compositional tool, as well as incorporating found sound into the music. The summer of 1981, when we were working in Toronto and at Grant Ave., was probably one of the most stimulating and creative times in the band's history. There were no limits."

Their third album, *This Is The Ice Age*, became Lanois's first full production credit as well as the first manifestation of what he had learned directly from Eno. *Ice Age* has the detached and clinical feel suggested by the title, and while Johnson and Gane's vocals have a distinctive early-'80s monotone, the dense musical backdrops perfectly capture the ambient sense of subconscious exploration. Although there were no hit singles on the scale of "Echo Beach," the album successfully followed the Eno pattern of being crafted as an entire piece and as a result achieved widespread critical acclaim, putting The Muffins back at the cutting edge of Canadian new wave.

Coming off this aesthetic success, Lanois plunged straight into recording Jon Hassell on *Fourth World Vol. 2: Dream Theory*, then assisting Eno with *Ambient 4: On Land*. This album would be the last in Eno's *Ambient* series, since by then the term had virtually become its own genre, with almost every post-punk artist now dabbling in global rhythms and sweeping soundscapes. Eno described the album as "an attempt to create something almost like a documentary film — each piece was an emotional documentary of a place I had been, music as figurative as I could make it. A lot of the sounds don't come from instruments, but stones, chains and wood, all sorts of things that make the complex noises that real things make — because most instruments make extremely focused noises. Classical music is weighted very much toward purity and distinction from normal sounds. What pop music keeps doing is shifting the other way, absorbing more and more of the world."

In 1982, The Muffins returned to Grant Ave., its line-up again depleted. They were now a four-piece band consisting of Martha Johnson, Mark Gane, Jocelyne Lanois and drummer Nick Kent. Their deal with Virgin was also over, which had led to the formation of their own label, Current, and a more necessary focus on Canada. The changes didn't seem to affect their

Martha and the Muffins at Concert Hall, 1981:
Martha Johnson, Jocelyne Lanois
(Photo by Bruce Lam)

working relationship with Lanois, however. *Danseparc* continued to mine the same sonic territory of *Ice Age* while putting the band back in pop's good graces with a return to their earlier songwriting style; the title track was their biggest hit since "Echo Beach." The positive reception also got The Muffins back on the road, where they toured the U.K., Canada and the east and west coasts of the U.S. The smaller core group allowed Gane to augment the sound with guest players, and Michael Brook was the first choice for lead guitarist, The Muffins having known him since their early gigs opening for The Everglades. "My best memory of that tour was playing the Ontario Place Forum with Michael in the band," Gane says. "We hired Comfort Sound to record it and had Dan engineer it. The tapes vanished a short time later during one of our record company's frequent moves and we thought they were lost for good. Fifteen years later, our manager Gerry Young was cleaning out his mother's house after her death and found them in a closet. It would be nice to release the show on CD, but it's all history now."

Following the tour, Brook remained a presence at Grant Ave., working on further projects by Hassell and Eno. On the other hand, Lanois was now balancing these sessions with the more commercial work he was being asked to do more frequently. In 1983, he worked with new Current Records signees The Parachute Club, a band formed almost as a manifestation of

Toronto's maturity as a centre of cultural and sexual diversity. The core of the band — singer/guitarist Lorraine Segato, drummer Billy Bryans and keyboardist Lauri Conger — first came together as Mama Quilla II in 1977. Bryans had been a journeyman drummer since the early '70s, but was attracted to the music of the city's large Jamaican community. Segato and Conger found common ground there as well, especially within reggae's political thrust, and Mama Quilla II subsequently became a fixture in Queen Street clubs like The Bamboo, until 1981 when a changeover transformed the band into the more militant V. That line-up lasted only a year, but Segato, Bryans and Conger quickly bounced back when they were asked to perform at a gala reception at the Festival of Festivals (as the Toronto Film Festival was then called). The Parachute Club was formed for this show and made an immediate positive impact through a more tempered Caribbean-flavoured sound.

When the band started work with Lanois soon after, the producer was enthralled by their emphasis on percussion and placed it at the forefront of the mix. The results culminated in the ubiquitous Canadian single of the era, "Rise Up." On paper it's a call-to-arms on the scale of "Get Up Stand Up," but the message is sugared by an unforgettable chorus, and the relentless rhythm created in part by Lanois's dense production. This was socially conscious pop music at the height of Cold War tensions, and part of the remedy, as South African demonstrators showed, was to simply dance in the face of their oppressors. The other side of the coin was using an openness toward other cultures as a symbol of solidarity. While Lanois's productions never bore a distinctive cultural stamp, they always implied that rhythm was the common global language.

The Parachute Club's self-titled debut would go on to be one of the best homegrown successes of 1983, but the band would steadily be sucked into a bland white-funk vortex after their next album, *At The Feet Of The Moon*, produced by Michael Beinhorn, followed by sessions with John Oates (the silent partner of Hall And Oates) on *Small Victories*.

As "Rise Up" permanently embedded itself as Canada's consciousness-raising anthem, Lanois was already onto his next pop success story. Luba Kowalchyk was a young Montrealer who had learned how to sing through the music of her Ukrainian heritage. By her teens she was reborn as a punk amid the always offbeat Montreal scene. She adopted a new persona using only her first name and assembled a band to effectively colour her fractured take on pop. In 1979, Luba released her first EP, *Everytime I See Your Picture I Cry*, and received a lot of attention as part of a new breed of

Canadian female singer. The wholesome image of Anne Murray was rapidly fading, replaced by the sexually aggressive and ambiguous Carole Pope of Rough Trade, and the consciously genre-defying Luba.

In 1983, she signed with Capitol and started work on her first album, *Secrets and Sins*, at Grant Ave. By this time, Lanois had gotten into a regular working pattern: complex rhythm tracks driving heavily processed guitars and backing vocals, creating a dense backdrop for the lead vocals. Luba's strength in this department made for a compelling combination. Her passionate, often religiously inspired words further added to the mix, yet Capitol's determination to ensure a hit led to two separate outside remixes of the sessions and an eventual narrowing of Lanois's soundscape. The label did get its hit with "Let It Go," a bouncy call to dance in a similar Caribbean style as "Rise Up," but elsewhere a remake of "Everytime I See Your Picture" fails miserably as an overblown power ballad of the sort that would soon dominate the airwaves. However, Lanois's stamp was not totally erased. It is most apparent on "Storm Before The Calm," a neo-gospel ballad that contains Luba's best vocal on the album, and an arrangement which closely mirrors the feel Lanois would later suggest on U2's "I Still Haven't Found What I'm Looking For." Luba's debut album would turn out to be another chart success for Lanois, aided by the inclusion of "Let it Go" on the soundtrack to *9 ¹/₂ Weeks*, but it remains a relic of its time.

At the end of 1983, Lanois welcomed a chance to work again with Eno, this time in a more collaborative capacity. Eno had been approached to compose a score for a new documentary of the Apollo lunar missions, comprised completely of NASA footage and commentary from the astronauts. It seemed the ideal project for Eno to tackle, and he and Lanois (along with Eno's brother Roger) transformed Grant Ave. into a lunar landscape over the course of a month. Taken in this context, *Apollo: Atmospheres & Soundtracks* vastly surpasses anything Pink Floyd may have accomplished in terms of "space rock," but otherwise its extreme tranquillity makes it a leading contender for the ultimate album to induce sedation. In terms of Lanois's development, the album contains the first examples of his new "infinite guitar" style borrowed from Brook, a combination of Hendrix at his most refined, and Fripp at his most soulful. It is heard most clearly on Lanois's solo composition credit, "Silver Morning," a brief track that distinctly points the way toward *Acadie*, and as Eno implies, a return to Lanois's roots: "I discovered that the astronauts were each allowed to take a cassette with them on those missions, and they nearly all took country and western songs," Eno says. "I thought it was a fabulous idea that people were out in space, playing this music which really belongs to another frontier — in a way, seeing themselves as cowboys. The idea was to try and make a frontier space music of some kind."

A few months after completing *Apollo*, Eno returned to Grant Ave., this time with minimalist composer Harold Budd. Although Lanois did not write or perform on the record, which is a cycle of mostly short piano pieces under the title *The Pearl*, he still received a prominent co-credit on the cover for his instrumental treatments and production work on this once again subdued album. Eno says, "Harold Budd's intention was to make what he called 'eternally pretty music,' and his way of composing was to write a piece of music, then take out all the notes you didn't like. It was essentially a kind of minimalism, but by then he had moved to more live improvisation. I would set up a sound, he would improvise to it, and occasionally I would add something; but it was mainly him performing in a sound-world I had created."

Just as it seemed Lanois would become completely engrossed in a balancing act between the avant-garde and mainstream Canadian pop, he received a call from Eno that would forever change his career.

From their earliest days in Dublin, the members of U2, Paul (Bono) Hewson, Dave (The Edge) Evans, Adam Clayton and Larry Mullen Jr. believed they could be the biggest band in the world. Upon convincing Island Records founder Chris Blackwell that their bombastic mix of raw new-wave, Catholic vs. Protestant dogma and Cold War hysteria could accomplish this, the band worked harder than any of its contemporaries to build an audience in North America.

By 1983 and their third album, *War*, they had cracked the continent with minimal radio support. After the attention surrounding the *War* tour and the accompanying live EP *Under A Blood Red Sky*, Bono gladly accepted the torch he imagined was being thrown to him. Riding the wave that followed *Rolling Stone* labelling U2 "band of the '80s," Bono constantly expressed a willingness to fall into the arms of America, as he ultimately would in a few short years. At the final show of the tour in Dublin, Bono warned fans that the band would be going in a different direction on their next album and to be prepared for it. It was clear from the outset that they wanted to expand their sound with someone like Eno. When asked, Eno balked at the idea since he no longer had much interest in working with rock bands, and others around U2 were equally unsure that such a pairing would make sense.

"Chris Blackwell thought I was completely the wrong person for the job," Eno recalled in 1990. "He thought I'd turn it into art rock. I thought this was a possible outcome myself, so I took out the insurance policy of bringing Dan along. I thought that at least if he were there it would be a good, well-produced record with good performances, because Dan has a very good way of working with musicians. He's very encouraging and he can get people to do fantastic things. I was never very interested in musicians until I met Dan."

Bono says that Eno initially tried to pass the project onto Lanois outright: "He said, 'There's a guy called Daniel Lanois I'd like you to meet. He's a young guy, he's worked with me for the last five years, and I think he should produce you, not me.' We cooked up an idea which was to build the studio around the band; let's find a room where the band feels comfortable with each other and their instruments and the sound they're making and have the recording take place around that. Eno said, 'Look, Daniel has been doing the exact same thing, almost perfectly in sync with what you're talking about. You've got to meet him; this is more than a coincidence.'"

Lanois arrived in Dublin thoroughly enthusiastic about doing the project himself, but soon found the task of harnessing the sonic possibilities of Slane Castle, the band's choice of recording location, too much to handle on his own. Eno was persuaded to participate and through the spring of 1984 the pair created what would become *The Unforgettable Fire*.

As the sessions progressed, the members of U2 drew upon Lanois's first-hand experience with folk, country, blues and gospel — music they were all just beginning to discover and incorporate — but also his love for unconventional approaches. Lanois encouraged The Edge to acquire one of Michael Brook's infinite guitars, and that sound immediately became a catalyst for the rest of the album. Another came through allowing Eno to manipulate the band's overall sound to the point of unrecognizability. While U2's label and management sweated over what would come out of the sessions, the band became thoroughly engrossed in their new direction.

"At the time, people had heard of U2 but they were not a pop item," Bob Doidge says. "They weren't heroes in the marketplace by any stretch of the imagination. Looking back on it, you can see all the intriguing things about how wonderful it must have been, but it wasn't. They didn't have the fame, so nobody knew what the album would become until it was out on the market. Doing a U2 project was certainly a marvellous break, but Dan went into it thinking that if it didn't happen to sell, that it would still be a killer recording, and that's how he's always worked. As it happened, everyone immediately wanted to know what kind of microphones he used."

Lanois admits that the album was a learning experience for everyone involved, and that fact limited the finished product. "It was not a simple record to make," he says. "It took quite a while for the lyrics to come together. Bono was looking for a different way to express himself. There's a song called 'White City' that never made it on the album. It had a few sections that were really seductive, but there were other bits that didn't work. At the end of one day, we all agreed that it was not going on this record. The next morning, Brian and I came downstairs and the band was warming up. Sure enough, they were playing 'White City.' At the end of the day we decided again that we weren't going to waste any more time on it. Two weeks were spent on 'White City' and it never got on the record."

The early controversy — Eno's involvement, a deliberate break from the band's past — came to a head upon the album's release in the fall of 1984. However, nearly all declared the album a triumph, if not a masterpiece, after the first listen. From the brooding, neo-orchestral opening of "A Sort Of Homecoming," this was indeed a new U2. The rhythm section still sounds enormous, but suddenly it is The Edge who has opened a Pandora's box of sound, while Bono sings with a voice he always knew existed but was afraid to conjure. Film shot during the sessions shows Lanois guiding Bono along toward this goal. While recording vocals for "Pride (In The Name Of Love)," the singer reaches for the climactic chorus but comes up short. The producer doesn't let him off the hook. They do another take and the singer nearly collapses from exhaustion. It's still too ragged, but the producer knows they've broken through to a new level of performance and now it's only a matter of time for the edges to be polished.

"Pride" was the breakthrough song U2 needed in America, a tribute to Martin Luther King Jr. and non-violent resistance. Moreover, *The Unforgettable Fire* was taken by critics as a response to the militancy implicit in the *War* album and tour. Aside from *Fire*'s reflections on America, Bono's new voice seems to come directly from his intense spirituality, something that could have only been encouraged through Lanois's — and surprisingly, Eno's — love of gospel music. At times, Bono even sounds as if he's mimicking fellow countryman Van Morrison circa *Astral Weeks*. Although several of the songs on side one of the album were radio hits in North America, the real centrepiece is "Bad," the slow-building hymn on side two, among the overtly Eno-ish sound experiments. Reportedly written for one of Bono's friends hampered by a heroin habit, "Bad" would become the highlight of U2's live show as well; its deceptively simple two chords hypnotizing the listener into hearing Bono's confession. It was while performing "Bad" that Bono inspired the most lasting image of the Live Aid concert the following year, when he pulled a young woman from the front row on stage and slow-danced with her while the world watched and the rest of the band briefly transcended the preaching and posturing of the day's other acts. It was at that profoundly human moment, no matter how contrived it may seem in hindsight, when U2 did become the most important band in the world. Now all they needed was another album to back up the claim.

It could be argued that the vacuousness of most early '80s mainstream pop and rock aided in creating the instantaneous myth surrounding *The Unforgettable Fire*. However, in light of U2's later output, the album now truly sounds like a "transitional" work. What does still shine through is the juxtaposition between avant-garde and classic rock attitudes, embodied in the rapidly developing Eno–Lanois working dynamic.

Someone who could distinguish the two approaches was Peter Gabriel. He contacted Lanois after his guitarist David Rhodes recommended him to help with a soundtrack he had agreed to compose for the film *Birdy*. Although Gabriel along with Eno, was considered one of the leaders in the British prog-rock community his solo work upon leaving Genesis in 1975 increasingly showed that a sensitive singer/songwriter was lurking behind the outlandish stage costumes. Like Eno, Gabriel had fallen under the spell of African music around the turn of the '80s and began combining its rhythms into his own heavily processed sound. In 1980, he inspired the creation of WOMAD (World of Music, Art and Dance), the first organization dedicated to the promotion of global music for a western audience. The experiment was an instant success, with surprisingly large numbers of people attending WOMAD festivals and buying recordings by artists from Africa, Asia and South America. Energized, Gabriel found his first real solo success with his 1982 album *Security* and its driving single, "Shock The Monkey." By the following year, he was ready to begin a follow-up, possibly combining world music with his love for 1960s soul in a deliberate attempt at expanding his new audience. However, director Alan Parker came along first and Gabriel couldn't turn down the opportunity to further expand his interest in soundtrack music.

In retrospect, *Birdy* sounds as if Lanois was enlisted to once again provide a stable musical foundation in the face of potential sonic excess. In fact, half the album consists of instrumental remixes of songs from previous Peter Gabriel albums. Despite this, the album was received as a minor artistic breakthrough for Gabriel, simply by being a soundtrack that stood on its own without the benefit of accompanying visuals. He would later repeat this success with his soundtrack to Martin Scorsese's *The Last Temptation Of Christ* in 1988.

With *Birdy* completed by the end of 1984, Gabriel returned to his post-poned new solo album, retaining Lanois's services over the next year at his home studio in Bath, England. As with those who had previously worked with Lanois, Gabriel found his collaborative abilities invigorating. For Lanois's part, he found the initial six-month sessions — with just himself, Gabriel and Rhodes — slow-moving, and only felt that progress was being made after he connected with yet another dynamic rhythm section, bassist Tony Levin and drummer Manu Katche. Suddenly the prospect of making Gabriel's notion of an electronic Motown album seemed entirely possible. "All the tracks were laid down in the absence of a full band," Lanois says. "The record was developed so slowly that it didn't make sense to have a drummer and bass player sitting there twiddling their thumbs while other people worked out whether this part should or shouldn't be in the songs. It's not a way I would normally choose to work. I would prefer to have everybody there."

It was evident as the sessions progressed that Lanois was once again faced with an artist in transition. Up to that point, Gabriel's work had been characterized by murky, highly abstract themes. With his growing interest in world music, the goal was now to make a fun album while remaining true to the expectations of his fans. Yet, as several deadlines came and went with Gabriel still working on lyrics, Lanois was eventually forced to take a stand. One day as Gabriel wrote in a back room of the studio, Lanois nailed the door shut and said he would not let Gabriel out until the lyrics were finished. Lanois says of the action, "It was meant to be a joke, but he didn't take it as a joke. He did a few hours later." Out of this growing tension emerged *So* (a coded reference to "sell out") and the new Peter Gabriel, pop star and global activist.

Released in spring, 1986, *So* caught everyone off-guard, from the first crisp portrait of Gabriel to ever appear on one of his album covers, to the playful first single, "Sledgehammer," and its equally playful video. The momentum continued with "Big Time," an even bouncier number and an ironic jab at the music business, which Gabriel seemed to be embracing and resisting at the same time. The video for "Big Time" had a similar car-toonish style to the one for "Sledgehammer" and their popularity eventually showed Gabriel that his new formula was working too well. After winning a number of MTV awards, he prohibited the channel from ever showing these videos on a regular basis again. Instead, focus was placed on the album's more serious tracks, as Gabriel prepared for a world tour that stressed his WOMAD connections. It would be in concert that songs like "Red Rain" and "In Your Eyes" would take flight, as the new Peter Gabriel opened himself up as never before. While some critics found it simply a variation on his old on-stage pretensions, *So* and its tour firmly placed Gabriel in the upper echelon of '80s artists, and established Daniel Lanois as a starmaker.

Although Lanois had never been short of work, even during his pre-U2 production career, his notoriety following *So* now threatened to keep him away from Canada for more extended periods. He was still able to find time to work with friends like Michael Brook (1985's *Hybrid*) and Jon Hassell (1986's *Power Spot*), but in 1986 he and Bob Lanois sold Grant Ave. to Bob Doidge and his then-wife Maureen, who had both kept the studio running as an everyday facility for local artists and commercial work. "Dan was going to be out of the country a lot," Bob Doidge says. "Bob was doing a really great job running the business, but eventually he started moving into other things when Dan got really involved in the music end, so they both felt it was time. When Dan was gone, things would obviously still be happening; that's when I became more involved. Brian Eno might be here one week, and the following week we'd have a country band in. The week after that would be a bagpipe band, and the week after that would be a classical pianist doing an audition tape for a symphony. We'd go through reams of music that no one's aware of."

With his home ties cut, Lanois immersed himself in his new position as a jetsetting producer, and set his sights on recording the new U2 album. The overwhelming success on all levels of *The Unforgettable Fire* made it inevitable that another crack at the Eno/Lanois formula would occur. What wasn't expected was that the band's new material would delve even deeper into their fascination with America, both musically and lyrically. With the magic of their Live Aid performance still embedded in many people's minds, Bono and The Edge set about writing songs that preserved that moment. U2 was now a stadium band and needed songs that could resonate with such a massive audience. The topics became more personal, and consequently more universal — the struggle for freedom focused inward. In 1986, the crew returned to Dublin to begin work. Gone immediately were the brash sonic experiments, the goal being instead to make an album that showed how the band had absorbed the innovation of *The Unforgettable Fire* into their traditional live approach. It was an atmosphere perfect for Daniel Lanois and he asserted himself even more than before in aiding arrangements.

Lanois says, "There was a certain confidence entering that album. We knew what to expect from different people in the band. The relationship had been established and we got to the point quicker. There was less searching and Bono was also better prepared lyrically."

From the cover artwork on down, the themes on *The Joshua Tree* would largely dwell on redemption from the wilderness of isolation. The influence of gospel music that had first manifested itself in the band's music through Lanois and Eno's urging suddenly bloomed, inspiring a song cycle that, unlike *The Unforgettable Fire*, never digressed from Bono's mission statement that rock and roll could indeed provide spiritual fulfilment. The vast sonic canvas that was needed to evoke the isolation inherent to the songs came in part from Lanois's experience.

The part of the producer in rock and roll has rarely been given the same aesthetic value as the artist's, since it is commonly seen as a technical role rather than a creative one: Sam Phillips came upon the Sun Records sound by accident; George Martin was a conduit (albeit a brilliant one) for The Beatles' abstract notions of sonic construction; and in much the same way, Brian Wilson found ways around technical limitations through sheer devotion to his muse. Instead, it was Phil Spector who defined what the rock and roll record producer could be. In his case, the song itself was secondary to nearly every other aspect of the finished product. First, a song would be matched with the right performer, then the real work began to build a soundscape around the singer, thereby creating space for the listener to place themselves in as well. The process was not about merely capturing a performance, but transcending a performance, thus making Spector, the creator of this temporary world, the focal point of the track.

Eno applied this idea to his own compositions and collaborations in a purely artistic way, but it was Lanois who became one of the few producers to apply the concept to other artists with any degree of commercial ambitions in the post-punk world. What makes Lanois's work so captivating — from *The Joshua Tree* on — is that his sense of space in many ways reflects Canada's own vast distances. Guitars echo from far away, while a hand drum beats up close like the rhythm of a car's engine or the listener's own heartbeat. It all added up to a panorama of sound that inevitably found the artists in a place they had never been before, and it is a further testament to Lanois that it became a place that many of these artists chose to return to, even when working with other producers.

"I think we allowed [U2] to hear some of their tracks being transformed and increased into a higher level of life," Lanois explains. "Song like 'In God's

Country' and 'Mothers of the Disappeared' were relatively plain in their basic state. With treatment, with atmospheres overlaid, contrast was introduced, which is always a wonderful quality to have in any piece of artwork."

As U2 decisively conquered America and the rest of the world in 1987, it became a period for Lanois to take stock of what he had accomplished in the previous three years. He could now pick and choose projects at will, but what presented itself was the prospect of doing his own album. He knew from the start it would be an exploration of his French-Canadian roots, a subject that had increasingly been on his mind now that he was searching for a new base of operations, and in that he admittedly never felt at home within Canada's Anglophone culture. Like the original search for Grant Ave., the new location needed to be a unique working environment away from the pressures of the major media centres, but still close to amenities. Lanois's dream of building a studio in Mexico was initially considered but was ultimately deemed logistically impractical. He instead struck the perfect balance when he found an old New Orleans mansion on the fringes of the city's famous French Quarter. There was a natural attraction of course; Lanois was well aware of the fact that much of Louisiana became populated by French refugees from Maritime Acadian communities, driven out in the late 18th century following Britain's takeover of the region. As exiles, they mixed freely with the African- and Native American communities, together creating a rich and thriving culture that by the beginning of the 20th century spawned jazz. The unique rhythm inherent to the city naturally attracted Lanois as well. With its wealth of uncommonly talented musicians, his fantasies could run wild. While preparations were being made to set up what would become Kingsway Studio, Lanois postponed his move and his album for the project that even from the outset suggested his career had come full circle.

Robbie Robertson was facing a crossroads in his life as well. As songwriter and guitarist for The Band, the Toronto-born Robertson had played a major role in American musicians re-connecting with their country's rich cultural heritage during the height of late-'60s musical excess. Following The Band's dignified final bow in 1976, he had overcome his own excesses and slowly began making music again with the help of his close friend, director Martin Scorsese. Now in his forties and facing lingering questions about his Native Canadian roots, as well as the recent death of former bandmate Richard Manuel, Robertson saw the time had come to make a new statement. He had developed a film treatment entitled *American Roulette* and planned a song cycle as its soundtrack. Lanois was first contacted to

be music director on the film, but after several months Robertson abandoned the film and decided instead to simply record the songs. In choosing
to work with Lanois, Robertson recognized a kindred spirit: someone familiar
with his uncomplicated approach, but also someone equally willing to
abandon traditional methods in order to forge a new path.

Lanois says, "A lot of those songs that applied to the film were not viable
to the record, and a lot of other ideas came around which I preferred. Had
he just recorded those songs we had at the time, it would not have been
as emotional a record. It would have been a record of songs about different
characters. It wouldn't have been songs about Robbie."

Once recording began, an immediate concern was the absence of a
backing band. Rather than relying on the usual session stars, Lanois assembled his own groups specific to the feel of each song. He called upon Manu
Katche and Tony Levin as well as Peter Gabriel himself; longtime Hamilton
friend Bill Dillon on lead guitar; all the members of U2; young American
roots rock band The BoDeans; firebrand vocalist Maria McKee; and in a
natural move, Robertson's former Band-mates Garth Hudson and Rick
Danko. Surprisingly, Robertson placed full trust in the producer's decisions.
"He was thrilled about working with U2," Lanois says. "'Sweet Fire Of Love'
was invented in the studio; it was a jam. There's a 22-minute version and
a 12-minute one. It was a nightmare editing that thing. I spent three days
of my life cutting tape."

Robertson was equally impressed by the work of Dillon, who had also
started out backing Ronnie Hawkins. "I had plenty of room to play with,"
Dillon says. His atmospheres on the mostly spoken "Somewhere Down The
Crazy River" were particularly effective. "When Robbie was telling stories
that led to 'Crazy River,' he mentioned the sound of chirping cicadas down
south in the summer. We worked up a setting, and by barely touching the
strings and using the volume pedal while Robbie was talking, we got the
exact sound he'd described."

While any new music from Robertson would have been a major event
at that time, praise for *Robbie Robertson* was unanimous, leading to strong
indications that it would mark a full-time return to the business that he
took such pains to depart from gracefully. He would make several television appearances backed by Lanois, Dillon, Levin and Katche, but it seemed
clear that he would not embark on the road once again without the aid of
the musicians that produced the unique sound on the album. Robertson
would instead devote his time to Native American causes, and sporadic
periods of recording and acting. His first solo album had strengthened his

legacy and there was no longer any need to prove himself.

Lanois now returned to the task of settling into his New Orleans digs. To help build and operate the studio he brought along Malcolm Burn and Mark Howard, two Hamiltonians who had cut their teeth at Grant Ave. and subsequently become part of Lanois's inner circle of trusted collaborators. Burn had started out in Toronto new-wave band Boys Brigade, who became nationally known through their debut album produced by Geddy Lee of Rush. Soon after, Burn would enter into a relationship with Lanois's sister Jocelyne and begin helping out on the new material Daniel was developing for his proposed solo album.

Howard came from a completely different situation. A high-school dropout, he first found work as a tombstone designer, often being called upon by bikers looking to mark a friend's plot with a stone emblazoned with a Harley-Davidson logo. In 1982, Howard started working as a soundman around the Hamilton club scene but nearly ended up with one of his own tombstones after a motorcycle crash three years later. "I couldn't lift equipment as a result of the accident, so I approached Bob and Maureen Doidge, who had just bought Grant Ave. Studio from Dan and asked if I could work for them," Howard says.

Despite Howard's lack of expertise, the Doidges took him on. "The more a person knows technically when they get here, the less chance they're going to turn into the kind of person that Mark eventually became," Bob Doidge says. "If they come in here and they don't know the regular routine in a studio, they're more apt to dream up a whole new one. If they have it in their mind to follow the manual of what an engineer or a producer should be, then things aren't going to turn out the same. They're still going to have their head in the board 10 years later, whereas the guy who doesn't have any rules is going to come to me one day and say, 'Look what I just did,' and he's got the weirdest contraption hooked up. He doesn't know it's wrong, and it turns out it sounds really cool. It's the making of some people to not have the proper backgrounds. Dan didn't, Bob didn't, and I certainly didn't."

In 1987, Lanois returned to Grant Ave. for some solo sessions and found Howard ready to help out. "He'd get around to doing a guitar part or some-thing, and I'd have the mics ready for him," Howard says. "It all went well, so afterward he offered me a job. I asked Bob and Maureen about it, and they said, 'You know, if you take this, you can't come back here.' I was taking a chance." Howard soon found himself in New Orleans where he would remain for much of the next decade, working on Lanois's projects and eventually producing many artists on his own.

As Kingsway Studio got under construction in 1988, Lanois gladly embraced the vibe of his new home. Among the first musicians he came in contact with were the city's first family of funk, the Neville Brothers. Since their re-formation in the early '80s, the brothers had been widely respected for furthering the New Orleans musical spirit on record and on stage, but Lanois heard something deeper in their music, a manifestation of the American spirit of independence and community that breathed within the New Orleans cultural melting pot. He again put his own album on hold and jumped at the chance to make an album with them. *Yellow Moon* emerged in 1988 as not just an assertion of the band's rhythmic expertise, but also as a powerful political statement. Many of the original songs, like "Sister Rosa" and "My Blood," dealt with the ongoing legacy of segregation, but a collection of covers suggested by Lanois showcased the power of Aaron Neville's voice in conveying a timeless longing for freedom. Two protest-era Bob Dylan songs, "With God On Our Side" and "The Ballad Of Hollis Brown," would draw appreciation from their composer when he was urged to drop by the sessions during a concert stop in New Orleans. Dylan immediately connected with how Lanois was handling the material and sessions were eventually scheduled around Dylan's "Never-Ending Tour."

Before this highly touted collaboration took place, Lanois finally found time to finish his own album. Also released in 1989, *Acadie* sounded like the labour of love it was all through its long gestation, with the songs touching upon nearly all aspects of Lanois's life. Backing musicians once again included members of U2, the Hamilton contingent, both Brian and Roger Eno, and not surprisingly, the Nevilles and their rhythm section, bassist Tony Hall and drummer Willie Green. The meditative "Still Water," with fragile harmonies between Lanois and Eno, sets the tone of simple folk structures drenched in ambient textures. There is also a strong devotional quality throughout the album, reinforced by "The Maker," Lanois's crowning achievement as a songwriter, and one of the few cases in the post-folk revival world where a new song became an instant standard. It would shortly be re-interpreted by Emmylou Harris, Willie Nelson and Jerry Garcia. The reason for this lies in the song's timeless simplicity and humility, two traits that also marked Robbie Robertson's work on The Band's first two albums. The speaker in the song is a man of the land, contemplating whether his life's work is in vain. He has a vision in the midst of this despair — as the angelic voice of Aaron Neville joins in — and realizes he will indeed receive his reward when the time comes.

The reference to "the fields of Abraham" in "The Maker" is in many

Daniel Lanois, Canada Day 1994 in Barrie, dodging the bottles
(Photo by Richard Beland)

ways a dead giveaway to its author's ancestry, but Lanois pays an even stronger tribute by including French lyrics in "O Marie" and "Jolie Louise." Surprisingly, these would become two of the album's most popular tracks among English audiences, and consequently prompt Canadian cultural critics to heap even more praise on Lanois for bridging the language gap. "My Canadian roots are a lot clearer to me now than they ever were, and I embrace those roots," Lanois said in 1993 upon the release of his second solo album, *For The Beauty Of Wynona*. "That's a bit of a contradiction since I'm not living there, but I've decided I can't shake what I am. I'll always be a French-Canadian kid." *Acadie* concludes with a haunting rendition of "Amazing Grace," sung by Aaron Neville, that didn't make it onto the Nevilles' album. Perhaps it was too obvious to fit onto *Yellow Moon*, but its message of personal redemption is perfectly in keeping with *Acadie*'s solemn tone.

Lanois was now a performer in his own right and began taking his first tentative steps toward playing live. Through the summer of 1989, Lanois played selected venues backed by Malcolm Burn, Bill Dillon and The Nevilles' Hall and Green, with trusty Mark Howard at the soundboard. The focus was on replicating the atmospheres for a live audience, and while this may have eliminated any traces of showmanship, Lanois made up for it in his fragile vocal delivery and soulful guitar playing.

If working with Robbie Robertson was a milestone bridging the generations of Canadian rock, then working with Bob Dylan could only be looked upon as the fulfilment of Lanois's personal dream. Lanois's final project of this monumental year found him back in New Orleans with Dylan, who was then mired in a career lowpoint and struggling with appropriate new material to bolster his exhaustive touring regimen. As with Lanois's previous clients, Dylan entered the project knowing full well that his usual recording methods would be modified, if not abandoned altogether. For the notoriously spontaneous Dylan, it seemed likely he would be at odds with Lanois's meticulous attention to sonic detail, but the resulting *Oh Mercy* again struck a balance. As Dylan's first full collection of original material in four years, the album (like *Robbie Robertson*) was seen as a successful updating of his sound, without losing its essence. Many critics were surprised by the amount of influence Lanois had on the album, considering Dylan's prickly attitude toward producers. Yet Lanois seemed to pull it off by once again relying on his instincts as a musician, rather than technician. The now-regular cast of Nevilles' players made up the core band, with Lanois and Burn providing the atmospherics. Overtop of this, Dylan intoned his most passionate lyrics in years, from the bitter "Political World," to the hymnal "Ring Them Bells," and the heartbreaking "Most Of The Time." Dylan himself said at the time, "From someone who has an ear like Daniel Lanois, it's more like someone helping you. He's a musician; that helps. My feeling and my hope is that we could work together again because he made it very painless." With credit added for rejuvenating another career, Daniel Lanois entered the 1990s as the most influential record producer in the world.

Lanois's success through the last half of the 1980s had energized Hamilton's musical community. The buzz was constant around Grant Ave., with musicians who previously had never thought much of the studio's possibilities suddenly embracing ambient sounds. The spirit of exploration was so great that a new space was needed. After selling Grant Ave., Lanois helped Malcolm Burn set up The Lab, an even more informal facility, intended solely for musical projects. More than a spill-over for Grant Ave. sessions, The Lab became a training ground for the next wave of the city's players. One of the regular faces was Colin Cripps, a young guitarist who had done a brief stint with The Spoons, who themselves had recorded their first album, *Stick Figure Neighbourhood*, with Lanois. As far back as U2's first record, Cripps had been won over by The Edge's effects-laden guitar sound, a love that ultimately forged his own technique after hearing Lanois's participation on *The Unforgettable Fire.* "I saw U2 in 1980 at [Toronto's] Maple Leaf Ballroom," Cripps remembers. "I'd seen a few punk bands already and thought that was pretty cool because it was so raw and straightforward, but when I saw U2 on that first tour they just floored me. There was no backdrop or light show, just The Edge playing in this really simplistic but really musical way. The band was really intense and they knew they were really good. I came out of there thinking, these guys have just changed my whole view of how to play rock and roll music, and in a way that was so naïve. Bono wasn't pretentious then."

As Cripps honed his skills, he began a regular gig at a popular Hamilton watering hole, The Gown & Gavel, with a loose band called The Heavenly Brothers that included guitarist Dan Achen and drummer Ray Farrugia. Every other Tuesday, they would play a mixed bag of covers and originals mostly for their own amusement, eventually attracting the attention of a local songwriter, Tom Wilson. "He was trying to re-discover himself," Cripps says. "He was doing solo gigs and then he'd come and hang out with us and play. Then he started showing up with songs he'd written for us to play. We'd all known each other so it wasn't like, 'Who is this guy?' It's in his nature that when he sets his mind to something, he's a very diligent guy. It was exciting for us because I'd never considered myself that great a front person, and here was this guy who could at least help me get through the shows."

Wilson was already a recognizable figure in the Hamilton rock scene with his imposing frame and voice to match. He had avoided the rush to jump on the punk bandwagon — his muscular presence masked a sensitive songwriter — and instead played in hard-bitten blues-rock bands that reflected both the city's blue-collar image and the immediate predecessor of British punk: pub-rock. His biggest success up to joining The Heavenly Brothers' jam sessions had been with The Florida Razors, whose mid-'80s releases, *Beat Music* and *Half A Rock 'N' Roll Record,* got their name partially known in Toronto through the support of hard rock station Q107. Yet that band's ultimate failure nearly drove Wilson away from music altogether. As a would-be journalist, he had literary aspirations and was a prolific painter as well. Wilson ultimately resorted to working construction for two years, before a trip to New Orleans to visit old friend Daniel Lanois convinced him to take another shot.

As Wilson plotted his new course with The Heavenly Brothers, Cripps was suddenly presented with a new situation. One night after a show,

Jocelyne Lanois approached Cripps with an invitation to play guitar on some demos her new band was working on. "I went to Toronto and met the band, which at that point was Greg Keelor, Michelle McAdorey, Jocelyne and Ambrose Pottie. I think they only had four or five songs on tape, so I just added stuff to what was already there. Musically, it worked immediately. Greg and Michelle were both really excited, so I joined the band."

Greg Keelor first met Michelle McAdorey during his pre-Blue Rodeo days in The Hi-Fi's in the late '70s. The teenaged McAdorey was already an aspiring pop singer with a love of folk music and found a common artistic sensibility in Keelor. However, like many other young Toronto musicians in the early 1980s, McAdorey felt unwelcome in the scene and set out to break into the British pop market at the age of 16. While she accomplished some sessions with British mainstays Kirsty MacColl and Midge Ure in the ensuing five years, nothing solid materialized and she returned to Toronto just in time to be part of Blue Rodeo's breakthrough by starring in their video for "Try." "It was a strange situation," McAdorey says about her days in England. "I met Kirsty MacColl and she asked me to do some backing vocals for her. Then I formed a band called Cold Fish that Midge Ure produced. CBS picked us up and changed the name to Corect [sic] Spelling for the Canadian release. We weren't happy with the recording, it sounded too much like [Ure's old band] Ultravox and we had more of an acoustic thrash type of sound. We did one EP and it was really a case of being totally naïve and ambitious. We didn't know what we were giving up for what we were getting until after the fact. I started asking myself, 'Who am I and what am I going to do with my life?'"

The answer seemed at first to lie in a renewal of her emotional relationship with Keelor, which soon produced some new songs that he earmarked for a band that he and McAdorey would lead. "I really don't know what he thought of it at the time," Cripps says of Keelor's plans for the band. "I think it was a songwriting situation for him. Blue Rodeo at that point were starting to take off, so the reality of it was they would always come first. That became the reason why, after seven or eight months, I had started writing with Michelle so that there would be some viable potential outside of having Greg in the band."

It was largely left up to McAdorey to put the rest of the band together. Pottie came from a jazz background and could adapt to any situation, while Jocelyne Lanois's appearance seemed more like an act of fate. "I had it in my head that I really wanted to hook up with other female musicians — it wasn't a sexist thing though," McAdorey says. "I'd always been in bands with males and females, and it was quite hard. But when I got word of this female bass player who had played with Martha and The Muffins, I was immensely excited. Jocelyne had heard about me too and wanted to get together."

The name Crash Vegas was a Keelor/McAdorey collaboration. "Greg and I couldn't come to a unanimous decision," she says. "We originally called ourselves Giant Tambourine, which didn't work, so we started bouncing words around and somehow we put Crash Vegas together. Eventually we

Michelle McAdorey of Crash Vegas, 1995 with Eric Cheneaux on bass
and Gavin Brown on drums
(Photo by Pam Westoby)

found out that the slang term for Nashville is Nash Vegas, but I liked Crash more for its abrasive vividness."

As Keelor became increasingly preoccupied with Blue Rodeo, the band spent most of its time writing and refining its sound without him. Cripps's influence started to take over, creating acoustic and electric ambient guitar sounds that perfectly complemented McAdorey's yearning vocals. It was obvious that this was now the essence of whatever Crash Vegas was becoming, and an uncomfortable decision had to be made. "We wanted to be more autonomous, so eight months into it we fired Greg," Cripps says. "We said, 'Listen, we want to be a band and have our own thing. He was actually quite supportive of that — he's always been a great supporter of music — and he realized his thing was Blue Rodeo."

Keelor's influence led to Crash Vegas securing a deal with Blue Rodeo's label Risque Disque/WEA, and they began recording with Jocelyne Lanois's then-partner Malcolm Burn in Hamilton and New Orleans. Released in 1989, *Red Earth* fit perfectly with the Queen Street folk-rock crowd, while retaining the atmosphere of a typical Daniel Lanois production. The album's unique moodiness in turn inspired Blue Rodeo to work with Burn on *Diamond Mine*, released the same year. It is the sound of a band playing together in a room, but there is an uncomfortable distance separating them from the listener. After nearly a decade of development, this was the Canadian sound if ever there was one.

"It was the first record I'd done for a major release, and it felt like the band had a future above and beyond just putting out an independent record and seeing if we could drum up some interest," Cripps says. "Obviously, Greg's connection lent a lot of validity to it at the start, but the songs are really what sold the band." It was hard not to be captivated by the smouldering beauty of "Inside Out," "Smoke," "Sky" and the rest, but many eyebrows were also raised by the stripped-down version of Neil Young's chestnut, "Down To The Wire."

"I'm a huge Neil Young fan," McAdorey says. "But I like how we did it completely different from the original version. I still love Neil's version but it sounds strange with all the psychedelic guitar on it. Colin and I were playing it one day in the studio and Malcolm said we had to record it after he heard us."

With a fanbase established almost immediately, Crash Vegas set out on their first serious round of live shows, but the experience of reproducing the sound live already began sowing the seeds of destruction, according to Cripps. "You have to lend a certain amount of your personality to the songs to make them believable to an audience. If you saw the band back then, there was an intensity there and it didn't always mean we lost it when we got off stage. That was the chemistry of the band; there were intense personalities and it fuelled the material. I think the whole legacy of the band is that intensity, or that certain moodiness that you expected when you went to a show. It wasn't a façade, it was the real thing, but it was also something that after awhile became too encumbering for me."

In the year after the release of *Red Earth*, Jocelyne Lanois left the band and their deal with WEA ended upon Risque Disque's closure. The intensity had to be expressed on a larger scale in order to save the band, and the next album would reveal a new Crash Vegas.

In Cripps's absence, Tom Wilson had commandeered The Heavenly Brothers in 1989, renaming them Junkhouse and introducing a new batch of tough original songs around Hamilton and surrounding area clubs. With a shaggy image that was more reminiscent of a motorcycle gang, the band hardly fit with the overall underground rock population. Instead, Junkhouse seemed to fully embody the experience of living in working-class Hamilton. Wilson's songwriting had taken a dramatic turn from recycled blues images to drawing upon his surroundings. These often dealt with scenes of alcoholism and domestic abuse. Even though Junkhouse was an unabashed rock band, Wilson continually developed his troubadour soul, drawing upon Gordon Lightfoot, Murray McLauchlan and Willie P. Bennett for inspiration. "The Canadian music business, and Toronto in particular, didn't know what to do with us because they were marketing techno stuff like Boys Brigade and Martha and The Muffins, all those bands," Wilson says. "So what were they going to do with a bunch of drunken louts from Hamilton? They didn't want to touch us at all at first. But by the early '90s, I felt part of a rediscovery as far as writing about things that went on outside my front door."

After logging several years on the bar circuit, by 1992 Junkhouse had caught the ear of Sony A&R rep Mike Roth. Upon signing, and given the choice of producer, they likewise opted for the widescreen approach of Malcolm Burn in lieu of Daniel Lanois. When their debut album, *Strays*, was finished by the fall of that year, the occasion was marked with a triumphant gig opening for Bob Dylan at Hamilton Place, an experience that was memorable for more than the obvious reasons. "We were all blown away by just being allowed to hang around backstage," Wilson says. "After our set, we were there celebrating when Dylan walked over completely unexpectedly and started talking to our drummer Ray, thinking that he was his drummer. I guess there was a bit of a resemblance. Bob told Ray about all these things he had to remember to do and Ray was just dumbfounded. So Bob said what he had to say and went back to his dressing room. It was unbelievable."

From there, *Strays* launched Junkhouse onto the international stage, with the raucous first single, "Out Of My Head," leading the way. With the rest of the album, Wilson established a kind of Southern (Ontario) Gothic storytelling style, exploring the dark corners of his surroundings on songs like "Praying For The Rain" and "Big Lake." Wilson was the most surprised when his songs found admirers in Europe and Australia. "In Australia, they were so happy to have a band from Canada because they want Canadian music down there badly. What was a real compliment to my writing was when I'd go over to Holland or somewhere and people would be asking me about the Niagara Escarpment and Lake Ontario and things that people might have taken for granted in Hamilton. The bullet went right through my head then, and it felt great.

"Down in the States it was another story; we were hoping for five minutes of fame and got about two and a half," he continues. "But I've always believed that you have to be honest to yourself. I'm from Hamilton and I know this area. I've travelled a lot now, but in those places I'm still just a tourist or a working musician; I can't talk about what those people are like. I can do that here. Some of the songs come from remembering trips down to Lake Erie and drinking on beaches."

As Junkhouse alternately thrilled and intimidated audiences across Canada in the early '90s, Crash Vegas was hoping a little volume would kickstart them as well. The addition of bassist Darren Watson had largely completed their transformation into a full-fledged rock band, and Cripps revelled in the opportunity to unwind his Les Paul. The band had found a new record deal with U.S.-based label London and recorded *Stone* in Los Angeles, once the personal turmoil that forged the songs had been straightened out. While McAdorey admitted that an acrimonious split with Jocelyne Lanois was part of it, she also conceded that much of album's bleakness was a result of a romantic split with Greg Keelor. "It was not an easy thing, but it was necessary," she says. "We know each other so well and there's so much love between us, but love is an intense thing and I don't think it's ever easy when you want to change it. My life felt fucked up during the writing and recording. Up until then it was like a mountain of energy and chaos in my head and my body, just swelling up and not knowing where to go."

That energy was evident from the first notes, as *Stone*'s pummeling first single, "You And Me," took them into previously unknown sonic territory. Also notable was a songwriting contribution from Soul Asylum's Dave Pirner,

"One-Way Conversation," which seemed to best spell out McAdorey's feelings, both musically and lyrically. "We were feeling more aggressive because we had been touring as well," Cripps adds. "Everything we'd done up to the first album had been in a controlled environment, but when we were on the road in '91 and '92, we saw a lot of the exciting changes that were happening in music and we wanted to be a part of that. Michelle was always a huge Patti Smith fan, so there was also that influence of trying to communicate a little bit more aggression."

The tour for *Stone* furthered the band's hard rock evolution with McAdorey casting a defiant stance at the microphone, deflecting any taunts from a male rockist audience with either a retaliatory remark or piercing glare. Meanwhile, Cripps led the rhythm section with churning riffs, and normally closed the show with his jagged treatment of The Velvet Underground's "I Can't Stand It." "The perception of the band after that second record was that people were going to hear a more aggressive show," Cripps says. "But at the same time we were trying to get into areas that probably seemed a bit indulgent to some audiences. I think for that reason, certain audiences weren't into it. They just wouldn't get it, or they weren't in the mood for it. I can't say I blame them because it wasn't something that was everybody's cup of tea."

If *Stone* showed a band fiercely overcoming its hardships, the tour ended with things once again in disarray. Their deal with London was terminated after general apathy in the U.S., and the overall strain had caused the departure of not only another bass player, but drummer Ambrose Pottie as well. Crash Vegas was now boiled down to the McAdorey-Cripps partnership, and initially it seemed as if things could not continue on such uneasy terms. For a while they didn't continue, until 1995 when Mike Roth of Sony began assembling a Neil Young tribute album by Canadian artists. Cripps had already contacted Roth about lending a hand in cleaning up the mess of their American deal, and the guitarist was offered a spot on the record if he and McAdorey could put something together. The song they chose was "Pocahontas," one of Young's many dream-like indigenous fantasies, and it was given a mesmerizing full-band arrangement not that far removed from *Red Earth*. The experiment proved so successful that Sony offered a one-album deal and the pair quickly found themselves back in the studio working on new material.

When it emerged shortly thereafter, *Aurora* possessed a coherence drawn from combining the extremes of its predecessors. The title exemplified the glow at the core of songs like "On And On (Lodestar)" in which McAdorey's voice and Cripps's guitar intermingled like leaves being carried on an autumn wind. The album was another pleasant surprise, but the *Aurora* tour also brought things back to square one as the band once again faced the task of recreating atmospherics in noisy club settings. The shows were admittedly a letdown after the magic they captured in the studio, and old tensions were rekindled. "Things were already unravelling by the time we went on tour," Cripps says. "It was getting to be too much work to get the results we wanted. I was at a point in my life when I realized it wasn't the path I wanted to keep going down. The touring aspect of Crash Vegas was always difficult for me; it was always imbued with a certain amount of difficulty. It came to a point where I frankly would not have continued if the record had done hugely well or not. That was a decision I made, probably three-quarters of the way through that record."

As Cripps and McAdorey parted ways, Tom Wilson was also realizing there was more to being a musician than playing the record company game. He had become obsessed with keeping his band's momentum going, after it appeared that *Strays* was one of the biggest homegrown successes of its year. Wilson pushed Junkhouse to tour tirelessly before recording the follow-up, *Birthday Boy*, an experience he admits was ill-timed. "The second album was full of conflict everywhere, not just within the band. It was between the band and me, our management and the band, our management and the producer, the producer and the band, the producer and the record

Junkhouse, final line-up, 1997: Colin Cripps, Tom Wilson,
Dan Achen, Ray Farrugia, Grant Marshall
(Photo by Mark Bartkiw, courtesy of Sony Canada)

company, the record company and everybody. It was an impossible situation to work in and if I could go back, I would have held off making that album until the air cleared."

Birthday Boy is a darker vision, with Wilson's tales of alcohol and self-abusers now without any hope of redemption, unlike on the previous album. "Burned Out Car," Wilson's desolate duet with Sarah McLachlan and written with Murray McLauchlan, summed it all up, although its sombre tone captured a spirit beyond Wilson's immediate state of mind. Between the lines was the sound of bands and songwriters who only a few years prior seemed to burn so brightly but were fading out rapidly, one by one. The song was tough medicine to take, but it still rang true. It became a place Wilson did not want to revisit, and not surprisingly his next venture was an informal collaboration with folk singer Stephen Fearing and guitarist Colin Linden to pay tribute to Willie P. Bennett. Dubbed Blackie & The Rodeo Kings after the second album Bennett recorded with the Lanois brothers in 1978, the resulting album, *High Or Hurtin'*, was a shot in the arm Wilson had needed. "When it all clicked for me was when we played the Edmonton Folk Festival and we were on the main stage in front of 10,000 people," he says. "I was doing one of the songs off the album called 'Has Anybody Seen My Baby Here Tonight?' and it was dead quiet. While I was singing I kept thinking, 'Fuck, I've been trying to sing "Burned Out Car" in front of Junkhouse audiences for a year and a half now, and I get the same reaction as if we were doing "Out Of My Head."' People were crawling on top of each other, stage diving, surfing, not really listening. After that I wanted more than anything to transfer that moment to a Junkhouse record."

In 1996, Wilson called Colin Cripps to see if he had time to write some songs. It was a new beginning for each and over the next year Cripps became a full-fledged member of Junkhouse and produced the band's third album, *Fuzz*. Despite including their biggest single yet, "Shine," the album could not lift Junkhouse out of the club circuit. By 1999, *Fuzz* would prove to be a final testament to the spirit of the post-punk Hamilton scene. Wilson would go on to another triumphant round with Blackie & The Rodeo Kings and a solo career, while Cripps would continue to produce other artists and work with Jim Cuddy on his solo projects. Michelle McAdorey would also eventually take the solo route, working on her own terms for the first time.

The focus in Hamilton had shifted from Grant Ave. to the upstart Sonic Unyon label, which almost single-handedly maintained Canadian independent music's credibility as the early '90s boom eventually went bust. On its roster was a Hamilton-area quartet adept at creating lengthy soundscapes, almost as if the Lanois/Eno experiments were as common a touchstone as Beatles songs are to every other fledgling songwriter. The original line-up of SIANspheric, guitarists Sean Ramsey and Paul Sinclair, bassist/vocalist Steve Peruzzi and drummer Matt Durrant, formed in 1994 and by the following year had released *Somnium*, an interstellar trip unmatched by any other Canadian band before. It displayed a sound that would come to be known as "post-rock" in international critic's jargon due to the general absence of any traditional concepts of rhythm and structure, but at its core was a simple head-on collision between ambient technique and punk fury.

As natural as it seemed to have Daniel Lanois become involved with SIANspheric, his discussions with the band after they approached him to produce their next album led Lanois to concede that they had enough ability to do it on their own. By this time guitarist Sinclair had left the band, and in the winter of 1998 the remaining trio recorded *There's Always Somewhere Else You'd Rather Be* in a makeshift studio built in the shed behind Durrant's house. The album was another critical success, as engagingly emotional as any other album released that year, but the power behind the music was also tearing the band apart. Four shows into their cross-country tour in the summer of '98, Peruzzi disappeared, presumably succumbing to a nagging drug habit, and was not seen again for several years. Ramsey and Durrant continued on with new line-ups, releasing an album in 2001, and still managing to carry the legacy not just of SIANspheric, but of almost everything that the Hamilton music community had come to be known for. Within their hypnotic sound collages could be heard Simply Saucer's primitive noise, Teenage Head's attitude and of course Daniel Lanois's pure creative abandon. It is hard to envisage what could come next.

In 1997, Daniel Lanois put Kingsway Studio up for sale. In the two previous years, he had helped create another masterpiece there, Emmylou Harris's *Wrecking Ball*, toured with her, and partially returned to his pop roots with Luscious Jackson's *Fever In, Fever Out*. However, the pressure to leave New Orleans was building. Some of it came from local DJ Barbara Hoover, who had launched a lawsuit against Lanois in the early '90s claiming she had never been properly compensated and credited for establishing the studio. Despite the lawsuit being an ongoing burden, many who knew Lanois assumed his choice to abruptly relocate was simply part of the pattern he had established long ago. "Dan's kind of transparent in a way," Colin Cripps says. "He'll still phone us up, but you never know where he is. He might come back to Hamilton for a month and we'll see him, but he doesn't hang out with everybody. That's always kind of how he's worked. You'll hear after the fact that he's worked with David Bowie or somebody. He's never made a big deal out of anything."

Lanois would go on to produce another album with Dylan in Florida, the glorious *Time Out Of Mind*, before setting up a new studio in the town of Oxnard, situated in the desert outside of Los Angeles. From there would come Willie Nelson's *Teatro* (including Nelson's interpretation of *Acadie's* "The Maker") in 1998, before Lanois was summoned once again to make a U2 album with Eno. By then it seemed working with the pair was a security that U2 could rely on to maintain whatever creative drive remained in the band. Following the nearly disastrous *Rattle & Hum* album and movie, U2 was on the verge of collapse until sessions with Eno and Lanois in Berlin produced the surprisingly affecting *Achtung Baby* in 1991. Although the accompanying Zoo TV tour proved innovative and put U2 back at the leading edge of mainstream music, the experience eventually led to the *Pop* album and tour which saw the band making overblown statements on consumer culture that weren't helped by the extravagant lengths Bono went to illustrate them. It was now established that with Lanois and Eno at the helm, the music never reached such levels, and news that they would produce what would become *All That You Can't Leave Behind* was welcomed with expectations rarely given to albums by the year 2000.

As he always had done, Lanois would manage to turn an untested situation into a work of art that anyone — casual pop consumer or cynical aficionado — could accept and even be moved by. As he stated in 1997, it came down to his approach. "I guess my sense of commitment is really what rubs off on people, what seems to hang in the atmosphere, and people respond to that. What I choose to work with project-wise will be something I care about. That promotes performance better than anything I know."

If anything still hangs in the atmosphere at Grant Ave., it is precisely this quality. The studio's list of memorable sessions continues to grow long, as well as more diverse. The '90s brought *Black-Eyed Man* by Cowboy Junkies, *Temptation* by the Holly Cole Trio, and the first recording of "Birdcage" by John Cage. Bob Doidge was also behind the board for influential albums by Ani DiFranco (*Dilate, Little Plastic Castle*) and American folk star Brooks Williams.

For Bob Doidge, running Grant Ave. has been more than just a good run in his hometown, it has encompassed an era that irreversibly changed the sound of music around the world. "Dan and I spent a lot of time together on the road talking about goals and ideas," Doidge says. "He had some, I had some. Musically speaking, they were probably night and day even though we were working closely together. But it dawned on me two years ago that I was producing Gordon Lightfoot while he was producing Bob Dylan at the same time, when thirty years ago we were both playing their songs in our little folk club in high school," he says. "But I find it kind of depressing when I hear records obviously imitating what Dan and Eno were doing back then. It's only natural if they're your heroes, but at the same time it's a little sad when people come here expecting to get that sound and spending so much time on it that a wonderful song might be lost because of it. The thing that makes Dan great is that he's always trying to do things in different ways. Music in general changes really fast, and I don't think you can be a truly great artist without understanding that."

In the Spirit of Crazy Horse

"I think you've got to look at every Canadian singer/songwriter as a folkie. Neil Young, Leonard Cohen, Joni Mitchell, Gordon Lightfoot — there's your folk pantheon. If Dylan hadn't grown up just over the border in Hibbing, Minnesota, you could make a case for all the important folk voices of the '60s being Canadian. Maybe in the U.S. and the U.K. they didn't really have that. In the U.K., the most famous songwriters are Lennon and McCartney, and in the U.S. they were busy with Motown, R&B and the San Francisco scene — which was also built on the folk thing. But give me Leonard Cohen over John Prine, and give me Neil Young over Jackson Browne, and give me Joni Mitchell over any female folk songstress in the U.S. The quality of the folk music we were listening to up here was so high."

These words might sound unusual coming from a dyed-in-the-wool punk like Groovy Religion's William New, but the message behind them is that the core of Canadian music has always been, like all great music, an individual voice struggling to say something truthful about the world in which it exists. In the folk revival of the early- and mid-1960s, Canadians took in their surroundings and translated them into song with a modern perspective; sometimes in a simple, nationalistic way prompted by the country's centennial, but most often in a self-effacing tone that suggested every Canadian must forge his/her own dream.

The abundance of great Canadian singer/songwriters in the 1960s has been well-documented, but the myth of their sudden appearance has rarely been questioned; as if Canadian rock and roll musicians did not exist previously. Of course, this was not totally the case, as Ronnie Hawkins discovered soon after arriving and drafting future members of The Band into his own Hawks, but on the whole Canada did not experience the cultural collision between country and blues that created rock and roll, nor the religious tenets and societal restrictions that created soul music. Instead, songwriters had the inherited folk music of their European ancestors, but more importantly, the isolation of their surroundings and their place within them.

For Roberta Joan Anderson, growing up on the prairies, this would manifest itself in perhaps her most important early song, "Urge For Going." Gordon Lightfoot's first signature song, "Early Morning Rain," is likewise an existential masterpiece — the narrator realizes his insignificance while watching a jet plane take off and knows he can't be on it. Lightfoot would quickly become an icon through writing about Canada, but Joni (soon-to-be-Mitchell) along with another kid from the prairies would leave for good, and create their best music as a result of coming to terms with what they'd lost in leaving.

For many in Canada, Neil Young will forever be someone who made it big by singing his heartfelt reminiscences about a town in north Ontario, set in the shadow of the mythical Sugar Mountain. But in a larger sense, his career stands as the template for rock and roll integrity no matter where you're from. Beginning as a British Invasion-styled rocker in Winnipeg, then a Dylan-esque folkie in Toronto, Young's own voice would systematically emerge out of a combination of the two following his introduction to international audiences with Buffalo Springfield. With his ensuing solo work backed by the visceral Crazy Horse and the Nashville-honed Stray Gators, as well as occasional flings with Crosby, Stills & Nash, Young furthered his image as a rock and roll iconoclast, never failing to follow an errant muse that invariably led him to create a string of deeply moving and often painfully honest albums throughout the 1970s.

For all the emotional strain that fuelled his many musical mood swings during that period — which also included divorce and fathering two children with birth defects — Young had emerged in the eyes of critics as the most consistently challenging artist of the decade. Yet it all seemed to be unravelling soon after Young took up old friend David Geffen's offer to sign to his new label in 1982. The troubles actually began three years earlier when Young publicly came out in support of Ronald Reagan's presidential bid. Although he would maintain it was a reaction to the malaise of the Jimmy Carter years, the incident was the first in a series of confounding moves that left even the most ardent Young supporters wondering what was going on in his head.

When word ultimately got out that the rapid, chameleon-like genre shifts between *Trans, Everybody's Rockin'*, and *Old Ways* between 1983 and 1985 were deliberate responses to charges that Geffen was rejecting his albums for not sounding "Neil Young" enough, it became clear that Young was once again rebelling. Unfortunately for fans, it was often too much to accept Young in 1950s greaser get-up or new-wave attire. A promising return to Crazy Horse in 1986 after the dismal *Landing On Water* could not be sustained at the height of image-obsessed '80s pop and the Third-Best Garage Band In The World tour of that year almost proved the band's undoing, as the few scenes shot backstage and later included in Jim Jarmusch's compelling film *Year Of The Horse* clearly show. The tension finally spilled out on *Life*, the final album for Geffen and a continuation of *Water's* limp, synthesizer-dominated production. The glaring exception was "Prisoners Of Rock 'N' Roll," a thinly disguised jab at Geffen's opinions of Young's work, punctuated by the off-key "That's why we don't wanna be good!" chorus, ironically the sound that many longtime fans were craving.

Neil Young and Crazy Horse in Barrie, 1996: Frank
Sampedro, Billy Talbot, Ralph Molina, Neil Young
(Photo by Richard Beland)

The *Life* tour in the summer of 1987 was still not yet a time to rejoice, even though Crazy Horse seemed back in top form. There was a point in the nearly three-hour show when the band was briefly joined by a horn section for a set that most only remembered for an odd little tune that, like Young's best accusatory songs, perfectly expressed the average person's bile at being at the mercy of forces beyond their control. Taken in such a context, "This Note's For You" is not dissimilar to the more revered "Ohio" and it showed those who had chastised Young for supporting Reagan just who he believed the real enemy to be. Even though it was sung from the perspective of a working musician faced with the realities of corporate sponsorship, the song fulfilled the potential that "Prisoners Of Rock 'N' Roll" had failed to accomplish by avoiding the latter's obvious connection between ragged rock and roll and commercial failure in the mid-'80s marketplace.

Instead, "This Note's For You" spurred the debate over the possibility of artistic freedom within the corporate domain through a brilliant video that parodied every major artist who had recently sold their talents for the sake of advertising, from Eric Clapton to Whitney Houston. The dicey scene re-enacting Michael Jackson's flaming hair during the filming of a cola commercial didn't prevent the video from stirring the emotions of even non-fans. In another of his career's great ironies, the clip was voted MTV's video of the year after the station had initially rejected it.

Yet this new sound showed Young once again stuck in a role, this time as leader of a full-blown R&B band, The Bluenotes. Their album, *This Note's For You*, was hardly an improvement from the Geffen years, but anybody who bothered to attend their 1988 tour, "Sponsored By Nobody," had more to be encouraged by than merely Young's biting statements about corporate greed. The shows were composed largely of the expected horn-driven revue of simple jump-blues variations, but each night there were at least three moments that completely transfixed everyone. The first came when Young stood alone with his acoustic guitar and pounded out "Days That Used To Be," an indictment of the baby-boom generation's loss of values, pointedly set to the melody of Dylan's "My Back Pages." Next, Young settled into a chair and the rest of the band tentatively joined in over the next 15 minutes as the seemingly endless string of scenes comprising "Crime In The City," — from the crooked cop getting "paid by a 10-year-old" to the cynical record producer controlling the pop assembly line — played themselves out in a brutal vision of modern life. Finally, picking up his electric again, Young then kicked the band up to full speed and led them even further into America's heart of darkness with "Ordinary People," still regarded by fans and critics who have heard it as the missing link between the idiosyncrasies of the Geffen years and the stunning return to form on *Freedom*. The song unravels much like "Crime In The City" — rapid-fire jump-cuts illustrating desperate loners, decaying inner cities, and suburban paranoia — 10 minutes that stretch into a sweeping panorama of the post-industrial landscape.

If these three songs — reportedly all written on Young's boat during one mammoth burst of inspiration — were indeed a turning point, it was almost stalled by his appearance on CSNY's *American Dream* album later in 1988. Although Young's participation was believed to be merely a favour to Crosby, who was recovering from his many addictions and a life-saving liver transplant, the album clearly showed Young's creative state was head and shoulders above the others. As with his career's other dark periods, Young returned to solo acoustic performing as a salvation. His 1989 tour was once again not so much a reclamation of his past, as another sign pointing toward the future. This was the summer immediately following the Tiananmen Square massacre, not to mention the twentieth anniversary of the Woodstock festival and the height of nostalgia for that event's trappings. For someone like Young it was not a time for quaint musical self-indulgence. He rose to the challenge as if it had been planned all along.

Audiences did get their fair share of what they wanted to hear, but only after Young had said what he came to say. Like "Tonight's The Night," "Hey, Hey, My, My," and "This Note's For You," Young knew from the outset that "Rockin' In The Free World" was a song that summed up his current state of mind better than an entire album possibly could. Subsequently, he would play it two, often three times throughout the show, each time driving its message home harder until the entire audience could no longer resist its call to arms. In some ways it was an act of hubris, considering his critical standing at the time, but by the end of the summer there were rumblings that a full-blown return to loud rock and roll was in the offing when the *El Dorado* EP snuck out inexplicably only in Japan and Australia.

The rebirth was officially heralded in September when the full album, *Freedom*, was released and Young chose *Saturday Night Live* as its launch pad. Those who had seen him re-energized that summer expected big things for this major television appearance, but hardly anyone expected what ultimately played out. Accompanied by Crazy Horse guitarist Frank Sampedro and Keith Richards's rhythm section Steve Jordan and Charley Drayton, Young appeared in a leather jacket and his old trademark patched jeans with the Toronto Maple Leafs logo prominently sewn on the posterior. The opening metallic crunch of "Rockin' In The Free World" immediately signified Young's

Neil Young at Exhibition Stadium in Toronto, 1993
(Photo by David Leyes)

return from the genre wilderness to a place of pure abandon that he had
not reached even during his best moments with Crazy Horse in the 1970s.
Possibly because it wasn't quite Crazy Horse, the performance barely held
together; the unfamiliar rhythm section pushed Young harder and faster,
but he managed to hold on even when the cameras sometimes couldn't.
The sheer thrill of the moment threatened to overshadow the rest of the
show. Reportedly, Young soundchecked the band with a brand new song
called "Fuckin' Up," then trashed his dressing room to get in the proper

frame of mind. By the time of his second segment, a run-through of "Needle & The Damage Done" straight into *Freedom*'s anti-drug plea "No More," there was no need to carry the point further. As he stood scarecrow-like for the show's sign-off, Neil Young had a lot to smile about. In a few glorious minutes he had been welcomed back into the popular consciousness with open arms after nearly a decade of derision.

Neil Young's first half of the 1990s thus became as admirable a renaissance as any artist entering his forties could possibly expect. The impact of "Rockin' In The Free World" quickly led to several other high-profile appearances. While Young had been among the founders of Farm Aid, his 1990 set at the Indianapolis Hoosier Dome debuted yet another new form: the solo folk singer with an electric guitar and overdriven Marshall amp. The song that stood as his message that day, "Mother Earth," based on the spiritual "The Water Is Wide," never did live up to its potential to pull together these two extremes of Young's sound, but that did not stop him from trying it again later at the massive Nelson Mandela Freedom Rally at London's Wembley Stadium. It was another transfixing moment, but for some it was pure caricature. The image of Young with long, scraggy hair, flannel shirt and torn jeans ran contradictory to the image of the '60s rocker on the comeback trail. The Who, the Stones and seemingly countless others were once again filling venues, but with few exceptions — notably Bob Dylan and The Grateful Dead — the events were more often obscured by the audience's expectation to relive an artist's classic youthful period since it was generally accepted that no musical progress had occurred in the meantime. Young's renaissance, on the contrary, became a celebration of not just a return to his high standard of creativity, but also a reaffirmation of the moral beliefs that fuelled his best music.

Unlike many of his contemporaries, the biggest of these was a belief in rock and roll's communal spirit to transcend the growing age gap; a gap that was first bridged, appropriately, by the 1989 album *The Bridge*, one of the first "tribute albums," and one of the most significant, since it included soon-to-be-legends like the Pixies, Dinosaur Jr., Flaming Lips, Nick Cave and Soul Asylum admirably injecting their energies into Young's songs. The gap was completely erased in late 1990 with the release of *Ragged Glory*, Young's first substantial collaboration with Crazy Horse and trusted producer David Briggs since *Rust Never Sleeps*. For most die-hards, the album was the fulfilment of the promise that Young had avoided, or forgotten for the sake of making an emotional point, since the mid-'70s. *Ragged Glory* was the musical equivalent of a victory speech addressed to all those who had doubted him. It didn't hurt either that the band suddenly rocked like never before. While the songs were a hodge-podge — "Country Home" and "White Line" dated back to the *Zuma* tour of 1976, and "Farmer John" was a mainstay of Neil Young's first band, The Squires — everything melded into Crazy Horse's new grinding attack, culminating in extended feedback codas to each song with Young wringing out every last drop of joy he obviously felt from the experience.

As an extension of the success of *The Bridge*, the alternative music press latched onto *Ragged Glory*'s deliberate rawness, putting Young in touch with a new generation of listeners. Young himself seemed to be feeding off the connection as well, and he threw down a challenge to older fans by offering Sonic Youth the opening spot on the winter 1990–91 *Ragged Glory* tour. The New York avant-garde punks, just hitting their stride after *Daydream Nation* and their major-label debut *Goo*, were harshly received in the arenas and it only seemed to strengthen Young's resolve to pummel the crowds with further sheets of feedback-laden solos. There was also the backdrop of the Gulf War to deal with, and instead of playing into the general consensus that the war was a just cause, Young instead pleaded for reason with a version of "Blowin' In The Wind" given the "Mother Earth" treatment.

The tour was preserved for posterity on the double album *Weld* and a long-form video, which successfully captured the energy of the performances by including almost as many crowd reaction shots as footage of the band on stage. More significantly, early pressings of the album contained a third disc, *Arc*, comprised entirely of the extended feedback endings that were now mandatory on each song. While some dismissed it as an example of Young's continually bemused attitude toward his audience, others heard a brilliant minimalist composition and a tip of the hat to Sonic Youth's advancement of the electric guitar. It was hardly lip service to the burgeoning underground movement, although Young remained one of the few old guard figures who seemed naturally at home with the new bands. By the end of the *Ragged Glory* tour, that album's unbridled fury had in many ways paved the way for the sea change that was shortly to follow.

Like the great genre-defining rock bands of the '60s — the Beatles, The Rolling Stones, the Jimi Hendrix Experience — the Crazy Horse dynamic (singer/guitarist backed by a three-piece rhythm section) is one of the easiest blueprints for young bands to follow. Young stated that at the outset he wanted the band to capture the interplay he'd heard between Keith Richards and Brian Jones, but what ultimately resulted was the perfect minimalistic sonic canvas upon which Young could unleash his most aggressive musical ideas. Despite the fact that Young's work with the band comprises more than half his catalogue, it is his acoustic output and scant work with Crosby, Stills & Nash that worldwide media are more likely to mention when describing his career. But with Crazy Horse, Young was more often in touch with his essence, whether it was reliving the glorious feeling of his earliest shows with The Squires, denouncing the false front of the hippie lifestyle, or reconciling his many self-doubts.

For a generation of Canadian kids who grew up hearing "Heart Of Gold" every time they turned on the radio, Neil Young was someone their parents listened to. But then maybe one day they heard "Cinnamon Girl" and something changed. When they got enough money, they might have then purchased the *Decade* compilation or *Live Rust* and begun exploring. If they wanted to play guitar, it would be Neil Young songs they would learn first for their simple yet distinctive chord patterns, and then move on to bashing out "Hey, Hey, My, My" or "Like A Hurricane" with some friends in a garage or basement. Eventually they might even hear the words with new ears and understand that the songs spoke not only of the author's life but of their own reluctance to embrace the adult world. As writer Kit Rachlis observed, "[Young's] songs, like those of all confessional songwriters, invite you into his house, but when he opens the door all you see at first is a goddamn mess."

Embracing Young as your icon meant acknowledging that your room was a mess too. Punk may have had flash and passion, but any sign of vulnerability would have undermined its message completely. The strength in Neil Young's music lay in the simple fact that he is able to express the pain without any bitterness. "Ohio" is most effective, not as a rallying cry for retaliation, but as a reluctant admission that transcends its moment. Or as a more personal example, in *Zuma's* "Pardon My Heart," the singer's aching reflection on his part in a failed relationship.

It may be short-sighted to proclaim Young's style a direct result of his Canadian upbringing, but something has to attest to his lasting influence in Canada following his escape. The imitators were always there, from Ian Thomas to Murray McLauchlan, but they were still part of the folk-rock crowd. It was not until the punks made their connection that Young's influence was finally brought back home.

In the mid-1980s, the Toronto scene was becoming fractured. Roots-rock was becoming the rage, but punk and new wave still got the most attention. Caught somewhere in between with his clutch of songs was John

Critchley, originally from North Bay, Ontario, and now plotting to form a rock band with his York University classmate Mike Robbins.

Raised in a musical family, Critchley was drawn to York through his brother Mark, an accomplished pianist who broadened his horizons in the school's music department and went on to form his own band, Itch. John found the program an easy way to get a post-secondary education, but the lessons on modern composition were soon shelved in favour of using the school's recording facilities for his own ends. "York had a big jazz department, but I was more of the anti-jazzer," Critchley admits. "I took that course mainly just to learn recording technique. It was pretty primitive — mostly four-track — although they had a more advanced studio that you got to use after you got through the introductory course, which I never did. I dropped out."

Instead, Critchley concentrated on writing songs and convinced Robbins to pick up the guitar to accompany him. The pair had become friends in 1984 after spending much of their time at the campus bar. Critchley had hoped to form a band out of more accomplished players, but once Robbins mastered the basic chords, they struck upon a competent rhythm/lead relationship. With a short-lived rhythm section, they became The Ikons by the spring of 1985, and attempted to record their slim repertoire after hours at the campus studio. Critchley recalls that even for that first session, the band was doing songs like "Come Back Lover," "The Reunion" and "Blue Smoke Curl" that would turn up on later albums. With this tape, The Ikons managed to get gigs throughout the summer, mostly at shady places like Quoc Te in Kensington Market. "There were things going on there that I didn't want to know about, but somehow I started going there to see bands," Critchley says. "There was a band called Madhouse that I really liked and a band called Living Proof that I liked a lot as well. There was a punk ethic involved, but it wasn't like brushcuts and jackboots, which wasn't really my scene at all. There was a bit of what the British press had called the Paisley Underground, which we felt a certain affinity for, although we liked a little Stooges mixed in with our paisley. We finally asked them if we could play since it seemed the only place where we could get a show."

The rhythm section didn't last much longer after that, leaving the two guitarists to struggle with a revolving door of other York musicians. One day they saw a poster stuck up on a pole for a band called Bubbling Over Jesus who were in need of a drummer as well, one whose influences should include Wire and The Fall. Critchley immediately ripped off a phone number and offered the band the opening slot for the next Ikons show. Critchley and Robbins

Neil Young

Sloan

Change of Heart

Steven Page of the Barenaked Ladies

John Kastner of the Doughboys

Jane Siberry

Spirit of the West

Bruce Cockburn and Blackie & The Rodeo Kings

Daniel Lanois

Sarah McLachlan

Dave Bidini of the Rheostatics

Greg Keelor of Blue Rodeo

Weeping Tile

Rick White of Eric's Trip

Joel Plaskett of Thrush Hermit

Hugh Dillon of the Headstones

Ron Sexsmith

Gordon Downie of the Tragically Hip

became friends with the band's singer/guitarist Jim Hughes after several more shows, eventually asking if he would join them on bass. Hughes accepted and the line-up was firmed when Grant Ethier answered a "drummer wanted" ad placed at Long & McQuade and passed an audition.

Critchley determined to get the new band on tape as quickly as possible and called upon his brother's help to get some free time at The Music Gallery, the avant-garde workshop that Mark Critchley was now part of. As with the experience of recording at York, sessions had to be done on the sly since the band's approach was contrary to the institution's mandate to create experimental sounds. Instead, The Ikons continued to bash out a growing set of anthemic pop-punk numbers like "End Of Your Chain" and "My Time." They were songs that raged but at the same time were crafted with the care of an established hitmaker, becoming staples of their live set.

The excitement that they felt with this recording extended beyond the mid-'80s Toronto underground scene. Critchley saw American independent labels as The Ikons' possible avenue out and sent tapes to anyone he thought might be interested. "We sent it to places in Canada, but there weren't too many independent labels and the major labels would have never considered what we were doing even remotely worthwhile," he says. "Later on I sent one of our first two albums to Capitol in Toronto and somebody there actually called me back. We set up a meeting and I went out there and she stood me up. I think the secretary felt bad seeing this kid waiting alone in the lobby, so she said, 'Tell me about your band.' I didn't really know what to say, so I told her what we weren't. I said, 'We're not Glass Tiger,' then I looked up and there's this giant picture of Glass Tiger and I realized they'd sold a million records for Capitol. I just said, 'All right, I'll see you later,' and got out of there."

The band received plenty of rejection letters from the States too, but when their tape landed at a Detroit label called Metro Records, employee Chris Varady found the opportunity he had been waiting for. Varady's job was to scour the piles of demo tapes in search of possible signings for Metro, but when he heard The Ikons, he was instantly convinced that this was the band that could launch the new label he had been forming with his brother Dave and friend Bob Doros. "Their sullen and brooding approach was a breath of fresh air amongst the stale stacks of musical retreads it shared the desk with. Right away I noticed something different with this band," Varady described. He called Critchley, who seemed interested in the prospect of working with a new label, and Varady got his first taste of The Ikons' live show a few weeks later at a Windsor club. After this formal introduction, The Ikons became the first band signed to Nocturnal Records and plans were drawn up to record an album.

"I guess we were fortunate," Critchley says. "Nocturnal was willing to pay for a recording and make an effort to get it out there. I was quite happy even though they were as green as we were."

The band set up at a studio that had once been a one-room schoolhouse in Ann Arbor, Michigan, just outside of Detroit and laid down *Before Our Time* during a week in the summer of 1987. Critchley was enamoured of the rustic surroundings, the fact that the studio was owned by the drummer from Brownsville Station — of "Smokin' In The Boys Room" fame — and the work of engineer Pete Bankert, who had cut his teeth with Detroit metal bands. "That helped get a certain toughness to the sound that I liked. That was normally how we did things, so we didn't have to fight with him," Critchley says.

A problem cropped up shortly before the album's release when Varady discovered an American band was already using a variation of the name The Ikons. Hoping to avoid any confusion with his label's first release, Varady urged the band to change its name. Critchley didn't have a problem with it. "It made sense because when we started The Ikons, it was a different band from what we'd become. When Jim was in Bubbling Over Jesus, for some reason they'd decided to change their name right before he joined us. They played one show as 13 Engines and then broke up. We always thought that was a cool name, so we used it."

Before Our Time was released in October 1987 in the U.S., and the newly christened 13 Engines found themselves back in Toronto in the unusual position of having their first album only available as an import. On the positive side, the situation attracted more than its fair share of media attention, but on the other hand, there were many cries of desertion and selling out to the U.S. as well. "I wasn't too bothered because I knew the album was good and the band was playing well," Critchley says. "I did get a sense of some resentment, as if we specifically bypassed Canadian labels, which is completely untrue. If Attic Records or whoever had offered us a deal in '86, we would have been happy. But nobody did, so what were we supposed to do? I think some people were a little jealous.

"That situation hasn't really changed. If you're a band in Toronto or Vancouver that's working hard and then you have a record come out in the U.S. and get some attention, it's part of the Canadian media psyche to suddenly sit up and say, 'This is now newsworthy, this could be important because it's not just a Canadian band anymore,' which I think sucks."

Toronto promoter Elliott Lefko echoes Critchley's sentiments about the band's reception once they returned home. "Critchley realized what was going on with Hüsker Dü and The Replacements and all these bands, and he wanted to be a part of that. He was doing what a lot of people failed to do, which was just go down there and knock on some doors. If you did that enough, eventually they would open."

The album got rave reviews from influential American underground music outlets such as *CMJ* and *Option*, leading 13 Engines to focus their initial attention south of the border. "We played a lot in Detroit, Minneapolis, Chicago — Columbus, Ohio was a big place for us for some reason," Critchley says. "When you'd go to these places, and any city in Canada or the U.S. really, if something was happening, it usually revolved around one person who was a true music fan. You'd go to their house and they'd have, like, 10,000 albums. It was serious for these people, and a thing grew out of their passion. It wasn't business, it was all fans."

The band's first tour of western Canada, on the way to the first Canadian Independent Music Festival in Vancouver in August 1987, had already thoroughly prepared them for taking on the U.S. "We bought an old junker van for the trip," Critchley recalls. "We had our sleeping bags and a tent, and it was pretty fun, the thrill of being on tour, but then the first drive was from Toronto to Thunder Bay and it was like, holy shit, this is a long way. We camped about halfway there. In Thunder Bay we played Crocks 'N Rolls, which every Canadian band has played probably more times than they'd care to admit, but that was the oasis between Toronto and Winnipeg. At least there was one club where there was a cool guy running it and they were happy to get bands. Our hope was to get shows on the way out when the tree planters were in town. I don't know if we ever did, because there was never a lot of people at any of them. But the ones who were there were receptive. A lot of the places were like the Royal Albert Hotel in Winnipeg, which were grubby old man bars. We'd play three nights and stay in rooms upstairs when I would have rather stayed in the tent. The younger kids wouldn't go there, but at the universities, word was getting around."

One problem that they hadn't anticipated was frequently crossing the U.S. border, which was becoming an inconvenience by the end of the year. No one in the band had enough money to get work visas, so in early 1988 — primed to record a new album — the members all agreed to move to Michigan until things got sorted out. "Nothing was too clearly thought out," Critchley admits. "We started out living at Chris Varady's house until his brother couldn't put up with us four hairy beasties hanging around all day

13 Engines, 1991: Mike Robbins, Grant Ethier,
John Critchley, Jim Hughes
(Courtesy Capitol Records)

long. Then we moved to Byram Lake where one of the guys at the label had a family cabin. We holed up there through the winter, writing songs and drinking copious amounts of Ernest & Julio — you could get a gallon jug for $3.99 — then we started recording the album."

Byram Lake Blues was also recorded in Ann Arbor, but the sessions did not go as smoothly as before. Tensions between Critchley and Varady over production threatened to drive a wedge between the band and the label. Even after recording was completed, the album's release was continually delayed over the next several months, leaving the band waiting impatiently in a rented house in Detroit for the chance to go on tour. When it was finally released in early 1989, the Engines were partially comforted by another round of rave reviews from the American press, including a review in *Rolling Stone* by David Fricke, a feat then unheard of for a Canadian band. A cheap video for "Beached" — with Critchley lip-synching to the record as it played on a turntable off-camera — even ended up on MTV accompanying an interview segment. With the buzz building, most of the band wanted to return to Canada. "It had been stressful living in Detroit," Critchley says, clearly downplaying the situation; the first day Chris Varady came to their house, his car was stolen within 20 minutes. "If the album had come out on time, it would have made more sense. The last show of that tour was a big show-case thing in New York, like the CMJ festival or something, and right after I was saying, 'Okay, we have to go back to Toronto now.' When we crossed the border and got CBC on the radio, I felt like, yaaa! That was about the only time in my life when I felt like that."

Their time at home would be short-lived. In March 1990, 13 Engines played at the nascent South By Southwest music festival in Austin, Texas with the backing of Minneapolis impresario Peter Jesperson. After beginning with the record store Oar Folkjokeopus, Jesperson started the Twin/Tone label to release records by local bands, eventually stumbling upon The Replacements in the early '80s. Recognizing their unpolished greatness, he valiantly attempted to help them achieve it, although by 1990, the effort had left most parties involved physical and emotional wrecks. Jesperson had known 13 Engines from their trips to Minneapolis, where he had let them sleep on his floor, and now saw them as a saner chance to get back into the music busi-ness. He became their manager and followed up on the interest generated in Austin by shopping them around L.A. The label with the strongest bid was Capitol — an amazing coincidence considering Critchley's earlier Glass Tiger incident. However, contractual problems arose over an industry stipulation that a Canadian band must be signed out of Toronto for worldwide distrib-ution. Capitol/EMI Canada was thus put in the uncomfortable position of re-evaluating 13 Engines at the suggestion of their parent office.

While this time they were immediately willing to do a deal, Critchley was obviously unimpressed by the abrupt about-face. "We were starting to feel comfortable with the people in L.A., then all of a sudden we had to deal with these people in Toronto and it was like, 'Who were they, why now?' It took a long time to do that record deal, and in the meantime the head of A&R we were dealing with in L.A. got fired. That put a big wrench into things. We ended up signing to a new subsidiary of EMI called SBK in the States, and then with Capitol in Canada."

Critchley admits in hindsight that their U.S. arrangement was an unusual one, as SBK was establishing itself with vacuous pop merchants such as Vanilla Ice and Wilson Phillips, yet the Engines were still given a degree of freedom when it came time to make their major-label debut. Critchley felt confident with his own skills as a producer but bowed to the label's wish that someone with a track record head the project. The band was given the opportunity to make its own suggestions and submitted a list of their favourite albums. Near the top was Neil Young's *Zuma*. To their amazement, the label had promptly contacted producer David Briggs and shortly thereafter, the architect of the

Crazy Horse sound was on a plane to Toronto to see the Engines.

"He was quite a character," Critchley says of Briggs. "By this time he was probably in his late forties, with long hair and a beard and aviator sunglasses on all the time; the dark side of the hippie dream. He wasn't what you'd call a mellow guy, with his 22-year-old German wife. They came up and saw our show and we ended up going to the Beverley Tavern afterward and it became quite a partying affair; Briggs was really carrying on. The next night we went out to see some band at RPM, and afterward we all went back to the hotel where he and his wife were staying. I'd heard he had pissed off someone in our group, and the night ended with him at his hotel door and me by the stairs with Jim in between us, trying to push David into his room and me down the stairs because we wanted to fight each other or something. Somehow out of that we decided to make a record together."

The process then sped up as Briggs decided on a studio in L.A. while getting the band started on pre-production. When the question arose of where to rehearse, Briggs suggested Neil Young's ranch near Santa Cruz where work on *Ragged Glory* had just been completed. They proceeded to set up shop for 10 days, commuting every morning from their San Francisco hotel. Briggs put the band through its paces during that time, banging rough rockers like "Big Surprise," "Another Toss Of The Coin" and the anthemic "You're Nothing If You're Not Strong" into shape. The scene then shifted to L.A. where recording commenced at Sound City, one of the hubs of the L.A. scene in the 1970s where artists like Tom Petty and Pat Benatar could often be found. Briggs lovingly referred to it as "the Spruce Goose," a big old airplane that was hard to get off the ground, but once it was in the air it soared majestically. Following the Engines' sessions, a dishevelled Seattle trio called Nirvana was booked to do their first album for the David Geffen Company.

If Critchley hadn't recognized who was in charge up to this point, he discovered it at the recording sessions. "David Briggs was very passionate," Critchley says. "You never got the feeling he was punching the clock, but there was definitely a feeling that the power situation was a little skewed, which is always there when you're a young band working with someone you consider a legend. But David Briggs was admittedly a loose cannon too. He had an us-against-them attitude, meaning the band and him against the record company. We hadn't been exposed to that way of thinking before; he despised anybody who worked for a record label before he even met them. He just assumed they were bad people."

When mixing sessions followed at Indigo Ranch in Malibu, an A&R rep from Toronto came down to check on the album's progress. After he heard a song Briggs had just finished, he casually asked to hear it again with the vocals raised two decibels. Members of the Engines slowly began exiting the booth, sensing the producer's volcanic temper rising. Critchley describes, "We could hear him from the other room screaming at this guy: 'I do one mix, and it's the right mix! I don't do no two d.b. up or down!' A half-hour later, the A&R guy came out looking at his shoes."

However, Critchley is quick to add that Briggs's attitude toward the band was hardly as tyrannical. "I learned a lot of good things from him. He was a smart man and he did things his own way through his life. I was talking to him late one night after recording and he started telling me that through his life he knew so many people who were now dead, or in his mind didn't stay the course of what they all originally set out to do. I learned a lot from him in that regard, but he had his own problems with substance abuse and other things."

A Blur To Me Now was released in spring 1991, with most of the press attention focusing on the Neil Young connection, both in the album's unadorned production and the obvious influence on the Engines' sound. Critchley was hardly put off by it at first, since he felt that fans of the band could easily distinguish his more ambiguous songwriting style, not to mention his distinct, deadpan voice. Yet the Engines' inherent full-throttle guitar attack and Critchley's fractured solos plainly echoed the Crazy Horse wall of sound, leading some to think they were doing more than simply emulating their primary influence. "That whole thing overwhelmed that album, and we were partly to blame. I really wanted to get away from any Neil Young comparisons right away," Critchley says. "The difference with us was we had an art school background — we felt that if a song might be lyrically opaque, that it wasn't a drawback; in fact, it might have been something to strive for occasionally. I definitely was a big Neil Young fan growing up, but the whole media angle blew it way out of proportion."

On the other hand, this perception had developed through previous comments Critchley had made such as, "We're not a noise band or anything, we're more like Crazy Horse," and, "We wanted a very plain sound because we want people to listen to the music and not the production. Frankly, we hate the way most records are produced." These statements drove a wedge between them and Toronto critics especially, who either supported this attitude, or dismissed it outright. Upon the release of *A Blur To Me Now*, one decried, "Does Toronto really need another quasi-'60s, folksy, hard-rocking garage band?" But soon these voices would be in the minority.

With record company support in Canada for the first time, the Engines set out across the country, following on the heels of steady video play for "King Of Saturday Night," a rather innocuous tale (by the band's standards) of a barroom rounder they would encounter at a typical club gig. The song's popularity became another unexpected burden to Critchley, who tried to avoid playing it as much as possible in the coming years. Despite establishing themselves as a powerful live act in Canada and continuing their inroads in the U.S. — which included a 40-date tour with Cleveland punk godfathers Pere Ubu — by the end of 1991, the Engines were facing the loss of their manager and their U.S. record deal. Peter Jesperson had already shown signs of cracking under the stress of recording *A Blur To Me Now*, prompting him to make another exit from the music business, while SBK Records ultimately became a victim of EMI cost-cutting.

"To their credit, EMI Canada stepped in and picked up the slack after SBK dissolved," Critchley says. "We had a new manager, Danny Goldberg at Gold Mountain, and right around the time we started the next album, he went to work at Atlantic Records, so through him we got a new deal with Atlantic in the States, but that didn't last too long either. All these changes were bringing new stress. To me the whole thing was to learn from the mistakes that surrounded *A Blur To Me Now*. The next record wouldn't be with some big-name producer and recorded at some really expensive place. I basically told EMI that either I'm producing this record or the band is toast."

In spring 1992, the label put the Engines together with engineer Glen Robinson who took them to Le Studio in Morin Heights, Quebec, best known as being the site of Rush's best recorded work. Robinson was also well equipped at capturing heavy sounds, having previously worked with Voivod and others in the Montreal hardcore scene. He and Critchley opted for the opposite approach to *A Blur To Me Now*, laying each instrument on separately, and building up a crushing, multi-layered guitar sound that nevertheless still complemented the band's melodic thrust. From the outset, the *Perpetual Motion Machine* sessions seemed the Engines' defiant response to the chaos surrounding them. "That was a fun time, we were all really focused," Critchley says. "In a way I wanted to redeem myself from what had gone on with the last album."

When *Perpetual Motion Machine* was released in 1993, the band was praised for showing precisely the improvements Critchley hoped to get across. The sound was extremely confident, with few overt Neil Young-isms; any that remained being long-absorbed into the overall effect. The lyrics reflected the aggressiveness in the music; the opening "Bred In The Bone" intones a theme of addiction and obsession that is carried through in "More,"

"Smoke And Ashes" and "The Estrangement." Even on the delicate "Moment Of Clarity," the setting is a Toronto graveyard in autumn. Only with the final song, "Lift You Up," does Critchley show a sign of hope and in that one instance brings the album perfectly full circle.

The Engines rode the wave of adulation back to extensive North American touring. Yet the collapse of their deal with Atlantic in the U.S., shortly after the release of the album, let a lot of wind out of the sails. "We were always in a position of being a critical success that never translated to a commercial success," Critchley says. "When the Atlantic thing fell through, it left us feeling like we couldn't make people buy our records. All we could do was keep making good records and playing good shows. We felt like we had done that, and that made us feel good, especially in Canada where it sold pretty well."

Perpetual Motion Machine was left stalled south of the border, but in Canada the work had paid off, making it the biggest commercial success the band had encountered to that point. As with many "critic's favourites," this seemingly never-ending grind on the club circuit eventually caught up with the band. In 1994, they set to work on a new album in Toronto. When released the following year in Canada, *Conquistador* lacked the overpowering energy of *Perpetual Motion Machine*, showing the Engines instead consolidating their strengths, and even softening the edges a little on songs like the country-flavoured "Tailpipe Blues." By comparison, the songs sounded like a band with little left to fight for. "The band had been together a long time at that point," Critchley says. "Even though I felt like we were successful, not selling a lot in the States after getting great reviews certainly was disappointing. When we started working on *Conquistador* there was some personal stress within the band, and the label started reverting back to their earlier ways, wanting to get some big name producer to come in, so there was stress in that respect too in making that album. It's a really good album and I stand behind it, but that was the beginning of the end of the band, really."

The Engines laboured on through another round of cross-Canada tours, but by the beginning of 1996, both Grant Ethier and Mike Robbins were out of the band. Ethier returned to his hometown of Kingston to work with younger bands at his studio The Funhouse, while Robbins set aside music for a career in the technology field. Critchley and Hughes attempted to continue with replacements and a new deal with Nettwerk Records, but the spirit of the band was irreparably damaged. The name 13 Engines was quietly put to rest that year, with Critchley eventually reemerging three years later as an independent artist displaying much of the same youthful vigour he had always had. His work now stood out among other albums that, on the surface, had lost touch with honest, straightforward rock and roll. It's not surprising that one song on his first solo album *Crooked Mile*, "For Worse Or Better," was one of the first that The Ikons ever recorded, and still sounded unmistakably fresh.

"I think of my songs as a floating body of material," Critchley says. "It's always good to keep writing new stuff and moving forward toward wherever you're going, but because you don't record a song when you write it doesn't mean it's not a good song and it won't sound good on another record. To me that's the definition of timelessness."

With Neil Young's restoration completely acknowledged by the early 1990s, it became easier to pick out the influence in Canadian artists, whether it was conscious or not. Once again, as a sonic touchstone it was one of the most accessible, and for some intrinsic aesthetic reason, the easiest avenue for many to inject their own artistic personality. If a band like 54·40 originally patterned themselves after British post-punk minimalists, the desire to embrace songcraft inevitably led them closer to home.

Significantly, the Vancouver quartet's name came from nineteenth-century American political sloganeering, led by President James Polk, aimed at pushing the northern U.S. border through British Columbia into what is now Alaska. About a hundred years later, Neil Osborne turned the message "54·40 or Fight" in the opposite direction. The genesis of the band began when guitarist/vocalist Osborne met bassist Brad Merritt at South Delta High in the Vancouver suburb Tsawassen in 1978. It was the height of the first VanPunk wave and the pair would spend their weekends at shows and haunting record stores. Osborne's immediate post-secondary plans took him to Boston to study at the Berklee College of Music, hardly the place for an aspiring punk. After some persuasion, Merritt convinced Osborne to come home and form a band with a drummer he had met, Ian Franey.

By the end of 1981, 54·40 had played its first gig, opening for DOA at Vancouver's Smilin' Buddha Cabaret, and made its first recordings for the Mo-Da-Mu label, a non-profit collective that helped bands set up shows and record themselves. These initial songs turned up on the compilation *Things Are Still Coming Ashore*, and in the following year, six more appeared on the band's own EP, *Selection*. "One of the founders of Mo-Da-Mu was Allen Moy, who became our manager," Osborne says. "There were other bands involved like Tin Twists, Animal Slaves, Jungle Run and Popular Front. It started out on the main floor of somebody's house, and that became the address and phone number. We just hung out there — we were always between jobs and collecting welfare or unemployment insurance — drinking coffee mostly, and staying up all night worrying whether we'd get anywhere."

With mainstream ambitions beckoning, 54·40 saw their viability as a working band becoming at odds with their associates in the collective. "One day we said we wanted to make T-shirts [to promote the band] and some of the people in the other bands thought that was a total sell-out," Osborne says. "We held off for a while, and couldn't help ourselves. We couldn't play bars [according to the collective], we had to play in halls. Radio and record companies were considered complete evil."

Merritt adds, "There was a total separation between mainstream and underground music. We were underground only because we were writing our own songs and there were influences from Britain there. There was no club that would hire bands like us; if there were, we could only play on 'New Wave Monday' or 'Punk Rock Wednesday.' We usually resorted to renting halls ourselves and paying for everything."

Although 54·40 were lumped into Vancouver's post-punk scene, their work ethic ultimately set them apart from most other bands that got mentioned in the same breath. They were one of the first bands of the era to create ties with Seattle — aside from bringing up producer Mark H. Smith for *Selection* — playing there more regularly than in their hometown. Yet shortly after *Selection*'s release in June 1982, Franey left the band, giving Osborne and Merritt an opportunity to expand the sound. "We'd just had our record release show where we got two guys to be the horn section that we had on *Selection*," Merritt explains. "One of the guys was Phil Comparelli, and when we heard what a great guitar player he was too, we automatically asked him to join because Neil had wanted it to be a four-piece all along. We knew Darryl Neudorf of the band Empty Set from Kelowna, so I went up there and brought him back and he lived with me for a couple years. He was just a kid, 17 or 18 years old."

With its new line-up in place, the band set out to tour in support of their EP, following the now well-established west coast route instead of the potentially arduous trek east where no one had heard of them. "The whole American thing was more open," Merritt says. "We opened for PiL in San Francisco at The Galleria, then in December we did a big headlining show there at the I-Beam, which was the centre of the punk/new wave scene in San Francisco. We were making quite a name for ourselves; the EPs all sold out, so by 1983 we wanted to make another one and started writing songs with Phil and Darryl. It was obvious that things were moving in a different direction."

54·40 recorded *Set The Fire* in late 1983 with Allen Moy producing. The sound still reflected stinging British post-punk, but the band's image now plainly revealed their homeland: publicity pictures showed four refugees from a logging camp or Depression-era vagabonds. Only as the band continued to tour at a furious pace did the actual essence of folk music slowly begin to seep into their work. "We were getting flak from the Vancouver punk community constantly," Merritt says. "Some of it made sense at the time, but most of it was sniping. In a sense we were breaking ground and whenever you get yourself in that position you are always opening yourself to criticism."

After hearing *Set The Fire* Keith Porteous, a friend of Allen Moy's from the band Popular Front, convinced Moy that the two should commit to managing 54·40 full-time and immediately booked more tours through to California. With pressings of the album selling out once again, most major labels from L.A. had checked out the band by this time. Osborne says that the underground stigma was still in full effect even though he also admits the money was sorely needed. "Sub Pop put one of our songs on a compilation called *The Sound of Truth*, and we started to get calls from labels like CBS. But everyone was wary then of signing to a major because you knew you'd immediately be branded a sell-out. The first band from the States to sign was The Dream Syndicate, and that's exactly what happened to them. Then X signed to Elektra, R.E.M. signed to IRS and Hüsker Dü signed to Warner, mostly because all of them were at the end of their ropes. When we realized that, it made it easier to deal with because we were at the end of ours too."

Osborne went back to his job in a print shop, while Merritt worked at an aluminum recycling factory, saving money to make the next record. The sessions unfolded slowly throughout 1985, as the band were only able to afford brief stints at Vancouver's Mushroom Sound with engineer Dave Ogilvie. The prolonged time in the studio and away from the road began frustrating Neudorf, whose own artistic side was beginning to blossom. Toward the end of the sessions, he informed the band he was leaving, forcing the others to scramble to find a replacement. They approached Matt Johnson, drummer for Vancouver new wave band French Letters. While they didn't particularly like his band, they knew Johnson was a great drummer and were relieved when he agreed to join and finish the record. "Many, many times in our career, things have come to a complete dead stop — totally out of money and options," Osborne says. "We were at one of those points doing that record and tensions with Darryl started to mount. But it was becoming obvious that he was on a different wavelength. He was much more interested in the technological side of things, and he's gone on to show he's a very creative guy in those areas.

"After we finished the record, we wanted to go back down to the States because the record companies were still interested, but we didn't have enough money to press the albums. We were thinking about going to our parents for loans to press 2,000 singles for 'I Go Blind.'"

A deal with Capitol in the U.S. almost came through, but the label's Canadian office nixed it, claiming — as in a similar case with 13 Engines — that it was their prerogative to sign a Canadian band, not the American head office's. By 1986, 54·40 had found enough money to put out the self-titled album, also known as *The Green Album* because of its cover, and the band was back in the U.S. shopping themselves around. They ultimately found a home at Warner/Reprise, which agreed to remix and re-release the album, although it was a deal that initially did not give the band everything they wanted. "When that record was eventually picked up by Warner, it was almost as a mercy mission," Osborne says. "A junior A&R guy made the deal, had it remixed and threw it out there without really putting anything into it. We played the I-Beam again right after that and some guy said to me, 'Why did you guys sell out?' and I was like, 'What?' He had no idea that if we hadn't signed, we basically would have had to break up. The label didn't even give us any money, they just released the record which created this perception that we could keep going."

However, the album had a much more profound effect when it was released in Canada. The lead-off single, "Baby Ran," was an instant classic; anthemic power chords and chorus, cut through with some brilliant lead guitar work by Comparelli. The song would prove to be 54·40's future touchstone in its deceptive simplicity, although their reputation at home would be solidified with the next single, "I Go Blind," an almost tailor-made campfire singalong whose seeming naïveté transcended any traces of punk rock the band might have still shown. "Around that time I realized that you can't be a Gloomy Gus forever. Let's face it, there are other things going on," Osborne says. "I think we got back to that childhood aspect of music — great pop songs, folk-based songs — as opposed to the teenage part. 'I Go Blind' is a folk-based song of the sort that I pictured Neil Young would write. In order to grow you have to let other influences through. Initially it was stuff like The Jam and Joy Division, but as we got more confident, we started to lean back on our roots. Neil Young albums are like God albums to me."

With a national profile for the first time, 54·40 quickly went back into the studio to record an album with the now-permanent line-up. With new-found financial contributions from Warner, the band set up to record *Show Me* in L.A. with Dave Jerden, who had re-mixed *The Green Album*. While they felt encouraged for the first time in making a "real" album, the harsh realities of the situation soon cast a shadow over the project. "Jerden and the A&R guy somehow decided without us that it would be good if we used sequencers and processors," Osborne explains. "We hopped in the van and drove down to L.A. where they showed us our condo, then the next day we're at the studio and it was, 'Meet so-and-so, your computer program-mers.' 'Pardon me?' I was freaking out. I called Dave Jerden and said 'I don't like this,' and he said, 'Fine.' The next day he was all mopey and the record company people were all mopey because I took away his vision, which I was never told about. I felt like a big heel so I said, 'Okay, let's do it,' which was a big mistake. Even though there are some great songs on that record, they're spoiled by the production. It sounds so out of date, it's not funny."

As the band struggled through the sessions, expenses soon became a major issue as well. "It was ridiculous. We paid Dave Jerden $40,000 U.S. and Warner had us on 12 bucks a day when we went on tour afterward," Osborne continues. "It was do-able, but we were eating McDonald's and burritos every day. If you wanted to see a movie before a gig, you didn't eat. That whole record ended up costing $250,000 U.S., which we had to pay back. We would have meetings where Keith [Porteous] would say that if the label is spending all this money on us then they'll damn well make sure records get sold, and of course that didn't happen. We were confident in selling two-or-three thousand copies ourselves, but at that level we had to give up control and that was a huge adjustment."

Show Me made up some ground in Canada where it carried on the momentum of its predecessor with two more major radio and video hits: "One Day In Your Life" and "One Gun." "'One Day In Your Life' is about putting your life in perspective," Osborne explains. "Rather than getting down, there's so much that you can convert into *up*. One time we were playing at the Anti Club in L.A. and this old street person, a black man with a friendly smile and a sax, started playing along with us. Then these two people in front of me, who were really digging the song, laid down a sticker at my feet that said, 'I have AIDS.' It really freaked me out — then I realized what I was singing."

"One Gun" displays even more of Osborne's latent hippie folksinger ten-dencies as the song unfolds like a mantra based on the "one gun added on to the one gun" refrain echoed in Cold War peace demonstrations. By the

54·40: Neil Osborne fights for love in Halifax
(Photo by Eric B. Brown)

end it builds to an unforgettably euphoric chorus that became the centre-piece of their live show. "It's my version of a Christmas song," Osborne says. "I wrote it when my wife was down in South America where the Reagan administration was sending aid in the form of guns and causing all this repression. It was around Christmas and it made me sad thinking that if there weren't any guns, there wouldn't be any Disappeared People and all that other stuff there." The song's success as a single left little doubt that 54·40 was now an established national attraction and their touring patterns quickly shifted to the eastern half of the continent. The schedule stretched into most of 1988 in an effort to recoup some of the expenses, but by the end of the year the band was back in the studio, this time in the safer con-fines of Mushroom Studios with Dave Ogilvie.

Prior to those sessions, the members agreed that the stress of playing the major-label game for the past year was affecting their creative process. As a remedy, they regularly convened at a house rented by Osborne's brother Dave (also the band's hired keyboardist) to practise with a clean slate. The new songs, which saw the light the following year on *Fight For Love*, reflected the re-emphasis on a live sound and group interplay. Subsequently, the album was 54·40's most cohesive rock record to that point, although in this context, some of Osborne's simple sentiments were drawing unfavourable comparisons to U2's recent output. Osborne maintains he has never been a politically motivated writer. "A lot of *Fight For Love* was inspired by the birth of my first kid," he says. "'One Gun' is a love song too. That's always been the juxtaposition I like: how a person can say they believe in these virtues at the same time as all this crap is going on in the world. In the '80s, the enemy was a little more clear — the U.S. government in Central America and things like that — but nowadays the enemy is the multina-tional agenda, and we're so behind in that war that it's occupational. The attitudes, the bands, the priorities, the culture, everything has totally changed. We've lost, but you still have to live."

Despite the band's personal satisfaction with *Fight For Love*, no single from the album made as much of an impact as previous releases, which finally brought their differences with Warner to a head as they set out on tour. "They only gave us some of the money they promised," Osborne says. "We were in L.A. and we had to meet up with Bob Mould in Richmond, Virginia, but our money ran out after three or four weeks. By this time the second single had died, so Keith stormed into [Warner head] Lenny Waronker's office and gave him a speech basically standing on his desk. He said, 'Look, these guys are the only ones out there working on this record, why aren't you? Do this with dignity. If this is it with them, fine, but let them finish the tour they started.' That was essentially it with Warner; they gave us the money to finish the tour, and it was pretty much understood at that point that that was going to be it. Admittedly, I would have dropped us too because we got put in a position where we had to spend way too much money to make records and we were in way over our head. That's the thing about record companies: when you're signed they tell you it's all about people and relationships, but it's decided by accountants."

As the '90s began, 54·40 found themselves in another state of limbo. Fortunately, their status as a gold-selling band in Canada didn't keep prospective new labels away very long. As their old label released a kiss-off best-of compilation, *Sweeter Things*, the band signed a longterm deal with Sony and started work on a new record. Eager to take advantage of the fresh start, the band tried the L.A. vibe again, this time with producer Don Smith, best known to Canadians for getting the no-frills rock sound on The Tragically Hip's first two albums. The choice reflected the band's new material, much of which was composed spontaneously on the previous tour. "Our philosophy is that anything you do spontaneously tells you something about the environment. It's an accurate reading, and that's all we're really after — to make something accurate," Osborne says. "You're on stage and it sounds so live, so you think, let's capitalize on the feel of that. At shows you see people going nuts and it's beautiful therapy."

The band had already been encouraged to pursue a more flat-out rock direction by the response that songs like "Nice To Luv You" had been getting in concert and when *Dear Dear* was released in 1992, it was evident that many others appreciated the change as well. The album would be 54·40's first to be certified platinum, adding further confirmation that the band was finally reaching its full commercial potential. While some of the appeal lay in the hard-hitting sound, the release of "She-La" as a single showed that Osborne's priorities still lay in more controversial areas. The song is an indictment of domestic violence, influenced by the work of Osborne's wife in the social services field.

Yet as the '90s unfolded, the casual fan's perception of 54·40 quietly shifted from an issue-oriented band to a mainstream rock band as their relationship with Sony resulted in a string of tepid but consistent-selling albums. *Dear Dear* was followed-up in 1995 with *Smilin' Buddha Cabaret*, a tip of the hat to their origins and a further extension of their new spontaneous recording process. Once again they chose to record with Don Smith, but the final results disappointed the band so much that nine of the album's

14 tracks were original demo versions of the songs. "*Dear Dear* was a record we had to make — we were sort of in a pop/rock vein," Merritt said at the time of *Smilin' Buddha*'s release. "We spent a long time on arrangements, on building songs up and tearing them down. This time around we said, 'Okay, if a song is not ready in 25 minutes, we won't do it.' Nothing was precious, everything was sort of under-realized and raw, with a spirit of fun."

As a capper to this seeming return to their roots, 54·40 hauled around the authentic Smilin' Buddha Cabaret sign as a backdrop on their extensive tour for the album, which culminated in an opening slot with Midnight Oil in their native Australia. Their sales figures also finally allowed the members to leave the world of day labour behind for good. If there were any doubts that this was the right decision, they were eliminated when multi-million sellers Hootie & The Blowfish faithfully covered "I Go Blind" in 1996. "I quit my job probably six to eight months after *Dear Dear* was released," Osborne says. "Things were too busy and there was actually real money to be made. We all had worked day jobs for 10 years. But I still remember sitting in someone's office at Warner when our mix of 'I Go Blind' was done. I was so excited and the guy took it right to the president's office and I could hear it blaring out from behind the door. It sounded so good, but they never released it as a single in the States. When the Hootie version came out, it was a vindication. It's a song that's always been a good song. It's unfortunate that a lot of people didn't think it was cool. Certainly, if we didn't get remuneration, I wouldn't have allowed it, but imitation is one of the sincerest forms of flattery."

The coming years would see 54·40 continue to prosper and tweak their sound; 1998's *Since When* presented an especially refreshing mix of country and classic R&B influences. Most importantly, the band's perseverance and ever-growing catalogue of memorable songs had earned them a place as one of the most respected bands in Canada. In a moment of reflection, Osborne summed up the band's legacy by saying, "We have a Canadian rock band sound; I don't know what it is, but it's there. It still happens where a hockey player type of guy will come up to us after a show and say, 'I'd sort of heard of you, but I didn't know those were your songs man!' I'd rather they remember the songs than us as individuals."

As a landmark of musical timing, Neil Young's *Ragged Glory* not only immediately foreshadowed the Seattle renaissance and a return to raw, guitar-based rock, but in a smaller way its acceptance by a new generation also marked a swing back to musical honesty in general. If the album focused anything in the alt-rock community, it was the viability of being a punk with a heart on your sleeve. On songs like "Love To Burn" and "Love And Only Love," Neil Young sang to the new generation with the wisdom of an elder, that things would inevitably turn out all right, but most still had to find out the hard way.

At that time a new generation afflicted with suburban ennui was given vindication through *Generation X*, the first novel by Vancouver native Douglas Coupland, which firmly established that a social and cultural inferiority complex was typical of those under 30. As the

Hayden listens to
Neil Young's advice at
Young's ranch, 1997
(Photo by William Tenn)

book's core ideas were soon blown out of proportion by media over-analysis, the task for young songwriters became to cut through the hype and further illuminate the bleakness that marked the early '90s for so many faced with a future of under-employment and unfulfilling relationships.

Hayden Desser wrote songs precisely about this bleakness, spurred by the sterile surroundings of his parents' house in the Toronto suburb of Thornhill. As buzzsaw guitars raged around him, Hayden — as he preferred to be called — emerged unassumingly with just an acoustic guitar in 1994 on a self-made cassette, *In September*. Although the novelty of his unpretentious demeanour and quietly explosive performances won him acceptance in the Toronto indie rock community, the clarity of his message reached much further. In 1995, Hayden released his first full-length album, *Everything I Long For*, through the emerging independent label Sonic Unyon. Once again the album was largely comprised of unadorned bedroom recordings. As a snapshot of post-teenage depression, it made an immediate impact. The opening track, "Bad As They Seem," set the tone, stripping away the façade that most things promised in life are unattainable in their ideal form. It resulted in the question, are these things worth working for at all? The song's video was equally unnerving as it showed Hayden in his assumed suburban setting, fantasizing about a young neighbourhood girl and her mother, then performing to a rabid audience in his bedroom.

From there, the album moved deeper into childhood nightmares ("Skates," "Bunkbed"), to the banality of day jobs and suburban life, as the singer alternated between hushed tones and near-unhinged rage, depending on the song's message. "The reason why I started singing like that was because of the way I started playing live," Hayden says. "I wasn't in folk clubs, I was in rock clubs opening for some pretty heavy bands, so that dynamic way of playing — getting soft then getting heavy, and actually screaming like that — was my way of getting people to listen. A lot of the songs where I'm yelling, I'm not really saying, 'Argh! My life sucks!' I do understand why it sounds aggressive but what I was actually singing wasn't so aggressive.

"All through school, I never liked being put into groups. Sharing ideas was fine, but getting to that point where everyone is happy is just so delicate and hard sometimes. Being in a band is like that every second you're together, so I guess I wasn't ready to do that when I started. It seemed so natural just to play my songs by myself, so suddenly I was a solo artist."

As one of the definitive documents of its time, *Everything I Long For* deservedly sold major-label-like numbers in Canada, which soon translated to worldwide distribution for the album after American critics discovered its fractured beauty as well. Hayden was now forced out of his perceived comfort in southern Ontario into the harsh world of international promotion. When commenting on his first trip to Japan, he says, "On the CD, the lyrics are translated into Japanese with liner notes where the writer adds his interpretations of the songs. They'll have 40 different meanings for each song, so the journalists would ask me these intense questions. I'd be sitting there going, 'Oh my god, what is going on?'"

Throughout the heavy schedule that ensued, Hayden kept his perspective, mostly by maintaining a solid base at home in Thornhill and remaining with Sonic Unyon as his Canadian label, where he released a follow-up EP, *Moving Careful*, in 1996. The songs retained his strict sense of intimacy and knack at capturing emotional details in ordinary scenes. "When people ask me about living in Canada or living in the suburbs and how it affected my music, I usually answer how it didn't affect my music," he says. "If I grew up in Ireland or the Middle East or L.A., there would be things about my environment that I would sing about, because my life would be in danger or people wouldn't be getting along around me. But living in Thornhill, I was never really in danger. There was nothing freaky going on. I sang about things that affected my life; they aren't necessarily earth-shattering, but to me — because that's what I was going through — they're just as important."

Although many who embraced *Everything I Long For* did so because of

Hayden
(Photo by Jordan Mitchell)

the frustrations expressed in the songs, Hayden admits that the album probably would not have been made if he did not see a way out of the malaise. "I remember in first-year university at Ryerson, all these knobs in residence, living on their own for the first time. They'd get drunk every night and think they were so hip and such exciting people because they weren't living at home. That got annoying, but maybe I was bitter because I had to take the subway home every night. Something that definitely saved me was two or three really good friends who lived in Thornhill. We'd get together a lot and hang out, play music sometimes. That made me not hate where I was. And I got along really well with my family, which helped out a lot."

As critical gushing continued into 1997, including a spot on *Spin's* list of the 40 most important new artists, the major-label bidding war began for Hayden's next album. Perhaps not surprisingly, one of the first to jump in was Neil Young, who, with manager Elliott Roberts, had just started Vapor Records. On paper it seemed a perfect cross-generational match, but after initial meetings, Hayden's team pulled out. "I met with Neil and Elliott and it definitely was like a dream, an out-of-body experience," he says. "Everything happened so fast, I didn't have time to think about the fact I was sitting there talking to Neil. Making the decision about what label to go with was a huge deal for me. There were a lot of issues at stake; it's kind of hard to talk about."

Hayden ultimately signed with Outpost/Universal which released *The Closer I Get* in 1998. Although it was a clear indicator of his maturity as a songwriter, and in many ways a better album than his debut, the production left many recalling the Cowboy Junkies' jump to the big leagues. Whereas the year before everyone was heaping praise on the primitive aspects of the music, those same people seemed to be recoiling from the fact that the artist was now in a position to make a professional recording. "I hope I've matured in five years," Hayden said at the time of the album's release. "If I haven't I'm in big trouble, I might as well end it now. But I'm still sort of like a kid."

Yet the critical backlash that followed, compounded by Outpost's dissolution the following year, seemed to hasten Hayden's retreat to the safety of Toronto.

If Hayden represented the folk singer as a reflection of this new environment, then it was no surprise that rock bands expanded this concept, just as Neil Young had done when he applied his songs to a four-piece band format. The simplicity he espoused in his creative process was tailor-made for the indie-rock movement as well, best shown through the rise of Treble Charger in 1994 from humble roots in Sault Ste. Marie, Ontario.

Originally called NC-17, but forced to change the name at the behest of an American heavy metal band, they had to hastily add "Treble Charger" to their debut album's artwork, and *NC-17* became the unexpected title. It made sense in a roundabout way, as the songs of co-lead vocalists/guitarists Greig Nori and Bill Priddle largely dealt with teenage regret, nowhere more evident than on the first single, "10th Grade Love." But it was "Red" that firmly captured the imaginations of those who at first believed the band to be another in the string of indie-rock pretenders. Over a simple, grinding chord progression, Priddle sings in a plain, high tone that immediately evokes Young, yet the song remains unmistakably locked in its time by revisiting innocent days which for many listeners were becoming as cloudy as the lyrics themselves.

These days would soon be gone forever when the band, once placed at the vanguard of the mid-'90s Canadian indie rock movement, quickly became just another radio and video commodity in the mainstream marketplace upon signing with BMG.

On the other hand, Kingston, Ontario's Weeping Tile forged an indie rock sound firmly rooted in the Canadian folk tradition. The band emerged as a loose contingent around singer/songwriter Sarah Harmer, a Burlington, Ontario native who first became recognized singing backup for Toronto roots-rock outfit The Saddletramps, and struck out on her own after moving to Kingston to attend Queen's. Weeping Tile's earliest recordings — first released on a homemade cassette in 1994 to sell at gigs, then in modified CD form a year later on *EePee* — were steeped in their surroundings. Harmer's sensitive touch on a confessional love song like "The Room With The Sir John A. View," could quickly be replaced by the accusatory tone heard on

"Westray," written in response to the chilling Nova Scotia mine disaster of the early '90s. A full-band cover of *After The Gold Rush*'s "Don't Let It Bring You Down," was a perfect fit in this mix; its coded message of hope losing all traces of cynicism in Harmer's confident interpretation.

Although Harmer initially struggled to find full-time musicians willing to constantly tour, the band won a small but loyal audience after its first cross-Canada trips opening for the Bourbon Tabernacle Choir and the Skydiggers. This quickly led to a deal with Warner in Canada and with the short-lived Atlantic Records subsidiary Tag in the U.S., whereby the band's line-up stabilized with the inclusion of lead guitarist Luther Wright, his former Kingston jam partner Cam Giroux on drums, and Harmer's sister Mary, lured away from Salt Spring Island in B.C. to play bass.

Members would continue to fluctuate, but it was this group that would create the first real backdrop for Harmer's increasingly haunting snapshots of rural Canada. A wider audience was introduced to Weeping Tile on their 1995 full-length debut *Cold Snap*, which seemed at the very least an indication that writing songs about Canada was no longer a defensive patriotic reaction to outside influences. The songs were placed within a history as old as Kingston itself, but at the same time flowed naturally as only a seamless four-piece rock band can sound. "It's not intentional patriotism," Harmer says. "It's more of a belief in the truism that you should write about the familiar."

Weeping Tile would continue to be a familiar opening act over the next year, both in Canada and the U.S., where they accompanied The Watchmen on an extended tour, but their music never seemed to get beyond the personal bond apparent when they played their own shows in small clubs across the country. Harmer herself seemed to accept that fact in refusing to change her approach on the next album, *Valentino*, released only in Canada in 1997 after Tag was shut down. "I think you have to examine the assumption that music has to be huge for the masses in the first place," she says. "Music can be regional. Small bands can entertain people within their own communities. There don't have to be supergroups, except that we're conditioned to expect them."

Unfortunately, Weeping Tile's community was not enough to sustain them in the eyes of Warner, which dropped them in 1998. The band drifted apart at that point, with Harmer moving on to a solo career. Although she has re-emerged as one of the most vital songwriters in Canada, the abrupt end of Weeping Tile was another point in the sad trend of a major label short-sightedly snuffing out one of its brightest homegrown hopes.

Of course, by 1998, the major labels were already consciously shifting their attention from volatile, independently-rooted artists, to easily marketable pop hitmakers and safe retreads of the Seattle sound. For bands like Treble Charger, the choice of sides was probably made not long after the moment Kurt Cobain pulled the trigger on himself four years earlier. When they found him, at his side was a note that ended with Neil Young's pronouncement on Elvis Presley and Johnny Rotten, "It's better to burn out than to fade away." Young never publicly commented on the quote. His response instead came several months later with *Sleeps With Angels*, a largely sombre album that echoed the elegiac *Tonight's The Night*, but with an overriding plea for sanity among the disaffected youth culture. Coming off the widespread commercial success of *Harvest Moon*, *Angels* was tough, yet necessary medicine to swallow.

By the end of 1994, Young had made the further step of consolidating with one-time Nirvana enemies Pearl Jam for the album *Mirror Ball*, which seemed to reinstill some joy to the music-making process for all involved. In the midst of this regeneration, Crazy Horse's guiding spirit, David Briggs, passed away in November, 1995. The band as a whole chose to cope by turning back the clock to the mid-'70s, playing loose, long and loud jams ostensibly for themselves; getting back in touch with the indefinable magic that Briggs always maintained was at their core. Nineteen ninety-six thus became the "Year Of The Horse" with the release of the slow-burning *Broken Arrow* and an international tour with marathon sets spanning the entire Crazy Horse catalogue. The shows also reaffirmed their place as the best live band in the world, as newcomers like Oasis were memorably taken to school when they appeared as opening acts.

Most significantly, the band did its first extensive cross-Canada tour that fall. Although Young had not been a stranger to the places he grew up in with past touring, having Crazy Horse along finally fulfilled the pact that so many Canadian musicians had made with their own careers. Young and Crazy Horse unabashedly displayed that pact on the tour without even having to acknowledge it. Only during an interview with MuchMusic did bassist Billy Talbot seem to grasp what many had accepted for years: "I never realized until now that we were a Canadian band."

Folk You:
Roots Revisited

Guitarist Steve Koch could be a poster boy for the chronology of Canadian punks getting turned on to roots music. Raised in Calgary, he had a fascination with punk-rock culture before he ever heard the music. His curiosity took him to London, England and then Toronto in the late '70s. After stints in seminal Toronto punk bands the Viletones and the Demics, Koch hooked up with pioneering Queen Street neo-traditionalist Handsome Ned, and today plays with other ex-punks in the John Borra Band. For him, the leap from one to the other wasn't that big.

"Everyone who was interested in punk rock was basically a musicologist," says Koch. "Their whole lives were music, and they were open to a lot of new sounds. There were some hardcore guys who went the other way and got into the thrash scene, which to me was a dead end." Today, connections between punk and country seem natural, but it was still cause for discussion right up until the late '90s. When Neko Case, of the Vancouver trio Maow, put out the Loretta Lynn homage album *The Virginian* in 1997, most of the media discussion focused on the novelty of a punk drummer transforming into a convincing country belter.

Margo Timmins of the Cowboy Junkies discovered blues in her early twenties. "There's a lot of bands that came out of the punk era whose roots are pretty much the same," she says. "They were teenagers in the late '70s and were very influenced by that scene, and yet have gone on to do different stuff, and there's that common feeling to them. That feeling — to me, what the punk era taught us — is to do whatever feels good, as opposed to trying to get on a label and trying to become the next Rolling Stones. As a teenager, you're into big rock-'n'-roll or whatever the big sound is at that time. Then punk came along, and that was your rebellious stage if you were 17 or 18, a 'bug your parents' kind of thing. But after that, you can't really go back to the big mega-bands, and punk was a roots thing — it was an expression of where you live and what you're feeling. A lot of people found country from that, for some strange reason. Or blues, or jazz, a more down-to-earth kind of thing, then they twisted that around to meet their own needs."

It was in the late '80s that a significant number of American punk and new-wave artists first starting coming around to the virtues of country music — honest delivery, straightforward acoustic instrumentation, direct and potent lyrics. American bands such as Uncle Tupelo would become canonized as leaders of an "alt-country" movement, when in fact experiments with country and roots music had been going on in Canada for years. The difference was that because roots music never encountered much antagonism from new-music audiences in Canada, there was no history of opposition that always spins into a better story for the media. Canadians were doing what came naturally in their culture, whereas Americans liked to inflate the importance of a punk artist crossing into country as a monumental shift in vision. Witness how revolutionary The Band sounded to American rock critics in the '60s, doing what came naturally to Canadian musicologists who didn't see any grand distinction between country, blues, soul and rock — they were all equally exotic Americana and Canadians were entirely comfortable melting them into a new sound — one that sent American heads spinning. While Gram Parsons was converting the Byrds to country-rock, Canadian folk pioneers Ian and Sylvia Tyson were forging an equally progressive fusion with their short-lived Great Speckled Bird project.

But because the Americans have always had the final say on the history of country-rock, Jr. Gone Wild will never take their historical place alongside Uncle Tupelo, and Blue Rodeo will always be overlooked next to minor players like the Jayhawks. And because the Cowboy Junkies morphed into a fairly conventional pop band, it's easy to forget how out-of-step and adventurous their first two albums sounded. Finally, because Canadians had a tendency to gravitate towards their rediscovered influences with enthusiastic levity — which could manifest itself in k.d. lang's campy performances, Jr. Gone Wild's wise-ass songwriting, or Handsome Ned's larger-than-life presence — it was easier to take the artists less seriously, much in the same way Stompin' Tom has been perceived as a mere novelty act. But the revisited roots music created during the CanRock Renaissance was rarely imitative, consistently inventive and extremely enduring.

On January 9, 1982, an imposing figure in a large cowboy hat took the stage in the back room of Toronto's Cameron House on Queen Street, one block west of Spadina. He called himself Handsome Ned, and he was about to start a five-year tradition that galvanized the Toronto music community. Every Saturday, Handsome Ned would put on a matinee performance that would be packed to the rafters with punks, rockers, country fans, new-wave refugees and anyone who knew that it was the place to be. Armed with a towering voice, Handsome Ned turned his audience on to the compelling charms of country, a form that was hardly in vogue at the time. He made no attempt to dumb it down, camp it up or fuse it with modern genres — instead, he tackled it straight on, with a fiery passion that was entirely convincing. Five years to the day, he would be struck down by his heroin addiction, shocking his peers and fans, and leaving behind a legacy that still sounds vital today.

Handsome Ned was born Robin Masyk in 1957 in West Germany, where his father was stationed in the Royal Canadian Air Force. Raised in Stoney Creek, Ontario, Masyk dropped out of high school after Grade 10 to hitchhike across the continent. During a stay in Banff, Alberta he became enamoured of a restaurant called Ned's, which would later provide him with half of his stage name. In 1978, he moved to Austin, Texas with his brother Jim, where they soaked up the outlaw country music indigenous to the region and talked about forming a band. Upon returning to Toronto the following year, the Masyk brothers started The Velours.

"The Velours used to do a lot of early Elvis, some originals, and Velvet Underground covers," says Jim Masyk. "It was a mix of influences. We also did 'Sleepin' With the TV On' by the Dictators, and various things that came out of pre-punk: the Velvets, the New York Dolls, all those people. We didn't play punk per se. When we formed, Ned had a cowboy hat and lambchop sideburns and we were going for rockabilly with a country edge, but targeting the new music audiences at the time. We weren't going after country music audiences; we were going after the people on Queen Street."

In early 1981, the Masyk brothers acquired a new punk-rock rhythm section consisting of The Next bassist Ronny Azzopardi and the Demics' drummer JD Weatherstone. They changed their name to the Sidewinders and attracted the attention of Steve Leckie and the Viletones. "Steve Leckie went nuts over us and blessed us, and then we started opening for the Viletones," says Jim Masyk. "We started taking their audience and pretty soon we started headlining. We were packing Larry's Hideaway, and it was the Demics' and the Viletones' audience that came to see us. We were the new punk in a way. We cranked it up, it was more rockabilly and fun, and less snarling and spitting."

The Sidewinders would also gig with another rockabilly band, the One-Eyed Jacks, featuring Steve Koch on guitar, who had just finished his stint with the Demics. The band was led by Chris Houston, who had just departed from Hamilton punks the Forgotten Rebels. True to just about everything Houston has done, the One-Eyed Jacks took a light-hearted approach to rockabilly. "Most of the Toronto rockabilly bands were very purist, and they really took it seriously," says Koch. "But we didn't. Most of them did 80 percent covers and 20 percent originals, and we did 80 per cent originals and 20 per cent covers. It was a bit irreverent, because I always looked at rockabilly as a dead art form. That's why I started to get into country when I met Ned. It was never a traditional part of my musical upbringing. But at that point I was ready to be turned around, because [country] struck me as *not* being a dead art form. It was happening right now and was really talking to people and wasn't all smoke and mirrors, wasn't all form and no content. It was the lyrical content and the dedication."

Koch had moved from Calgary to Toronto in 1978. "My dream was to get into a punk rock band, if possible the Viletones," he recalls. After a short-lived band — Crash Kills Nine — with future Shadowy Men drummer Don Pyle, Koch's dream was realized when he was drafted to be one in a series of Viletones guitarists, for one year between 1979 and 1980. "We weren't learning any new songs, there weren't that many great gigs and it totally lost direction," says Koch. "The original Viletones went back to '76; they'd been doing those songs for a long time. It was time to move on to something else."

Before he did, however, Koch helped the band with their transition to rockabilly. "At that time," says Koch, "there was a feeling that doing that old-fashioned punk was dead, which Steve [Leckie] knew as well, so that version of the Viletones went rockabilly for a while. That was okay, because I knew how to do that stuff by getting my chops playing blues at coffeehouses in Calgary. It was not terribly popular at the time. There was a rock-abilly influence in Toronto music, because Teenage Head did all those Eddie Cochran-type songs in a revved up style and everybody loved them. The Viletones started doing rockabilly stuff in 1979, and it was not terribly well-received. We opened up for the Buzzcocks and people threw bottles at us. That was one of the last shows they did with me in the band."

In 1983, Koch and Ned formed a band called the Running Kind, which focused on Merle Haggard-influenced outlaw country. "I can't think of anybody else on Queen Street that was doing that at that time," says Koch. "There was definitely rockabilly, but nobody was doing downtown country music. There were certainly the real professional bands playing country, just like there always was and always will be. But they weren't downtown, and we brought a different perspective to it, having been through the musical upbringing we had been through."

That same year, the Sidewinders broke up when Jim Masyk left for the stability of a day job. Before the split, the band recorded nine tracks with ex-Stampeders guitarist Rich Dobson, two of which ended up on a 7" single: "Put the Blame on Me" and "Cryin' Heartache Misery." "Put the Blame on Me," perhaps Ned's strongest composition, would be used to great effect in Bruce McDonald's 1989 film *Roadkill*, where it plays over the opening credit sequence featuring the annual Good Friday parade down College Street — the title phrase amusingly juxtaposed with shots of an actor portraying Jesus carrying his cross. Aside from Ned's promising songwriting and compelling vocal delivery, the recordings are also notable for not falling into the trap of most '80s production — there are no thunderous drum sounds, no processed vocals, no fakery.

By 1984, Ned's Saturday matinee was the weekly social hub of Queen Street. "There was this whole scene built around Ned," says Jim Masyk. "You could depend on him being there every Saturday, and you knew the faces. I can't imagine how many people he knew. Once he met people he remembered them. He was very street level — 'Hey, you coming out to see me?' — just a promotional machine."

"Ned was the king; he was a scenester," says Greg Keelor. "Because of Ned, [Blue Rodeo] had something to do, that didn't seem like we were doing something on our own. We did a show with a band from Vancouver, the Rocking Edsels, at the Bathurst St. Theatre. Ned just put it on for something to do. And he was an artist; he was always doing an art show, and we'd play that. A Valentine's Day show he did was our first or second gig. We didn't have that facility as a band. We didn't know how to do that.

Luckily, there was something there for us to step into and for our music to be heard. Every Saturday, at his fantastic matinee, he just played on and on until the band [playing later] that night had to say 'Get off!' He was really legit, and committed to amphetamine country. He had a very exciting voice and a great, cool band."

Ned's vocals were central to his appeal. In his voice you can detect traces of all the rockabilly greats to come out of Sun Records in the '50s — the grit of Johnny Cash, the sweetness of Roy Orbison and the unshake-able swagger of Elvis Presley. In a 1986 *Nerve* review of his regular Cameron

Handsome Ned (right), Jim Masyk (left)
of the Sidewinders
(Photo by Ross Taylor)

show, critic Tim Powis wrote: "No matter how many times Ned's done a song, he never seems to fail at grabbing it by the gizzards. His plain-tive prairie-dog voice doesn't just carry a tune, it pushed the dog-gone thing along like a ranchero herding cattle. Same goes for his hard-attack strumming style. . . . This is a band that could give you the impression the west was won with a saddlebag of bennies."

Steve Koch would become Ned's right-hand man for the next three years, first with the Running Kind and the cajun side project Handsome Ned and the Hayseed Hellions, which also featured future Blue Rodeo drummer Cleave Anderson. In 1984, the Handsome Neds were formed, with Koch, upright bassist Rene Fratura, and drummer JD Weatherstone carrying over from the Sidewinders.

Fratura had moved to Toronto from Vancouver, where he had been playing with rockabilly songwriter Herald Nix. Nix's band arrived in Toronto for the first time in 1983 "with the greatest pre-packaged buzz," says Koch. The post-punk rockabilly and roots enthusiasts all turned out to see the show, and Koch still claims that Herald Nix had "the greatest band on earth. They had an unbelievable drummer, Russ the Bus, and a crazy man piano player [Mike Van Eyes] who was a musical genius. Herald Nix is a bit of a musical genius himself, and Rene is in a class of his own," says Koch. "Rene met Ned and was very impressed with him, so he decided to quit Herald Nix, move to Toronto and join Ned's band. It was like me moving from Calgary to join the Viletones — that was what he wanted to do. When he came along, that added a lot of credibility, a real roots feel to it." Fratura would also act as a visual counterpoint to Ned, rolling his eyes, contorting his face and attacking his stand-up bass.

The first summer after forming, the Handsome Neds headlined the First Annual Handsome Ned Picnic on Toronto Island, which over the next three years would feature Blue Rodeo, Shadowy Men on a Shadowy Planet, the Razorbacks and other Ned friends. Although well-attended, the picnics were a private affair out of necessity. "It was word of mouth, because they were illegal," says Koch. "They were open-air speakeasies, so it was pretty audacious."

In 1985, the Handsome Neds recorded a 7" featuring "In Spite of the Danger" and "Ain't No Room For Cheatin' (In a Song About Love)." It was received well at Toronto campus station CKLN, on the CBC, in certain smaller markets across Canada such as Red Deer and on the two major country stations in Ontario, Hamilton's CHAM and Toronto's CFGM. The latter became a big supporter of the Handsome Neds, inviting them to play on their syndicated Opry North program, recorded live at the Birchmount Tavern in Scarborough. "Apparently, we got the first encore that was ever allowed [on the program]," says Steve Koch. "That was a step into the mainstream, but Ned was never really interested in going into the mainstream. He definitely knew what he was doing — and what those people were doing was not where he was going."

Ned hosted a radio program of his own on CKLN, the Handsome Ned Honky Tonk Hardwood Floor Show, which he started in 1982, the same year his Cameron residency began. The popular program featured studio guests, including Greg Keelor and Murray McLauchlan, and a varied playlist that placed vintage country artists and Ned influences like Lefty Frizzell alongside newer roots-informed music such as R.E.M., Steve Earle and the True Believers. His listenership was so dedicated that 12 years after Ned's death, a loyal Honky Tonk Hardwood Floor fan brought Jim Masyk a box full of tapes documenting every show Ned ever broadcast.

While everything seemed to be moving forward for the Handsome Neds, the band broke up on the eve of the third picnic in 1986, after two full years together. Ned played his disastrous final picnic as a solo act, abandoned by his band. To make matters worse, Ned's guitar was stolen and the police busted the event, seized all the money and charged him under the liquor act. "All of us were supposed to go, and we said 'That's it, we're not going,'" recalls Steve Koch. "Nobody likes to say it, but there were dope problems, which leads to 'not getting paid' problems. We were losing a bit of focus as to what's important. Between Ned and the drummer, JD, there was a lot of tension. JD didn't think that Ned was doing the right things for the band, which could have been true. Tempers flared, but after that, everyone made up. I don't know about JD, but Rene and I were on speaking terms with him. He knew he had gone too far and was apologetic, and wanted to play with us again."

In the meantime, he had assembled The New Neds, featuring future Razorback guitarist Tony Kenny, ex-Sidewinder bassist Ronny Azzopardi and ex-Johnny Thunders drummer Billy Rogers. The band recorded one song for a Christmas-themed TV movie starring Loretta Lynn, and were scheduled to record demos for a full-length album in January, 1987.

But that same month, the night before his Cameron matinee was to celebrate its fifth anniversary, Handsome Ned succumbed to a heroin overdose in the back of his beloved Cameron House. "It was a real shocker," remembers Steve Koch. "We'd pretty much figured that all of that stuff was in the past, that he was headed for new and bigger and better things."

"His band loved him," says Greg Keelor, whose Saturday night social circle included Ned, Koch and former Demics frontman Keith Whittaker. "But because of the drugs in that period, there was a certain frustration [for Ned's band] in maintaining some sort of career momentum — whatever *that* is. The funny thing about drug deaths is that there's a period of time before they die when they've pissed everybody off. I hear that a lot. Ned and I were barflies together, but we weren't confidantes in a big way. We played a lot of music together and hung out all the time, but for the people that were closest to him, those were the ones who had been the most hurt for a period leading up to his death. There's that combination of being pissed off, angry and incredibly sad."

Once news of Ned's death broke, his friends and fans congregated at the Cameron. "It was an immediate wake," recalls Steve Koch. "Everyone knew where to go, right away." After his funeral, there was a procession of cars down Queen Street; like the death of a mainstream public figure, people lined the streets to pay their respects. "Hundreds of people were standing around who knew him," says Koch, "and that's not including the people who actually went to the funeral; there must have been 50 cars."

"I don't remember going back to the Cameron," says Greg Keelor. "The only thing I can remember is that a guy walked in and asked me, 'Is this where I can get some skag?' I don't remember what happened after that. If he had asked [scenester] Mohawk Bob, he would have got the shit kicked out of him. It would have been ugly, because people were just so angry." Years later, Keelor's Blue Rodeo bandmate Bob Wiseman would write a song borrowing a title from Ned, "In Spite of the Danger," with the lyrics: "I know who killed you / And everyone else knows who killed you too / They found the murder weapon behind your bedroom door / Found an empty syringe next to your arm on the floor."

Ned's death was covered in the media with a mixture of drug sensationalism and fond musical memories. "The media needs some kind of sensationalist angle," rationalizes Steve Koch. "That's how they sell papers. You can't deny that he died of an overdose — it's true, you can't gloss it over. But a lot of papers also reflected on the importance of the music and what he'd done."

"The day after he died," Jim Masyk recalls, "someone from the CBC came to my parents' house. They interviewed everyone. They came out a few days later with this thing that was just awful, and so painful for us. I wanted to kill the fuckers. We learned a lot from that. Obviously writers need something to write about, and of course, 'Underground star dies of drug overdose' is a story. Not having been through anything like that before, I was naïve — shouldn't have been, but I was. I'd been screwed around enough by the music industry, which was why I wanted to get out of it, but I never expected people would take our words that they recorded and say things before and after it and warp it to whatever message they wanted."

Musician Kurt Swinghammer was working at the Cameron during that time, bussing tables. "The scene at the Cameron was pretty much headquarters for everybody in the arts scene: writers, artists, musicians," he says. "It was the main watering hole. And when Ned died, the whole tourist thing kicked into gear, because everybody wanted to see where junkies hung out. The Cameron became the most incredibly packed room. The *Toronto Star* did a full-page story called 'Mean Street West,' and it was all about heroin at the Cameron. There were needles in the john, and people were getting dragged outside because they passed out. There was a lot of experimentation, a lot of people were goofing off and thought it was hip or something. When Ned died, a lot of people woke up."

Two years later, a posthumous compilation was issued by Virgin Records Canada, whose president Doug Chappelle had been a Ned fan and had conducted preliminary conversations with Ned about a record deal before his death. *The Ballad of Handsome Ned* consisted primarily of Sidewinders recordings, as well as the two songs from the Handsome Neds' single. It was promoted with a video for "Rockabilly Girls" and by the appearance of "Put the Blame On Me" in *Roadkill*; in 1989, Handsome Ned was posthumously nominated for a Juno award in the Best Country Male Vocalist category.

In 2000, after two and a half year's work of researching Ned's audio archives, Jim Masyk compiled a two-CD set titled *The Name is Ned*, featuring remastered versions of every studio session he ever did, as well as live tapes from his Cameron House shows featuring the Handsome Neds, and live solo radio performances from CKLN. The fact that Masyk convinced EMI Canada to release it is a testament to the fact that Ned did have fans in the industry, who could have helped bring him to larger audiences had he not met an untimely end.

"It's helpful to reflect back," says Masyk of the compilation. "Not only for me personally, having grown to understand better and seeing where his music went and listening to the influence. This was for me and his fans. If other people like it, great. This is Ned, this brings him alive. This is what he said and how he was. It was his character that came through not just in his singing or his activities like picnics and radio shows, but on stage — how comfortable he was. To take what he was really like when he was sitting around with friends and a few beers."

After Ned's death, the Cameron tried to distance itself from heroin associations. By that time, another band that started off in its back room was beginning to move beyond Queen Street with a controversial name: the Cowboy Junkies.

The Cowboy Junkies were also enraptured with roots music, specifically blues, but they had a decidedly more unorthodox approach to their chosen form than Handsome Ned and Blue Rodeo. "I don't even know if we recognized it as roots music at the time," says guitarist Michael Timmins. "I don't know what we thought it was. We came into that scene but we didn't have a country side at that point, it was more of a blues thing. [Handsome Ned and Blue Rodeo] were leading the way, which was nice. I went to [Blue Rodeo's] first show at the Rivoli and it was jam-packed, and it just took off from there."

Although the Cowboy Junkies would eventually tour the world and sell millions of records, their beginnings sounded like a marketing nightmare: somnambulate, frightening blues music played at minimum volume, fronted by an intriguing yet painfully shy female singer, backed up by her two brothers and a family friend who all hid in the shadows with their heads down.

The four children in the Timmins family were raised in Montreal in the early '70s, as was bassist Alan Anton, who met Michael Timmins when they were both five years old. "I've known Alan longer than I've known my brother Pete," says Michael. "We became music fans together, sharing a record collection. We were the two music heads in the school, who bought every new obscure record that came out, and went to all the concerts down at the Forum together."

The Timmins family moved to the Toronto suburb of Etobicoke in 1977, after Michael had left to attend the University of Western Ontario in London. His friendship with Anton persisted, and they formed the band Hunger Project in Toronto in 1979, with singer Liza Dawson-Wisker and drummer Geoff Railton. Railton was the lead singer and bassist in the Popular Spies, "which was a fairly big underground band in Toronto at the time," says Michael. "It was a very power-pop band, and he was a bit of a heartthrob. He quit that band to become our drummer."

The Hunger Project were influenced by British goth-rock of the day, such as Joy Division and Siouxsie & the Banshees — "basically rhythm and noise," says Michael. "Our singer had an antagonistic stage presence. There was no bass, just two guitars, drum and vocal. It was very mid-range and aggressive."

Because the band perceived the Toronto club scene as drying up, they moved to New York City in 1979. While down there, they hooked up with their Toronto friends Greg Keelor and Jim Cuddy, who were fronting a power-pop band called The Hi-Fi's. The two bands shared a practice space in Toronto and the Hi-Fi's moved to NYC two years after Hunger Project. "Greg had grown up in the same suburb of Montreal that Alan and I did, and was a good friend of my older brother John," says Michael. "I knew Greg as a kid; he likes to tell a story about the time I speared him in the stomach with my hockey stick because he was bugging me. Alan and I went to see the Demics play one night, and the Hi-Fi's were opening for them. I recognized Greg, so we re-introduced ourselves."

After a year in NYC without much progress, the Hunger Project packed up again and moved to another musical headquarters, London, England. "Liza, our singer, was English," says Michael, "and her mother had a place in Notting Hill that she rented out. It was cheap rent and a place to go to. Plus, my grandmother was born in England, so the minute I landed there I was able to sign onto the dole. I was like, 'You gotta be kidding!' But we broke up as soon as we got there. It was a bit of an illusion; we thought we were coming to Mecca, and it was just like any other city where you had to know who to talk to and what clubs to get into."

Although the Hunger Project had come to an end, the three men decided to stay on in London and form Germinal, a free-form noise band that Alan Anton describes as "more therapy than music."

"We stopped looking at pop music altogether," says Michael. "I got a job at a record store, where I was turned on to some very weird music, improvisational jazz like Cecil Taylor and Anthony Braxton. We started playing very abstract stuff. Not that we had the chops to pull it off, but it was a very excessive form of punk music: make whatever noise you want and just play. We did that for three years."

Michael's sister Margo had been a big fan of Hunger Project, helping them haul equipment around and working the door at their Toronto gigs. Her reaction to Germinal was a bit different. "Germinal was what it was," says Margo. "I tried to like it, being Mike's music, but I never really got it. He sent me his Germinal tapes and I thought he was having a nervous breakdown. I got on a plane and went over there and realized, 'Oh my god, you *are* having a nervous breakdown — but there's nothing I can do about it, see you later!'"

Germinal never performed live, although they recorded one cassette, *Germinal 1*, and an LP, *Din*. Although performers like Evan Parker and Derek Bailey were playing around London at the time, Germinal didn't have the confidence to announce themselves in the presence of those innovators. "We'd go see them in places like a basement of a church with 10 other people there watching," says Michael. "We'd go to these gigs all the time, but never got the guts to force our way into their scene. We'd see them, and then go back to our space and just pretend. But it was very cathartic, and gave us an appreciation for the lack of limits that music has." Germinal splintered when Railton remained in London, Timmins returned to New York briefly, and Anton travelled before he and Timmins eventually settled back in Toronto.

In 1985, Michael Timmins and Alan Anton rented a house in Toronto's Little Italy, with the youngest Timmins brother, Peter. They converted the garage into a rehearsal space and Peter decided he wanted to learn how to play drums. The eldest brother, John, started sitting in on second guitar, and soon their sister Margo would cautiously enter the fold on vocals. "We knew she could sing because she'd done school plays, but she'd never pursued it," says Michael. "We all remembered back when she was six that she had one of those voices that when she walked on in the *Oliver* play she'd blow the theatre away."

In the early days of the Cowboy Junkies, Margo struggled to find her voice by belting it out. "Like any singer," says Margo, "when I started to sing I felt — especially at that time — that you had to sing loud, and you had to be aggressive. So of course that's what I started to do." The only recorded evidence of this appears as the hidden track on the band's 1996 live album, where Margo tries to be heard above her noisy brothers on a punk version of Carl Perkins's "Bad Boy."

"We had songs that would go for 45 minutes with me just making weird noises," she recalls. "When we listened back to tapes, and I'd hear myself sing loud, it was just terrible and embarrassing. I began to realize that when I sang quietly I liked the sound better and I could do more. I also saw Emmylou Harris sing at the Horseshoe, and when she sang it looked like she just opened her mouth and it came out. It didn't look like she was pushing anything; it was as if she was just breathing. I'd always been a big fan and admirer, so I thought, I'm gonna do that too. I'm not going to force it.

"I started to do that and of course all the soundmen just went insane and started yelling at me, telling me to sing loud," she continues. "It was a nightmare for them with feedback, and I could never hear myself through the monitors. Then the boys had to turn down so that they could hear me in rehearsal, and Mike liked playing in that style and Pete had to use brushes instead of sticks while we were rehearsing. We also rehearsed in a neighbourhood so we didn't want to be too loud anyway."

The family affair wasn't entirely harmonious, as Peter's older brothers decided that his novice drumming wasn't cutting it. Michael explains, "We told him, 'You can play with us as long as you want, but you have to dedicate yourself to it, otherwise we're not interested.' He lacked dedication, so we fired him!"

Michael and Alan enlisted their old friend Ian Blurton of Change of Heart. "We knew Ian was a wanna-be drummer, and he was pretty good, so we asked him if he wanted to play with us," says Michael. "He played with us for several months. It was a different thing, because Ian's a real whacker, whereas Pete is a very soft drummer, so it certainly changed our sound for a bit. At that same time, Pete decided to pick up the drums again and hired someone to teach him. After five or six months, Ian had tendonitis in his wrists and wasn't sure if he could keep it up. Meanwhile, Pete was working away, so we invited him back in the band."

By the time Peter returned, John Timmins became a father and moved to Montreal with his new family. The band chose not to replace him. "We liked the space created by not having the extra musician there," says Michael. "At that time Margo was singing a bit quieter, and the whole hushed aspect of the band began to develop."

The Cowboy Junkies had little in common with Hunger Project or Germinal — or, for that matter, anyone else on Queen Street in 1985. It was delicate and spooky music, driven primarily by Alan Anton's undulating bass lines and featuring Michael's feedback-drenched textures and jerky leads. Michael's playing was worlds away from what blues had become in the '80s. Instead, it brought back a haunting quality, ripe with tension, dancing around the rhythm section and Margo's sparse vocals.

"Near the end of our stay in London another record-store friend introduced me to the blues," says Michael, "I'd never been introduced to it by a real enthusiast, which he was. I began listening to his records a lot, and began to appreciate a structured song. During all these years I didn't listen to rock or pop music at all and this was the way back into it; there was structure but still a lot of improvisation."

Although their material consisted entirely of covers — by the likes of Lightnin' Hopkins, John Lee Hooker and Robert Johnson as well as Bruce Springsteen, the Velvet Underground and Nick Cave — the Cowboy Junkies took liberal license with their interpretations, often sounding only remotely like the originals.

"Writing wasn't something we were focusing on," says Margo. "We were focusing on learning our parts, Pete drumming and me singing. I was listening to a lot of blues at the time. At rehearsal, the boys would be jamming and I would have to do something other than going 'ooo-ooo-ooo.' I'd pick up a blues line that I heard that afternoon and would throw in lines that didn't have to make sense. Then we'd listen to tapes and pick out good areas of the jam and focus on that part."

"We weren't really covering the song," says Michael. "We were just taking the lyrics and creating our own music and then putting the two together. We'd do these bar shows where we had to do three sets, and we'd only have enough material for one and a half, so the second set would be 40 minutes of one song."

One of the oddest factors in the Cowboy Junkies' take on the blues was Margo's personal interpretations. She relayed tales of paranoia, fear and longing through a voice that sounded tender, frail, and sometimes scared, bringing a new perspective to songs written by men from a different era. "When you're in your twenties it's not so hard," says Margo. "You're so lost and wondering what the hell you're supposed to be doing. Most of those blues tunes were written by guys who were 20 years old. In those days we were all living together, travelling in a van and sleeping on people's floors. We had no money and no idea whether the band was going to work or not, and didn't really care very much, and wondering how we were going to pay the phone bill. That's what we needed to sing about because that's where our heart was — that lost feeling."

As sung by Margo, several of the songs underwent a gender role reversal in which a done-wrong woman sought revenge on an unfaithful man. Delivered by a firm, quiet voice, a song like John Lee Hooker's "Forgive Me" became even more harrowing. "I never was a gun person, so I've never shot anybody — not yet anyway," laughs Margo. "I'm not trying to be that person, I'm just trying to understand fear, and I've experienced some levels of fear. I've never played with guns, but I was trying to capture the mood of being desperate or down and out. I had a nice family around me. I never pretended to be from the streets, and yet these lyrics were written by people who really knew what a hard life was. If I didn't understand the song, I approached it by listening to what the boys were doing with the music, the rhythm, and how the words fit in, and went with that as opposed to trying to express something specific."

Margo also had to become more comfortable on stage, which wasn't easy at first. "I was a very reluctant singer," she says. "I didn't turn around, let alone talk to the audience or look at them. I was not an angry young person and everything then was angry and in-your-face. Ours was very laid back — take it if you want it, if not, that's okay."

She also couldn't find much inspiration locally, as female-fronted bands were few and far between. Early on, Margo recalls seeing Sherry Kean of The Sharks, a band that also featured Blue Rodeo's future rhythm section. "She was so good," Margo gushes. "I wasn't watching with any interest in becoming a singer at the time, but she had a real presence about her. She had her own style too; she didn't look like another Siouxsie, which most other girls did.

"Most of the bands we played with were male. The first female we worked with was Michelle Shocked," she says, discussing a late '80s tour the two shared. "There was a bit of a threat to it; I remember thinking, 'Oh god, I have to go on stage after her.' She's a good singer and she has her own style, and I had a lack of confidence. Then we did a tour with Lucinda Williams in the early '90s. That was hard to do every night, to listen to her and what she can do with a song, and then I'd have to get up and sing 'Blue Moon.'"

Margo Timmins and Alan Anton of Cowboy Junkies, 1988
(Photo by Bruce Lam)

Within a year of forming, the Cowboy Junkies hit the road around Ontario and across Canada. They also set out to discover the United States, the country that provided so much of their musical inspiration, and the country that to this day has been more responsive to their music than Canada. Toronto promoter Elliott Lefko says, "They saw themselves maybe not as an American band, but they never saw themselves as a Canadian band. That's why they were successful. These other [American underground] bands would play all over the world, and the Junkies realised they wanted to fit on the same map, even if they were only making 50 cents and sleeping on people's floors. A lot of the other Canadian bands didn't do that: they were scared to do that, or didn't want to do that. To Michael Timmins's credit, he didn't really care. He was going to do it, and if people didn't come, they didn't come; if people came, then people came."

"There were hardly any people there," says Michael. "There were always two or three people who were really into it, who freaked us out and kept us going. It was exciting because all the music we were listening to and taking from was from down there, if not all of it, and there's a romance to going down there."

The Hunger Project had toured the eastern seaboard and southern States, so Michael and Alan already had some experience booking tours on the fly. "As we'd go along we'd call ahead and get contacts in different communities," says Michael. "It was all the hardcore scene then. Every town had one. We weren't hardcore, but [hardcore audiences] didn't really care, it was just a term. If we didn't have a contact for a specific town or didn't know the club there and we knew it was a good music city, we'd call information and ask for the number for The Horseshoe. Every town had a Horseshoe, whether it was a club or a bar or whatever. We'd call up and say, 'Hi, we were told that you guys book live music there.' 'Oh no, we don't have music.' 'Oh, well can you tell me who does?' And they'd give us a list of clubs, and we'd keep phoning places until we got a gig. It worked all the time! There was definitely a scene across Canada, and in the States as well, of people looking for something different."

After improving their sound on the road, the Cowboy Junkies were ready to make their first recording, but weren't sure how to go about it. They knew that they didn't have enough money to work in a proper studio, and that almost anything else would leave them with an unsatisfactory recording. Peter Moore, a Toronto sound engineer and an old Hunger Project acquaintance, solved the band's problem when he met them at a dinner party at Greg Keelor's house. Michael recalls, "We'd reached the conclusion that what we liked was what we heard in our rehearsal space; that was what we wanted to capture. Peter knew what we were looking for, so he came over to our space a week later and recorded to see if it would work. And it did; we liked it, so he came back the next week and went from there."

On the blistering hot day of June 26, 1986, the band assembled in their garage with Moore and a single Calrec Ambisonic microphone. After Peter Timmins accidentally knocked over the $10,000 microphone, giving Moore a near heart attack, the day went smoothly. The band positioned themselves around the microphone in the same fashion that any early blues band would have, creating a warm room sound without separating the sound of each individual instrument. Twelve songs were recorded in seven hours, including "Take Me," which was improvised between Michael and Margo on the spot, and became the band's first original composition. A version of The Velvet Underground's "Sweet Jane" was also put to tape, but discarded. The highlight was Bruce Springsteen's "State Trooper," a song from the likewise lo-fi *Nebraska*, his darkest album. The ominous paranoia of the lyric, told by a mysterious narrator escaping a police chase, is accented by Michael's tense release of howling feedback and the insistent pulse of the rhythm section; Margo's delivery refuses to betray the narrator's guilt or innocence, making the song more unsettling.

To celebrate their first recording, the band held a pool party at their parents' house, inviting a bevy of guests, including Greg Keelor and Jim Cuddy, who were now fronting Blue Rodeo. Cuddy's work at a film company had provided him with an unlimited supply of Polaroids, four of which would provide the gaudy portraits of the band that would grace their first album, titled *Whites Off Earth Now*.

"The phrase comes from a San Francisco group that Alan and I came across, and their slogan was 'whites off earth now,'" says Michael. "They figured if they could get all the white people off the face of the earth, then all the earth's problems would be solved. We thought, 'Well, that's one way to approach it!' When we did the record, it was a bunch of white suburban kids covering the great black bluesmen, once again ripping off these greats. Plus there were these beautiful, ugly pictures of these white kids on the cover. I thought, that's gotta be the title of it."

Upon the album's release on their own Latent Recordings, the Junkies hit the road while maintaining day jobs when possible. During their next trek across the States, the band found themselves exposed to classic country music — on the radio, at every truck stop and in the record collections of their gracious fans who gave them floor space to sleep on. "That was totally unfamiliar to us," recalls Margo, "because here in Canada our roots were folk, not really country. We went to the Country Music Hall of Fame in Nashville, which was a big influence on us. This was a big tour we were on, but we didn't have many dates, and we were just in a little van, so we spent a lot of time either doing nothing or touring around doing some sightseeing. When you have four people in a van discovering a new kind of music, it's going to influence the way you play."

They started adding some of these songs to their repertoire, such as Hank Williams's "I'm So Lonesome I Could Cry" and Patsy Cline's "Walking After Midnight." At the same time, Margo and Michael were bit by the writing bug and started to compose songs together in a similar vein, such as "Misguided Angel" and "200 More Miles," the latter a classic road song documenting their long journeys across the States.

With an album to promote, their time on the road brought them more attention — and sales. In the first year of release, *Whites* sold 3,000 copies, which by independent standards of the day was a formidable number. Reviews were extremely positive and the band found strong supporters in the staff of the new late night CBC radio program *Night Lines*, based in Winnipeg at the time. "On our first tour across Canada we met [*Night Lines* producer] Ross Porter," says Michael. "We had a three-night stand in Winnipeg and by the third night there was one person in the audience, and that was [*Night Lines* host] Ralph Benmergui. It was a good person to have." On their way back across the country, *Night Lines* broadcast a live Hallowe'en show from Winnipeg's Blue Note club, with Cowboy Junkies and Deja Voodoo.

Kim Deschamps was a northern Ontario musician who was doing free-lance broadcasting work for the CBC in Toronto, and interviewed Michael for a series he was doing on independent Canadian music. The two got to talking after the formal interview, and Deschamps told him he played pedal steel guitar. "At the time, I had no intention of ever hiring a pedal steel player," says Michael, "but we traded numbers and he said if I ever needed one to give him a call. Sure enough, a year later, we were moving to the country side of things, so I called him."

The Cowboy Junkies figured they'd need plenty of help to flesh out their new fascination with country music and they stumbled across a unique cast of characters. Kim Deschamps recommended an accordion player from Sudbury, Jaro Czerwinec, who led one of northern Ontario's most popular east European polka bands, the Black Sea Cossacks, and had also played with art-folk singer Daisy DeBolt. Steve Shearer, a blues harmonica player, had played some shows with the band before. Shearer was one of 20 people at their first gig, and introduced himself backstage as "honky white trash."

They also invited their brother John back for the session, who in turn recommended a fiddle player from Guelph named Jeff Bird. Margo knew Bird's work in the Canadiana folk trio Tamarack; John Timmins had given her the band's debut album *A Pleasant Gale.* "I could sing every song on it," says Margo. "I was a huge fan. I went backstage one day at [Guelph's] Hillside Festival in the early '80s. Never in my life had I gone backstage, but I just wanted to tell Tamarack how much I really liked them. This was way before the Junkies started, way before there was ever any hint of music being in my life. I went up to Jeff Bird and he snubbed me — he turned around like he couldn't give me the time of day!" she laughs. Bird's harmonica and mandolin playing — and his incredibly versatile multi-instrumentalism in general — would be a signature part of the Cowboy Junkies' sound from 1988 onwards. Margo jokes about meeting Bird again: "Years later I said, 'Okay, I'm gonna get you! You will *follow* me around in a *van* for the rest of your *life*! I *curse* you!'"

With their collaborators chosen for their next record, the Cowboy Junkies wanted to continue the single-microphone experiment of the first album, and called on Peter Moore to once again organize the session. Moore suggested recording in the Church of the Holy Trinity, near the Eaton Centre in downtown Toronto, for a more spacious room sound. Moore had recorded classical and jazz music in the venue, but never anything with vocals, a drum kit, or electric instruments. To avoid any potential controversy with church officials regarding the band's name, they booked the space as The Timmins Family Singers, and told the church officials that they were recording a Christmas radio special for the CBC.

There were a couple of warm-up gigs with Jeff Bird, Kim Deschamps and Steve Shearer to work out arrangements; they couldn't afford to pay Czerwinec to come down from Sudbury for rehearsals, and although they exchanged tapes, the first time they ever met him was on the morning of the recording session. Everyone else had rehearsed beforehand, with Moore present and making extensive notes for song arrangements. Because they weren't allowed into the church until the recording date, the band considered the whole project a gamble.

At this point, the Cowboy Junkies were far from seasoned players — although their exploratory amateurism was part of their appeal, they were suddenly in a new league of expertise when professional musicians were hired. "We were intimidated by the stature of players," says Michael. "These guys knew how to play their instruments and that was a bit intimidating. But then you think, 'Fuck, we've been doing this a long time!'"

On November 27, 1987, the four core members and Peter Moore assembled at the church to begin recording. "Rearranging to get the sound and getting everyone sitting in the right spots was quite exhausting and frustrating," says Michael of the six-hour process. "That took half the time. In the first couple of hours, we thought, 'This isn't going to work. It sounds like a huge wash.'" Instruments and musicians were moved inch by inch until the perfect balance was found. As with the *Whites* session, Margo sang into her own microphone, which was patched through a PA system to add to the room sound, outside the twelve-foot diameter musician's circle. The other musicians showed up one by one, and were sent off to the Eaton Centre or were told to sit still while Moore arranged the sound. Czerwinec had taken an overnight train from Montreal, and curled up in a corner of the church to catch some sleep, lulled into dreams by the band's lilting sound.

Once the tape started rolling, "Sweet Jane" and "Dreaming My Dreams of You" were recorded first because they didn't require any extra musicians. The side players were added cumulatively as they were required. Because one of the conditions of renting the church was that it couldn't be closed, several takes were ruined by tourists who bumped into Peter Timmins's drums while gaping at the architecture. Otherwise, the day ran smoothly, although the security guard had to be bribed to let the band stay an extra two hours. "Misguided Angel," featuring Jeff Bird on harmonica, was recorded in one take, the first time that group of musicians had all played the song together. Likewise, "Walking After Midnight" — the closing song of the album and of the day — featured all nine musicians and plenty of solos, and was entirely unrehearsed.

All the players, as well as Moore, were working on "spec," or a percentage of profits if anything should come of the recording. When the session was finished, the total bill was $250. "I think the church was $125," recalls Michael, "then we had some tape costs, and we got some pizza. Everybody eventually made decent money off it; Peter made a fortune off it, and rightfully so. But our out-of-pocket expenses at the time totalled two hundred and fifty bucks."

Upon finishing, the band realized they had forgotten to record their simplest song: "Mining For Gold," a traditional song melodically re-arranged by Tamarack's James Gordon, that Margo wanted to sing a cappella. A couple of days later, Moore was back in the church recording the Toronto Symphony; Margo came in during their lunch break and recorded several takes of the song in front of the munching musicians.

The next day, their accomplishment became clear at an impromptu family gathering. Margo recalls, "My mother was driving my brother John to the train station, and she came by my house. It's not so strange, but she normally calls, and this time she just showed up. Five minutes later, Mike came running down the street from his house with the tape of *The Trinity Session*, and he said, 'You gotta hear this.' It was early in the morning; everyone was there for breakfast. We put on the tape and started listening to it. I certainly didn't think the rest of the world would hear what I heard; you don't know what people will hear, but I remember being amazed that I was a part of it, that it was my voice and I was a part of creating this thing. My mother was blown away that this was her offspring."

Released in early 1988, the reaction to *The Trinity Session* was instant, and not just from the extended Timmins family. It immediately went into high rotation at *Brave New Waves* and *Night Lines*, and topped the charts at Toronto's CKLN and other campus stations across the country. Daily papers like the *Toronto Star* and the *Montreal Gazette* were effusive in their praise. "We were very shocked by it," says Michael. "It generated a buzz, and as an independent band, it was huge. We could get any gig anywhere we wanted. We went to Montreal every third weekend and sold out clubs, and we were playing in Toronto pretty much every weekend."

Between the time that *The Trinity Session* was released on Latent and when it became a mainstream success, the Cowboy Junkies didn't take anything for granted, even while they were caught up in the new flurry of activity. "Things started changing pretty quickly," says Margo. "I remember going to my mom and saying, 'As soon as my life gets normal, maybe I'll take a course at Ryerson.' My mother looked at me and said, 'Your life will never be normal again.' And it hasn't — I'm still waiting to take that course. It wasn't bang out of the box; there was always something planned for our future that you couldn't have a regular nine-to-five job anymore. Even when *The Trinity Session* did break loose and I was on the cover of all these magazines around the world and people were taking my picture, I never even knew what was happening. I was just doing what people were asking me to do. 'Oh yeah, another cover, sure.' It never struck me as 'Oh my *god*, it's *People* magazine!'"

The idea of approaching a major label seemed equally ridiculous. "We were going to release it with a goal of selling 5,000 albums, which would mean we'd have enough money to do the next one," says Michael. "The only reason it got sent to a major label was because we hooked up with Graham

Henderson, who was starting out as an entertainment lawyer. He used to come see us at the Rivoli a lot, although he never introduced himself. We met with him, and he said, 'Give me 20 tapes and we'll see what happens.' We thought, 'Sure buddy, whatever. Here's 20 tapes, good luck!'"

When the majors did come calling, a dream situation for most struggling bands, the Cowboy Junkies were less than eager to jump into the fray. "That was a terrible time, actually," says Michael. "We had a really fun time as an independent band, and all of a sudden there were full bars and it was a really high time for us. Then the majors came around, and there was a shift because there were suddenly a lot of major decisions to be made. Nowadays you think, 'Well, of course you're going to sign a deal.' But there was a real good chance we weren't going to sign back then. We talked a lot about the idea of keeping it to the music side of things. A lot of people wanted us to change the name of the band, and some of them wanted us to re-record the album. It was like, 'What are you people here for?' It was because there was a bit of a frenzy going on, and people felt they had to get in on it. They didn't understand what the hell they were listening to. But they knew other people wanted to sign us, and therefore they did." Although the media buzz was primarily Canadian at that point, the label interest was exclusively American. "The Canadians passed on it, basically," says Michael. "One of the Canadian A&R guys called up and said, 'What is this, a demo?'"

The band settled on RCA, where they met an A&R rep and the label's new president, both of whom they felt they could trust. "There was definitely a point where we thought, 'We can't work with any of these people that we're meeting. We can't stand talking to them, never mind working with them,'" says Michael. "The lucky thing was that we created *Trinity Session* by ourselves without anyone around us, and it was released as it was on a major label, and it did very well. Therefore we had a lot of pull and power, because we could say, 'Look, you guys had nothing to do with this record; we made it ourselves and look how well it did. So back off!' That was really lucky. We didn't have to make our first record for these people; it had already been made."

The Trinity Session was re-released on RCA in November, 1988, with the tracks missing from the Latent version. "Sweet Jane" was the first single and immediately caught on with radio. It didn't hurt when Lou Reed was quoted as saying it was his favourite cover version of any of his songs.

The band soon entered a bubble, where they became quite oblivious to how well they were doing. They had been on the road since the indie release of *Trinity*, and that routine didn't stop upon its re-release. "We didn't really pay attention to what was going on with the record or at radio," says Michael. "That was all kind of meaningless to us, and we focused on what we knew, which was playing gigs, and figuring out how to play to these audiences that were growing. It was hard, because at that point *Trinity* was the buzz album, so lots of people showed up at shows who had no idea who we were. Whereas when we were an independent band, people would show up because they're music fans. Now, they were there because we were 'the band.' The audiences were really loud and noisy, and unfocused. It was weird, and a big learning experience for us."

"We slowly started to play bigger clubs and there were certain nights when I realized that I wasn't doing a good job," says Margo. "The first thing I started to do was talk, which was really hard, to get the people in the back rows to notice. In the early days when people were lying on the dance-floor, you didn't have to pay them any attention, because they'd fall asleep and be happy." Margo insists that a snoozing audience was a flattering thing. "I'd think, 'Oh, I wish I was down there.' I still have that sometimes; I'll look out at the audience and they're cuddled up with their boyfriend and I'll think, 'Aww.'"

The Cowboy Junkies were becoming a much more professional band, due to the cumulative years of rigorous touring and the boost from their new sidemen. For industry people and their fellow musicians, the improvement was welcome. Lewis Melville, who would play pedal steel and banjo on later albums, says, "They benefited a lot from the people they had playing with them, in terms of establishing credibility as a band, because they had some pro players who really held it together and gave it what it needed for people to pay attention. In their early stages, Margo could hardly sing her way out of a paper bag. She was a good singer, but in terms of a live show, they didn't have that figured out. A lot of times it just didn't go across at all. But they got that together eventually. When they started touring for real, they had to get better, and they did."

Kim Deschamps, who doesn't recall his experience in the band with much fondness, says, "It was an interesting ride, but none of us around our house really got it. It was very bizarre. I would be apologising for my gig. I'd be out there playing to people all over the world, with people like Bruce Springsteen in the audience, and I was meeting childhood heroes of mine like Bonnie Raitt. In a way I was a little embarrassed by it. There I was playing my butt off every night, trying to put a little excitement into this show that was, by definition, not very exciting."

Following up such a unique album as *The Trinity Session* was a daunting task. Playing constantly on the road with the full band had prompted Michael to write many new songs that sounded much louder — comparatively — than their hushed beginnings. Their initial plan was to once again use the single microphone recording technique, but in a series of different sessions and venues, whenever they'd be home in Toronto in between legs of their tour. The best versions from the different sessions would comprise the next album.

The first session, using an actual studio but not using the studio's equipment, proved disastrous due to road fatigue. The second was recorded over three days in April of 1989, at the Sharon Temple — located just north of Toronto in the town of Sharon, and pictured on the cover of the album that would become *The Caution Horses*. Because Moore was unfamiliar with the building, the set-up time was considerably longer, and exacerbated by the fact that the weather was unseasonably cold. The building was unheated, and the band was forbidden to bring in heaters because the structure was made entirely of wood. The band had also added percussionist David Houghton, and the road-worn arrangements of the new material were considerably more expansive than the *Trinity* songs.

Although the band and Moore were initially discouraged, listening to the tapes at home they decided that, although strained and obviously quite different, the Sharon session was just as intriguing as their earlier recordings, and created by a much more confident band. The Junkies informed RCA that their next album would be titled *Sharon*, and went back out on the road, thinking their work had been done. During that time, the songs' arrangements continued to develop, and newer material was added to the set. "By the time we got back," says Michael, "it was six or seven months later. We all felt that we should go back and do some more recording, because the other sessions were six months ago." For the first time in their career, the Cowboy Junkies checked into a "real" studio in December, 1989 — Toronto's Eastern Sound — and modified their approach to recording. Peter Moore used a combination of the old one-microphone approach with each instrument individually mic-ed as well.

The other key change was that Michael was now the principal songwriter, and only two of the 10 songs on *The Caution Horses* were covers: Neil Young's "Powderfinger" and a very liberal interpretation of Mary Margaret O'Hara's "You Will Be Loved Again." Margo contributed lyrics to only one song ("Witches"), the last one she'd co-write for the next seven years.

"I had written a few [songs on *Trinity*]," says Margo, "and I never loved doing it or felt strong about it. Michael started writing beautiful songs that I loved; he had always written poetry since we were kids, so writing was definitely part of his expression. We went with our strengths. I'd rather sing a Michael Timmins song than one of mine any day. They're more interesting, and they don't all rhyme. People would say, 'you should write more' and there'd be a hint that Michael doesn't want me to. But Mike would always be saying, 'Do you have anything? Just give me a line!' But over the years I've tried not to, because I feel silly about it. It doesn't make me feel good, so why do it?"

While the poetic narratives of Michael's lyrical vision were evident in songs like "Sun Comes Up It's Tuesday Morning" and "Where Are You Tonight," *The Caution Horses* was uneven, the sound of a songwriter and a band both in a period of transition. The Junkies were not playing sparse blues anymore, instead creating a pleasant, country-tinged pop sound that was still unique but much less surprising.

Michael Timmins of Cowboy Junkies, 1988
(Photo by Bruce Lam)

Fans may wonder what the outcome would have been had the band released *Sharon* instead of *Caution Horses*, and while Margo admits that *Sharon* might see the light of day as a low-key fans-only release, she doesn't regret the decision. "I never try to second guess things," she says. "There are some things in our career that I think, 'we should have done this earlier' or 'we should have gotten rid of this person earlier or got off that label' or whatever. But as far as how you record a record, no. *The Caution Horses* is one of my favourite records. It's the misunderstood one. It was after *Trinity Session*, so people either accepted it or they didn't, but I don't think they ever really listened. For me, it's a very beautiful, lush, well-played record, and it's really pretty. We did that after having done *Sharon*, and *Sharon* is much more edgier than what *Caution Horses* was. *The Caution Horses* is a more mature version of *Sharon*, more well-rounded."

After an exhaustive tour for *Caution Horses*, everything ground to a halt — partially because the band needed a break, but also because Margo had come down with pneumonia. "It was quite shocking, because I had never been sick before and now I was quite sick," she says. "It all came to a stop, and we hadn't stopped in years. We'd done everything everybody asked us to: all the press and all the touring, and just kept going. But I learned that when it *did* all come to a stop, that it didn't end. It was a good lesson. We all realized that if we say 'no' it doesn't all come crashing down. A lot of us at that point were married, and we hadn't seen our spouses for three years. I got married in '89, and the *Caution Horses* tour ended in late '90, so for the first two years of my marriage I didn't really live with my husband. Our third year of marriage, when I came home, was our hardest year ever. [The band] realized, 'What are we doing? Our home lives are very important to us too.'"

For the next five years, the Junkies spent much of their working time touring in the U.S., which has always hosted their biggest audiences, as well as Europe and Japan. The *Trinity* band was dismissed in 1991, except for Jeff Bird, who has been the only constant presence to this day, his versatility and virtuosity a key asset to the band in any setting. Michael would continue to grow as a writer, greatly influenced by a friendship he struck up with legendary Texas songwriter Townes Van Zandt. The band would score worthy middle-of-the-road radio hits with "Southern Rain," "A Horse in the Country" and "Anniversary Song," but there was a nagging feeling among some fans that something was always missing.

In 1996, after releasing a double live set and switching record companies to Geffen, the Cowboy Junkies released *Lay It Down*, which marked a return to basics: additional instrumentation was kept to a minimum; it sounded like the band was listening to the Velvet Underground again instead of lush country music; Michael was once again playing angular lead guitar; Alan Anton's bass was brought to the fore; and the all-original songwriting — a first for a Junkies album — was Michael's best yet. It was the perfect balance between the haunting quality that originally defined the band, and a more refined pop sound that they had been aiming to achieve ever since *The Caution Horses.*

"*Lay it Down* was a result of getting off RCA, getting a new label and a new beginning," says Margo. "At the end of our relationship with RCA, it was really dead, like a bad marriage, just stale. Nobody understood what we were trying to do. They didn't like us, we didn't like them. When we left them — again, like a marriage — you wonder why you didn't do this earlier: 'I don't hate myself! I don't hate my music!' Whenever we'd get into a crunch, we'd get together and literally verbalize: Do we want to continue to do this? Do *we* want to continue to make music? And the answer is always yes. We still enjoy being together and writing music and we still think it's good."

Lay It Down rightfully became the band's second-best-selling album, granting them a new lease on life. It was a boost they badly needed when their short Geffen affair ended two years later, resulting in their next album, *Miles From Our Home*, being stillborn in the wake of the Universal/Polygram merger in 1998.

"The question then was, what do we want to do next?" says Margo. "After Geffen I remember flying on a plane with Mike and I said to him, 'If we continue this way, I'm going to have to quit. I don't like this anymore. I love playing with you, but I hate these politics. I don't like this dance. I'm too old. It's so draining and it makes me crabby, and I'm not a crabby person.' I wanted Mike not to take this the wrong way, but as soon as I started to talk he said, 'You know, I feel exactly the same way.' He was in the exact same place. It was, let's get out of here and figure something out."

The solution was to return to their independent roots, kick-starting the Latent imprint again and re-connecting with their strong fan base around the world.

"I would like to be global instead of local," k.d. lang told *Vanity Fair* in August, 1993. "As everything — as an artist, a spiritualist, a cook, a singer." Today, k.d. lang is known around the world as an international icon of celebrity lesbian chic, but from day one she never pretended that she was from anywhere else in the world than Consort, Alberta, Canada. She never changed her appearance to become more palatable to mainstream audiences, never toned down her image, and never kept her mouth shut on issues that mattered to her. Everything about k.d. lang positioned her as an outsider to American country music, including her nationality.

"I think being 'alternative,' which most people think holds me back, actually helps [in the music industry]," she said, upon becoming "Miss

Chatelaine" — *Chatelaine* magazine's woman of the year in 1988. "If I'd been an ordinary singer, I'd still be trying to get noticed in Canada. I'm an alternative in every way. I'm a country singer who's a vegetarian for health reasons and because of compassion for animals. I'm also alternative because of Canada — there's something romantic about being Canadian. I always push the fact that I'm Canadian. I'm not self-righteous enough to think I'm unique and I'm not being overly rebellious," she continued. "But I've learned that to go your own way and be yourself, which is what I'm trying to do, is alternative to a lot of people."

When she came out of the closet to the gay magazine *The Advocate* in July, 1992, she provided two marginal cultures — lesbians and Canadians — with a pivotal moment of celebrity. It wasn't a shocking revelation to most, but especially not to Canadians, who knew in the first few seconds of her debut indie album, when she belted out an ode to a female lover, "Bopalena." Rather than hurting her career, after the revelation she sold two million copies of her post-country makeover, the torch song cycle *Ingenue*.

But it did overshadow just how different and what a threat k.d. lang was to the mainstream country music industry of the '80s, and made it easy to forget that her approach to country was once as exciting as everything else about her personality. According to publicist Richard Flohil, who made lang's 1984 Toronto debut a media sensation, "It's interesting to see people like Neko Case and Carolyn Mark who are treading the same path today, and meanwhile k.d. is now famous for being famous."

Growing up in Consort, Alberta (population 650), Kathy Dawn Lang didn't have many cultural outlets, and did everything she could to *not* listen to country. She was an athlete, excelling in javelin and volleyball, and a thespian, getting a head start on her gender-bending by playing Gilbert Blythe in a high-school production of *Anne of Green Gables*. Although lang would later alienate some of her neighbours with her vegetarian activism, she recalls Consort as a town where it was easy to establish a unique personality, where eccentricity was normal.

In 1981, she moved to Red Deer to attend college, and it was there she started participating in avant-garde performance art, painting and playing music influenced by Joni Mitchell, Kate Bush and the Allman Brothers — at that point, the latter was her closest brush with country music. In January 1982, after she had moved to Edmonton, she met a drama professor who wanted to cast her in a musical called *Country Chorale*, about a woman's fantasies of becoming a singer like her favourite country star. Lang played the part of the country singer.

On her 21st birthday in 1982, lang received a copy of the Patsy Cline album *Stop The World I Want To Get Off*, as well as the soundtrack to the Loretta Lynn biopic *Coal Miner's Daughter*. "I had started playing guitar and singing comedic avant-garde folk music like Jonathan Richman or The Roches," she told *Mojo* magazine. "I knew I was a singer, it was my destiny, but I didn't know where to place myself. When I listened to *Stop the World*, it was this instantaneous click. The songs definitely connected my upbringing in Consort with my theatrical sense, my sardonic side, my kitsch side. And the way Patsy delivered them, they were way beyond country — they were multi-dimensional performance. I never wanted to emulate Patsy, but I felt that I owed it to myself and maybe to her to take country further out. I connected with it on such a deep, intensely all-encompassing level that I got this flash of inspiration: 'Okay, I'm gonna start a country punk band.'"

Her connection to Patsy Cline was so strong that lang started to tell friends that she'd been dreaming of plane crashes and that she thought she was the reincarnation of Cline, who died in a plane crash 18 months after lang was born. In the ensuing years, lang tried to downplay the reincarnation claim. Her first national exposure, an article in the *Globe and Mail* in November, 1984, read: "While she claims 'a real sense of psychic connection to Patsy Cline,' she puts the hype into quick perspective. 'Well, if some idiotic interviewer asks me if I'm really the reincarnation of Patsy Cline, of course I'm going to say yes.'"

The same month she was given the Cline record, she auditioned for a western swing band called Dance Party, managed by Larry Wanagas. The band split up after one show, but lang started singing jingles in Wanagas's studio and she soon asked him to be her manager. Their initial plan was for her to become a jazz singer to showcase her range, but figuring jazz was a dead end, they went with her newfound love of country. "I dedicated myself to country music because I love it," she told *Network* magazine. "But also, in performance art there were no limits, nothing to argue or challenge. In country music there's so *much* to challenge and so *much* to change."

lang and Wanagas hired a band, chose some songs, and she started playing around Edmonton in 1983, beginning at the Sidetrack Café. From her first gig as k.d. lang, she abandoned her formerly shy, introspective folk singer persona, and adopted a love for outrageous performance — due in large part to her on-stage apparel: second-hand clothing with plastic cowboys and Indians sewed on to them, long skirts, cowboy boots cut above the ankles, self-inflicted spiky hair cuts and horn-rimmed glasses.

In Nashville culture, there's a saying about female country singers that goes: "the higher the hair, the closer to God." Although k.d. lang always had ambitions to make it in Music City, her punkish haircut — which attracted more attention than her singing when she first went there — was rooted in a practical decision of a different kind. "I look goony in long hair," she told *The Advocate*. "If I have hair that's long, it covers up what I think are my best features, my sharpnesses, and I end up looking very plain. A more practical reason for having short hair is when I'm onstage I sweat and my hair goes flat, and it looks really awful."

The most shocking thing about k.d. lang was her sexuality, or rather, her androgyny. Although she was boyish, she wasn't entirely butch, as she chose to wear long skirts and had a feminine manner. She sang like any of the female country greats, but with a fuller lower range, decidedly more swagger and a cocksure strut. "I would hope I can attract both men and women," lang told *The Advocate*, "and that when a person is attracted to me, they're not thinking about my genitals. The stage gives you the emancipation to do things. Because there's always been cross-dressing onstage, since theatre began. It's the place to do it. It's about art transcending sex, but still retaining sexual elements."

In 1988, Miss Chatelaine told Canadian women, "I'm a very androgynous-looking woman, and my goals are not to be a wife or necessarily a mother. Androgyny is important in my life because I can deal with people on a human, not a sexual, level; it's important on stage, because both men and women are attracted to me. They were to Elvis Presley too. It's important not to eliminate possibilities for people."

If for some reason her appearance wouldn't attract an audience's attention, her stage antics would. A staple of her set was "Johnny Get Angry," a wife-beating tale where she would enact a fight with the imaginary wife-beater, at one point falling down on the stage, and after a dramatic pause, finishing the rest of the song on her back. She performed Nancy Sinatra's "These Boots Are Made For Walking" carrying a rocking horse on her head. For Cline's "Stop the World I Want to Get Off" she cavorted about the stage with a globe as a prop. In the press, she admitted that she acted ridiculous to release hip audiences from their inhibitions about sentimental country music. "I don't think people could take the passion in my singing if I didn't present this bizarre exterior," she told the *Globe and Mail*. An editor of the arch-conservative *Alberta Report* magazine commented on her early performances by saying, "I thought she was talented, but she was so weird it was hard to tell."

lang's stage performance was in step with her approach to country,

k.d. lang, 1985
(Photo by Richard Flohil)

which alternated between revved-up rockabilly honky-tonk with unbridled screams and yelps, and intense, off-kilter ballads like "Pine and Stew." She wasn't aggressive enough to be part of the nascent cowpunk scene, too irreverent to be a neo-traditionalist and too charismatic to define exactly what it was she was doing for, or to, country music. It was corny, but behind the artifice was something more real than the mainstream pop scene. "Sure it's corny," lang told the *Globe and Mail.* "But people are beginning to get smart enough to realize most emotions are corny, that corny is real life."

In December, 1983, lang released her debut 7" single, "Friday Dance Promenade," backed with a cover of The Roches' "Damned Ol' Dog." In homage to Patsy, she named her band The Reclines and started playing around Alberta, including a gig opening for Rank and File. In April, 1984 the band — which included Gord Matthews, who would stick with her until her country days were through — recorded *A Truly Western Experience*. The 26-minute album was pressed right before the Edmonton Folk Festival, the biggest of its kind in Western Canada.

On August 10, 1984, k.d. lang announced her arrival in the big time when the headlining act at the Edmonton Folk Festival that night got lost on the way to the gig. What was supposed to be a 25-minute set was extended to 50 minutes, with lang continually upping the energy level as if each song was her last. Richard Flohil recalls, "She grabbed it by the balls and ran with it. She had a big stage to work, she was wearing her get-up, and for her show-stopper she'd do an old Leiber and Stoller song called 'I'm Saved'; Laverne Baker had done an R&B version. Here was k.d. with a bass drum strapped around her chest, marching around and belting it out.

The place went nuts. Then she segued into 'Amazing Grace' and the place was in tears." lang got a standing ovation.

Flohil booked her into Albert's Hall in Toronto at the end of October, 1984, for what would be her central Canadian debut. "It was a blues club, a place where you wouldn't expect to see her, the same way Benny Goodman went into Carnegie Hall," says Flohil. "She played from Tuesday to Saturday, and by Thursday there were line-ups outside by 6 p.m. [At the end of the set] she did 'I'm Saved' standing on a table halfway into the audience and then left the room — the place was banging and demanding more. She came back, with no band and a guitar — which she rudimentarily plays — and no glasses, and she did [Patsy Cline's] 'I Fall to Pieces.' Then she walked away, out of the room, and the audience left. They knew she couldn't follow that, and they got the feeling that suddenly they've seen the real person, not the act, just because she took her glasses off."

"I don't need them to see," she told the *Globe and Mail* when asked about the glasses. "They don't have any glass in them, but I just liked them. They make me feel stately, like my mom. But they're so ugly. They help lower my self-esteem on stage, and I think that makes me more accessible. Or maybe it just puts people off, and then I like to win them back."

A Truly Western Experience soon sold out of its first pressing of 1,000; it would eventually sell 11,000 as an independent release. MuchMusic, an obvious sucker for a great image — not to mention desperate for good CanCon videos — started playing live lang footage to compensate for her lack of videos. She embarked on her first Canadian tour in April, 1985, with a slightly different band that included longtime keyboardist Teddy Borowiecki. It was here that, for the first time, she had to face audiences that weren't as enamoured with her as the Canadian media was. In Kenora, Ontario, she sold one piece of merchandise: a vinyl album bought by a heckling fan who immediately turned to his laughing friends and broke it over his knee.

By the time the tour hit Albert's Hall for an encore appearance, a major label bidding war was underway. On May 2, in the middle of her tour, lang debuted at The Bottom Line in New York City, where word had spread in the music industry about a hot talent that had jaws dropping in Toronto. *Rolling Stone* was impressed, although they ended their rave review with an odd comment: "At a showcase at New York's Bottom Line, she turned in a kinetic performance, do-si-do-ing primly around the stage at one moment and bellowing into the mic with the range of Johnny Rotten the next." In the middle of the show, lang jumped on one of the tables filled with record executives and sang to them, dripping sweat everywhere.

Sire Records' Seymour Stein, the man who signed the Ramones and Madonna, heard about the Bottom Line show, and after inquiring about her with Warner Canada, he flew from London, England to Edmonton to see her play. Jet-lagged and exhausted, Stein got up in the middle of the show and danced with her, then walked back to his seat, announced to his guests that he was going to sign her, and promptly fell sound asleep. At her next Bottom Line gig, where he was more alert, Stein told her, "You're what country music would've been if Nashville hadn't screwed it up."

On November 4, 1985, now signed to Sire Records, k.d. lang won the Juno Award for Most Promising Female Vocalist. She bounded up to accept her award in a wedding dress, joking to friends that it was the only time in her life that she'd be wearing one. In her speech, she said weddings were about promise, and then made some of her own: "I promise to deserve this award. I promise to work hard next year. I promise to always sing for the right reasons."

Some of those reasons got lost during the journey to her major label debut, *Angel With a Lariat*. While discussing possible producers with Sire, lang suggested either Elvis Costello or T-Bone Burnett, who had recently produced Los Lobos and the BoDeans. Sire, however, wanted British roots rock mainstay Dave Edmunds, who had worked with Johnny Cash and Everly Brothers and therefore might have more credibility with country radio. Edmunds reluctantly took the project on, and it was a gamble for all the parties that didn't entirely pay off. The album has energetic moments like "Pay Dirt," the mostly instrumental "Watch Your Step Polka" and the fiery "Turn Me Round," all of which would have made great cowpunk songs if the production didn't gloss it all over with an '80s sheen. Having only just begun working with her new collaborator and violinist Ben Mink — a former member of prog rock band FM that lang met while playing Expo '85 in Japan — there was a shortage of new material, not to mention considerable friction between Edmunds and lang.

She later told *Rolling Stone*, "I like that record now, but I hated it for years. Tons and tons and tons of reverb, 150 milliseconds on everything." One can only imagine how different the results could have been had the production job gone to Costello, who proved his empathy and love for country music on *Almost Blue*, and helmed vital and raw records by The Specials and the Pogues.

Angel's best quality, of course, is lang's voice, which soars through all the album's highs and lows, and is mind-blowing on her cover of one of country's greatest melodies and lyrics: Lynn Anderson's "Rose Garden." Sadly, it's the last time that lang would sound so exuberant, before she settled down and discarded her abandon in order to perfect her craft. She had already grown to despise the term cowpunk and started using her own phrase. "Call me torch-'n'-twang," she told *Graffiti* magazine. "The whole cowpunk thing is in the process of crawling under a rock and dying, and I was never really a part of it. I wasn't even vaguely aware of bands like Rank and File and Jason and The Scorchers until after we'd started playing around Alberta. They were important groups that broke ground for a new generation of rock-'n'-roll, but it has nothing to do with what I'm talking about. Basically, those bands are taking rock-'n'-roll energy, throwing in a Duane Eddy guitar lick and calling themselves country. I'm trying to reach further into a 30-year legacy of wonderful country music and see if I can avoid all the clichés."

Lang had trouble convincing not only mainstream country fans that her aim was true, but also the alternative press. Writing in Toronto's *Nerve* monthly, Dave Bidini wrote about being unimpressed with lang on both her first two albums: "k.d. became an affront to everything I had learned was right about country. With tunes like 'Hanky Panky,' the music sounded forced, the idea seemed untrue, and the schtick looked ridiculous, at least to someone who had previously found honesty and wisdom in the music of Stompin' Tom and the Flying Burrito Brothers. After listening to *Angel With a Lariat*, I'm still not convinced that k.d. means it . . . I don't find value in an artist who effectively feigns country music while ignoring its virtues. This is souped-up, perma-pressed country-pop that forgets the rigour and the heartache of the real stuff. That it's being marketed as true Canadiana makes me feel embarrassed and sad."

Everyone else knew that she had great records ahead of her, and the next year was full of promise. She would make Johnny Carson her biggest fan, landing her an open invitation to play on *The Tonight Show* that she accepted three times in 1987 alone. *Angel* went gold in Canada in October, 1987, and she was named Entertainer of the Year by the Canadian Country Music Association. She played a two-song showcase at the Grand Ole Opry in Nashville and was called out for a rare encore. In February, 1988, lang performed "Turn Me Round" at the closing ceremonies for the Calgary Winter Olympics before 60,000 people plus millions more worldwide on TV. And in a career-defining, hair-raising performance, she sang a magical duet with Roy Orbison on a transcendent remake of his classic "Crying."

Her next album, *Shadowland*, was her most conventional foray into country, and allowed her to face the legacy of Patsy Cline that she'd waltzed with for five years. In June, 1987, the man who produced Cline's classic records, Owen Bradley, was lying in a hospital bed recovering from a massive heart attack when he saw lang perform Cline's "Three Cigarettes In an Ashtray" on *The Tonight Show*. He immediately sat up in bed and started making plans to come out of retirement and work with lang.

For *Shadowland*, lang left the Reclines at home at Bradley's request, and recorded with the Nashville players who had helped define Cline's sound. The material consisted of solid torch and twang classics like "Black Coffee" and "Lock Stock and Teardrops," as well as Chris Isaak's "Western Stars" and a resurrected "Busy Being Blue," a *Truly Western Experience* song written by lang's ex-keyboardist Stuart MacDougall. Bradley coaxed magnificent vocal performances from lang, who for the first time was singing material she could sink her teeth into. The songs were dressed up with lush instrumentation that sounded timeless, and just on the right side of syrupy.

For the closing track, Bradley hooked lang up with his former clients Loretta Lynn, Brenda Lee and Kitty Wells for the "Honky Tonk Angels Medley," which showed that even if lang wasn't accepted by country radio, she was by her mentors. At the album release party, Bradley made a speech in which he praised lang for restoring his faith in music and placed her in the same league as his old friend Patsy Cline. "You're lucky if you find someone like that once in a lifetime," he told the crowd. "I guess I'm a very lucky man."

Shadowland was the success that *Angel* wasn't. It was a classic country record in every sense, and the torch songs meant that it appealed to a middle-of-the-road pop audience as well, perhaps signalling to lang that if she was going to be a crossover, it was going to be as a balladeer with an older audience, and not a cowpunk who's hip with the kids. Working with Bradley meant smoothing over all her rough edges, and after *Shadowland* she never went back — perhaps it was a natural maturation, perhaps because she felt she'd found her calling. She described the album as "the end of a dream, the end of the rainbow."

She had won over audiences everywhere, fellow artists and the print media, but she still had battles to fight with the Country Music Association and radio. "Politically, this album is very correct," she told *Spin* upon *Shadowland*'s release. "I was working with Nashville session players, in Nashville, with Nashville's most celebrated producer. It's going to be very interesting to see how they swallow the next Reclines record. I've gotten the first taste of acceptance, but the game's not over."

"I don't eat meat," she continued, "and I'm not a Christian and I don't have big fluffy hair, which basically stands against a lot of the Americanisms and the fundamentalist values on which country music is based. But at the same time, I understand and appreciate all those values. I just see wide, or beyond those things. . . . I would like to bring the country audiences a little closer to the middle and the people on the left a little closer to the middle, too, and people who are too artsy to like country and people who are too country to like art."

Ben Mink was less diplomatic when asked by the press why he thought k.d. lang wasn't fully embraced by the country music industry. "At its worst, Nashville is an inbred family that's won the lottery," he said. "They're threatened by what they don't understand — like Rosanne Cash or Lyle Lovett, people who think a little bit too much and write about that thought in words that aren't blatantly about beer drinking or cars."

Comments like these fuelled the idea that lang was just slumming in the world of country music before moving on to something else. The accusations seemed a bit absurd: why would an artist continue to try so hard to be loved amidst such resistance unless her heart was truly in it? "It's because she really loves the music," manager Larry Wanagas told *Chatelaine*, before pointedly adding: "And it's a challenge. She could shoot to the top of the charts with a pop song anytime."

Her next album, 1989's *Absolute Torch and Twang*, was as good as mainstream country could expect to be. Huge, soaring ballads ("Pullin' Back the Reins" and "Trail of Broken Hearts"), western swing numbers ("Full Moon Full of Love") and rockers ("Big Boned Gal" and "It's Me") formed a complete snapshot of lang's capabilities within conventional country music. Her songwriting work with Mink sounded more assured, less gimmicky, and held its own with the album's covers.

The album was an immediate success, going platinum in Canada in its first month, and becoming 1990's best-selling female country album in the U.S. It also landed lang her first Grammy award. She launched the album with a CBC-TV special in which she convinced Stompin' Tom Connors to make his first public appearance in 10 years; he sang his tribute to her, "Lady k.d. lang," and the two duetted on "CA-NA-DA."

The love-in with the public didn't last long, however. In 1990, lang appeared in an ad for the People for the Ethical Treatment of Animals standing beside a cow and asking, "We all love animals, but why do we call some 'pets' and others 'dinner'? If you knew how meat was made, you'd probably lose your lunch. I know. I'm from cattle country. That's why I became a vegetarian." The ad never actually aired, because it didn't have to. Once the tabloid TV show *Entertainment Tonight* picked up on the story, it spread like wildfire and became a media sensation. Radio stations who didn't play k.d. lang music in the first place now felt that they had a real reason not to, considering her statement an insult to their listeners and the beef industry. But the cruellest backlash was the one closest to home, in the country that had tolerated and embraced lang's eccentricities from day one: a road sign welcoming people to "Consort, the home of k.d. lang" was defaced with the statement "eat beef, dyke."

The incident slammed the door shut on lang's country career, and made her later decision to come out of the closet look like a walk in the park. "We got well over 1,000 letters attacking her on the meat thing," Larry Wanagas told *Vanity Fair*. "I could have filled my trunk with the CDs and cassettes that came back. When she came out, there was not a phone call, not a letter; somebody sent back one of her records, and that was it."

In mid-1990, after her tour for *Absolute Torch and Twang* had finished, she said: "The time has come for me to let go of the idea of being a country singer. Country will always be a major influence on me. But I've also been influenced by everything from opera to Ofra Haza, and I'm not prepared to make the kind of compromises that would be necessary for me to be accepted by [country] people. At one time I did very much want to prove to them how much I honestly loved country music. But they make their own assessments whether you're honest or not."

Lang retreated to her Vancouver home and began work on her next record, *Ingenue*. The languid melodies and panoramic production approach sounded unlike anything lang had ever done, unlike anything else in the horribly bland world of adult-contemporary and more daring than the paint-by-numbers *Shadowland*. "Season of Hollow Souls," "Miss Chatelaine" and "Save Me" sounded huge, exotic and captivating, and with "Constant Craving" she had her first hit single, aside from the Orbison duet.

Her public turmoil of the last year was matched by a painfully pro-tracted unrequited love, and as a result her lyrics were soaked with universal longing and pain. *Ingenue* became her most personal album to date, a glimpse of the woman, not the performer. Her decision to come out of the closet in *The Advocate* was in line with her new approach to clear the air, strip away all artifice and focus on the music. "Now you know all the rumours that have been circulating in the press," she joked with live audiences just before her *Advocate* interview hit the stands. "And I have to say it's true. It's true, I am a L-L-L-L-Lawrence Welk fan."

Ingenue became a smash hit, selling two million copies and making her music as well-known as her celebrity. But she didn't feel secure, as a *Rolling Stone* article pointed out: "She says that the two things she fears the most are that *Ingenue* will turn out to be the career pinnacle that precedes her losing her creativity and that she won't ever find a true love." lang would find love, a domestic bliss that she celebrated on her 2000 album *Invincible Summer*. But since *Ingenue*, she has struggled to find musical and lyrical ground, and only its immediate follow-up, the overlooked soundtrack to the film bomb *Even Cowgirls Get the Blues*, has been remotely memorable. In the age of over-reaching divas, she's become highly underrated for her impeccable vocal talents, perhaps because she hasn't used it on worthy material, and clearly needs a creative kick. Perhaps it was the challenge of conquering country audiences that fuelled her fire, and without that she's rudderless.

"Even though I was never accepted on country radio and I was never embraced by the Nashville political establishment, I could play the Grand Ole Opry once and I could be a part of their big outdoor festivals because I drew people and I could be on their TV shows because I was good viewing," she told *The Advocate*. "But they never wanted to embrace me. And I understand why. I didn't want to ever be embraced. They didn't want someone who looked like me, who thought like me, who spoke out like me. They wanted to take the value of me involved in their system.

"And that's fair, because I did the same. I used them too."

By the time k.d. lang was giving up on country music, a group of her former peers in Edmonton were almost a decade into their own mission to update the genre. Between 1983 and 1995, Jr. Gone Wild — Mike McDonald, Dove Brown and a revolving door of musicians — took the low road through Canada's dingiest clubs, fusing country and punk, fed with a rugged determination and a dangerous amount of alcohol. Jr. Gone Wild were well ahead of their time in Canada, something that McDonald approaches with a slightly bitter satisfaction.

"Jr. Gone Wild felt quite alone for most of their career," he says. "We were a hard band to classify. We had no music scene to fit into so we made our own. Alt-country exploded almost the very next day after Jr. Gone Wild split up [in 1995]. Being ahead of your time sucks.

"There were very drunk appreciative fans backstage after shows analysing what we just did," McDonald continues. "I remember three drunk guys at three different times in three different places coming up with the term 'cowpunk.' 'Thatsh what you guysh are! *Cowpunk!!*' In each case the guy was so inspired by his epiphany I was certain he was going to the copyright office the next day. Being a punk rocker, a part of me liked it. The other part of me didn't like it, because I wasn't about fashion and clever little catch phrases. What we did, we did naturally. There was never a band meeting where we agreed to experiment with country and western."

As a teenager, Mike McDonald was influenced equally by Neil Young and Moe Berg's local power-pop punk band, the Modern Minds. McDonald's first band in high school was Joey Did and the Necrophiliacs, which featured drummer Ed Dobek, who would be a tumultuous figure floating in and out of McDonald's life for the next 10 years. When Joey Did and the Necrophiliacs changed their name to the Malibu Kens in 1981, the Modern Minds' drummer Kim Upright produced their 7" single *Be My Barbie*, with the songs "Crude City" and "Wednesday Morning." The single's cover was designed by Kenny Chinn, soon to be of venerable punk band SNFU.

In 1982, the Malibu Kens released a cassette featuring "High Plains Drifter," the first sign of a country influence in McDonald's work. "I'd been listening to country and western all my life" says McDonald. "My mother tended to listen to '50s and '60s rock-'n'-roll when the old man wasn't around, and when he'd get home it would be '50s and '60s C&W. By the time I was a teenager and in The Malibu Kens, I was in the middle of rebelling against my parents as all faithful and true blue punk rockers did, so out of rebellion alone I was not listening to *any* C&W at the time. I was actually developing a fierce Bob Dylan fetish."

The Malibu Kens broke up in 1983, just when a song of theirs was featured on *It Came From Inner Space: The Edmonton Compilation*. A few months later, McDonald hooked up with guitarist Graham Brown, bassist Mark Brostrom, and drummer Kim Upright. McDonald named the band Jr. Gone Wild, and started playing original material penned mostly by Graham Brown. Both Brown and McDonald were into Neil Young, and had a fusion of punk and country on their minds, however subconsciously. "I had seen Neil Young's *Rust Never Sleeps* about a million times," says McDonald. "The whole idea of starting acoustic and building to the wall of distorted sound seemed amazing to me. The problem was, everyone I knew was getting into the L.A. hardcore punk scene. Black Flag's *Nervous Breakdown* was the hit of the day. Everyone was making a hardcore band, and they all sucked, except for SNFU. I worked at a store in Edmonton called Saveco with SNFU front man Kenny Chinn." Chinn introduced McDonald to Rank and File's first album, which featured punk-influenced country with a clean Telecaster sound, which opened McDonald's ears to new possibilities. "I came away with a little less fear regarding my music plans," says McDonald. "It was as if I was given permission to proceed with my ideas." Jr. Gone Wild's first important show was opening for Rank and File in Saskatoon. "It was an honour I felt unworthy of at the time," says McDonald.

Jr. Gone Wild's first line-up lasted less than a year. After frequent road trips to Vancouver to play with their friends in the neo-psychedelic garage band the Enigmas, Graham Brown and Kim Upright were enticed to move there. "I chickened out because I didn't want to move again," says McDonald. "I'm an army brat. I don't come from anywhere; I was born in Hamilton, Ontario and moved around all my life — always the new kid, and I hated it." Upon returning to Edmonton, bassist Mark Brostrom decided he'd had enough of music, leaving McDonald alone with the band name and a determination to continue. "It seemed important to me that after a solid year of building the reputation and learning what to do, that I keep the momentum," he explains. "I always believed the idea of the band was bigger than the people in it — a pattern of behaviour I've been very consistent with."

The second incarnation of Jr. Gone Wild brought in McDonald's best friend Ed Dobek on drums, and a fellow Neil Young fanatic named Dave Lawson. The final addition was bassist David M. Brown, a.k.a. Dove, who was close friends with McDonald's brother Patrick. He had seen the band play in the fall of 1983 at the Army Navy Club, and had a premonition of his future. "Immediately I thought, 'I can play bass better than that guy, and I should be in this band,'" says Dove. "I was impressed by the songwriting of Mike and Graham Brown. Over the next year I ran into Mike a couple of times, and during the summer of '84 I made my pitch, not knowing that there was no longer a bass player to replace. In September I auditioned, joined, and the rest is history."

Dove would remain with the band until their final gig 11 years later. His tastes were much more steeped in country than punk. "I'd always had a lot of country music around me growing up," says Dove. "My dad had instilled a great love of the Carter Family in me and Willie and Waylon were standard listening around the house. I was never really interested in the punk thing until shortly before joining Jr."

On the Edmonton scene, there were few punks dabbling in country, with the exception of Jerry Jerry and the Sons of Rhythm Orchestra, with whom Jr. Gone Wild shared a practice space, alongside SNFU and Moe Berg. McDonald also shared an apartment with Jerry Jerry's guitarist Ronald Ramage, a.k.a. The Rockin' Rollin' Reverend Rockin' Roland. Ramage and McDonald started a straightforward acoustic country act called the Dusty Chaps. McDonald's stage name in the band was Mike Sinatra; somehow this fact caught the attention of Frank Sinatra's management, who issued McDonald a cease-and-desist order.

"The Dusty Chaps were a response to the rockabilly idiocy that went on for awhile," says McDonald. "Like the Celtic craze, every band did the exact same songs the exact same way, wearing the same style of clothes — just a bunch of fashion plates. There were some of us who did not sport quiffs and painted flames on our leather jackets, who knew so much more about rockabilly music than any of those assholes who were always stealing our girlfriends. The Dusty Chaps was the first overt country and western thing I did. We covered everything from Johnny Cash to the Sons Of The Pioneers; we would always bring the house down with our version of 'Tumbling Tumbleweeds.' Rockin' Roland always wore a minister's collar, never shaved and drank like Bukowski."

By this point Jerry Jerry had been signed to Montreal's Og Records; through Rockin' Roland's connections, the Dusty Chaps' song "Yukon Buddy" — a heartfelt ode to Roland's dog — ended up on Og's *It Came From Canada Vol. 1*. McDonald wanted the band to capitalize on this and move to Montreal, something Jerry Jerry himself did shortly after. The rest of the Dusty Chaps didn't share McDonald's ambition and gave him the boot.

Edmonton being the small scene that it was, McDonald was also singing back-up vocals with Jerry Jerry, as a result of jamming at parties held at their practice space. He appears on Jerry Jerry's debut, *Road Gore: The Band That Drank Too Much*. At one benefit gig for campus station CJSR, McDonald performed in three out of four bands on the bill: Jerry Jerry, Jr. Gone Wild, The Dusty Chaps and Idyll Tea.

There was also a slight overlap between Jr. Gone Wild and the pre-sensation k.d. lang. At wasted social gatherings hosted by Tim Folkman, creativity would run rampant between artists of all different stripes. "It was an excellent cross-pollination," McDonald recalls. "Everyone was an artist of some kind or another, and we would do some very stupid art stuff that fortunately only the people involved know about. Everyone was shaking or banging something, and k.d. and her girlfriends were wailing away the lyrics of Dion's 'Teenager in Love' or something, and every now and then k.d.'s operatic voice would soar above the chaotic racket. They were fun times. The people involved in this fellowship were not tight friends, but we got along well.

"She came over to my place once to hear a couple of my songs; she hadn't put out her first album yet. Nothing came of it, but she was courteous and listened at least. The last time I saw her was backstage in Vancouver at some long-defunct club in Gastown. It was after a Jr. show.

k.d., who was quite famous by now, comes backstage and says, 'Howdy boys!' Very nice and cheerfully. Ed Dobek looks up and says in a sneering tone: 'Oh, hi, k.d. How does it feel to be rich and famous?' She got real turned off and split. I never spoke to her again. Thanks, Ed."

Although lang never claimed to be cowpunk, her earliest performances obviously tapped into some of the same energy that Jr. Gone Wild was exploring. "I liked her a lot at first, but when she started to change the original Reclines I started to cool off towards her stuff," says McDonald. "And when she became mainstream — well, I'm a punker, what can I say?" Dove adds, "In the early days I found it hard to tell the difference between the sizzle and the steak. She had lots of both but it was a pretty blurry line."

With a small fraction of the hype that lang was receiving, Jr. Gone Wild hit the road through the primitive Canadian touring circuit of the day. "With my perceived nobility and romance of the lifestyle, I was really into it," says McDonald. "We were playing a lot of dives and community halls, with no accommodation or meals. My ideal of a good band included road seasoning, and I was hungry for it." Dove adds, "Before our first album came out touring was extremely difficult and financial rewards were none. Fortunately, if you were drunk and naïve it was a lot of fun and adventure."

Their first tour was booked by SNFU's manager Gubby, who pitched a Jr. Gone Wild demo to Southern California punk label BYO. The label had already released two SNFU albums, and was run by three expatriate Canadians, the Stern brothers. The attention came at an odd juncture for the band. "We were thinking of breaking up when Gub called us to say that BYO in Los Angeles wanted to make a record with us," says McDonald. "So we stayed together. We figured, what the fuck."

The album, *Less Art More Pop*, was recorded in L.A. with engineer Brett Gurewitz of Bad Religion, and mixed by Thom Wilson, whose sound would later become signature to SoCal punk. "We had no input on personnel," says McDonald. "That a guy from Bad Religion worked on it had nothing to do with us. Brett confessed years later that he has no recollection at all of the recording. He was into a lot of cocaine back then."

"California was a weird strange trip," says Dove. "We lived in an old WWII aircraft factory in Venice and lived on a diet of bad cigarettes and worse beer. The studio was nice, the engineer excellent, and the results pretty good. *Less Art* is still my favourite Jr. album — lots of energy and enthusiasm."

Despite the punk connections, *Less Art More Pop* sounds much more like early R.E.M. recordings, with jangly Byrds-like guitars and multi-layered vocal harmonies. The Bangle-ish, Paisley Undergound-inflected vocals are one of the album's strong points, showing that Jr. Gone Wild was much more interested in craft than many of their contemporaries.

The songwriting is surprisingly enduring, featuring three classic McDonald compositions: "Slept All Afternoon," "Day of the First Snow" and "Martha Quinn." Dave Lawson's "It Never Changes" kicks off the album on a strong note, while Dobek pens two songs, including the rave-up "Cosmos," and Dove makes his first contribution. The surprise comes from McDonald's brother Patrick, who pens another album highlight, "Fine Scotch." *Less Art More Pop* confirms that despite McDonald's role as bandleader, Jr. Gone Wild was a songwriters' collective from the start.

Yet it was a collective that was soon to splinter, with the "departure" of Dave Lawson and Ed Dobek. "The split in the band had gotten pretty big," says Dove. "Childish, petty warring factions, like little kids drawing a line down the centre of the sandbox. Dave and Ed were going one way and Mike and I were going the other." McDonald adds, "You can't kick guys like Lawson and Dobek out of a band. I simply called Dove and told him I was leaving the band, taking the name and my songs, and was wondering if he wanted to come with me. He did. Lawson didn't leave the band, the band left him, because he was a loose cannon and a constant embarrassment."

Dove continues, "At this point [drummer] Duke Paetz had just arrived back from Montreal where he had been playing with Jerry Jerry. We grabbed him and guitarist Terry Cox. Our first gig with the new line-up was at some community hall in northeast Edmonton. Mike and I were both nervous, wondering if the crowd would approve of the change. Just like a made-for-TV movie, we went over like gangbusters."

It was the second overhaul of the Jr. Gone Wild line-up, and it certainly wouldn't be the last. McDonald would develop a reputation as a caustic bandleader with a low tolerance for slackness or any less dedication to the project than his own. For this, he is unapologetic. "I have been caustic on stage and verbally abusive, but no more so than a football player or a construction worker is when they are working," he says. "True, some people couldn't handle it, but I wasn't there to have friends. I was there to realize a rock-'n'-roll dream." With the exception of Lawson and Dobek, most members left of their own volition. Dove says, "As far as I recall only one person was ever fired from Jr. It was a girl we referred to as The Beast, who had no talent and little ability — the worst hiring choice in Jr. history. All the others quit, either because they hated the road or they hated working with Mike. Both can be difficult and odious for the uninitiated."

The late '80s were spent entirely on the road, with only *Less Art More*

Pop to sell off the stage. "*Less Art* got old in a hurry," says Dove. "We toured and toured, made three videos — only one saw the light of day — and fought and drank and played. We got stale, started to run into dead ends, and never did make any money. I still worked for the government half the year and toured the other half."

On the road they met many valuable friends, such as Montreal road-hounds the Doughboys, who would cover Jr. Gone Wild's "What's Going On" on a 1992 EP. "On our first couple Canadian tours the Doughboys were our saviours," says Dove. "They loaned us gear, fixed our van, and gave us places to crash. I once had a dream that a bunch of skinheads were beating me up, when from over the hill came thousands of John Kastners to the rescue. Just like the cavalry — with dreadlocks." Jr. Gone Wild also shared numerous bills with like-minded American roots-punk band the Beat Farmers, featuring the late Country Dick Montana, "Whom I got drunk with many times and enjoyed more of his witty repartee than was maybe good for me," says McDonald.

Jr. Gone Wild got a vicarious thrill when their childhood hero and Edmonton expatriate Moe Berg finally found success with his new band, The Pursuit of Happiness. "I was the happiest guy in the world to find out Moe had finally made it," says McDonald. "Sure, TPOH didn't do the same things to me that the Modern Minds did, but I feel Moe deserves everything he can glean from this material world. I love the first album; I'm kinda cool on the subsequent stuff." Dove concurs, "Moe is awesome. If he made an album of farting noises I'd probably buy it, like it, and wish that I could fart like that. The first time Jr. played with TPOH they warmed us up for free in front of 30 people. A few years later we warmed them up for $2,000 in front of 5,000 people. Go figure."

In 1988, Jr. Gone Wild travelled to Toronto for something called The Independence Festival, where they played a packed show at the Silver Dollar before a crowd of homesick former Edmontonians. William Tenn, who was working A&R for the Canadian division of Island Records at the time, stumbled into the gig and was duly impressed. "He flew out to Edmonton to see us and had a private meeting with me," McDonald recalls. "He suggested I ditch the band and go to Toronto and they would make a record with me. The jury is still out on whether I did the right thing or not, but I declined respectfully, citing six years of work already invested, and the cursed loyalty to my friends. Plus, I had never really seen myself as the main songwriter.

"We ended up going back to Toronto to be examined by Island," he continues. "We were stuck there for five weeks while they wondered what they wanted. In the meantime, we were starving and bored, so every Monday night we would play Elvis Mondays. We did it five weeks in a row. You didn't get paid, you got a beer. We did it anyways, and we came out of that with a following in Toronto. Island jerked us this way and that, then wanted us to sign a letter of intent, which we did when they agreed to give us $5,000 to wait the year or so and rehearse and write. Finally, they decided they did not want to sign us, so they said they would tear up the letter and we could keep the $5,000. Our feelings were hurt, but it was kind of funny."

"We learned a lot from the Island fiasco," says Dove, "We learned a bit about how the big boys play and learned that polite avoidance might be our best bet. We certainly enjoyed the money and the notoriety, but we didn't have the stability or the infrastructure to make the best of the relationship. Looking back, they didn't either."

McDonald also received a call from Holger Peterson of Edmonton roots label Stony Plain, whom he had to respectfully turn down because of the Island negotiations. When the Island deal went south, Peterson's offer still stood and the band accepted. Stony Plain was beginning to have some success in the pop world with Spirit of the West, and had distribution through Warner Canada. It seemed like the perfect home for a roots/punk band, allowing them to reach a larger pop audience with one foot in the folk world; Peterson also ran the Edmonton Folk Festival.

"After we had signed to his label, we were suddenly the darlings of the roots music world," says McDonald. "We lived two lives: we functioned and moved freely in the folk circuit, and simultaneously did the shitty bars and marginal rock clubs, with the odd high profile opening slot on big shows. Back then, the new thing was roots music, whatever the hell that is. I went from thinking I was a punk-rock survivor to roots-rock visionary, according to [Stony Plain publicist] Richard Flohil — Christ our press kits were embarrassing!"

"Folk festivals loved us," says Dove. "We were rootsy enough that we didn't scare the old folkies, and rockin' enough to wake up the younger crowd. Although, as I recall, Peggy Seeger didn't approve of us playing Mariposa in 1991. She complained to Richard Flohil that it was a disgrace to have Jr. Gone Wild, a rock band, perform at a folk festival. Odds are that she never heard us and just saw the leather jackets and attitude."

Dove continues, "For the couple of years before the grunge thing took off, things were looking kind of rosy for the country rock sort of thing we were doing. Then Kurt Cobain told the world we were too slow and too clean. Funny — before that everyone said we were too fast and distorted."

Just before signing with Stony Plain in 1989, Jr. Gone Wild released their first album in three years, a cassette of odds and ends called *Folk You: The Guido Sessions*. Most of the songs would later reappear on Stony Plain releases, but the live recordings such as "Slept All Afternoon" and especially "Tin Can," as well as the demos, have a rough charm that make them essential listening. There are also gems like two songs by new guitarist Steve Loree, an acoustic version of Patrick McDonald's "Rhythm of the Rain," and "Six Pack," a funny country weeper by Dove about a highly dysfunctional family, and one of his best compositions.

Around this time, Jr. Gone Wild's influence was beginning to be felt on a new generation, particularly in western Canada. Carolyn Mark of Victoria — formerly of the Vinaigrettes, now of the Corn Sisters and with her own solo career — recalls a revelation she had. "They made me want to play in a band," says Mark. "In 1989, I was riding up Mount Tolmie with my friends in a baby blue '58 Chevy. My friend Jeremy was playing a tape and the song 'Slept All Afternoon' came out of the speakers. As we circled higher and higher up over the city at dusk, lyrically and rhythmically the song made me feel like time had stopped and it 'spoke to me.' A few months later Jr. Gone Wild came to Harpo's in Victoria for a weekend and I saw them every time they came to town. I had never heard music like it before. Later, I found out the stuff they were influenced by — Gram Parsons, Lucinda Williams — but they were the vehicle that brought it to me."

Stony Plain wanted to hook up Jr. Gone Wild with a known producer, someone who could provide them with some discipline in the studio. They chose Bill Henderson, who was best known for his pop/rock band Chilliwack, but who also created some of the most fascinating Canadian psychedelic pop of the '60s as a member of The Collectors. The experience was quite different for a sloppy road band who hadn't been in a studio in four years. "For one thing we were blown away to be signed and working with a Canadian rock legend," says McDonald. "For another we had a label taking an avid interest in *everything*. It was the first time we worked with an omnipresent producer. Bill was at pre-production, and he was there for every single minute of tracking and mixing. His stamina for the tedium is amazing. He wanted 'Tin Can' live off the floor. It's a twelve bar [blues structure], and we played that song for 12 hours. I've hated the song ever since. Years later I understood what he was up to. We were out of control, and he had to bring us down a notch or two. I learned an awful lot in those four weeks. The education I stole by working beside Bill Henderson serves me almost on a daily basis. He was kind, yet firm with me, and he tolerated a lot of naïve ego."

Other than solid production and a well-stewed bunch of songs, the first

Stony Plain album benefited from the addition of keyboardist/guitarist Ford Pier, who years later would become a coveted side player for diverse acts such as DOA and Veda Hille. Pier first joined the band as a roadie, and at one small town Ontario gig, he came across an old piano at soundcheck and started playing a classical piece; no one in the band knew he played before that. McDonald told him he was "the worst fucking roadie in the world" but that he should join the band instead. Pier was a manic stage presence, attacking his keyboards like a combination of Jerry Lee Lewis and Bob Wiseman.

Released in the fall of 1990, the album was titled *Too Dumb To Quit*, a phrase that Canadian rock critics like to recycle to this day when describing CanRock road warriors. Says McDonald, "That was my romantic view of the band — the show must go on and all that rot. We really were too dumb to stop. People quit the band or got kicked out all the time: fighting, bad health, drinking, playing shitholes, getting robbed, being cold. We'd been through all that hell before we made *Too Dumb*. I knew bands who broke up over things that occurred to us on a daily basis.

"Once I referred to Jr. Gone Wild as dysfunctional, but Ford disagreed. He said he has never been in a band that was more like a real family. We didn't treat each other as fragile things. We were brutally honest with each other. No one in Jr. had any reason or desire to lie about much, including our feelings for each other, which were manic and all over the place. If you were in Jr. Gone Wild, you were part of something that not everyone can handle. It may have destroyed my mental health, but it did wonders for my self-esteem."

Two other members were added to the band upon the release of *Too Dumb to Quit*: pedal steel guitarist Chris Smith and fiddler/vocalist Jane Hawley. With the exception of Hawley's fiddle, both were covering parts from the album. Vocalist Bernice Pelletier sang on the record and had a standing offer to join, but became pregnant before recording began. McDonald liked the idea of female vocals, and when he found out about Hawley's instrumental prowess and her willingness to tour, she was a shoo-in. Chris Smith was McDonald's roommate and a budding guitar wizard who had just picked up the pedal steel. "With the fiddle and pedal steel and piano, we got that cowpunk thing down to a science," says McDonald.

Of the new players, Dove says, "As well as a lot of energy they both brought varying amounts of sanity to the mix." That was becoming a bit of an issue, as prankster drummer Ed Dobek had rejoined the band for *Too Dumb To Quit*. His return was brief, and his exit was unforgettable.

Jr. Gone Wild stands on guard for Alberta, on the steps
of the legislature, 1991: Dove Brown, Chris Smith,
Jane Hawley, Mike McDonald
(Courtesy of Mike McDonald)

Jr. Gone Wild was headlining a sold-out show at the University of Alberta's Dinwoodie Lounge, a gig McDonald had dreamed of ever since his first band. Dobek "got so fucking drunk he could hardly stand," says McDonald. "He had put a lot of mustard in his hair — don't ask me — and it was his buddy Ian's birthday. There was a rumour that he had promised Ian he would sabotage our show as a birthday present. Whether that is true or not, he did fuck the show by playing the [syncopated, unusual] drum beat from XTC's 'Making Plans For Nigel' for the whole night. It was weird and challenging to keep my cool. Our soundman and Steve Loree told me in the set break that if Ed was at the next gig, they weren't gonna be. Chris Smith took his Strat and smashed a hole in the side of Ed's kick drum. Even Ford got mad at Ed. It was the last time I ever played professionally with him. Ed and I saw each other every day for eight years. You always give your brother third and fourth chances. Sadly, it ended all wrong." Dobek was replaced by Larry Shelast, who stayed with McDonald to the present day.

Steve Loree also left the band to focus on his new project, Greyhound Tragedy. With Hawley, Pier and Smith on board, McDonald had his strongest line-up ever, although that too wasn't going to last long. By 1991, Pier had an offer to join Vancouver reggae/funk band Roots Roundup, who were favourites of his at the time. His amicable departure was followed by Hawley's, who had gotten married and was also beginning to focus on her solo career; in 1992 she released an excellent traditional country album called *As We Walk On Thin Ice*, on which McDonald plays harmonica. Although her departure was also amicable, it came just before a much-anticipated seven-country European tour in 1992. It was one of many things that would soon go wrong.

"It was the hell tour from hell," recalls McDonald. "Our promoter fucked up royally. We landed in Amsterdam to find out immediately that a) our van just got towed and b) half the gigs were cancelled. We made the mistake of doing the entire continent in one month. We were very broke, and went three days without food at one point. Our soundman was hypoglycemic and losing his mind. Larry Shelast was used to his three square meals a day. I was the only one who was used to not eating for three days; by this time I was an amazing alcoholic. It was a shitty situation all around.

"However, though we were not getting along, and hardly ever got paid, whenever we did get to play we made the most of it," he continues. "One highlight was in Lund, Sweden. We opened for the local fave band, who were too relaxed and pandered to their crowd. We were tired, broke, hungry and frustrated Canadian rockers who had no real idea where we were geographically, and we played like we were possessed. It was shameful how badly we blew those guys off the stage, and we sold a lot of CDs that night. We went over well pretty much everywhere we went.

"When we went back a couple of years later to play Berlin, there was an awful lot of kids that were in cowpunk bands who came to see us. We had Lance Loree with us then. I guess they all knew what pedal steel sounded like, but they had never actually seen one in the hands of a master, so they had the treat of their musical lives. I was surrounded by guys asking questions about us, country music, the Beat Farmers — they were duly impressed to find out I was friends with them — and when I brought up the name Gram Parsons, they all fell silent and listened with reverence to anything I had to say about the man. It was great. I guess we were seen as prophets in Europe, whereas back home we were seen as radicals."

Immediately following that tour, in the middle of four months on the road, Jr. Gone Wild went to work on their second Stony Plain album, *Pull the Goalie*. It was recorded near Barrie, Ontario, in a mansion owned by the Christie family, of the cookie dynasty. It had been run down and available to rent, and at the suggestion of producer Peter Moore — who had lured the Cowboy Junkies into a church to make their definitive recording — the band rented it and converted it into a temporary studio.

Perhaps because of their extended stay on the road, *Pull the Goalie* sounds like a band at their peak. The guitars snarl and crackle, McDonald sings with more conviction than ever before, and the rhythm section propels songs like "God is Not My Father," Chris Smith's definitive road song "1000 Miles to Go" and Dove's gospel punk "March into Jerusalem."

"I wrote 'March into Jerusalem' about the night we found out Mike's brother Patrick had committed suicide," says Dove. "It was a long fast maniacal drive from Winnipeg to Edmonton through the night. About two weeks later when the smoke had cleared, I wrote it in a couple of hours."

As with *Too Dumb to Quit*, three *Pull the Goalie* songs are oldies dating back to *Folk You* and earlier: "God is Not My Father," "What's Going On" and the late Patrick McDonald's "Rhythm of the Rain," which is given a fiery makeover, with soaring backing vocals by Kathryn Rose. "I was always resistant to re-recording things that were already released," says McDonald, "but we weren't the only ones involved in song choice. I have always regarded it open season on any song I wrote that hasn't been released yet when it comes time to choose material for a record." McDonald's sharp wit continued to develop on "Just the Other Day," "Where the Hell Are You" and "(You Didn't Leave Me Baby You Just) Beat Me To the Door."

In 1993, McDonald celebrated his 30th birthday at the Power Plant club in Edmonton, with a three and a half hour set featuring plenty of Jr. Gone Wild alumni. Shortly after, at a three-night gig in Jasper, he realised that he might not live to see his 40th unless he tackled his chronic alcoholism. "I had alcohol poisoning and was doing a bad job," he recalls of his moment of clarity. "I hated everyone and everything. Rock bottom. Something had to change or I would die. I had already contracted alcoholic hepatitis and gastritis, and I hadn't taken a solid dump in two years. It came down to quit or die. It nearly killed the band."

Since their inception, Jr. Gone Wild had developed a reputation for being a hard-drinking band, a reputation that always seems to enhance a band's appeal with the predominantly campus crowds they play for. "It may be entertaining and it may be fun to hear and read about that stuff," laments McDonald. "But if you could experience even five minutes of the misery someone enslaved to a substance goes through, you wouldn't find it so amusing. I refuse to believe you need an altered mind to create good art. There are people I knew who read *The Basketball Diaries* and ran out and tried heroin, and they are idiots.

"Over time I think it was expected of us — our schtick if you will," McDonald continues. "We were selfish and evil about it. We all had our own dark reasons. I was avoiding a lot of stuff, so denial is definitely a part of it. We were basically a bunch of twisted individuals who made their own therapy and got busy instead of going on psych pensions. Plus we were rock-'n'-rollers with rock-'n'-roll heroes we were dying to emulate. Mostly though, in my case, it was clinical alcoholism. I needed a certain amount daily to stop the shakes. I never ate, guzzled Maalox — not a good way to be."

Dove says, "Mike was like most drunks: angry, self-centred, and often belligerent. When he quit drinking he became what they call a dry drunk: angry, self-centred and often belligerent. Now, he's mellowed with age, experience and sobriety. He's less angry, less self-centred and less belligerent. He's still Mike. But sober, he's far more useful to himself and all of us."

McDonald muses, "Things were never the same after I quit booze. I started writing better and playing better, and our audience packed up and went home. They deserted us. Even today I am the guy who suffers for the sins of Jr. Gone Wild. People with long memories do not hire me, while they hire anyone who used to be in the band."

It was also a time when an explosion of new independent music shoved some veterans off to the side in favour of new faces, a time when cowpunk was considered dead and alt-country had yet to become a catch phrase. The three-year gap between *Pull the Goalie* and its follow-up, 1995's *Simple Little Wish*, didn't help either. It's a gap McDonald doesn't attribute to his battle with sobriety, or anything else in particular. "I honestly don't know," he says. "I don't think three years between records is a long time. We made *Simple* when it was the right time to do it. The three-year gap was probably an artistic issue."

Simple Little Wish was a mellower, more adult record, with most of the punk influence and sardonicism stripped away for a straightforward approach. Past members and associates Bernice Pelletier, Jane Hawley, Ford Pier and Carolyn Mark help flesh out the record. Most noticeably, *Simple Little Wish* is full of songs about resilience and survival. "The record itself and a lot of the songs were made when I was a relatively new sober person," says McDonald. "I was also having to leave sessions early once a week to see a shrink and attend anger management classes. I suppose I was demonstrating how I hadn't lost my 'edge.' There were a lot of emotional ups and downs in my environment at the time. 'Dropping Like Flies' is about all the people I knew who were dying of heroin overdoses at the time. 'Guy Who Came In From The Cold' is me getting sober and comfortable with myself that way. 'Downtime' is an 'enough is enough' type of tune. For me, *Simple Little Wish* was my statement that I'm not done with this shit yet."

The album did garner some good press, most of which dealt with McDonald's sobriety and survival skills. He was quoted in the *Globe and Mail* as saying, "I'm embarrassed by 50 per cent of the stuff I've said and done and I don't remember the other 50 per cent." The band played 11 shows on the way to Toronto in February, where they were going to have a big launch. To promote the Toronto show, they were booked onto CITY-TV's *Breakfast Television*, where Dove slipped on some ice in the parking lot and broke his wrist. McDonald assesses: "End of tour, end of album, and as it would turn out, end of band. We lived on in a coma for another few months. It all got off with a bang, but after Dove broke his arm, folks stopped coming out to see us. Our last tour that summer was pathetically attended, coast to coast. It was the end."

The official end came that fall, on a less-than-inspiring note. "Our last official gig was October 27, 1995 at the MacEwan Hall Ballroom at the University of Calgary," says McDonald. Jr. Gone Wild was the middle act between the Gandharvas and headliners She Stole My Beer. "There were a few Edmontonians who knew we were splitting up that showed. It was down to just me, Dove and Larry. Oddly, I recall it not being all that sentimental, although I was very aware of the 'last gig-ness' of things. I remember thinking when we did 'Tin Can' that I would never ever have to play that stupid song again, and I haven't to this day. We were typically stoic about it. No tears, not in front of the guys, anyways. I bawled my eyes out later while re-reading the final interview in [Edmonton weekly] *See* magazine."

Jr. Gone Wild's death was protracted by an obligation to appear in a musical theatre production called *Messiah*, which they had co-written with their friends in the Edmonton comedy troupe Three Dead Trolls in a Baggie. The last performances of the play were in Winnipeg, November 25–27, 1995. "Dove, Larry and I were still in our silly costumes," says McDonald. "After the play we did [*Too Dumb To Quit*'s] 'I Don't Know About All That.' And that was all she wrote. It was a poorly attended gig. Jr. Gone Wild died a cold and lonely death."

The decision to pull the plug rested with Dove. "Over the years Jr. had run into a lot of brick walls, but we always had a ladder or a battering ram or shovel or something to get us past it," says Dove. "During Jr.'s last year the signs were all there. Just looking out at the crowd each night, I could feel it coming and I knew we didn't have — and couldn't get — the implements to get past it. It was time for all of us to make a change."

"Dove and I were never great friends," says McDonald. "He even once told me to my face that he never did like me very much. While that kind of hurt my feelings, I was moved by his honourable sense of loyalty to what we were doing. He was like me that way — the band was bigger than the people in it. It worked, and being friends was a petty concern next to the music, the shows and the travelling. It's kind of like the anecdotes from the Vietnam War where guys hate each other as people, but have absolute faith and trust in their abilities in a fire fight. I wouldn't trust Dove with a girlfriend or to speak kindly of me, but I would, without hesitation, trust him with my life."

For his part, Dove says, "More than anything it was the love of the music and belief in the project. We both knew we had great songs and made great music. Through shared experience, we formed a sort of brotherhood. Common experiences create common attitudes and common goals. Like brothers growing up together, we developed similarities. Families are not created by genetics alone."

"I was so fucked up when Jr. Gone Wild quit it was like quitting booze all over again," says McDonald. "Jr. Gone Wild was how I defined myself. I was terrified of being on my own. I am certain now that I kept Jr. together so long because I had an emotional need for it. We were a fiscal nightmare. We could have made it if we had done certain things, but I was fulfilled having a surrogate family to belong in. I never wanted to be the dad, though. That part of the plan backfired on me."

In the years following Jr. Gone Wild's break-up, McDonald formed a punk trio, recorded an album and scrapped it on the way to the printing plant. He then formed a more pop-oriented band featuring two female back-up singers and a synth player, while becoming a staple solo performer on the Edmonton scene. Dove also became a solo performer, and acted in some musical theatre. McDonald watched the rise of so-called "insurgent country" or "alt-country" with much bemusement. "I had a musical agenda," he says. "Over time I started to look at the rock/country fusion with an eye towards changing the face of modern country music. Pure hubris, and the band died before I had a chance to beak off about it. I regard Ford Pier's song 'Raisins' from *Simple Little Wish* as the definitive alt-country song of all time. It was my suggestion of where C&W ought to be going." The song is a 135bpm barn-stomper with heavy guitar, furious banjo picking, choppy fiddle and pedal steel. "On weaker days, I am slightly embittered that we missed out on the audience," he continues. "But over time one gets used to a fate of being a conduit — always a bridesmaid and all that shit."

Jr. Gone Wild's role on the Stony Plain roster always seemed a bit incongruous, amidst reverent roots artists steeped in tradition. Fans of Stony Plain artists aren't the type of listeners to be on the lookout for innovative new sounds, and one must wonder if Jr. Gone Wild could have been marketed to a different audience on another label. McDonald says, "Stony Plain was more or less a blues/C&W/folk label, and we fell slightly out of that purview. I always sensed that Holger Peterson was more concerned with historically important work than large sales, even if only by a little bit. After all, he did eventually drop us. But as he said when we parted company, 'We got three great Canadian albums out there.' And I really hope they are. There are all kinds of factors, but I'm not the kind to blame the label for all my shortcomings. We had a lot to do with our failures, as well as our successes. I'm convinced that some of it has to be our fault."

Today, McDonald focuses primarily on his solo performances and continuing to hone his craft. He approaches his role in the history of Canadian roots music with a mixture of pride, modesty, and bewilderment. In Bruce McDonald's movie *Hard Core Logo*, loosely based on a book by McDonald's friend and peer Michael Turner of the Hard Rock Miners, there is a shot of an Edmonton map; the highway leading into the city is renamed the Mike McDonald Freeway. "We are part of the local folklore now, at least the name is," he says. "Whenever a junior league sports team wins a championship, the *Edmonton Sun* in particular always uses the headline 'Jr. Gone Wild.' That tickles me pink. Sometimes I feel smug when bands tell me their cute little road and drinking stories. I still have better ones than all those guys! I am amused by the bands who do a western swing for two weeks for the first time and come back acting all road-weary and 'experienced.' It pleases my ego when some people treat me with respect just because of who I am and what I've done. But only rookie band guys do this: don't worry, I am not seen by my actual peers as anything but that guy who used to be in that asshole band, especially by Jr. vets!

"For the most part, Jr. Gone Wild seems like a great story I was told by someone. It really seems like it happened to someone else. Sometimes I reflect and go, 'Did all that really happen?' My deepest hope is that we get at least a footnote in the history of Canadian rock-'n'-roll. It would be good to know that it all really mattered. We put everything we had into it. I won't bullshit you and say we did it for our fans. We did it because we felt we had to. We were driven to do it. For what it's worth, we were glad to do so."

"The band that we are trying to create is this
four-way democracy, which is really hard.
I would argue if there were any bands in
Halifax that were influenced by us, it was
less musically and more so politically. There
are a lot of bands dividing things up and
having multiple writers, which makes for a
really volatile group."
— Chris Murphy

The Importance of
Being Sloan

In the spring of 1994, Chip Sutherland was between a managerial rock and a hard place. He had just met with the heavies at Geffen Records and they were not happy with the results of the sophomore album by his client Sloan, *Twice Removed*. To put it mildly, they hated it. Furthermore, they had just informed him that they wanted Sloan to return to the studio to re-record the album. Alone in the label's Los Angeles office, Sutherland now had the unenviable task of relaying this news to the band.

The "Sloan" that Geffen had envisioned were to be the Canadian grunge lords of the Nirvana monarchy. Like Nirvana and the rest of that band's Seattle contemporaries, Sloan was the largest diamond of a smaller cluster of pop-punk bands from a newly mined musical centre. The band's debut full-length album, *Smeared*, was far from a commercial colossus, but it had gained Sloan an exceptionally broad profile in their home country. Armed with killer alternative pop rockets like "Underwhelmed" and "500 Up," the band's sound was certainly in line with the Geffen world view. With the success of other like-minded acts on the label, Geffen predicted a sweet future for Sloan.

The album that the Haligonian quartet had delivered to their bosses did not reflect this future. If anything, *Twice Removed* echoed the past. With all four members in the band having a vocally and creatively distinct presence on the album, the dozen tracks hopscotched over the popular music palette like a K-Tel compilation record from the '70s, and this certainly was not Nirvana. As it was consistently pointed out in the press, this was closer to the Beatles. The label was certain that fans would not buy into this, and rock radio was unlikely to kick Seattle grunge out of bed for Sloan's retro-pop. If the success of Stone Temple Pilots — an L.A. band aping Pearl Jam — was any indication, *Twice Removed* would have a fleeting commercial lifespan.

It put Sloan's manager, Chip Sutherland, in an awkward position. Sitting in that L.A. office, Sutherland conference-called his band to deliver the grim headline. "Boys, I'm going to meet [Geffen president] Eddie Rosenblatt in half an hour and he's going to ask us to re-record the record. I need to know what to tell them." The band was conscious of the fact they had taken on a different musical mindset, but they never fathomed this artistic barricade. Bewildered and frustrated, the band sought their manager's opinion.

"I think you should tell them to go fuck themselves," replied Sutherland. "It will be the end of your career here at Geffen, but you made a good record and you know it. If you start trying to make records for record companies then you're fucked."

In agreement with their manager, Sloan directed Sutherland to follow that path, only without the profanity. Geffen A&R rep Todd Sullivan, responsible for Sloan's signing, and high off his recent success with Weezer, symbolically threw his jacket over the mud in front of Sutherland, and insisted on handling the situation. He was in agreement with the Sloan camp and did not feel that they should re-record the album. Sutherland was resistant at first, as he did not want Sullivan to suffer the repercussions of not supporting the company line. The A&R rep, however, was insistent on delivering the news because, as he saw it, they were "his band."

Geffen was told that under no circumstances would Sloan be re-recording *Twice Removed*. As Sutherland puts it, "[Geffen] said, 'Okay, we'll put the record out anyways, but good luck.' You don't tell a record company that we're not re-recording and expect them to do anything with the record."

Admits guitarist Jay Ferguson, "It was taking a chance at the time, and our career was potentially destroyed. Geffen didn't really understand the album, but I'm glad we didn't change it. I think it's relatively timeless."

The album and the scenario are both indicative of the integrity that has marked Sloan's decade-long career. *Twice Removed* was about taking a chance, and firmly establishing the band as a four-headed democracy. The band's mandates were, and continue to be, quite straightforward: take the democratic governing systems of your favourite bands, explore the history of rock as you will, and let everyone have a voice so that nobody — audience included — gets bored. When Geffen quashed *Twice Removed*, the band opted to break up rather than conform. In early 1995, after a couple of albums, an EP and a few singles, Jay Ferguson, Chris Murphy, Patrick Pentland and Andrew Scott announced Sloan would no longer exist.

The biggest coup, after the massive amount of media coverage of the band's 1995 separation died down, was that in 1996 they would land the top spot in *Chart* magazine's first-ever poll of the Top 50 Canadian Albums of All Time. Surveying over a hundred people from the industry and media, the votes were strongly in favour of *Twice Removed* as the best Canadian album of all time. This was a year-old album that had yet to even break Canadian gold status (50,000 copies), and it had beat out CanRock staples and career-defining albums like Joni Mitchell's *Blue* and Neil Young's *Harvest*. Sloan would downplay the poll's importance, calling it "jock talk" and "flattering but stupid." Naysayers attributed this accomplishment to collective pining for a prematurely deceased cult band. Yet this poll reflected the opinions of musicians, the media and the industry; this was not derived, as is usually the case, from a fickle teenage vote-in poll. In the 2000 *Chart* poll, *Twice Removed* would place third, perhaps justifiably ousted by the aforementioned Mitchell and Young albums. Interestingly, with the hype long behind them, four of Sloan's five albums occupied spots on the list.

There have been, and continue to be, plenty of talented acts in Halifax, but it was these four — mainly suburban, university-bred and far from cookie-cutter rock stars — who drew significant national and international attention to Canada's east coast alternative scene. Sloan is a cult band of the highest order, enjoying the support of rabid fans and a series of near hits, but only selling modest numbers of their albums. The band's appeal is derived from a winning combination of brilliant pop songs and clever lyricism, without the seedy notoriety normally associated with the rock world. There is also an attractive garden of folklore that surrounds them, including the placement of heavy media broaches such as "Seattle of the North" on Halifax and "Canada's Beatles" on their name, the arena sports allure of the David vs. Goliath conflict with Geffen and the survival of both a band break-up and their exodus to Toronto.

In the end, the media excitement subsides, and it's the music that determines whether or not the band stands the test of time. "What makes them attractive to people," observes Sutherland, "is that they told Geffen to go fuck themselves and their record gets chosen as the top Canadian record of all time. They stuck to their guns and the people who know the story love that. It's a thing that a movie is made of."

Christopher Michael Murphy was born on November 7, 1968, in Charlotte-town, Prince Edward Island, to Joseph and Pat Murphy. His father's path to becoming a university professor took the family briefly to Virginia, and then to Scarborough, Ontario, where Chris and his younger sister Alison completed their first years of school. From a young age, Chris was given the chance to explore his creative boundaries. His first exposure to a low wattage of limelight occurred when he was selected to star in a variety of television commercials, the most noteworthy being for a prominent Canadian meat producer. He also accomplished a stint as a junior model in the pages of various Sears catalogues in the '70s. His musical germination, however, began in front of the television set on Hallowe'en night in 1976. At nine years old, Murphy was introduced to the pyrotechnic rock posturing of KISS on the Paul Lynde Hallowe'en special, and he was immediately convinced that he had found his calling. He needed to pick up the guitar. He also needed make-up.

Elsewhere in downtown Halifax, Jay Ferguson had also witnessed the same Hallowe'en special. He too was turned on by KISS's rock and roll presence, though it would become only one of many favourites in Ferguson's musical toy box. Born John Howard Ferguson III on October 14, 1968, to architect Howard and financial bookkeeper Phyllis Ferguson, he had what some may term an accelerated music education — at least in the context of music history. Most post-1970s adolescents discover artists like the Beatles, The Beach Boys, Otis Redding and Motown after many awkward teenage years of being a victim of current trends, or the unwilling recipient of their parents' record collection. Remarkably, Ferguson had never gone through such phases. As a young child he expressed a keen interest in music and sound. He was given a portable tape recorder that he would often use to tape things off the TV. As his appetite grew, he started dragging his mother to Woolco to pick up actual records: the *Grease* soundtrack, ABBA's *Greatest Hits*, and KISS's *Destroyer*. But his true music-history apprenticeship would happen when he landed the dream job of every young music fan.

While most 12-year-olds were babysitting or delivering papers, Ferguson worked at Ol' Dan's Records. The store was situated in a house on Dresden Row in downtown Halifax, and Jay's employment there from 1981 to 1985 gave him a head start on his record collection and made him far more musically mature than most of his peers. Recounts Ferguson, "[Ol' Dan's] had this thing called Beatlefest one summer, the summer after John Lennon died. I went there for this thing and I kept going back and hanging out there. I was in there one time and this guy got fired, and the guy who ran the store asked, 'Do you want to work here?' It was around the corner so [my mother] didn't care. It was basically babysitting me, but I was getting paid."

Through four years at Ol' Dan's, owner George Zimmerman and his clientele exposed the young Ferguson to the likes of the Beatles, the Stones, The Stooges, Roxy Music, Motown, Big Star, The Beach Boys and a variety of other classic genres and albums. *Switchback¸* a youth-centred program on CBC-TV, was drawn to the anomaly of the 12-year-old record store clerk, and interviewed the precocious Ferguson about his job and his knowledge of the Beatles and The Beach Boys.

Growing up as an only child with a single parent in the city's downtown, Ferguson attended Halifax Grammar School. This was a private school not only notable for its affluent student body, but also for its utter lack of heavy metal fans. The inside joke in Sloan surrounding Ferguson concerns the epiphany he felt when he first saw the rivals of the "greasers," the wealthy "socs" (short for socials) in the movie adaptation of S.E. Hinton's *The Outsiders*. Agrees Ferguson, "It's true about private school. Nobody I knew, except a couple of people, liked heavy metal. There were a lot of people into punk. I don't know why. Maybe it was kids with more money or affluence. It was all The Jam, The Specials and The Style Council. They were all very big [on] sharp-dressed punkers."

Ferguson, like most of the students attending Halifax Grammar School at the time, was turned onto punk music through his classmate Matthew Murphy. Matt's older brother, Luke, would access the punk imports of the Sex Pistols, The Clash, Sham 69, 999 and Madness through the family's connections in England. "Matt was bringing these records to school dances in Grade Seven. I was like 'Holy shit, this is awesome!' We all would take them home and tape them. I was hearing different stuff at Ol' Dan's Records, but from Luke Murphy's hand-me-down records I discovered punk."

In eighth grade, Ferguson's mother gave him an acoustic guitar for Christmas. After his mother listened to Jay play out of tune for nearly a year, she enrolled him in guitar lessons with Phil Black who would, incidentally, also briefly teach Chris Murphy. Jay stuck it out for a while, but was fairly vocal about the direction he wanted to pursue. "I didn't want to learn anything that my teacher provided," he admits. "I kept on bringing him R.E.M.

songs: 'Can you teach me how to play this? Can you teach me how to play "This Charming Man" by The Smiths?' I read interviews with Peter Buck at this time and he talked about guitar playing and being in a band as if anybody could do it if they had the will. He was very down to earth and reading things like this really inspired me. I would often buy records that he name-checked in interviews: the Velvet Underground, Nick Drake, Richard Thompson, Hüsker Dü and Sonic Youth, and I love them to this day."

Chris Murphy began attending Clayton Park Junior High School a year after his family moved to Halifax, and by this point he was far from listening only to KISS. He had discovered the more intellectual end of the hard rock spectrum by listening to Rush. He too discovered the American and British tributaries of punk through a friend's older brother's record collection. His interest in playing music was mounting, though his resistance to formal training meant that his skills would develop mainly through self-instruction. Murphy discovered through a couple of experiences that he was simply not suited for the traditional approaches to music education. "I took lessons for two months [in Toronto], but it was all this ta-ta-ti-ti-ta shit and they made me clap. I hated clapping. I also wanted to show up in makeup, so I quit." In eighth grade, his mother managed to pass down her knowledge of the guitar, albeit limited, after another aborted attempt at proper lessons. Later, in ninth grade, he took a stab at percussion through a school music program, but was kicked out for not bringing his music. Part of his problem was that he was not too excited about being stuck on the xylophone. He was set on learning the drums.

High school proved a fruitful time for Murphy — at least musically. Through friends at Halifax West Secondary School, he was introduced to Minor Threat, and Ian MacKaye's Dischord label. Murphy became infatuated with MacKaye's anti-rock star image, his support of the community and his straight-edge movement in punk music — a philosophy that celebrates abstinence from alcohol, drugs and smoking. It was the polar opposite to the overindulgence of KISS that first lured Murphy to the music world. Explains Murphy, "It's more of a teenage thing. For me it was like a peer pressure defense mechanism. It wasn't that I don't drink and I'm cooler than you, it's that I don't drink and I'm just as cool as you."

Punk rock was a force that existed outside of Chris Murphy's own environment until a young band that attended his school caused a minor tremor throughout the city's music scene. "Jellyfishbabies put out a 12" record and it was just blowing my head off. They were a grade younger than me. On 'punk rock day' back in Grade Nine, I went to school as a punk and they all came as preps. I was incredibly embarrassed. I was so into being a punk, but I wasn't there yet. They were all so over it. Jellyfishbabies, to me, were the big band." The fact that a group from Halifax was making music Chris Murphy held in the same esteem as his favourite bands showed him that the music he championed could be made in his own town. In essence, it pushed every competitive button in his head. And so began Chris Murphy's evolution in a variety of punk bands: Wit-out gave way to Aware, and then Murphy traded the guitar to play drums in Aware's later incarnation, Spent.

Spent made a minor dent in the city's small hardcore scene. The band, which featured a vocalist also by the name of Chris Murphy, made a fabled hardcore pilgrimage to Washington, D.C., to track down Dischord hero Ian MacKaye. The warmth that MacKaye displayed when the Haligonian quartet knocked on the door of his home made a permanent impression on Murphy that would influence the way he would deal with people throughout his career.

After graduating from Halifax West in the spring of 1986, Chris started working as a porter at Victoria General Hospital. Through this job he met Matt Murphy and formed what would become a long-term friendship. That summer Chris was introduced to a couple of Matt's schoolmates, bassist Henri Sangalang and guitarist Jay Ferguson. Ferguson had played with Matt Murphy in the Deluxe Boys after the band's original drummer Walter Kemp left for university in the fall of '86. Matt Murphy joined guitarist Ferguson, singer John Gould and bassist Stephen Cooke as the band's drummer. The band was a training camp for all the musicians involved, and marked their development from covering "Wild Thing," "Tequila" and Jellyfishbabies songs to writing original material.

Over this time, Chris would moonlight from Spent, and performed at a few summer parties with Matt and Henri under the pseudonym the El Caminos. Both the El Caminos and the Deluxe Boys disbanded in 1987 as a result of post-secondary education pulling the musicians in different directions. In the fall of 1986, Chris had started a B.A. in English at Dalhousie University, and Jay enrolled in a history program at King's College. They were token degrees to appease their parents; both students were rock and roll dreamers pining to be in a band — especially Ferguson, who years later earnestly admitted, "I had no back-up plan. This basically had to happen. It was either luck or else."

The trio of Jay Ferguson, Chris Murphy, and Henri Sangalang finally solidified a year later in October 1987 in Sangalang's basement, and casu-

Chris Murphy, before the fame, in
Kearney Lake Rd.
(Photo by Eric B. Brown)

ally named their band after a street sign in Chris's house. The resulting music was not quite so trivial. In 1988, Spent lived up to its name, and Kearney Lake Rd. became Chris Murphy's musical focus. Murphy describes Kearney Lake Rd.'s sound as a combination of Sangalang and Ferguson's pop rock influences, his hardcore punk values and a NoMeansNo brand of drumming. "We began with Led Zeppelin covers in Henri's basement and quickly wrote our own stuff. Jay and Henri did most of the writing at the beginning. Jay was into R.E.M., and Henri was into 'mod' stuff, and I was still full-on into hardcore. Our first tape was an ugly mix of these three things — made ugly by me for the most part."

The recorded work showcases every one of their musical touchstones, and arguably foreshadows some of the devices that would become part of the foundation of Sloan: strong multi-strata pop songs, multiple songwriters and killer harmonies. Songs like "In Your Eyes" featured Ferguson's Peter Buck/Johnny Marr style of guitar playing and the band's Minutemen/Hüsker Dü influences were predominant on "Every Trip and Fall." Of particular note is "Painting a Room," which is an eerily perfect acoustic anthem for Halifax's inbred music scene, a phenomenon just beginning to intensify.

The trio's live show was also explosive, with the twin attack of the long-haired Ferguson and Sangalang playing co-frontmen and Murphy exercising his unique rhythmic style and penchant for unconventional time signatures. It wasn't long before the band had made a name around town through the airplay of their self-produced tapes on the Dalhousie University radio station, CKDU. The fact that they were one of the city's only bands playing melodic riff-oriented rock also drew attention to the band. Most of the bands that had attracted some attention had either folded or traded the isolation of Halifax for hopes of breaking into a bigger musical centre. Musical drought aside, the band was impressive in its own right, and their impact is still felt throughout the Halifax music community. "They were the best local band," affirms Halifax's No Records head Waye Mason. "The photocopied cover and hand-dubbed tapes on their dads' dual cassette deck were in my tape collection right next to whatever major label release I was into at the time. They were a big deal."

While Kearney Lake Rd. was carving a niche, so too was Peter Rowan in Fredericton. An avid music fan who had moved from Edmonton, he had begun to make a name for himself by booking local shows and bringing in decent Canadian acts. He later formed one of the east coast's first independent labels, DTK Records, named after the Johnny Thunders lyric "dressed to kill like a motherfucker." Rowan released a variety of LPs from local bands like the Vogons, and later Halifax's 100 Flowers and Jellyfishbabies, which carried his reputation with the scene's young bands. "Peter Rowan was seen as big time," admits Murphy. "He was from Fredericton and he had put records out. It was like 'Holy shit, Peter Rowan's at the show! Act cool!'"

There was little need for such worries. Rowan was immediately turned on by what he had heard of Kearney Lake Rd. He laid out an invitation for the band to play Fredericton, and later to record there for a release on DTK. In the fall of 1989, Rowan took the trio, along with two other Maritime bands, Hector's Body and the Stratejackets, on a brief tour to Toronto where they ended up playing a showcase at the Rivoli. This event was covered in a short MuchMusic news segment that showed the three acts playing to a sparsely populated audience. VJ Erica Ehm interviewed Sangalang and a mute Ferguson, with Sangalang accepting the role as ambassador from the east coast alternative scene. He informed the nation that there were good reasons to pay attention to the development of music in the Maritimes, but the rest of the world would not realize this for at least a few more years.

This poor showing did not go unnoticed by Murphy. Between the effort of working for popular success outside Halifax and band in-fighting, Kearney Lake Rd. was laid to rest after a final show at King's College in early 1990. Rowan's label, unorganized and lacking a financial pulse, would never release the record, but a posthumous tape copy of the unreleased DTK album still ended up placing fourth on CKDU's year-end poll. Recalls Murphy, "We broke up and it was kind of hard because we had a record ready to go, and I was too chicken to take the next step. I didn't know where we were going. Peter didn't seem to offer a lot of direction. As we got to know him better, it was obvious he wasn't a business hound. He was just a guy, only a little older."

In 1989, Murphy met Andrew Scott, a local DJ at The Flamingo Club whom he quickly befriended after discovering they shared mutual musical interests. When they ended up at the Nova Scotia College of Art and Design (NSCAD) together in 1990, the pair would schedule jams in Scott's bedroom whenever possible. Using Scott's father's old drum kit, Murphy played the role of the teacher; however, in a short period of time Scott would excel beyond whatever Murphy could impart.

Though Andrew Scott enjoyed playing music, his primary focus was NSCAD. Unlike Murphy, Scott went because he actually felt that art was his calling. "Chris probably enjoyed fucking around at NSCAD for a year or so, but he never seemed comfortable there," says Scott. "He felt like he didn't belong there, but I really did. When he would bug me to paint pictures of KISS, I flatly refused, and almost felt insulted. Perhaps I took things a little too seriously, but I still don't see any paintings of Ace Frehley as future subject matter."

Andrew Walter Gibson Scott was a relatively late bloomer in terms of playing music. As much as he grew up an ardent music fan, he didn't entertain the same dreams of rock stardom as Ferguson and Murphy. His goal was to become a painter, and he came by his first love of visual arts honestly. The third child and only son born to Walter and Diane Scott on November 15, 1967, in Ottawa, Ontario, Scott was raised in an environment where fine art and music were always present. His Scottish migrant father, a trained naval architect and engineer, was the predominant artistic influence in his formative years, although the world Walter Scott presented did not include rock and roll.

When Andrew was six the family moved to Halifax's sister city, Dartmouth, N.S., where Walter would hang up his architect's cap and accept a civil service position. An accomplished artist and a fine musician, Walter used this two-pronged artistic escape to relieve the frustrations of his unfulfilling job within the Department of Fisheries. "When he moved away from the design aspect of ship building and became caught up in the bullshit of government, the art was the only way to relax him," notes Scott. Any chance he could get he would indulge in the enjoyment or creation of art or music. He was a realistic painter, and was often commissioned to paint warships and planes for military veterans. A self-taught drummer, pianist and guitarist, his love for music was focused on jazz. Along with six other friends,

Walter created the Dixi Tech Seven and recorded an album. Walter's drum kit was almost always set up in the house, though surprisingly, his son never expressed an interest in playing it.

Andrew's early exposure to rock and roll came through his elder sister Kristine, who introduced him to the primal joys of Van Halen and Black Sabbath when their father was out of earshot. It was not that Andrew did not appreciate his father's musical interests; in fact he played trombone in the junior-high school band. However, he soon realized that when it came to playing music, he was pining to be Black Sabbath's Tony Iommi, and not jazz trombonist Kid Ory. "I would walk to school in a jean jacket with pyramid studs flanking my shoulders, a bullet belt and a huge patch of Tygers of Pan Tang on the back, all the while carrying a trombone case just wishing it was a guitar."

At 14, Scott experienced a tragic loss when his father suffered a major cardiac arrest and passed away at the age of 48. Alone in the house at the time of the heart attack, Andrew watched his father slip from his life. "I was the only one there and had to call my mother at work," reveals Scott. "I was 14 and his last words to me were, 'Well, I guess you've got yourself a drum kit.' This wasn't the sentimental impetus for me taking up the drums — it was simply the last thing he said to me."

School also produced its share of difficulties in Andrew's life. An admittedly poor student, Scott ended up repeating both Grades Six and Twelve, though he adds, "This didn't affect me too much. I wasn't exactly popular, nor was I unpopular. I had a lot of good friends and the notion of failing a grade or two was almost inconsequential. I was interested in sports and drawing way more than schoolwork. Girls also figured heavily in the reasons for my constant failing grades. I don't mean to infer that I was a Romeo or Ladies' Man of any sort — I was a daydreamer and had no interest in learning math or grammar. I just wanted to play spin-the-bottle in the woods, play soccer and draw pictures."

Scott placed most of his extra-curricular attention on sports during high school, especially basketball. Through his Afro-Canadian friends on the team, Scott became a fan of various forms of rap. Between this, his love for British metal (Motorhead, Judas Priest), and post-punk bands (Swans, Sonic Youth and Joy Division), his influences became what he terms "a confused dog's breakfast, but in a good way." Recalls Scott, "There I was on my way to basketball practice on my skateboard listening to tapes of MC Shan, wearing homemade T-shirts with the K-422 record label [home of the Swans] emblazoned across the front. I had a terrible time of shifting looks and changing identity for whatever the circumstance might require. I didn't know who I was."

After a short-lived attempt to learn the piano in Grade Three, Scott quickly figured out that he would not excel by reading music; he could only pick things up by listening and watching. When a friend taught him how to play "Paranoid" on the guitar, he was immediately sold on the instrument. Scott's first live appearance in a band came in the form of lead-guitar duties for Oreo Reverse ("two white boys and a black guy"), a one-off high school hip-hop-act, aping the Beastie Boys for a Queen Elizabeth High School variety show. He admits that his playing at this point had grown to reflect his admiration for rockabilly, namely Brian Setzer and the local rockabilly combo The Lone Stars, but he only lightly entertained the idea of forming a serious rock band. His attention would be focused on his studies at NSCAD.

Scott says, "Art school was the best thing I ever did. It was an environment not unlike Romper Room, but I learned so much and gained so much experience that I know I never would have received from a straight academic university."

Creatively, this was a fertile period in Scott's history. He discovered his major passion for painting, he was jamming with Murphy in a combo Scott dubbed Furious George, and through longtime girlfriend Fiona Highet, he joined No Damn Fears after the departure of original drummer Pete Digesu. They became the first serious, gig-playing band that Scott participated in. Led by Halifax mainstay Dave Marsh, No Damn Fears also featured Chris Murphy's high-school sweetheart and future Jale member Jennifer Pierce on vocals, and soon became one of the city's most well-regarded acts. Eventually Scott would find himself moonlighting in various acts with Chris Murphy.

A short while after Kearney Lake Rd. broke up, Murphy started playing in the popular local roots rock act Black Pool. He became interested in joining the band after he heard that Black Pool had been selected to be a guinea pig for a recording workshop with famed Rush producer Terry Brown, where as Murphy explains it, "goons are going to pay a hundred dollars to watch him work." Black Pool was the antithesis of everything Kearney Lake Rd. had stood for. They played melodic mainstream roots rock that earned well-paying gigs and a record deal. The band earned more money in a single high school show than Kearney Lake Rd. had cumulatively earned over its entire two-year lifespan. Led by singer/songwriter John Chisholm, Black Pool's primary intent was to become a lucrative pop act. This wasn't exactly in line with Murphy's Dischord label-based ideals, but he discovered it was a decent way to put himself through school. He also found it novel to work with the infamous Brown.

Reminisces Murphy, "I was interested to meet Terry Brown because I had been a Rush fan as a kid. It was humiliating, because Terry Brown had to hold every bass string I wasn't playing because they were all ringing. I could barely play, and I was surrounded by people who paid to get in. They're like 'His string's ringing, Terry!' 'I think he's flat, Terry!' I was beet red and sweating."

The album that resulted from these sessions was *We The Living*. It features compositions by Chisholm and guitarist Phil Sedore, but nothing from Murphy. A couple of his compositions made it into the live show, including the Kearney Lake Rd. song, "Painting a Room" and a song called "Kiss Me, Kiss Me" which was later recorded by Sloan as "I Am The Cancer." His songwriting was honed through his jams with Scott and Jay Ferguson.

Both Murphy and Ferguson had managed to set past differences aside and focus on creating a new band. This developing collective would be one of the many reasons that would lead Scott to leave his position in No Damn Fears after a year-long stint with the band. Says Scott, "Dave [Marsh] and I bickered all the time and it was not a particularly healthy band relationship. I quit because of Sloan and my schoolwork. I really sweated the fact I had to tell Dave, but he was great and let me out easy. We are very close friends today." As these jams progressed into an actual side-project, Murphy envisioned a quartet in which everyone would write and have a creative input, and that would allow him to play guitar. The search began for a bass player.

Patrick Pentland worked in a magazine store around the corner from the Sam The Record Man store where Jay Ferguson now worked. He would often visit Ferguson at the record store and engage in small talk about music. Though a member of various area bands such as the Ripping Convulsions and Happy Co., Pentland had never truly felt a part of the same Halifax music scene that Murphy and Ferguson were a part of. Pentland was well aware of Kearney Lake Rd.'s legacy, and he had even once interviewed Murphy for a piece on Spent in the King's College journalism school paper. Murphy knew of Pentland's vocal and guitar abilities from his previous bands, and the two had met occasionally when visiting Ferguson at the record store. When Murphy offered a membership in the band, Pentland jumped at the chance. Reflects Pentland, "I felt he was a bit pretentious, something that I now know for a fact, but I was getting more into the Halifax scene."

John Patrick Thomas Pentland was born on September 20, 1969, in

Newtownards, Northern Ireland, to Richard and Patricia Pentland. After Richard's career as a civil engineer moved the family between Ireland, Nova Scotia and Jamaica, the Pentlands finally planted roots in Sackville, Nova Scotia, in 1977. Patrick Pentland, like Andrew Scott, was heavily influenced by his father's musicality, and like all four members of Sloan, school shaped much of his listening habits. "I was very interested in music from birth," claims Pentland. "My father played in rock bands in Northern Ireland right up until we moved to Canada, and then played in a few here as well. School exposed me to what was popular about music, and later, what was rebellious about music."

Throughout the early half of his junior high years at Sackville Heights, Pentland began his first serious instrumental study on the tenor saxophone, his father's instrument, and played in the junior-high school band. It was through his peer group that Pentland was drawn into the rebellious side of music, and he began a steady listening diet of Black Sabbath, Van Halen, Def Leppard and AC/DC.

After a failed attempt to learn the guitar a couple of years previously, Pentland was re-inspired to pick up the instrument by AC/DC's Young brothers. "Even at 14 I was mesmerized by the simplicity of the emotion being conveyed. The striking of one chord with the right temperance of volume and tone made my heart beat faster. I was in love with the very essence of rock music: loud, basic and looked down upon. I've always been able to relax in that shade."

While attending Lower Sackville District High School — drolly nicknamed "L.S.D. High" — Patrick met his future best friend on a ski trip to Quebec City. Pentland first encountered Cliff Gibb in a Quebec City record store vying for the last available copy of Metallica's newly released *Master of Puppets*. Pentland nabbed the copy, and the accompanying bragging rights, until its release in Halifax a week later. "We had both been eyeing each other in school, but hadn't gotten up the nerve to introduce ourselves. We became fast friends on the trip, smoking hash off a pin in a hotel room the first night, and passing out after two beers."

When Pentland discovered that Gibb was a drummer and had a basement with a free rein to make noise, the pair soon began jamming out various fractions of metal songs, while creating a few of their own. Soon punk, gothic and electronic influences seeped into their jams, and in 1986, the pair formed a hardcore band known as the Ripping Convulsions with vocalist John Johnson and bassist Scott Hiltz. The Convulsions made a few home recordings on Gibb's four-track, played a few parties and gigs, but disintegrated by summer's end.

As high school waned, both Pentland and Gibb grew out of hardcore and gravitated toward college rock. Dinosaur Jr. and Sonic Youth became their new musical templates, and by the time Pentland commenced his studies in journalism at King's College, he and Gibb had joined an old grade-school friend, bassist Melanie Rusinak, and formed Happy Co. This trio's sound was described as straightforward pop, but they kept an edge with Gibb's quick-tempoed, punk-influenced drumming. Happy Co. once again put Gibb's four-track to work, and demo'ed various pieces from their set list. They made a minor name for themselves playing Peter Rowan's Two-Buck Tuesdays at The Flamingo Club and at other area gigs with other baby bands like No Damn Fears, Tetris and Coffee in Madrid. When Rusinak introduced her boyfriend Brad Baxter into the mix as a second guitarist, the result was disastrous. The band dynamics became discordant when their romantic liaison ended, and Gibb and Pentland cashed in their chips. Says Pentland, "It was around this time that Chris asked me to join [what became] Sloan, which I jumped at since he and Jay were tapped into a whole different level in the Halifax scene — something I was very interested in becoming a part of. Cliff was great about it all, but I felt a bit strange for a while."

Sloan was officially born in late January 1991 in Andrew Scott's bedroom practice space. Their name was taken from a friend's sobriquet "Slow One," which when said in a French accent translates into the monosyllabic, Sloan. This friend, Jason Larson of the Stratejackets, is honoured with a close-up of his face on the cover of Sloan's first release, the *Peppermint* EP. Two weeks after Pentland joined, the band played their first show at NSCAD. Their live debut featured the band's full repertoire — all eight songs — and the set ended with a 15-minute strobe light freak-out by art school peer Kirk Sabeen shaking a muppet doll through a seizure-inducing puppet show. "That was the only truly art-type rock show I was ever involved in," remembers Scott. "It was all pretty stupid, but it was really fun and certainly made for a memorable first gig."

Ferguson was absolutely thrilled to be playing with Murphy again, and to be involved with a project that was based on influences that excited him. Though Scott is often cited as the symbolic bridge between the band's hard rock and alternative influences, Ferguson remains the undisputed music authority in the group. He is largely responsible for influencing what the band listens to — Murphy in particular. Ferguson remains the archetypal music geek, collecting import singles and religiously reading music maga-

zines. Through his experiences working in music stores and hosting a radio
show at CKDU, Ferguson had discovered the shoegazer/noise pop scene
coming out of the U.K., especially the flagship artists of Alan McGee's
Creation record label, My Bloody Valentine. It would be through Ferguson
that this influence would begin to creep into the quartet's songwriting.
Concurs Ferguson, "I really loved all the new records and singles on the
Creation label like Ride, Slowdive and Swervedriver. They all seemed to echo
'60s pop melodies, and buried harmonies with loud distorted guitars. I
wanted to be like My Bloody Valentine. They were the best band of that
scene — noisy with excellent songs."

"Jay knew all the latest shit from everything from Nirvana to Happy
Mondays or whatever," says Murphy. "British stuff and American stuff. To
me that's what the Sloan thing was." While working one night at the hospital, Murphy was listening to Ferguson's radio show and was completely
stunned when Ferguson played a selection from the Irish quartet. "I called
him up and said, 'What the fuck is this?' It was My Bloody Valentine's 'You
Made Me Realize.' In a lot of ways Jay takes me, the Rush/punk fan, and
shows me all this other music. Without him, I don't know what I'd be."

Pentland was also a fan of sculpting a barrage of noise, something that
he was able to further explore in the band once he traded his bass for
guitar duties. By Sloan's eleventh live appearance, Patrick knew that he
would not remain the bassist of the group, and handed over the honour to
Murphy, who was honing his bass-playing skills in his concurrent stint with
Black Pool.

Murphy's divided focus definitely irked Ferguson. He had been in a
similar situation before when Murphy considered Kearney Lake Rd. his side
project to Spent. "I was upset," confesses Ferguson. "It was like once again,
'Are you serious? Sloan is way more important.' I thought our songs were
so much better. I don't want to put Black Pool down. They were a roots
rock band in the style of The Band or Creedence or Blue Rodeo. There's
nothing wrong with them, but [Murphy's decision to play with both bands]
blew my mind. It makes me look like I'm bragging by saying Sloan was
going to be big, but I felt that. I thought we would be as good or as big
as the Pixies in Halifax."

Murphy simply couldn't see Ferguson's vision at the time, admitting,
"Nobody had any expectations that were that big. Black Pool, to me, was
the ultimate money-making scheme and I didn't think a band like [Sloan]
would ever happen."

In September 1991, that ceased to be a worry. Murphy left Black Pool

Black Pool: Phil Sedore, John Wesley Chisholm,
Chip Sutherland, Chris Murphy
(Courtesy of Chris Murphy)

acrimoniously, making Sloan his top priority. After Black Pool couldn't collectively decide whether they should take an opening gig with The Tragically
Hip, Chisholm broke up the band to make Black Pool into a born-again Celtic
act. Chisholm is diplomatic when recalling his feelings, citing that, "I've always
tried to surround myself with the best possible musicians, and I've been
lucky. It's not like people came into the band and became smart. It was that
I was able to see perhaps earlier than other people who these people were.
Whether they were in Black Pool or not, they were destined to be stars. There
was no frustration at all." Murphy remembers the disintegration of Halifax's
favourite pub act differently. "I was in Black Pool while Sloan had been playing
for about a year trying to decide where to put my energy. In the end I wasn't
too jazzed by John Chisholm and when that band broke up it was like a huge
epiphany for me. It was like: *This is what I'm doing.*"

Without the distractions of playing in other bands, things started to progress
quickly for Sloan. Through a battle-of-the-bands-type gig, Sloan scored a
spot on the DTK Records compilation *Hear and Now*. The prize allowed them
to have a session with local producer Terry Pulliam at his Soundmarket
Studios. The band decided to make the best use of their time, and Murphy
and Ferguson kicked in some extra cash to record an album's worth of
tracks. The song "Underwhelmed" was selected for *Hear and Now*, and

would end up driving Sloan onto the Canadian music scene.

"Underwhelmed" started as a poem Murphy wrote in a journal in 1987. According to Chris Murphy, "The lyrics were written mostly about Jennifer Pierce, who is the letter writer and she still can't spell, but also about Fiona Highet who skipped her classes and got good grades." Murphy pieced together a few actual events into a single narrative, painting the uneven landscape of teenage relationships. The song would become a Canadian generational anthem akin to Nirvana's "Smells Like Teen Spirit." "Underwhelmed"'s clever script touched on personal truth about Murphy's abstinence from smoking or drinking, but the song had enough universal themes to reach beyond the composer's diary entry.

The song's clever string of events also bore a regional trademark. Murphy trades a line about his subject rolling her eyes at him for a later line about her swearing at him and rolling her Rs. This not only reveals the female protagonist's east coast accent, but is a cheeky double entendre. The first attempt to transfer the poem into a song resulted in a folkie version with different lyrics. The idea was shelved until Murphy and Scott were compiling a tape of demos for Patrick to learn. Placing his book of lyrics in front of him, the song's structure was composed on the spot.

Peter Rowan knew all four of the young men from their former musical incarnations, and expressed an interest in helping out the band. Along with The Flamingo Club's Greg Clark, Rowan was one of the few proponents of the city's alternative scene at the time. With Rankin Family manager Mickey Quayce, who was working with Chip Sutherland at the time, Rowan had helped kick in $500 for No Damn Fears to record a demo, and helped the group land the first slot for an alternative group at the East Coast Music Awards. No Damn Fears fell apart just before the gig, leaving the showcase vacant. Through Rowan's persistence and verbal wrestling with the ECMA organizers, he eventually scored the spot for Sloan. Whether it was this gig, or the pre-show showcase organized by Chris Murphy and John Chisholm at the OO (Double-O) Gallery with Thrush Hermit, outside interest was ignited that evening. Among those who were infatuated with the young band were MCA Canada's Cam Carpenter and Nettwerk's Ric Arboit.

Nettwerk really wanted Sloan. Ric Arboit, then in A&R at Canada's largest independent record label, felt that the Haligonian quartet was a perfect draft for the Vancouver label, and was immediately intent on signing them. Rowan and the band thought this was a big deal as well. "We were freaking out," admits Rowan. "I was faxed an offer from Nettwerk and almost signed it.

Being from Halifax, the concept of getting offered a recording contract was absolutely unbelievable." Interest in the band was gaining momentum, and decisions became more complex when a larger cast of characters moved in to the scene. Cam Carpenter, then working for MCA Canada, had made it to Halifax on an invitation from Jay Ferguson. Based on the recording of "Underwhelmed" and on the band's live performance at the ECMAS, he wanted to talk contracts. As Carpenter puts it, "I met Peter Rowan the next morning and I said, 'What do you want to do? Here are seven things we could do conceivably.' He said, 'Ideally we want to sign to the U.S.' I said, 'Okay, let's see what we can do." Carpenter started a campaign for the band around the MCA offices, and one day found himself ping-ponging artists with Geffen A&R rep Todd Sullivan. When he played Sloan's music, Sullivan raised an eyebrow.

"I was sitting at home," recounts Rowan, "and the phone rang and I picked it up and it was, 'Hi, I'm Todd Sullivan from Geffen Records.' I thought to myself that I'm going to tell whatever asshole friend of mine to fuck off because this is not a funny joke." It was no joke, and when Sullivan expressed his serious interest in the band, Rowan made sure that a copy of Sloan's DAT of the Pulliam sessions was on the A&R rep's desk the next morning.

Once contracts started to creep into the picture, Chip Sutherland held out a hand to the band's growing legal affairs. Sutherland met with Nettwerk heads Terry McBride and Ric Arboit in an attempt to hammer out an acceptable contract for the young band, but playing the sport of low ball, Sutherland couldn't see a binding document or numbers that interested him. Most of the band, on the other hand, was very interested in signing with Nettwerk, and according to Sutherland, preferred signing with the Canadian independent to Geffen. Geffen's size intimidated some members of the band, but Sutherland refused to let them sign with Nettwerk. He had experienced a bad record contract first hand when Black Pool signed with Justin Entertainment/MCA. "This is where I get my credibility as an entertainment lawyer because I signed the worst deal you could possibly sign," confesses Sutherland. "I said, 'No boys, you can't sign it. The Nettwerk deal is too shitty.' I was in Vancouver and I tried to work it out with [Nettwerk], but they learned the hard way. Todd [Sullivan] called me when he got the tape and he said 'Okay, let's get going. I'm really serious about it.'" Sullivan was told that Sloan was heading to Vancouver for the Music West industry festival. He would check them out there.

Despite the excitement of the label interest in the band, the journey to Music West wasn't pleasant. Chris Murphy remembers, "Geffen called and said, 'Don't sign a deal until we see you,' and we were like, 'whatever.' Geffen is interested in small things, but they're interested in a lot of things. For the punchline of the whole thing, we were travelling in a caravan and our first tour was Montreal, Regina, Calgary and Vancouver. We had no shows. We drove from Montreal to Regina. But this was all about 'Geffen is going to come see us.' It was pretty exciting."

The band faced more troubles than simply a lack of filler gigs between Halifax and Vancouver. Their Music West show was scheduled for The Commodore, the largest concert hall venue in Vancouver, and the festival was happening at the same time as the Los Angeles riots. Reports filtered to the band that the L.A. airport had delayed or cancelled flights, and there was a certain level of uncertainty as to whether Sullivan would show up. When the band arrived at The Commodore, there were only 20 people in attendance. In addition, Sloan contended with a surly venue staff, a keyboard amp for Ferguson to play through and those in the band who drank had imbibed considerably.

Rowan recalls it with fervour. "I'll never forget this. Patrick was loaded and his pants were three quarters of the way down his ass. He took his shirt off and two songs into the set it was just this drunken 'fuck this.' Jay looked at his guitar amp and did this perfect karate kick on his microphone. Then another microphone was broken by accident. To this day I have never received a higher compliment than when this jerk stage manager goes, 'Who the fuck do you think you are, Malcolm McLaren?'"

Pentland laughs when recalling the evening. "Essentially it was: 'Nobody's

Sloan recording *Peppermint* at Sound Market:
Jay Ferguson, Andrew Scott, Patrick Pentland,
manager Peter Rowan
(Photo by Chris Murphy)

here, let's be as outrageous as possible because we came all this way. This is our big shot and it's not really going to happen so let's try to blow away these 20 people.' It was a weird time because that summer everyone was looking for the next Nirvana and I guess we fit the bill."

Their antics worked. Of the 20 in attendance, over half were A&R from various labels, and the band was swarmed with offers. As promised, Todd Sullivan had made it to the performance, and to the following day's showcase at the Town Pump. He was ready to exchange vows. Chip Sutherland flew in from Halifax and took Sullivan skiing at Whistler. The deal was mapped out on the chairlift, and the band was officially signed to Geffen three months later. In the meantime, Sloan took on Chip Sutherland and Peter Rowan as a management team, and released their first recording.

The *Peppermint* EP merely hinted at what was to come. The Pulliam sessions were recorded with the intention that the band would have something to sell at shows, but the release soon amplified the buzz. Released on their own Murderecords label, the predominantly Murphy-penned sextet of songs reflected much of what the band had been experiencing over the past couple of years. Whether it was clever and troubled love songs ("Sugartune," "Torn") or songs that reflected the activity in the band ("Pretty Voice," "Lucky For Me") the EP captured a lot of change happening in Sloan. Pentland had left his journalism program and finished up his studies at King's College with a B.A. in History, and Scott semi-reluctantly dropped out of NSCAD in his fifth year of study to be with the band. "Underwhelmed" was once again selected to be a single, and was released along with a video — a spin-the-bottle motif starring a young Thrush Hermit — directed by Murderecords/Cinnamon Toast Records manager Colin MacKenzie. Almost immediately, MuchMusic, modern-rock radio and campus radio started to liberally expose the public to Sloan's charm.

When their major label debut, *Smeared*, finally hit stores in the fall of 1992, there was little question that the industry was taken with what had come out of Halifax. The mystique of coming from an unlikely musical centre benefited the band in many ways. Once the rest of the world realized there were a number of talented acts in the city, the media latched onto Halifax as they had with Nirvana and Seattle or R.E.M. and Athens. Soon, labels were flocking to Halifax trying to find an equivalent band to sign. Sloan would become the figureheads of this scene, and would stand as the height chart against which all Halifax acts would be measured for the remainder of the decade.

Smeared was culled from the same sessions with Pulliam, with a few

Peppermint tracks replaced by a couple of new songs ("Take It In," "Median Strip" and "Lemonzinger"). It also featured a wise reworking of "Underwhelmed" which consisted of a new drum motif, a faster tempo and a razor-sharp harmony between Murphy and Pentland. As the listener would immediately gather from the other tracks, however, there would be a lot more to this band than "Underwhelmed." The mixing work of Dave Ogilvie (Skinny Puppy) helped beef up the sound and consolidate what the band was aiming for: the union of British noise pop with American grunge. "Marcus Said" and "I Am The Cancer" captured the feel of My Bloody Valentine, not only with brush strokes of feedback over pop structures, but also with the gender-mix harmonies created by Murphy and guest star Jennifer Pierce. On the other hand, the American influences reared their respective heads on songs such as "500 Up" and "Two-Seater."

Though the band was striving to portray itself as a four-way democracy, with all parties writing and singing, Murphy soon found himself regarded as the frontman. He had written two-thirds of the material on *Smeared*, and the bassist's comfort in front of the audience was something that Geffen wanted to encourage. Admits Murphy, "It's hard to market a band with four people. It was suggested to me to sing Andrew's songs. I did sing some songs on the first record like "Median Strip," and Patrick sang "500 Up," which is partly Andrew's." The band had compensated for this early on in their history by swapping instruments on stage. If it was Scott's turn to sing a song, he'd pick up a guitar, Murphy would hand his bass to Ferguson, and Murphy would then take Scott's position. Sloan's idealistic objective was to have no frontman, but it was happening regardless. This pressure was not without its side effects.

"When we signed to DGC they were very into the idea of pushing one guy as the leader," says Pentland. "Chris, with the most songs and the biggest grin, got the tag. That really held me back through the second record."

In 1993, the fault lines in Sloan broadened when the band engaged in a 10-week North American tour for *Smeared*. Scott remembers the tour as a sobering experience for all, "even those who didn't need sobering." The tour started off on an unbelievable high as the band spent the first two weeks playing alongside the encouraging Lemonheads and their large and equally supportive audiences. The reality of the following eight weeks would be the polar opposite. The band was still very green to touring, and they were thrown into their travels without a lot of preparation. There had been some introductory games on their 1992 jaunt to Music West and brief touring of southern Ontario. But what Pentland jokes as becoming "a real hating the way you chew type of thing" started to eat away at the flesh of the band. "We didn't realize that we didn't all see eye to eye on everything until we were forced to spend weeks together," says Pentland. "The cracks started to show. There was a real growing up factor that we had to face, and it took a while to feel comfortable."

The personal acclimatization, in conjunction with playing to virtually no one in the States and poor tour planning on Geffen's part, was enough to inspire a few nervous breakdowns. "Everyone took turns crying," recalls Murphy, "even Matt Murphy, an amazing musician who was reduced to selling T-shirts for us. I took my freak-out after we had played great shows with the Lemonheads in the Northeastern States, and then did some sparse American shows on our own."

Ferguson's meltdown occurred when the band was excluded from playing in their home country as their travels across Canada conflicted with Seattle's Screaming Trees' tour. The band had been advised by their label not to book shows in Canada during this time because Geffen felt there would be too much competition. When the Screaming Trees gigs were cancelled, Sloan couldn't put a tour together in time, and they ended up driving across Canada to Seattle without a single gig or in-store appearance. Ferguson lost it. "I talked to someone at Universal and was furious and asked, 'Why can't we do something?' It was this feeling of helplessness and being on tour and not being able to do something with your own band."

Additionally, some personal seismic shifts were occurring during the tour. All of the members suffered varying degrees of homesickness, while both Murphy and Pentland dealt with floundering relationships. On the business end, the band experienced the defection of their promotional team, and aside from staple supporter Todd Sullivan, the new squad in radio promotion and publicity at Geffen did not share the same enthusiasm for the quartet. With this negative reinforcement, "Take It In," the second U.S. single, was a radio stillbirth. The biggest shake-up came when the band was informed midway through the tour that Chip Sutherland had fired Peter Rowan.

Both Sutherland and Rowan admit that their philosophies were not suited for a business partnership, and in particular, Rowan's excessive spending did not sit well with Sutherland. Sutherland explains, "We had a deal with the Sloan guys that they could fire us at any time if either one of us wasn't involved. I said to Peter, 'Look, I'm quitting. We're not going to be able to work together because we have diametrically different views on how to run this business." Sutherland and Rowan agreed to a cash settlement, and split the management's roster. Rowan took Eric's Trip and Hardship Post, while Sutherland remained with Sloan. Understandably, Rowan was disappointed at the time, and the band was uncomfortable with the shift as they were certainly grateful to Rowan for igniting their career. Years later, both Sloan and Rowan realize that he had played out his role. Admits Rowan, "These American multinationals will literally eat you up and spit you out. I was really intimidated. I knew Sloan for so long. They knew what they were doing. They needed an asshole to deal with a record company, not a buddy to go out on the road."

Even though it was a wise decision in the long run, it was a major wake-up call for the band at the time. "Once Peter was gone, that was a big signal of a decision that was made principally because of business and not because of fun," reflects Murphy. "To me it was like, 'Mom and dad are divorced. Mom's gone, and we live with dad. There's no love in the house, but we'll be very efficient. We are going to do great on the sports team, but we'll cry in the locker room.'"

The cumulative effect of this tour and the tensions caused by the band's rites of passage were evident throughout the recording of their second album — both thematically and aurally. The band was intent on moving away from the shoegazer grunge rock they explored on *Smeared* and giving their distortion pedals a rest, partly due to the early '90s influx of noise pop bands, and because of the prolonged experience of playing loud music in small venues. Says Ferguson, "It was a retreat into something that was easier on the ears, the idea of taking a bit of a turn, but still representing influences at the time like Fleetwood Mac or the third Velvet Underground album, which was really quiet. That tour had a real effect — playing music like that for a year straight without much variety led to a certain direction with *Twice Removed*."

Twice Removed showcases a completely different side of the band. The only sign of Nirvana on the album is Murphy's coy use of two Nirvana fan letters he stole from the Sub Pop offices and used verbatim for lyrics on "Penpals." The '90s musical influences have been exchanged for classic devices from the '60s and '70s. Ferguson's "I Hate My Generation," a brilliant duet with Murphy, trades cheeky lines over treble-heavy guitar arpeggios until its pure '60s pop chorus. "People of the Sky" bolstered its refrain with harmony-laced "bah-bah-badda-bah's" while his melancholic piano-based "Before I Do" was a nod to the quieter side of the Velvet Underground.

Along with the musical shift, the band opted to record their second album away from home in a New York studio with producer Jim Rondinelli. Having recorded their first album for $1,500, Sloan was a little intimidated by *Twice Removed*'s six-figure budget. Rondinelli was also a very different character than the laissez-faire Pulliam, and he didn't create an optimal creative environment. He did, however, make the band listen to one another, and all but Pentland are proud of the final product.

"The record is great but none of us had a great time," comments Murphy. "We weren't getting along with each other and seven weeks recording seemed too long. So much time was spent dicking around. I was also terrified to be spending someone else's money [Geffen's] in a way that I thought was quite wasteful. I did not enjoy myself much."

Scott views the difficulties as a result of personality conflicts and failed expectations. "The addition of Jim created problems because we were a very selfish kind of band with regard to our 'process.' He had many suggestions that were flatly shot down; he also had a real New York impatience and his energy didn't sit well with us. I don't know if the record indicates this friction. We were so young and new to the whole thing. We all had different ideas of how it should be, but few of these expectations were met."

To Pentland, the album's opening track, "Penpals," is the only song that represents his perception of Sloan on the record. The track was captured late one evening after Rondinelli had left the studio for the day. After Murphy and engineer Todd Childress returned from a Rush concert at Madison Square Garden and found Pentland alone in the studio, the three began jamming out their favourite Rush songs. This led to the trio revisiting their work on the vocal tracks to "Penpals." The trio ended up staying up until eight in the morning perfecting the song. It would be the first and last moment that Pentland would enjoy working on the album, claiming, "It was like a light went on over our heads: 'This is actually fun!' It changed the way we saw the making of the record, that we could have been more productive, except that Jim was so hard to get any fun out of. I'm not that fond of the record, but I really like that song. It's the only one on that record that really sounds like Sloan to me."

Pentland has often expressed a disdain for *Twice Removed*. In addition to his feelings of inadequacy within the group, and what he perceives as a creative low point, it was a chaotic personal era in the guitarist's life, having split from Jennifer Pierce (who he was dating during *Smeared*) and formed a new romantic link with Sandra Kingsley. All of Pentland's contributions reflect this unrest. "Loosens," a tear-jerking piano ballad, details the universal feelings surrounding a break-up, and the uneasy rocker "Worried

Now" reflected the theme of Pentland's life over this period. Pentland discloses, "The lyrics were about how I perceived my failings and why my relationship with Jennifer Pierce had ended, and how I was relieved that the wait was over." "I Can Feel It," the only glimmer of hope on the album, was ironically a duet with Pierce that was directed at Kingsley.

There are still moments of fun on the album — such as Ferguson's paean to an older girl on "Snowsuit Sound" and Murphy's geek-love sing-a-long "Deeper Than Beauty" — but the sombre tones of Pentland's work carry through most of the album. Scott's glorious "People of the Sky" was written about a couple he was close to, and detailed the disintegration of their relationship at the hand of betrayal. The drummer admitted this was his attempt to "write a song like Bob Dylan's 'Ballad in Plain D.'" "Before I Do," a dark epic track that combined his basic verse structure with Murphy's unrelated choruses used Scott's father's passing as a partial theme. Murphy's songs were, for the most part, closely personal as well, with "Bells On" and "Shame, Shame" painting scenes of bumpy relationships with his characteristic use of sarcasm and puns.

The album's first single, "Coax Me," was the most metaphorical of the unrest with Geffen. As Murphy explains it, "Coax Me" was "the idea of trading love for money as your motivation — in this case for writing music. We are the 'widow' who has lost her husband, 'love,' but has received an inheritance that she would trade back if she could." His apprehension, which is expressed in the song, would soon be further justified.

Twice Removed earned many critical accolades, such as being one of *Spin*'s Top 10 Records of 1994 That You Didn't Hear, but these victories eluded Geffen. Geffen had more or less promised to do nothing with the album, and they followed through. Released in August 1994, *Twice Removed* was a dead concern by October. For a band that was already borderline dysfunctional, Geffen's lacklustre support was essentially the match that incinerated the family home. According to Sutherland, in December of that year, Geffen held an A&R meeting to discuss the future of the band. Their response after the brief, impotent campaign for *Twice Removed* was: "We're convinced that Sloan will make the right record at the right time. If we just let them make enough records, they'll eventually connect with the industry and their fan base and they are going to be huge. So let's just put this little thing behind us and just keep going." Sutherland remembers the band's response to that as being, "Fuck that, how long is that going to take? We're going to kill ourselves making not as much money and being frustrated and having them not working on projects we believe in. If we have to be

Sloan on the road, 1996
(photos by Catherine Stockhausen)

on Geffen then we quit."

Somehow that news quickly found its way from an employee at the Halifax club The Birdland to an Internet rumour on James Covey's Sloan.net discussion group, to a *Halifax Herald* reporter. Much to Pentland's chagrin and despite his personal request not to take the rumour seriously, the reporter let the media virus out. Sloan released a new single, "Stood Up"/ "Same Old Flame," and spent the remainder of 1995 explaining the break-up to the Canadian media. They engaged in an extended separation process of a string of farewell gigs. The "official" final show was the 1995 Edgefest headlining slot at Toronto's Molson Amphitheatre, an event that showcased every substantial indie rock band of the time, including most of the Murderecords roster. Despite being a final gig, Sloan would be lured to play a few lucrative gigs after this well-publicized performance.

While Scott remained in Toronto, biding his time with various ensembles such as The Sadies and The Maker's Mark, the other three members returned to Halifax to focus on Murderecords. Along with ex-CKDU director Colin MacKenzie, Murphy and Ferguson decided they could spend some time building the Halifax community through their success. By the time of *Twice Removed*, the band's Murderecords label had released a fair number of recordings of area artists — largely EPS by Thrush Hermit, Eric's Trip, Hardship Post, Al Tuck, and hip-hop artists Stinkin' Rich and Hip Club Groove. Debuts from Matt Murphy's new band The Super Friendz, and Montreal's Local Rabbits — the latter which Ferguson also produced — became new priorities for the label. "The idea of running a record company appealed to me immensely," admits Ferguson. "Of course, the romanticism isn't always there — not enough money to do something the way you really want to, or not always agreeing with the artist about how things should be done. Most of the bands eventually broke up, or moved to other labels. It also became hard running Murder when all the members of Sloan owned the same shares and not everybody was jazzed about releasing records that would potentially lose money. It's unfair to spend Sloan money on what was becoming a pet project."

Some time after they played one of their last 'farewell shows,' while they had been focusing a fair amount of their energies and finances on other bands, the quartet started to realize the benefits of being in Sloan. Talk started to circulate between the members about recording an album 'for posterity's sake.' It would be nothing too elaborate, probably just something for the few thousand hardcore fans — something released on Murderecords. Says Colin MacKenzie, "The sum of the total is greater than the one. I think they realized that they had something; that it isn't just writing songs, it's about getting along together. You realize you can make a living at something you really enjoy and maybe it's worth making a few concessions here and there depending on who you are. Looking at Jay and Patrick in particular, when they came back from their meeting where they decided to call it quits, they were devastated. Chris feels that he can do anything, which he quite possibly could, and Andrew is a talented guy as well and will always fall on his feet. Whereas Patrick and Jay, that's what they always wanted to do and now it had been pulled out from under them. The interesting thing that happened was when *One Chord To Another* came out, the first two singles were Patrick's songs. That also solidified what everyone knew in the back of their minds. It was about Sloan and making it happen."

"*One Chord*," recounts Scott, "was and still is my favourite. It was our 'let's get back together, but never really admit it' album. I lived in Toronto then, and the feeling of the 'three against one' was pretty prevalent. I did not move to deliberately derail whatever process we had going, but I did it for personal reasons. I felt no real guilt, and still think I made a good decision."

Recorded and engineered with Laurence Currie at his Idea of East Studios in Halifax, *One Chord To Another* stands as the pinnacle achievement by the band. Not only did it hint at a future for Sloan, but also it proved the band could have success on its own terms. To this day the album remains the band's biggest seller and with an approximate recording budget of $8,000, as opposed to *Twice Removed*'s $120,000 price tag, their financial kickback was even sweeter. The Geffen ordeal had left its share of scars on the band, and the healing factor of *One Chord*'s success saved them.

It's a work that took their musical time machine back another few years beyond *Twice Removed*. If there was ever a time to tie Beatle boots to the band, this was it. The songs themselves are reminiscent of the Fab Four's *Rubber Soul/Revolver* period, particularly "Autobiography," "A Side Wins," "Can't Face Up" and "Anyone Who's Anyone." Ferguson's radio single, "The Lines You Amend," is an undeniable first cousin to "The Ballad of John and Yoko" and the lyrical citation of "'Photographs' sung by Ringo Starr" did little to distance the Beatle analogies in the media. The retro-production gave the album more than simply a melodic similarity. Experiments in radical stereo separation, use of four-track analog recorders, backwards guitars, boxy drums and a variety of instrumentation nominates this album as a great, lost '60s pop classic.

Recorded over Christmas of 1995, *One Chord to Another* was far from a conventional recording experience. It was assembled with the same "he who writes it calls the shots" philosophy the band had always stood by, except that Scott was not present for the process. Scott's only studio appearance with the band happened when he flew in from Toronto and, in a single afternoon, proceeded to quickly record all of his drum parts on a four-track. However, Scott had neglected to pack his contributions to the album — something that became a source of anxiety for both the Halifax contingent and Scott while in Toronto.

Confesses Scott, "I had been saying, 'Yeah, I've got some stuff — it will be great.' I had nothing. I had no ideas, and I basically had to say I'm really going to have to do this in Toronto by myself. I was terrified. This is after we had supposedly broken up and we were still under the impression that we aren't really getting back together; we're just making a record to put out on Murderecords and it will be fun. It was nerve-racking for that reason alone." With Sloan's live engineer Brenndan McGuire helping in the studio and on bass, Scott ended up penning and recording two tracks that fit in perfectly with the retro-vibe of the album: the piano-based "A-Side Wins" and the guitar-oriented "400 Metres." Even Murphy, the most vocally blunt of the group, was pleasantly surprised both with the songs and the fact that he could stop considering a new drummer for the band. "I was expecting Andrew to send up shit, but when I heard Andrew's songs, I was blown away. We had talked about getting a new drummer, and especially then it was obvious we should never do that."

If anyone benefited from the fan response when the album was released in June 1996, it was Patrick Pentland. Having gone through a particularly dark period during *Twice Removed*, Pentland was out to prove himself — if *One Chord* was, in fact, going to be the band's final release. He justified his place in Sloan by scoring the first two singles on the release. The lead-off track and first single from the album was "The Good in Everyone," a two-minute rocker with a unique intro and outro featuring crowd noise from the band's final gig. CFNY DJ Brother Bill prematurely introduced the band before they were actually ready to start playing; some band members came out to sound check, but Pentland's amp wasn't working, and Murphy was still in the washroom. The crowd noise that bookends the song is a fitting acknowledgement of the past by kicking into the future with a confident simple pop rocker, or as Pentland describes it, "The first song on our 'comeback' record fits in over the amount of time the crowd waited for us to get our shit together."

Radio and video gold came in the form of another Pentland song, "Everything You've Done Wrong." The buoyant ditty, tattooed with an instantly recognizable trumpet riff, became the band's brief passport into the mainstream. The glossy wedding-themed video earned a fair amount of play on MuchMusic, and the song landed outside the typical modern rock station support, debuting the band on middle-of-the-road stations. Pentland admits he felt the song's commercial potential early on. "I played around with another version of this song that had a more 'Lust For Life' feel. It went through a few different wringers. Then one day I was at home watching TV and playing the guitar when I came up with a melody line that would become the horn part. Within minutes I had rewritten the whole melody structure, and I called Chris and said that he could stop worrying, because I'd just written the single. It was a cocky boast, but I was so excited. It was like nothing I'd come up with before. I was literally holding on to the guitar for an hour not wanting to let it go in case I forgot it all."

Murphy wouldn't score a single on the album, but two of his selections would be important for their reflection on the band's rebirth and possible future together. "Anyone Who's Anyone" was a parade-like anthem for the reformed band who was looking for another shot at the music game. "Nothing Left To Make Me Want to Stay" was a literal thematic sibling to *Smeared*'s metaphorical "I Am The Cancer" in his "leaving Halifax series." Murphy's songs would strangely symbolize the album as a bridge to the band's gradual relocation to Toronto. "*One Chord* to me is the transition album for the end of our involvement in the Halifax scene. We were two feet in for the first two records, and one foot in for *One Chord*, and then essentially out of it ever since."

If a band claims they are breaking up, leaves a record company contract and then reforms and releases an album a couple of years later, it's nothing short of illegal. This was Sloan's dilemma when they had originally presented the idea of *One Chord to Another* to Chip Sutherland. In his wisdom, Sutherland had kept Murderecords going as an "insurance home" for the band, and he kept Geffen informed from the beginning of the album's recording. "I thought they were going to get dropped," he admits. When the album was a concrete reality, he sent a copy of the final mixes to Geffen. Always a supporter of the band, Todd Sullivan wanted Sloan back on the label. Sloan, on the other hand, were not as thrilled. Their scars had yet to heal, and they had little confidence that the label would be a good home to start the band up again. For a label that wanted the band to return to their roster, they certainly didn't make it easy. After a frustrating negotiation period with Geffen that lasted close to five months, Sutherland felt like he was back dealing with Nettwerk again. This was further magnified when the band played a showcase in New York and a number of labels showed up offering them more attractive offers. Sutherland knew that they were too far into the negotiations with Geffen. After a long paddle in his canoe trying to brainstorm some kind of Houdini act, he called upon a legal friend in L.A. Sutherland was essentially told that if he ever wanted to work in L.A. again, it would be in everyone's best interest to be straight with the label. Sutherland explains, "I called Todd up and said, 'They're not happy. Why don't you make a gesture of some kind? Give us some money, buy them a guitar, I don't care what it is. Here's what these other labels are offering us, and you're not even close.' Todd's a practical guy himself. He said, 'All right, let me go have a serious talk. [When he phoned back] he said, 'I talked to everyone and they don't want to let you go, and they feel we have a deal, but I know what you're saying, so we'll let you go.' Ultimately there was all this bad blood between Sloan and Geffen, but they couldn't be nicer to us in spite of what their wishes were."

When the dust had finally cleared and the contract nullified, the band signed an American deal with Tom Zutaut's fledgling label The Enclave. Zutaut was part of the old Geffen guard, and had been Todd Sullivan's boss when Sloan initially signed with DGC. Eventually Zutaut jumped ship from Geffen and started The Enclave label at EMI.

To celebrate the delayed release of *One Chord To Another* in the U.S., the band recorded a bonus disc, *Recorded Live at a Sloan Party*, for their patient American fans. In the spirit of *Live at a Beach Boys Party*, the band quickly recorded nine songs with various friends, including members of Jale and Thrush Hermit, in the studio, leaving in all screw-ups to give the recording a more authentic live feel. They subsequently added crowd noises recorded at the actual Sloan party — which also happened to be Murphy's birthday — to lead everyone to believe this was actually a true live recording. The Sloan songs are enjoyable, especially Chris Murphy and Jennifer Pierce's acoustic update of "I Am The Cancer," but it's the covers that make this disc worthy of the band's discography. Particular stand-outs include the Pentland-led version of The Hollies' "I Can't Let Go," Murphy singing Jonathan Richman's "Dignified and Old," Ferguson's take on Roxy Music's "Over You" and Scott and company's gang vocals on The Everly Brothers' "Glitter and Gold." The in-between song chatter is also worth a chuckle, with such classic moments as Pentland informing the party that "Chris is going to get back on the traps. Bear with him, he's a little drunk." Murphy later reciprocates the slag, with the command: "Patrick, get in *tune, PLEASE.*"

Collector's items aside, Sloan were to be a top priority with the label, and The Enclave pledged to sink plenty of money into the radio promotion of "Everything You've Done Wrong." Unfortunately, neither the label nor the band had a chance to prove the song's worth in the States. When EMI decided to slice 20 per cent of their company, The Enclave went belly up. Sloan was again without an American home, but the situation would garner them a few consolation prizes. The band left the dead label with full rights to the album, *and* their paycheck for a yet-to-be completed fourth album.

Having been in this place before, the band decided Murderecords would remain the band's home and that they would worry about American distribution through licensing deals. With the help of *One Chord*'s success, and the money they received from The Enclave, the band bought back *Smeared* and *Twice Removed* from Geffen, thus owning their complete catalogue. Between November 1997 and January 1998, Sloan hibernated in Toronto's Chemical Sound Studio with Daryl Smith to make the band's fourth record. They would spend a little more time and money than they did on the thrifty *One Chord to Another*. Most importantly, this time they would all be together.

When Patrick Pentland finally moved to Toronto with his girlfriend Sandra Kingsley in 1998, it marked the beginning of real hope for the band. The quartet had subsisted with members scattered between Halifax and Toronto, but it was never good for the band's morale. Scott had felt the brunt of the blame for this since he had resided in Toronto from 1993 onward. During the band's hiatus, his decision to remain there was one of the oft-cited media hypotheses for the band's split. Soon after the release of *One Chord To Another*, Ferguson and Murphy made their way to the Ontario capital to join their girlfriends in 1996 and 1997, respectively. This had left Pentland the sole remaining member in Halifax, and the classic three-against-one scenario began to brew all over again. It had also become very clear that the long distance relationship was far from beneficial to the band's live show.

In late April of that year, the band did a couple of "practice gigs" at the Trasheteria clubs in Kingston and Peterborough, Ontario, to cram for their MuchMusic *Intimate and Interactive* special which celebrated the release of their fourth album, *Navy Blues*. Those gigs, and the subsequent MuchMusic performance were loose, to say the least. Hit-and-miss live experiences were typical for Sloan, but the band's live inactivity in the clubs was particularly evident after being holed up at Toronto's Chemical Sound and not rehearsing for a few months. The band's sense of humour and the strength of their material had always made up for this looseness, but television audiences are not always as forgiving as hardcore fans. Regardless, the band appeared comfortable with each other, all taking turns at the microphone to perform their material, answer questions or contribute a one-liner. The attention vortex that is Chris Murphy continued to feed the camera with a series of smartass quips hovering between hilarious and patronizing. He pulled out all the stops, especially when he commandeered a vehicle on Queen Street during the evening's finale of "Underwhelmed," and sang the end of the song while the driver took him around the block. Given the complexity of the material on the newly released *Navy Blues*, it was also a brave step for the band to reproduce live — especially at such an early stage in the album's campaign.

On *Navy Blues*, Sloan continued to display their well-established character traits, but in many ways, they were demonstrating a maturity beyond their years. The album is a paean to classic rock, with all four members of the band exhibiting their evolving tastes. The songwriting arrangements were more complex, and the studio experimentation and tape splicing wielded some incredibly creative results. The majority of the material on *Navy Blues* underlined the fact that many of the band's composers were not going to let up on their Beatles fixation. Ferguson himself admitted that he was looking to recreate the feeling of Lennon's "Instant Karma" with "C'mon C'mon (We're Gonna Get It Started)," while "I Wanna Thank You," his salute to the passing of The Enclave, echoed the cello arrangement of "Eleanor Rigby."

Scott contributed a psychedelic couplet of keyboard tracks, "Seems So Heavy" and the wonderful "Sinking Ships." Even "On the Horizon" came close to a revved up mix of "Drive My Car," with its car horn harmonies and smart riffs. This song provided a straight-ahead guitar kick in the pants to the album, and one that had yet to be delivered by the drummer on a recording. "Sinking Ships," a tape-spliced opus that featured a multi-instrumental arrangement and creative wordplay is, in Scott's estimation, "an attempt at piecing together opposing parts and connecting them cohesively to make a psychedelic 'masterpiece.'" It worked.

Murphy's "Suppose They Close The Door" was assembled in a similar vein, merging together the tapes of two separately recorded pieces in the studio to create his masterstroke of *Navy Blues*. Where his catchy "Keep On Thinkin'" would have found a comfortable home on the Beatles' *Red Album* compilation, "Suppose They Close The Door" could be a perfect bonus track for the *Blue Album*.

As this description of Beatle-influenced material would suggest, the rumours of a Sloan hard rock album prior to *Navy Blues*' release were greatly

Sloan, *Navy Blues* era, 1998:
Jay Ferguson, Andrew Scott,
Patrick Pentland,
Chris Murphy
(Photo by Catherine Stockhausen)

exaggerated. There certainly was a tip of the hat to certain members' fist-pumping pasts. Murphy's "She Says What She Means," the lead-off track and second single, fell somewhere between Aerosmith's ass-shaking riff rock, and Boston's gang harmonies wrapped in Murphy's traditional weave of puns. As strong as the song is, it was too clever for its own good, and neither the initial radio play, nor the clever, big-budget video based on the obscure film *Privilege* caught fire.

Pentland's "Iggy and Angus" was both a literal ode to his hard rocking heroes, Iggy Pop and Angus Young of AC/DC, and a self-conscious reflection on Sloan as well: "We're still the same after all these years / It's funny how you get a feel for it / When you finally lose your sense of fear." This was an affirmation of Pentland's sense of security, which had finally started to materialize since the band's second phase began. "We were getting pushed around a lot, and *One Chord* is a rebirth of independence," revealed Pentland at the time. "It was like becoming adults and standing on our own. With this record I feel we are a mature band now. When we did *Twice Removed* and *Smeared* we didn't know how to act as a band. Now we do and we're more comfortable."

The radio adrenaline shot — and the most blatant homage to hard rock — came in the form of the aptly titled "Money City Maniacs." The hit single's creation remains one of Murphy's much-loved moments of Sloan's history. "This is my favourite Sloan song because it is pure collaboration," he admits. "The basic riff and feel is Patrick's, but I changed his chorus and added the nonsensical lyric: 'and the joke is / when he awoke his / body was covered in coke fizz.' I made the line up on stage in Buffalo." Right from the opening sirens to the thumping eighth notes of Murphy's bass, this song was a pure tribute to the anthems everyone but Ferguson had grown up listening to. "Money City Maniacs" was an amalgam of AC/DC's "For Those About to

Rock" and the melodic, harmony-filled pop that had been a staple quality of this band's music since its inception.

It was the perfect, perhaps only, choice for a first single. It is the type of radio song that insists on being played at top volume, and it was no surprise that this song landed Sloan a considerable sum of money for a Labatt's Blue advertisement and would by default become a hockey arena anthem. None of the band was particularly thrilled about aligning Sloan with a corporate beer giant, but it allowed them to survive and remain independent. (Scott's "Sensory Deprivation" from the next Sloan album, *Between the Bridges*, would later make its way into a Labatt's Stanley Cup playoffs spot.) With Murderecords having already bought back *Smeared* and *Twice Removed* from Geffen, they were looking to secure all aspects of their career to ensure full independence. As Ferguson explains, owning their publishing rights was the biggest incentive to agree to license their music this way: "Because we are a self-run band/company with no person or major label backing us with financial support, we have to fund all our endeavours on our own. At the point we were offered the commercial, we were in the process of buying back the songwriting publishing rights to two albums [*One Chord to Another* and *Navy Blues*] from a company that we signed with and had a slight falling out with. It probably doesn't look too cool from a fan's perspective — perhaps assuming we're selling out to beer companies to purchase sports cars — but the money actually helped us become more independent than we were."

Chip Sutherland is quick to emphasize the importance of how distinctive the band's situation has been since leaving Geffen. "They are one of the few bands in the world that owns their own record label. They never have to ask permission to make a record. They never have to have an A&R man near them. They never have to play a song for anyone before they finish a record. You talk to 90 per cent of the bands and they'd just shit their pants if they knew what Sloan was able to do. They have all the things that all bands dream of that you don't get until you are Paul Simon. All these people slobbering at the mouth to be superstars — the Sloan guys are so smart. They just want to be happy. They don't want to be superstars. That's why they are beating the music business at their own game."

Being music fans first and foremost, the band was extremely sensitive to the needs and wants of their following. After four albums and a wave of popularity and confidence, the band was ready to release its own classic rock double live album. A mere nine months after the release of *Navy Blues*, Sloan released *Four Nights at the Palais Royale* (a play on the Knights in

KISS), culled from the band's sold-out engagement at Toronto's Palais Royale in November 1998. One of the nights was Murphy's 30th birthday, which made itself known throughout the evening, most notably in the form of a surprise reunion set by Kearney Lake Rd. When Henri Sangalang, now of Matt Murphy's mod combo The Flashing Lights, appeared with his bass to play three numbers he had prepared with Ferguson, Murphy was knocked off his confident perch, forever redefining the concept of a surprise party. Unfortunately, the Kearney Lake Rd. reunion is not included on the disc. With 28 songs amassing all stages of the band's career, the live album displays what they do best: two-hour concerts that don't cheat their audiences, witty between-song banter and audience participation that would make any *Rocky Horror* fan smile. It displays honest performances with some minor glitches, but they have enough integrity to leave them in.

Given the pace and output that the band had maintained over 1998–1999, it was quite a surprise when Sloan announced it would release another album of original material in September 1999. Produced by Sloan and Brenndan McGuire, *Between The Bridges*, the band's fifth studio album and third release in 18 months, maintained the band's sense of independence, democracy, and further explored classic rock landscape of the 1970s. Combined with a tip of the hat to such artists as Television, the Bee Gees and The Smiths, the album never veers too close as to risk being labelled *Navy Blues Part II*.

With rock radio championing generic punk and oatmeal rock, Sloan did not stand much of a chance with their retro chic. There was some minor support of Pentland's "Losing California," and to a lesser degree his Cheap Trick-rocker second single "Friendship." Critically, it is as good as anything they had produced in the past. Ferguson's triptych of songs was his strongest batch to this point and displayed far more from the shy guitarist than had been consistently proven in the past. The Gibb Brothers vibe of "Don't You Believe A Word," the Johnny Marr guitar-playing exercise of "Waiting for Slow Songs," and rock-solid "Take Good Care of the Poor Boy" indicated that Ferguson had tapped a creative well. Unfortunately, too few people heard them; *Between The Bridges* failed to catch on commercially as the band's previous two albums had.

It would be unfair to call *Between The Bridges* a failure. Sloan was at the top of their game in all areas of the music business. It would have been very easy for the band to focus on copying past keys to success, but the band had continued to write eclectic, strong material, and released it on the completely self-sufficient Murderecords. Of particular note was that their live show had finally risen to their creative altitude. During this period they officially embraced the idea of being a tight, professional band, and the critical applause for the band's live events extended to pockets all over the globe, as Sloan spent a considerable amount of time cultivating their audiences in Japan, Australia and Europe.

Though not all members of the group consider *Between the Bridges* a concept album, there is a self-reflective theme focusing on Sloan and its relationship to its hometown which surfaces throughout the record. "The N.S." (a.k.a. "The Nova Scotian"), Scott's Floydian opening to the album, begins with the cryptic lines "Lost the fight, but won the war / But no one's really sure what it is we're fighting for" — a reference to their short-lived Halifax music scene and Sloan's survival. Murphy's songs are all home-based and self-interested. "So Beyond Me" and "All By Ourselves" are very much his soundtracks for *The History of Sloan*, with their musical nods to KISS and The Beatles, and pseudo-autobiographical lyrics. His most delightful song in this vein, however, is the multi-layered "The Marquee And The Moon." The song managed to reference the Television album *Marquee Moon*, the Halifax night spots The Marquee Club and the Misty Moon, as well as reflect upon the activity of Halifax circa 1992, and Halifax now: "To me buzz is onomatopoeia / Will something be happening soon? / To settle the difference / Between the Marquee and the Moon." These songs reflect Murphy and Scott's disillusionment with what Sloan and the Halifax music scene accomplished in the early '90s. These concerns, however, are inconsequential.

Regardless of whether Halifax continued to be a hotbed for musical activity or not, Sloan forever changed the city's musical landscape, and gave a whole music scene a sophistication and a profile that previously did not exist. The early '90s "Halifax Pop Explosion" may not have been as big a deal as it was, had the scene been led by a less altruistic force. It is extremely rare for a band with such early success not to capitalize on their commercial potential for their own good. Sloan had always been smart about prioritizing the important things in music — whether it was building a community, tending to their fans, ensuring their independence or creating music they know will stand the test of time. They are CanRock survivors, and by reflecting on the band's career, it's clearly evident that Sloan left music listeners with a lot more than hype.

Andrew Scott concludes, "*Between the Bridges* was exciting because now we are starting to build a strong legacy of music. That is the most important thing: your history and what you leave behind. So many bands make one great record and then can't hold it together, or they put out one piece of shit and follow it up with many other pieces of shit. We have a pretty strong background and we've held on to our ideals and philosophies. We know what we are capable of, so the most important thing is just keeping it together. The current musical climate is unforgiving and abysmal. We have to block all of that out and carry on as we have for a decade now."

Never Mind the Molluscs:
The Halifax
Underground

It's 3 p.m. Atlantic time, on a Sunday in late August 2000. Greg Clark is obviously victimized by the toll of working in a bar scene that closes at 4 a.m. He's had many of these Sundays, not only as the recent co-owner of Halifax's Marquee Club, but also through a succession of the city's most notable clubs since the 1980s. Clark is widely recognized as the Godfather of the Halifax underground. He has nursed the city's music scene for over two decades, and he has seen it all.

His state of sleep deprivation has left him alternately curt and apologetic, but he has no problem finding his way through his Sunday fog and reminiscing about the musical generations. Years after Sarah McLachlan moved to Vancouver, Sloan relocated to Toronto, and many other artists in the scene broke up or quit music entirely, the question of how Halifax's underground gradually rose to international heights is still of interest to the club owner. "It can only be like it was once, right?" Clark says rhetorically of Halifax's time in the spotlight in the early '90s. "It's easy to lose perspective as to whether the scene is [now] better or worse. It will never be as it was. That was the time that people were starting to realize that we definitely have the seal of approval from outside attention. That only lasts so long."

Clark pauses to organize his words, and then he reflects on the opportunities for his city's children in the future. "One of the things that sticks out in my mind is that if the music business would be a more perfect thing; this is the easy part. You need management and people like me, but without the bands there's nothing at all. I definitely have pet peeves against people like me who are in the non-talent part of it that begin to think they're bigger than that. For me there's always another band: a band breaks up, there's more coming along. I've basically provided the stage. I can always make a living at this, but it's hard to see a band like Thrush Hermit breaking up. You see these people and you're like, 'Man, these guys should be making a living at this.' They want to and this business just sucks, and it's not getting any better."

Halifax, Nova Scotia, is by default the metropolitan musical capital of the Canadian east coast. There are pockets of activity going on in New Brunswick (Moncton, Fredericton) and Newfoundland (St. John's), but it was Halifax where the infrastructure gradually grew to accommodate musicians of all sorts, and where most of the recognized activity has taken place. Though the music of the east coast often brings to mind Celtic influences, kitchen parties and platinum sellers like Rita MacNeil, Ashley MacIsaac, The Rankin Family and Anne Murray, the city's history is rich with many genres of music; more than tourist handbooks would lead you to believe.

There is the influence of blues and jazz, as well as a credible hip-hop/DJ culture, for Halifax is a city with a large African-Canadian population.

The underground rock community in Halifax always had potential. Like Vancouver, its bi-coastal counterpart, it's a multiple-university town (including The Nova Scotia College of Art and Design), draws staggering numbers of tourists and is relatively isolated from other key cities and the music industry at large. The common joke regarding the city's bearings on the map is that Halifax is only a convenient stop if one is en route to Europe. The nearest major Canadian metropolis, Montreal, is an arduous 15-hour drive away, and even the more convenient three hours to Moncton, New Brunswick, can be an impossibility if Mother Nature gets ugly.

This explains the inherent lack of live-music events. Well-established rockers like Bryan Adams, Metallica and The Cult sometimes made the trek to the east coast, but most Canadian bands avoided it because they couldn't reap the financial benefits of the bigger acts. Only some of the nation's rock road warriors who could live off ridiculously low budgets would make the attempt to play the city, which is why most of the Halifax underground from 1985–1995 cite punk bands from Montreal (the Nils, Doughboys) and Vancouver (DOA, NoMeansNo), indie rockers (Change of Heart) or local heroes as their favourite Canadian bands. They were simply the only ones who made the effort.

By necessity, Halifax bred its own heroes. This, coupled with a small population, explains why the scene is so inbred and fiercely proud of its own. There are no major labels in Halifax, and thus, there is little to gain or lose by taking a stab at the music business. For years there was no infra- structure to support the underground bands. Playing in a Top 40 cover band provided the possibility of some success, but if one dabbled in the alter- native sphere, any success would be limited to a small portion of the city. All of these factors resulted in artists who had no choice but to remain true to themselves and create their own rules. Local musician Barry Walsh says, "What made Halifax stand out from other small cities is this weird dichotomy between this artistic community being fostered by the art college in a pretty conservative little place. There is a conservative mentality there, but there's also this artistic side that is responsible for some amazing stuff all across the board, not just music. That dichotomy is what helps make things inter- esting. When you are making stuff based on reaction, you have to have something to react against."

Throughout the '80s, musicians in Halifax existed unto themselves, eyeing Toronto with looks ranging from antipathy to infatuation. The early philosophy within the city was that bands needed to move to Canada's musical industry headquarters to get anywhere with their careers. Thus, the Jellyfishbabies, the October Game's Sarah McLachlan and Basic English all made the trek to bigger music centres. However, this exodus often resulted in extinction. Between 1985 and 1995, Greg Clark, along with the talent of the music makers themselves, provided a good reason to be proud of being an artist in Halifax. In the early '90s, the collective work of artists like Black Pool, Sloan, Eric's Trip, Jale, Hardship Post, The Super Friendz, Rebecca West and Thrush Hermit — admittedly propelled with some luck because of being in the right place at the right time — made it possible to exist as a band living in Halifax. "I don't think anything would have happened with respect to the success of the punk rock and alternative scene without Greg Clark," states Peter Rowan, another primary advocate of the scene. "The percep- tion of the east coast as being nothing but fiddlers and fishermen was always wrong. There just wasn't anywhere to play but people's basements."

Greg Clark was born and raised in Waverly, a town known as "the gateway to Nova Scotia's Annapolis Valley." In 1970, he moved to Halifax's twin city, Dartmouth, and began high school, where it became clear that he was a natural social convenor. "I had a very social last couple of years of high school, organizing parties," he admits. "From there I left high school because they wouldn't let me play football anymore. At the time I thought I wanted to open a record store. I always loved music, and that was the first idea which indirectly led to Backstreet in 1980."

Backstreet Imports, like many of Clark's endeavours, would go through a number of name changes, but the initial shop that sold used records, as well as rock and roll and smoking paraphernalia was, in essence, the incubator of the Haligonian Underground. Clark's business soon became the unofficial clubhouse for the city's punk and teenage hipster population. "I hired a few cool kids that seemed to have lots of friends," says Clark. "Backstreet was in the middle of downtown in this tiny little place, basically underground. A lot of the appeal was because of the music we were playing and the kids I hired to begin with. All these kids were hanging around and not buying anything. It was a cool atmosphere and there were no coffee shops at the time."

Clark soon realized that the Asteroids video game he had stuck in a corner of Backstreet was actually making some money, and gradually he phased out the T-shirts and used records and transformed the hangout into Backstreets Amusements. But this would not be enough to satiate his musical appetite. In the early '80s, The Grafton Street Café was the only establishment in town that hosted the occasional punk show. When this ceased to exist in 1983, Clark had a brainstorm. The teens at Backstreet had been decorating his spot with gig posters for some time, and the music had always been part of the draw. Perhaps he could transfer their loitering into an all-ages live music club.

Clark opened the low-budget Club Flamingo on Grafton Street. It was an extremely modest set-up which featured picnic tables, pop machines and a cheap PA system. The venue, which was just up the street from his arcade, lasted a short four months due to conflicts with the fire marshal. There was also some difficulty transferring the teenage herd to the new hangout. "All the kids would rather hang out in that hole in the wall," Clark laughs. "I was competing against Backstreet. Even the big Flamingo Club we had on Gottingen Street, we had some pretty decent bands up there. NoMeansNo would be playing The Flamingo and I would go down to Backstreet and it would be just jammed with people."

From the 1970s onward, Halifax had a history of punk rock bands. *Halifax Herald* writer and longtime scenester Stephen Cooke cites Halifax West Secondary School specifically as the birthplace of the city's punk community. "Halifax West is supposedly ground zero for Halifax punk rock because Bill MacGillivray was an art teacher there and he put on a talent show in 1977–78. A bunch of local kids put together a punk band because one or two of them had been to England in the summer of '77 and brought back all these great records." The first generation of Haligonian punk included the likes of The Trash Kanz, The Hopping Penguins and Nobody's Heroes, but nothing really consolidated the scene until the mid-1980s.

Halifax's true 'ground zero' can be found between 1985 and 1986, when a few developments instituted the beginnings of a scene framework. In 1985, Dalhousie University Radio's CKDU was granted an FM license. A year later, two official recordings were released, gradually making the city's musical underground visible to the public eye. Clark took over the old Cove Theatre on Gottingen Street, opening up his second Club Flamingo with Keith Tufts and Derek Honig on Hallowe'en of 1986. It unbolted the door to a new realm of possibilities for the city's scene, as the series of shows Clark and his partners produced prior to the official relocation/re-opening of the Flamingo inspired many of the local bands to take their craft more seriously. With this influx of bands, the opening of the club coincided with the release of a compilation album of local artists entitled *Out of the Fog: The Halifax Underground 1986*, released on the club's own Flamingo Records. Stephen Cooke notes, "That's where things really got going. There were all kinds of things bubbling under, but up until that point nobody put out a record and nobody had access to a studio or anything like that. *Out of the Fog* was the first time anyone got their act together and got these bands into a proper studio."

The celebration of the album's release remained within the city limits. The *Halifax Herald*'s review of the LP was polite and extremely telling of the infancy of the underground music scene. The paper noted, "You won't see these bands performing anywhere in town but at Halifax's newly-opened Club Flamingo, which is deliberately dedicated to promoting underexposed local talent. The compilation album reflects a degree of accomplishment that Halifax should be — but isn't — proud of. To be sure, compilation albums are just that, and the result is therefore somewhat uneven. But one thing is sure: these bands are singing and playing their hearts out, and most have matured greatly since the album tryouts were held via a series of concerts last winter."

Considering the scene had few acts that toured outside the city or the Maritimes, some of the outside assessments of Halifax's burgeoning scene were less than flattering. Philip Bull from Toronto's *Nerve* magazine wrote in January 1987, "*Out of the Fog: The Halifax Underground 1986* is a smart package with nifty graphics and clever photos, all of which promise more than the record can deliver. Dull bar-band goop and gormless hardcore are in conspicuous evidence. Someone should have spoken firmly to almost all these bands about the virtues of brevity." There are honourable mentions to the Karma Wolves, The Lone Stars, Ridge of Tears and The Killer Klamz, but the writer's overall tone is less than supportive. In all honesty, few of the songs hold up, but along with Jellyfishbabies' eponymous debut released only months before *Out of the Fog*, the album was an affirmation to musicians in Halifax that music could be made in their own backyard.

The Jellyfishbabies, who contributed "Running Out of Time" to the compilation, made history as the first band of this era in Halifax history to release a record of their own. They would become the pop/punk template from which many of the local bands would draw. "I think that's why there's a Halifax sound to some degree," says Waye Mason, head of local independent No Records. "If the songs hadn't been recorded on an eight-track, and if the drums didn't sound like wet paper bags, that first album would have had some solid pop hits."

Formed by a motley crew of four teens hanging out at Backstreet's — singer/guitarist Scott Kendall and guitarist/singer Peter Arsenault from Halifax West, drummer Colleen Britton from Queen Elizabeth High School and bassist David Schellenberg from Dartmouth — the Jellyfishbabies quickly became the city's buzz band. Greg Clark says, "Certainly anyone with taste realized that they were the best band to come out of the city at the time."

"This was the coolest band," acknowledges Black Pool leader John Chisholm, who spent a fair amount of time busking with Kendall in the '80s. "I pride myself on being able to pick people who have that thing that makes them attractive to other people. Scott Kendall was one of those people. They had Scott, who had this perfect thing going on, they had Peter Arsenault, they had the heroin addict bass player, and they had a girl drummer. How cool could that be?"

"At the time I thought Scott Kendall was so cool on stage," admits Sloan's Jay Ferguson. "He had this really long straight hair and it was always hiding him. He was really skinny and tall and he had these hoop earrings and a bandanna. I think that's what elevated these bands in our minds. Because there were no other bands, you get excited about having a rock star in the north end of town."

After a couple of demo tapes recorded by Killer Klamz leader Steve Moore, the Jellyfishbabies made their first album while Arsenault and Kendall were still in school. The album cover was extremely reflective of the time: on the front is a simple picture of a lighthouse, probably one of the most stereotypical images of the east coast, but also a symbolic beacon to welcome the Haligonian underground. The back pictured the four members standing by a car looking like a bunch of hippie punks, which, given the sound of *Jellyfishbabies*, made perfect sense. Colleen Britton remarks, "I think me and Dave were the most punk in the band. I guess I looked the most punk with a nose piercing and spiky hair. Scott was more of an activist. Jellyfishbabies played many benefit gigs."

Jellyfishbabies, second line-up: Mike Belitsky, Dave
Schellenberg, Scott Kendall, Peter Arsenault
(Photo by Eric B. Brown)

The eight songs on *Jellyfishbabies* balanced American influences like Hüsker Dü and Soul Asylum with the Canadian folk of Leonard Cohen and certain elements from the U.K., including early Cult ("Diamond Joe") and U2 ("Can It Be"). The explosive introductory couplet of "Messiah" and "Blue Eyes" displayed the band's talent for fusing memorable melodies with punk arrangements, which included Kendall and Arsenault's frenetic vocal and guitar interplay and the rhythm section's creative breaks and time shifts. The explosive anthem "Never Really Knew" tapped into the same psychosomatic magic that U2 had created with their 1980 debut *Boy*, with its tapestry of guitar harmonics and its call-to-arms chorus.

Aside from being the only band in town with a record, Jellyfishbabies would be one of the few Halifax bands to head out on tour. The only other bands that attempted touring the vast country were The Killer Klamz and antagonistic rockers Dogfood. In the latter case, Dogfood's biggest accomplishment during their trek was chasing an audience of 200 people out of a Vancouver club. It was Dogfood members Curphey Forrestal and Sean Murphy, along with friend Moritz Geda, who created the short-lived local independent Plot Records that released *Jellyfishbabies*.

The Jellyfishbabies made their first tour in 1986 in a station wagon, and performed at venues in Fredericton, Montreal and Toronto. The band would make a second excursion in 1987 with Britton suffering through a deadly 104-degree fever. Yet throughout the two tours, the Jellyfishbabies shared the stage with other scene-making bands such as the Nils, Change of Heart and Jr. Gone Wild, as well as various hometown bands.

After their second tour, the band recorded a follow-up album, but unhappy with the quality of the recording, the band didn't release it, and it sits in a box in Greg Clark's residence. Along with internal politics, other roadblocks started to get in the way of the band's evolution. Britton fell ill again after a pilgrimage to Washington, D.C., which became a catalyst in her decision to leave the band. "My kidneys failed a month later in Halifax. I thought it might have been from drinking the water down in the States, but I found out I was pregnant," explains Britton. "I decided to stay in Halifax because of this fact and because I didn't enjoy the Jellyfishbabies' music or the direction they were headed in."

Others report that Scott Kendall pushed Colleen Britton out of the band. "I was there the day Colleen was told that they were moving and she wasn't coming," recalls John Chisholm. "It was a sad day. The plan was made to leave town and they were going to move to Toronto and make it big. The day before, Scott told Colleen, 'You're not coming, Belitsky's going to play drums.'"

Ex-Lone Star drummer Mike Belitsky, who was attempting to go to school in Montreal, was torn away from his studies and enlisted as a new member before the band's relocation to Toronto. "When I met [Scott] he was really young and just discovering who he was," says Belitsky. "Lord knows that was a process. We all lived together in Toronto and we practised in the basement. We toured a lot for a band back then. It wasn't about comfort. It was about trying to get better. We would practise four hours a day, five days a week as a band and then individually everyone would practise all the time. It was a really integral part of my musical development."

During the band's stay in Toronto they produced a 7" single of covers (Velvet Underground's "Here She Comes"/Leonard Cohen's "Famous Blue Raincoat"), contributed to Leonard Cohen and Bruce Cockburn tribute albums, and donated "The Erkling" to the soundtrack of Bruce McDonald's *Highway 61*. In 1990 they released their long-delayed sophomore album, *The Unkind Truth About Rome* produced by Michael Phillip Wojewoda. It signalled, among other things, a grave change in the band's direction. *The Unkind Truth About Rome* reflected Kendall's recent interest in poet musicians, primarily Lou Reed and Jim Morrison. The album would inevitably distance the band from its original followers. Stephen Cooke says, "Scott was trying to do this weird gypsy-type folk punk stuff. He really went off in a weird direction. The record is all weird tempos, it's not melodic and it's really odd. It really wasn't the same band. Scott's lyrics were really dense and poetic. It was hard to get into what he was thinking about, whereas the first album is pretty straightforward."

"I think Colleen was a good foil for Scott," states John Chisholm. "She's a real cut-the-crap sort of girl. She inhibited him from going into too much of this airy-fairy 'I am the poet' sort of guy. Once she was gone, there was nobody to stop him."

Peter Arsenault would part ways with the band before Kendall, Schellenberg and Belitsky moved to New York in 1990, and there the band lasted long enough to record another album that would remain unreleased entitled *The Swan City*. Eventually New York would take its toll on the band. Belitsky, a dual citizen, was used to the stress, but Kendall and Schellenberg escaped to Vancouver and Toronto respectively. Arsenault would go on to play on the final albums of Montreal's Doughboys, Belitsky would join the otherwise all-female outfit Jale, and Schellenberg would play bass for Toronto's Squirrel until his tragic death from a drug overdose in 1995. Schellenberg's memory was appropriately preserved in the acknowledgements of the book *Please Kill Me: An Oral History of Punk*.

Other artists in the late '80s — like rockabilly legends The Lone Stars, new wavers Staja/TANZ and The October Game and post-punks Ridge of Tears — would also make their mark, but they remain like footnotes. Of all the '80s Halifax bands, The October Game continues to be the most frequently referenced. This art/new wave group played only a handful of live gigs, and had only one recorded song officially available to the world — a Siouxsie & the Banshees' derivation "Grind," on *Out of the Fog*. Formed initially by guitarist Barry Walsh, keyboardist Patrick Roscoe, bassist Jeff Semple (later replaced by Jim Parker) and a drum machine (later replaced by Creighton Doane) The October Game drafted a 17-year-old named Sarah McLachlan from Queen Elizabeth High School into their ranks as a vocalist, landing them a permanent place in pop music history.

Sarah Ann McLachlan was born on January 28, 1968, in Halifax, and became the adopted daughter of Dorice and Jack McLachlan. The youngest of three children, Sarah grew up in a strict but loving home that offered her 12 years of classical guitar, eight years of piano and five years of voice. Though disciplined in her study of classical music, she soon discovered that her heart yearned for other genres. McLachlan says, "As a child, I was never passionate about classical music, even though I put so much energy into it. From the age of four, I preferred to improvise on the stuff I was learning. And the moment I hit puberty, I got into popular music instead.

"The music my parents brought into the house was old jazz and a lot of traditional folk," she remembers. "Joan Baez, Mary O'Hara, Cat Stevens, and Simon and Garfunkel are my earliest influences. They were my first loves in music, and that's what stuck with me — the memories of those chords and melodies, and the places they would take me."

McLachlan became one of the many arcade rats to frequent Greg Clark's Backstreet Amusements. She would eventually be hired by Clark to work at his Club Flamingo, and soon the influence of punk and alternative music would filter into her musical vernacular. "Sarah used to play Dead Kennedys and various punk songs on her acoustic guitar on the school lawn at lunch times," remembers schoolmate Colleen Britton. "The October Game was more 'techno' and I was not a fan of the band, although I did attend a few of their shows. Sarah is a great musician/composer, it just wasn't my style of music."

Clark recalls his first exposure to the young McLachlan, "I knew she played a bit of music, but I didn't realize she sang. I was really blown away when I first heard her sing. The October Game had really good players in it. It would be recognizable as Sarah because of the voice, but it definitely wasn't her thing at all. She wasn't involved in the songwriting process. It was frustrating from my standpoint because I thought these guys should realize what they've got. A couple of other band members would do the in-between song patter. I wanted to throw something at them."

Though Walsh remembers there were stronger personalities in the band that may have eclipsed the young singer's stage presence, he notes, "I do recall her being kind of shy about the performance aspect. She had an incredible voice and wasn't shy abut using it, but she didn't seem like the type to crack jokes between song like, 'All right, Halifax! You ready to rock?' That wasn't really her style. But again, as time went on and we got more gigs under our belts we all got a little more comfortable and stopped looking at our shoes."

McLachlan's now-legendary first step on the path to superstardom occurred after The October Game's first gig opening for the Club Flamingo's presentation of Moev on March 27, 1986. On a whim, Moev guitarist and Nettwerk Records partner Mark Jowett decided to check out the opening act of the evening. The October Game's young vocalist knocked Jowett off his feet. "I was just amazed at this kind of glow she had," recalls Jowett. "It's hard to describe — a warmth exuded from her towards the audience so magnificently. She was also technically so great as a vocalist and also as a guitarist. 1 was completely captivated."

Immediately after the show Jowett approached her about singing for

October Game, in one of their live shows.
From left to right: Jeff Semple, Sarah McLachlan,
Patrick Roscoe, and Barry Walsh
(Photo by Jennifer Raven/ Metaphortography)

Moev. He would later send her some of the band's demos to experiment with some vocals. When McLachlan's parents uncovered the Vancouver label scouting their daughter at the age of 17, they put their foot down, and told Sarah she wouldn't be going anywhere until she finished school.

In the ensuing two years, McLachlan would graduate from high school and spend a year at NSCAD. During this time, the loose collective of The October Game began to unravel. McLachlan says, "We sort of fell apart. We all lived at different ends of the city. We didn't have cars. We didn't have any money for rehearsal space or studio time and there were very few venues that we could play. I went to art college and the others were doing university and other things. We stopped for a year. We still talked once in a while, but it wasn't like we were breaking up. We didn't have any big plans, at least I didn't. I was just this young singer thinking, 'Hey, this is fun.'"

Allison Outhit, who led the early '80s Halifax new wave band Staja/TANZ and later formed Jeffrey's Wake and Flags for Everything with Barry Walsh, says, "I think the other guys from The October Game were pretty bitter about the whole thing because they lost their singer and she was a pretty good singer. She was very nervous and had no stage presence whatsoever. It was funny for me because they started while I was living away [from Halifax in England], but when I came back it was like, 'Yeah, there's this girl who's totally copping your thing.' The band was largely based on what I had been doing [in Staja/TANZ] which was kind of funny. It predated them for a fair stretch. I only saw them once with Sarah as the singer and I did think she had a good voice, although it wasn't the kind of voice I liked. It was really high."

"I don't think it was a case of anyone wanting to keep things going past the expiration date," says Walsh. "After I got a call from Nettwerk early on about our first demo that I sent them — where they expressed an interest in the band — we worked hard and recorded a few other songs in an 8- or 16-track studio. And after that we played a couple of gigs, but as Sarah said, we just kind of stopped. Nettwerk wasn't really interested in the newer material for whatever reason, we were all starting university — it wasn't possible to play the same venue every week. It was hard to sustain things, and in the end we didn't."

McLachlan remained in town living next to Club Flamingo, and made the occasional solo appearance at events like "Lawn Jam" at the TUNS School of Architecture in the summer of '87. It was during this fateful period that she met Nettwerk President Terry McBride while working the door at a Skinny Puppy concert, and she would soon sign with his innovative label.

"Of course the folks in The October Game at that point decided they should have her be more involved in the band," notes Greg Clark. "It was too-little-too-late. Certainly at that time too, a lot of people wondered what she should do and I was like, 'Get the hell out.' It wasn't the time to stay in Halifax. The music scene was pretty much dominated by Toronto and Vancouver and somewhat Montreal."

Though Walsh won't speak for the rest of the band, he notes, "Personally, I wasn't too broken up about the band stopping. It was more like, 'Okay, where to now?' So contrary to what the outside opinions might be, and in spite of all the weird shit that's occurred years later — trials, phone calls from nefarious authors — I think most of us have mostly good memories about what we did. We had some fun, learned some lessons, and we got our sea legs."

While McLachlan would eventually ascend into the limelight as a high-profile pop star, Walsh continued on in a series of well-received bands, the most renowned being '90s pop band Cool Blue Halo, who released 1995's *Kangaroo* on the No Records label.

The last band to emerge from the *Out of the Fog* roster was Basic English, comprised of vocalist/guitarist Tim Armour, guitarist John Davis, drummer Roger Whyte, and bassist Sean Ryan. Like the Jellyfishbabies, Basic English relocated to Toronto with hopes of a career break. Given their Stones/roots rock sensibilities, the prospect of success was certainly higher. They started off well by winning two high-profile Toronto radio station awards — a lucrative Q107 new band contest as well as a CFNY 102.1 FM CASBY for "Best Non-Recording Act" in 1987. Their subsequent signing to Risque Disque and the Bob Wiseman-produced single "Images of Love" resulted in brief renown. After the release of their 1990 debut *Sweet Panic*, however, Risque Disque folded, and the band would suffer a similar fate in 1991.

Nonetheless, Basic English made an impression on John Wesley Chisholm. "I thought that was the best thing there could be. I thought they would be the number one band, but people didn't take the same interest in them. They left town a little early before they truly consolidated their Halifax audience. That really struck me because the Jellyfishbabies were gone and Basic English was gone — Staja/TANZ, and all the new-wave bands were gone. That's when I was pretty sure I would make a rock band, but a huge part of it for me was to not leave town. I had only ever seen the process work where a band leaves town and goes from being a big popular band to being nothing. It wasn't clear yet about Sarah McLachlan. At that time it just seemed that the record company guys had come in and screwed up a good band by taking this girl away."

Chisholm, like Greg Clark, was a transplant from Waverly, Nova Scotia. He had made his way into Halifax after seeing the Halifax punk band the Defects, and he was introduced to Clark's Backstreet gang. Over time he made the acquaintance of Jellyfishbabies' Scott Kendall, who became a close downtown friend, and between 1985 and 1986 the two busked nearly every evening. At this time in Halifax there were few buskers, and the city's now-famous Busker's Festival was not yet a reality. The only other buskers in town at the time were Chip Sutherland and Al Wilkie. The two busking duos would often meet for breakfast and, through Wilkie and Sutherland, Chisholm met guitarist Phil Sedore. Sedore eventually moved to Halifax and joined Chisholm's first version of Black Pool.

Historically, Black Pool is notable for its revolving door line-up, which made the band the training school for many of the Halifax scene's major players. The band is also important for bringing a sense of professionalism to the independent community. From the start of Black Pool, Chisholm straddled the line between mainstream aspirations and community ties. His university business degree reflected his approach to running a band. Chisholm's holy grail was simply to compete head-on with the town's Top 40 cover bands, and become the biggest original band in Halifax. With an accessible roots rock sound in the same vein as Blue Rodeo, Black Pool became one of the few bands in town at the turn of the decade to warrant the top slot on local bills, or one of the coveted opening slots for the bigger Canadian bands that came to town. Their 1989 album, *Cemeteries*, also reflected this approach, as the album was the first local independent release to be recorded in a professional studio.

Chisholm is also one of the few Halifax artists from the independent scene who champions the role of the East Coast Music Awards, created by Rob Cohen in 1991. "One thing I was always bummed about was that there was no star structure. There was no way of placing people. There were no charts, no accolades. Out of sheer willpower, Rob created that whole thing which now is the central feature of the music community here. It's those music awards that give definition to the community." However, most of the independent community fails to regard the awards in such high esteem. "The ECMAS are mostly an establishment thing, like most awards shows," says *Halifax Herald* writer Stephen Cooke. "They're more for the Rankin Families and Rita MacNeils of the world."

For Black Pool's second LP, 1991's *We The Living*, Chisholm, Sedore and

Chip Sutherland were joined by future Sloan bassist Chris Murphy. Less than a year later, this line-up parted ways due to conflicting interests. "We all left in 1991," says Chip Sutherland. "We left because Chris kept saying we should turn our guitars up and distort them a little more and we should all wear flannel shirts and have thumpier bass lines, and we were like, 'Chris you're crazy!' He had a different musical direction; he was working on Sloan at the same time. It was his hobby band."

"I was trying to create this Celtic version of my band, and Chris was trying to create a band specifically to play for lots of kids," says Chisholm. "He had his idea and I had mine. His idea worked out better for him, but my idea worked out better overall and sort of became this Celtic rock monolith. Now I can go out any night of the week and see a band doing what I was doing in 1992. That's weird, and of course Great Big Sea is the ultimate incarnation of that. Not that I'm taking credit for that, but I did that in 1992."

Guitarist Matt Murphy (The Super Friendz), violinist Catherine McKinnon, drummer Dave Marsh (No Damn Fears, The Super Friendz) and bassist Tim Brennan (The Lone Stars) would round out the Celtic incarnation of Black Pool and, according to Greg Clark, would be the strongest version of Chisholm's band. After the release of *Seahorse* in 1993, Chisholm ditched both rock and Celtic music for a stab at the mid-'90s swing revival with the Johnny Favourite Swing Orchestra. He would write and play guitar in this 17-piece band for five years, before he decided to stay at home with his family, and was, in his words, "screwed out of my own band."

In 1988 Greg Clark left the Club Flamingo over a disagreement with partners concerning the philosophy of running a club and how staff and clientele should be treated. "I foolishly signed a non-competition clause, so I spent the next year and a half not being able to do anything," he says. Eventually Clark survived his exile from the club scene and was hired as the promotions manager for Waldo's. Though the venue lasted only three months, this experience opened Clark's eyes. "Waldo's was when I first got the idea that the local scene was starting to change. There were a lot of new local bands that were quite good and there really seemed to be a much bigger audience for it. Having started as an all-ages club, a lot of those kids we had dealt with at the Flamingo before it became a bar were now of age. I thought I would like to get a smaller club that would focus more on local music."

Between the activity at Waldo's and the Two Dollar Tuesdays run by Clark's roommate Peter Rowan at the Flamingo — a showcase evening that provided a stage for burgeoning talent — there was a significant change in the level of musical activity occurring in Halifax. As a result of this boom and Sloan's ascent and eventual record deal with Geffen, Clark opened the Double Deuce on Hollis Street in 1992 and it became the first club that could actually support itself predominantly on local talent.

Clark says, "When the attention started to happen outside the city, suddenly for a lot of the audience here in Halifax it was like the stamp of approval. Up until then, with the exception of Sarah there had never been anybody from the alternative scene that had done anything at all, so bands had tended to come and go. When the attention started to happen with Sloan, the inferiority complex lessened a bit. People began to think there was a reason to be doing this. The Deuce was a small club and I was pretty amazed that we were doing Thursday, Friday, and Saturday night runs with mostly local bands. We were about 70 per cent local. The purpose that we served was giving the bands the prime nights to play."

Through two 1992 compilations on Peter Rowan's DTK Records, *Hear and Now '92* and *Cod Can't Hear*, the earliest evidence of this germination can be witnessed. All of the talent that made a name outside of the city (Sloan, Thrush Hermit, Jale, Cool Blue Halo), the other mainstay players who would surface later in the decade playing in larger profile bands (Matt Murphy, Dave Marsh, Lukas Pearse, Allison Outhit) and those whose popularity remained within the city limits (Al Tuck, Aimless, 100 Flowers, Leonard Conan, and Quahogs) can be found on these recordings. *Cod Can't Hear* is an audio archive of the first Halifax Independent Music Festival. This festival became an annual event celebrating local, national (cub, Zumpano, Doughboys, etc.) and international talent (Stereolab, Redd Kross, Elliott Smith, Yo La Tengo, etc.) run by Peter Rowan, Colin MacKenzie and Thrush Hermit/Rebecca West manager Angie Fenwick under the name The Halifax Pop Explosion, and later, Halifax On Music.

Barry Walsh, who at this point was leading Cool Blue Halo, remembers a distinct change in the perception of his hometown. "When we would leave Halifax and play shows in Ontario, there did seem to be some sort of exotic thing about Halifax which struck us as really funny. It probably struck the people of Athens, Georgia as funny too. I know people who made their pilgrimages to Athens to spot R.E.M. Sometimes you would see that happening here. People would come down and look for Sloan. Using their vacation time they would hang out at the fabled Double Deuce. For us, it was as natural as breathing salt air."

"The blueprint for me was Washington D.C.'s Dischord Records; we really wanted to be community-minded," says Sloan's Chris Murphy. "We had the best luck and the most fortune first, and we were able to bypass Toronto, but we were interested in other bands. There were other bands going on [in Halifax], and that's what made it larger than life. If we were the only band from there, it wasn't that interesting a story. What we tried to do in early interviews was talk about other people [in Halifax]. I don't think it's just our selflessness. Part of it is the fear of: 'when this fails in six months, I want to come home and look my friends in the face.'"

After Sloan signed with Geffen in late 1991, Sub Pop — the Seattle label that gave Nirvana, Soundgarden and Mudhoney their start — became eager to unearth what other gems were buried in the city. This, of course, would draw further reasons for the prevalent media analogies between Halifax and the "grunge capital."

Peter Rowan remembers, "Around August of 1992 I got a phone call from Joyce Linehan from Sub Pop. She called and said, 'I just heard this band called Sloan, are they signed?'

"'Yeah they're signed to Geffen.'

"'Cool. My mother's from Matega, which is just outside of Yarmouth, and I'm coming to visit the family. Is there anything else going on?'

"'Yeah there's lots of great bands up here.'

"'Well I'm coming up this weekend, is there a show going on?'

"'Yeah, as matter of fact there is a show going on.'

"I hung up the phone and called the Double Deuce and said 'Greg, we have to have a show.' I got Eric's Trip, Bubaiskull and a band called Tag, who became Jale. Joyce came and saw the show and they gave Eric's Trip an offer." It was an offer that the Moncton quartet would turn down.

In 1984, a New York art-rock quartet made the trek to Halifax to play a show at NSCAD in the art college's cafeteria. Comprised of guitarists Thurston Moore and Lee Ranaldo, bassist Kim Gordon and, at the time, drummer Bob Bert (replaced by Steve Shelley a year later) Sonic Youth slowly challenged and extended the boundaries of popular music. Combining punk rock with art rock, and just enough of a fascination with pop, Sonic Youth are regarded as pioneers of alternative guitar rock of the early '90s.

Sonic Youth's 1988 release, *Daydream Nation*, was an ambitious double album, foreshadowing the American mainstream's acceptance of punk rock three years later. Perhaps this is why Rick White, a Moncton, New Brunswick native, took the title of a song on the record's second side — "Eric's Trip" — to represent his band. In many ways, they were the rock and roll pioneers of the east coast.

The story of Eric's Trip centres on guitarist/songwriter Rick White; the three other members — drummer Mark Gaudet, bassist Julie Doiron and guitarist Chris Thompson — all acknowledge that it was White's creative vision that really propelled the band. Even though his approach could be called primitive, from the band's basement recordings to album artwork, it all bore his unique trademark. "It was all Rick and we just followed his path," admits Gaudet. "He's probably improved because of different talents he's worked with, but it's basically all him."

After White's early love affair with metal, he acquired a taste for early 1980s hardcore. His first bands — Bloodstain, T.C.I.B. and finally The Underdogs in 1987 — were modelled after this style. Doiron says, "He went from metal to hardcore. That happened when he became a skateboarder."

"Moncton's always had a kind of heavy, hardcore-type scene, with Discharge-sounding kind of stuff," says White. "When I started going to shows, that's what I heard a lot of. I was around 16 years old, and I had lots of energy. It was like, try to go as fast as you can for a while and you release all that. Teenagers always have to have some extreme form of music, depending on the times."

Chris Thompson was another misfit exploring the underground scene in the mid-'80s, though in a different mindset than White. "I wasn't really in hardcore bands. We had a mixture of Shadowy Men and Deja Voodoo kind of stuff. My first band was Dang where we were basically just making up songs about people we didn't like. After that we had this band called Clarence and we were doing surfy stuff and slow punky stuff."

Thompson met White in 1988, when Clarence began playing at the same house parties as the Underdogs. By 1989, White and Thompson had formed a new band called The Forest and were compelled to move in new directions. "Chris and I were getting into stuff like early Dinosaur Jr. and My Bloody Valentine records," says White. "It gave us a different perspective of music. We tried making this full-volume guitar band and then that turned into Eric's Trip once Julie joined."

The full-on sound was tempered by another new influence on White's songwriting. "I first got into Sebadoh because someone got me a copy of *Freed Man* in the late '80s. I'd been doing those little home tapes the way Lou Barlow had been doing it too, but never really thought of it in the way his came out. It connected with me when I first heard that."

In 1990, White met Julie Doiron, a disarmingly shy but charming person who until that point was happy working on her own songs at home. "I started playing guitar when I was 15," she says. "I was into the Velvet

Underground all through high school, and The Smiths, The Cure, that kind of thing," she says. "I played around at home a whole bunch, then I started playing classical guitar for a while. When Rick and I started hanging around, that's when I wanted to buy an electric guitar."

White and Doiron's relationship, both musically and emotionally, provided the foundation for Eric's Trip. Each used the relationship as the basis for often heartbreaking lyrics set amid song cycles of mind-numbing thrash and hushed ballads. The first line-up got together in June 1990, and featured Doiron on guitar, Thompson on bass, and Ed Vaughan on drums. Taking another cue from the lo-fi four-track recordings school of Lou Barlow, White began recording the new band in Thompson's basement immediately. Doiron says, "We were borrowing four-tracks from the Moncton high school and finally Rick got one for Christmas and it all went from there."

According to Thompson, "We'd recorded our first cassette and never played a show. I think our first gig was at an Earth Day celebration [April 1991] in Moncton. We played four songs, and people in Moncton were really in for something new because there weren't many bands around at that time that were doing anything new. Not to sound conceited, but when we came along people really loved it."

"We'd just put out our second cassette when we played our first show," remembers Julie Doiron. "It seemed like people took right to it because they already knew the tapes and they were really excited about seeing us. We'd sold a lot of tapes before that show. People had heard about us in Fredericton so they invited us to play there, too. That's when Peter Rowan heard us and invited us to play in Halifax. People always seemed to hear about us before we got there, so there were always people at the shows and luckily they didn't say anything bad."

Peter Rowan, who was working with Sloan and would become Eric's Trip's manager, had heard rave reviews before this initial encounter. "A guy I knew from Fredericton named Chris Vautour had told me about this band from Moncton that blew people away. He gave me a number to call and I got this incredible tape from them. I remember sitting at my desk thinking, 'What am I doing with this dead end job?' since nothing had happened with Sloan yet. I put on this tape and the first song was a cover of Madonna's 'Open Your Heart.' My copy had these incredibly complex liner notes — 'Please Madonna, don't be mad at us' — and all these classic Eric's Trip drawings. I got on the phone and said, 'You guys have to come down and play The Flamingo.'"

Someone else who had been following the band's progress was drummer

Mark Gaudet, a fixture in the "Punkton" scene since the early '70s. Gaudet began playing in Purple Knight in 1974 with Ray Leger before discovering punk in 1977 and later forming The Robins. That band played Halifax and gave Gaudet his first perspective on how hardcore was affecting different cities. "When The Robins played Halifax in '81–'82, the only punk bands that were happening down there seemed to be Clash or Who-style stuff, but not really punk or hardcore. In the Maritimes at least, the Moncton scene was real street-level kind of punk rather than an imitation. But it's hard to say because we all imitated."

Gaudet's image as a father figure to Maritime punks is well-deserved since his job at Moncton's Sam The Record Man made him one of the few sources of imported records. Looking at his career, Gaudet can not only claim to be one of Canada's most experienced punk rockers, but one of its most experienced musicians, period. "Everyone else who's been around that long usually tames after a while, but I'm still pretty raving nuts," he says. "When I first started with the punk scene in Moncton there were only about six or eight people. Then in '85 a band called Syntax Error brought it to about 50, and then in '91, Eric's Trip brought it to about 200. You could put a demo out and sell that many. It was the biggest band that Moncton has had in the underground."

White was attracted to Gaudet because of his punk history, and invited him to play in the band in November 1990. According to Gaudet, it would take a while before he would accept White's offer. "About a year after they'd been asking me to join, I said, 'I'll do a few gigs with you until you can get Marc Doucet [Thee Suddens] on drums.' He really had more freedom than me so I figured it would be a good gig for him. Then when *Warm Girl* came out I realized I liked what Rick was doing so I didn't feel like quitting anymore."

Warm Girl was the fourth Eric's Trip self-released cassette in a year and it marked the beginning of the band's wider appeal. After debuting Gaudet on drums at the Kacho at the Université de Moncton in January 1992, they moved on to gigs in Halifax set up by Peter Rowan. "The first one was a little weird because we were playing with a band that people didn't really like," admits Thompson. "I think we were second last. A lot of people came out to see us who were from New Brunswick and who had heard a little about us. At the end of our first show, I smashed my bass because the headstock broke on it accidentally so I just went nuts. That helped a little bit."

"The beauty of Halifax is that it's so small that when you have something that's really great, it takes no time to catch on," attests Rowan. "I gave

Eric's Trip, final show in Moncton, 1996: Rick White, Julie
Doiron, Mark Gaudet, Chris Thompson
(Photo by Catherine Stockhausen)

Chris Murphy my only copy of that Eric's Trip tape and Eric's Trip packed the place two weeks later because this tape had totally circulated. We couldn't believe what we were seeing. During their last song, Chris [Thompson] was banging his bass and he noticed he had broken the neck. He didn't know what to do and was mad and all of a sudden he just picked it up and fucking smashed it. Halifax thought they had seen the second coming of Christ. Everyone from all the bands was at that first Eric's Trip show. They quickly became the darlings of Halifax."

After several more tumultuous shows, Rowan and his business partner Chip Sutherland began managing the band and worked on getting a CD out on Sloan's Murderecords. Sloan and their management had kept their hobby label open to release recordings by their east coast colleagues, including Thrush Hermit's *Smart Bomb* EP, Al Tuck and No Action's *Brave Last Days* CD and *Arhoolie* cassette, Hardship Post's *Hack* EP and Eric's Trip's *Peter* EP.

At the end of the summer of 1992, Eric's Trip's landmark east coast tour with Change of Heart and Sloan prepared the band for recording the *Peter* EP, named for their friend Peter Holt. Created on a four-track in White's basement, the seven-song disc was the first wide exposure for Eric's Trip outside of the Maritimes, and by the time of its release in April 1993, the

hype about the Halifax scene had reached a fever pitch. Yet *Peter*'s unchar-
acteristic rawness took some getting used to, even though songs like
"Happens All the Time" were pop-punk treasures.

"We'd get a lot of reviews that said, 'This band's all right, but they sound
like they recorded this in a trashcan,'" says White. "We'd get all those reviews,
but then to hear Sebadoh, it made us feel there was someone else doing
it, and he was getting a lot of good response to it. We figured people would
just get used to it after a while, and they did." Says Thompson, "If we had
a 24-track studio in our basement, we'd be recording on that."

Though Eric's Trip would turn down Sub Pop's initial offer after the release
of *Peter*, the label still gave the band their Toronto debut in October 1993,
opening for Sonic Youth, and then invited them to play at the label's
Vermonstrous Festival in Vermont soon after. "We were really lucky to get
that Sonic Youth show," states Doiron. "A lot of people I've spoken to since
then have said, 'I was at that show and that's the first time I ever saw you
guys.' I didn't realize that a lot of the talk about us came from that show,
because when we came back in March there were a lot of people there and
we'd never done our own show in Toronto before. It was very nerve-wracking.
We only played about seven songs for a 20-minute set."

At the Vermonstrous Festival, which featured Sub Pop signees such as
Pond and Six Finger Satellite, the label made another offer and this time
the band accepted. According to Gaudet, "Right after we played, the owner
of Sub Pop, Jonathan Poneman, approached us and asked, 'Why did you
turn us down?' I told him we were scared of a 40-page contract with all
these big words we didn't understand. He just said, 'Wait a minute; what
you do is what we want. We're not going to tell you to do anything.' I asked
him if we could believe him on that, or if something would go weird that
we'd be forced to do stuff, and he said no. So we signed with them."

The Sub Pop connection immediately intensified with the release of
Never Mind the Molluscs, a four-song compilation of "Halifax" bands reminiscent of earlier compilations that launched the "Seattle scene." However,
the "Halifax band" classification on *Never Mind the Molluscs* was debatable,
given that two of the four bands on the compilation were from New
Brunswick, the other being Idée du Nord.

"We never really felt like we were part of [the Halifax] scene," admits
Doiron. "We were always lumped in with it. Because Moncton had a completely different scene that no one seemed to know about, we felt more
like a part of that."

White concurs, "We saw a real difference between the music scenes and there was some subtle joking about the heaviness factor and how people in Halifax were scared of people from Moncton, because they thought we were all rude, foul-mouthed people. We'd always end up freaking them out with weird stuff."

Shortly after the release of *Peter*, the band began work on its first full-length album for Sub Pop. Released in 1993, *Love Tara* was recorded over three days in White's parents' basement, like all previous releases, but somehow this collection of 15 songs touched a different nerve in people. Perhaps most prominently, The Tragically Hip's epochal "Put It Off" from *Trouble At The Henhouse* included the line, "I played *Love Tara*, by Eric's Trip, on the day that you were born."

Yet at this time, White and Doiron were splitting as a couple and the lyrics took on a different confessional tone. The images of a spring rebirth throughout the record are juxtaposed with lines filled with honest pain and loss, especially in such songs as "Secret for Julie" and "Behind The Garage."

Doiron described the work as simply the sound of the band maturing as people. "The older I get, the more I feel like, 'What was I doing? Was I crazy?'" she muses. "Now I'm a little more conscious about it. I feel like if I sing too much, people are going to think I'm crazy. Because sometimes you feel a certain way, and you write a song about it, but you're not always that way. Now I think maybe we did say quite a bit in the songs, especially when it came to what was going on between me and Rick."

Understandably, the band members look back on *Love Tara* like anyone would look back on an old diary entry, with a mix of wonder and self-consciousness. White admits, "I can see why people like that one, because we still had that energy and this weird creative thing. It was done our way — we were really naïve about everything and we were blurting out the most emotional lyrics we possibly could back then."

This trend continued on the band's 1994 recordings, *The Gordon Street Haunting* EP, and their second full-length, *Forever Again*. Both contained a new, slightly more professional sound, but also a creeping darkness as suggested in songs like "My Bed is Red," "Hate Song" and "My Chest Is Empty," resulting from the aftermath of White and Doiron's break-up.

"Eric's Trip was essentially a diary of their lives together," says Peter Rowan. "That's the thing about Eric's Trip records. There were no analogies going on there. What you hear was it. This is what happened. As soon as I listened to *Forever Again* the first time, I called Rick and said, 'Are you okay?' It was incredibly powerful, because this is how he deals with life. It comes out in music."

"At that time in our lives, that's what we thought about a lot," says White. "We were at the age when it seems the most important thing is all this relationship stuff — between us as friends, and us as part of the whole scene of friends who were always swapping each other. Eric's Trip documented all that time, up until *Forever Again*."

Further events assisted in raising the band's profile after the release of *Forever Again*. A quirky video for the album's infectious single "ViewMaster" got the band some exposure on MuchMusic. Most of their previous videos were done with a super-8 camera in one shot — White being the model of consistency that he is — and were virtually ignored. The band's biggest exposure came in 1995 when The Tragically Hip invited the band to play on their Another Roadside Attraction tour. It was an experience that came as a total shock. According to White, "We got a call from Gord Downie, and we didn't know what to think, if it was even him or not. It's bad to say, but none of us were really fans of The Tragically Hip. We didn't hate them, we just never thought of them too much. But he said he was a fan of ours so we did it, and it was kind of bizarre the whole time."

"It was fun though," remembers Doiron, "because going on in the afternoon meant that people who wanted to see us were there early and the people who couldn't care less only showed up later in the day. We didn't have to play for thousands and thousands of people who wanted us off the stage."

Gord Downie says, "If someone else had picked the bill, they would have never been there. We handpicked all of that and felt really good about that. It was very hard for them in broad daylight. Then at the tail end [of the tour] we took Eric's Trip and the Rheostatics — we couldn't afford to take the whole production out to Newfoundland — but we took them to Memorial Auditorium for two nights, and the first night Eric's Trip went on in the dark and it was like a switch had been flipped. The power and intensity there was making my hair stand up on my arms. It was like they were waiting in the weeds until the second-last show of the tour."

Aside from that tour, seeing Eric's Trip live was always something unique. With three painfully shy faces at the front of the stage hidden by uncommonly long hair and the stage usually illuminated by a single light, the shows could either become otherworldly or extremely trying for both the band and the audience.

"We were an up and down kind of band," admits White. "But even on bad nights something came out, even if it was just weirdness. We never got down after shows too much. Sometimes we'd come off the stage thinking we were the shit and everyone else can fuck off, but then some nights we were just like, 'Well that was weird.' We'd leave the crowd in this kind of silent lull."

The use of songs as a diary was not confined to Eric's Trip. This phenomenon would exist throughout much of the city's scene, which was notoriously inbred. Though it's common for songwriters to inject personal issues and reality into song, the footnotes of interactions within the city's music scene — emotional or otherwise — are cleverly preserved in song throughout the albums of Sloan, The Super Friendz, Hardship Post, Thrush Hermit and Jale. The Super Friendz' Matt Murphy referenced the scene's Cinnamon Toast Records on "Prattle On" from 1996's *Slide Show*. Hardship Post further perpetuated the use of the term "sizzleteen" from Sloan's "Snowsuit Sound," placing it in "My Secret Life" from *Somebody Spoke*. Thrush Hermit's Joel Plaskett would pay Hardship Post a similar favour when he referenced their aforementioned album on "At My Expense" from *Sweet Homewrecker*. Plaskett, however, notes the majority of this practice is "mainly 'You're So Vain' kind of stuff."

Most of Sloan was guilty of this practice, leaving snapshots of their relationships on recordings. Chris Murphy went as far as mythologizing ex-girlfriend Laura Borealis's erotica in *Smeared*'s "Median Strip" — a reference to *Inherit The Median Strip* — and *Twice Removed*'s "Shame Shame," alluding to *Dames Dames*. Murphy's "G Turns to D," from *One Chord To Another*, was essentially a song about all the women he's taught guitar to, and how it's come back to haunt him in songs by Borealis and Jale (which included ex-girlfriend Jennifer Pierce). Murphy explains,"[Borealis's] record isn't as anti-me as Jale's is. I tried to make my song ambiguous enough about Jale. It could be [Jale's] Jenny [Pierce] because she writes 'fuck you' songs to me all the time. I wrote a whole bunch about her, too. It's a very healthy dialogue."

"I know I wrote some response songs," admits Jennifer Pierce. "'Nine Years Now' [from Jale's *Closed* EP] has lyrics that mimic a Sloan song ["Coax Me"]. These are by no way a comprehensive assessment of the scene though. It's sketchy at best and very elite.

"I suppose I'd rather not spoil them by revealing their true meaning," she continues. "It is safe to say that a good percentage of what I wrote was not so much directed at Chris, but me working through some of my confusion about Chris, right up to *So Wound* when I switched subjects."

This emotional honesty was part of the allure to the scene's first all-female band. Jale wore their hearts on their record sleeves — though with a slightly thicker veil than Eric's Trip — and despite the fact they were late bloomers as musicians, the quartet created some of the finest pop music to leave the city. Jale would eventually become the second Halifax signing to Sub Pop, though like Eric's Trip, Pierce admits she never really felt a part of the geographical collective into which the media often lumped her band. "We weren't part of the scene, and then we were, but we were always out of the loop. People were always kind to us, but there was always a void between us and the real band — real or perceived."

"It surprises me to this day that we had the gall," remarks guitarist Eve Hartling of the band's beginnings. "If you don't know anything, fine: you're ignorant and you can go up there and do it. As soon as you learn about skill and performance, it was like holy fuck, we went up there! That's what everyone was so excited about. People said that it looked like we were having so much fun and everyone kept encouraging us. That's why we kept going. No one said we sucked. We just played three-chord stuff and people liked it for whatever reason. People told me to write songs and to not be afraid. To write songs seemed so ridiculous. It was so ominous."

Originally named Tag during its first incarnation — with Melanie Rusinak (Cool Blue Halo, Happy Co.) playing bass, and Laura Stein playing keyboards — Pierce describes Jale as simply "an idea formed over coffee." Four art school students — guitarist Jennifer Pierce, drummer Alyson McLeod, bassist Laura Stein and guitarist Eve Hartling — took their first initials to form their band name and instituted Sloan's democratic rule of sharing singing and songwriting duties. Pierce, Hartling and Stein were all roommates at one point, and McLeod was introduced to Pierce through her NSCAD schoolmate Chris Murphy. Eventually the women all ended up in Pierce's living room with acoustic guitars, sharing their developing skills and trading harmonies.

"It started off as a joke," remembers Hartling. "All the boys we knew were in bands. It just started off as something to do. Sloan had a lot to do with it. Their rise to fame was unbelievable for them and a lot of bands. They were good musicians, but they were just normal art school kids and that's why we thought we could do it too."

Sloan would help the neophyte musicians find their feet by donating gear and providing them with opening slots, though this would also lead to similar media barbs that scraped Lava Hay when touring with The Grapes of Wrath. Alyson McLeod says, "In one way or another they've helped everyone here. I've heard things like it's because we went out with some of them. That's not why. They were very supportive and they were recognizing something that was worth being seen. They let us open for them and use a lot of their gear and were very encouraging. Andrew would give me little hints with drumming. To see them go through things was like having an older sibling and watching them."

Upon the release of some early singles ("Aunt Betty," "A Sort of Grey") on independent labels Cinnamon Toast Records, Genius and Derivative, Jale started to get some attention from the majors. After turning down what manager Colin MacKenzie refers to as "your typically worst major label deal" from Island Records, all involved with Jale essentially resigned themselves to a city-bound existence. However, when Sub Pop came to town, and the label's *Never Mind The Molluscs* EP was in production, the label's A&R rep Joyce Linehan pulled MacKenzie aside and told him that she wanted his quartet for the label. "She said, 'We want to sign Jale because they've improved substantially since we last saw them two months ago,'" remembers MacKenzie. "Sub Pop was doing the same thing [as the major labels]. They were picking up a lot of acts at that time and not paying them very much, but the allure of Sub Pop was theoretically their artist-friendly approach to music. The strange thing was that shortly after *Dreamcake* came out, things changed at Sub Pop to an indie approach with a will to operate within the realm of a major label, which became very frustrating to watch and to be a part of. But we were happy to have them think that for a little while Jale was going to be the band next to Sebadoh that was going to do something. We were lucky in that respect."

Jale, 1994: Laura Stein, Alyson McLeod, Jennifer Pierce, Eve Hartling
(Photo by Zellers, courtesy of Colin MacKenzie)

Released in 1994, *Dreamcake* is testament to the idea that some artists write their most interesting material in the early part of their career. Produced by Brad Wood (Liz Phair, Veruca Salt) and recorded by Brenndan

McGuire in a cabin in the woods outside Halifax for $6,000, *Dreamcake* showcases all four voices and songwriters in Jale — though McLeod is the most prominent in the latter regard.

Dreamcake combined a host of subtle influences including the Pixies ("River," "Emma"), The Breeders ("Not Happy," "Nebulous"), Joy Division ("Again") and even locals Al Tuck and Sloan ("Promise") into a dozen alt-rock bullseyes. All four women adeptly laid out their emotions. Alyson McLeod, who lost both her parents at a young age, opened up to the ghost of her mother in the song "The Unseen Guest." Pierce, whose "Promise" was picked as a single, also aches as she begs her subject to stay close to her heart. But it's not always vulnerability that is expressed. "I'm Sorry" contains one of the iciest stares in Halifax history with its opening lines that express a shivering hate for her subject.

The quartet spent the majority of 1994 and 1995 touring Canada, the States and England, and made a guest appearance on Ashley MacIsaac's *Hi™ How Are You Today?*, but there was unrest within the band, predominantly with McLeod, who never enjoyed the position of drummer. Hartling says, "She was always unhappy in the band. She was in a role that she didn't like, and she was playing an instrument she didn't like. We told her to play drums because no one else wanted to. She's very talented and she worked really hard. She wanted to sing and play guitar like everyone. I know she wanted to quit from the beginning on. I know the rest of us didn't. We loved it and we got along in our own way."

Recorded in three days by Brenndan McGuire and released in 1995 on Murderecords, the *Closed* EP seemed to mark the end of an era for the band. Though all members claim the album's title is simply a coincidence due to the selection of Pierce's black and white cover photo, it was oddly prophetic. It would mark the last recording with McLeod in the fold, and according to MacKenzie, it would be the point where the relationship between Sub Pop and Jale "began to crumble at an accelerated rate."

"Joyce [Linehan] and a number of other people at Sub Pop said [the EP] was awful," claims MacKenzie. "They gave us absolutely no support for it and ironically it was the most successful tour they have ever done. They got the most amount of press and halfway through the tour Joyce phoned me and said, 'Listen, what are you doing for press? Sub Pop press is never this good.' I said, 'All I've been doing is phoning the club and asking what four papers I should send stuff to. That's all I did, which is pretty sad. One of the low points was when we went to Seattle and they didn't have any support for the band. They didn't put any ads in the paper. They didn't willingly put them up in a hotel. This is, of course, the hometown of their label."

"I found it was very difficult when we went to do that recording because we weren't very prepared," remembers McLeod. "I'm not a very big fan of that recording. Stuff didn't turn out as well as I thought. Looking back it's not so bad, but at that point I knew that it was going to be pretty much it for me. It was important for me that it was written down that I wrote the song that I wrote. That caused a bit of an uproar, and that's when I knew there was no room for growth. I didn't want to feel like a jerk for wanting to have my name put on it. It seemed like we always had to be 'Written by Jale' and it wasn't. I was getting tired of 'you're just the drummer' and initially that didn't bother me, but then it was like I was working really hard and the songs were very personal to me and my experiences."

Despite the internal difficulties, the remaining three members would continue the Jale legacy and work on material for their second album for Sub Pop while they searched for a new drummer. According to Alyson McLeod, Sub Pop also asked her to stay on the label as a solo artist. Not feeling ready for this commitment, McLeod would pass on the offer and briefly play bass and sing with her friend Sebastian Lippa in The New Hardship Post. This would exist for a mere 1995 single on Squirtgun Records and a few low-key gigs. She would join Lippa in a outfit named Speedo, but other than live appearances in the city, there would be no official recording or appearances outside of Halifax. McLeod has remained outside of the music world, while Lippa returned to school to do a degree in philosophy.

Though the lazy Canadian journalism analogy of "the new Nirvana" was often bestowed upon Sloan, it was associated with the wrong band. In actuality, it was Hardship Post, a trio from Newfoundland who were more suited for the tag. They were the biggest live spectacle, and explosive on stage. "Those guys blew up the city when they came here," states McLeod. Like Eric's Trip, these transplants would erroneously be billed as a "Halifax band," though admittedly, the majority of the band's lifespan was spent in Halifax.

"It wasn't really much of a scene there," Sebastian Lippa says of St. John's, Newfoundland. "Audiences were small and the clubs didn't really like having bands play. We would always have to play with groups who I didn't feel much affinity with. I felt way closer to the scene in Halifax artistically. It was the pop influence. The first record I owned, and it's my favourite to this day, is [Simon and Garfunkel's] *Bridge Over Troubled Water*. It was always trickling through, whereas all the other groups that we played with in St. John's were more metal."

Hardship Post in
Halifax, 1995:
Sebastian Lippa, Mike Pick,
Matt Clarke
(Photo by Catherine Stockhausen)

Formed in 1992 by guitarist/ vocalist Lippa with drummer Matt Clarke and bassist Mike Kean — replaced by Mike Pick in 1993 — Hardship Post remains the most notorious alternative band to hail from Newfoundland. As suggested by the band's 1993 recordings — the independent cassette *Moodring*, the Mag Wheel single "Sugarcane" and the Murderecords EP *Hack* — the band fit neatly into the next-Nirvana vein the entire music industry wanted at this time with nuggets like "My Only Aim" and "Colourblind." As the tightest of the tribe of east coast bands in the early '90s, they quickly won the attention of the industry.

In 1994, Hardship Post followed Jale's footsteps, and became the third Sub Pop signing from the east coast. Prior to the release of their debut LP, they pulled a 180-degree turn as Sloan had on *Twice Removed*, and left scant traces of Seattle in their body of work. Lippa literally announces his jump to "new wave" on the lead-off track from 1995's *Somebody Spoke*, and he means it. It was obvious from the clean guitar sounds that the band had traded their copies of *Nevermind* and *In Utero* for used copies of British new wave/post-punk pioneers Wire, Joe Jackson and Elvis Costello. The introduction of bassist Mike Pick's songwriting skills and baritone vocal also provides a counterpoint to Lippa's tenor, often recalling The The's Matt Johnson ("My Secret Life") and Leonard Cohen ("Capability").

Though well-received critically, the band's new colours placed speed-bumps in the band's developing career. This would not be the only thing to sabotage the band's commercial potential. "They passed on a huge American record deal [with Elektra] to sign with Sub Pop," explains Hardship Post manager Peter Rowan. "They decided to go with Sub Pop because Seb knew he wasn't comfortable with what was going on. They recorded their record and two weeks before their first six-week tour, they fired Matt the drummer and the bass player took over drums. I don't think Seb really knew what he was getting into when he agreed to be in a band and it got way ahead of him."

Lippa carried through with the tour with Pick as a two-piece. "A lot of people would come up to us and say, 'What the hell was that?'" he recalls. "We had been in a totally antagonistic mode, which was stupid in a way. When we started we really kicked ass. We became pretty popular around here because of that. As we were in the infancy of our career and picking up fans we changed our sound. Our shows were always a collection of one record at a time. It wasn't really inclusive of our earlier stuff, which had made us popular. We were so anti-career that it gained the impression that it was credible, but it certainly doesn't sell T-shirts."

"That was pretty hard on me," admits Rowan. "At that point you cannot *imagine* trying to survive on managing two bands on Sub Pop."

As the Halifax scene's profile had increased exponentially by 1994, Greg Clark moved his focus from the Double Deuce and took over the Trade Mark Building. Originally dubbed Brunswick Hall, and later The Birdland Cabaret, this 1,000-capacity club was probably a little big in retrospect, but the buzz was still strong. Sloan's Murderecords, described by then co-owner Colin MacKenzie as "built on passion, not profit," was widely known as the flagship label in town. To the rest of the nation, Murderecords represented what was going on in Halifax. CBC's *Brave New Waves* host Patti Schmidt told *Shift* magazine, "The Murderecords mafia are the best networking pro-motional team in indie Canada." Murder also extended a hand outside Halifax and picked up Montreal's Local Rabbits and Kingston's Inbreds — who had moved to Halifax by this time — as well as one-off releases from Vancouver's Zumpano and Australia's Richard Davies. It would be The Super Friendz, however, who would become the city's next great pop hope.

Like other democratically minded pop bands consisting of guys with guitars, The Super Friendz suffered Sloan comparisons throughout their career. In their case, it didn't help that the band had a direct link. Chris Murphy often acted as the band's fill-in drummer during their tours, and guitarist/vocalist Matt Murphy had been a longtime close friend of Chris Murphy since their late teens. The congruent surnames and similar vocal qualities would also prompt erroneous claims that the two were brothers. This aside, Matt Murphy doesn't deny the Sloan bassist's influence on his career. "He's pretty responsible for getting me to take some chances, fin-ishing some songs and getting in a band," says Matt Murphy. "I wasn't really filled with a lot of confidence in my songwriting. As far as referencing some of the songs I write, he's a pretty good model. I don't want it to sound unnatural. It's just who you're hanging out with, and who you went to school with at the time."

The Super Friendz was formed by Matt Murphy and Ontario transplants Charles Austin and Drew Yamada while they were all attending King's College. They were a democratic three-piece with a rotating drummer's chair. Early on, this position was filled by Dave Marsh (No Damn Fears), Thrush Hermit's Cliff Gibb and the aforementioned Chris Murphy. Matt Murphy had a history of band experiences ranging from The Deluxe Boys to Black Pool to Leonard Conan. Austin had played with Jale's Alyson McLeod in a short-lived side project named Skreech, and he first met Matt Murphy after Murphy replaced him in Al Tuck's band when Austin left Halifax for a summer. Yamada was the late bloomer and hadn't participated in a band until hooking up with Austin in the relatively unknown Hüsker Dü-influenced Rhinoplasty. Eventually the three started to craft their own pop releasing "By Request," a 7" on Murderecords as well as their own independent cassette, *Sticktoitiveness*. "By Request" was recorded in the same cabin where Jale had created *Dreamcake* when Brenndan McGuire had his portable studio in town.

The opening gig for Sloan on their *Twice Removed* tour brought the band to the attention of those outside of Halifax, but it would be 1995's *Mock Up Scale Down*, the band's first true album, that would draw the most

The Super Friendz, 1996: Drew Yamada, Charles Austin,
Matt Murphy, Lonnie James
(Photo by Catherine Stockhausen)

attention. Once again enlisting McGuire and the drumming assistance of Dave Marsh, the trio committed 15 tracks to tape, ranging from Murphy's sugar tunes ("10 lbs," "One Day") to Austin's jagged rock and killer choruses ("Rescue Us From Boredom," "When They Paid Me") to Yamada's Neil Young/Dinosaur Jr.-tinged folk ("Undertow," "Fireflies").

"We figured out where our common goals are," said Austin at the time. "We want to do something that is not alternative rock, and something that has a lot of retro influences, but we want to make something new out of it. Most of the stuff we listen to is a little older. I like a lot of angular new wave stuff like Wire. Those guys really like Led Zeppelin. Matt is very musical and good at arranging things. Drew and I would be a little bit left field. Especially between Matt and I, there would be that occasional friction between pop classicism and wanting to be a little more arty. That's what makes the band."

This polarity was particularly evident on 1996's *Slide Show*. Recorded at Chemical Sound in Toronto with the Dambuilders' Eric Masunaga using vintage equipment and saluting a variety of artists from the '60s British Invasion to '70s new wave, there was a definite line between Murphy's prolific pop and Austin and Yamada's art-rock introspection. Though Murphy continued to pen a couple of classic rock hits ("Up and Running," "Stop-Start"), he pushed modern rock radio's patience with creative arrangements and complicated shifts in "Everything Writes Itself" and "Forever a Day." Austin and Yamada bring on most of the departure from the band's early work with the former's Floydian psychedelic country on "Fooled At First," the Jonathan Richman nod of "No Good Reason," and with Yamada's well-textured "Citizens Banned."

Despite landing a permanent drummer in Lonnie James (The Lawn, the Nils) for 1996's 10" *Play the Game, Not Games* and *Slide Show*, and finding an American home for *Mock Up Scale Down* in March Records, the band parted ways in the fall of 1997. Matt Murphy initiated the breakup, claiming that The Super Friendz didn't offer him enough of a forum to satisfy his prolific songwriting. He spent the first part of his post-breakup time in Halifax with his joke country project Lil' Orton Hoggett. Eventually he convinced former Kearney Lake Rd. bassist Henri Sangalang to move with him to Toronto and drafted Toronto drummer Steve Pitkin (Mrs. Torrance) and Hamilton keyboardist Gavin Dianda. As The Flashing Lights, Murphy released 1999's *Where The Change Is* to thunderous praise. Austin and Yamada acted as fill-in players for various bands (The Vees, Speedo) before they launched their new project Neuseiland in 2000, and opened their Ultramagnetic Studios in Halifax.

Cinnamon Toast Records would be regarded as Murder's sister label. The label was a hobby farm run by Leanne Gillan, Shawn Duggan, Walter Forsythe and Colin MacKenzie, and released 7" singles from virtually every notable area act — including Eric's Trip, Hardship Post, Bubaiskull and Jale — but its primary focus was female artists in the city. The teenage all-girl troupe named Plumtree would be their longest staple on the label, but Rebecca West's work is the defining moment of both Cinnamon Toast Records and Allison Outhit's music career. Chris Murphy echoes the sentiments of many artists in Halifax when he notes, "Allison Outhit is the godmother of the Halifax scene."

"If you could condense her into one role in Halifax it would be the 'keeping everyone honest role,' for doing things with integrity and intelligence," remarks then-manager Angie Fenwick. "I don't think she gets what she deserves from the Halifax community. I find it's very much backwards in their attitude towards women. It's a town of boyrock and it has been for some time. Allison is the bridge between the art rock and the *rock* rock. There's a whole thing of just music for music's sake — bands that you would have never heard of at all. Rebecca West are very much the heroes of that group of people."

Alyson McLeod recounts, "When I first moved into Halifax, [Outhit] was the first female musician that I was in contact with, ever. She definitely influenced me. She's like a mom to me in some ways. She's a very important person in my life."

Rebecca West: Lukas Pearse, Allison Outhit, Dale Hussey
(Photo by Catherine Stockhausen)

Born in Halifax, Allison Outhit started writing songs at the age of 10 and never stopped. Influenced by songwriters ranging from Carole King to Cole Porter to rockers Led Zeppelin to new wavers Echo and The Bunnymen and Kate Bush, Outhit displayed the uncanny ability to write wonderful music, whatever the genre. She was a major part of the Halifax scene since new wave's heyday in Staja/TANZ, to the late '80s in Jeffrey's Wake and Flags for Everything and in the early '90s as the lead guitarist in the otherwise all-male Bubaiskull. She would do all of this while earning a law degree and being a single mother to her son.

After the fall-out of Bubaiskull in 1994, Outhit decided her time had come to take the driver's seat and began work on her own project. Taking the name of a feminist author, she formed Rebecca West in August 1994 with P.E.I.–born drummer Dale Hussey (Merge) and her producer brother Stephen Outhit. Lukas Pearse (Les Gluetones, Black Pool) replaced Stephen Outhit only weeks before recording *Burners On*, the band's debut album. Pearse's intricate playing occasionally incorporated a steak knife for effect, complementing Outhit's eclectic songwriting.

Burners On is a landmark album that encapsulates almost six years of songwriting. Outhit says, "*Burners On* is like the end of something rather than the beginning, which is peculiar because it's a first album. It's a closure for me because it represents several years of songwriting and I had the opportunity to get a band together and record them."

Her lyrical prowess is demonstrated with the album's tales of ageing ("30 and Falling"), self-evaluation ("Save It"), relationships ("7 Days," "Sick") and observation ("I Love The Way You Talk About TV") — all of which are delivered with a kick of equal parts confession, metaphor and humour.

Though Rebecca West had pop intuitions, the band was always more inclined to put itself under the art rock umbrella. Rebecca West didn't quite fit into the "Pop Explosion," as they didn't write Beatlesque pop and they weren't offered a spot on the Murderecords roster. *Six More Weeks of Winter*, a low-key EP produced by Change of Heart's Ian Blurton, shows Rebecca West as a band in synchronicity and at their artiest.

"What we wanted to do was create an ambience that was about winter, loss and desolation," explains Outhit of the EP. "I was trying to draw the analogy of the idea of the winter of a relationship and also the same feeling of never-ending coldness and misery. I was married for a while and we were breaking up when I was writing most of the songs on the record." The EP is a chilling counselling session far removed from the guitar pop normally associated with the scene. "Bullseye" and "Geranium" are hypnotic and eerie, "Mystery Bird" expresses the frenetic anger of the breakup. The concluding track, "State of Grace," is pure pathos and the sad reflection of a deceased relationship spearing the soul with its final refrain.

Despite an admirable touring ethic that saw the band traverse the nation a few times, the EP would be the final moment for the band. Personal issues, public disinterest and the death of indie rock would make it impossible for the trio to continue. Outhit would end up in film production with Salter Street Films, and sadly put her musical talent on the backburner.

In November, 1995, Jale convened at Idful Studios, a strip mall studio in Chicago, with producer Brad Wood to create *So Wound*. Drummer Mike Belitsky, a friend of Jennifer Pierce, occupied the spot McLeod left vacant. "He was a very reassuring person to have. He was very professional," says Hartling. "We made a really good record and he had a lot to do with that. Alyson and I didn't like touring. Mike and the other girls liked touring. With Alyson, we were always kind of worried about her. It was like 'Oh my God, is she going to quit or freak out or cry?' Not that any of those things happened. We just knew she wasn't settled. There was a big difference, but Alyson for me was always the original Jale and I never felt the same."

Regardless of the changes, the three remaining women loaded *So Wound* with potential radio hits. Pierce's jangly love songs "Hey Hey," "All Ready" and her duet with Belitsky, "Despite" — along with Hartling's peppy ode to her sister "Ali" and the gorgeous Warholesque ballad "Superstar" — are all standouts. Laura Stein also took a more prominent role on this release, with her deep voice and quirky contingent of songs, including the Throwing Muses-like "Sign of Life" and the slick punk of "Mosquito" and "Blue."

Sub Pop expected this album to break the band open to a mainstream audience. Sub Pop had recently sold half of its ownership to Warner Brothers for $20 million. The result was a bigger budget for the album, though Colin MacKenzie admits most of the $50,000 went into the band's hotel bills and a big budget video. After minimal radio and video play for "All Ready," Sub Pop pronounced *So Wound* a casualty a week after its release. In Canada, the album's lifespan was somewhat sustained thanks to distributor Warner Canada's support and a video for "Ali," which squeaked on to MuchMusic. But another challenge would make it difficult for the band to continue to promote the album.

Just prior to the release of the album Eve Hartling discovered she was pregnant, and she would be unable to tour with the band after the fall of 1996. Upon the birth of her and Chip Sutherland's daughter Kate, Hartling split from the band, leaving only two of the original four members remaining in the band. "I didn't decide that I didn't want to be in Jale," admits Hartling. "I went to the band and said I could do this and this. They said that wasn't good enough. The decision was made. It was more them, but I couldn't be in a road band and play shows. Not with a baby. It just isn't feasible."

In 1997, the house of Sub Pop would also undergo an extensive remodelling, dumping the majority of its Canadian roster and closing its satellite offices in Canada and various other American cities. Peter Rowan says,

"When I found out that Jale was off I went up and congratulated Colin [MacKenzie]. They are the most arrogant bunch of fucking Americans you will ever face in your life. They present themselves as something they are not. They are a major label in every aspect in terms of the way they take advantage of the artist. The only way that they are not like a major label is in the amount of money that they pay their artists to sign their deals. Other than that they are equally as heinous as any."

Though Jale was a fatality, Pierce doesn't share Rowan or her manager's frustrations toward the Seattle label. "They were genuinely enthusiastic about the music and supportive of us. I recognize the potential commodity of an all-female band, but they were always respectful towards us, and provided us with wonderful opportunities to see the world and put out records. I wouldn't change a thing."

Pierce, Stein and Belitsky would rename themselves The Vees, and continued long enough for a couple of tours and a self-titled EP on Murderecords. Unfortunately, the difficulty of Belitsky living in New York, Pierce in Montreal and Stein in Halifax would mark the end of this band.

Oddly, Rowan's client, Eric's Trip, was the only Canadian signing to survive on Sub Pop, although they would soon be releasing records under new configurations. All four had side projects and travelled down different paths in their lives, which had diverted their full focus from the band. Rick White had married Tara S'Appart from Orange Glass — the "Tara" of *Love Tara*. The couple formed Elevator to Hell with Mark Gaudet. Doiron — also a newlywed and a new mother of a baby boy — recorded under the name Broken Girl, and Thompson found an outlet for his back catalogue with Moonsocket. As they regrouped to record *Purple Blue*, rumours began spreading of an impending break-up. Although most of these rumours hinged on past tension between White and Doiron, the band members insist that a desire to pursue the side projects signalled the end of the band.

According to Thompson, "Rick and Julie broke up about a year and a half or even two years before that. That didn't kill the band then, so it couldn't have done it when we actually did it. I think Rick had been thinking about it for a while, but I thought he was just getting down on himself, not being able to write the kinds of songs he wanted to do. Then he wrote all these great songs for *Purple Blue* and I thought it was going to go on forever, then all of a sudden it was over."

Released in January 1996, *Purple Blue* has more similarities to the heavier material White went on to produce with Elevator. The band moved further away from their past influences and closer to a fascination with '60s psychedelia and the culture attached to the music.

Notes Doiron, "Those musical influences started coming out more because of Mark's presence. To him, '60s and punk are the best. Honestly, drugs didn't have any role to play with me, but with Rick and Mark, that's what started to change his lyric writing, and the music too. Chris and I were not into that, so we were split half and half, but we still got along. Occasionally Chris would get drunk on tour and eventually I had a beer. I can't say that I never did anything, but I never became really into it like they were."

"He definitely likes his weed," says Chris Murphy of Rick White. "I heard somewhere that some people are the lightning rods and some people are the lightning. I am a lightning rod and Rick White is the lightning. He's the real thing. I'm just someone who surrounds myself with the right people. I still trust my talent, but I'm not a genius. He's a complete music head. I'm not. It's more romantic: the idiosyncratic weirdo who lives in the basement. I love him for it."

The growing lifestyle and creative rifts prompted the decision to disband Eric's Trip shortly after they began an American tour in support of *Purple Blue*, as another Canadian tour loomed on the horizon in the spring of 1996. "We were all doing our own things, so breaking up wasn't really a sudden thing," says Doiron. "However, breaking up right in the middle of a tour was sudden because we were supposed to do a Canadian tour in June. Rick wanted to cancel the American tour and then I refused to do the Canadian tour. I guess it's my fault the Canadian tour didn't happen, but I didn't think it was fair to do it just because we were getting paid well."

"It wasn't a fighting thing," says White. "It was more of an over-emotional thing that none of us could bear after a while. We got halfway through the tour and I ended up saying, 'I want to go home, I'm splitting.' Then there was a fall-out between me and Julie because she wanted to finish the tour. But it wasn't too bad once we got over it and played our last two shows. There was that long drive home to talk to each other and that was it. We missed half of our tour in the States and we're still hearing about that when we meet people: 'I was at that show and you guys weren't there!'"

After one final farewell show with Sloan in Moncton, each devoted themselves to their side projects full time. They maintained casual friendships and insisted in interviews that there were no hard feelings. The legacy of Eric's Trip is a document of a specific time and place, yet one that, for years to come, will speak to kids going through the rites of passage.

Rick and Tara White and Gaudet would continue on with their "Elevator" project through three more albums on Sub Pop until they parted ways with the label before moving to Toronto label Teenage USA in 2000. Chris Thompson would be the only member not to remain on Sub Pop, but continued to record under the name Moonsocket and release work independently. Julie Doiron, the dark horse of the band, would end up retaining the largest profile. After her Broken Girl record and 1997's *Loneliest in The Morning*, Doiron would make her pet label Sappy Records her home. She would release more solo releases as well as 1999's *Julie Doiron and the Wooden Stars* album, for which she earned a Juno. She would also honour longtime Eric's Trip fan Gord Downie by singing on three songs on The Tragically Hip's *Music @ Work* album released in 2000, as well as on his 2001 solo album.

To many involved in the scene it was no real surprise when the attention on Halifax began to wane after 1995, and bands would slowly splinter. Catherine Stockhausen, who photographed many of the bands in Halifax, looks at the scene as a victim of its media description, "The Halifax Pop Explosion." "Explosions don't last for years," she says. "They are an explosion and then it's gone and hopefully you're left with something, which I think we were. And now things are changing, which is a good thing instead of 'it failed because it changed.'"

"Most people around here put really stupid spins on that — that there was all this hype and we bought into it and now we're fucked," says Sebastian Lippa. "To me that seems so stupid to base it on the alternative scene. Let's see who got signed in the alternative scene: Sloan, Eric's Trip, Jale and us. That's pretty much it. We fell apart for personal reasons. Jale fell apart for personal reasons. Eric's Trip, if you want to say bad stuff happened to them it's totally their own doing. It's like misusing statistics to prove some theory: 'All these bands are not as successful and it's all because the evil industry duped the naïve Haligonians. Now we are all crying in our beer.' I don't think it's like that at all. I guess I don't look at the music industry as evil. I think they gave the community around here a great opportunity to construct, that for our own reasons we didn't capitalize on. We could have put out another record. If Alyson would have stayed in Jale and they maintained the momentum they had built up with the first record, who knows what could have happened."

Colin MacKenzie concurs with Lippa, though with an air of frustration, "I've come to think there's something in the water out here that people take a shotgun and blow their foot off just when things were getting going — Hardship Post being the prime example." Chris Murphy adds, "In the beginning it was like we opened everybody's eyes to the possibility, but in the end we ended up showing everyone the improbability."

Allison Outhit doesn't see the dissipation of the regional excitement as negative. "People will often ask me, 'Is the scene dead now?' I say, 'No, of course not.' The music scene is a lot like the stock market. It's like you buy low and sell high. The market is low now, and this is when people should pay attention because what's going on is all the same activity that's ever been, without the hype. It's not all Sloan. There's only one particular gene pool to be drawn from at one time."

In 1996, the Pop Explosion's youngest sons, Thrush Hermit, became the last band of this gene pool to sign with a label. The tale of Thrush Hermit is not terribly different from some of the other acts, except that it begins with teenagers dying to be a part of a new music scene, and ends with adults laying an era to rest.

Joel Plaskett met Robert Benvie and Ian McGettigan when he moved from Lunenburg to the middle class Clayton Park suburb of Halifax. All three attended Clayton Park Junior High School, and later Halifax West High School, where all three shared a love for rock music. At the age of 14, they took a silly pop culture amalgam Nabisco Fonzie, and the trio started jamming together with Benvie on drums, Plaskett on guitars and McGettigan as the vocalist. In late 1989, drummer Alex Grace joined the trio, moving Benvie to guitars and McGettigan to bass, prompting a name change to The Hoods. They renamed the quartet Thrush Hermit in March 1990 and played their first gig at the Shearwater Yacht Club. The 15-year-olds were paid in pizza for the gig and indulged in some rock and roll shenanigans by pilfering an empty beer keg from the establishment.

Soon after this petty crime, Mike Catano replaced Grace, and the precocious teenagers started gigging within the scene. Full of nerves from taking the band out of Benvie's garage, they approached Peter Rowan and handed him a demo tape for a chance at playing a Two Buck Tuesday at the Flamingo Club. "It was probably the first time Peter had ever been called 'Mr. Rowan' in his life," recalls Benvie. Thrush Hermit would eventually land a gig, and an association with the city's top act would soon elevate the band's profile.

Plaskett remembers, "I saw Sloan's second show at the Green Room at Dalhousie University in early 1991. They were noisy as hell and very scrappy, but they blew my mind and left an indelible influence on me. I was 15. After that I saw any of their shows I could get into. They could be a pretty ramshackle unit but I was enamoured with their whole approach, so in those early days they could do no wrong in my books. When the Hermit played our first headlining gig at the Flamingo in 1991 we packed the place because we postered the city like madmen. I met Chris Murphy for the first time in the bathroom after we played, and he said we should play a show with Sloan and do KISS covers. After that we started playing shows locally with them. Chris was always supportive of us and took us under his wing, despite the fact that we were quite young and made him feel like a child molester."

Benvie notes, "As a young kid who lived in the suburbs, having a chance to hang with these older interesting people really broadened my scope. Of course, I later grew to realize that they were just poor schleps like me, but for a short time Sloan et al. seemed like genuine rock stars to me. A lot of the opportunities we got were because of [Sloan]. At the time we were like 'We're not like Sloan.' We had guys calling us *Clone* and stuff like that. Now I look back and I think deservedly so, but we were also ripping off a zillion other bands."

After releasing the "Marya" 7" single on Genius Records in 1993, the band attracted the slightly older Cliff Gibb to the fold. Gibb had played with a variety of bands including Cool Blue Halo with Barry Walsh, and Happy Co. with Sloan's Patrick Pentland, and he would remain with Thrush Hermit throughout all of their future recording projects.

The first of these, an EP released on Murderecords in 1994 entitled *Smart Bomb*, was compiled mainly from reworked tracks from their indie cassettes and vinyl singles. Opening with Plaskett's kick-ass anthem "Hated It," it's clear the band wanted a part of the "Halifax Sound" as the immediately catchy song is wrapped up in the same teenage smarty-pants culture of Sloan's *Smeared*. The song would end up on the soundtrack of Kevin Smith's teen culture indulgence, *Mallrats*. Benvie's "French Inhale" and "Cott," sung by McGettigan, are no less infectious. The former would become one of the first Thrush Hermit videos to get some rotation on MuchMusic.

After watching their mentors land deals throughout the peak years of the Pop Explosion, Thrush Hermit met with Seymour Stein, then of Elektra Entertainment, at the Five Fishermen Restaurant in Halifax, and signed with the label in 1996. Recorded in Memphis with Doug Easley (Pavement), Thrush Hermit's 1997 debut full-length, *Sweet Homewrecker*, continued what the band had started on its second EP, 1995's *The Great Pacific Ocean*. That Steve Albini-produced EP showcased the band entering their twenties and trying to distance themselves from the Sloan associations. What becomes even more pronounced on the band's first full-length recording is the difference between Benvie and Plaskett's songwriting. Whereas the songs on

Thrush Hermit's first two EPs don't show a huge chasm between the two songwriting styles, *Sweet Homewrecker* starts to showcase Plaskett as the rock hit writer ("Skip The Life," "North Dakota," "Darling Don't Worry") and Benvie as the risk-taker, matching his clever lyricism with a post-punk sneer ("Noosed and Haloed Swear Words," "Snubbed") or introspection ("Strange To Be Involved"). McGettigan's sole contribution scores the honour of the coolest track on this release. "On The Sneak" captures the rock posturing mentality of the band that they often celebrated live with a $2,500 electric sign that simply flashed "ROCK AND ROLL." It is an awesome riff-rock moment featuring a great sing-along chorus.

Benvie remarks, "That album is weird because there are interesting songs, but overall it's a bit sterile. We practised every day for months beforehand, really putting ourselves through the grinder, so when we got to making the album it wasn't a very creative process. Our A&R man unabashedly preferred Joel's songs over mine, as did most people associated with the band, so my ego took a beating. When we were in Memphis recording I had personal issues back home, and with the way we had wound ourselves up so tight it wasn't a lot of laughs. It's too bad, because our producer Doug Easley was a world-class gent.

"There's nothing like getting paid to do something you love, but as a band you have to have confidence to make good music. We spent months in fruitless touring, mostly in the middle and southern States. In Canada, where we thought things would fall easily into place, we were received worse than when we were on Murderecords. Elektra didn't even pay to make one video, that was how little regard they had for us."

After Elektra bought the young band out of their contract Thrush Hermit decided to focus their live show on jamming out new ideas during performances. The band was known to occasionally take certain liberties on stage. When they played on a Toronto Edgefest gig at the Molson Amphitheatre in 1995 with various other east coast acts, the quartet tossed their original material to play an entire set of Steve Miller covers. "That was such a beautiful moment," says Elliott Lefko. "To have the sense of irony that they had, and for the biggest moment in front of their biggest crowd — instead of going for it and playing a set to do that, that's when you realize you have a sense of community here. A band with a guy like Joel, a superstar singer like that who said, 'You know, I don't care if I sell a million records. This is my moment and I'm going to enjoy it.' And for him to make the audience enjoy it that much, everybody understood the joke at that point."

"The idea of pushing our last record had become laughable," says Benvie of using their 1997–1998 touring experiences for workshopping new material. "That gave us the confidence to make *Clayton Park*, which is our only actually good record."

Clayton Park, named after the Halifax suburb where they honed their rock and roll skills, was exactly what the title implied: a return to their youth. The band had always admitted that they were influenced by the '70s rock of Led Zeppelin and Steve Miller, but this claim never translated into their music — until this album. *Clayton Park* is a glorious celebration of classic rock right from Cliff Gibb's opening drum roll on "From the Back of the Film" to the rousing choruses of "Songs For The Gang" and "Before You Leave." "From The Back Of The Film" and "The Day We Hit the Coast" — both underrated Canadian singles — signify Plaskett's maturing pop sensibilities, and his trading of Americanisms like "North Dakota" from *Sweet Homewrecker* for namedropping Canadian places like Lake Louise.

Sadly, the future of this band would be victimized by a variety of factors working against it. Cliff Gibb, who had married manager Angie Fenwick, departed after the recording of the album to accept stable employment in the computer field. Ben Ross would fill in for the band's live support of the album. There was also the issue that they were merely surviving as an independent band. *Clayton Park* was recorded with Dale Morningstar at the Gas Station studio and only after its completion did they find a home in Hamilton independent Sonic Unyon. The majority of the album is Plaskett's, which furthered the songwriting divide between him and Benvie. This didn't reassure a long future for the band after the release of the album.

As the band prepared for a national tour with the Flashing Lights and the Local Rabbits, Plaskett fell seriously ill. Their tour would be delayed, but the rumours began to fly that this was a farewell jaunt. Once the guitarist recuperated, Thrush Hermit embarked on a quick final set of gigs, which culminated with a performance in their hometown.

When Thrush Hermit played their last gig at Greg Clark's Marquee Club on Saturday, December 11, 1999, they were the last major remnant from the Pop Explosion to remain in Halifax. Some of the city's smaller acts such as Plumtree would hang on for a little longer, but the fragmentation of Thrush Hermit at the turn of the century officially closed a chapter in the city's history. Sloan had moved to Toronto, Eric's Trip splintered into various new projects, Jale's second and third incarnations were long dead, senior players like Allison Outhit and John Chisholm both traded music for jobs in film and TV production companies, and others, like Sebastian Lippa, completely vanished.

Plaskett explains, "Rob wanted to go on to other things, I wanted more control, the money had run out and we had sold around 3,500 copies of *Clayton Park*. It was disappointing to break up, but we didn't want to turn into a part-time band and become a mere shadow of our former self. Money might have greased the wheels, but that shouldn't be what keeps a band together — although most of the time it is. We had seen the future of successful rock and roll in Canada and it had more to do with music videos that look like beer ads, and bands we couldn't relate to. At least we went out on a high note and that's more than most bands can say."

Subsequently, Plaskett released a 1999 solo album, *In Need of Medical Attention* that he had recorded prior to the *Clayton Park* sessions, and then started The Joel Plaskett Emergency. Benvie made his own record under the name Tigre Benvie called *Year of the Mutt*, and would join McGettigan as members of the Rick of the Skins. Today Benvie maintains it was the right thing for this group of high school friends to grow in different directions. "All of us have nothing but fond memories, and I feel that we did it all in a fairly dignified fashion," he concludes. "Altogether it was an amazing experience, but none of us are the type to keep reliving adolescent glories for the remainder of our days. Perhaps that's a Halifax thing — there aren't as many ageing leather-clad rockers here as you'll find in Toronto or Montreal or Vancouver. People keep moving on."

The Path of Thorns:
Nettwerk Records

On December 13, 1999, Sarah McLachlan felt like she could actually breathe again. After over a decade of endless touring, recording, and headlining a marquee of a high drama, McLachlan and Nettwerk spent the last few months of the '90s dealing with a legal tourniquet on compositions she had written when she was 19. It was an intensely public battle, meticulously documented in the press, which placed a huge question mark over her artistic credibility and raised similar issues over the label's practices. But 17 days before the year's end, this legal nightmare would conclude, and leave McLachlan and her label with one less worry as they entered the next century.

In 1998, Darryl Neudorf, a longtime player and studio hand in the Vancouver scene (54·40, Moev), slapped both McLachlan and Nettwerk with a legal suit. He had worked on McLachlan's first two albums, and claimed he had not been credited properly for four songs he had worked on from her debut, *Touch* ("Vox," "Steaming," "Sad Clown" and "Strange World"). The plaintiff claimed that in 1987 Nettwerk A&R head Mark Jowett hired him, as well as a variety of other Vancouver musicians, to work on what was nicknamed "The Sarah Project." Along with musicians such as Darren

Phillips — who *is* credited for co-writing two songs — Neudorf's job was to help McLachlan in the creative process during her initial recording sessions. It was his understanding that he had assisted McLachlan in both a songwriting capacity as well as the "pre-production" and "inspiration" role that he was credited for on the album. And he would go to great lengths to prove that Nettwerk had wronged him.

According to testimony during the trial, Nettwerk wanted to market McLachlan as a prodigy — for her talents as a performer and as a singer/songwriter — despite the fact she had never written a song until the *Touch* sessions. "The idea was to have Sarah as a figurehead for all these different voices," testified Phillips when asked to describe the creative process for *Touch*. The trial disclosed many of the voices — the governing bodies of the label (Terry McBride and Mark Jowett), former Nettwerk staff, session musicians, studio hands, ex-roommates and even bandmates from McLachlan's early Halifax band, The October Game — all of whom were called to testify for or against the superstar. In many ways, this trial was not just a battle between a former employee and a record label and artist. It was a record label's clash between its past and its present.

Though firm about its innocence, Nettwerk attempted to settle out of court to bypass a costly struggle that would only succeed in filling the pockets of the lawyers. Neudorf flatly refused a healthy settlement, and proceeded to stand by his claims in the Vancouver courtroom for 39 days. He could have walked off with a sum reported in one paper as being "equivalent to 20 years worth of wages" for just dropping the issue. Neudorf, however, was adamant. Over the course of the trial, Neudorf would claim that he had previously attempted to reconcile this issue with Nettwerk and McLachlan, something that he alleged had been met with resistance on each occasion. "I think a lot of people are looking at me as some kind of opportunist who came out of the woodwork, out of nowhere, and I'm a has-been," stated Neudorf to the press. "There's a lot more to the story than whether or not I co-wrote songs with Sarah. It's kind of complicated for the press to fit into two sentences."

Moev's Tom Ferris who ran the Limited Vision studio where parts of *Touch* were recorded still supports Neudorf's claims. "She had so many people helping her," says Ferris. "People were helping her write tunes. I can't believe what the fuck was going on with this lawsuit. I can't believe she said Darryl had nothing to do with her songs."

In the end, it was well-documented how Nettwerk had enlisted many people to assist the troubled McLachlan sessions, and Neudorf did prove he made a significant contribution on one track, "Steaming." But the law favoured the defendants, stating that there was never an intention for McLachlan and Neudorf to merge their works into a unitary whole or to joint-author any of the songs. The British Columbia Supreme Court would find Sarah McLachlan and Nettwerk Productions of Vancouver completely innocent of songwriting fraud. Neudorf's sole consolation was that he would be awarded unpaid wages of $4,500 for his work on McLachlan's 1991 sophomore recording *Solace*. This was a mosquito bite on the label's ankle compared to the royal beating Supreme Court Justice Bruce Cohen would deliver to Neudorf in August 2000. Since Neudorf had refused a settlement and dragged the trial on for over a month on liability alone, Cohen ordered him to pay half of Nettwerk's legal bill as punishment — a sum of $250,000.

"They persisted with very serious allegations of quasi-criminal and fraudulent conduct throughout the trial in the absence of any evidence to support those allegations," Nettwerk lawyer Jennifer Conkie told the press. "To allege fraud is a very serious thing and I said [to the judge] it was damaging or potentially damaging to the reputations of the personal defendants, particularly in a case that attracted such intense media interest."

Neudorf would respond to the court order via a simple statement: "I guess I had some kind of belief that the Canadian judicial system was less favoured toward the rich and famous. Which I guess in hindsight was pretty foolish." The musician had already filed for bankruptcy prior to the court order.

Nettwerk Productions, the successful Canadian independent record label, would remember this December day as one of vindication, and another chapter in their 15-year survival. It wasn't just McLachlan's name at stake; it was Nettwerk's as well. "The reputation of this label means a lot to us," admits McBride, "so we spent the last five years fighting him. In the end we won. It was a stupid thing and it should have never happened. There's no ill wishes to Darryl, but he made a big error in judgement."

Small wonder that Terry McBride protects his label and his prized artist like a diplomat's bodyguard. No other independent label in Canada has generated the global attention Nettwerk has throughout its history, and few can attest to even existing for a fraction of Nettwerk's lifespan. Very few independent labels in Canada have boasted a roster of artists comparable to Nettwerk's, and most definitely, no other independent label has had a superstar artist that has sold 10 million copies of a single album. For reasons of capitalism alone, it is perfectly understandable why Nettwerk's drones have gradually reconfigured their hive around McLachlan — the label's incontestable Queen Bee. Nettwerk helped make McLachlan, but McLachlan would become Nettwerk. They're symbiots, and neither party would disagree. Mark Jowett, head of A&R says, "It certainly changed the infrastructure of Nettwerk, because when you have an artist with that much potential and it starts to really take off, you can either license it away so someone who is bigger can handle it, or you have to develop your own infrastructure so that you can help it reach its full potential. We decided on the latter course."

"If we didn't have Sarah McLachlan, what else would we have?" label president Ric Arboit asks rhetorically. "We'd have a Skinny Puppy catalogue, some great Consolidated records, some great MC 900 Ft. Jesus, a really good Delirium record and some great Mystery Machine records that not a lot of people heard." For Arboit to describe the label this way should bring a feeling of sadness to any music fan that has followed the label throughout its growing pains. Between 1985 and 1995, Nettwerk was responsible for the careers of a cross-section of the finest artists from Canada and beyond, a list that merely *included* the exceptionally talented McLachlan.

This was the crossroads the innovative label faced when it was obvious McLachlan had more than a cult status after 1991's *Solace*. The brain trust of Terry McBride, Mark Jowett and Ric Arboit all maintain that they're still working with what they love, but since the early '90s, Nettwerk's focus diverted from putting out records to developing Nettmanagement, a venture which has grown through working with commercially successful artists such as Barenaked Ladies, Moist, Dido and Treble Charger. This has left many wondering what happened to the groundbreaking label that began the careers of a variety of notable artists including The Grapes of Wrath, Skinny Puppy, Lava Hay and Moev, as well as a variety of international talent such as Consolidated, Front 242, and Severed Heads. McBride sees this shift in direction as a natural evolution of the label.

"For the longest time, the three owners of Nettwerk had three other jobs," he says. "I would pay the rent, I'd have my food, and whatever I made from working either DJ'ing, record stores, working at a fish plant or lifeguarding went into this company to keep it alive. Sarah was no different from some of the earlier artists. In a roundabout way, we had blind passion for certain things. We're very fortunate that for the first five or six years, three things worked, and one of those things worked in a really big way. Nowadays I don't go into things with that blind passion — at least not as much fiscally. I have to hope that what I like and what I believe in becomes mainstream fodder."

The core of Nettwerk — McBride, Jowett, Tom Ferris and Cal Stephenson

— began inauspiciously with a $5,000 bank loan to release their friends' music, which no other label would touch. This group was like the typical high-school clique that came together in a living room party, attended the same shows and traded tapes back and forth. Eventually they became more widely known by hooking up with likeminded pen pals from the musical centres that influenced their tastes — namely Europe and the United States. As the label grew in both size and success, that initial clique split into different factions and directions. Some stuck it out for the long run, others grew apart and a couple died prematurely. As time went on, many started to question where it was exactly they were heading.

The head triumvirate learned through trial and error. In some cases — with artists like The Grapes of Wrath, Skinny Puppy and Sarah McLachlan — Nettwerk earned impressive sales and notoriety. In other cases, the risk taking and on-the-job training came back to bite them. Their love of music, combined with contractual ignorance and the unstable and lethal mix of friendship and business, ultimately led the label into legal wrestling with McLachlan's collaborators, former signees and one-time partners. "The whole thing about the lawsuits is that I think it's a consequence of not being very together when we first started Nettwerk as business people," says Jowett. "We never had contracts. Everything was done in a good faith way which is good, but you do have to have things on paper."

Michele Gould, whose two bands — Lava Hay and Taste of Joy — experienced life in Nettwerk over the course of the label's first decade, describes Nettwerk's three-headed partnership: "Ric is the muscles, Terry's the brains and Mark's the ears." But she credits the label's longevity solely to McBride's shrewd business sense and work ethic. "He's the genius behind the entire label, and he's a rich man," claims Gould. "I remember Terry as always working, working, working. He would start Wednesdays at four in the morning to do his books. Nobody else would do the books, and he would do all the accounting for the label. He's probably the most calculated and focused person I've ever met in my life. I think the sheer success of Sarah had a lot to do with Terry. In some ways I miss Terry managing me because he was so like that. I really wonder whether he's a happy person. He takes joy and pleasure in his successes, but I don't know if he really enjoys the journey."

Terry McBride's journey didn't start in music. He was on the road to becoming an engineer, but his hobby soon interfered with that plan. For the Vancouver native, born in 1959, it was really a complete accident that his full-time career eventually became an independent record label. "It was just the love of music," states McBride. "One doesn't set out to be an artist manager. One doesn't set out to start a record label. The record label was purely a hobby because some local artists were doing the same sort of music I liked."

McBride had always surrounded his life with music. While studying Sciences and Engineering at UBC, McBride DJ'ed at CITR, the UBC campus radio station, and made some extra money spinning records at various Vancouver clubs. It would be through his employment at Vancouver's trendiest import record stores — first Cinematica, then Odyssey Imports — that McBride would gradually become a player in the Vancouver music scene. As the only retail conduits for European imports and new underground music, McBride rubbed elbows with a variety of music types, including many of the city's artists. When he met a developing electronic act named Moev, he found the impetus to trade a secure career in engineering for an uncertain place in the music business.

Moev was a rare species in Vancouver during the early '80s. As a band influenced by the European electronic underground, and not the popular New Romantics like Duran Duran, Moev was a mere progressive seedling in the 'hair band'-dominated landscape of Canadian rock. At the time the only other Vancouver band in line with Moev's philosophy was Images in Vogue, and like that band, the only thing Moev's Tom Ferris and Cal Stephenson wanted to do was make music that was akin to the albums they were buying from Vancouver's 4th Street record shops.

Moev: Tom Ferris, Cal Stephenson,
Madeleine Morris, Mark Jowett
(Courtesy of Kevin Komoda)

Ferris met Stephenson during their school days in Coquitlam, B.C. and at the dawn of the '80s channelled a mutual love for synthesized music into Moev. Left guitarless after original member Steven Mulder quit, the pair spotted an ad in the Vancouver weekly *Georgia Straight* placed by a guitarist looking for a band. Ferris and Stephenson discovered a like-minded soldier in Mark Jowett during a meeting in a Granville Street coffee shop, and he was quickly invited into the band. "We had extremely similar interests," says Ferris. "Back then it was Ultravox before Midge Ure, Fad Gadget, New Order, Joy Division and Magazine. Magazine was a heavy influence."

Jowett grew up an international nomad, moving with his parents from Johannesburg to Liverpool to Montreal and finally landing in Vancouver in his teens. He had developed an ear for eclectic music, and he also had band experience through playing bass in E, one of Vancouver's first electronic acts. Once again scouring the *Georgia Straight* classifieds, Moev found a lead vocalist in Madeleine Morris. Now all that was needed was a home for their music — something Terry McBride was looking to provide.

Ferris recalls meeting McBride: "He would always give us amazing deals on records — way below cost. That's how we got hooked up with him." On top of discount vinyl, McBride would provide Moev with their first gig at a friend's house party. He became the band's manager after that night. McBride's first attempt to release their music resulted in a label called Noetix, which he formed with a few investors. This venture lasted long enough to see Moev's "Cracked Mirror" single hit the stores before the label quickly folded. Not to be deterred, McBride sent some copies of the Noetix recording to various labels in hopes of attracting further interest in the band. Go Records, a small San Francisco label looking to expand its roster, signed the band and released Moev's 1982 recordings: the *Rotting Geraniums* EP and *Zimmerkamph* album.

The members of Images in Vogue were also frequently found at Cinematica Records. A local band based on the model of Japan, Kraftwerk and Ultravox, Images in Vogue had made their live debut along with Moev in 1981 through an innovative marketing tool concocted by Terry McBride and Images member Gary Smith. "Elektra: The Fashion Dance," as it was named, was a live event featuring both bands, where members of the audience participated in the show by modelling their new wave fashions. "Everyone had a whole lot of mascara on," remembers Ferris. The Fashion Dance introduced both bands to Vancouver, and it also foreshadowed a future working relationship among many of those involved with the event.

Over the next couple of years, Images in Vogue progressively mainstreamed their music and signed a major label deal with WEA in 1983 after opening for Depeche Mode at the Concert Hall in Toronto. The band's artistic shift from their original mandate was a signal to drummer Kevin Crompton that his artistic appetite wasn't going to be satisfied in the band's future. As a sideline pursuit, he constructed a makeshift demo studio, and started sculpting sounds in his apartment influenced by the experimental noise of Throbbing Gristle and Test Dept. Admits Crompton, "Images in Vogue was an idea of [members] Gary Smith and Don Gordon, and I was really into the idea of learning a lot of new things at that point, but I have to say that I was naïve as to what sort of music I was making, even though I felt like I was doing the right thing at the time."

Upon his introduction to Kevin Ogilvie, Crompton discovered a mutual fan of horror films and the various tributaries of non-mainstream music. Unlike Crompton, Ogilvie had neither a background in music, nor the slightest inclination to ever form a band. Ogilvie had been an ardent fan of the theatrical goth of Bauhaus and the poetic apocalypse of Joy Division, but his involvement in the music scene was simply an unintentional progression of his recreational experiments with Crompton.

The two Kevins regularly convened in Crompton's apartment, and after ingesting various illegal substances, Ogilvie would proceed to "gargle" over some sounds Crompton had recorded. It was Crompton's vision to form a band around the concept of "life through a dog's eyes," hence their partnership's tag, Skinny Puppy. In order to reduce the confusion of two Kevins in one band, they adopted stage names. Ogilvie took on the alias "Ogre," an apt choice, given his vocal delivery and ghoulish live presence. Crompton renamed himself "cEvin Key," which also distinguished him from his identity as Kevin Crompton, who would remain the drummer of Images in Vogue until that band's relocation to Toronto in 1985. Ogre would later credit their union as a escape hatch out of Images In Vogue for Crompton: "He was looking for something to break out of [Images in Vogue], and maybe I was it, considering the way my life was going. I became this distempered piece of mental steel that created the darkness, but that character was a darker side of me that I wanted to explore. It became all-consuming; I certainly got my full share of my character."

The pair released a self-produced, home-dubbed cassette entitled *Back and Forth* in 1983. Only 35 of these were made, but they were soon traded among the Vancouver underground. Skinny Puppy's live debut, during the closing of an art gallery in March 1984, brought out a jaw-dropping 300 people to the show, and it was evident the band's home experiments started to interest more than its peers. Not surprisingly, one of Skinny Puppy's tapes would land in the hands of Terry McBride and Mark Jowett.

After McBride had a highly contentious falling out with the owner of Cinematica, he ended up working down the street at Odyssey Imports with Jowett. Moev was once again in search of a label after Go Records died in 1983, and their vocalist had split for another band. Together, the remaining trio and their manager envisioned a label that would learn from the mistakes of both the ephemeral Noetix and the Go Records experiences. Nettwerk was plotted solely as a means to get Moev into the public eye. "No one was interested in Moev and that was the problem," admits Ferris. "That's where the idea came from so we said, 'Screw it — we'll do it ourselves.'" Through McBride and Moev, Nettwerk was born in the winter of 1984, and Moev's *Toulyev* EP was its first word.

All parties involved knew that if Nettwerk was going to survive, the label needed more than just Moev. They were intent on making a label with an image that would reach outside the restrictive ears of Vancouver, which meant bolstering their roster with other unsigned acts they enjoyed. On the strength of the *Back and Forth* cassette, Skinny Puppy was offered a place on the label, and signed on for two albums. The next signing, a wise move in retrospect, was a non-electronic band, The Grapes of Wrath. They would firmly establish Nettwerk's initial interest in a variety of musical styles, despite the label's predilection for electronic music.

McBride and Jowett's careful study of other independents had also reinforced the importance of image, thus local artist Steven R. Gilmore was enlisted as the resident artist to design a distinct look for the label's promotional material and album covers. The look of the label would be a staple characteristic throughout Nettwerk's history, with John Rummen filling Gilmore's shoes in the '90s. Explains Jowett, "We looked at some of the European labels like Factory Records, and in particular, 4AD Records, and there was this strong unison. For a music enthusiast it gives a knowledge that there's going to be a certain amount of quality [to the artists on the label] — specifically something about the sound of the label [overall]. The visual element really helps to concretize that."

The follow up to *Toulyev* in the fall of 1984 was a simultaneous assault of three EPs: Moev's *Alibis*, Skinny Puppy's *Remission*, and The Grapes of Wrath's eponymous debut. The three EPs were reissued in 1985, and sent as a combined package to international labels throughout Europe and the States to attract licensing agreements outside of Canada. Nettwerk's focus, unlike that of their Vancouver independent contemporaries, Mo-Da-Mu and

Zulu, was to concentrate on an international audience first, rather than establishing a following in their home country.

Vancouver journalist Tom Harrison notes that this was an intuitive move on Nettwerk's part: "They instinctively realized, 'We're going to make a record, but we're not going to rely on people keeping us in business in Vancouver because there may not be a thousand people interested. We're going to distribute through a cartel [i.e., Play It Again Sam] — large distributors of independent labels in Europe and England and elsewhere.' They made their records, leased with these companies around the world and they found their audience. At the same time those records were getting in the hands of the media in England and Europe. 'Who's this Skinny Puppy and Moev?' The people in Vancouver were reading in these magazines from England and elsewhere what they're saying about their own little label, Nettwerk. So Nettwerk automatically had this cache of smarts."

Part of the label's "smarts" included recruiting a label staff with individual strengths. In mid-1985, Brad Saltzberg, the co-owner of Odyssey Imports, was brought in for a brief period. Saltzberg offered the label a retail connection, and not surprisingly, Nettwerk releases would often find their way to strategically placed displays in his record store. At this point, Brad Saltzberg was being presented as Nettwerk's third partner — the other two being Terry McBride and Mark Jowett — and apparently replacing Moev's Tom Ferris and Cal Stephenson. "I didn't really get off on Brad [Saltzberg]," admits Ferris, "I thought he was bad news. He ran Odyssey — that's why me and Cal got the boot. Brad wanted to be involved and he wanted me and Cal out, but it wasn't brought to us that way. It was very convoluted and it was like a shell game. They still wanted us involved, but they didn't tell us what the fuck was going on until way after the fact."

Despite this confusion over early internal affairs, Saltzberg's role at the head table was also short-lived. Eventually his commitments to Odyssey eclipsed his responsibilities in Nettwerk, and McBride and Jowett bought him out. "Terry and I felt that he wasn't really into being the third part of the label that we needed him to be," explains Jowett. "We parted on quite good company, actually."

Ric Arboit began crossing paths with various music types as one of the main live-sound engineers in town. Along with Greg Reely and Dave Ogilvie (no relation to Kevin), Arboit had honed his sound craft in clubs and studios for Images in Vogue, DOA and various other Vancouverites. In 1985, Arboit left Vancouver to follow Images in Vogue's exodus to Toronto. While Jowett and McBride were in Toronto for a business meeting, they scheduled a visit with Arboit to lure him back to Vancouver with a position at Nettwerk. The label heads were attracted to both Arboit's sound engineering skills and the fact that he owned a PA. Arboit was offered a road managing position and a partnership in the company, both of which he accepted in 1986.

The band Arboit was assigned to road manage, or at least attempt to manage, was Skinny Puppy. "I called that hell on wheels," confesses Arboit. "There was a lot of chaos going on and only one straight person in it all. That was me. I didn't smoke before that. It was fun; we were making a hell of an impression everywhere we played." From its early beginnings, Skinny Puppy carried a strong reputation for excessive tendencies, on and off the stage. Tearing a page out of Alice Cooper's handbook, Ogre often incorporated B-grade horror movie visuals into the act with buckets of fake blood, plaster bones and audience-staged events.

The vocalist recounts, "We did an assassination where someone came out of the audience and shot me. I wore this chest plate with flash pots,

Ogre of Skinny Puppy
(Photo by Eric B. Brown)

gunpowder and condoms full of meat and blood which exploded when triggered. It worked very well, but turned out to be too dangerous. During the show, my shirt was ripped off and I was sweating profusely, so when I fell to the stage the vest started shorting out and I got three zaps in the chest. The next thing I know cEvin is yanking me off the stage."

Skinny Puppy's music fed off a similarly adventuresome philosophy as it was generated through any sounds, synth or rhythm cEvin Key could create, find or sample. This, along with Ogre's varied vocal delivery, often resulted in music that resembled a dance remix of a Kubrick or Tim Burton score. In fact, Key admits this cinematic mindset permeated Skinny Puppy's sonic black magic. "Remember the eerie feeling of *Eraserhead* and the initial horror of *The Exorcist*? People who've seen those particular movies will understand that the combination of the two, for me, is like potion."

Regarding the band's penchant for shock gore, Key justified this as simply mirroring society. "What we're presenting isn't that much different from what [the audience] is subjected to in everyday life. For instance, a commercial is a very plastic view of existence and reality. When you watch a TV show and you see a world with picture-perfect endings, all you have to do is switch the station and watch the news. And you don't have to see something like war to see the difference. You just have to see a bunch of fat old ladies who've gotten together to fight their school board. There's so much reality out there." With this mindset, the duo of Ogre and Key set out to change the parameters of electronic music, and, as they became more popular, the social consciousness of those who came in their path as well.

Skinny Puppy followed up the 1984 *Remission* EP with the 1985 album, *Bites*. Now a trio with Wilhelm Schroeder on bass synth and backing vocals, the band's European influences and appearance brought to mind Kraftwerk sung by Tolkien characters. Thanks to underground goth disco hits like "Smothered Hope," "Far Too Frail," and "Assimilate," Skinny Puppy became an underground buzz band. However, it would take a while before Canada knew what to think of them.

Greg Clow — a Toronto music writer, DJ and promoter of electronic music live events — remembers his first introduction to the band came through MuchMusic, and even the music channel had difficulties describing the band. "I recall [VJ] Michael Williams introducing one of the early Skinny Puppy videos and referring to them as 'Canada's answer to Depeche Mode,'" says Clow. "I saw the video for 'Smothered Hope' or 'Far Too Frail' — I can't remember which as they're quite similar — and was totally blown away by the sounds. It was one of those 'I don't know what this is, but I sure do like it!' type of moments."

The band's "noisecore" — as was the journalistic cliché at the time — quickly found admirers in the gothic and electronic underground contingents of most major urban centres, but unsurprisingly, not everyone warmed up to Puppy's uniqueness. Dressed in jet black as if they were The Cure's biker cousins and shunning Top 40 conformity, Skinny Puppy stood out —

visually and aurally — as the antithesis to what Key would describe as "the Bruce Springsteen mentality of music." Recalls Arboit, "I'll never forget being in Edmonton and some guy walking up to me and saying, 'There's two things that I don't like in this world: punk rock and faggotism, and you look like you have a bit of both in you.'"

Just as Moev had hit brick walls trying to cultivate a substantial Canadian audience, Skinny Puppy would have been doomed had they been marketed strictly in Canada. "They didn't rely on the local scene," journalist Tom Harrison says of Nettwerk's marketing tactics. "They went into the market-place internationally. That's where they found their audience and it enabled them to grow very quickly and establish a broad base of acts." Jowett concurs, "The only other label in North America that was releasing music like that of any kind was WaxTrax, who had Ministry. They were a label we quite revered, and were like a sister label. It got us on the map so that artists like Severed Heads, SPK, Chris and Cosey — a lot of electronic acts that were looking for a home for release in North America — would approach us. It helped establish us as an electronic industrial label."

The Grapes of Wrath turned out to be the other side of Nettwerk's musical coin. The addition of this Kelowna-bred trio rounded out the label and pro-vided a rock highlight to the electronic focus of Nettwerk, and would provide a base for the label's future rock or folk-based signings. The band came to McBride's attention through a tape of their debut EP that producer Greg Reely had recorded at Inside Trak and Mushroom Studios. After The Grapes of Wrath had been turned down by Mo-Da-Mu, the trio planned to self-release the recording, but days before the first pressing of the EP, McBride contacted them and offered them a spot on Nettwerk's roster.

The band transplanted themselves from Kelowna and took up residence in McBride's apartment, which until 1987 was the Nettwerk office. The promise of artistic independence and control of their music was a big factor in the band's decision to sign with the fledgling label. According to drummer Chris Hooper, "We pretty much always knew what was going on with the company, which at that time, was just a phone and a P.O. Box."

Hooper remembers McBride had big plans for the label and the band right from the beginning of their relationship. "He definitely had an idea from the start of what he wanted: a big record company built on the model of European labels like 4AD and Factory. At the start he ran and oversaw everything that Nettwerk did. He believed in us and really put in the time and effort to make it happen. Some of the first pressings of our first album

[*September Bowl of Green*] had the word 'Dreamer' scratched into the vinyl in that blank space next to where the label is. He did this, because we used to laugh at some of his predictions for us and how the band would do, so we started singing that song 'Dreamer' by Supertramp."

The Grapes of Wrath on back stairs of Changes in Kelowna, February 1984: Chris Hooper, Kevin Kane, Tom Hooper
(Courtesy of Chris Hooper)

The Grapes of Wrath was a product of three school friends who had shared a penchant for the '60s British Invasion and punk rock. Brothers Chris and Tom Hooper first spotted Kevin Kane during a re-release of *A Hard Day's Night* at their local movie theatre. Kevin and Chris later attended the same secondary school, and given their mutual musical interests they formed a basement band in 1978 with the younger Hooper rounding out the line-up. Chris was a drummer, Tom had a guitar and amp, but Kevin was already a proficient player. Reluctantly, Tom handed over the guitar his mother had recently purchased for him to Kane, and he took up the bass instead.

As Kane remembers, "We grew up together and learned to play together. When you look at a lot of bands, The Zombies are like perfection. They all grew up around the block from each other. That's the weird thing with bands; it's such a pain in the ass trying to find people. At that point you're not thinking about musicianship, you're thinking about other things — like in Kelowna there were a few bands we were all into: The Jam, The Beatles, Barrett's Pink Floyd and The Who. When we were 14 and 15 years old, every Friday night we'd play The Who's *Live at Leeds* from start to finish. We played it so badly."

In 1979, barely into their teens, the trio gravitated towards new wave and punk and paired up with a twenty-something Scottish punk named Chuck McDonald. Together they formed Kill Pigs with "Chuck Unpleasant," as he preferred to be known in his role as the front man. "Chuck was 24, tattooed, had dyed hair and scars from soccer brawls in England — not typical Kelowna, B.C.," reminisces Chris. The band rehearsed religiously every night after school, and developed a set-list of 50 songs. Despite their rigorous practice ethic, they would only play a single gig at a house party. Shortly after, McDonald took a job in northern Alberta working on the oil fields in order to make some money for the band to go into the studio and cut an EP. Months went by and the boys heard nothing from their front man. Eventually the trio was informed by McDonald's mother that Chuck had perished in an oil-rig accident. The Hoopers and Kane split, and pursued other avenues for the next two years.

The Hooper brothers began playing with bassist Don Walchuk, and became Kelowna's inaugural hardcore band, The Gentlemen of Horror, producing the limited edition single "Sterling Death." At the same time, Kane formed Empty Set, an art-rock collective heavily influenced by British post-punk, with classmate/drummer Darryl Neudorf, his kid sister/vocalist Adele Neudorf and bassist John Brotherton. Though it was Kane's creative voice fronting the group, his performance role was strictly relegated to guitar duties. "I wrote the words, but I didn't step up to sing at that point," says Kane. "Even after Tom, Chris and I got back together, neither one of us wanted to sing, so we were trying out singers. They were just too awful, so I said, okay fine, I'll sing." A month after Kevin Kane and Darryl Neudorf graduated from high school, Neudorf was drafted to Mo-Da-Mu's most successful band, 54·40, and Empty Set disbanded.

The small number of musicians in Kelowna ultimately brought the Hoopers and Kane back together. The reunited trio played a few cover gigs under the name Honda Civic, and eventually decided to give a creative partnership another try. Recalls Chris Hooper, "When we started recording demos and entering battles of the bands around our town, people couldn't figure out why we weren't playing covers, so we knew we were on the right track." Being an avid film fanatic, Chris lifted the name The Grapes of Wrath from the John Ford film based on John Steinbeck's classic novel, and the band was born. After an introductory live show on August 27, 1983, in Kelowna, The Grapes of Wrath immediately set to work on a recording. They booked studio time with Greg Reely and picked four songs on the basis of their length to fit on a 16-minute long reel of tape. The debut EP was financed with money raised from yard sales and flea markets. Not long after the completion of the debut EP, Nettwerk offered the band a deal and the trio moved to Vancouver in a station wagon.

Following the self-titled Nettwerk EP, the band's first album, *September Bowl of Green*, along with the single, "Misunderstanding," would catch the interest of Capitol, which offered Nettwerk national distribution in return for The Grapes of Wrath. The deal would have the trio make the transition to Capitol when all parties were ready. The interest was initially the result of classic word-of-mouth. With the popularity of Images In Vogue, Capitol's Deane Cameron was in Vancouver to scout a synth-rock outfit named Fabulon. When this band failed to make an impression, Tom Harrison suggested that Cameron check out The Grapes of Wrath, who were also playing that night in Vancouver. Recounts Kane, "Between sets they walked down the street to the little bar that we were playing at. Having grown up on The Byrds and The Zombies, [Cameron] was always really into the folk-rock type thing."

Treehouse, the band's second record, was different from Nettwerk's previous projects for several reasons. It was the first to be recorded during normal day hours, but more significantly, it was the first to use the services of a name producer. Tom Cochrane not only stepped into the producer role, but also adopted the role of The Grapes of Wrath's "band dad," as he treated the financially challenged trio to meals and fatherly lectures on various subjects. Cochrane became a key factor in the refinement of the band's brand of folk rock. Songs like "O Lucky Man" and Cochrane's personal favourite, "Backward Town," illustrated the Grapes' talents for spinning folk-pop gold and a knack for articulating coming-of-age angst. Interestingly, "Peace of Mind," the band's breakthrough hit, was the track Cochrane felt was their weakest. Recalls Ric Arboit, "Cochrane hated that song. We were taking a day to mix each song and Tom turned to me and said, 'Okay, hit

The Grapes of Wrath recording *Treehouse*: Chris Hooper, producer Tom Cochrane, Tom Hooper, Kevin Kane. Who's in charge here?
(Courtesy of Chris Hooper)

the record on the two track.' He figured the mix was done and he wanted to print the master. I said, 'No, it's not finished yet. I laid down on the ground in the studio and refused to turn the tape machines on." Consequently Cochrane departed from the project, leaving some of the final mixes in the hands of Nettwerk's Arboit and Dave Ogilvie. "Peace of Mind," a paisley pop gem, would find its way on to rock radio throughout the country, and encapsulated the defining qualities of The Grapes of Wrath: jangly, '60s-influenced folk rock coupled with incredibly earnest lyrics.

Capitol was ecstatic about the recording, and they covered the $40,000 studio cost that Nettwerk had fronted. The Grapes of Wrath made the transition to being a major label band, with Nettwerk Productions maintaining the band's management. For Nettwerk it would mean national exposure for their releases. For Tom Hooper it was the beginning of his band's self-sufficiency. "When Capitol bought the record, we were basically on welfare," he says. "All I cared about was that we each got a cheque for 7,000 bucks. I remember Terry taking me to the bank and withdrawing this money. To me it was like, 'I'm fucking rich. This is the big time!'"

This business move resulted in some changes for Nettwerk, beginning with a move to an actual office — a tiny one on the 17th floor of a Granville Street building. Nettwerk expanded its roster picking up domestic talent like The Water Walk, Pretty Green and After All, as well as international acts like Norway's Bel Canto and Australia's Single Gun Theory. The distribution deal would also help Skinny Puppy establish a larger fan base across Canada. As they were the cash cow during Nettwerk's early years, mainly due to their large following in Europe, McBride admits that Skinny Puppy's sales would total a surprising two million worldwide by the end of the century.

It became clear to Wilhelm Schroeder there was little room to grow as a musician in Skinny Puppy, and he left the band to forge his own career in electronic music. Changing his name to Bill Leeb, he would go on to form such acts as Front Line Assembly and Noise Unit. Leeb would later gain considerable commercial success with Nettwerk in a group called Delirium. That band created an easy-listening electronica/world-music hybrid that drew most of its attention from its various female guest vocalists as heard on 1994's *Semantic Spaces*, and 1997's *Karma*. Leeb's successor in Skinny Puppy was Dwayne R. Goettel, a quiet, technically trained Alberta musician who added an element of sophistication on *Mind: The Perpetual Intercourse* and all of the band's subsequent releases.

With the success of Skinny Puppy's third album *Cleanse, Fold and Manipulate*, Nettwerk decided the time was right to document what the band was notorious for: the stage show. *Ain't It Dead Yet?* captured the trio's June 1, 1987, appearance at Toronto's Concert Hall. It's an apt representation of the band's early live drama, complete with Ogre's in-your-face theatrics, his visual mosaic backdrop film clips, shadow puppetry, and gore props. All the while, cEvin Key and Dwayne Goettel continually fire their electronic artillery. The concert film documents the majority of the band's best-known tracks from 1984–1987, including inspired performances of "Dig It," "Assimilate," "Deep Down Trauma Hounds" and the set-closing "Smothered Hope." Though fake blood and organic-looking stage props remained a mainstay of Skinny Puppy concerts, the impact of the Skinny Puppy live experience would become more realistic, and according to Greg Clow, "more surreal and psychological."

This was particularly clear on the tour for 1988's *vivisectvi* (Vivisect Six). Ogre had promised that this would stand as the band's most overtly political statement to date concerning animal rights, with both the album and the tour infused with the singer's concerns. Animal rights had always been an issue with Ogilvie since his youth in Calgary, where he had been exposed to animal cruelty when fellow adolescents pressured him into hunting gophers. It would leave a scarring memory on him. "My friend was the first to spot one and when he shot, he only wounded it in the leg and it ran back into its hole. It stunned me. I just kept thinking, 'Wow, that gopher's going to go down there and slowly die. It'll never see daylight again.' The feeling of sadness and horror overwhelmed me." Ogilvie would end up purposely missing his shot or firing into the air to scare the animals away. "I lost a lot of friends that way," he admits.

vivisectvi was filled with themes of animal cruelty, human atrocity and disease, some of which was surprisingly combined with some of the band's most accessible musical material ("Testure"). That said, one single, "Dogshit," would have to be re-titled "Censor" due to record company pressure. Some of these concessions were made as Ogre was no longer content to preach to the converted; he wanted to get the band's concern to a wider audience. Even in his stream of consciousness lyrics, the message is clear in the song "Testure." "Brain break the skull again smash price research rat lab rent pain in flesh more ill drug store sales sharpen the knife emphasis on money new disease everyday end is seen and coming research turns its back to gain crush the spine genocide kitten drags its dead limb continuing all."

The accompanying tour included film montages of horrific animal testing, and thanks to some realistic puppetry by Ogre, a vivisection on a dummy canine the band dubbed CHUD. This act made such an impact on a female audience member at a show in Cincinnati on October 23, 1988, that she rushed to call the police, thinking Ogre was performing on a live animal. When two plain-clothes officers entered the Skinny Puppy dressing room and demanded to see the reported dog, the band greeted them with some less-than-welcoming words. Ogre, Key and manager Dan McGee were immediately arrested and spent the night in jail. They would be released the following day and fined $200 for disorderly conduct. Ogre released a statement through Capitol Records upon his release: "I find it paradoxical that the police can justify arresting us on the assumption that we mutilate and experiment on live animals for a theatrical performance when the inhuman reality is that it occurs in over 300 laboratories a day."

Many of Skinny Puppy's videos reflected the visuals displayed in the live show, which became an issue when it came to airplay. James Booth, who worked at MuchMusic at that time, claims that Skinny Puppy's main problem with getting into rotation wasn't so much the content of their videos as it was the music, which did not fall into the station's format except for the late night alternative showcase *City Limits*. He claims the only video that was ever banned was "Worlock," a video composed of over 80 deleted scenes from horror movies that were deemed too graphic to be released. "I know because I got in trouble for it," says Booth. "It had a shot of a guy hanging himself, and it got used for a concert listing. It was something that Moses [Znaimer] saw, and he just freaked out. To a certain extent, because the audience at Much was a younger demographic, we were constantly under scrutiny from the CRTC and other groups, who were looking for imagery in the videos that they didn't feel were appropriate."

"Worlock" would appear as one of the more identifiably Skinny Puppy tracks from the band's *Rabies* project, co-produced by Ministry's Al Jourgensen in 1989. Jourgensen was enlisted after he formed a friendship with Ogre. The union looked phenomenal on paper: Here were the most influential '80s electronic acts from the two most notorious labels in North America, Nettwerk and Wax Trax. Sadly, the result was a mongrel of Ministry ("Tin Omen") and Skinny Puppy ("Worlock.") "Unfortunately," says Greg Clow, "from a creative standpoint, the timing of Al's involvement was bad, at least in my mind. Had it occurred a couple of years before, when Ministry was doing their most interesting work, it might've been great. But since *Rabies* was recorded while Al was starting his slide towards the world of uninspired sludge-metal, it ended up being a real mess — along with *The Process*, it's my least favourite Skinny Puppy release."

Rabies also marked an extremely difficult time for the band's dynamics.

Ogre had bonded with Jourgensen as a result of feeling shut out by Key and Goettel's musical kinship. Not only were Key and Goettel solely responsible for Skinny Puppy's music, but they were also involved in a variety of side projects without Ogre: Hilt, Doubting Thomas, Tear Garden, and later on, Download. Ogre would have the equivalent of a revenge affair on his bandmates when he joined Jourgensen on the tour for Ministry's *The Mind Is A Terrible Thing To Taste*, and briefly held a membership in the industrial supergroup Revolting Cocks. This union would end after personal differences surfaced and Ogre began to fear the excessive drug use on tour. "I personally felt I flopped on *Rabies*," reveals Ogre. "I was near a nervous breakdown in a way. I was really unsure of myself and unsure of what I wanted to say or do. The work and artistic environment really weren't there at all. It was completely negative. With mud being thrown back and forth, there was no trust between the members."

"I understand why Ogre was doing it," confesses Key. "We had been doing Skinny Puppy for eight years, and we needed a break. What I really got pissed off about was Al, although I don't have anything against him personally. His motive for the whole thing was to break this band up. . . . At least that's what I feel."

Besides Ogre being one of the most distinctive front men in Canadian rock history, the band's influence on what became known as "industrial music" — aggressive electronic music — remains undeniable. Future successes such as Marilyn Manson would liberally borrow from the Skinny Puppy model, in terms of the band's song structures, vocal delivery, shock gore and even the members' erratic lifestyles. Throughout the late '80s, Skinny Puppy and Nettwerk's track record with them would eventually help the company to form relationships with other electronic notables: Belgium's Front 242, and America's Consolidated and MC 900 Ft. Jesus. One electronic act led by then-unknown New Jersey native Trent Reznor would approach the label about releasing his project known as Nine Inch Nails. Nine Inch Nails would open for Skinny Puppy on their 1987 tour, but legend has it that Reznor's band would be asked to leave after the tenth show due to their weak performances. Moev's Tom Ferris claims that the label flat out rejected Reznor's demo, but McBride remembers it differently. "It came down to one clause that they could not agree with their lawyer," he says. "It wasn't a money thing or dollar figure, it was a contractual clause — the composition clause. If you give a certain thing to a new and unknown artist it can sometimes cause you problems with the more established artists."

Still, it would be an unfortunate loss for the label, as Nine Inch Nails would become one of the biggest alternative acts of the 1990s. At this time, however, there were other roads the label would take that would make up for the loss. And they led directly to Halifax.

In 1987, Terry McBride met Sarah McLachlan while she was working the door at Halifax's Flamingo Club. McBride had ended up in Halifax while rescuing Skinny Puppy from an inept tour manager, and McLachlan just happened to be working that evening. The label had monitored the young woman's progress from afar since Mark Jowett had first witnessed her opening for Moev in 1986. When she was 19, and a year into her studies at the Nova Scotia College of Art and Design, McBride and McLachlan mapped out a five-record deal that would alter both of their futures. In half an hour, McLachlan quit school and bought her ticket to Vancouver to begin a career as a recording artist, even though she had never written a song.

This didn't seem to faze Mark Jowett. He had waited nearly two years for McLachlan to turn this age so he could persuade her to leave her parents. When she finally signed the deal, he was simply happy to have her on the label. Incidental details like her untested songwriting ability could be worked out in time. "Call it naïve, but we never really thought that way back then," admits Jowett, who by then had left Moev to concentrate on his A&R duties for the label. "If we loved something or felt it had a lot of potential, we would just do it. In the latter stages of recording [*Touch*] it became a bit of an issue because it had been going on some time and we had very little money. There was some pressure that we had to deal with, or I had to deal with. We never thought things through in a very formulaic way."

McLachlan spent her first few months in Vancouver during the fall of 1987 like a wide-eyed child absorbing a theme park for the first time. She took up residence in the back offices of the label's new Homer Street location, and worked part-time at a coffee shop in the Bentall Centre. Most of her free time was spent socializing and getting to know her new city. Eventually, Nettwerk clamped down on the singer and informed her that they expected an album to be recorded in March of 1988. Confined to her new apartment, McLachlan undertook a crash course in songwriting. At first, all she had guiding the process was the influence of her musical idols, Peter Gabriel and Kate Bush, and Nettwerk's overwhelming belief in her untapped talent.

Only months before the recording sessions were to begin, it became obvious that the material wasn't pouring out of her, and that McLachlan was in need of some assistance. Jowett enlisted a cast of Nettwerkians and

Sarah McLachlan in Halifax, 1988
(Photo by Eric B. Brown)

Vancouver musicians to assist in her creative gestation, and the nine official tracks that made up the album *Touch* were eventually completed. The
label made it clear from the start that regardless of any contributions others
may have made, McLachlan was to be presented as a singer/songwriter
who did it all. "That was the line there," says Moev's Tom Ferris who ran
the label's Limited Vision Studio. "'She was a solo artist. She writes *everything. Okay? You got it?'*" This would be thoroughly examined in the 1998
court battle; the biggest revelation at that trial would be what contributed
to the album's flaws.

Like many artists' first recording experiences, *Touch* was an obvious sign
of a young singer being 'produced.' Producer Greg Reely had done the same
thing to The Grapes of Wrath's *September Bowl of Green* by washing their
folk rock in effects. The result was a sound akin to The Cure's *Seventeen
Seconds/Faith* period. McLachlan's debut demonstrated her vocal flexibility
over a lush, medieval tapestry, and the influences of Kate Bush, Sinéad
O'Connor, and Enya were apparent. Although there was enough musical
talent to draw the listener, McLachlan's talent for lyrical honesty isn't exposed
until the concluding track "Ben's Song." This was a touching eulogy to the
passing of a young friend, but McLachlan openly admitted the majority of
the recording's lyrics were constructed by scotch-taping together lyrical
phrases chosen for their phonetic, and not their semantic, appeal. McLachlan
says, "With *Touch*, I didn't have anything to say, so I tried to create a mood
through words and imagery. It was very nebulous what everything was about."

However, the public didn't seem to mind, as a growing audience also
saw the overwhelming potential of the 20-year-old. *Touch* quickly earned
gold sales status through McLachlan's opening slots for The Grapes of Wrath
and the underground support of the radio and video singles "Vox" and
"Steaming." "I was surprised by that first record," admits Ric Arboit. "My
gauge was that when she went out to play there was a crowd already there
for her through college airplay. When I was touring with The Grapes I would
always play her record before the band came on. People were always asking
me who she was. Word of mouth spread quickly. I was amazed that this
girl could go out on her first tour and draw what she would draw."

A year later, her debut would attract an American deal with Clive Davis's
Arista Records, and with a remixed re-release, McLachlan's Stateside noto-
riety would soon reach an equally respectable level for the Haligonian rookie.
It was a startling accomplishment given the popularity of starlets like
Whitney Houston and Mariah Carey, and the rarity of the female singer/song-
writer at the time.

In the midst of touring *Treehouse*, The Grapes of Wrath's core trio had added keyboardist Vincent Jones, who became an integral part of their next album, 1989's *Now and Again*. It would establish the band as a rock radio staple and CanRock pin-ups, due to heavy rotation on MuchMusic. Listeners latched on to the masterfully performed acoustic pop songs with lyrics that ached of lost and unrequited love. They were no longer simply a band with university appeal, but the type of act that whipped teenage girls into a frenzy from the minute they set foot on stage. Though all members admit they could have done without the degree of hero worship, the adulation had its effects.

"I thought I was God," laughs Kevin Kane. "I think anyone would when you're young and you're looking for acceptance in your life and then all of a sudden, boom. I didn't go crazy. When I look back on it, it obviously affects your psyche, but I didn't take advantage of my position."

The success of the album took everyone by surprise, and Kane was especially surprised that the first single took off. "I didn't even think 'All The Things I Wasn't' was going to make it on the record," he admits. "I thought it was one of those throwaway little tracks you put at the end of the album." In a succinct two minutes and twelve seconds of acoustic bliss and relational disillusionment, The Grapes of Wrath had created a pop hit out of well-produced minimalism and universal pathos on par with the finest Simon and Garfunkel singles. Complemented with a simple video co-directed by Kane and Chris Hooper, this was the band's passport into the mainstream. Tom Hooper would sustain the momentum with his "What Was Going Through My Head," a thinly veiled account of a bad mushroom trip he and Jones had experienced while seeing a Pink Floyd concert in the States. Commercial success aside, *Now and Again* was a creative high, and from start to finish the record is a gorgeous realization of the folk rock The Grapes of Wrath had been honing for years. However, it was not an easy realization.

The band had hired Anton Fier to produce the album because of his work with The Golden Palominos, and he brought them to Dreamland Studios in upstate New York. Fier was largely responsible for pushing the band to greater performances, but his social skills hardly endeared him to his clients. This should have been clear when Fier came to Vancouver for pre-production. Recalls Tom Hooper, "We thought we were pretty good. We played him our songs in our practice space and we were all proud and pompous. He didn't say much and then after a while he said, 'That was horrible. I have to go for a drink.' He just left. He's a drummer and he's really good so he was really hard on my brother. He was also really hard on Vince, who had just became a member."

"I will always remember what an asshole he was," states Chris Hooper. "I can laugh about it now, but we went through hell. He was a classic manipulator of people and an esteem destroyer. His way of working was to completely destroy you, so you'd be nothing but someone doing what he wanted. He'd get pissed and start crying to us, saying he couldn't believe how he could be that way to us. Then the next day [it would be] the same old thing. He'd scowl and say, 'That's shit.' Then it would get to the point where all he ended up saying when we'd record was, 'Again.' It made me stronger because I'll never take shit like that again in any project I work on with other people, so I guess I can thank him for that. He'd pass out in the bar during pre-production and we'd keep running up the bar tab on his VISA all night."

Every member has their own memories of making *Now and Again*, whether it was because of Fier's harshness, the absence of certain band members on particular songs or the overbearing cabin fever. While making the album, two cars were totalled, Jones left in frustration for Toronto and smashed his accordion, pot and alcohol were abundantly consumed, various members had near-nervous breakdowns, and Fier nearly abandoned the project. Despite the painful process, both Kane and Tom Hooper admit that Fier was needed to push them to the professional level, and Tom Hooper claims that he could handle Fier again in the studio. "We're the same kind of people," he says. "I don't think I'm as harsh or bitter as him. We could argue and then have a big hug, and then go have a drink. I'd work with him again, for sure. I think the end product is just great. You listen to it now, it seems so pro — not in a bad way, but on par with a lot of world class stuff."

While touring *Now and Again*, the band was paired with Lava Hay, an acoustic pop duo consisting of Michele Gould and Suzanne Little from Toronto, and Nettwerk's latest signing. This initial pairing, the eventual romantic liaisons that bloomed between the bands and the media's inane fixation with their twin blonde hairstyles would undoubtedly underscore the band's music throughout their career. Tom Hooper and Suzanne Little began a long-term relationship that has included parenting two sons, while Vincent Jones was married to Michele Gould for seven years. What many failed to realize was that Lava Hay was one of the pioneering DIY female acts from the mid-'80s in Canada, and they were far from a couple of cute puppets controlled by male musicians.

"I felt bad for Lava Hay because they got a lot of shit for that," says Tom Hooper, "[There were] a lot of bad reviews and ridiculous things that people were saying [that] this band was basically formed by the Grapes and they do everything for them. One critic said, 'They even got the same person to do the video as the Grapes did.' What really happened is that we saw the video this guy did for them, so we got him to do our video. That was in *Now* magazine. We were on the road and I was so pissed off I wrote this big letter basically to the tune that this was so typical of [the view of] women who play music. People always assume that it's always a guy behind it. They never printed the damn letter, which really pissed me off."

Michele Gould and Suzanne Little met while working in the classified section of Toronto's *Now* magazine in 1986, and became friends through a mutual interest in acoustic music, though each embraced the music via entirely different avenues. Michele Gould was born to teen parents and spent her earliest years in poverty. She was constantly immersed in music while living in Newfoundland and Toronto. Gould sang in choirs, and eventually taught herself to play guitar. Her musical talents were innate and self-honed, but she knew from a young age she wanted to be a musician. As a teen, she worshipped Chrissie Hynde, and later developed an interest in underground music. She later absorbed the Queen Street music scene while attending York University in an arts program, where she met the likes of the Rheostatics' Dave Bidini and 13 Engines' John Critchley through the university radio station. Eventually she was drafted into her first band, playing pedal steel for The Ten Commandments. She played her first show opening for The Gun Club at Larry's Hideway. After the show, The Gun Club's leader Jeffrey Lee Pierce would crown Gould a "rock and roll woman," a compliment that she would forever wear with pride.

On the other hand, Suzanne Little balanced an extensive musical education with a huge affection for folk music. Born in Scotland, Little grew up in Scarborough listening to Neil Young, Joni Mitchell and her ultimate hero, Bob Dylan. From the age of 14, Little used her musical training to earn money teaching guitar. Following high school, she pursued journalism at Centennial College in Scarborough, and subsequently landed an internship at *Now* magazine. As with her folk idols, her love of language would become a huge focus in her songs. "It was really important to me to write meaningful lyrics," admits Little. "I was more into the thoughts behind things. I taught guitar, I studied music, so I had that background, whereas Michele came to things completely fresh having never studied. It was interesting to me because she'd play a chord which wasn't even a chord and I'd go wow, that sounds really cool. Michele had a lot of inventiveness which was good for the group. We both respected where we each came from."

"She was the total opposite of me," says Gould of Little. "She was like this hippie girl, and my whole style thing was like Nico from the Velvet Underground. That's where my longhaired image came. We started playing music together and everyone seemed to remember us because we had similar haircuts. It was never my intention to be folk-rock, but that's what got pinned on us."

The pair developed their musical relationship over a couple of years playing at the Cameron House. The Cameron had offered the duo a weekly show on Monday nights that they named "The Living Room Show." Gould and Little adopted the name Lava Hay and carved a memorable acoustic rock sound with a strong emphasis on vocal harmonies. Gould, who borrowed a guitar from a friend for her first few gigs, ended up scoring a cheap acoustic for $30. The instrument had a crack in the back and she was unable to use a conventional E tuning, so Little would tune down a semi-tone, creating part of Lava Hay's signature sound.

Due to their short set-list, the duo filled their "Living Room Show" with other players from the Queen Street scene including Handsome Ned, Laura Hubert of the Leslie Spit Tree-o, Bob Snider, Greg Keelor of Blue Rodeo, Bobby Wiseman and Molly Johnson. "The scene was really small and everyone went to see everybody else's bands and hung out with everybody," says Gould. "It was a really cool time. It was like Yorkville in the '60s." With a little help from these friends, the duo managed to record an eponymous EP at the Danforth Music Hall, which was self-financed through gig money and from their own paychecks. Now armed with a recording and a video for the track "Waiting For an Answer," Lava Hay began shopping their vision.

A lucky marketing opportunity arose when Little's roommate got the duo a gig at a Roots clothing party. The company would often throw parties for celebrities who appeared in its advertising campaigns. In this case the party was for Robbie Robertson. Lava Hay would make an impression on the famed musician. Remembers Little, "We felt a little bit out of place because it was such a schmoozy kind of class, so we went upstairs to where the caterers were and Robbie Robertson was sitting up there because he didn't feel at home either. The three of us are at a table and he said, 'You have angelic voices.' It actually got us a lot of mileage in the press. Things like that perked up a lot of people's ears."

Lava Hay was soon courted by Capitol and Nettwerk, but signed with Nettwerk because it was more willing to offer the artistic control they desired.

Lava Hay, 1992: Michele Gould, Suzanne Little
(Photo by Siobhan O'Keefe, courtesy of Nettwerk Records)

The pair relocated to Vancouver to be closer to the label, and to record their first full-length record. The benefits of Nettwerk became apparent when the band signed an American deal with Polygram a year later. Says Little, "One of the people at Polygram in the States couldn't figure out who we were appealing to, and the only thing they could think of was Wilson Phillips — because it was three dolled-up girls singing harmonies. That's their sense of marketing female music. They had no sense of what we were doing and where we were coming from. That's why we were really lucky to be on an independent label at the time because they saw we were into doing our own thing. You don't get signed to a lot of labels that will let you do everything. Nettwerk was good about that."

Lava Hay's North American introduction finally happened in 1990 with a self-titled debut that culled tracks from their 1988 EP, along with new material. The band co-produced the album with Greg Reely and Steve Berlin, and it featured appearances from several members of the Nettwerk family including Kevin Kane, Tom Hooper, Vincent Jones and The Water Walk's Dave Kershaw and Ike Eidsness. The result was a cohesive, finely textured folk-pop recording with gorgeous singles like "Baby," "Won't Matter," and "Wild Eyes." Lava Hay's debut would sell respectably and get the band widely noted in both the U.S. and Canada. They spent most of the *Lava Hay* campaign touring, playing shows with many of their friends from both Queen Street and Vancouver such as Blue Rodeo, The Grapes of Wrath and The Skydiggers. After a political reshuffling at Polygram U.S., the duo was dropped, and ended up the sole responsibility of Nettwerk. But at this point in time, Nettwerk would be paying attention to another one of its female acts and her difficulties with an American record company.

Not surprisingly, Sarah McLachlan felt an enormous amount of pressure when she commenced work on 1991's *Solace*. The singer/songwriter's mission was not as simple as topping the sales of her debut and pleasing her record company. It was an attempt to strip away her perceived image. "I didn't know what 'image' was," McLachlan told the *Globe and Mail* in 1991, "But people told me, 'This is what you are' so I figured I better play along. My manager at the time thought it was a good approach to be this ethereal, whimsical waif. It wasn't particularly easy to live up to. I think I disappointed a lot of people when they actually met me."

Solace became a bid to reveal the real Sarah McLachlan. Throughout the album's 10 songs, McLachlan's voice danced gracefully and naturally, complemented by acoustic instrumentation and an organic texture. There were few signs of vocal grandstanding or the '80s production indulgences found on *Touch*. Admits McLachlan, "I was kind of showing off [on *Touch*]; I was going 'Wow, my voice can do all these neat things!' I'd never been recorded before, and it was really exciting. With the second record it was, 'Yeah, yeah, okay, I can do that. Let's buckle down and sing a song.'"

This 'stripped-down' approach was also pervasive thematically throughout the record. From the blurred nude couple on the back of the album cover to McLachlan's own naked self in her videos for "Into the Fire" and "Drawn to the Rhythm," *Solace* carried a clear message: McLachlan wanted to figuratively bare it all and reclaim her autonomy. "Into The Fire" was an especially telling sign of McLachlan taking control of her art through the single's "rebirth" theme, and the accompanying video displaying the nude singer tastefully immersed in mud, hardly the image of a perceived Celtic princess.

Though many writers compared her to Jane Siberry or Sinéad O'Connor, McLachlan was actually picking up the torch of folk pop that Joni Mitchell had dropped in favour of jazz in the mid-'70s. Songs like "The Path of Thorns (Terms)," "I Will Not Forget You" and "Drawn To The Rhythm" touched a cross-generational audience with tales of the heart and the bittersweet journey for a sense of place and being, much like Mitchell did on her early records *Ladies of the Canyon*, *Blue* and *Court and Spark*.

McLachlan would describe *Solace* to one journalist as "the mourning of lost innocence," something that perfectly expressed the steep learning curve regarding her understanding of the music industry during the three years between her debut and its sequel. *Solace* would reflect her transition from a teenager to young adult, and the consciousness-raising that can occur through an individual's first experiences living on their own. It would also subconsciously reflect the harsh realities of being an artist signed to a major label.

The making of the album was a challenging nine-month process, as the initial demos for McLachlan's new material were not met with enthusiasm from Arista. Says McLachlan, "We'd send them stuff that we just felt great about and the label would call and say, 'That's not it.' I'd say, 'Doesn't it make you feel something?' And they'd say, 'That's not the point.' But then what the fuck is the point? I got so heartbroken. At one point I wanted to stop making music."

What saved her was the beginning of what would become a long-term working relationship with the Montreal-born producer Pierre Marchand. He can be credited for keeping McLachlan focused, and helping her complete *Solace* despite the adversity. Marchand, a disciple of Daniel Lanois who had started playing keyboards in the '80s with Luba, had but a sole production credit — Kate and Anna McGarrigle's *Heartbeats Accelerating* — when he was suggested to McLachlan. She hired Marchand because of his decision to include a tape of his own compositions with his resumé. The idea of a musician/producer who understood the creative process as opposed to being solely a technical studio engineer was attractive to McLachlan.

"I love working with him," gushes McLachlan. "I love every element of it. We are actually two peas in a pod. We're so alike it's frightening, so we drive each other crazy. He's the perfect mirror for me. He's really forced me to see a lot of things in myself and to work through a lot of things. Musically, he's just fantastic. He has great ideas, great sounds and he loves making music. He works so hard, and he's in it for the right reasons."

Though the album successfully established McLachlan and Marchand's creative alchemy, and sales significantly trumped the numbers of *Touch*, this was not enough for Arista. The album had failed to make a serious dent in the U.S. for the label that expected the pop chart muscle of Whitney Houston, and *Solace*'s promotional campaign was a short party. On the other hand, Nettwerk didn't share Arista's sentiments. When the American label pulled the plug on pushing her sophomore record, Nettwerk invested large amounts of money to keep McLachlan on the road and visible in the United States. Eventually, this tactic worked.

If there was anything the Grapes of Wrath learned from making *Now and Again*, it was how not to make an album. All members of the group are unanimous that inviting producer John Leckie to Vancouver for 1991's *These Days* was a godsend. His even-tempered manner was welcomed after the emotionally scarring experience with his predecessor. Leckie was an ideal choice, as his résumé spanned decades of the band's favourite records, including studio experiences with George Harrison, John Lennon, Pink Floyd, XTC and The Stone Roses. As a '60s survivor, Leckie easily adapted to the vintage gear at Mushroom Studio in Vancouver, and worked the band hard with charming social graces. Says Tom Hooper, "He was a real character. He didn't produce us the way Anton did. The songs were basically our creation. He's a wizard at getting groovy sounds. He's such an eccentric guy. He loved Mushroom because it's all old stuff. People like that don't come around much anymore. Anton would take a song and just rip it apart where John was like, 'That sounds really good. Let's record it. Let's smoke a joint.'"

Leckie further impressed the quartet when he suggested the album should be mixed at The Beatles' famed Abbey Road Studio. This was the realization of a childhood fantasy for all in the group. "We brought our girlfriends over and we lived in a flat next door," says Tom Hooper. "For me it was a dream come true, being a screaming Beatles fan. John would always let us go into the Beatles' studio and he knew how excited we were about it. He gave us a tour and let us hang out there all night. We got wasted and we were playing Beatles songs and it was just incredible."

The resulting recording, *These Days*, displayed what happens when a band spends enough time on the road: the performances were better, the songs featured inventive solos and creative arrangements and virtually every lyric longed for home. The songs built on the sound of *Now and Again*, adding the multi-layered traits of Led Zeppelin, Allman Brothers and CSNY. The Grapes had never been more prepared to go into the studio, and their confidence and direction were rock solid. It's unfortunate that their personal lives didn't reflect that as well.

The band does not cloud most of their songs in metaphor, as usual wearing their hearts all over their sleeves. Kane begins the album with a series of questions in "Away": "Does it matter what I say when I'm far away? Does it matter what I do when it's without you?" The theme of homesickness carries through many of the tracks: "Travellin'," "I Am Here," "I Can't Find My Home" and "Miracle," indicating that this band was in need of a long break.

Unfortunately, The Grapes of Wrath would never get the break they clearly required. The toll of their schedule was evidenced as early as the Abbey Road sessions. "It became [obvious] that people's egos and people's lifestyle and everything turned," says Vincent Jones. "When we were mixing

These Days I had a feeling that it was the end at Abbey Road. We almost broke up there, actually. We had a pretty heavy conversation about some business stuff that we had to deal with and you could tell that [Kane] was thinking it wasn't the way it used to be."

The business area was always a sore spot for Kevin Kane. He had tired of the constant touring that would result in putting the band in the red — even when they were selling out large venues across the country. Recounts Kane, "As things went along and got more complicated, I started becoming enraged about certain things — like, 'How is it that we go on the road and the guy who tunes my fucking guitar gets paid more than I get paid for playing in front of thousands of people? No, fuck it. I will not tour unless I'm getting paid more than the crew.' Even then, our soundman was still getting paid more than any of us. Nettwerk saw me as a real pain because I actually cared about my career. I realized that the money was being made — a lot of people rode on our backs. That's the truth. Nettwerk got a distribution deal because Capitol was interested in us. Nettwerk said 'Oh no, we have a contract.' Whatever, I have absolute proof they rode on our backs. I'm sure Sarah McLachlan is carrying the company through a lot of stupid stuff."

The other three would claim Kane's ego had become troublesome. Chris regularly fought with Kane over the guitarist's issues. Both Jones and Chris Hooper attest that Kane had a "big problem" with the three singles from *These Days* — "I Am Here," "You May Be Right" and "A Fishing Tale" — coming from Tom Hooper's pool of songs. Kane refutes this, claiming, "As it went along, Tom started bringing more stuff in, which in itself wasn't a problem. What got to be a problem was when I was bringing my songs — and Tom felt this too — other people wanted to have their say. Before, we would just do a song. It was obvious. Why change things just to change them? It just got really uptight."

Throughout the tour, the bus was partitioned into two sections. Kane and Tom Hooper would sit in the back and Chris Hooper and Jones in the front. Tom Hooper attempted to be the intermediary between the two dividing camps given his creative bond with Kane. This unhealthy situation further resulted in spending nights in different hotel rooms, and only being together to play on stage. Sadly, nothing was reconciled. To conclude the touring for *These Days*, the band played a homecoming gig at the Commodore on October 30, 1992. By all accounts, it was an amazing gig that received numerous post-show accolades. However, it would be the last time the band was collectively on-stage as The Grapes of Wrath. The next day, Terry McBride fired Kevin Kane from his own band.

The Grapes of Wrath at Town Pump in Vancouver, 1988:
Kevin Kane, Vincent Jones, Tom Hooper
(Photo by Paul Clarke)

McBride is diplomatic, but can't hide the regret in his voice when he recalls the event. "Kevin had a very strong personality. His point of view didn't match the point of view of the other three people. It just came to a point where it was either him or us. As the manager I was stuck in the middle and it wasn't an enjoyable place to be. Kevin took it differently when I tried to stay with the other three guys. He took it personally and that basically killed the friendship."

"Essentially they killed an aspect of me," Kane confesses. "I wasn't like Syd Barrett or something like that. I wasn't a complete fuck-up. I was a professional doing my job, but there were a lot of little bullshit things going on around the band. I remember sitting in a lobby of a hotel thinking, 'Where is everybody?' And I found out they had all gone to the airport without me.

"I saw the band coming to an end, but the way that it was done — I didn't see that [coming]. If someone has a terminal illness, and foresees dying, you go through all these different things like anger and sadness and finally acceptance. But what you may not expect is your entire family bursting through the door and killing you. It's like, you're going to die anyways, you're depressed and bugging us, so we're going to kill you. I don't think that would stand up in court for a defence of murder."

"I think we grew and changed as people," says Chris Hooper. "What someone said I may have thought was funny when we were in high school together, I now thought was stupid or embarrassing. Our musical influences were starting to change and not coinciding anymore. [Kevin] always complained about money, [and] of course the ego thing. At one point Kevin let it affect him. Everyone saw a change, and I think it went to his head a bit. It's the classic story — as soon as a band has gained some success, there isn't that drive to reach a goal anymore. There's no more 'us against them' that a band needs to keep going."

Adds Jones, "Splitting up the band was very hard and a lot of people thought it was a very stupid thing to do. We were at the ultimate height of our success. We hadn't stopped, we were on a roll and we ended it. It was a very bad situation. We didn't even talk about it. We just ended it."

But not everyone is quick to point the finger at Kane. Tom Hooper admits that he took the band's situation for granted, and should have tried harder to communicate. "You don't realize what you have. We were doing very well and I would sit and complain. I think maybe we should have tried to make this work."

Michele Gould, who at the time was married to Vincent Jones, denies that the band's split was entirely the result of Kane's personality clash and career demands. She lays equal blame on Nettmanagement and the band's inability to communicate. Says Gould, "A lot of people aren't being honest. In this industry, you say one bad thing about one person they'll shit on you for the rest of your life. With The Grapes of Wrath it was really a shame because of a lot of people weren't getting along with Kevin on a personal level because of the management. The management was focusing on Kevin being the star — and he was. He's probably the most talented guy in that band as far as songwriting goes. His personality — he's not the easiest guy to get along with, but to me, when I first met Kevin, I thought he was the nicest guy. He was so helpful to Suzanne and me.

"Things got crazy because Suzanne was dating Tom and I was dating Vince. [Kevin's] girlfriend became really good friends with us. The situation changed. You have the record company heralding him as the star of the show and then playing all the boys against each other. I totally saw that. 'We'll talk about so and so behind their back.' The next thing you know they're all fighting amongst each other because they're all fighting for attention. Musicians have huge egos. It was a drag, the way that ended. I tried to advise Vince, 'Do not break up that way. Don't do it through management. Talk.' None of them would talk to each other. They were young and they were treated like the Beatles. A lot of people didn't realize that because they didn't get the hype that all the other bands got. They were literally huge."

The Hoopers and Vince Jones soldiered on together under the name Ginger and released a self-titled EP and the full-length *Far Out* — expanding the band to a quintet with Lanny Hussey and Sean Ashby on guitars — to modest critical and public acclaim. Kane, on the other hand, remained incognito. The five years after the breakup would be spent with acrimonious litigation suits over songwriting royalties, the band name and wrongful dismissal. During this time fans were left in the dark as to what had happened. The ardent ones would keep an eye on the fractured pieces that were left, but the vast majority would agree that that's all they were: pieces of an invaluable whole.

Lava Hay would suffer a similar fate a year later. In 1992, they released *With a Picture in Mind*, an album with some of their strongest work and great guest appearances, including Bob Wiseman and Randy Bachman. There was, however, an evident polarity to the songs. No longer were the compositions unanimously reflective of retro-folk. Suzanne Little remained true to her roots ("3 O'Clock," "Find My Way") as Michele Gould started to indulge in her long-term Chrissie Hynde adulation ("Don't Tell Me," "This Pain").

Explains Little, "Michele just got to the point where she wanted to do a rock thing. That was in her system, to be aggressive, hard — that's where she came from. I was not into that. I moved to Salt Spring Island. I was into organic farming, kids and a way more earthy thing. It wasn't going to work artistically for another record. Our lives were going in different directions. A collaboration only works when you're on the same track."

This inevitable end began in the Stoney Creek, Ontario, studio of Daniel Lanois guitarist Bill Dillon. The duo both claim he had his talents, but admit he was the wrong producer to work with. "He was super-moody and extremely weird," remarks Little. "He would tell us, 'You hired me to be your producer and this is what's going to happen.' No one had ever talked to us that way before. It was our thing so that didn't work." In the end, the band parted with Dillon, and returned to Vancouver to self-produce the remainder of the album.

Though "Don't Tell Me" and "This Pain" received some radio play, *With a Picture in Mind* was a commercial disappointment. After an obligatory tour, the duo parted ways. "To me it's the trip, it's not the end product," explains Gould. "In Lava Hay I stopped enjoying the ride. There was a lot of pressure and due to the naïveté of our management, and the lack of maturity, they caused a lot of problems between Suzanne and me, as they caused with The Grapes of Wrath. Because it's a small company and people knew each other personally and would play on everybody that way, there was no professionalism. There was no liaison between your management and your record company because it was so small. Your A&R guy could talk to you about your record instead of talking to your management. 'We need a hit. We need this and that.' We started getting that direction. 'You guys should harmonize less and write more up-tempo songs.' They should have let us do what we liked to do."

Jowett sees things differently. "We really tried to support them and make it grow. Making records is a difficult thing. There's no formula. Sometimes if you put them with a producer or a different situation and if they aren't very well connected themselves, it can pervade their music and diminish what's special about it. I think that happened to Lava Hay in a sense. The second record was one of the most difficult albums I've made with an artist. Unfortunately it didn't help with their future."

Both Little and Gould would resurface in 1995 with new projects. Little's solo album *Be Here Now* would display her folk roots intermingled with layers of instruments, and intricate songwriting. It was a critically acclaimed debut, but it wouldn't find its way into many homes. Little would admit that she chose to be a mother over devoting herself to the promotional grind of pop stardom, and she has few regrets about her decision.

Gould would answer her rock calling, and move on to front a power trio called Taste of Joy. *Trigger Fables*, the band's sole recording, was often compared to Tanya Donelly's Belly project or Juliana Hatfield, but the album was an honest reflection of Gould's adolescent rock fantasies given a mature foundation. After falling out with Nettwerk, she signed a brief deal with the EDEL label in Germany, and toured Europe.

The Grapes of Wrath and Lava Hay were not the only losses tallied by the label in the early '90s. Nineteen ninety-two would mark a year when most of the label's international electronic roster uprooted for various reasons. Among others, Consolidated jumped to London Records, and MC 900 Ft. Jesus moved to American. Nettwerk's staple Canadian electronic artists also started to come apart at the seams.

Moev had, for the most part, been a studio-based band. They attained some minor success later with their albums *Yeah, Whatever* and *Head Down* — both on Atlantic Records in the United States — but the band's alternative/dance charting was never anything to make Moev into a primary concern for the label. Tom Ferris had spent most of his time working at Nettwerk's studio, Limited Vision. Upon the premature death of Moev's third vocalist, Dean Russell, Ferris decided that both Moev and his relationship with Nettwerk were over. "Everyone wanted to keep going at it. I really didn't want to go to Nettwerk. I didn't like anyone there. It was so phony and fake. It reminded me of Grade 8. It was really sick."

The next time he would partner up with a member of Moev occurred when Ferris launched a lawsuit against Nettwerk with Cal Stephenson in 1995 over their role in the founding partnership of Nettwerk Productions in 1984. In a press release, Nettwerk called their claims "vexatious and without merit."

Explains McBride, "That was a nuisance lawsuit done by a lawyer who put three lawsuits on us all at the same time to try and scare us. By the time Ferris and Stephenson hired a different lawyer who looked at all of the evidence, he went 'You're nuts.' We had it in writing that they weren't partners any more. It was obvious from the evidence trail that exactly what had been said from day one was, in fact, what had actually happened."

The plaintiffs eventually settled out of court in 1998 for $7,500, with Arboit stating, "It is unfortunate whenever past business dealings lead to such acrimony. I believe we have always been fair with Tom and Cal. The settlement is very generous and I am confident they would agree."

Ferris still remains extremely bitter and confused over the outcome. "There was this meeting when we all got together and we were very concerned about the cost of recording. I understood [the subject of] the meeting, way back in 1985, was that we have to control the cost of recording. So we wanted to invest in a small studio set-up. That's where the confusion sets in because it wasn't spelled out what the fuck was going on. That was Terry and Mark's advantage to keep me and Cal fucking confused. With our little lawsuit, it's basically [that] Terry had us sign this paper that we had nothing to do with Nettwerk's day-to-day operations from mid-'85 onward. I thought we did because we were recording bands and we basically made no money."

McBride continues, "You decide to leave the company and just become an artist. The company isn't doing much. Everyone is struggling along just trying to live with the dream and so forth and six years later the company hits it. [Ferris and Stephenson] are simply going, 'Why did we do that?' 'Maybe we should have got more.' Maybe if they stayed in the company and it had gone under, maybe they would have had to pay money to creditors. That can go both ways."

Skinny Puppy was the last of the original signings to sever ties with the label. Though Nettwerk continued to release compilation records of hits, b-sides and rarities, 1992's *Last Rights* was almost too intentionally prophetic a title for this infamously unstable trio. Even in the record company biography that accompanied the release, Ogre was quoted as saying, "There's always a new beginning after something dies. It's too early to tell yet what shape things will take. If this is the last record and the beginning of a new direction for all three members, I can't say."

Though both *Last Rights* and its predecessor, 1990's *Too Dark Park*, contained some of the act's artistic highpoints, it was obvious the band's direction was headed downward, and fast. The band had never been shy about discussing their drug habits; Key had informed *High Times* magazine that every single Puppy song was written under the influence of marijuana,

Skinny Puppy, 1995: Ogre, cEvin Key, Dwayne Goettel
(Courtesy of American Recordings)

but it was when the harder narcotics entered the picture — especially heroin — that the band went into steady decline. "At the beginning the band was fuelled by a lot of excess," admits Key. "We started sort of based around drugs, or a replacement for drugs. Everybody knows about Ogre's drug history. In trying to deal with him, you had to accept that this person was not gonna be 100 per cent normal to work with. I think through drug-related situations I would end up on Ogre's paranoid delusional side, and I would become more or less the victim of the whole experience. I should say that I'm not trying to persecute Ogre for how it all started, but essentially the root of the issues between us always had to do with the fact that he had to be fogged over by a glazed outlook from a drug perspective. And since I was always the one that dealt with the business, I was probably always the one seen as being the deliverer of the negativity."

Drug problems aside, those who worked around the group were surprised Skinny Puppy existed as long as it did. "I never thought they'd make it past the first record," claims Arboit. "It had to be the music. They couldn't even stand to be in the same room together." In the end, the band's ongoing public feuds and hard living had become too much for the label to manage. It was decided after *Last Rights* that a change would be good for everyone involved. "They internally combusted to some degree," states Jowett diplomatically. "It got out of hand. It was very difficult for us to manage them. It wasn't fun or inspiring anymore."

Unfortunately, this twisted soap opera would only worsen when Skinny Puppy moved their affairs to Rick Rubin's American Recordings in L.A. — a change they believed was a good idea at the time. During the next three years they'd rack up a studio bill of over half a million dollars, Ogre would again wrestle with heroin, and the trio would learn American Recordings wasn't the most welcome home for their new start. According to Key, the label withheld money, caused political strife within the band by offering Ogre's W.E.L.T. project a deal if he left Puppy, and demanded multiple reworkings of the recording. It was amazing that the band's swansong, 1996's *The Process*, ever saw the light of day. "To them there was always a problem," claims Key of the label. "It's almost like one of those habitual abuse things that you have in relationships where people can't leave each other alone. I'm not trying to blame it all on American, but they definitely hold a major part in the destruction of the band Skinny Puppy."

Amidst this chaos, Ogre left the band, and on June 12, 1995, an official statement surfaced which confirmed what Internet rumour-mongering had known long before: Skinny Puppy was officially dead. Sad as that was for any fan of the band, there would be more serious matters to mourn when two months later, on August 23, 1995, Dwayne Goettel died of a heroin overdose in his parents' Edmonton home. According to Key, Goettel had never dabbled in heroin before this period. He was the last member to fall victim to the needle, and it was something he used to numb the pain of a painful separation from his girlfriend. It was a shock to all, not only because of the loss of a creative talent, but because it was Dwayne that was heroin's casualty, not Ogre.

The Process was posthumously released in 1996, thanks in part to the return of longtime studio collaborator, Dave "Rave" Ogilvie. Although this album was not warmly received from Skinny Puppy's fan base, it was, in Ogre's eyes, a suitable eulogy for the 13-year-old dog that pioneered much of the electronic landscape. "It's a fitting final record because it does mash together what has been going on for 10 years, which is fine. We were always a totally schizophrenic band."

From Nettwerk's stormy beginning to the '90s, the pathway would be cleared for a new roster, and a new focus for the label. In February 1995, Nettwerk celebrated its tenth anniversary with a special concert at Vancouver's Vogue Theatre, which featured various members of the label's past and present.

The label also marked the occasion with the release of *Decadence*, a five-disc box set compiling the majority of the artists from the label's history. *Decadence* featured an extremely impressive multimedia component including videos, biographies, photo essays, sound clips and interviews with artists and Nettwerk staff. It was a document that reaffirmed the label's survival, and observed its contributions to the global music sphere in the past as well as where it was heading in the future.

A new breed of Canuck talent was signed to Nettwerk throughout the early half of the '90s including Mystery Machine, Rose Chronicles and Wild Strawberries. With the exception of the last, these signings seemed to be indicative of current musical trends, rather than future ones. Mystery Machine provided the label with a typical early-'90s noiserock quartet that spent most of its career being frequently compared to Sonic Youth, My Bloody Valentine and Ride. They were certainly in line with Arboit's preferences, as he still felt stung by losing Sloan to the David Geffen Company. Rose Chronicles, featuring the alluring vocalist Kirsty Thirsk and guitar-effects addict Richard Maranda, fit in perfectly with the label's 4AD fixation. This Vancouver quartet framed itself around the likes of the Cocteau Twins and early Lush, and Jowett would take on the band as a pet project, co-producing their first release, 1994's *Shiver*. Rose Chronicles hold the distinction of being the first group to ever receive the Best Alternative Album Juno. Their second record, 1996's *Happily Ever After*, would also be their last.

Toronto's husband/wife duo of Ken and Roberta Carter Harrison, a.k.a. Wild Strawberries, had already built a solid following on their own with their meticulously crafted eclectic pop on their Juno-nominated *Bet You Think I'm Lonely*. Signed in 1995, they delivered gold that year with *Heroine*, an album that charted three consecutive singles. Though they continued to build a following playing to Lilith Fair audiences, they would eventually tire of being tied to their chosen milieu. The band showed their more experimental leanings on 1998's *Quiver*, which resulted in a fraction of *Heroine*'s sales. Eventually, the couple became dissatisfied with Nettwerk's financial control of their record-making process and with having their career eclipsed for three years by McLachlan's promotion schedule. They parted with Nettwerk before the release of *Twist* in 2000. There would be few other Canadian artists to name-drop on the label after 1996, with the exception of the label's two-album affiliation with Toronto's By Divine Right.

It's important to note that the label's spotlight on Sarah McLachlan was never a point of denial for Nettwerk. It had been clear since *Solace* that she was the label's priority, and this was further reinforced when the company restructured to best suit her rise. Arboit moved from A&R to label president, which McBride gave up to focus on making Nettmanagement his main concern — primarily breaking McLachlan into the mainstream. It would consequently benefit McLachlan's profile greatly. After completing a rigorous touring schedule, her third album, *Fumbling Towards Ecstasy*, would go on to sell over four million copies.

Released in 1994, *Fumbling Towards Ecstasy* is a pinnacle moment for McLachlan. It boasted some of her strongest material, which combined the acoustic charm of *Solace* with the electronic brushstrokes of producer Pierre Marchand. "I do believe *Fumbling Towards Ecstasy* was our best album," confesses Marchand. "I was determined to make the best record ever — in my book, of course — and I think 'Fear' was my highest achievement. The end result still sends shivers up my spine." The words, music and production all work together in a mystical way that perfectly captured segments of McLachlan's most extreme memories: desire, apprehension, loss, betrayal. "I look at music as a bit of a diary for myself, as a cathartic way of working through my own neuroses," says McLachlan. "Whether it's obvious to the listener or not, a lot of these songs are very therapeutic in the process of writing them. It made me forgive on a lot of levels."

There are moments when the simplicity of McLachlan's diary entries veer too close to finding their way into an anniversary card ("Ice Cream") but the majority of this work is so finely textured ("Wait," "Plenty," "Fear" and "Elsewhere") that the result is timeless.

The combined effort that Nettwerk and McLachlan put into *Fumbling Towards Ecstasy* had finally resulted in the widespread success they all had originally envisioned. It was clear from some of the drama surrounding McLachlan's life that she was about to join the lofty ranks of multi-million-selling artists — and experience all of the associated pressures. The combination of the singer's soul-baring with the beauty of her music had a powerful effect on her audience. Some fans chose to start Web pages and chat groups, some were inspired to pick up the guitar themselves, while others were a little more extreme with their devotion to McLachlan. One man, Uwe Vandrei, penned hundreds of creepy letters to McLachlan, and informed her that the two of them were meant for each other. Most of the press would claim that this experience translated into the record's opening track and first single, "Possession." It was one of the singer's most haunting works with her lyrical imagery painting the point of view of an obsessive fan. However, despite reports in various large-scale publications, McBride denies that Vandrei was the muse for the song, or that "Possession" was inspired by a single fan. "Magazines are not the gospel truth," he states. "Some of the media spun this story early on and only inflamed the situation and it was the farthest thing from the truth. 'Possession' was written about a year before *Fumbling* came out. She played it on some CBC program [that featured] just her and a piano. It was after all the Uwe packages that came flying in with an intensity that we noticed [him] to be more than any other [fan]. Previous to that he was one of many and didn't really stick out. After that he stuck out as more than just an overzealous fan."

The popular legend of the origin of "Possession" was also believed by Vandrei. He claimed his letters had been used to pen the song, and consequently set his sights on bringing McLachlan into court, as he insisted McLachlan had used lines from his letters in the lyrics. The suit was Vandrei's attempt to meet with her face to face, but it would not happen. In late December, 1994, while McLachlan was touring Europe, Vandrei was found dead in a Quebec forest — minutes away from Marchand's Wild Sky Studios.

"This one person wasn't the only guy," McLachlan told *Rolling Stone* in 1997. "Thankfully this is the only fellow who committed suicide, but there were a lot of letters from other people saying the same kind of thing. For a while there I looked over my shoulder every time I walked out the door. Writing the song 'Possession' was very therapeutic. Almost every letter I get these days, the writer says, 'I'm not one of those psycho fans.' But ever since then I haven't gotten any letters that were freaky like that, which is great, because I used to get them all the time."

Both McLachlan and Nettwerk would fall into more traps of celebrityhood when they were victims of an incredibly sloppy and indulgent unauthorized biography *Building a Mystery: The Story of Sarah McLachlan and Lilith Fair* by Judith Fitzgerald. The book, among other things, interviewed McLachlan's supposed birth mother, examined skeletons in McBride's closet regarding his firing from Cinematica Records, and spent most of its pages tracking down the life of Vandrei. Fitzgerald also inexplicably dedicates the book in part to the memory of McLachlan's stalker. With people now capitalizing on McLachlan's fame through items of such questionable merit, it was obvious she was no longer a mere singer/songwriter.

In 1995, Kevin Kane finally appeared in the public eye again. He released a solo album, *Neighbourhood Watch*, and produced the pop-wizardry of Zumpano's debut, *Look What The Rookie Did*. Between 1992 and 1997, Kane existed as a musical hermit for the most part, choosing to spend most of his time on his house, and working various jobs in amplifier and guitar factories. Occasionally, he surfaced for a low-profile solo gig. After his eviction from the house of Nettwerk, his presence in the music community was greatly reduced. "I had a few friends who would listen to me moan and complain who were really supportive," confesses Kane. "One guy — a famous old-guard musician, Paul Dean — was telling me how Streetheart kicked him out of the band. He said, 'I can't believe how heartless they were, what a bunch of bastards.' He told me this little story, and then I told him my story. He shook his head and said 'Okay, you win. You are the most fucked over guy ever in music.' Thanks, that's not the kind of prize I was looking to win."

Eventually both Kane and Tom Hooper realized that there were no prizes to win in their bitter situation. Ginger finally called it a day in 1997 after 1996's *Suddenly I Came To My Senses*, as all involved believed that the band had played out its role. In Tom Hooper's eyes, "it was no longer a band." Vincent Jones had already left the band after 1994's *Far Out* because Tom's writing didn't leave a lot of room for keyboards. He moved on to produce various records by Mystery Machine and Taste of Joy before being drafted into Sarah McLachlan's touring band in 1997 as full-time keyboardist. With the exception of some recreational drumming for Vancouver beatnik revivalist Ralph Alfonso, Chris Hooper left music to work in film and multimedia. Tom Hooper realized that something had been missing from his life since that fateful Hallowe'en of 1992. The Lennon/McCartney vibe that existed in The Grapes of Wrath never carried on during Ginger, and five years later, he was still left with an empty feeling. After $15,000 in lawyer's fees and five years of not making any inroads towards resolving issues with Kane, Tom Hooper decided it was time to begin communication.

Hooper wrote Kane a letter inviting him to meet to try to solve the quagmire of bad feelings and litigation that had built up. Says Tom Hooper, "I didn't hear anything back for three months and one day the phone rang and it was like, 'Hi Tom.' I hadn't heard his voice in five years. We talked back and forth for a few weeks and we decided that we were going to meet. We met at this restaurant and bar in Vancouver. It was weird — it didn't take long at all. It was just like the old days. We had a bunch of beer and got drunk and had a big hug. It still makes me pinch myself that we're playing together again. The bottom line is that he has a son [Severin] that is a month older than [my son] Owen. When you get feelings like that, children are more important than stupid things like this. That's the main reason I wanted to get back together. You only have one life and you can't keep up grudges like that. We have home movies together and it's just ridiculous. I couldn't watch these things after all that time."

"I guess I'm not good at holding a grudge," adds Kane. "There's always been something with Tom and I. That's where any chemistry was." The Grapes' creative figureheads mended fences and regrouped under the pretences of forming a power trio with a hired gun drummer. This time, Kane and Hooper would run the show. Over the next three years the duo would eradicate the lawsuits, mark their return with various gigs and spot tours, and finally in September, 2000, they released their phoenix album, *Field Trip*, through the Song label. The album, like their reconciliation, was a reaffirmation of their musical strengths.

Interestingly, the other two acts from Nettwerk's original roster also resurfaced by the end of the millennium. When Skinny Puppy stitched its dismembered limbs back together in 2000, it sent fans into a state of shock. After the band split, the remaining pair continued to work on their various projects. Key focused on Download, Tear Garden and Doubting Thomas, while Ogre moved onto W.E.L.T. and Rx. Though Skinny Puppy's return was unofficial and brief, no one ever expected any resurrection of the band — especially after Goettel had passed away. On August 20, 2000, the band played a one-off reunion show headlining the Orkus Doomsday Festival in Dresden, Germany. Key would admit to the press that this was the result of coaxing from their fervent fan base. At the time of the show, neither member would commit to whether the will of the fans would push the group to officially reform, but it was certainly a better way to officially close the book on the history of Skinny Puppy given the rancorous split in 1995.

Tom Ferris reactivated Moev in 1999 with wife/vocalist Julie, guitarist Drew Maxwell and original creative partner Cal Stephenson back in the fold. They released an EP, *Suffer*, on their own independent imprint. Though his acrimonious relationship with Nettwerk would not see the return of Moev to the label's roster, Ferris still can't help looking back on how the groundbreaking label that had provided his band with a home changed as drastically as it did. "I really like the time when we first started Nettwerk off," reminisces Ferris. "I thought that was a really good show. People in Canada were basically snubbing us and weren't giving us the time of day and [we thought] that we could do it. After things got rolling it got stale and predictable. That's were it ended up now with Nettwerk. I don't think they're progressing; they're regressing. It's just like a major label — getting anything commercial."

The success of Sarah McLachlan's *Surfacing* in 1997 can be looked at as a major catalyst in Nettwerk's gradual shift toward working with more economically viable artists than artistically notable ones. *Surfacing* would essentially set McLachlan and the label up for life by selling over 10 million copies worldwide, an amazing accomplishment for any major-label artist, never mind one on an independent label. The record's success was a sign of the phenomenon that surrounded McLachlan rather than a result of the album itself justifying the massive sales figures. Unlike *Solace* or *Fumbling*, it is simply a well-produced, pleasant album of ballads and mid-tempo pop similar to that of the company McLachlan was now keeping on tour. Coupled with the release of *Surfacing* in 1997, Lilith Fair banded together the collective efforts of Sarah McLachlan and a mix of women in music — pulled for the most part from similar artistic ground — including Sheryl Crow, Natalie Merchant, Jewel, Indigo Girls and Erykah Badu, and it would make the artist and label wealthy. The media would jump all over this "little sister" touring festival that trumped Lollapalooza's male-dominated line-ups. Lilith Fair would be regarded as the vehicle that brought new awareness to female artists, but also narrowed the scope of how the term "women in music" was perceived. Over its three-year run, Lilith Fair spawned numerous CD and video compilation spin-offs, extensive published documentation, and a whopping $65 million in revenues for Nettwerk and McLachlan. Still, this was an impressive feat to the music industry because, in 1995, concert promoters had grimaced at the thought of a full female bill when McLachlan took neophyte Paula Cole as a touring partner.

Despite McLachlan's behemoth success — and despite being a recipient of the Order of Canada, along with numerous Grammy and Juno Awards — she has remained with Nettwerk for 12 years based on her undying loyalty to the label. Says McLachlan, "I love their integrity and I love the people within the company. I really believe they do things for the right reasons and they gave me a huge opportunity. They've really let me discover my musical identity without trying to force me into any particular musical direction and continue to do so — which gets harder when you have the huge pressures of 'We want her to have an even bigger record than the last time.'"

To the label's present fans most of the old names in this chapter are nothing but historical footnotes. The name 'Nettwerk' is essentially regarded as the home for a singular talent, not as an artistic community. Though change occurs — and Nettwerk can't be blamed for supporting McLachlan's rise, or reaping the benefits of their hard work — it's a shame the label had to trade its original mandate for a major label tunnel vision. Says Greg

Clow, "Even with the eclectic nature of their catalogue early on, there still seemed to be a unique Nettwerk 'identity,' and a feeling that there was a real love for the music they were releasing. But that feeling has been gone for quite some time. After the rise of the cult of Sarah, the imprint lost pretty much everything that made it unique and is just another medium-sized record label."

Nettwerk's metamorphosis may not have kept every hardcore fan they initially drew from underground sects around the world, but they remain an unparalleled Canadian success story. In the eyes of Terry McBride, it's because of this success that Nettwerk continues to exist at all.

"This is the way I look at it," he says. "Probably one per cent of the records released account for 25 per cent of the overall sales. The bottom line is: if we do not have successful artists, I don't have the funds to finance the other ones. The success of Skinny Puppy allowed us to have money to work with Sarah. The success of The Grapes of Wrath allowed us to work with Lava Hay. Those bands didn't make the other bands. If we hadn't put our money into that band, then maybe we wouldn't have put it in another band later. I don't think The Grapes of Wrath can look at being instrumental in Sarah's career. Maybe as a part of 1200 different people who have touched her career, they have definitely helped. Anyone who has made it in this business and who has longevity knows how much it takes within that person to actually pull it off. Sarah sacrificed basically 12 years of her life. Only now is she getting to be a normal person. She's sacrificed more than I think anyone really understands.

"If we hadn't put out Skinny Puppy records no one else would have. If we hadn't put out Grapes of Wrath records, no one else would have. Sure, two or three albums later people would have, but they sure wouldn't have put out those early records. Sarah — the exact same thing. If there's one thing that we gave from day one it was artistic and creative freedom. That's what you get when you sign to an independent."

"They're great songwriters with undeniable
songs. In 1988, here was a band that's
unpretentious, doesn't dress up, and
probably played with three lights over
their heads. In Canadian music, that was a
turning point back to what's real, what has
longevity — what's going to make people think
in five years that these songs still have relevance to their everyday life."
— Colin Cripps

Trust Yourself:
Blue Rodeo

The 1988 Juno Awards marked a watershed for Blue Rodeo. The notoriously conservative and industry-driven institution bestowed the band with
honours for Group of the Year, as well as single and video awards for the
ballad "Try." Three years earlier, "Try" was one of four songs on a demo
tape that was rejected by the same A&R rep who would later sign them;
the tape featured two other songs that would be singles from Blue Rodeo's
multi-platinum 1987 debut *Outskirts*. Blue Rodeo had assumed that their
hybrid of psychedelic-tinged country rock would never break through to
the mainstream. On this night, they had received the first of many affir-
mations that would grant their career a longevity that previously didn't
seem feasible in the Canadian music industry.

"From the outset we knew that we were at the beginning of something
different in Canada, which was the beginning of a real domestic scene,"
says Jim Cuddy. "That domestic scene was not defined by how well that
music travelled, but only by how much it represented people within the
confines of the country. We understood that at the '88 Junos. All the bands
that played that night all had double platinum records and they were all
Canadian. It was apparent that a change in Canadian music had happened."

That year's awards ceremony would name Robbie Robertson Male Vocalist of the Year and his debut solo work the Album of the Year; his alma mater The Band were also being inducted into the Juno Hall of Fame. The Band was a frequent point of comparison when critics tried to describe *Outskirts*, and although Blue Rodeo's creative core of Greg Keelor and Jim Cuddy dominated the group's output, Blue Rodeo boasted a group of individual characters not unlike The Band: keyboardist Bob Wiseman's wildly inventive work sounded like a hallucinogenic Garth Hudson; Bazil Donovan's melodic and soulful bass work recalled that of Rick Danko's; and versatile drummer Cleave Anderson anchored the band with a deceptively simple style in the style of Levon Helm.

The Juno organizers had decided it would be a great idea if The Band and Blue Rodeo performed together on the televised program. Jim Cuddy recalls the first meeting between the underdog newcomers and the legendary group of musicians who launched the notion of CanRock in the first place. "We got set up in the room at the CBC for rehearsal, and in walked Robbie, Rick Danko, and some guy who looked like a piano tuner but was actually Garth Hudson," says Cuddy. "The first thing Robbie said was, 'There's too many people here. We only need a bass player and a drummer.' We thought wow, in typical fashion, this hasn't even been okayed with this guy.

Blue Rodeo at 1988 Junos with Robbie Robertson: Bazil Donovan, Cleave Anderson, Robertson, Greg Keelor, Jim Cuddy
(Courtesy of Jim Cuddy)

He didn't want to do it, and we knew the song better than they did; we'd learned 'The Weight' backwards and forwards. Maybe they hadn't played together in a long time, but they didn't really know the harmonies anymore. The guy who put it all together was Rick Danko. He was the nicest, friendliest guy, who was so open to anything. He'd say, 'Yeah, two bass players!' He was completely into it and broke the ice, because there was a lot of ice formed by that reception. We had lots of meetings with Rick over the years. He was really a gregarious, open soul you liked the moment you met."

During the remainder of their career, Blue Rodeo would have more in common with the amiable Danko than the aloof Robertson. Blue Rodeo was the hard-working, low-key Canadian band that created great art in pop songs and played every small town in Canada in the process. That Juno night in 1988 after their performance with The Band, the normally cynical Greg Keelor was caught gushing on MuchMusic: "Robbie played my guitar!" Cuddy, always keeping his creative partner in check, turned to the camera and said, "Isn't rock-'n'-roll pathetic?"

Greg Keelor was raised on a steady diet of music and hockey in the "suburban paradise" of Mount Royal, Montreal in the late '60s, where two of his hockey pals were John and Michael Timmins, later of the Cowboy Junkies. Keelor finished high school in Toronto, where he met Jim Cuddy at North Toronto Collegiate in 1971. "We weren't the greatest of friends in high school, but we hung out in the same crowd," says Keelor. Neither one of them played music in public. After graduation, Cuddy and two friends had renovated a school bus as a mobile home and planned to discover western Canada. When one of the friends dropped out, Keelor took the seat and the bond between the two began. The bus broke down in Moosomin, Saskatchewan, and the high school buddies headed to Alberta to earn money and wait for its repair; Keelor went to Lake Louise, and Cuddy went to Banff, where he met another Ontarian named Robin Masyk, who would later move to Toronto and call himself Handsome Ned.

Independently, both Keelor and Cuddy nurtured their musical muses in the Rockies. Cuddy started playing guitar in coffeehouses, while Keelor learned how to play guitar from songbooks of Gordon Lightfoot and the Everly Brothers. Cuddy also shared an affinity for Lightfoot; the first song he learned how to play, at age 10, was the Canadian folk legend's "That's What You Get For Loving Me." Cuddy had been passionate about music ever since, but wasn't sure it would be a large part of his future. "A lot of the struggle for me when I was younger was accepting that I wanted to define myself as an artist and a musician," he says. "There were no artists in my family. Music was a hobby, and that way of life was temporary. Committing yourself to being an artist is in one way a vow of poverty. So until I found some reasonable job that I could do while still doing music, I was very conflicted about doing it."

In 1975, Cuddy returned to Ontario to attend Queen's University in Kingston, and when he landed in Toronto in 1978, he and Keelor formed the Hi-Fi's with bassist Malcolm Schell and drummer Jimmy Sublett. Michael Timmins recalls, "They were a power pop band, very influenced by the Beatles and The Jam. They were a really good band, really exciting — very high energy."

Keelor says, "What we sounded like and who I think we sounded like are two totally different things. But in terms of our major influence, it was The Clash. They were the band who survived the whole punk thing; they were the band with the integrity and the sound. Locally, it would be bands like the Secrets or the Demics. I used to love the Mods, but they couldn't really play, although they had the greatest drummer in the world."

For Keelor, the Hi-Fi's goals were modest. "We made an independent single ["I Don't Know Why (You Love Me)" on their manager's Showtime label]. We just wanted to make a record and hang out and live the musician lifestyle," he says. "We did a weekend gig in Kitchener at this big rock place. Goddo had been there on the weekend. Then we came in to play Monday, Tuesday, and Wednesday, and the owner said, 'Goddo just filled this place!' We had 40 people in this bar that held 1,200 people. Our manager came to one of those shows, and we had a really bad night that night. His line was, 'The phones aren't ringing off the wall for you guys.'"

The band was approached by Ready Records, an independent Toronto label that was home to Blue Peter, Santers and The Spoons, although at that time the Hi-Fi's were experiencing hometown bringdown. "By '81 the scene — punk, post-punk, new wave — was evaporating, or at least as far as we could see," says Keelor. "There was no place to play, and it didn't seem that record companies were going to sign bands like that."

The Hi-Fi's disbanded after the Ready deal fell through, and Keelor and Cuddy packed up for New York City. Cuddy's brother lived near Washington Square and his girlfriend and future wife, Rena Polley, had been accepted to theatre school there. "Going to New York was such a conscious choice, of getting out of Toronto and getting away from personal history," says Cuddy. "Like many other places in the world, New York is a place where there's so much encouragement to turn your inclination into expression —

whether you're an actor, painter, sculptor, street artist, anything."

While down there, they hooked up with Michael Timmins and Alan Anton, who had also moved there with Hunger Project. "They were over in Alphabet Town, because the rent was so cheap. You could get a big apartment in those days for three hundred bucks," Keelor recalls. "[New York] was very intimidating then. It felt like a war zone; it looked like Beirut.

Fly to France in New York City
(Courtesy of Jim Cuddy)

You'd look down the road in the winter, and on every block there'd be a barrel with a fire burning in it and all these street people standing around collecting scraps of wood to burn to keep warm. The first day [Timmins and Anton] went out, they hadn't put bars up on the windows; they locked it up and they came back and the blaster [radio] had been stolen, so they realized they had to make their place a little more secure. They cut a hole in the floor which led to this little bunker that we both rehearsed in."

"We learned a lot of musical stuff from [Hunger Project]," says Cuddy, "because they used to jam a lot and we didn't. We were pretty pop-oriented at that point. When we would jam with Hunger Project, we'd do these long, mesmerizing jams and learn things about that. New York was the most extreme part of our learning curve. The good part of it was that we didn't know what kind of band we were. It was a pretty confused musical scene at that point too, between 1981 and 84, unless you were into the New Romantic stuff, which we certainly weren't. You could do rock, ska, pop, anything. We weren't very good at any of them, but we learned a lot."

Keelor and Cuddy dubbed their new project Fly To France, which Cuddy admits "was a truly stupid name," as was its successor, Red Yellow Blue. The revolving line-up was rounded out by musicians they found through a *Village Voice* ad; Keelor and Cuddy eventually hooked up with a New Zealand band, The Drongoes, and recorded four new songs — "Try," "Floating," "Outskirts" and "Rose-Coloured Glasses" — to shop around to labels. The songs were greeted by a round of rejection, including one from Warner Canada's A&R manager Bob Roper which read: "I felt that the songs were well crafted and presented in a pop vein that was too soft for our current direction. At the present time, I am only developing much harder-edged rock artists who are currently touring live on a national basis."

While in New York, the band met Howard Wiseman, a Canadian expatriate who helped them out with management. Wiseman introduced his younger brother Bobby to Keelor, whom he befriended. Bob Wiseman had studied avant-garde piano under Casey Sokol at York University, and his manic jazz-inflected keyboard work would be too much for Keelor and Cuddy to ignore. "Bobby and I were hanging out and started talking," Keelor says. "He said, 'Yeah, I play music too.' The first tune I remember playing with him was 'Rose Coloured Glasses.' He was playing piano and I was playing acoustic guitar and singing. He was playing along to the chords, and I'd only ever played with conventional rock-'n'-roll keyboards at this point. Then we got to the solo point and he just started being Bobby. It was like, 'Fuck, this is fantastic!' I'd heard music like that, but I'd never played with anybody like that. We'd start playing in the afternoons, and then Jim would come over and we'd rehearse songs together with Bobby. It was very exciting to play with somebody who had that musical capability, being way out there but still connected. And taking a song from one place to another in eight bars, then bringing it back in."

Overall, New York City didn't seem to be treating the pair much differently than Toronto had. "It's a tough city to live in if you don't have any money," says Michael Timmins. "It's fun, but it's tough. They had a tough time, because while we were there they never really formed a band. They did a lot of writing, and just did a lot of living, basically. They absorbed the city and I know they wrote a lot of songs. I don't think there was much structure or stability to it."

By 1984, Keelor was becoming disenchanted with New York. "While I was there I thought for sure I'd be there for life, but I wasn't sure whether I'd be a musician or just an alcoholic waiter," he says. "By the end of it, the life I had created for myself didn't seem that pleasant. It felt like a skin that I could shed. On the Fourth of July, a friend of mine had a bag full of mushrooms and I ate the whole thing. I had been reading a Carlos Casteneda book at the time, too, so my head was geared towards that psychedelic magic, and New York was not a fun place for me to be in that state of mind. Everyone was drunk on the street, with all these rooftop fireworks displays. It was definitely a nightmarish trip. New York felt like the crack in the earth where hell had spilt onto the surface. By the end of that, I really wanted to get out. I hadn't been thinking too much about Canada; I was quite happy to be [in New York], but it was that day I realized I wanted to be [in Canada]."

"Greg was done," says Cuddy. "For him it was all Sodom and Gomorrah down there. My wife was finished acting school and wanted to come back, so I came back kicking and screaming. I wept when we left. I thought we were making the biggest mistake of our lives. New York represented this unbounded imagination, this incredible unstructured pursuit. Toronto represented everything that was uptight. I felt like we were giving up. When we came back, Greg became 'Mr. CBC Farm Report boy,' driving around just happy to be living the slower life and saying how much he loved it. I thought, this is a fucking nightmare! We came from New York, where you'd step into the street not knowing what challenging situation you were going to encounter, to this dull, low-rise city. Ultimately, I was very wrong. Within a very short period of time, we had a band together that was a way better band than we'd ever had before."

Upon arriving home to Toronto in the spring of 1984, Keelor and Cuddy placed an ad in the Toronto weekly *Now*, looking for a rhythm section. It read: "If you've dropped acid at least 20 times, lost three or four years to booze and looking good, and can still manage to keep time, call Jim or Greg." Bassist Bazil Donovan, who was playing in the reggae band Strike One and the punk band Scab, decided to answer the ad. By that time they had already hired drummer Cleave Anderson, who had played in the Battered Wives and had a brief stint with Handsome Ned; he also played in The Sharks with Bazil Donovan, guitarist David Baxter and singer Sherry Kean. "When we were the Hi-Fi's between '78 and '81, The Sharks were a big band," says Cuddy. "But we didn't have any fraternity with them. They were a popular band and being courted by record companies. We were just a band that did Cabana Room gigs and nothing else."

On Anderson's recommendation, Donovan got the Blue Rodeo gig without an audition. "I walked into the rehearsal space," says Donovan, "which also doubled as Greg's apartment, and we started right in working on 'Rose Coloured Glasses.' There was no audition, no meeting or anything." The first line-up of Blue Rodeo was born.

"When we came back from New York, I thought we were playing with more edge," says Keelor. "After witnessing all the bands we were going to see down there and the records we were listening to, we were singing with a bit more conviction and writing songs that meant something to us. When Jim and I first started writing songs together, we weren't really writing songs, just putting pieces together. I'd steal a few pieces from something, he'd steal a few pieces from something, and then we'd put them together in a song. By the end of the stay in New York, we were still writing together a bit, but we'd gone through the process of writing our own songs and enjoying the process of finding our voices."

The new songs moved away from the sound of the Hi-Fi's or Fly To France and displayed more of a country influence, without ever being explicit about it. Keelor had a recent conversion to Patsy Cline, as well as Elvis Costello's *Almost Blue*, which partially inspired the new band's name. In 1988, the name got them dropped from an American tour with the BoDeans because of its country associations, which the BoDeans' management thought was a kiss of death.

"There was a time in my life when I was into the hippie country thing," says Keelor, citing Jerry Jeff Walker, Bob Dylan's country albums, John Prine and Willie P. Bennett. "But when I first started playing music, I discarded all of that stuff. I wasn't a very good guitar player; I relied on volume and energy, and country music didn't fit into it. But when Costello did that record, it showed that it does fit. There were a couple of books that came into my life around that time, too: *The Unsung Heroes of Rock'n'Roll* by Nick Tosches and *Lost Highway* by Peter Guralnick. It all justified that whatever I thought the punk thing was, country worked really well in that context; it was actually the granddaddy of them all.

"Leaning towards a more traditional country thing was sort of exciting," he continues. "Plus, our playing was getting better. I was always so loud that doing anything traditional was impossible. I played rhythm guitar louder than a traditional player would play lead. By our natural musical inclinations, we couldn't do that sort of music until we'd matured a bit."

"What we understood as country-rock," says Cuddy, "was formed by either rock musicians of the '60s discovering country and getting so tripped out by the beauty of it and the sound of wide-open spaces, or '50s Sun recording guys who were hepped up on amphetamines and playing stuff so fast and driven and intense that it no longer resembled country music. Either form left the origins of country music so far behind that we never considered doing a straight country song. We used to do a cover of [George Jones's] 'Good Year for the Roses,' which we would do fairly straight, but with electric guitars. We never even played an acoustic guitar on stage until our third record."

Blue Rodeo's first gig was at the Rivoli on February 12, 1985; their second was opening for Handsome Ned at the Horseshoe on Valentine's Day. Right away, Keelor and Cuddy realized that Handsome Ned had been sowing the seeds for a band like Blue Rodeo to come along. "There was all this encouragement to play and there was an already-realized scene," says Cuddy. "When we were in New York, as fun and as inspiring as it may have been to write songs, we rarely got gigs. It was really tough to get people together to rehearse. Up here, as soon as we started getting gigs, we could play five nights a week, playing original music. We were very fortunate to come back when we did, because of Handsome Ned and because he had carved out a style, this *Lost Highway* '50s-inspired rock/country music. Everybody was coming out of the woodwork, like [the Handsome Neds'] Steve Koch, who had been in punk bands, got sick of it, and had retired to work in Xerox shops. That was the first time we had ever been associated with a scene that we felt we were a vital part of. It was so easy from then on. You didn't have to make much money to live in Toronto, and you could spend most of your time playing. We could never do that in New York."

Their decision to finally leave New York City behind was confirmed by Blue Rodeo's third gig. "When we first got to New York," says Cuddy, "we sent a tape around and got one call back from someone who said they would put it out. It never happened, and not another thing happened until we left. The day before we left we delivered a Blue Rodeo tape around, and we got a call back when we were back in Toronto. They said, 'When are you playing New York?' We said, 'We just moved! We lived there for three and a half years!'

"We did one gig on the 15th of February, 1985 at CBGB's, and it was nightmarish — a five-band night with everybody fighting about when they were supposed to go on. Our slot got changed, and the guy who was supposed to come see us never came," Cuddy continues. "We thought, 'Fuck this, this is a waste of time.' If we never get a record contract, at least in Toronto we could play music. We could play all the time. Handsome Ned was the one guy who kept the fire burning about record companies. He had a bit of a Don Quixote-ish dream. We'd say, 'Ned, no one is ever going to sign us. Look at the kind of music we play and turn on the radio — do you hear anything like it?' Only by virtue of the crowds did that change. For whatever reason — you can postulate whether people were just sick of artificial music or whether it was just such a fun live scene — people were really enjoying the music, and there wasn't a saturation point on Queen Street. You could fill every club on a Saturday night, and then they opened the Holiday [The Big Bop], which was another 500-capacity place, and that would be filled every night."

Blue Rodeo's sound was very much a hybrid, with Wiseman's dissonant and experimental keyboard solos making the band uncategorizable, subverting their traditional pop songwriting and adding psychedelic overtones not heard in alt-country before or since. "The band was dominated by a keyboard player who was all over the place," assesses Keelor. "There were some nights where he would play sort of straight, some nights he'd be out there, and some nights he'd be way out there.

"You had a bass player who came from a prog rock school who played country music all the time, because that's how he made his living. Bazil played in hardcore country bands since being a teenager — where you'd show up at the gig that night, no one had met each other before, and the lead singer would just call out the numbers. He'd play all over Ontario: a week in Kapuskasing, a week in Blind River. But he came from prog rock — that was his love.

"And then there's Cleave, who was the first punk I ever saw. I went to a show at the El Mocambo, and I saw him with this group of guys who were all drunk and pushing each other and throwing beer on each other. It was like a clip from a British movie, and I thought, 'Ah, that's punk! They're small — punks are short!'

"Then Jim and I, who were poppy singer/songwriter type guys, very Beatle-influenced. Jim and I were discovering the way we would sing together; we were starting to hear the buzz in our voices and enjoying that. It's funny, when I listen to the opening lyric of 'Outskirts,' I can hear this fake twang in my voice.

"All of that made for a pretty interesting match. I'm sure there are people who went to see Blue Rodeo who thought it would be — well, more like it is today. That's the band they expected and wanted to see. Back then, they didn't get much chance to rest. Bobby was either taking you into dreamland or assaulting you somehow."

Such was Blue Rodeo's early eclecticism that one of their songs paid a musical tribute to local psychedelic goth band A Neon Rome. "They were my favourite band for a while," says Keelor. "There was one song we used to play a fair amount called 'Railway Crash' that was our A Neon Rome epic, with time-signature changes and dramatic changes and scraping. It was an incest/murder/drugs sort of song. The original [Blue Rodeo line-up] would try anything. Bobby could be pretty chaotic; the rest of us maybe weren't capable of that chaos, but we tried our best. 'Railway Crash' was sometimes a pretty impressive performance. We even opened with it when we wanted to make an impression."

In 1986, they were approached by Bob Roper of Warner Canada, who had seen the band several times after his initial rejection letter and grew to be convinced of their commercial potential. At a rather unglamorous gig at Nag's Head North in the suburb of Markham, Ontario, Roper offered them a record deal. They recorded *Outskirts* with producer Terry Brown, best known for his work with Rush, and who was a partner in the subsidiary Risque Disque label with the band's manager, John Caton. Keelor remembers Brown as "a bit of a tyrant. He didn't seem that way; he was very mild-mannered. His sounds were quite different than what I expected our record to be. There are mixes that I liked so much better, with more guitar. But it was our first record, so we lost sight of it a bit."

Although the band may have felt that their rougher edges were smoothed out, *Outskirts* did sound remarkably different from any other pop album or "new roots" artist of the day. The first thing heard is Cuddy and Keelor harmonizing the lyric "Don't you know that we're out of touch." Wiseman was granted two solo showcases: a prolonged Thelonious Monk-ish piano introduction to the six-and-a-half-minute "Piranha Pool," and two long Acetone organ solos in the seven-and-a-half-minute "Floating." Keelor's lyrics display a Costello-esque verbosity rich with vivid and cinematic images, critiquing cults of celebrity and militaristic materialism. Donovan and Anderson are an impeccable and melodic rhythm section, capable of slipping into rockabilly, reggae, jazz, and soul, even in straightforward pop songs; their touch in "Try" has more in common with an Otis Redding ballad than any of Cuddy's later country heartbreakers.

One of the album's key songs was Cuddy's "Underground," written with the death of Handsome Ned in mind. "Handsome Ned died a week before we started making *Outskirts*," says Cuddy, claiming that he was shocked and ignorant of how pervasive heroin was on Queen Street at the time of Ned's overdose. "It was definitely an end to the scene as we had known it.

It certainly wasn't innocent anymore, and the stakes were higher because some people got a contract and others broke up — but certain things had been determined that for the longest time had been so gloriously *unde*-termined. Ned wasn't the only one; there were a few other deaths at the time of people who were fixtures on the scene. It cast a pallor over the whole happy scene, that some of us should have known was there all along.

"It was a cruel irony that we got a record contract and started to make this record, when [Ned] was the one that really wanted it," Cuddy continues. "We didn't really want [a deal] when we started; we thought it was more trouble than it was worth. He wanted it so badly and he was such a defining part of the scene that nurtured us. 'Underground' was about the disappearance of all these people who had been so key to us. I felt ungrateful. I felt that we shouldn't be doing this and that it didn't seem right, like we'd cut some people adrift."

The album garnered good reviews but minimal airplay for the first — and rather unlikely — single, the title track: a Keelor song about Robert Kennedy's son David, who committed suicide in a Florida hotel, surrounded by photos of his doomed father. The band's first big splash was opening a national theatre tour for k.d. lang, who had just released her major label debut, *Angel With a Lariat*, and who didn't say a word to Blue Rodeo for the entire tour, though Keelor still found the experience inspiring. "That seemed like a big change in Canadian music to me," says Keelor. "To me,

Blue Rodeo on the set of "Outskirts" video: Jim Cuddy,
Bazil Donovan, Cleave Anderson, Greg Keelor, Bob Wiseman
(Courtesy of Jim Cuddy)

that tour was very encouraging, just to see that you can do it, that she could go from Albert's Hall to Massey Hall."

Through Cuddy's connections in Toronto's film community — where he had a day job in a props department — Blue Rodeo was able to call in some favours to shoot a video for the second single, "Try." Directed by Michael Buckley, who would frequently collaborate with the band throughout their career, the video was shot on the cheap by the company Cuddy worked for. "They took an interest in the band and were incredibly generous," says Cuddy. "It was shot on 35mm, edited by some of the best guys in the business, and shot with full crews. We had horseshoes up our ass."

"Try" eventually became their breakthrough hit, a prom-night staple, and a fan favourite — not to mention that it established Cuddy's reputation as a heartthrob crooner, adding some sex appeal to the band. However, "Try" was also ignored by radio, at least until MuchMusic took a liking to it. Keelor explains, "[MuchMusic Programming Director] John Martin says he liked the song, hated the video. But because he liked the song, he played the shit out of the video, made it a popular song, and then radio picked it up and it became a popular single." The single was certified gold in the same month as the album, in January 1988, six months after *Outskirts'* release.

Even before *Outskirts* was released, it was apparent to the band that "Try" was a special song. "We'd play it twice in a night," says Cuddy, "because we were usually doing three sets and people would always ask us to play it again. We were very aware that the song had a strange effect on people for some reason." Cuddy says the reason "Try" wasn't their first single boils down to one reason. "Because Greg's a bully — it's simple," he laughs. "But we didn't want to lead with a ballad; we didn't think of ourselves as a ballad band. That was a big reckoning for us when we got known for a ballad. Certain people would come and think, 'Oooh, what's the rest of this shit? What's that keyboard player doing?' We had a year of really confusing people just because they heard 'Try,' or because of our name they wanted to see a country band. People felt they'd been tricked."

As the band's popularity rose, they would select their gigs carefully, often flying out west or east for three shows in a weekend, because everyone in the band wanted to maintain their day jobs, which they did until after the release of their second album. "We hung on to them much longer than we needed to, because it was a good life," Cuddy admits. "It took away any of the decisions that had to be made about making money. We never had to take a gig for money, because we all had jobs. We just took things that were good for us, that we liked, that we wanted to do because they were musically exciting. That was very beneficial; we never got a jaundiced view of what we were doing."

For Keelor in particular, it was a very prolific time for writing. "I was always writing," he says. "I was a waiter at an Italian restaurant, and my pay slips — that you balance out at the end of the day — would have tons of lyrics written on the back of them, that I would write when I was waiting for table 15 to come up. Waitering was not bad for songwriting, because there's a certain amount of frustration and anger in being a waiter."

Musically, Keelor was also writing with his girlfriend, Michelle McAdorey; together, they named their new project Crash Vegas, with bassist Jocelyne Lanois and drummer Ambrose Pottie. "She had notebooks and notebooks of lyrics," Keelor recalls of McAdorey. "She had such a strong idea of where she wanted to be melodically. That used to be a lot of fun writing those songs."

McAdorey's first post–Crash Vegas solo album, 1999's *Whirl*, featured melodically abstract compositions, which relied more on atmosphere than structure, which Keelor says she was interested in even back then. "It's probably where she wanted to be," he says, admitting that they heavily influenced each other's approach to music. "I, as a structured songwriter, would have tried to keep her out of that. But she also pulled me in that direction. I always appreciated having somebody like Bobby and Michelle around, and listening to the records they played, pulling me in a certain way. It helped me musically."

Jocelyne Lanois was going out with Malcolm Burn, a protégé of her producer brother Daniel, and Crash Vegas would develop their recordings at Burn's eight-track studio in Hamilton. It was then that guitarist Colin Cripps became more heavily involved, when it became clear that Keelor's Blue Rodeo commitments were beginning to accumulate. For a while at least, both Keelor and Cripps were in Crash Vegas. The band's first show was at the Cameron House in Toronto; their second was opening for Blue Rodeo at the Diamond.

Keelor was impressed with Burn's approach to recording and Blue Rodeo hired him to record their second album, *Diamond Mine*, in December, 1988. They set up shop in an abandoned theatre — the Donlands, in Toronto's east end — chosen for its roomy acoustics, due largely to the 100-foot ceiling. They were inspired partially by the Cowboy Junkies' *Trinity Session*, as well as the Lanois approach of creating a conducive recording environment, instead of settling for a concrete bunker. Cuddy, who had sung lead on only three of *Outskirts*' 10 tracks, beefed up his contributions to six out of *Diamond Mine*'s 13 tracks. Together, Keelor and Cuddy were at their peak as songwriters. They were at a critical juncture where every song is a crafted gem, just before the inevitable stage where it becomes easier for an artist to fall back on clichés and past tricks. Keelor displayed the first sign of his fondness for dead quiet material on the closing track, "Ballad of the Dime Store Greaser and the Blonde Mona Lisa."

Anderson and Donovan once again made a world of difference to the arrangements, and Anderson in particular became more of a driving force on songs such as "God and Country" and "Love and Understanding" — the latter an obvious nod by Keelor to Nick Lowe's "(What's So Funny About) Peace, Love and Understanding." Wiseman was unleashed on two songs: a jarring, gurgling organ solo on "Fuse" and an extended tour-de-force during the mid-section of the title track, which appeared to be a nod to the psychedelic section of Led Zeppelin's "Whole Lotta Love." It was edited out of the eight-minute song for the radio single, but it was often the highlight of the band's live shows during Wiseman's tenure in the band, a challenge that would split audiences between the enraptured and the bored or annoyed.

"If I had to choose one, *Diamond Mine* would be my favourite record," says Cuddy. "I've often listened to our catalogue of records, and each one record represents a certain phase and has its own charm, but *Diamond Mine* is the least manipulative record. It's the most honest expression of musical interest. When I listen to it, I don't feel pushed in one direction or the other."

Critical response to the album was gushing. Toronto's *Metropolis* magazine wrote, "Call it Western Pop, New Country or anything else you like, but nobody, not Dwight [Yoakam], or Steve [Earle], or Lyle [Lovett] does anything as complicated or as interesting. . . . *Diamond Mine* is nothing short of a triumph of songwriting and a victory over complacency."

While the band was mixing the album at Lanois's new studio in New Orleans, Cleave Anderson announced that he would soon have to leave the band. When the news was announced to the press, much of the surprised reaction centred on the fact that Anderson was leaving Blue Rodeo so that he could hang onto his work as a postal carrier, but it wasn't a shock to the band. "In one of the first conversations we had with him about playing in our band, he said, 'I can only go so far,'" says Keelor. "It's a lifestyle. He likes being at home with the kids, and he quite enjoys his mail route."

"When Cleave left, a lot of the fun went out of it for Bobby," says Cuddy. "Cleave was the glue of that [incarnation of the] band. He was a taste arbiter, and the mediator between the poles that would inevitably be established on certain issues: between Greg and me, or between us and Bobby.

Drummers are key in bands; they have to be the driver of the band and Cleave was. Stylistically, he was very important for all the different music we did. He determined how closely to the original [form] we would go. His was a choice; ours was by virtue of our talent or lack of it."

Anderson was replaced by Mark French, who ably imitated Anderson's drum style, but whose two-year contribution to the evolution of Blue Rodeo was like that of George Lazenby to the James Bond series.

The *Diamond Mine* tour, with a loaded bill including the Skydiggers, Jack DeKeyzer and the Razorbacks as opening acts, found the band playing theatres for the first time. Hushed songs like "Dime Store Greaser" were no longer "mass exits to the bathroom," in Keelor's view. But they still found themselves playing less-than-inspiring shows, mostly in America, and one such occasion spawned the song "What Am I Doing Here?"

"That song is about an infamous gig we did at the Erie County Fair just outside Buffalo," says Keelor. "We'd been on the road far too long, and we were playing on a dirt racetrack, last on the bill after seven high-school groups in a battle-of-the-bands contest. By then there was hardly anyone left — maybe 200 high-school students who were more interested in drinking and throwing up than they were in watching us. I looked around at the rest of the band and every one of them was just playing away, staring at the Ferris wheel going around and around, and it sure seemed like a good metaphor for us; a circle going nowhere!"

During the *Diamond Mine* tour in early 1989, the band hit another setback when their manager, John Caton, made an abrupt decision. "John developed a heart condition that seemed to parallel his financial problems, and he got out of the business in one afternoon," Keelor recalls. "It was some big deal he was trying to put together for everything. Jim and I were with him at the time. He got this phone call, hung up the phone, and said, 'I'm out of the business.'" This meant the end of Risque Disque, whose only other significant act was Crash Vegas. Because of Blue Rodeo's success, their deal with Warner remained intact.

With the help of their new American manager Danny Goldberg, a powerful industry player who would later manage Nirvana and run Atlantic Records, the focus shifted to breaking into the U.S. market for the new record, *Casino*. Blue Rodeo had made some inroads there when they were hired as the on-screen band backing up Meryl Streep (at her request) in the film *Postcards From the Edge*, and the American wing of Warner was interested in developing them. They turned to producer Pete Anderson, who was popular on the "new roots" scene for moulding the careers of Dwight

Yoakam and Michelle Shocked. Although each artist had distinct differences, Anderson used the same studio musicians for both, further insisting that each of their records had 10 songs and was no longer than 35 minutes. He told Blue Rodeo that he liked some material from *Diamond Mine*, but couldn't sit through the whole hour-long album.

Keelor downplays the notion that their work with Pete Anderson was a concession to the American market: "We had a pretty good collection of songs, and we were in the frame of mind to work with a producer. Part of working with a producer is that you gotta trust them. You respect the work they've done up to that point and you think it will help you in this collection of songs. We did a lot of rearrangements of the arrangements we already had, and editing, paring them down. Some were good and some were bad."

There's nothing wrong with the material that ended up on *Casino* — it's Blue Rodeo's purest pop moment, recorded on equipment tailor-made to make it sound good on '70s AM radio, and the economical arrangements mean there isn't a wasted note. If *Diamond Mine* was the sound of expansiveness, *Casino* was the sound of compression, both sonically and materially. And although Cuddy scored the album's two big singles ("'Til I Am Myself Again," "Trust Yourself"), he and Keelor drew upon their harmonies together to propel songs like the two-step "What Am I Doing Here," the Beatle-esque "Two Tongues" and the blistering "Time." The latter is the only place Wiseman is unleashed, attacking a 22-bar solo with everything he has, because that's all he was getting. In some cases, he and the rhythm section got even less — "After the Rain" was recorded with Anderson's staple studio musicians.

"Bobby was completely lost on that record," admits Cuddy. "He wasn't utilized at all. I think he was terminally disappointed at that point anyway. Bobby didn't really speak for the last couple of years in the band. He was over it and was trying to plan an escape. I don't really remember his participation in *Casino* very much."

Keelor and Cuddy realized that in sanding off their edges, they had compromised what made the band special. And because *Casino* sold as well as their first two albums without making a significant dent in America, the editing process didn't appear to make them any more successful than they already were. Consequently, every Blue Rodeo album after *Casino* was self-produced. "The last record where we were told what to do was with Pete Anderson," says Cuddy. "It became apparent to us that we had way too much that we wanted to accomplish with our music to allow ourselves to be told what to do. What we ended up with was what Pete wanted out of the record, but it wasn't what we wanted out of the record."

That said, the band did briefly consider working with Pete Anderson again. "It got to the point where he was going so studio crazy weird," says Keelor. "For what would have been *Lost Together*, we had talked about doing it with him. He came up for a visit and heard the demos and was talking about drum machines. We thought, 'What happened to you?'"

Pete Anderson wasn't the only part of the American plan that wasn't working. Despite their new management, the only American touring they did was opening for Edie Brickell and the New Bohemians, who were promoting their less successful second album; they also toured Germany with Brickell. She hit it off with Wiseman, who started to produce sessions for her third album. It was one of a number of increasing signs that Bob Wiseman was envisioning his future outside of Blue Rodeo.

Bob Wiseman was too talented and too opinionated to remain in a pop band, and as he branched out beyond Blue Rodeo, it was obvious to everyone that he couldn't acquiesce to someone else's vision forever. There were many Blue Rodeo fans who didn't mourn his departure from the band in 1992 — the same fans who would grow audibly agitated at shows when Wiseman would engage in mind-blowing keyboard solos that could easily extend beyond five minutes. Wiseman brought a sense of danger to the band, a sense of true unpredictability. In the glossy, blemish-free music of the '80s, chances were infinitesimal that a listener could hear experimental music from a mainstream band, not to mention one ostensibly rooted in country music.

Wiseman's piano talent was fully explored on the 1990 independent cassette *Hits of the '60s and '70s*, solo improv performances recorded by Toronto avant-garde staple John Oswald. Wiseman had been one of the few live musicians on Oswald's controversial and innovative sample-manipulation project *Plunderphonics*.

In 1991, Wiseman told *Saturday Night*, "My whole thing now is to look at [the keyboard] as though it's something I don't know how to play. I pretend that I don't know how the thing works. The improvisations are really about life and death, about the earth spinning, and the galaxy. It's about listening to other musicians. It's a spiritual thing. Music is a bigger deal than most other things. If you show a painting to a dog, it doesn't mean anything to him. Play him a flute and his head turns."

In the fall of 1989, Wiseman had launched his solo career with *In Her Dream: Bob Wiseman Sings Wrench Tuttle*, released through Warner, who had right of first refusal on any Blue Rodeo solo material. Wrench Tuttle was a typical Wiseman construct, a fictional poet Wiseman dreamt up and

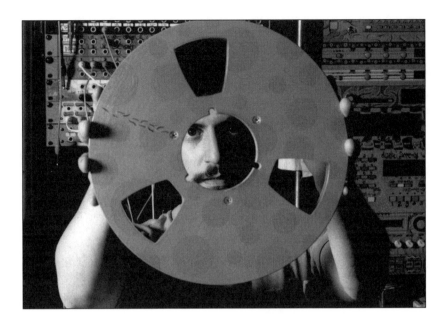

Bob Wiseman in his element
(Photo by Graham Kennedy)

claimed to be the author of the album's lyrics. For the entertainment of
television reporters, Wiseman went so far as to produce letters apparently
written by Tuttle, only to claim that Tuttle had died a year later. It was one
in a series of memorable Wiseman pranks. In the liner notes to a later
album, he invited fans to "call his parents collect," providing the Warner
Canada phone number. He frequently credited aliases such as Hugh Manoid
and Dame Julia Nesbelch on his albums. He attracted plenty of publicity
when, after Prince legally changed his name to an unpronounceable androg-
ynous symbol in 1992, Wiseman tried to legally change his own name to
Prince — arguing that a good stage name shouldn't go to waste.

Whether or not a man named Wrench Tuttle penned the lyrics to *In
Her Dream*, they were remarkably deft, shifting from the whimsical ("Older
Brother," "Dog on a Leash"), to the romantic ("We Got Time," "Ship at Sea"),
to the existential ("All the Trees" and "Blind Horse"). But it was Wiseman's
searing political indictments that made Bruce Cockburn sound like Bryan
Adams; he tackled the French government's bombing of Greenpeace's
Rainbow Warrior ("No Commotion," "Just Tourists") and provided a detailed,
harrowing history of the 1984 Union Carbide disaster in Bhopal, India.
Wiseman also penned a song called "Rock and Tree," which pointed fingers

directly at the complicity of Richard Nixon and Pepsi-Cola in the assassination of pre-Pinochet Chilean socialist president Salvador Allende. This song was deemed too controversial by Warner's lawyers, and was removed from *In Her Dream* at the last minute.

Musically, Blue Rodeo fans who did get off on Wiseman's keyboard escapades were shocked to discover that he primarily played guitar on all of *In Her Dream*, with only "Cockroach" — a short blues song he dismissed as simply "a piano exercise" — to satiate them. And although Wiseman could sing sweetly when he tried, he preferred instead to revel in the nasal and raspy aspects of his voice, the vocal equivalent of the keyboard dissonance he loved to inject into Blue Rodeo material. *In Her Dream*'s best vocal moments are when he duets with Mary Margaret O'Hara on "If I Knew" and the poignant title track, both of their voices darting around an elusive harmony that's all the more satisfying when it actually resolves.

Mike O'Neill of The Inbreds recalls, "Bob Wiseman's early records were really influential. I once walked up to him and said, 'Thanks, Bob. You showed me that you don't have to be afraid to sing with your own voice.' Then I thought, boy, what a backhanded compliment that was! But he took it in stride."

Wiseman's *modus operandi* of avoiding the obvious was no more apparent than on "Airplane on the Highway," a catchy blues progression that he laced with backwards guitar and feedback-drenched harmonica. The lyrics were a direct metaphor for his frustration inside Blue Rodeo: "I'm an airplane on the highway / and I know something's wrong / Yeah, I'm an airplane on the highway / that's why I'm singing this song / I've got to know if it's true / they say there once were airplanes / and in the sky they flew." Ironically, in an attempt to pacify Wiseman's separatist tendencies, Blue Rodeo learned the song and would often encore with it, with Wiseman playing guitar and singing, Cuddy moving to bass, and Donovan playing keyboards. "We did that quite regularly," says Keelor. "I think he hated our version, though. We wanted to do it because he had some pretty great songs at the time. But after a while, he said, 'I don't want to do this with you guys anymore.' He had his own way he wanted to do it."

It was around this time that Wiseman also became a prolific producer, mostly for peers spawned from the burgeoning songwriter's scene at Toronto's College Street watering hole Fat Albert's. Ron Sexsmith, Bob Snider, Kyp Harness, Sam Larkin and Wiseman were the principal regulars of the venue, and Wiseman produced the first cassettes by each of them. They were all singers with idiosyncratic voices, and Wiseman stumbled upon the ideal blend of instruments and arrangements for each, to bring out their narratives and highlight their melodies. In the case of a Dylanesque singer like Kyp Harness, Wiseman encouraged him to fully explore his vocal peculiarities on the *Nobody's Fool* cassette.

Bob Snider's *You* cassette was a feat of minor ingenuity. Snider was an older performer who wrote funny and heartfelt songs with elementary guitar accompaniment and a Maritime drawl. Wiseman recorded Snider's voice and guitar alone in 1989, and then disappeared with the tapes, promising that he would do something special with them. In 1992, Wiseman returned to Snider with a fully formed, kaleidoscopic '60s-tinged pop/country album, complete with horn sections, backing vocalists, full bands, and Wiseman's keyboard prowess.

"He was a total inspiration to me," says drummer and recording engineer Don Kerr, who would later play in Wiseman's band. "Bob didn't know anything about EQing or anything. We went to mix Ron [Sexsmith]'s record, and I had to tell him, 'No, that's not volume, that one finds the frequency and the one in the middle turns it up or down.' 'Oh, really? Wow!' He'd record one day with the DPX turned off and the Dolby turned off, and then play it back with it on and say, 'Why does the piano not sound as good today as it did yesterday?' He was a total musician who didn't care, because he was going to learn one way or another. That's why you get these wonky sounds on his first records. He has that 'I've got a didgeridoo, who wants to play it?' approach."

Wiseman applied his learning curve to his most fully realized album, 1991's *Presented by Lake Michigan Soda*. Featuring performances by Jane Siberry, Edie Brickell, drummer Andy Stochansky, longtime bassist Hugh Phillips and American avant-garde audio prankster Eugene Chadbourne, it is a sonically diverse collection of more acerbic politics ("Gabriel Dumont Blues") and sweet heartbreak songs ("Me an Arrow"). "Frost in Florida" loops UIC's rhythm section run backwards, with Michelle McAdorey's out-of-focus vocals adding to the eerie tale of environmental decay. Wiseman also penned his most commercial pop song, a zydeco blues number obtusely titled "What The Astronaut Noticed and Then Suggested," better known by its chorus, "Let's not be separated tonight." When the Barenaked Ladies launched their family-friendly *Gordon* album, they invited Wiseman to open an Eastern tour, where audiences had their eyes and ears opened to songs about Leonard Peltier, elephant poaching and the plight of South American farmers caught in the drug war.

Upon leaving Blue Rodeo, Wiseman's solo records became less diverse and slightly less interesting. The 1993 release *City of Wood* was surprisingly subdued, musically. His guitar and voice drenched in reverb, Wiseman's romantic songs never sounded so longing ("Real Thing," "Didn't I Get My Wish"), and his attacks on anti-Semitic apologists such as Canadian lawyer Doug Christie are scathing.

Beware of Bob, an independently released improv live performance at Waterloo campus station CKMS with Don Kerr and Hugh Phillips, was the last time he would indulge his instrumental prowess. In fact, most of his recorded solo work downplays his keyboard dexterity, perhaps to focus critical attention on the songwriting instead of inviting accolades like "the next Glenn Gould." Wiseman says, "I've always known, since I was a little kid, that the thing I could do on the piano is like a dog that I own, and it's like I'm showing it off to everyone: 'Look how beautiful it is!' But, if you have a conversation with me, I'll be just as stupid as the next person. If someone calls you a genius and you start to believe, 'Yeah, I knew that all along,' you're stupid. The same person could have called you a jerk, then you'd have to be telling yourself, 'Am I a jerk?' You have to be focused on doing your thing, and you have to have a thick skin. Some people aren't going to get it, and some people are. It can't be about the compliments or the insults, it has to be about the work. It has to be about the joy of creating it, and enduring, and the joy of meeting other artists."

The disappointing and overproduced *Accidentally Acquired Beliefs* (1995) was his final release on Warner, which he left later that year. After a couple of years touring America and Europe, Wiseman resurfaced with a stellar return to form, 1997's *More Work Songs From the Planet of the Apes*. Although Wiseman's abrasive non-mainstream music was obviously more suited to the independent route, the album met an obscure fate. Wiseman has charted his own course ever since, and looks on his major label foray with bemusement. "It was a waste of time," he says. "The first record I made, I didn't think [Warner] would put it out, but they put it out, and I didn't argue because at the time, 1989, I thought this is a great advantage, that Warner's going to distribute it, but I paid for making it. I came to realize there are independent distributors, and my work is not mainstream. Over the years I noticed the rise of Ani DiFranco and NoMeansNo. Both of them have totally embarrassed me because they're both doing it [independently], and they're totally free. It's a much happier world, for me, doing it myself. Of course, it's much more difficult too, but life's short. I'm happy with pursuing this. I would regret a lot if I didn't."

Wiseman's dissatisfaction wasn't the only internal problem Blue Rodeo had to deal with in 1991. During the demo process for the next recording, *Lost Together*, it became obvious that drummer Mark French didn't have a musical future in the band. They immediately turned to Glenn Milchem, who had been a Queen Street staple for years, playing with Vital Sines, Groovy Religion, Plasterscene Replicas, Colin Linden, Malcolm Burn and hard rocker Andy Curran. He played with Andrew Cash around the time of Cash's *Boomtown* album, and also held down a residency at the Cameron as part of guitar-less local trio The Garbagemen.

"He was always intense and a great drummer," says Cuddy. "I wasn't sure that he was suited to our band, and then I saw him with Andrew Cash. He gave that band a majesty that I was very impressed with. I'd only seen him with superfast rock bands or heavy duty bands; I'd never seen him play behind-the-beat stuff, or whatever our style is."

Milchem had just joined Change of Heart when Cuddy called him in December, 1991, asking him to audition for Blue Rodeo. Milchem recorded *Lost Together* in January, 1992, just after he recorded the *Smile* album with Change of Heart, and joined Blue Rodeo permanently.

Kim Deschamps, who had lent his signature pedal steel guitar sound to the Cowboy Junkies for three years, was also hired by Blue Rodeo to contribute to *Lost Together*, and subsequently to play a series of shows after the album's release. He stayed in the band for the next seven years. "It's a funny record," Keelor muses. "Starting off with Mark, ending up with Glenn, Bobby saying he's leaving, then the Cowboy Junkies influence of getting Kim in to play some pedal steel. It was a bit of a roulette wheel there for a while. And also no producer — Jim and me steering the ship, oh boy!"

Even if it hadn't come on the heels of *Casino*'s conciseness, *Lost Together* sounds indulgent, something the band admits themselves. "A couple of songs shorter and I think it would be a much better record," says Keelor. "If we were to drop 'Willing Fool,' which gives me shivers, and Jim's song 'The Big Push' — that might have been the only time we ever played that song." For the first time on a Blue Rodeo album, there are throwaway tracks that would have been better served as b-sides, and five tracks linger past the five-minute mark. Keelor assumes control of the best material, such as the rocking "Restless," the pure honky-tonk country of "Western Skies," and the understated power balladry of the title track.

The album opens with "Fools Like You," a song explicitly in favour of aboriginal rights, an issue Blue Rodeo had supported since their beginnings. They were also now regulars at benefit concerts to save B.C.'s Stein Valley rainforest from development.

"Just after *Diamond Mine*, we did a few Stein Valley benefits," says Keelor. "That was a real eye-opener for all of us. We'd go to these Stein Valley benefits and there would be all these great speakers. Especially Chief Ruby Dunstan, talking about what was going on in her land. It was a real education and a humbling experience. We were singing all our songs, and they didn't seem to address anything. ['Fools Like You'] was trying to address something, how we felt about all that and aligning ourselves to it. It's the first song on [*Lost Together*]; we wanted it to be a thank you to all those people, and a jab at everyone else."

The song was also informed by an experience Keelor and Cuddy had during the Oka crisis in 1991, when they went to play on the Kanesatake reserve in the middle of the standoff. "That was an incredible eye-opener," says Cuddy. "We had played plenty of benefits and had situations described to us and had worked to try to help land claim settlements, but those were very invisible battles. With this one, what we'd read about in Toronto was so different than what we experienced when we went through all the battle lines — barbed wire, tanks and troops. When we got inside, we saw this impoverished, sparsely populated reserve and talked to the people and heard their stories. Like anybody would be, we were just enraged at the imbalance of the battle."

The catchy, fiddle-driven song closes with an ode to Elijah Harper, the Cree Manitoba MLA who single-handedly defeated the Meech Lake Accord: "God bless Elijah / with a feather in his hand / stop stealing the Indian land." It would also be the last time they would be either directly or indirectly political, with the exception of "It Could Happen To You" in 1997 and a benefit album Keelor organized to raise awareness about the wrongful imprisonment of American Native activist Leonard Peltier.

The most indicative *Lost Together* song is the closing track, "Angels," an eight-minute epic that sees all three guitarists stretching their chops, and closes with a gorgeous solo piano coda by Wiseman. It also serves as his last moment with the band. "A lot of things came together on that record," says Keelor. "Bringing Kim in legitimized more of the traditional country sound, Glenn gave more authority to the rawk, and it was Bobby's swan song, and he played some beautiful stuff. The ending of 'Angels' was very fitting."

Wiseman announced that he was quitting when *Lost Together* was completed, and his departure was probably overdue. "By the time he left I was so mad at him that I was glad he left," says Cuddy. "He's a fucking genius; he can come in for three hours and put stuff down that's incredible and memorable and perfect for every song, but his total lack of involvement was infuriating. When we finally arranged a session just for Bobby, he couldn't even stay — he had to leave after three hours, and I was raging: 'We gotta get rid of this guy, he's fucked off.' Greg was calming me down, and then Bobby quit that night, so it didn't matter. I'll be the first to admit that Bobby is probably the best musician I've ever played with, but it was impossible to be around that dark cloud. It was ridiculous. Bobby was so miserable by the time he left, whether it was the band or his personal life, I don't know. It was not a good situation."

Wiseman's departure affected how Blue Rodeo saw themselves as a band. Although his parting was not a surprise, Keelor says, "The shock was, 'How do you replace Bobby?' It seemed pretty daunting." Because Wiseman was such a unique presence, it would have seemed callous to replace him with another improv specialist, and for a new keyboardist to immediately step into Wiseman's shoes would have been a formidable task. Deschamps's presence in the band deflated expectations by turning Blue Rodeo into a completely different entity, one that now boasted three loud guitarists and a heavy-hitting drummer. "That was a critical change for us," Cuddy admits. "We became more guitar-oriented without having the chops to do it well." Keelor adds, "I don't know how much the audiences enjoyed it, but it was a lot of fun for us taking a stab at doing the solo on 'Diamond Mine.'"

After doing 40 shows with Deschamps, the band got the itch to hear keyboards back in the band. Keelor recalls the pressure of the immediate post-Wiseman shows: "There wasn't a comfort zone. There wasn't a place where I could just lean back and let somebody take it. With Bobby, you could zone out for a half-hour sometimes." The band auditioned new keyboardists and the job went to James Gray. Gray had played in Whitenoise with Milchem, as well as serving time in Chris Bottomley's funk band, with ska/reggae band the Hopping Penguins and a very brief stint as an early Rheostatic. His father was in the '60s folk band The Travellers, who played at the first Mariposa Festival and are best known for Canadianizing Woody Guthrie's "This Land Is Your Land," altering the second line of the chorus to read: "From Bonavista to Vancouver Island." Gray debuted with the band during a three-night stand at the Ontario Place Forum in Toronto, an annual hometown summer gig.

Later that year, Blue Rodeo travelled to Australia for the first time, and it was there that they began to amass the material that would form their next two albums. "During that trip to Australia we had a fair amount of time to sit around and play music acoustically," says Keelor. "With Kim there and James noodling around on things, there was a very nice acoustic music thing that was starting to emerge. And for myself, there was a deep-ening of my emotion toward how the singing was, and even the songwriting — more personal. There's a certain weight to some of those songs, like 'whew, I gotta sing this one.'"

The appearance of mostly acoustic new material also came as a reaction to the rock onslaught the band was then offering. "In terms of physicality, by the time we finished the *Lost Together* tour, we were such a loud band," says Cuddy. "Doing 150 of those loud shows was too fatiguing. We planned on doing an acoustic record because we were interested in it, but it also provided us with an enormous relief on stage — things that were interesting to us that didn't involve pounding our eardrums. We wouldn't have considered that 10 years [prior]; it wouldn't have occurred to us that we needed relief."

In June, 1993 the band hired Doug McClement and the Comfort Sound Mobile studio to record some demos at Greg Keelor's farm in rural Kendal, Ontario, between Port Hope and Peterborough, in what turned out to be a heat wave. "We had a lot of songs, most of it acoustic, but also a big pile of electric songs," says Keelor. "We were out here for about a week and recorded everything, electric and acoustic. And it became evident that what-ever it was — the combination of the truck, the house, the pot, the sunshine — the acoustic instruments and those songs sounded fantastic. The elec-tric stuff sounded really good, but it didn't have the same thing as the acoustic stuff, which really sounded great. It was obvious to everybody. It was kind of funny to get Glenn Milchem in the band, and then say, 'Play brushes for the whole record!'" Even more surprising is that Milchem doesn't even play on the album's last three songs, which act as an extended lullaby, a series of hushed duets between Keelor and Sarah McLachlan.

Blue Rodeo had befriended McLachlan at the Stein Valley festivals, and when she was in Toronto putting some finishing touches on *Fumbling Towards Ecstasy*, they invited her out to the Keelor farm while they were recording demos. "She was really focused, musically, because she had been working a lot," says Keelor. "She came just to hang out and have a little party, and whenever she'd pick up the guitar or play the piano, we'd be like, 'holy shit!' and then she started singing."

Realizing that they were on to something, the band booked the mobile truck for another week in July, and opened the doors to a feast of friends, including McLachlan, guitarist Colin Linden, members of the Skydiggers, and Milchem's girlfriend Anne Bourne, best known for her skilled and diverse contributions — on cello, keyboard and vocals — to Jane Siberry, Change

Blue Rodeo with Sarah McLachlan, 1995
(Courtesy of Jim Cuddy)

of Heart, and Loreena McKennitt. The initial idea was to record covers or re-work older material, but the strength of the new songs took precedence. The band finished two songs a day, informed by their social surroundings. "The idea was to have a big party, and have everyone sing," says Keelor. "A lot of musical friends hanging out gave that record a little lift. It felt really special. It's nice when you don't have to steer the boat and the boat's going to a better place than you could ever take it. That record had a very pleasant sort of stoner vibe. A lot of stoner stuff can go weird and strange, or sometimes it dovetails into something where the focus is way better than you could have ever imagined, and that record definitely did that."

Initially, the farm recordings were intended to be an EP to act as a stopgap before the next "proper" Blue Rodeo release, but it quickly became obvious that there was a whole album's worth of work that the band was proud of. *Five Days in July* was premiered at another Ontario Place Forum show in August, 1993; after opening with 10 older favourites, the band played their as-yet-unreleased album in its entirety. "We did an hour of absolutely brand new material," laughs Cuddy. "It went on too long, there's no doubt about it, but people loved it."

Upon its release, *Five Days in July* slowly crept its way into the hearts of old and new fans. Because subtlety is its strong point, it wasn't the type of album that bowled you over on first listen, and its appearance in November, 1993 didn't mesh with the lazy, hazy summer night vibe of the recording. Compared to Blue Rodeo's other albums, it sold relatively slowly,

but has become their best-selling album, having been certified over quin-
tuple platinum.

There are obvious reasons why. If *Diamond Mine* demonstrated their
diverse songwriting skills and *Casino* proved their pop smarts, *Five Days in
July* is a pleasant, reassuring work that sounds as comfortable and familiar
as one of Neil Young's country albums, as essential to a Canadian cottage
weekend as a warm sweater and a case of beer. There's also nothing threat-
ening about it: no psychedelic weirdness, no raging guitar solos, no caustic
Keelor lyrics. There's none of the tension that often otherwise informs Blue
Rodeo's most creative moments; in its place is the sound of a unified group
of people, not six individuals in a band with a few guest stars. The presence of Gray and Deschamps — unlike Wiseman — never overwhelms the
rest of the band, and yet they subtly supply the most important textures,
such as Gray's piano on "Five Days in May" and Deschamps's pedal steel
on "'Til I Gain Control Again" — the latter a Rodney Crowell song and the
only cover Blue Rodeo has included on an album. Keelor and Cuddy split
the songwriting evenly; respectively, "Hasn't Hit Me Yet" and "Bad Timing"
are two of their strongest compositions.

Yet even by the time *Five Days* was released, Blue Rodeo was expecting
to quickly return to the studio to record their "real" album. But the album's
popularity kept spiralling, and the band became busier than ever. Although
they had always spent a lot of time on the road, it was around this time
that Blue Rodeo started to veer off the traditional concert route and play
smaller towns, as well as larger big-city shows. "Those civic things are great,
because it's the thing that's happening in town that season," says Cuddy.
"We do those because we want to play, so we find these places. And then
when you're known for that, all these opportunities come up. I can't understand why somebody wouldn't want to. If you do a Toronto gig, there's a
lot of pressure. You know you're going to get critiqued, you know your family
is going to come, you better have enough seats."

Keelor says it's been part of their work ethic from the beginning. "A lot
of other people look at their careers differently. The Hip don't have to [play
small towns]. They can go out and make a ton of money the way they do,"
he laughs. "They've got a pretty good thing going. Maybe a band like Sloan
likes to make their shows more event-y. There was a time when we had the
same thing. But when we started Blue Rodeo, we thought, let's just play the
shit out of it, even on Queen Street. At the time there was this notion that
if you play here then you can't play over here, and so we said, fuck that,
we'll play there and there. And because we were popular, we could." Cuddy

adds, "When we were first coming up, it was so Torontonian to plan an event for a year and then have the event. We thought, 'Well, then what do you want to do? Don't you want to play tomorrow night?' We always thought the best thing to do is play and learn as you go."

As the laid-back feel of *Five Days* caught steam while Blue Rodeo was on tour, audiences were confronted with an incredibly aggressive opening act, Change of Heart. "They became a big influence on that tour," says Keelor. "They were getting pretty proggy at the time. I really loved [Ian Blurton's] guitar playing, and I liked the way his songwriting was going. I definitely took a couple of pages out of his book."

Ian Blurton recalls, "In a lot of cases they're a very straight audience, so it's really challenging and fun to see what you can do to them. We played a show in Kapuskasing, Ontario with Blue Rodeo in this community centre — a bingo hall, basically. There were a whole bunch of kids there, because there hadn't been a band there in two years, so their first show was going to be Change of Heart. You want to freak them out so that they remember you."

Cuddy was also won over by the loud upstarts. "To my mind they seemed to be an illogical pick, but one hundred per cent of the time audiences loved them. Part of it was because Ian was so funny with the audience; he was so abusive and yet he looked like the kid next door. He'd say things like, 'What, is there some fucking city ordinance against clapping here?' They would laugh and start to get into it. Change of Heart was a band that took me a while to come around to, and when I did I just flipped. I really tried to get them signed to Warner, I kept pushing for that."

When it came time to focus on the next recording, the second incarnation of Blue Rodeo was in top form. On the album that became *Nowhere to Here*, over half the material had been in the live set since before *Five Days* was recorded. They once again retreated to Keelor's farm at the tail end of the winter of 1995, only this time there was no mobile truck, and all the recording equipment was squeezed into the living room along with the band. The album's claustrophobic sound was quite authentic.

"It was a tough record for me and Jim personally, as collaborators," says Keelor. "I wanted to go somewhere and he wanted to go somewhere else. I wanted to take it further into a darker, rock way. There were conflicts there. *Five Days* was like a cloudless sky on a beautiful August day with 50 nice people hanging around. And it only lasted a week. *Nowhere to Here* was the end of winter, and it was all of us locked in that house. It didn't have the space to it. A lot of the songs are a lot darker, or a steady stream of them are. I like the music a lot, and the band was playing great. But it was a lot of work."

For Keelor, it coincided with the most intense time of his life. Shortly before the recording began, Keelor discovered that he had been adopted and that his birth name was Francis McIntyre. He was determined to find the whereabouts of his Nova Scotian birth mother, and when he did, the news came at the most awkward moment possible. "The day we started *Nowhere to Here*, these two big brutes were carrying in this tape machine," he says. "All our crew were bringing in all our gear. There was this Laurel and Hardy scene of people coming in, just all over the place. The phone rang in the kitchen, and it was a friend of mine. I had just smoked a joint, I was very stoned, and there was all this stuff going on, and she says, '*I found your mother.*' As soon as that phone call came, I didn't want to be there. More than anything I wanted to get in my car that minute, go out there and start looking. But all this stuff was going on: I had to make this record, and the record ended up being this big undertaking."

After the bed tracks were finished, Keelor fell from a loft in his house, landing on his back and suffering cranial and rib injuries, which prolonged the recording process, closing the gap on the time he had available to drive out east and search for his mother. On the drive to Nova Scotia, his eyesight started to weaken due to the effects of diabetes, triggered by the fall. The effects of the injury also meant that he had to record all his vocal and guitar overdubs with broken ribs, barely able to breathe in. "That really put that record in the shits," he admits. "I would just sit up there for at least 14 hours a day singing and playing guitar."

The tone of *Nowhere to Here* is set on the opening track, a beautifully beige and dirge-like Keelor song, "Save Myself." It once again features Sarah McLachlan, on a track in an entirely different plane than anything else she's ever lent her vocals to. Glenn Milchem plays a gloriously sloppy *Harvest* drum pattern on a kit that sounds like it's tuned as low as it can go. It's a jarring beginning, and immediately signals that this isn't going to be a Blue Rodeo album for the grandmothers who might have enjoyed *Five Days*. "Yeah, great opener," Keelor laughs sarcastically. "I love it, but it's anti-'what a record is supposed to be.' You're supposed to have your three hits as your first three songs, and instead, we've got this funeral, then this space-out jam ['Girl in Green']."

Coming on the heels of the commercial success of *Five Days*, *Nowhere to Here* is certainly Blue Rodeo's most misunderstood album. Its darker sound calls to mind the famous Neil Young quote, in the liner notes to *Decade*, referring to "Heart of Gold": "This song put me in the middle of the road. Travelling there soon became a bore so I headed for the ditch. A rougher ride but I saw more interesting people there." And if *Five Days in July* was Blue Rodeo's *Harvest*, then *Nowhere to Here* is similarly akin to *Harvest's* forgotten successor, *Time Fades Away*. Both follow-ups feature material drawn from the same writing period as their forebears, and — like Neil Young's — some of Keelor's songs detail neglect and a quest for a lost parent.

Musically, *Nowhere to Here* is the typically awkward mid-career album intended to prevent being taken for granted; the catch-22 being that if it is followed by something conventional, like Blue Rodeo's next album, *Tremolo*, then accusations of stagnation arise. *Nowhere to Here* is anything but stagnant. Over a funky beat in Keelor's "Girl in Green," the elements fighting for space include a wah-wah rhythm guitar, skittering organ, an anthemic chorus, Cuddy screaming his backing vocals with a surprising grit, and two guitar solos — one recorded backwards, and a blistering closer worthy of Wiseman's psychedelic pyrotechnics. With "What You Want" and "Better Off As We Are," Cuddy delivers his most convincing rockers ever, while his ballads "Sky" and "Blew It Again" stand miles above some of the clichéd vocal showcase slow songs he may be guilty of composing. The songwriting, the guitar textures, the drum sounds, the backing vocals and the bleak vibe make *Nowhere to Here* Blue Rodeo's most interesting record, if not necessarily their most artistically successful; the final three tracks, especially "Flaming Bed," drag it down to a complete stop.

Fan reaction was decidedly tepid. Although the album shipped platinum in its first month, it never picked up steam after the initial post-*Five Days* frenzy. "I think that's a really good record, but everybody wanted another *Five Days*," says Keelor. "They wanted the Blue Rodeo/Sarah McLachlan experience and that acoustic thing. It's like the other side of the coin. But in our minds, we had already committed to that batch of songs. It's a more complex record. There's lots of layers of music on there, and it's one of my faves."

Cuddy counters, "I found *Nowhere to Here* to be this all-over-the-place, random, vibe-y thing that culminated in our show at Maple Leaf Gardens, which in my estimation was a disaster. We played like shit, we didn't know what we were doing, we didn't have a set list, and there'd be two-minute pauses while we conferred on stage. For the longest time we believed that our aesthetic was randomness. That wasn't working for us anymore. It didn't feel spontaneous; we knew what songs followed each other, so we were doing set lists in our head, and yet we weren't getting the full effect of having a set planned."

Keelor concurs about their hometown Maple Leaf Gardens arena show. "That was a pretty horrendous show. I had an abscessed tooth that night, just horrible. And my guitar tech was off on a cocaine bender and didn't show up; I had to use the opening band's guitar tech. He didn't know any of the guitars that I used. My amps weren't grounded, and as soon as I went up to sing my first note I got a jolt of 120 volts into my abscessed tooth. Then my pedals weren't working properly because he hadn't set them up properly. I just hated it. I thought, fuck this. There was no flow to the show, it was just horrible. It was funny, because it was supposed to be 'Maple! Leaf! Gardens!' — our first time there, and the review said, 'Keelor throws a hissy fit.' It was just so foul."

Keelor admits that the *Nowhere to Here* tour "was probably the most strained we'd been" as a band. It was the enthusiasm of their opening acts that provided them with inspiration, and perhaps encouraged them to soldier on. "We did a long tour of America with Weeping Tile that was great," Keelor recalls fondly. "They were very inspiring. Their spirits were so high all the time. We'd be playing a shitty little bar somewhere with 14 people in it, and they'd put on a great show, and then they would stick around for our show all the time and make it so much fun, dancing around. Touring with a band and hearing them every night, it's a lot different than listening to a record. You hear where they're going as a band, and their commitment every night to the kind of music they play; it doesn't matter how many people are there.

Blue Rodeo, second incarnation, 1999: Kim Deschamps, Cuddy, James Gray, Keelor, Donovan, Glenn Milchem
(Courtesy of Jim Cuddy)

"And when we went out east and did a tour with Great Big Sea — that was a blast," Keelor continues. "They opened for us on our Eastern leg, and we did about 20 shows with them. Especially hanging out at Allan Doyle's house when we were in Newfoundland. They're such great after-show hosts and partners, singing songs and initiating good singing parties after the show."

After the *Nowhere to Here* tour had concluded, it was time for a break. "Greg and I were completely and gratefully apart at that point," says Cuddy. "We'd had enough of each other. What we really needed was to have substantial time away from being Blue Rodeo, which we had been a part of since 1978, basically."

Keelor went on a trip to India to study with a guru, at the recommendation of his doctor. While sitting in the plane upon his return to Toronto, he decided that he had to make a solo record to deal with all the emotional turmoil he had undergone in the recent months.

"I didn't know what I was going to do," says Keelor. "When you go to make a solo record, you can make yourself out to be anything. I thought, okay, at last I can put on a Nudie suit and be Gram Parsons. I contemplated that, then I thought, no, I'll put on a plaid shirt and do a rockin' country thing." What ended up happening was entirely different from either. Keelor booked time with Sarah McLachlan's producer, Pierre Marchand at his Quebec studio, and invited McLachlan, her drummer and soon-to-be fiancé Ashwin Sood, Anne Bourne and Michelle McAdorey to hang out and contribute. Marchand played bass. "All these mother songs were coming out of me at the time, and then after the trip to the guru, there were all these contemplations, meditations and prayer songs," he says. "Partially it didn't feel fair to make Blue Rodeo try to record another whole pile of 'Flaming Bed's; I don't know if they wanted to do a whole pile of that. So I showed up at Pierre's with my nylon string guitar, we started recording and started to see where it would go."

It went to a place deep into the soul, and far away from what people knew of Blue Rodeo, even the lullabies of *Five Days*. The album, titled *Gone*, rarely rises above a whisper, with Keelor crooning like Leonard Cohen or Chet Baker over sparse accompaniment. McLachlan shines on muted piano — the recording is so intimate that you can hear her feet shifting the pedals — and lets loose on the mildly honky-tonk "Star of the Show." McLachlan, McAdorey and Bourne provide a celestial choir on a waltz re-arrangement of the Talking Heads' "Heaven." The album's snowflake delicacy is broken only by the Krishna rock of "White Marble Ganesh," which was chosen as the album's single; the video featured an extremely bearded and grey Keelor singing Hare Krishna chants, which was a little too George Harrison for most, and it immediately deep-sixed the record's commercial appeal. *Gone* is hardly a "difficult solo album," but its shimmering beauty is destined to be the most sadly overlooked element of the Blue Rodeo oeuvre. A few select theatre dates followed *Gone*'s release in January 1997, featuring John Borra on bass, Glenn Milchem on drums, and Anne Bourne on cello and vocals.

While Keelor was putting the finishing touches on *Gone*, the workaholic Cuddy was getting itchy, and in September 1996 started to prepare his own solo record. Unlike Keelor, Cuddy stuck closer to home: his band included Bazil Donovan on bass, James Gray on keyboards and John Whynot (*Nowhere to Here*, *Tremolo*) in the producer's chair. Drummer Gavin Brown (Phleg Camp, Big Sugar) and guitarist Colin Cripps rounded out the core line-up, with guest appearances from Michelle McAdorey; violinists Melanie Doane, Adele Armin and Curtis Driedger; Wilco's Jeff Tweedy and Jay Bennett; and vocalists Sarah Harmer (Weeping Tile) and Andy Maize (Skydiggers). If Keelor's album was a very private meditation, Cuddy's was drawn from an extended family of friends, and was nowhere near as drastic a change.

"Even if this didn't work out, I wanted this to be an enjoyable experience," said Cuddy at the time of the album's release. "We work hard at Blue Rodeo, and we don't need to add another stressful, hard-working situation. When I first started thinking about doing a solo record, I wasn't sure that I could handle all the elements of expression myself, because I had never had to," he continued. "There had always been some point when there'd be some deflection off to my partner. We'd both written songs that were representative of our personal states of mind, and that we then brought to the band. That's a more fearful moment — bringing songs to a collection of people who are expecting something from you and who know you — than it is to bring to strangers. Strangers will cut you a lot of slack. They're willing to go along with something."

Cuddy's *All in Time* was recorded in increments, and wasn't ready for release until September, 1998. Although it had solid songs such as the "Disappointment" single, featuring a trademark Colin Cripps riff, it was sadly predictable, suggesting that Cuddy's work benefits from the creative tension that drives Blue Rodeo. "My worst habit in Blue Rodeo is that I over-refine," Cuddy admits. "I'm suspicious of experimentation. I've always thought my role in Blue Rodeo is trying to make things coherent. But that's an imagined role. What happens is that everyone participates to some degree in every aspect of the music, the aesthetic of the sound. I have to resist being the one who wants to tidy up the edges all the time.

Sometimes that's fine, but in the initial stages, it's not."

At a preview performance of the album at Toronto's NXNE festival in June, 1997, Cuddy debuted his band before a packed room at the Reverb club. Keelor could conspicuously be spotted in the middle of the room, beaming with the pride of a brother watching his sibling grow up and move on. Cuddy had a similar reaction upon his first exposure to Keelor's album. "I remember sitting in his car and listening to mixes of his record, and thinking, 'This is really nice — and I'm so glad I don't have to play on it,'" says Cuddy. "I really enjoyed sitting there and listening to Greg's music without thinking about where I fit in.

"We were lucky to be able to do our solo records and go off and come back to each other gradually, with some new offerings," Cuddy continues, discussing the ease with which 1997's *Tremolo* was recorded. "We were tired of sorting out the minutiae of our relationship. *Tremolo* was the 'getting back together' record. We knew we couldn't put much stress into it, and we have to enjoy the band again. Then we can delve deeper and tear it apart again.

"The times that were the most difficult for us had preceded the times that people actually thought were the most difficult. By the time we were doing solo records, we were on course to be committed once again to what we do together. When we were making *Nowhere to Here* and touring it, we were trying hard to be civil. There was a lot of pressure and it wasn't working out. When we were reconstructing, that's when most people thought we were breaking up. Of course, no amount of reassurance makes people think you're doing anything but lying."

It would have been hard for Blue Rodeo to fake the enthusiasm they showed on stage at *Tremolo*'s Toronto launch — but they had a few other things to celebrate that weekend as well. The inaugural Stardust Ball, the beginning of an annual tradition for the band, took place at the historic Fort York near Toronto's waterfront in early July, 1997. Staged by the band without corporate sponsorship, the Stardust line-up featured Blue Rodeo headlining over Steve Earle, Victoria Williams, the Skydiggers, Great Big Sea and Oh Susanna, as well as a side stage with local independent bands. In 1998, the line-up was even better, with Neko Case, Ron Sexsmith, 54·40 and Cowboy Junkies. The event's success was testament to their taste and their talent, and their respect for their audience.

"Any time we've taken back control of what we do, there's always the possibility that it will be an inspiring and joyous occasion," says Cuddy. "Stardust was definitely that. It's as much the whole atmosphere as the concert itself. People really respond to that, which I suppose is a desperate thing meaning that they're so used to the opposite: they're so used to feeling compromised, ripped off and sponsored to death. And we're just as subject to that, too."

Stardust was an attempt to replicate the intimacy of Blue Rodeo's annual shows at the Ontario Place Forum, which was gutted in the early '90s and replaced with the cold and corporate Molson Amphitheatre. Recalling the time the band launched the then-unreleased *Five Days in July* at the Forum, Keelor says, "You couldn't do that at the Amphitheatre. You have to put on a show. The first show we did [at the Amphitheatre], I was lipping off and I was putting it down pretty bad. I got in a lot of trouble for that, from the band, friends, everybody. So we wanted to find an alternative to it. Fort York came up; it's not Ontario Place, but it's pretty good. The band felt refreshed at that point, more united."

Blue Rodeo had become a familiar fixture for their legions of fans, and although they may have lost the edge of Bob Wiseman's playing, they continued to write timeless songs that won their way into people's hearts just as their debut album did. "There is something extremely deep about the work we can do in this band," says Cuddy, "although it's not always reflected in what we do. The solo stuff is a break and a challenge, but the work that we do in the band is our life's work."

Two Solitudes:

The Tragically Hip

July 1, 1994 — the nation's 127th birthday. Its traditional collision of introspective pride and overt, alcohol-inspired patriotism is appropriately
concentrated in Barrie, Ontario. Home to one of the two major brewery's
largest production facilities, in the past few years the corporation has clued
into the benefits of tying its name to the country's burgeoning homegrown
rock industry and now celebrates this connection with an annual Canada
Day concert at its affiliated outdoor concert venue. Canada's most popular
band, The Tragically Hip, have been part of these shows from the beginning, but the promoter's original plans for this year have been altered since
The Hip have agreed to headline only on certain conditions, not the least
being the banishment of any beer company advertising inside the grounds.
The band also feels that if this is indeed a Canada Day concert, it is only
natural to have it reflect the best in Canadian music.

Vocalist Gord Downie, one band member not comfortable with the status
their financial gains have granted, seizes the opportunity to recommend
artists he feels are equally worthy of sharing this stage. Since moving to
Toronto from Kingston in the wake of the band's meteoric rise over the previous five years, Downie has become enthralled by a musical community

which, partly because of his origins, had always seemed closed off to him. Even as the figurehead of the new populist CanRock voices, Downie initially saw himself as an interloper in the established Toronto scene; his band's tough, blue-collar sound was often deemed retrogressive in comparison to those artists. This, despite Downie's increasingly impressionistic poetry drawing him — consciously or not — closer to Queen Street. Since his relocation, he displays a fan's appreciation and eventually discovers a mutual respect.

Having staged the Another Roadside Attraction festival tour the previous year, The Hip's managers Jake Gold and Allan Gregg feel no qualms about putting together a one-day event, but with Downie's input, the show soon resembles a CanRock time capsule: The Mahones, Treble Charger, Change of Heart, Eric's Trip, the Odds, Jane Siberry, the Rheostatics, Spirit of the West, Daniel Lanois, and The Tragically Hip. The mere presence of The Hip attracts a sold-out audience, even though the band has not played extensively in Canada since the previous year, and will not again until the beginning of the next. This feat casts the band's influence in an even more impressive light as only a few short years ago they were virtually in the same position as the others on the bill — playing clubs, campus halls and modest soft-seat theatres. But if it wasn't clear up until now, this day proves that The Tragically Hip's music has tapped into a well of youthful Canadian energy. It has become a unique entity which embodies the long-held virtues of rock and roll, but more importantly, the indelible qualities that each person in attendance feels identifies them as Canadian. For some, it is in a song that evokes a familiar surrounding that shaped their own personality, be it a small prairie town or their local outdoor hockey rink on a frigid Saturday morning. For others it is in the deeper experience of hearing The Hip in the wider context of their fellow artists throughout the day, and having the amorphous concept of a "Canadian Sound" suddenly take shape.

Yet as the day unfolds, the contingent of those wishing to hear only The Hip's version of Canada slowly takes over. Most of the artists on stage in the afternoon come through unscathed, but with the energy level constantly rising in relation to alcohol consumption, the appearance of a moody Daniel Lanois just before The Hip cuts some fuses short. The subdued beauty of songs from his two solo albums is callously disrupted by flying water bottles and the now-common chant, "Hip! Hip! Hip!"

Those watching from backstage are torn. "Daniel had it real rough that day. He sort of insisted that he go on before us," says Hip bassist Gord Sinclair. "It was tough for him to go on after Spirit of the West too, because they were playing so hard and they're such a great band."

In Jake Gold's pragmatic view, "There were certain acts that we suggested play at certain times, knowing that the audience could get unruly at a certain point in the show. But they insisted on playing at the times they wanted to play at, so some of what happened was as much a part of when they went on stage. I mean, we knew when the beer gardens were going to close.

"I remember Daryl Johnson, Daniel Lanois's bass player, said, 'If you don't stop throwing bottles, we're gonna leave the stage.' Well, as if that isn't an invitation. All he had to do was not say that. There were a few mistakes that shouldn't have been made, but the interesting thing was, it wasn't ugly. For us, it was still this great gathering of Canadian musicians. Backstage, no one was walking around going, 'This is shitty.' All the bands were in great moods. The funny thing is, after that show we never saw that happen again. I think Gord said something from the stage like, 'Anyone who throws something at a musician is an idiot.' At that point I think all those people realized The Hip were saying, 'These are our friends, they should be respected.'"

Downie obviously takes the display more personally than the others. As the band opens with the as-yet-unreleased "Grace Too," he dedicates it to "the asshole who throws things at musicians," and throughout the set peppers his between-song comments with anti-Canada Day sentiments. "I stood there and it was really difficult," Downie says. "If it wasn't before that point, then it was definitely then that I put myself toward trying to instill in the crowd — which is ultimately futile, standing on stage and telling people to act in a certain way — but trying to reflect my love of music, and bands, in other people. However, that day it struck me that I didn't really know why those people were there; July 1 being a celebration of beer and money and Canada, in that order. I maintain that if we'd done that show on July 2, everything would have been totally fine."

Downie's allegiance to what he and the other bands represented, rather than to the orchestrated significance of the event, ultimately grounded The Tragically Hip — once the most sure-fire bet for international rock stardom this country had seen since The Guess Who — to the place they and their peers actually came from, a place they were all just beginning to discover in their music. It also drew a line between those who got the message and those who didn't. In Canada at least, a majority had formed their own understanding.

As then-Rheostatics' drummer Dave Clark remembers, "The first time I heard The Hip, I thought to myself, 'I don't like this band.' It was around the time we were recording with Neil Peart and one day he gave us tickets to the show where The Hip were opening for Rush at The Gardens. Gord Downie blew me away, with what he had to say more than anything — his take on the world. Then they invited us to play on Canada Day. I don't know how many people were there, but I guess it was our biggest gig. Everyone was nice, and we were on early enough that nothing got thrown at us. Then watching Daniel Lanois and Daryl Johnson and Brian Blade that night, I was in tears listening to them play this beautiful music with such majesty amidst the most ignorant behaviour from a crowd I'd ever seen in my life. They were such a calibre above every other musician there that day in many ways, just in the command of their instruments. I was completely inspired by it. Then I watched The Hip go on and saw Gord deal with that negative situation in a way that was very diplomatic. It showed his capacity as a person."

The Tragically Hip's story begins with Gord Sinclair and Rob Baker. As neighbours since birth in the early 1960s, the pair grew up across the street from each other on Kingston, Ontario's Churchill Crescent. It was a neighbourhood of relative privilege in a city still rooted in its origins as a Loyalist stronghold, as well as a rich hockey history. The city also had Canada's largest prison community, providing a dark counterpoint to the longstanding traditions of Queen's University. Sinclair's father, Duncan, was Dean of Medicine at Queen's, and along with his wife Leona, shared a love of bigband music. Young Gord began his musical education playing bagpipes with the Rob Roy Pipe Band, then later the fife during a stint in the Fort Henry Guard. From there he moved on to studying piano and eventually picked up stringed instruments.

Baker's father Phil was a provincial court judge and allowed his sons to indulge in artistic pursuits as well. Rob was always admiring his older brother Matthew's achievements and when the elder Baker got a guitar, it was only a matter of time before 13-year-old Rob got one too. Although naturally left-handed, Rob learned to play by mimicking his brother's right-handed style and his enthusiasm for the instrument eventually persuaded his parents to buy him a Fender Stratocaster. From there, Baker and Sinclair became even more inseparable, spending most of their free time in each other's basements, learning songs and jamming with other novice rockers.

With Sinclair opting to play bass, the pair first received inspiration to form a band from the staples of FM radio, which led back to hard-edged British R&B bands like Them and The Yardbirds and, eventually, the first

The Tragically Hip, 1999: Rob Baker, Paul Langlois,
Johnny Fay, Gord Sinclair
(photos by Janice Dunn, courtesy of The Management Trust)

wave of punk. In high school they made their first public appearance as part of The Rodents, and immediately other students took notice.

One was Gord Downie, a product of much more humble origins in the town of Amherstview, outside Kingston. His parents moved from Toronto in the 1960s to take advantage of land development opportunities. The man who found their house in Amherstview was Harry Sinden, then a real estate agent, but whose sideline pursuit as a semi-pro hockey coach would soon find him guiding the Boston Bruins to Stanley Cup wins, as well as the 1972 Team Canada to their legendary victory over the Soviets. The Downies' friendship with Sinden gave him the honour of becoming godfather to young Gordon, their fourth of five children. Not surprisingly, the three Downie brothers' early years revolved around hockey and their beloved Bruins, especially the star defenceman Bobby Orr. Gord played goal for the town team, which would win a provincial championship in its division, but sport was abruptly put aside by the time he started at Kingston Collegiate and became aware of rock and roll's mystique. "The Rodents were kind of like a punk band and very revered," Downie says. "Robbie walked the halls and people definitely knew who he was. It was an amazing thing. I came from a rural area; I wouldn't say it's given me a stigma, but it's something that's always stayed with me, not actually being from Kingston."

Although Downie too was partial to '70s FM rock at first, not knowing an instrument forced him to join a band called The Slinks as vocalist and learn contemporary material by The Clash, The Sex Pistols and Talking Heads. As part of the small Kingston musical circle, Downie ultimately crossed paths with Sinclair and Baker, and they soon developed a friendship through their shared love of blues-inspired rock. In fact, the seeds of several bands were being sown at the same time in Kingston high schools. Future Headstone Hugh Dillon was rapidly wearing out his welcome at several of them. "It was very incestuous. I grew up with the guys from The Hip and we all started playing in bands together," he says. "Finn McConnell from The Mahones was a soundman at one point and he was in a band with Gord Downie. Grant Ethier, who ended up playing in 13 Engines, was the drummer in my first band, The Rattlers. We were actually more into music than we were drinking back then."

One of the first friends Downie made in high school was not a musician at the time. Paul Langlois's parents were both teachers and it was understood that his first priority would be his education, even though his mother Terry encouraged him to develop his musical talents. His father Adrien also coached the Kingston Collegiate football team, which Paul finally agreed to join in Grade 13 after years of avoiding the sport. By then he had already set his sights on a career in journalism, but during his first year at Carleton he gave in to his desire to play guitar and made the tough choice to tell his parents he was dropping out to play music. He took a job driving a taxi while waiting for the right band to come along.

Sinclair, Baker and Downie had begun their post-secondary careers at Queen's by the early '80s, which put an end to The Rodents and The Slinks, although Baker and Downie continued to play with McConnell in The Filters. This configuration didn't last long, and Baker and Downie eventually brought Sinclair back into the fold upon deciding to form a new band that would reflect the music they all loved. For a drummer, they recruited Johnny Fay, still at Kingston Collegiate, but who already had a reputation as a solid player. Fay began taking lessons at the age of eight after his parents John, a heart surgeon, and Loretta, recognized their son's passion for the instrument.

Rounding out the line-up was Davis Manning, a veteran saxophone player, 15 years their senior. They chose the name The Tragically Hip after hearing it in a clip shown on *Saturday Night Live* from Michael Nesmith's innovative 1982 music video/movie *Elephant Parts*. "For our first few rehearsals it was Rob and Johnny, Gord and me, doing bluesy, R&B kind of stuff," Sinclair explains. "We knew Davis through a friend of ours. He played with us for the first couple of years, and really helped us learn how to play that kind of music — Little Richard stuff, lots of Yardbirds, and lots of old Stones that people didn't really know."

The band made a conscious decision to stick with covers that weren't recognizable so they would be able to eventually blend in original songs. This led them in several directions during their first few years. "We started writing right away, sort of modest ideas," Sinclair says. "At that time no one was playing original music in the clubs; it was totally frowned upon. In Kingston it was a tribute to Genesis one week and tribute to the Stones the next. Bands like The Northern Pikes and 54·40 had just put out their first records and when they played on campus it was pretty cool, but it was more of a campus event. The town kids didn't get exposed to a lot of original music.

"That's why we started playing really, Kingston being what it was. A lot of our early songs were more acoustic-based so we wouldn't really perform them. Some of them were quite beautiful though, and Davis kind of pushed us to start writing more as a band and start expressing ourselves. He'd done quite a bit of writing when he was younger."

After providing his encouragement, Manning dropped out of the picture by 1985, at which point Sinclair and Downie brought in their new housemate Paul Langlois on rhythm guitar. He had been playing in a band with Hugh Dillon — an unusual turn of events since Langlois had initially been the target of the singer's bullying at hockey games during their high-school days. His new attitude helped earn Langlois the nickname Rock, one that also reflected his slight but unshakeable figure on stage. It was Langlois's unrelenting guitar style, and presence as Downie's on-stage foil, that immediately freed up Baker and Sinclair to weave melodies and thus provide the crucial element that had been missing from the music. From this point on, The Hip would begin developing a local following through their often manic interpretations of garage rock staples. "It was easier for us to learn the basic gist of a song," Sinclair says. "We'd learn the main riff and Gord would learn the first verse, then the rest we'd kind of jam out and try to make it our own. When we started writing, that was definitely the vibe we were working under: you get a cool-sounding riff and write a blues progression around it and go from there."

By his third year, Downie was finding the university experience unrewarding and the band was becoming his primary creative outlet. "I was in film school at Queen's, which sounds stupid to say because I wasn't really," he says. "I had a student card, and did pay my tuition eventually. Once we got together, formal education was the first casualty." Downie instead focused his energy on finding his voice. From the start he admired full-throated blues wailers like Free's Paul Rodgers, but also felt a pull toward the dramatics of the two Morrisons, Jim and Van. With the band cutting its teeth on early Van Morrison standards like "Gloria" and "I Can Only Give You Everything," Downie was able to capture the rough, Howlin' Wolf-inspired growl perfectly, and at the same time turn the performances into mini-movies through dark monologues that expanded upon the song's characters. Even though Downie was not yet writing many structured lyrics, these ad libs would ultimately show him a way inside the process.

The Hip's gigs at bars like Lakeview Manor and Zorba's were generating a lot of excitement, but general opinion remained divided. Downie says, "Within Kingston, there were some who thought we were a university, frat-boy band, too smart for our own good. And then obviously others who thought we were working-class bums."

Sinclair adds, "We started out doing a gig a month, which progressed to a weekend thing. Only gradually did it start taking over what we were all doing because people started coming out. There were a couple bands based out of Queen's that were trying to do the same thing we were doing, and we felt that we were in direct competition. One group in particular would do a Them song, while we were doing another. They were always a couple months behind us. Original music was just so remote from what we were exposed to."

As Downie's performing skills developed, other members of the band set about writing songs. Sinclair was the most prolific at the outset, adding several of his folk-inspired numbers to the set. These included the unreleased "Times Are Passing Us By," "Running For My Life" and "Waltz For Juliette," as well as what would become their first singles, "Small Town Bringdown" and "Last American Exit." If these songs represented anything, it was a deliberate attempt to overcome the one-dimensional perception many had of The Hip. "Back then being a band meant literally every man for himself," Sinclair says. "We were the only band in Kingston trying to write their own stuff. People thought we were kind of dumb to do it. We kept getting pushed to be a clone band — 'You guys should be a Doors clone band. Gord kind of looks like Jim Morrison.' We had that told to us a couple times with the reasoning that we'd make more money."

Sinclair's reaction can be heard in "Small Town Bringdown," a swipe at songwriters like John Mellencamp who at the time were glorifying the parochial experience, when all that young musicians like Sinclair wanted was to break out of their regional boundaries. The Hip's first attempt at this depended on recording primitive demos of their original material in hopes of getting it into the hands of anyone that could help. The goal was to get out-of-town gigs, and when the Blais Agency in Toronto showed some interest, Downie and Sinclair eagerly made the trip down the 401 for a meeting. "I think we went to anybody and everybody at some point," Downie says. "Sinclair and I put together a list of 300 songs that we knew and could play to show this guy in Toronto, and I remember him saying, 'Next time, could you guys bring me a list of 40?'"

Sinclair adds, "We were really flailing at that point. There were a couple modest studios where we could lay stuff down, but we were really rudderless. We'd make demos and enter them in the CFNY Battle Of The Bands and stuff like that and never hear back from anybody."

Tapes were even sent to the small independent labels that were beginning to pop up in the major centres, although even this proved more ambitious than the band anticipated. Several began landing on the desk of Tony Dewald at Og Records. "Back then we were getting 50–60 demo tapes a week in the mail," he says. "At one point The Tragically Hip sent us, like, five or six in a row, and we had to start sending them letters back saying, 'No, we hate you. Please don't send us stuff anymore!' Their stuff was always

Gord Downie, 1989
(Photo by Eric B. Brown)

the most professionally packaged. They were religious about sending out demo tapes to us, and we kept saying, 'No, don't bother. You're just not our style. Don't you understand? Go away!'"

However, the tape that found its way to artist manager/political pollster Allan Gregg forged an unlikely marriage. After failed attempts at becoming a musician as a teenager in Edmonton, by the late 1960s Gregg had moved into management and promoting, his biggest coup coming through booking an appearance by the fledgling Led Zeppelin. By the early 1970s he felt the pull of finding steady employment and found himself lingering in the halls on Parliament Hill while completing his Ph.D. at Carleton. In 1979 he started a polling firm, Decima Research, which maintained ties with the Progressive Conservatives up until Kim Campbell's disastrous 1993 campaign. Yet the music business always remained a passionate sideline venture for Gregg, and it was through Tory strategist Hugh Segal, whose brother-in-law had been casually assisting the band at gigs, that he first heard of The Tragically Hip in the summer of 1986.

The previous Christmas, Gregg had met Toronto band manager Jake Gold at a party thrown by the magazine *Music Express*, another of Gregg's ventures. The pair immediately began discussing the possibility of setting up some showcase gigs for Peter Panter, an artist Gregg was then managing. The New Jersey–born Gold first became involved with the Toronto music scene in early 1981 when a friend, Coleman York, lured Gold back from a job in L.A. to work with his band, The Numbers, as a road manager/lighting technician. Around the time of Gold's return, the band renamed itself Hot Tip and asked Gold to become their manager. "I said, 'Okay, I don't know anything about it, but I'll try.' That was sort of the beginning, and the last time I did anything but management — the last time I had a straight job — was the end of November, 1981."

The band cultivated their following among the Jam-inspired mod revival crowd, and strengthened it further after personnel changes led them to become The Purple Hearts. This band drew upon one of their older songs, "Sideways Elevator," and gained some notoriety after it started getting regular spins on CFNY. While The Purple Hearts kept Gold busy, he also became interested in a new-wave band called New Regime, which often opened for the Hearts. When The Purple Hearts finally disbanded, Gold refocused his energies on New Regime, as well as a company he had formed with Dave Kirby, manager of The Tenants and later a high-profile booking agent. Although Gold was able to secure an RCA recording contract for New Regime, his partnership with Kirby soon proved unfeasible. Instead, not long after, Gold and Gregg's business relationship would bloom, and they formed an official partnership in January, 1986.

In August, Gregg received The Tragically Hip's demo, and upon hearing it, urged Gold to investigate. The tape actually sat on Gregg's desk for about a week until one afternoon when he threw it on as he and a radio consultant were passing time in the office waiting for a third person to arrive for a meeting. "It was really, really rough," Gregg says of the demo. "It was live-off-the-floor on a four-track, but both of us looked at each other and said, 'Holy mackerel, is this ever raw and dynamic, a really exciting sound.' It was all their original stuff."

The partners determined the clincher would be the band's live show, and Gold scrambled to set up a gig. "I called up the guy at Larry's Hideaway and said, 'I need to see this band next week, can I have them play on Saturday night?' The guy said, 'Yeah sure, there's this Stones cover band playing.' I said, 'That'll be okay, we just need to see them.' They came into town and did a 40-minute set, and after the first 30 seconds, I just looked at Allan and said, 'We gotta sign these guys.'"

It wasn't just the band's sound that caught their imagination, Gold elaborates, but how Downie won over the sparse, and initially ambivalent audience. "[Downie] was a great communicator. The first time we heard him open his mouth, we just went, holy shit. At the end of their set that night, the whole place stood up and clapped. It was like a standing ovation, and it was undeniable if you were in the room that night that this was something special."

After the show, Gold and Gregg took the band to another bar for drinks and presented their management offer, one that the band readily accepted. Although big plans were discussed, the initial task was to get The Hip playing more often and to record their most time-tested original material for release as an eponymous EP. To accomplish the latter, the band was paired with Tom Cochrane's right-hand man Ken Greer, who accentuated the heartland-rock elements of the songs. Overall though, the rowdiness of their live show was preserved in songs like "I'm A Werewolf Baby" (based around a borrowed Hendrix riff), the manic "Evelyn" and the Stones-inspired "Highway Girl."

"Those songs that we ended up recording for the EP had been around for a while and they were certainly the most rehearsed," Sinclair says. "Working with Ken Greer was an attempt to get us with an established songwriter and get some guidance. When we went in for that session, it was literally a demo, in hopes of getting a recording contract. At the time we weren't even thinking that big; just hoping we'd get more gigs out of it."

In retrospect, it is unusual to see individual songwriting credits on the EP, notable for Downie's limited contribution, although he says that was already changing. "The EP is a compilation of all the first things we did, things we were doing in our live set, in and amongst the cover tunes," he says. "We had sentimental attachment to them and in the studio they wouldn't do anything but be what they were. When it came to decide who wrote what, that's what we did, but it spawned the need to come up with a better way of doing it so that we could actually be more productive and as prolific as a five-headed monster can be."

As these recordings proceeded, New Regime was finishing their second album for RCA. The plan for The Hip was to simply press a small run of the EP independently through Gold and Gregg's imprint — Rock Records — for sale at shows and for promotion purposes. But when an RCA rep heard The Hip's tapes, he was immediately enthusiastic about taking on the project. The managers worked out a licensing deal with the label that secured national distribution and promotion for the EP, and a release was slated for the beginning of 1988. However, this schedule did not sit well with the band, and they let it be known. "It got released December 11, 1987 in Kingston," Gold explains. "Everyone in the band had told all their friends and families that it would be out for Christmas. We were like, shit, what are we gonna do? The record company's telling us, 'You can't just release it in Kingston,' and we kept saying, 'Yes we can.' What ended up happening was Allan and I went to the six record stores in Kingston and said, 'Would you stock this record?' and they all said yeah. So we went back to the record company and said, 'Look, put them in your car and deliver them to the six stores.' They were all caught up in central buying and catalogue numbers and all these layers of getting it out. We just told them, put this many records in each store, and the record went to number two in Kingston after *The Joshua Tree*. When we did release the record in January, we had a story."

The Hip had spent most of 1987 on the road, building up their fanbases both at home and in other cities along the 401 between Windsor and Montreal. In Toronto, their managers took the risky step of booking a monthly residence at the Hotel Isabella. The shows started out as low-key affairs on Wednesday nights, mostly opportunities for Gold and Gregg to invite friends and colleagues to see the band in a casual atmosphere. The stage was so small that Baker had to stand to one side on the floor. After six months, word had spread to the point that line-ups became a common sight before the shows and the venue began booking the band regularly on weekends.

The Toronto press had trouble making up its mind. "There was a review of us when we first came in that basically talked about us playing Doors covers. There's a certain history of dismissal in Toronto that still exists today, which is fine," Downie says. In fact, acceptance was slow to come in most places when the band appeared for the first time, although by the time the EP was released in Kingston, The Hip were able to draw close to 1,000 home-town fans to a gig.

"We had a record-release party, and we shot a video for 'Small Town Bringdown' at this strip club in Kingston called Lakeview Manor that we used to play all the time," Sinclair says. "It was a big deal because we were now outside the borders of southeastern Ontario, which for Kingston bands was unheard of. We were rock stars at that point, and it was very, very weird, but cool."

Sights were now set on points west of Ontario, the first stop being Winnipeg. The five members, along with road manager Boyd Bailey, arrived expecting a week's worth of shows at the city's two major rock clubs. Both were owned by the same individual who demanded two longs sets per night, something the band were only too happy to supply. Yet, with an estimated 15 people in attendance the first night, The Hip were fired after the first set; the owner protested that he hadn't hired a punk band. "All of a sudden we had a week blown out, like a massive torpedo to our midship, and we were looking down the road thinking, 'Wow, this is going to be rough,'" Downie says. "But it didn't feel altogether horrible; in some ways it made me feel great, like we were doing things right."

As the band spent the rest of the night pondering their next move, by the morning they had received some unexpected support. One of the few in attendance had been longtime *Winnipeg Sun* rock critic John Kendle who was already aware of the buzz surrounding The Hip and was anxiously looking forward to seeing them. His glowing review of the band — pointedly headlined "Hip Get Gypped" — concluded with a diatribe against the short-sightedness of the club owner, and of the city's music community in general in not welcoming the out-of-towners. The words struck a chord, and by the next day several unlikely people had come to the band's rescue. "The Hell's Angels had a couple clubs in Winnipeg and they put us up in one of their hotels," Sinclair says. "Then the boxer Donny Lalonde had a place called Cornerboy's and he gave us a gig, even though it might not have been the most suitable place for a band. We were out there and had zero money, so right away we became popular in Winnipeg through sympathy. It worked out really great and people started coming out to the shows."

The Hip continued to ride the high and low tide of their notoriety throughout the rest of the tour. In Edmonton, plans to film the show for use in the video for "Last American Exit" had to be altered when only 10 people showed up at the club. The clip instead turned into an authentic glimpse of their life on the road; packing and unpacking their gear, doing the promotional rounds at radio stations and record stores, and viewing the world from the windows of their van. It was hardly a new story, but in a country where touring was such a daunting prospect for so many bands, the video became a romantic ideal.

A constant each night was the new batch of songs, growing rapidly through new contributions from individual members, as well as Downie's spontaneous musings. Langlois had written "She Didn't Know" and "When The Weight Comes Down," and one night, during a swampy jam out of the blues standard "Baby Please Don't Go," Downie began relating the story of a trip to New Orleans he and some friends had taken. Once completed, "New Orleans Is Sinking" became The Hip's first successful encapsulation of their initial influences, just as the British R&B bands needed several years to finally filter American music through their own experiences. The song itself is a simple blues variation, but played by a ragged bunch of Canadians weaned on punk and '70s hard rock, it somehow balances all these styles. And while Downie makes a valiant attempt to create some original blues verses, his abstract recollection of the city makes the song more akin to the Mardi Gras acid trip scene in *Easy Rider*.

The new songs overall reflected a fascination with the darker corners of American culture. This exploration eventually led back home with the prison-break tale, "38 Years Old," which for many across the country seemed to typify the Kingston experience upon first listen. Downie would explain that the song sprang from the opening line, "Two men broke loose in '73 / From Millhaven Maximum Security," a memory from his childhood, but that the rest was pure speculation as to what happened next. The brooding "Opiated" also seemed to evoke the hard life in small-town Ontario where drugs are often the only respite.

As The Hip earned fans one town at a time, it was a surprise that by the spring of 1988, both mainstream FM radio and MuchMusic had jumped all over "Small Town Bringdown" and "Last American Exit." From a narrow-minded point of view, the songs were manna from heaven for radio programmers dying for new music that fell in between insipid pop, post-punk nonconformism, and heavy metal excess — and which, more importantly, fulfilled their CanCon requirements. While it may have been for these reasons that the Toronto media suddenly claimed The Hip as their own, it was clear that the timeless qualities of both the band and the music exemplified the overall shift back to no-frills guitar rock which had been building through the slow re-acceptance of original live bands.

"The EP only sold 11,000 copies in its initial release, but the band was selling-out 1,000-seaters everywhere," Gold says. "They were way bigger than their record sales. I think it was a writer in Calgary who said, 'Save the five bucks for the record and go see the show instead.' Our original deal with the EP was just a license so when it was over we could walk away, and that's what we did. When we started talking to other labels, nobody was really interested, but we still had this thing going."

The EP had also received some attention from U.S. college radio and in the fall of 1988, The Hip earned a slot in the CMJ New Music Festival in New York City. One of those tipped off to the band's appearance was MCA A&R rep Bruce Dickinson who was as equally blown away by The Hip's set as Gold and Gregg were two years earlier. Dickinson came to Toronto in early December when the band performed at the Toronto Music Awards, and by Christmas The Tragically Hip were signed to MCA, ending speculation that they would sign a multi-album deal with RCA.

With the arrival of the new year, things accelerated as the band and their label determined how to approach their first album. "Every day, something new was coming down the line that was awesome," Downie describes. "'Well, Bruce thinks you should go down to Ardent Studios in Memphis. That would be a great spot, and he knows this guy Don Smith. He worked with Keith Richards. . . .' And you're just like, 'Ah, you're kidding right?'"

The decision to record in Memphis with Smith — fresh from working on Keith Richards's first solo album *Talk Is Cheap* — was nearly irrelevant since the band members felt thoroughly confident in their new material. All the songs that would comprise *Up To Here* were road-hardened, and the goal was simply to translate their energy onto tape. "It was our first recording experience in a way, like making a true record, in Memphis," Downie says. "My most vivid recollection is a round table in the studio totally covered in beer cans. Not a space on it, except for an ashtray. But we had the stamina to record like that because we'd come off of playing the songs three hundred nights in a row. Sometimes we'd be, like, 'Why is this not working?' which is where the producer comes in to sort of guide you along."

Sinclair agrees that *Up To Here* was the only record they could have possibly made at that point. "The humility of playing in shitty clubs night after night made us a better band. I wouldn't say we were ignoring the

crowd, but in order to have a good performance it was up to us to inter-
nalize what we were doing and let the songs speak for themselves. While
we were doing this we were writing, and that's what we brought in when
we made *Up To Here*. The songs were born of that, not necessarily navel-
gazing, but about digging in and trying to play really hard; trying to make
a good evening out of a bad evening with 20 people."

The album was snapped up by eager fans upon its release in the fall
of 1989. The lead-off single, "Blow At High Dough," was more hard-driving
than anything on the EP, and as a result it could not be removed from FM
playlists for months, at least until it was challenged by "New Orleans Is
Sinking." That song's popularity largely stemmed from the fact that it was
now the climax of The Hip's live show. They had turned this one-time
product of a loose jam into the window of opportunity every night where
anything could happen; where the sketch of a new song could be embell-
ished, or Downie's improvised monologues could meet the crowd's energy
head on, creating an often extended, catastrophic narrative. Although the
band had relied on improvisation all along to varying degrees, it was not
until "New Orleans Is Sinking" was transformed into what Downie calls a
"workshop," did it firmly alter the course of The Hip's creative process.

Reflecting on the song a decade later, Downie said, "In order for a show
to be great something has to happen, and that is the type of song where, if
you're feeling right, something can happen. No matter who you are, you love
a glimpse into the workshop. At the Big Apple in Colborne [Ontario], there's
the window where you can watch them making pies, and there's something
about that. It's only the big corporations that have created this clandestine
world where you're not supposed to see how something is made. In a weird
way that song shows we really have nothing to hide, that it's an ongoing
process when we're writing songs and that's the thing we care about most."

By 1990, *Up To Here* was a mandatory part of the soundtrack for high
school and university beer-drinking binges, and that was also reflected in
their hands-down claim to the Most Promising Artist Juno award that year.
Expectations continued to grow when the band got back on the road with
a set heavily stacked with new songs yet to be recorded. Some like "Crack
My Spine Like A Whip" and "On The Verge" upped the ante in terms of
energy, while others like "Get Back Again" and "Long Time Running" echoed
their first attempts at writing acoustic ballads. A MuchMusic broadcast
during the summer of a show taped earlier at Halifax's Misty Moon, whetted
an already voracious appetite for new material, but by the time that new
album would be released, The Hip had realized they had turned a corner.

Sessions for what would become *Road Apples* were undertaken in New Orleans upon the recommendation of Crash Vegas guitarist Colin Cripps. As a recent friend of the band, Cripps spoke highly of the casual atmosphere at Daniel Lanois's converted mansion at Chartres and Esplanade, which had greatly contributed to the mood of the first Crash Vegas album, *Red Earth*. Much like the experience of recording in Memphis, The Hip jumped at the chance at working in a place that seemed another of their spiritual homes.

"It was around that time that Daniel was dabbling with the idea of opening the studio up as a commercial venture," Downie says. "We'd approached him about working there, and we got in there right at the point where we could see into his workshop. But he wasn't around. His assistant, Mark Howard, was there and Malcolm Burn. That was thrilling down there in the French Quarter, kind of the same vibe as Memphis, but this time the difference was that we were developing songs."

With Don Smith once again producing, The Hip arrived in much the same state as they had in Memphis, with a large cache of road-tested new material that could quickly be recorded, although their surroundings eventually seeped into their work habits. Some of the flat-out rockers like "Crack My Spine" were ditched in favour of moodier pieces like "The Luxury" and "Fight." However, these songs had been played live as well; the real breakthrough came one day when "Last Of The Unplucked Gems" emerged fully formed out of a lazy jam session. "That was something we wrote in the studio which was just a vibe," Sinclair says. "We weren't really considering it at the time, but Don was into it and had the machines rolling. The lightbulb went on at that point where we all thought, this is kind of cool, you can goof around in the environment. Maybe it doesn't have to have a start and a middle and a bridge and a chorus and an ending, maybe it can just be open-ended."

Downie felt extra affirmation when a few outside the band recognized it as well. "There was a review at the time in the *Globe & Mail*. It was generally derisive — I don't know who wrote it, but I can think of maybe a half-dozen guys there who didn't like us — but it said 'Last Of The Unplucked Gems' was a good sign of things to come, and that it's appropriate that it's the last song on the record. I totally agreed with that, and the whole review really. The record was okay, but that was a new direction — getting together and being stimulated by a time and place. It ushered in a new era of being able to write diaphanously."

Downie continues, "Back then our immediate acceptance kind of created this impostor syndrome, this fear of fraudulence, that took about 10 years to eradicate. I couldn't catch up with it for a long time. I was waiting at any moment for the door to burst open and someone say, 'You didn't make this happen.'"

Indeed, Downie was getting nearer to a voice more his own rather than his heroes. In large part this was due to his personal exploration of images that were closer to home, something that was largely put aside for the sake of traditional rock and roll storytelling on *Up To Here*. His best moments on *Road Apples* occur when an indefinable menace is accentuated by the music, as in "Little Bones," or when the listener is suddenly challenged by the appearance of Canadian iconography — the doomed painter Tom Thomson in "Three Pistols," and the ongoing language debate in "Born In The Water." This approach could have gone even deeper if the album had included "Montreal," written after the December 6, 1989 Ecole Polytechnique massacre, but never recorded. The album's most moving image was instead saved for the acoustic vignette "Fiddler's Green," written as a tribute to Downie's young nephew Charles Gillespie, who had died of a heart ailment the previous September.

It was with the release of *Road Apples* in the spring of 1991 that critics in Canada began recognizing that Downie was a more complex figure than his on-stage image suggested. With young Canadian songwriters now assuming the mantle of cultural caretakers, the reasons for Downie's ascension as the most popular of these voices became a compelling debate. The songs were not overtly political, nor were they byproducts of the confessional ballad form. In some ways they were pure cut-and-paste pop art with roots in surrealism. The Canadiana references therefore became guideposts into a song's depths, and the resulting marriage of language and music became an invigorating experience that had never been so directly aimed at young Canadians before.

"The voice I use is the voice from the stage, which at that time was a voice maybe bent on obfuscation," Downie explains. "I don't want to call it a persona, because I believed in everything I did, perhaps at the risk of being precious or earnest. But it's the voice of a host, saying welcome. You know, when you're standing in a room full of people, you're always surprised at the voice that comes out. In my case it goes on tape, then you listen back and retool and set your course toward finding your voice. That's a long process of writing and singing."

In 1991, The Tragically Hip unquestionably became The People's Band in Canada. That August, in the wake of winning the Juno for Entertainer

Of The Year, their hometown took the unusual step of handing them the key to the city in return for "the honour and glory they've brought to Kingston," in the words of Mayor Helen Cooper. It was a timely gesture since most fans there and across the country were beginning to feel it was only a matter of time before The Hip gave themselves over to the rest of the world. This seemed an unfamiliar twist to the traditional Canadian stance, in that instead of abandoning a homegrown artist who was obviously attempting to assimilate into the global pop market, Hip fans seemed so secure in their idols' representation of Canada that it became almost necessary that The Tragically Hip carry the banner in other parts of the world. This was obviously a responsibility the band was not prepared to bear. Instead, they set about gaining new fans in the U.S. and Europe with the same humility they had shown at home.

It came easiest in northern U.S. border cities like Cleveland, Detroit, Chicago and Seattle where the buzz was easily translatable. Yet, there were also cities like Tucson, Arizona and Dallas, Texas which embraced The Hip as well, mostly through support from local radio. Their early touring experience in the U.S. was just as hit-and-miss as it had been in Canada. Stories — truthful or not — had filtered back since their first forays in 1989; like the night in Bloomington, Indiana when the total number of musicians and crew, which now included trusted road manager Dave Powell and soundman Mark Vreeken, outnumbered the five people in the audience.

At a club in Madison, Wisconsin, The Hip arrived to find they had been mistakenly double-booked with an indie band called Nirvana. The road-weary young trio were there to meet with local producer Butch Vig before beginning work on their first major-label album, and agreed to open the show. Downie recalls, "I remember playing pinball in the back after soundcheck, and what-would-be Kurt Cobain was lying on a table curled up in a ball. I was trying to make conversation — 'Pretty tired, huh?' They attracted a crowd of about 150, which dwindled down to about 40 when we went on. That was yet another of life's cruel lessons, never go on after a band from Seattle!"

The Hip found a more receptive response in Europe, where they played before their biggest audience to that point at the Pink Pop Festival in Holland, and took the first of many trips to Germany and Scandinavia. The open-minded concept of the European rock festival had slowly been finding its way to North America where, until the early '90s, simple logistical and financial constraints had prevented many from attempting to put on similar events. When Perry Farrell daringly launched Lollapalooza in 1991, it firmly marked modern rock's ascension in the mainstream North American marketplace, and instantly revolutionized large-scale touring in the process. It became clear to The Hip after being part of the massive multi-city Canada Day concerts in 1992, that with the right line-up, a Canadian equivalent of Lollapalooza could be staged, hence expanding the fan bases of all the bands involved. Plans were hatched for the tour that fall as The Hip prepared to record its next album, one that MCA America was counting on to match Canadian sales with equivalent U.S. numbers.

The songs were once again being written on the road. Much of Downie's

Gord Downie at Another
Roadside Attraction in
Markham, Ontario, 1993
(Photo by Richard Beland)

travelling time was passed with his nose buried in books and two in particular had made a strong impact on him during the *Road Apples* tour. One was *The Book Of Laughter And Forgetting*, by Milan Kundera that spurred Downie's stream-of-consciousness writing. It would directly contribute to a new song that built on a simple one-chord riff which gathered into a fury around a brief Downie interpretation of existence. "Fully Completely" was a logical extension of the ephemeral qualities of "Last Of The Unplucked Gems," although here the band sounded entirely uninhibited. The song became a cornerstone of the sessions, eventually earning its place as the title track.

Another arrived after Downie read Hugh MacLennan's *The Watch That Ends The Night*, the story of a love triangle set in pre- and post-WWII Montreal. Although the book's main theme was the effects of the Depression on the generation that survived it, how the characters each survived was both quintessentially Canadian and genuinely moving. MacLennan had been one of the first internationally known Canadian novelists, revered for his grasp of the country's ingrained socio-political attitudes, and *Watch* was arguably his most personal work. It inspired Downie's writing of "Courage" to the point that the song would not only bear a personal dedication to

MacLennan, but also contain a key line from the book as its final verse. "I lifted that passage. I just couldn't resist," Downie says. "Right or wrong, I put it in. There are some nights when I sing it and think, it's inappropriate because you're placing the words way above the music."

Other songs sprung from unusual sources. While visiting the Smithsonian Air & Space Museum on tour, the band saw an exhibit about the tiny cameras that were mounted on pigeons to take aerial photographs during the First World War. This unwieldy concept was translated to the song "Pigeon Camera" which examined human beings as similarly unmanageable objects sent out into the world.

There, they also saw the hat that bomber pilots in the Second World War earned for successfully completing fifty missions. Over a crunching rhythm that recalled The Stooges' "Down In The Street," Downie somehow combined this piece of recent archaeology with a straight re-telling of how young Toronto Maple Leaf defenceman Bill Barilko became an unlikely hero by scoring the 1951 Stanley Cup–winning goal, only to disappear that August as he flew home to Timmins, Ontario from a fishing trip on James Bay. He and the pilot would not be located until 11 years later when the wreckage of their plane was found 60 miles north of Cochrane. As the lyric describes, Downie took the story almost verbatim from a Barilko hockey card, but it was a legend that already loomed large in the annals of hockey history. Among the rumours that circulated prior to 1962 was a story that Barilko, of Russian heritage, had ordered the pilot to fly to the Soviet Union where he began coaching young players the hard-hitting Canadian style. The eventual song that emerged from these two ideas, "Fifty Mission Cap," would indelibly align The Tragically Hip to Canada's game, reinforced by their presence at a ceremony honouring the 50th anniversary of Barilko's historic goal. But for those who had been following Downie's evolution as a writer, the juxtaposition of images revealed a lot more.

"'Fifty Mission Cap' and 'Courage' are pretty good examples of an attractive image, or a salient idea, and trying to make a song out of it. And not necessarily succeeding; just the constant singing of it is all that's necessary for it to exist," Downie explains. "A fifty mission cap on its own signifies experience, talent, and luck. Then I put that together with the Bill Barilko story. Generally we'll throw everything into the mix and start seeing what happens. I probably put both images in and just couldn't take either out, so I had to figure a way to loosely stitch these things together. It's the stitching that provides any kind of meaning.

"[Barilko's story] is almost the greatest example of being struck down in your prime after you do something great and unique. Then you have this idea of a kid having a fifty mission cap, and wanting to get to fifty missions faster than it actually takes, but working it in to look like it is; to look like you've had that experience and to appear to be beyond your years. But then, if you like to hear someone say, 'won the Leafs the Cup,' then that might be all it takes."

Coincidentally, the Toronto Maple Leafs retired Barilko's number on October 6, 1992, one week before his story would be presented to a wider audience with the release of *Fully Completely*.

Sessions for *Fully Completely* took place in London, England during the summer of 1992. This time the band was paired with producer Chris Tsangarides at the behest of MCA in the hopes of getting a more American radio-friendly sound. Tsangarides had a proven reputation in this area through his recent work with Concrete Blonde. For The Tragically Hip, it was an abrupt change from their previous recording experiences.

"Chris was a real schooled producer," Sinclair says. "He had his way of doing things, so there wasn't a lot of ensemble writing and playing on that record. It was by-the-books. He was pretty hot off of working with Concrete Blonde so we were happy to work with him, but in retrospect we realized how incredibly naïve we were at the time that we were making that record — 'What? The band shouldn't be around for the mix? Oh, okay.'"

Downie adds, "It was a very cold kind of experience. The five of us were really brought together because there was nothing else to do. We stayed in a really depressing hotel in a nothing area of London, then went off every day to another nothing area of London to work. The actual in-studio time was a great experience, all very organized. It seems with every record we invent a new process of writing. I was definitely moving into the cockpit in terms of writing the words, so I was getting more diligent about my note-keeping and all that kind of stuff."

With immediate attention once again focused on its Canadianisms when *Fully Completely* was released that fall, two other songs quickly came to the fore. The story of David Milgaard had changed every Canadian's perception of the law after the Saskatchewan man, convicted for the rape and murder of a young Native woman in 1971, finally had the many vehement protests of his innocence heard after nearly 20 years behind bars. Through the tireless work of his mother Joyce, Milgaard was eventually granted a new trial on the basis of a DNA test. As more and more information emerged concerning flaws in the Crown's case, the entire country waited in anticipation of the conviction being overturned. When Milgaard was ultimately set free to seek a new trial, the elation in seeing justice finally served quickly turned into a hollow victory in knowing that so much of his life had been lost in the meantime. Downie joined in the ambiguous celebration with "Wheat Kings," still the song with the most obvious origins in The Tragically Hip catalogue, and one that continues to beguile its author. "I realized the thing I like about that song the most is the line, 'Late breaking story on the CBC / A nation whispers we always knew he'd go free.' At the time I thought, that's so us [as Canadians]; for a person to stand there and say to someone, 'Oh, we'd always knew he'd go free.' It's like telling people what they already know, even though that's not what you really intended."

In another case of impeccable timing, Milgaard was released from prison in 1993 in time to meet the band at the Vancouver Another Roadside Attraction show. As the second ARA tour began in 1995, Milgaard met them again to mark the commutation of his sentence.

On the other hand, "Locked In The Trunk Of A Car" represented a darker aspect of the Canadian psyche that had rarely been touched on in song. It sprang from an on-stage monologue describing a fictional double suicide, but its eventual popularity forced Downie to acknowledge the dangerous territory he was potentially entering, especially in the wake of subsequent high-profile violent crimes. "I've had concerns about that song since," Downie admits. "Jake [Gold] was actually contacted by the RCMP at one point because of a guy who was a suspect in a case where a woman was abducted from a flower shop in Toronto, and she and her husband were both later found in the trunk of a car. It was totally coincidental, but it was shaky ground because the guy told the police he knew me, or that I wrote the song about him. And because he was still a suspect, it was all considered evidence. I've never really looked at the song the same since. It's a big fan favourite, although we don't play it much anymore because it kind of gives me an uneasy feeling. But I also look at it in terms of the American murder ballad; there's not a lot of violent, bloody song history in Canada that I know of, so maybe this one can maybe go in that file, but it's not really about any one thing."

Nevertheless, the reception given "Trunk Of A Car" and "Courage" on radio and video brought The Hip an even more broad-based audience in Canada, and firmly moved them out of the club and campus circuit. The *Fully Completely* tour would find them playing Massey Hall in Toronto and small arenas in other big cities. The momentum that was expected to carry over into the album's U.S. release the following spring, did not, however, manifest itself. There, *Fully Completely* received lukewarm reviews despite favourable radio reaction, prompting MCA to cease its promotion of the album after only a few weeks. "We were still holding out hope for the equivalent American success," Sinclair says. "'Gee, we sold 300,000 copies of this record in Canada. There's 10 times as many people in the States, so 10 times 300,000 is. . . . I think I'm going to move next door to Bruce Springsteen. We're going to be huge, just wait!' Two weeks before the record comes out, all the record company is saying is, 'It's gonna be big boys, look out!' Then the week after, no one returns our calls. That's the way it is."

Part of their record company troubles stemmed from Bruce Dickinson's departure from MCA after *Fully Completely*'s release. Without his backing, Gold and Gregg could not come to terms with the label in renegotiating the band's U.S. contract, prompting a new deal with Atlantic while keeping ties with MCA in Canada and the rest of the world.

Still, this was all a minor distraction as energy had to be focused on their summer festival tour, now given the name Another Roadside Attraction from the Tom Robbins novel. It would be a massive undertaking, rarely seen in Canada since the Festival Express tour of 1970, featuring The Grateful Dead and Janis Joplin, and to a lesser extent, the Heatwave and Police Picnic festivals of the early '80s. Building on the Lollapalooza model, the tour would hit several of the country's large outdoor concert parks with an all-day line-up stacked with Canadian artists. As a bit of insurance for this risky venture, The Hip invited their Australian counterparts Midnight Oil to co-headline. The pairing seemed natural, since the Oils had likewise built up a loyal grassroots following at home and abroad. In singer Peter Garrett, the band had a bona fide Australian cultural figurehead thanks to his tireless political activism. Their current album, *Earth And Sun And Moon*, was expanding their North America fan base, and as fans themselves, The Hip saw the Oils' participation as both an honour and a challenge.

The bill also featured the main cast of Crash Vegas, Daniel Lanois, Irish group Hothouse Flowers, and other supporting characters in each city. If there were any doubts that The Hip couldn't pull the entire crowd themselves, they were erased after the first show in Victoria. "The first night, right after Midnight Oil finished their last song — after literally the last note they hit — the crowd started chanting 'Hip! Hip! Hip!'" Jake Gold says. "This was our favourite band; it was unbelievable for all of us to be playing with Midnight Oil, and it made us all feel a little weird."

Sinclair concurs that their crowd's growing zealousness heightened the energy of the shows. "The first couple of shows going on after Midnight Oil was the hardest thing we'd ever had to do, because they were by far one of the best live acts on the planet. The overall quality of music on that tour was amazing. Daniel was inspiring every night, as was Crash who we'd known for two years, but every night the Oils were so intense and so good musically. Nice people too, but you knew they were out to steal the audience every night. Their credo always was that they never opened up for anybody, and they never had. We assured them that this was not like an opening thing. We all got to know each other and there was no ego involved, but you knew they wanted to take us down every night, and they played like it. I don't think we ever got close to being as great as they are, but certainly the effort we put into it made us a better band in our minds."

As the tour progressed, a major political issue of that summer — the proposed cutting of old growth forest at Clayoquot Sound on Vancouver Island — began dominating the atmosphere. As outspoken supporters of environmental causes in Australia, Midnight Oil immediately threw their support behind the protesters, going as far as playing an impromptu set at one of the logging road blockades. Feeling the urge to follow up on this example, the main participants of the tour rallied around a song Oils' drummer Rob Hirst offered called "Land." Following an Oils on-air performance in Calgary, Lanois organized a makeshift session in the radio station's recording studio, and much of the touring party aided in laying down the song, each singer contributing their own verses. The single came to represent not only a spontaneous show of support for the protests, but a snapshot of the camaraderie that had quickly developed during the tour. By the time of the final show in Edmonton, members of The Hip could feel a new sense of purpose.

"We really got a sense of what the power of the music is all about, especially from the Oils," Sinclair says. "Garrett would get down on the people that were moshing every night and remind them about the humanity that was involved. We really learned a lot from those guys about the responsibilities up there regarding the safety of the crowd, and also the message that you're getting across. We went from being this little barroom band to being more grown-up by the end of that tour."

These responsibilities would ultimately extend to The Hip's commitment to several charitable organizations in the coming years, including Camp Trillium, in aid of kids with cancer, and their memorable United Way benefit show opening for Rush at Maple Leaf Gardens in December, 1993. This was The Hip's first appearance at the hallowed arena, and most pundits saw it as a symbolic passing of the torch since it had taken Rush almost up to that point to earn even a modicum of critical respect outside of Canada, a situation that The Hip were now facing themselves. Rush had overcome their underdog status through a consistent re-evaluation of their songwriting process without ever tampering with their original goals as musicians, or the bond with their American fan base which had built up steadily over years of touring. For The Tragically Hip, their evolution as musicians was also ongoing, but their relationship to the fans was much more complicated. When *Fully Completely* failed to conquer America, the band resigned themselves to the U.S. club circuit once again, although this reality only seemed to strengthen Canadian fans' resolve to see them win out. Some of the most determined would drive hundreds, often thousands, of kilometres to see The Hip play in the U.S., and then make it known they had made the effort. Likewise, Canadians already living and working in these U.S. cities would drag their friends out to the shows in an attempt to educate them about Canadian culture. This led to some uncomfortable situations for the band who, in true form, were just trying to put on a good rock and roll show.

"We were playing to a lot of expats and the homesick and student travellers abroad, almost like the USO," Downie says. "I'd make jokes about performing for the troops in these far-off places. They'd make themselves known, and in ridiculous ways. I would only notice it until after the show when I'd be standing around talking and there would be one American saying, 'You guys were pretty good,' and then a guy from Canada going, 'Yeah, fuckin' right! They're Canadian boys, they're more than pretty good!' — really defensive. I understood it; the homesickness mixed with alcohol is a pretty potent brew. It might have been a guy who took a job down in St. Louis and all his friends think he's a hoser because all he talks about is Canada and they're getting tired of it, so he's going to show them something from Canada.

"They're not necessarily Hip fans, I've noticed," Downie continues. "All I was really concerned about was my sisters up front, the girls that regardless of where they were from got there first. They were there early on and a performance was speaking to them, and they didn't seem to care where it came from, and they were elbowed out after two songs. That's when — rather than trying to figure out what we were — I tried to figure out what we weren't. I had no affinity for people that would do that, for whatever reason they were doing it."

As always, The Hip were previewing new material on the road. One was a tough rocker called "Thugs" with a lyric that got to the heart of bad relationships: "Everyone's got their breaking point / With me it's spiders, with you it's me." Another was a blank verse poem about a nautical disaster that fit seamlessly in the middle of "New Orleans Is Sinking." Each night, the song's churning chord progression would cautiously appear, then build as the narrator recalled a dream of a shipwreck off the coast of France, until the details promptly shifted to an unwanted phone call from an ex-lover. The song followed in the tradition of Gordon Lightfoot's "Wreck Of The Edmund Fitzgerald," and the Rheostatics' "Saskatchewan," but the last loaded image of fingernails scratching on a hull lifted the song even further beyond any standard comparisons. It remains the perfect example of how the band's music and Downie's poetics could be interwoven to create a thoroughly moving experience.

Downie explains that the band had been toying with "Nautical Disaster," as it would be known, ever since they spent some time in an Amsterdam studio during a break in the European leg of the tour. "That was us dumping out our shoeboxes and trying to get some things onto tape so we wouldn't forget them, and that song came out very quickly from a circular bass line. I had to figure out where I was in the song and how to blurt this thing out. To this day if I even get remotely distracted, I'll forget the lyric. If I forget a line, I just can't pick it up again so the song might as well end. I find that very interesting; maybe the song's haunted."

Several theories as to the inspiration for "Nautical Disaster" immediately sprang up, the most popular being the battle of Dieppe, one of the most horrific missions of the Second World War for the Canadian Army. However, Downie says he was thinking mostly about the sinking of the great German warship Bismarck. "That's where the factual backbone comes from, if there is one. It was a compelling story; it was such an über-ship that had downed a lot of other ships, and in the end it went down in a way that was brutal. And the treatment of the sailors that were still alive by the Brits was equally brutal. All's fair in love and war, obviously, but in the end you feel a remorse for the actual sailors. I've always maintained that the lyric was spontaneous, but recently I was going through my notes and found endless drafts of it. Endless, but they don't really change."

Following Another Roadside Attraction and some time off, The Hip holed up in Kingston to work out new material. It was accepted that their approach this time would be more spontaneous compared to the experience of recording *Fully Completely*. With the pressure off to please MCA America, the band desired a return to the freedom they had found recording in New Orleans, and developing songs outside of a live setting. The band found the appropriate collaborator in Daniel Lanois protégé Mark Howard, and upon his arrival at their Kingston rehearsal space they began recording rough sketches of the songs. It was Downie who preferred this method most, as the band's personal interplay brought out the best in his voice as it attempted to fit somewhere in the mix. It was even hotly debated at one point whether or not to release the demos as they were, as Howard's contributions were having an immediate effect. "If you could have heard that record three months before we finished it, it was really out there," Downie says. "We probably sanded a lot out, but it was all Mark's influence in terms of the different sounds that he was working with, which at the time were cutting edge."

Sinclair adds, "Mark's experience with Daniel was what drew us to him, and a lot of what Daniel does, Mark's a big part of that. He messes around with gear all the time and gets cool sounds. The biggest thing about it is that he's not afraid to get them down on tape. That's what we really needed."

With the scene shifting to Howard's more familiar New Orleans digs, The Hip dug into the most abstract material they had written thus far. Unlike previous albums, no one song — apart from perhaps the indefinable "Nautical Disaster" — emerged as a clear indicator of what the overall tone of the sessions would be. Instead, songs began blurring into one another, with the traditional Lanois techniques of ambience and layered percussion remaining a constant. The songs changed radically from day to day as well; "Daredevil" starting as an almost formless mantra, until finally emerging as an angular rocker. "So Hard Done By" was the opposite, beginning as something that wouldn't have sounded out of place on *Road Apples* until being transformed into a swampy blues stomp.

Overall, what came through most was a darkness that Downie had only hinted at in the past. The album's title, *Day For Night*, seemed a perfect expression of the mask covering whatever meaning lay within each song. An echo from Downie's film studies, it was also the title of Truffaut's famous exploration of inner conflicts on a film set.

There would be no overt Canadian iconography on this record. Throughout the songs, images moved as elusively as the music, providing glimpses of what can only be described as a collective subconscious; places that were familiar but never fully explored, whether it was the metropolis noir, funeral home and kitchen window of "Greasy Jungle," or Springside Park, with its coffee-coloured ice, peeling birch bark and sound of rushing water in the dark, in "An Inch An Hour."

Since the songs stemmed directly from the subconscious, they therefore took time to seep back in, as suggested by the recurring line, "But your finger starts to wiggle and landscapes emerge." The impact of "Grace, Too" would reveal itself slowly, as the listener begins to question whether to praise or fear the song's subject. It was all part of the added attention Downie was giving to the lyrics, where boundaries between the political and the personal were completely eliminated. "All of our songs are about war," he says. "You can use them for any situation you desire, and I love 'Grace, Too' because of that. It has that resonance to the affairs of the day. It's just UN peacekeeping language — 'rules of engagement' — but definitely, the enlarged bits have their roots in the tiniest relationships."

Even "Scared," arguably the most direct song on the record, turns on its acoustic ballad arrangement with an uncomfortably clinical exploration of the nature of fear. When Downie sings, "Now there's a precious few that can prove, that at the root this is all nothing but cold calculation," the juxtaposition of the music and the message is indeed unnerving, as if the lilting melody is merely a distraction in order for the listener to submit to the experiment. Even more profound is "Titanic Terrarium," a lyric that Downie considers to be one of his best. It envisions the planet as the great unsinkable ship, likewise at the mercy of those who built and steer her. The lesson lay in avoiding human arrogance, illustrated by the song's simple example of staying off a Canadian highway in bad weather, and the aphorism, "If there's a glory in miracles, it's that they're reversible." The song was one of the few that appeared on the album in its original demo form, accentuated by some spooky ambient guitar from Bill Dillon, and its primitive qualities sent a message that despite their success, The Hip were determined to do things their own way — even if everyone else might not have been prepared for it. "After *Fully Completely* I read something that said we were poised to go in a different direction," Downie says. "I guess that's always been the case, but when we put out *Day For Night* it was perceived as being introspective, moody, dark."

When *Day For Night* was released in the fall of 1994 the initial response was mixed. Not helping matters was the lack of an obvious single; some stations settled on "Fire In The Hole," the album's most tension-filled song and perhaps the most raging song The Hip had ever done. "I think the reason people decided to go with that was because the rest of the record was so far removed," Sinclair says. "For them, 'Fire In The Hole' was the closest thing to a rock and roll song we had on the record."

In Canada, the album once again built upon previous sales, positioning The Hip for a year that would firmly establish their myth. It began with the announcement of a two-month cross-Canada arena tour. Although the

The Tragically Hip circa *Day For Night*, 1994
(Photo by Clemmens Rikken, courtesy of The Management Trust)

band were no stranger to arenas, this would mark the first time since Rush that a Canadian band would sell out all the major hockey rinks. With the Odds and Change of Heart in tow, the tour started in the Maritimes in January, slowly building up to the most anticipated show, Maple Leaf Gardens on February 10, 1995. The Hip's set list rarely changed from the first show, the vast selection of *Day For Night* songs blending well with the older material, but everyone in attendance that night held back for the moment when "Fifty Mission Cap" would kick in and the ghost of Bill Barilko would momentarily be resurrected on his home ice. The band struggled to compete with the crowd's roar throughout the song, yet for many this was the moment that would finally codify The Tragically Hip's place in Canadian culture: the biggest band in the country, playing its most prestigious rock venue and doing a song about a Canadian legend.

In true Canadian fashion, the members of The Hip could hardly believe it themselves. "We were surprised," Sinclair admits. "We were really worried and questioning the judgement of Jake and Allan in booking us in arenas. In that particular case the shows sold out right away, and we were left picking our jaws up off the floor because we'd never really had a sense that things were at that scale. I mean, we learned to do what we do by playing the half and quarter-sold rooms and trying to go over well, and that's much more of a challenge than playing a sold-out hockey rink."

For Jake Gold, the tour, and the Gardens show in particular, turned out to be the pinnacle of everything he had been working toward. "I was standing at the soundboard when they went into 'Fifty Mission Cap' and I looked at my friend and said, 'Man, this is why I do this.' You can't really describe the feeling because here I was, at the altar of rock in Toronto, and Canada as far as I was concerned, and for the first time a band I was working with was headlining. It was a real special moment. I was standing with a guy who was in the business and during that song he turned to me and said, 'Do you think the guys would want to play with The Stones this summer?'"

The Hip would not only accept those shows, but also join the Jimmy Page/Robert Plant tour in the U.S. immediately following the Canadian dates. Furthermore, March 25 found them on *Saturday Night Live* at the behest of the host and fellow Kingstonian, Dan Aykroyd. The band performed "Grace, Too" and "Nautical Disaster," the latter quoting a line from the Skydiggers' "A Penny More." Gold summed up this flurry of activity by saying simply, "If you were a band that was growing up in the '70s, to be on *Saturday Night Live*, play with Led Zeppelin, and play with The Rolling Stones all in one year; that was it, you know?"

The experience seemed to have profound meaning especially for Sinclair and Baker, in putting their own success into perspective. Sinclair admits, "That was definitely the biggest aspect, going from pretending to be the Stones and Led Zeppelin to suddenly, here's me with Keith Richards backstage. What the fuck am I doing here? We did a series of shows with the Stones over a couple weeks in Europe. They would do the über-stadiums with 85,000 dudes in black leather coats standing there. That was a real challenge for us because there was maybe 10 people in that audience that had heard of us before, and you had to live to tell about it."

Sinclair proudly adds they drew some rare attention from Mick Jagger during the shows and received similar admiration from Robert Plant. "Robert's a big music fan and he really made us feel more than welcome. I don't know whether it was a good idea for us commercially to support them, because how many records did we sell as a result of that? Probably not too many. But when Robert Plant phones you up and asks if you want to do it, what are you supposed to say? It's an opportunity of a lifetime, and we learned a lot from being in that position where you have to convey what you're trying to do in front of an audience that's not really user-friendly. That's what makes you a better band."

While all this was going on, everyone was scrambling to put the finishing touches on the second Another Roadside Attraction for that summer. It would build on the success of the first one by including a stronger Canadian contingent, which simultaneously would erase whatever ugly memories remained of the Canada Day '94 show. The Rheostatics, The Inbreds, Eric's Trip and Spirit of the West would join Blues Traveller, Ziggy

Marley and Matthew Sweet. The Hip were clearly the hosts this time, although their closing set resembled more of an expected denouement rather than a rousing climax. With each familiar song, the entire crowd would shout back every line in tribute to whatever personal meaning it held. The shows therefore became a testament to the power of both the language and the music that propelled it. One could only be left wondering to what extent this devotion was having an effect on the band as artists.

"It's overwhelming to certain people," Downie states bluntly. "I want to say that I have a disdain for ceremony, but I think I just naturally take my nana's approach; she said, 'I wouldn't go to the lobby of my building to see Frank Sinatra.' It was hard to thrill her. So I probably thought, 'These people are really fucking up my timing here.' It also really started to push my pitch around, and that was probably the point where I decided there's room for only one demagogue tonight, and it's me. I'll go after anyone else that tries to take any portion of my space."

Whether the notion of fully engaging an audience had grown beyond their control, or simply that the personal and artistic maturing process had firmly taken root, after 1995 The Tragically Hip seemed to already be settling into the role of CanRock elder statesmen. The year saw them accomplish more than any other Canadian band of their generation could ever hope to without compromising their values. But instead of once again attempting to use these as a springboard toward further international attention, the band discovered that Canada was in fact their only safe haven. Despite the increased exposure south of the border, *Day For Night* had barely dented the U.S. charts.

All along, Gold and Gregg had hardly been consumed by The Hip's fortunes. Even back when the first EP was hitting stores, Gold was placing equal bets on Plasterscene Replicas, a Queen Street outfit with ties to producer Michael Phillip Wojewoda. The band's only album, the independently released *Glow*, remains a classic piece of late-'80s paisley-pop, featuring equal songwriting contributions from the three constant members Chas Salmon, Stephen Stewart and Brendan Cavin. The band's inability to keep a drummer forced Wojewoda behind the kit once he started recording them. "They were a nation of three, and they were very innocent kind of people," Wojewoda explains. "In rehearsal, the three of them would face each other, away from the drummer; they literally wouldn't let anybody in. They were eccentric, all of them, in their way. We'd done some demos with Glenn Milchem and Ambrose Pottie, and then they had another drummer who furiously quit a few weeks before the recording session. I didn't really want to get that involved because of my workload, but I figured we had momentum and the tunes were well-rehearsed so I snuck in there and did it. But during rehearsal when I was behind the kit and started critiquing, they would get really stand-offish. If I stood up from the stool and leaned against the wall to talk to them, they were much more receptive."

The regional success of *Glow*'s two singles, "We Can Walk" and "All I See" brought interest from Gold, who immediately discovered he was dealing with an entirely different group of personalities from The Hip. Wojewoda explains, "That's when it all went downhill. Not because of Jake at all. I actually think he's a really sweet guy; old-school as hell, but a good guy. It was weird because the first time he called me he said, 'The band isn't happy with the way things are going,' and I'm like, 'What the fuck is going on? First of all, who the hell are you?' They wanted to renegotiate the arrangements they'd made with me and it got very messy. In the end it all collapsed under its own weight, for a whole bunch of personal reasons that didn't have much to do with music."

In the wake of this failure, Gold and Gregg, now working under the banner The Management Trust, focused their attention on more straight-forward rock bands that could follow the trail The Hip had blazed. One was a hard-working quartet from Winnipeg attempting to break into Toronto through a weekly residency at The Horseshoe. The Watchmen formed in 1987 with cousins Danny Greaves and Sammy Kohn, along with childhood friend Joey Serlin who had all started playing music together in their early adolescence. With Greaves and Kohn going on to university, Serlin started playing guitar in a full-time bar band that included bassist Pete Loewen, eventually coaxing Greaves back when a singer was needed, and Kohn when a drummer was needed. Serlin took charge of the new line-up, renaming them after his favourite comic book series at the time, writing original songs, and trying to carve out a place in Winnipeg's tough rock scene.

"At the time there were only two clubs in town where you could play original music," Serlin says. "Winnipeg was the last stronghold of heavy metal and there were a shitload of rocker bars. But it was exciting at the time; we'd play one weekend and the Crash Test Dummies would play the next. But there were only two clubs so quite often you'd play at the university or get together with some people and rent a hall.

"We were an interim band. When we started, the popular bands in the city were The Cheer, who were the first I'd heard of that had an indie release. I thought that was incredible. There was also a band called Monuments

Galore who were signed and recorded an album with Mitch Easter, but they kind of fizzled out. We came in at the same time as the Dummies and Acoustically Inclined."

The Watchmen marked a return to the blue-collar approach that always personified the Winnipeg rock aesthetic going back to The Guess Who and BTO, but with a lot of punk attitude thrown in as well. During the city's long, harsh winters, the quartet would barricade themselves in their rehearsal space in the basement of the McLaren Hotel, banging out new material in anticipation of getting on the road with the first sign of spring. After producing several cassettes on their own, The Watchmen found a strong ally in Ralph James, former bass player for Harlequin, now breaking into the talent-booking game. James took the young band on as his pet project, sending them on regular trips to the west coast and back to the point where by 1990 they were doing 150 shows per year. "We bought a cargo van from the city," Serlin remembers. "Just a standard-sized yellow van. It had no backseat, so we took this old loveseat out of my parents' basement and put it in there and it would roll around a lot. It was so hot in the summer that we'd keep the side door open, going down the highway. We were so young, it was so exciting to be out of the city and playing music every night. Just getting a case of beer in return was the biggest thing in the world."

By 1990, James was bringing The Watchmen to Toronto on a regular basis, starting modestly at a sports bar called Cadillac Jack's — where Barenaked Ladies opened for their first appearance — and working up to their Horseshoe residency. The band had already done some opening slots for The Hip in western Canada, so James assumed it would be a natural fit to hook The Watchmen up with Gold and Gregg, and urged the managers to check them out. "Ralph had brought Jake out to see us at one of the first gigs we did in Toronto. He thought we were good but we were too young and needed some seasoning," Serlin says. "Then he came out a year later to see us at The Horseshoe — we were opening for the Skydiggers — and thought it was great. Allan was there too, smoking a cigar, and afterward he just came out and said, 'Boys, we're gonna make a record.' Then we had to get in the van and drive back to Winnipeg, and I think we were up for the whole 20-hour drive just talking. It was a very exciting time."

The managers opted for an approach similar to the early Hip recordings, simply capturing The Watchmen's raw live sound. When *McLaren Furnace Room* was released in 1992, this unfortunately led to many initial comparisons to The Hip which were further fuelled when MCA licensed the album from Gold and Gregg's new Sumo imprint. Fans ultimately detected

The Watchmen at Ontario Place Forum, July 1, 1994:
Ken Tizzard, Danny Greaves, Joey Serlin, Sammy Kohn
(Photo by David Leyes)

an entirely different dynamic in The Watchmen, as songs like "Cracked" and "Run And Hide" brought out more aggressive tendencies within their audience. Serlin, the chief songwriter at the time, admits, "I was a pretty angry kid. I don't know why. I drank a lot and had a lot of fights. At the same time I had music, so it crept into what I was writing. I guess a lot of other people felt the same way. There's a lot of that on that album; I was hurting, angry, all that stuff, and it all made it into the music. I really don't know what it was, I came from a comfortable home. It was probably an internal thing in that I didn't know quite where I belonged, which is something that most people at that age go through. Danny would deliver it in a very energetic and exciting way while we were bashing it out, and people dug it."

The Watchmen would go on to become one of the most successful homegrown bands of the 1990s, pausing to replace Loewen with Newfoundland native Ken Tizzard before going on to record *In The Trees*, *Brand New Day*, and *Silent Radar*. Throughout, the band fought to maintain its no-frills sound and image within the changing commercial climate. It remains an ongoing battle that Serlin admits comes with the territory. "There came a time around *Brand New Day* when it started feeling safe, like we felt we could do whatever we wanted and we'd be okay, which wasn't the case. I lost my fighter's edge a little bit."

With Gord Downie now living permanently in Toronto, his influence became apparent when The Management Trust began working with Andrew Cash in 1992. Downie and Cash had become good friends, leading to the one-album licensing deal that produced *Hi*, Cash's powerful return to the national scene. His eventual decision to move back to the band format that would become his next project, Ursula, ultimately strained relations. Gold diplomatically states, "Andrew made great records and is a great songwriter. We worked with him for quite a while. Then he got a new band and things in the end didn't quite work out for both of us, but we remain friends. We always believed in Andrew as an artist, but the times were starting to change, and it wasn't let's say, as commercial as the way things were going."

In the late '90s, The Management Trust would find commercial success with other bands, most notably Big Wreck, and lend further helping hands to old Kingston cronies. This largely stemmed from an addition to the management team, Bernie Breen, adolescent friend of both Paul Langlois and Hugh Dillon, who would allow the latter's larger-than-life persona room to grow as frontman for The Headstones.

Dillon had always seemed just out of step with his friends in The Hip. Whereas they always remained tied to their comfortable surroundings, Dillon fully embraced the outlaw punk image, initially dealing drugs to support his goal of being in a successful band. Even though he had managed to get into Queen's to study history, his sideline business was leading him down a dark path. "It all blew up in my face," he says. "I had connections in Montreal and all over the place. I thought I was indestructible. Then I got into a bad situation where I ended up at the Y with two black eyes and a gun to my head. It was pretty heavy duty. I made a deal with my parents that if they paid off this guy, I'd get out of town until things blew over."

Dillon and Finn McConnell (later of The Mahones) took off to England where they spent the next year trying to make ends meet. Dillon finally settled back in Toronto, and discovered that his old friends in The Hip had been making their mark outside of Kingston. Dillon already had plans to put a band together again, and The Hip's success made him even more determined. As a frontman, Dillon shared a lot of Downie's charisma, but being the epitome of everything dangerous about rock and roll allowed even his most overbearing on and off-stage tendencies to be embraced by those around him. Dillon's frame of reference was hardly limited to punk, although his initial stance was almost an equal combination of Johnny Rotten and Teenage Head's Frankie Venom. Instead, he combined his anti-establishment desires with a caustic wit that appealed directly to unpretentious sensibilities. If Canada was searching for a rock star, Dillon was more than qualified for the job. Yet the singer also recognized from

The Hip's success that he needed to front a powerful band, not merely a confrontational one, and found the right combination in guitarist Trent Carr, bassist Tim White and, eventually, drummer Mark Gibson. Originally called The Tombstones in honour of Bob Dylan's "Tombstone Blues," their name was quickly modified to The Headstones upon discovering The Tombstones had already been taken.

They began a semi-regular residency in the late '80s at the Blue Moon Saloon, before the final line-up had been settled. Often 13 Engines' Grant Ethier and Copyright's Pete Bourne would be on drums for the long, rowdy evenings that saw the band and Dillon go to any lengths to make the experience rewarding. Dillon says, "It was one of the few places that would give us beer and a hundred bucks. We would do three sets and throw in some covers. Sometimes we wouldn't have a bass player so we would just crank up our amps. I would get on the tables and just be belligerent."

Eventually, The Headstones' flat-out rock and roll show moved on to places like Sneaky Dee's and Ultrasound, drumming up interest from management and labels. When they signed with MCA in 1992, Dillon admits it was partially a result of some outside influence. "The Hip opened the doors because they had such integrity. We aspired to that, to write songs as good as theirs and to have the kind of control they had. Both Paul Langlois and Gord Downie were a big influence on us getting a record deal because when we did showcases in Toronto, they would show up just to be supportive. People would see that and would be, like, 'Fuck, The Hip are here. Maybe we should look a little closer.'"

The Headstones' debut, *Picture Of Health*, stood on its own as one of the most potent slabs of melodic hard rock of its time. Dillon presented himself as a barroom hero, bloodied but unbowed, in songs like "When Something Stands For Nothing," but also as a reluctant prisoner of the drug culture in "Heart Of Darkness" and "It's All Over" where he describes the experience unremorsefully. In fact, Dillon had never completely left the hard drug world, continuing to dabble with heroin for the next several years. With the release of 1994's *Teeth & Tissue*, it was clear that Dillon was not presenting a contrived image; The Headstones represented rock and roll in the basest form that the mainstream market would allow, and maintaining this position without losing their punk ideals is what made them unique. "I hate people who are elitists and think that's the way to go," Dillon says. "We're actually pretty decent, down-to-earth guys. It's aggressive music that we're into, but I find our stuff incredibly well-written. It's something that we dig and that lends itself to why our fans like it. I remember seeing

posters all the time for Platinum Blonde and Honeymoon Suite and literally thinking, 'There's a way to beat these fuckers.' It was just poorly written
music for the masses, corporate rock."

Bruce McDonald had a similar attitude toward the film industry when he
began, and had no hesitations when in 1995 he cast Dillon as Joe Dick, lead
singer of Hard Core Logo, the subject of the final instalment of his rock 'n
road trilogy that began with *Roadkill* and *Highway 61*. While reactions from
fellow musicians to the film's rockumentary-style portrayal of the Canadian
touring experience were mixed, the reason it worked at all was because of
Dillon's compelling performance as the fading punk looking for one last shot
at glory with his old band. The authenticity Dillon brought to the complex
inner workings of the band's relationship was the real focal point of the film,
and the line between fiction and reality became extremely blurry for those
with only an inkling of Dillon's own musical career. "I gave Bruce a lot of
ideas in terms of how to make it more real, as opposed to how the book and
the first draft of the script went," Dillon said at the time of its release. "It's
not glossed over, it doesn't have a shiny little stupid message. It speaks for
more than rock and roll, I think it talks about relationships and desperation."

Overwhelming praise for Dillon's performance in the film fuelled speculation that he would make acting a full-time career. This seemed almost
assured when Quentin Tarantino bought the rights for *Hard Core Logo*'s
American release. The director had immediately become a fan upon seeing
the film and invited Dillon to take an audition for his follow-up to *Pulp
Fiction*, *Jackie Brown*. Dillon ultimately lost the part to Michael Keaton, but
the glowing press surrounding the situation made his return to The
Headstones a little easier to bear. In 1997 they released *Smile & Wave*, continuing their trademark grind but expanding it with some sonic
improvements on songs like the Nirvana-esque "And" and the slow-building
"Cubically Contained."

This growth seemed to position the band for bigger things, but a subsequent two-year layoff was marked by rumours of Dillon once again
indulging in heroin use. When they re-emerged in 2000 under the guidance
of The Management Trust with *Nickels For Your Nightmares*, Dillon remained
his usual unrepentant self. He still had an obligation to be Canada's rock
star, and few would be able to challenge this claim. "I don't bullshit, and I
don't like talking to people who bullshit me," he maintains. "The song 'Smile
& Wave' for example, goes back to the kind of people who call The Hip and
us hoser bands. They're people who come from fairly well-off backgrounds
and make judgement calls when it's not their place to do it. Instead of

arguing the point, it's just easier to say everyone's entitled to their opinion, however wrong they may be."

By 1996, The Tragically Hip were ready for a fresh start. The pressures of the previous year's touring schedule had prompted a retreat to the comfort of more familiar surroundings. In Canada at least, their career was secure; all four of their albums had sold close to one million copies each, a feat that no other band could claim. Yet, every time their name was brought up in the media, they faced the nagging question of why they weren't just as popular in the U.S. Their most common answer was to simply continue doing everything on their own terms.

The winter of 1996 saw the completion of their own studio in the town of Bath, just outside of Kingston. Here, along with longtime soundman Mark Vreeken, the band finally had the same freedom to record that they had found in New Orleans, much closer to their families. The relaxed atmosphere inevitably brought out the more subtle aspects of the overall sound and a greater willingness to try different songwriting approaches. The most surprising of these was Downie's new grasp of the guitar. While he contributed only rudimentary parts, it dramatically changed the dynamic of the band from one fronted by a dramatic vocalist to one fronted by an emerging singer/songwriter.

"I just felt like playing guitar, as well as wanting to become a better singer, and there was no better way to do this than to play with a band," Downie says. "It was a real trial by fire. The first bunch of gigs were very embarrassing because it was hard to sing and play. You totally get lost, and I still do sometimes. But a small decision begat a whole new landscape where I'm plugged into the band in a way I never was before and I like it. All of a sudden I'm able to converse with them."

The first breakthrough of this new configuration came with "Ahead By A Century," a song they had been experimenting with during "New Orleans Is Sinking" since the arena tour. Originally it was a striking description of a young boy and girl sitting in a tree talking innocently about forming a lifelong union through touching each other sexually as their parents do. But over the course of the year it emerged as a poignant examination of the effects of love growing from its initial ideal into a quiet, unspoken bond, punctuated by the refrain, "No dress rehearsal, this is our life." The largely acoustic arrangement of the song, when it came to be recorded, exemplified the band's new reflective approach, which also sacrificed much of *Day For Night*'s moodiness.

While that record seemed to be driven by a conscious effort to make creative inroads, the songs that would comprise *Trouble At The Henhouse* turned out to be a mixed bag of far-flung ideas, assembled with homespun care. Its best moments could clearly be picked out, but moments were all they were. Among them are the overall majesty of "Gift Shop," the fragility of "Flamenco," the sly appearance of Kurt Cobain reincarnated as a sled dog in "Don't Wake Daddy," and the solitary image of someone creating a backyard skating rink in "700 Ft. Ceiling." However, there were one too many examples like "Butts Wigglin'" (written for the Kids In The Hall movie *Brain Candy*), "Coconut Cream" and "The Apartment Song" that seemed bound to a narrow, unfulfilled idea.

Only in the closing "Put It Off" did any sense of real tension show through. Written upon the birth of Downie's first child, as the lyric suggests, the song in the end gives the impression that it represents the polar opposite of emotions such an event would bring. In it, the singer searches for a means of marking the occasion, finally settling upon simply listening to Eric's Trip's *Love Tara*. "I wouldn't say I was being flattering or unflattering in that song," Downie says. "Saying, 'To prove that words cannot touch beauty' is totally flattering. In other words, I'm trying my best to come up with anything and can't. Hence, *Love Tara* because I did listen to it on the way home from the hospital. There's a point when you have your first child that you feel you have a solemn duty to write a song about it. But afterward I didn't like the line 'find the cuteness.' I was like, 'find the cuteness,' what? But Eric's Trip just seemed so cute to me, always did and always will."

If anything, the album was summed up in the tag line to "Springtime In Vienna," "We live to survive our paradoxes." It was an ongoing challenge to sell the fact that they were the most popular band in Canada to apathetic American media, while at the same time trying not to allow their popularity to place them above their peers at home. In interviews during this time, band members grew frustrated with assumptions that they could actually explain these realities simply because of what people heard in the music. "I'm not a nationalist," Downie says. "I started using Canadian references not just for their own sake, but because I wanted to pick up my birthright which is this massive country full of stories. We wanted to go down to the States because that's your birthright as a musician, getting to see those places. You go to Memphis, and as a musician it's like going to the moon. At the same time, being from Canada, we were suffering from either false perceptions or no perceptions down there. We weren't thinking about it because we were cruising around North America in a tour bus."

Of course, Jake Gold has his own view of the situation. "The lack of success in the U.S. really is a myth, because one of the things The Tragically Hip never wanted to do was play the game. We always tried to do things that the band enjoyed doing. They weren't image-based, they weren't necessarily the pretty faces that go on magazine covers. At the same time, they managed to sell over 100,000 records every time they put one out and play to a really loyal following in America. To make a comparison between how The Hip are in Canada to how they are in the States is really unfair, because you have to look at other bands in the U.S. and compare them to that. In a lot of ways they're bigger than most bands are. They're still in the top 10 per cent of bands that tour and make records, but that can never match the fact that there's never been a bigger band in Canada as The Hip, ever. I don't know if there ever will be; I don't think the market allows for it anymore. Things get so over-exposed in today's market, and no one's out there building loyalty to these bands. That's one thing we always talked about as an organization, building band loyalty, not song loyalty."

That loyalty was clearly in evidence when The Hip played two surprise gigs at Massey Hall to mark their ninth release, *Music@Work*, in May 2000. They were welcomed to the stage each night with spontaneous renditions of "O Canada," an increasingly common occurrence that initially made Downie cringe. "That's something that has always given us a tinge of, 'It's a Canadian thing,' especially in the U.S.," he muses. "People once sang the national anthem when we played in London and afterward I asked a girl, 'Why do you guys do that?' I was just curious, and she said, 'I think we do it because we want you guys to know we're there. We know you're in the dressing room and this is the only way we can let you know that you've got some Canadians here.' I found that very touching, and I've started to be less cynical about it."

In the last two months of 1996, The Hip embarked on their second cross-Canada arena tour, this time accompanied by the Rheostatics. There would be no doubts this time as to whether the band belonged on these stages, and the decision was made beforehand to preserve the tour for posterity with a live album. Each show was recorded with the intent of releasing the best one instead of compiling performances from several. As the creator of each night's set list, Gord Sinclair made the final selection, going with Cobo Arena in Detroit, November 23. *Live Between Us* may not have been a hard-core fan's idea of the perfect Hip concert, but the band staunchly stood by its honesty and spontaneity. The album's appeal lay in how they had now fully incorporated its several stylistic domains, hard rock, folk balladry and experimental sound and poetry, into a compelling form of performance art.

The album also fulfilled the task of building excitement for 1997's Another Roadside Attraction. With a third stellar line-up that included Ron Sexsmith, Change of Heart, Ashley MacIsaac, along with Sheryl Crow, Los Lobos and Wilco, it was a much-needed respite in the increasingly corporate-minded touring battleground. Players joined in during each other's sets, and that cross-pollination led to The Hip recording their next album with Los Lobos'

Steve Berlin. The resulting *Phantom Power* was a much more cohesive effort, while still sticking with the *Henhouse* homemade approach. Much of its strength lay in the reappearance of strong Canadian overtones that are apparent throughout: "Something On" was written in the aftermath of the ice storm that crippled eastern Canada the previous winter; "Fireworks" hearkens back to Downie's hockey-obsessed childhood; and "Thompson Girl" is a poignant vignette set in remote northern Manitoba. The album's best-known song would be the lilting "Bobcaygeon," named after the small town north of Toronto. Although this superficiality immediately made it a summer cottage anthem, the lyrics play out like an enigmatic Raymond Carver short story; one man's struggle between his job and his relationship.

Julie Doiron of Eric's Trip and Martin Tielli of the Rheostatics, two of The Hip's favoured opening acts, backstage at Canada Day 1994 in Barrie
(Photo by Dave Clark)

After a further successful round of international touring throughout 1998 and the spring of 1999, The Hip appropriately rang in the year 2000 with a massive two-night stand at Toronto's new Air Canada Centre, which they had opened only months earlier. Once the initial hype of the event died down, what remained on stage was not just a party for the circle of friends The Hip had gathered around them over their career; instead, it was the closest that the CanRock Renaissance had come to its own personal celebration. There were the Rheostatics, Hayden, Skydiggers, Sharkskin (featuring former members of the Odds), Ottawa's Starling, Chris Brown & Kate Fenner, the Mahones, the Watchmen, Treble Charger, Blurtonia, the Cash

Brothers, the Headstones, Julie Doiron & the Wooden Stars and Sarah Harmer.

It was a gesture that no other band could have made, and a further testament to how The Tragically Hip indelibly altered the course of Canada's cultural history through both their music and their actions. By this time, critics looking for a new angle on the band had started questioning whether these lofty claims still held true. They pointed to musical complacency on recent albums, and Gord Downie's desire to carve out a solo career, as signs that The Hip were on the verge of collapse. The biggest surprise that came with these petty jabs was how long it had taken such opportunistic commentators to attempt to knock the band from its lofty perch. The fact was, in 2000, The Hip were still well into a remarkable 15-year creative run — one that few other bands of their generation could boast — during which they had built unshakeable loyalty in both their fans, and the rest of the Canadian music industry. Whether they accept it or not, The Tragically Hip are and forever will be Canada's band.

Even as their tour in the fall and winter of 2000 once again affirmed this notion for fans, and consequently silencing the critics, Gord Downie was still searching for new forms of expression. A constant companion on the tour bus was a copy of Al Purdy's *The Caribou Horses*, a foreshadowing of his own forthcoming poetry collection. In December, during a day off in Halifax, Downie attended a gig by tourmates Chris Brown & Kate Fenner at a tiny café. He joined them for a couple of numbers halfway through the set, then later on they tentatively began "Tears Of Rage," the song written by Richard Manuel and Bob Dylan that led off The Band's first album, *Music From Big Pink*. Downie took the second verse, aided by a lyric sheet, and suddenly he embodied everything Canadian rock and roll was and is; his own rich body of work merging seamlessly with a past that had never faded away, since its simple tenets of humility and community still lived and breathed within every musician who felt a connection to their own time and place.

And as is somehow always the case, only a precious few witnessed it.

Epilogue:
Where the Change Is

In the year 2000, two years after her band Weeping Tile was dropped from their label, Sarah Harmer launched her solo career with an astounding album that had critics, fans and fellow musicians drooling, even making the Top 10 year-end list in *Time* magazine — the American edition. The album bore the nostalgic title *You Were Here*. While there was certainly a reflective tone to her lyrics, the album acted as a musical summation of the gains made by the CanRock Renaissance that spawned Harmer's for-midable talent. *You Were Here*'s hit single, "Basement Apt.," had appeared on the first Weeping Tile cassette in 1993; another song on that cassette bore a coda with the lyrics "my hopes exceed my expectations."

Harmer and Weeping Tile were nurtured along the way by The Tragically Hip, Blue Rodeo, Rheostatics, the Bourbon Tabernacle Choir, Change of Heart and many others — the professional and personal relationships formed along the way benefited both sides, and most of all the listeners. As her solo star began to rise, Harmer retained her modesty and spirit of cooper-ation. In the press and on stage, she would vocally champion bands from the next generation imbued with the same spirit that inspired her.

"It's amazing in Canada," says Harmer, of the longterm effects of the

CanRock Renaissance. "I was a fan of a lot of bands that would come through Kingston and I would see them in Toronto, and then I got to the point where I had enough songs to get a set together and there was the prospect of opening for Change of Heart. You'd get acclimatized, and there would be so many bands and musicians doing the same kind of things that there was instant understanding. There's so much great stuff. I could listen to Canadian records alone and be fulfilled on a lot of musical levels, and most of it would be from people that I've met. That's really exciting."

While Harmer's deserved success was heartening, it also acted as a needed reassurance and a welcome sign of a coming thaw. The icy five years that followed 1995 saw several gains of the CanRock Renaissance begin to slip away: Live audiences started to dry up; media began to either narrowcast or pander to the lowest common denominator; major labels decided to stick with safe and uncreative investments; indie labels folded and the brightest new faces struggled to be heard.

The proliferation of business opportunities wrought by the CanRock Renaissance simultaneously enhanced and poisoned the atmosphere. In 1995, the same year Weeping Tile's *Cold Snap* was released, a viciously talented and very young east coast fiddler named Ashley MacIsaac was plucked from the campus and festival circuit and groomed to be a pop star, building on the groundwork laid by Celtic forerunners Spirit of the West and others. To help capitalize on MacIsaac's non-traditional image while making his traditional music sound hip, a rally of independent musicians was assembled — Chris Brown, Ian Blurton, Jale, Bob Snider, Gordie Johnson, Al Cross, Graeme Kirkland and others — to make an incredibly commercial album. A promising idea turned into the final corporate co-opting of the CanRock Renaissance, and attained multi-platinum status in the process.

Michael Phillip Wojewoda was one of three producers who guided the Ashley MacIsaac project to completion, along with Pete Prilesnik (Sarah Harmer's *You Were Here*) and Matt DeMatteo. "The idea of working with [MacIsaac] was really appealing to me," says Wojewoda, "because he was talking about making a really whacked-out record. We had conversations about these elaborate concepts, involving all sorts of stuff like jungle tracks and 'how many ways can you dress up this fiddle tune?'

"But then something happened," he continues. "Once it actually formalized and we hit the studio, Ashley grafted on to me and figured I was now an authority figure that he was going to rebel against. I said, 'You don't understand. It's you and me, and we can do this.' He was doing crack, and was supposed to show up at noon and he might show up at eight p.m. I'd stick around long enough to go, 'Fuck you, I'm out of there.' It turned into this fiasco where I ended up saying, 'Ashley, just play well for me for three days — three days, and then I'll build a record around you and we can part company.' I don't know why I didn't just walk away. I was clinging to some of these ideas we had discussed before that I wanted to enact. Because I had done so much indie stuff, I was still learning about how to serve the bureaucracy that surrounds label money."

Wojewoda refers to MacIsaac's A&R people as "really invasive and not very pleasant. The 'we're-really-not-happy-with-how-the-album-is-going' speech threw me for a loop. I attach so much emotion to what I do that I couldn't be neutral and started freaking out. They ended up using the tamest stuff, the CBC-style tracks I did. The stuff I was really interested in never got used."

Quick ascents to fame aren't always problematic, as the longevity of Sloan proves. Yet that kind of early success also tainted perceptions for young musicians and raised financial expectations for everyone involved. Waye Mason of Halifax's No Records, says, "When Sloan signed such a massively moneyed deal, that changed the way people perceived why they should be doing music. I think Sloan was extraordinarily lucky. You don't get handed a major label deal and only have played under 30 shows and never toured coast to coast. That's a phenomenal rarity. A lot of people think that's the way it's supposed to be. We [indie labels] all spent way more money than what was ever realistic to make, and now you see this recession in indie rock which was coupled with one of the worst retail dips since disco collapsed."

Mark Milne of Sonic Unyon, one of the few indies of the early '90s that survived the boom and bust, says that the success of a few indie bands led to a sense of entitlement among younger artists with delusions of grandeur. "People saw a small number of bands doing really well and thought, 'Isn't that the case with everybody?'" says Milne. "This is probably true of a lot of industries, but people will see advertising or records charting or see someone on TV, and they'll think, 'Whoever's responsible for that has a lot of money.' It's not the case. So people thought that we would give them $30,000 or $100,000 advances, and we'd look at them and say, 'Are you fucking on crack?' People's awareness of the reality of it is very skewed. We're not a charity, but we're not the opposite of a charity either; it's not like we're a massively profitable company."

In 1996, Sonic Unyon saw two of its star acts — Treble Charger and Hayden — poached by major labels, not long after both artists had gone out of their way to hang on to their "indie cred." In 1995, Treble Charger staged a press conference at Honest Ed's bargain emporium in Toronto to launch their new Sonic Unyon EP, *Self=Title*, and to flaunt their independent status in the face of the offers they were fielding from majors. The EP featured a multi-media CD-ROM component with features on fellow indie acts the Wooden Stars, Thrush Hermit, Banned From Atlantis, By Divine Right and several Sonic Unyon bands. It appeared to be a celebration of the community that spawned Treble Charger's success, when in fact it was a Dear John letter. Milne says that the band's manager "had a plan from the beginning: 'These guys need indie credibility.' He got them that, and once he had enough of it, he moved on."

Similarly, Hayden signed an international deal with the Universal-sponsored boutique label Outpost, one that opted out of Canada and granted Sonic Unyon exclusive Canadian rights; it was seen as a payback for Sonic Unyon's help in building his career, and as a vote of confidence in their ability to market him better in his homeland than a major could. But mere weeks before the release of his next album, Hayden's management reneged on the deal and left Sonic Unyon in the lurch; the album came out on Universal Canada.

That both Treble Charger and Hayden ended up on major labels isn't unusual at all. But by defiantly waving the indie flag while it was convenient, and then tossing it aside for the larger game plan, both acts lost some loyal fans. *The Closer I Get*, although far superior to Hayden's indie work, was a commercial failure. Meanwhile, Treble Charger spent the next several years courting an entirely different, image-based audience and facing difficulties with their American label. By 2000, the concept of "indie cred" seemed ludicrous. "It's gotten to the point where you can have no credibility," laughs Milne. "You can manufacture a band on television and it will still sell — I mean, you can't have less credibility than that! 'We're not even a real band, we don't write our own songs, we're not even real people but we can sell millions of records!' It's swung to the complete opposite, which is baffling to me."

Milne says that some of the indie solidarity was duplicitous and ultimately damaging to overall quality control, creating a glut of indie product that saturated consumer interest. "The more fashionable it got to be indie, you could do anything," says Milne. "You could pick your nose and record it on a 7" single and it was indie so it was cool, therefore someone would buy it. I always felt that if you were a part of that scene, then you weren't supposed to go around slagging other people on the scene, in the same situation as you. It wouldn't be cool to say, 'That band sucks,' because you shouldn't say that if they're on a cool label. Meanwhile you're thinking, 'Well, they may be cool people, but that record's fucking crap.' There would be so many records like that, and I'm not going to lie — our warehouse has some of it. I don't think any of the other labels that are still around are the ones I'm talking about here, but a lot of people started putting out anything, and 'as long as it's indie, it's cool.' Well, it's junk and it's taking up space on the rack. And the majors were doing that too, creating these crazy imprint labels and saying, 'We'll put all our junk on this imprint label, call it indie, and it will sell.' Sometimes it did, sometimes it didn't."

"Sometimes I identify with these dot-com people and their sordid tales," says Mint Records' Bill Baker. "I remember what it was like in '94 and '95 where every independent label was the biggest deal in the world. It was the same thing as the Seattle/Sub Pop thing a few years earlier; it got really gross for a while there. There was a perceived carrot at the end of a stick that everyone was really excited about — which really turned out to be nothing. During that boom period of 1994 to '95, everything seemed so fake. It was almost like if you had a job where someone is paying you tons of money to sit around and do nothing. You would be going, 'I've got a great job, but I'm going to lose this job because somebody is going to figure out that I'm not doing anything.' Everything was so shiny and exciting. The spotlight was on for a second and everyone was thinking, 'We're going to make it.' When one person does, the spotlight goes off and we were in the doldrums that followed."

Tara White, of Moncton's post–Eric's Trip band Elevator, agrees that saturation led to overkill. "After the whole grunge/Nirvana thing, every Tom, Dick and Harry jumped on the bandwagon and wanted to start a band," she said in 1998, "and so we were constantly being bombarded by this corporate thing, and that killed it really quickly. I think [now] it's maybe a bit of a weeding process, or survival of the fittest. It's been rough. I find you really have to dig deep to get to any substantial music, especially if your only resources are radio or MuchMusic. It's a sad state of affairs. There's always going to be an underground, but to find any substantial music you have to keep up with the underground. I can't even say I do that, because living in Moncton we don't have any bands passing through here." White would move to Toronto in 2000.

As the indie boom turned to bust, live audiences began to decline and clubs began to close. "The club scenes in Vancouver over the years have been so difficult to read sometimes," said Tom Harrison in 1998. "There are times when there are numerous clubs playing original music and they were doing okay. It began to change after a while and it's just got sicker and sicker. We've lost a lot of crucial clubs. Because there are so few clubs where a rock band can play, you are seeing more of the independent aspect coming back again and more privately done all-ages shows. The do-it-yourself mentality is creeping back in because of necessity."

The decline of rock audiences can be blamed on a variety of factors, including shifting youth trends towards hip-hop and electronic music, but artists themselves can't be entirely let off the hook. Reflecting on the declining live music scene, Ian Blurton asks, "Is that an influx of bad bands, or are people actually getting sick of going to see shows? If you're a good live band, people are going to see you."

CBC *Radio Escapade* producer Grant Lawrence acts as a judge at Vancouver's annual Shindig live talent search, and bemoans the dour nature of most young bands. "I was watching these bands, and they're not confident — mind you, they're young — and they're not entertaining the crowd, and their songs are mediocre," says Lawrence. "I asked these bands, 'Are you ready for this? Who are you doing the favour to that we have to watch you practise?' I feel bad about that, because bands have to get out of the basement eventually. But I feel the stage is elevated for one reason only, and that's so that people can see what's on the stage — and what's on stage should be entertainment. When a band isn't entertaining, it's a complete slap in the face to anyone who shelled out a couple of bucks to get into the club. It's almost some weird form of indie rock torture: you got a room that's painted black, smoke, booze and a lot of people who are usually agitated for some reason — and then you have a band that's horribly boring."

Lewis Melville, who now performs with the inclusive noise orchestra the Woodchoppers Association as well as bluegrass and rock bands, believes in the communicative nature of performance. "If you have a really good band that's dedicated to playing and you know how to get that across to people, then you will succeed," he says. "But you have to be prepared to follow it up. There are a lot of bands who are good but are missing that magical ability to really relate to their audience. They relate to themselves and their own music, but not to their audience. That doesn't mean you have to compromise, it just means you have to figure that out. It doesn't just happen."

Until that band finds that audience, the economics of touring means that many singer/songwriters are staying close to home and are wary of forming bands. "It's a side guy market these days," says ex-Jr. Gone Wild bandleader Mike McDonald. "Around here [in Edmonton], cover bands are getting all the work. The poor songwriter who wants to work in a band is fiscally enslaved.

There are lots of cases whereby the lead singer/manager/songwriter/agent-band-mother does not get paid because all money made at the gig has to pay the side guys. If you don't pay the side guys, you've got no band. Myself and a few other writers I know do all the work, and get nothing for it. Maybe it's because we're older, but it seems to me there is a shortage of true believers out there. And then there is the price of gas."

The commercial CanRock stars of 1995–2000 were usually those who ached to be larger than life. Yvonne Matsell recalls the first time The Tea Party played her Ultrasound club in Toronto, an intimate venue; they brought a drum riser with them. Matsell, who retains an affection for the band, says, "I was going to see if I could get a floor for them to stay on because I knew they'd come in from Windsor. I asked, 'Where are you staying?' And with all seriousness, they said, 'The Royal York' [one of the most expensive hotels in Toronto]. I just fell apart laughing. They were absolute rock stars right from the beginning."

Robert Benvie, whose band Thrush Hermit disbanded in 1999, sees today's climate as much more challenging than when he started in the early '90s. "As this country is so much smaller in population yet broader in size, the artist has little margin in which to prosper. That's how it's now become this Edgefest/ Summersault/ MuchMusic festival–dominated environment. The fans are so scattered and divided it's almost impossible for a little company like Sonic Unyon to get its stuff heard. But with the money of Feldman's or Much or Universal or House of Blues or whoever, it's easy to convince kids that they should go see crap that in any other country would surely be ignored. It's now this huge chasm between glossy pop and the live music crowd. As far as the future, I think Canadian bands would be wisest to look to Europe or Japan to make fans, because the rock scene in Canada will probably still be shitty for another five, maybe 10, years."

Tom Harrison says, "There was a certain point when alternative music became self-sufficient and it became a competition among the bands to play those [kind of] clubs. People became more aware of the business aspects of it — that you could put together a career making independent music. When managers and independent labels and a business structure for that music came along, that camaraderie and solidarity broke down and was replaced by rivalry."

Yvonne Matsell laments the sense of community she saw at Ultrasound in the early '90s. "I've never seen that time recreated since. It was a very supportive community, musically. You could guarantee that you were going to see several different musicians in the audience for their favourite bands.

You don't see that anymore. Every band wants the middle slot on the bill. They all think, 'I really need the prime slot, because if I'm going to get anyone out, this is the time they'll come to see me.' I was telling one musician off because I got fed up with him. I said, 'You've got to start going out to other shows, because if you don't, why do you expect real people to come out to yours? You're not going out to support live music, why should anyone else?' They need to go out and see bands themselves. Nobody seems to be able to find an opening band, either. They say, 'Oh, you just find somebody.' Well, do you go out and hand tapes out or connect with bands you'd like to play with?"

One of Matsell's favourite performers, Ron Sexsmith, slipped right through the cracks during the CanRock Renaissance, and only came to most people's attention after his first album on an American major label in 1995. In the early '90s, Matsell would often book him at Ultrasound, though the first adjective that comes to her mind is "heartbreaking. You could count three people in the room, that would be me, the soundman and [producer/songwriter] David Baxter — he was a huge fan. That would be it for Ron's audience. I would be racking my brains trying to find out why nobody was there to see him. It was very hard for me to keep putting him on as an opener, because obviously he was not drawing any people. I would have hairs standing up on my arm listening to him."

The career of Ron Sexsmith reflects the old axiom that the more things change, the more they stay the same. As he sang on his self-titled major label debut, "There's a rhythm, not cruel or kind / Though you feel that it's left you behind." One of Sexsmith's primary songwriting idols is Gordon Lightfoot, and it's a sad coincidence that 30 years after Lightfoot left the country to find fame, Sexsmith would have to take the same route; in Canada, he couldn't even achieve the modest success that his peers Bob Wiseman and Bob Snider enjoyed.

"On my very first trip to New York, I was offered a record deal," says Sexsmith. "The night before, I was playing a show to three people. I was very depressed. At that time I had a publishing deal, and there was some guy at Polydor Records who liked the demo that I made. I flew in there, and played three songs for him in his office, and he said, 'How would you like to sign with Polydor?' I couldn't believe my ears. My life in Toronto had gotten so bad that I would book a gig, show up and wait for people, and then ultimately no one would come and then I would end up packing up my guitar and going home without playing.

"There was a time in Toronto when there was a buzz and people would come out. Some labels would be excited, but nothing would ever happen. This happened two or three times. When I finally did get the publishing deal, I thought that was all that was ever going to happen and it felt like getting second prize. I was very happy. After the Polydor offer, I found myself in the middle of a little bidding war in the span of a week. It was an amazing time for me, because I always felt it would happen."

Sexsmith started writing in 1985, after the birth of his first child and several years of playing covers in Niagara bars. After short stints in Victoria, northern Quebec and Halifax, he moved to Toronto in 1987. Sexsmith recalls, "The only reason I moved to Toronto — I wanted to live in St. Catharines — was that I got some interest. A manager appeared, and said, 'Well, I can't manage you if you're down there.' We had to make the big move, but he ended up abandoning us. He didn't have any time for me. So I was like, 'Okay, what do I do now?' The whole family had just made this big move. It turned out to be the best thing I ever did, though."

Sexsmith fell into a productive peer-support group based around Fat Albert's bar on College Street. "When you move and you just have a guitar, you have to find out where the open stages are," says Sexsmith. "The first day I walked in [to Fat Albert's], I didn't know you had to sign up. Bob Wiseman — I didn't know who he was — had seen me a couple of nights before at Sneaky Dee's, so he offered one of his [allotted] songs, because everyone got to do two songs. I thought 'Wow, this isn't bad. I'll have to help him out one day.' Then it turns out he's in Blue Rodeo. I started going there, and Kyp Harness was there, Bob Snider, Sam Larkin. It was scary, because at the time I thought I was pretty good — then I heard those guys and I just thought I was the worst. I've been influenced more by those guys than anybody famous, just by knowing them and hanging out with them."

When Sexsmith's publishing deal led to a contract with Interscope Records in 1994, he was forced to leave the Fat Albert's crowd behind and work with L.A. studio musicians favoured by producer Mitchell Froom. Bob Wiseman — who had produced Sexsmith's debut cassette *Grand Opera Lane* — was Sexsmith's first suggestion to his new label; they insisted on a name, rather than another obscure Canadian. Before hearing his music, Froom was skeptical of Sexsmith, based solely on his nationality. "I went through a period of five years where every time I got a tape from Canada, it would be the most dreadful stuff I'd ever heard," says Froom. "When I'd talk to Ron, it became an inside joke. It's really not fair that people in America will say things like, 'Oh, that's very Canadian.' When I first got his tape, I listened to it with the worst possible attitude, just from the nature of the stuff I'd received, but I was completely won over. In America, what have we got to hear, Glass Tiger?! And then there's a lot of these goofy bands."

Froom and Sexsmith got along personally and musically, but even Froom's inventive, sympathetic production didn't meet with the label's approval. Daniel Lanois was brought in for a few sessions, with one song making it to the final album. The whole project was in jeopardy before Sexsmith got an unexpected endorsement from an idol. "Before my album came out, Elvis Costello got a copy. He ran into Mitchell at a bar, and asked, 'What are you working on?' Mitchell said, 'Oh, this Canadian thing' and gave him a cassette. At that time, there was a very good chance that my record wouldn't even come out, because they wanted me to scrap the whole record and start over. It was just a nightmare."

Costello sang Sexsmith's praises in an interview with Britain's *Mojo* magazine, which suddenly legitimized the troubled album in the eyes of Interscope. After its release in 1995, Costello appeared on the cover of *Mojo* holding up a copy of Sexsmith's album, heralding it as his pick for album of the year; five years later, Costello would include it in a list for *Vanity Fair* of the "Top 500 Albums Of All Time"; the only other Canadians on the list were Neil Young, Kate and Anna McGarrigle, Joni Mitchell, The Band and Leonard Cohen. Sexsmith toured with Costello and soon became a "songwriter's songwriter," with Paul McCartney, Squeeze and Sheryl Crow singing his praises. Mitchell Froom says, "He's the greatest talent to come out of Canada in recent years. Most people that talk to me say that he's the greatest living songwriter." Steve Earle, who first fell in love with Sexsmith's music in 1988 when he stumbled into an El Mocambo gig, called him "one of the best songwriters in the world, and one of the few I know who make me jealous."

Sexsmith would use his critical attention to return his debt to the people who supported him early on, namely his friend Kyp Harness. Harness distils the romanticism of Sexsmith, the political awareness of Bob Wiseman and the simplicity of Bob Snider into biting folk-pop songs. Sexsmith covered Harness on his 2001 album *Blue Boy*, and frequently sings his praises; Sexsmith himself may have been a hard-luck case who made the world pay attention, but there's always a hometown hero like Kyp Harness who still needs a break. "I don't know what it is with him," says Sexsmith. "It just takes someone with ears to come along. If a Leonard Cohen or a Dylan came along today, they'd be having just as hard a time as Kyp is. But it takes imagination to be able to see that, and nobody around here in terms of label people seems to have it. Somebody out there has got to pick up on it."

Sexsmith's profile increased slightly after two more albums with Froom and a spot on 1997's Another Roadside Attraction tour, but his Canadian appeal remains restricted to hardcore music geeks and critics; he has modest success in Japan, the U.S. and Europe. Sexsmith's career in the wake of the CanRock Renaissance proves that the climate of adventure and commercial risk — even for seemingly unrisky, well-crafted, traditional adult pop music — had dried up, and once again artists had to seek external approval before Canada took them seriously.

Sexsmith recognizes the harsh business reality of the situation. "I would get really frustrated when I was a courier," he admits. "You keep thinking, 'Why not me? What's the problem?' I would phone label people and ask them, 'What would I have to do before you would sign me?' Because people would say nice things, and then it's like, 'Okay, why don't you do something?' Their job is hard too, because they have all these people to answer to and people wanting their attention all the time. Being on the inside, I can see that it is quite complicated. Especially in Canada, where there's not a lot of money going around for bands. In America, they seem to sign more often and throw money around a bit more.

"I would have been just as happy to sign up here, but it didn't happen. There was interest for me, but nothing ever seemed to follow through. But what ended up happening turned out to be better. There's a lot of great albums that get released here that don't get outside of Canada. It seems that the way it's set up now, you can have a career and do well here now — The Tragically Hip have proven that — whereas before you had to go to the States. I may be one of those guys who never has that kind of success here, or any kind. I don't know why it matters so much to me, but I'm from here and you want people to know."

"It's really strange in Canada," says Steve Earle, who produced *Blue Boy*, which was held up for almost a year in label wrangling. "There was a time when Canada supported her best singer/songwriters, and there's a tradition of that there. Ron Sexsmith is not *just* good. Lyrically, he's better than most people are, and melodically he has no peer. He's been a huge influence on me melodically. Not supporting that is a crime."

In 2000, Ron Sexsmith was finally dropped by Interscope, a fate that befell many artists who weren't significantly improving a corporation's quarterly financial statements. Manoeuvring in a major label climate became even dicier for artists everywhere, not to mention Canadian ones. But for Canadian artists who had already learned how to operate on their own, the fall was cushioned somewhat.

Michael Timmins of the Cowboy Junkies recalls the short honeymoon they had upon switching major label deals in 1995, 10 years after they had started their career with their own indie label. "Geffen did a fantastic job on 1996's *Lay It Down* [which sold 500,000 copies]," says Timmins. "Then, with 1998's *Miles From Our Home*, [the parent company Universal] were going through their big merger and transitions. Everyone from the *Lay It Down* era had been fired or left. Before *Miles* came out we knew it wasn't going to sell anything, because we couldn't even get a call returned from the label. Since we got the official release from Geffen, we've been reconfiguring and this is a really refreshing period. We don't have to ask anyone's permission to do anything anymore, we just do it. We don't want to get into a big international contract again, because we've explored the pitfalls of those and we don't need one right now. We're going to maintain the [independent] side of things and license to different territories. The general idea is to keep it as close to home as we can.

"The whole industry has shifted," Timmins continues. "There are more artists of our stature — people who aren't superstars, but who can sell a few records — and there's no room for them on [major label] rosters anymore. For whatever reason, the major labels don't think they can make money by selling 300,000–500,000 records. Maybe they can't, I don't know. It's a very weird time right now. There's a whole new level forming, which is exciting in a way."

For those outside the mainstream, it has once again become necessary to look beyond Canadian borders to find any kind of audience. Especially if your music had trouble fitting into the CanRock landscape in the first place. King Cobb Steelie, a rock band whose genuine assimilation of dub, electronica, jazz and hip-hop influences set them far apart from most other CanRock bands when they started in 1991, should realistically have been sending their music to innovative indie labels in the U.S. or the U.K., instead of attempting to assimilate into the Canadian mainstream via a major label deal with EMI. Bassist Kevin Lynn recalls, "At EMI, we'd be talking about remixes, and we'd tell them that we had some connections to [innovative electronic artists] Amon Tobin and Coldcut, and the EMI people would roll their eyes and say [sarcastically], 'That's great.' It's not the public, it's the Canadian music industry as a whole." Lynn also laughs at the memory of renowned underground producer Bill Laswell coming from New York to see the band play at the Albion Hotel in Guelph, and the doorwoman didn't want to let him in.

Ironically, the success of the Canadian music scene in the early '90s may have cursed a band like King Cobb Steelie, by making it seem possible that they could crack the Canadian market. "We never thought to send [the first album] to Dischord or to someone in the U.K.," says Lynn. "I don't know why; it didn't seem viable at that moment."

"We've always been learning as we go along," says singer/guitarist Kevan Byrne. "Quite often it was simply a case of someone wanting to put out our record and us saying, 'Oh really? Well, let's go with them.' Then someone would call you wanting to be your agent or manager and you think, 'Oh, maybe we should have a manager.' We blundered along in a lot of ways, but it was a lot easier to do at that time than when I was in Heimlich Maneuver [Byrne's mid-'80s punk band]. By the time King Cobb Steelie started, there were a million places to play, a million bands around, all kinds of independent labels, people like Phleg Camp were making 7" singles. There was an infrastructure in place for us."

When King Cobb Steelie signed to EMI, the Laswell-produced *Project Twinkle* album "sold terribly, really badly," says Byrne. The follow-up, 1997's *Junior Relaxer*, was the band's masterpiece and even yielded a minor video hit, "Rational." "We thought the fact that it sold 10,000 copies was unbelievable," says Byrne. "The problem wasn't Canadian, but that we couldn't get released outside of Canada. It's kind of an old story for Canadian bands. We couldn't get released in the U.K., and we got a cursory release in the States, in places where we thought we should potentially have a good audience. So is there a glass ceiling for adventurous music in Canada? Commercially, yes. That's true everywhere; the only difference is that there's 30 million people here, not 300 million."

Byrne says that corporate culture's tolerance for unconventional music had dried up by 1997. "After they signed all the more eclectic things and discovered that only one sound was selling, all the other stuff got dropped and everybody sounded like this godawful, earnest grunge pop thing," says Byrne. "*Junior Relaxer* came out in 1997, and by that time we were feeling the screws from the record company to write something that they could sell. To their credit, they gave us total creative freedom and let us work with whomever we chose, and gave us money to mix it in England. When they got the record, they said, 'What the hell is this?' The song 'Rational' was the only thing they could relate to, and the success of that video is what kept them hanging in there. By the time we gave them new demo material, it wasn't hit material for them. The clamps had come down: they were not interested in our critical acclaim or building the band to a level of a cult band like the Pixies. They had direct orders to drop everything that didn't recoup. They told us, 'We're dropping everything that didn't recoup except you guys, and we're going to wait to hear your stuff.'"

The demo material they submitted to EMI Canada would form the bulk of their next album *Mayday*, which yielded two hit singles, "Below the Stars" and "Home." But by that time, King Cobb Steelie had wrangled their way out of the EMI contract and signed to Ryko in North America and Cooking Vinyl in Europe, where they toured with the likes of Cornershop and Laika. After years of floundering, they had finally found labels who could market their music throughout the international underground more successfully than a Canadian major could.

Other bands take a more DIY approach to international relations, with a dogged dedication to overcome all obstacles with minimal outside interference. Grant Lawrence and his garage-punk band The Smugglers have a fairly low profile in Canada, but they regularly tour America, Australia, Europe and Japan; their tenth anniversary live album was recorded in Spain, and their association with the California punk label Lookout has caught the attention of punks worldwide. Lawrence maintains that what has kept the Smugglers going since 1989 is the triumvirate of "ambition, denial and good times."

"Denial is when you've been together for 10 years and you follow up a great show in Seattle with a show at a vet's hall in Montana," says Lawrence, describing one particular gig. "It was just Vietnam vets — it was sad, they're a rough bunch and they hated us. There were 10 people there and maybe one of them said, 'Hey, rock-'n'-roll, man!' The denial comes in when you're driving away from the show, and you say, 'Well, you know, hey, that was, you know, that one guy, the guy with the eye patch and the cane? He liked it!' That's denial. It was an awful show, nothing good about it, and the promoter charged us $50 for the soundman — the denial is what keeps you going.

"But ambition is the most important thing," Lawrence continues. "There are a lot of things that we've done that a lot of bands are constantly asking, 'How'd you do that?' It's just the will to achieve it, and having a phone, fax and e-mail. I booked our tour of Japan without ever seeing a guy's face; it was all through e-mail — it didn't even cost anything. So many young bands depend on labels to put out their music, and if they don't get a label, they figure they're doomed."

Montreal's Local Rabbits benefited greatly from their association with Sloan's Murderecords, and in 2000 found themselves struggling to find an indie label to put out their third album. They burst onto the national indie scene in 1995 when they were still teenagers, and went on their first national tour with Sloan. Sloan's Jay Ferguson produced their 1996 debut full-length *You Can't Touch This*, and released it on Murderecords. While the Local Rabbits found an instant audience because of that link, things would soon change when Sloan had to devote more time to their own career than nurturing younger ones. "When our first album came out in 1996, Murder would do all sorts of things they didn't even have to," says Local Rabbits singer/guitarist Ben Gunning. "They'd make a fan newsletter and print pictures of parties we'd have, and you almost felt like you were part of a club and protected in that way. It helped a lot. When *Basic Concept* came out in 1998, it was more every band for themselves. Sloan was just concentrating on their own band and there wasn't that camaraderie.

"A lot of bands were getting disenchanted about not reaching the next economic level," Gunning continues, noting that many of the Local Rabbits' Murderecords peers were breaking up by that time: Super Friendz, Jale, The Inbreds. "A lot of teenagers who go to see shows think it's really square to talk about how much money you're making. But after you grow up and have been playing music for years, if you don't see any progress in terms of making a living out of it, it's discouraging. You don't want to be scrounging your whole life."

On the Local Rabbits' second album, Gunning wrote a song called "Play On," about the frustrations felt by many children of the CanRock Renaissance. The first verse documents a brilliant performance by a band in "a black-walled club on skid row" before an unappreciative and small audience; the second verse is about a band playing before "frantic crowds who hear but do not listen." Each chorus is sung in the voice of a fan who understands the beauty of both bands despite the differing surroundings, and urges the musicians to "sing these songs with all your soul / and do not let all these conditions drag you down / because among this frantic crowd is one who listens."

Gunning explains the origins of the song: "There's a place in London, Ontario, called The Embassy, and we were playing there with Zumpano. There was an opening band who brought all their friends, and then I was watching Zumpano play — such great music and they were totally giving it their all — and no one was watching. It seemed at that moment that it would be so easy to throw up your hands and say, 'What the hell are we doing?' We've been in that situation so many times, where we're playing a city once again for five people.

"The second half of the song is about discouraging aspects of being a more commercially viable band, and Sloan was on my mind because we played with Sloan many times, and one big show for us was with them at the Concert Hall in Toronto. When you're making a living off music, you have to realize that maybe 15 per cent of your fan base are people who are really into music, not just people who buy CDs because they have a CD player or watch MuchMusic. There's nothing wrong with casual listeners, but it could be discouraging if you're just a transient part of their life. You'll be playing something you think is really good, and then you see someone giving you the devil-horn salute and you wonder, 'Do they think we're being facetious? Are they actually listening to the details?'

"Part of 'Play On' is about people who might be enjoying your music on a level that's frustrating for you, but that there are always the people who study the records at home and those are the people that make you happy about what you're doing. Otherwise, what's the point of even trying to write good lyrics if all you need is cool hair and you jump around?"

"Live audiences aren't what they used to be," says Mark Milne of Tristan Psionic. His band took a hiatus between 1997 and 2000 to focus on running their Sonic Unyon label. They returned with a new album called *Mind the Gap*. "I was surprised on our tour in April 2000. We thought it was going to be really grim, because our band had been inconsistent and it had been four years since we had toured or released a record. In Ontario, it was okay, with a couple of hundred people out each night. But out west, where I thought it would be completely grim, it was our best tour ever. We were astounded. Maybe we waited out the drought. We were lucky though, and for new bands it's harder to get people out to shows."

Bill Baker, whose Mint Records was revitalized in 2000 by albums from Neko Case, Carolyn Mark and Huevos Rancheros, says, "When [the hype] all dried up and everyone looked elsewhere and that interest faded, you end up with people being in a band because they legitimately want to or they have talent. There's things to see [now], as opposed to, 'Oh God, I saw the worst three bands of my life last night.' It's like after a forest fire and the little trees start to grow again. The kind of career paths where you would see in the early '90s where people would play to 50 people for weeks or months and slowly build a following — I see little things like that happening again. People aren't expecting that overnight, superfast trip to Toronto — a lot of those kinds of bands aren't playing. The people who are willing to do the work, play the music and just have a good time are willing to do it again."

Baker was the midwife for one of 2000's sure signs of a thaw in the post-Renaissance ice age, a powerful Vancouver pop collective led by Carl Newman called The New Pornographers. In the space of a year, The New Pornographers went from being a Vancouver secret to the buzz of the Canadian underground to international acclaim. Newman had spent the '90s in relative obscurity in critical favourites Superconductor and Zumpano. Although Zumpano was signed to the once-powerful American indie Sub Pop in 1995, they had arrived too late to catch the end of the CanRock Renaissance and struggled to be noticed by anyone other than fellow musicians and the national monthly music magazine *Exclaim!*, who had faithfully championed Newman's every move and put him on the cover three times — once for each band. The New Pornographers showcased Newman's finest hour to date, both critically and commercially, and it was done with a little help from his friends, exemplifying a new community spirit.

A self-admitted archetypal music geek raised in White Rock, B.C., Newman grew up devoted to R.E.M. and the Pixies, and was frustrated by the original music created in his hometown. "There were some lame reggae or ska bands," Newman says of White Rock. "But it was the kind of thing where I said, 'I could do better than this in a fucking second.' And that was completely true."

As his high-school career concluded, he and school cohort Warren Weslink started the framework for Superconductor — "a loud six-guitar band" — with a revolving line-up of Vancouverites, which at times featured three bassists, and for a short period, Mecca Normal's Jean Smith on noise guitar.

In 1992, Newman formed Zumpano, which existed simultaneously with Superconductor. The four-piece pop band also included guitarist/keyboardist Michael Ledwidge, bassist Stefan "Scream" Niemann and the band's namesake/drummer Jason Zumpano. Their complicated orchestral pop echoed Burt Bacharach and The Zombies, forming a strong contrast from Superconductor's three albums of noise rock, including 1996's *Bastardsong*. "I had a weird epiphany in 1991 when I bought the *Best of Dionne Warwick* and I couldn't get over how much I loved it," says Newman. "Zumpano came out of my obsession with that album. I began to think all the indie rock around me was complete shit and I wondered, 'How could people like that garbage when there's Burt Bacharach and Hal David?'"

Though various international artists like Richard Davies, Eric Matthews and The High Llamas would pick up the "orch-pop" aesthetic, Zumpano was a lone Canadian entity in this pursuit. The band caught the attention of Sub Pop in 1993, with the Kevin Kane–produced *Look What The Rookie*

Did finally released in 1995, and the superior sophomore *Goin' Though Changes* hitting shelves the following year. Throughout this time, Newman toured with both Zumpano and Superconductor, the latter drawn out of retirement at the behest of Guided by Voices to accompany the band on tour. Newman spent some time in Halifax and developed relationships with many of the bands from the Halifax Pop Explosion, eventually touring with Hardship Post, and being regularly championed by Sloan. But the public neglected to fall for the pop excellence on *Goin' Through Changes*. Zumpano never moved beyond their status as critic's darlings, and entered an undetermined hiatus after a 1997 tour.

Later that year, Bill Baker says Newman told him about "a solo project that would involve friends of his that he recognized as being particularly talented in certain ways, and that he wanted to write music with them in mind." Dubbed The New Pornographers — a trivial name that Newman later justified after discovering televangelist Jimmy Swaggart's book *Music: The New Pornography* — Newman leisurely began work on his pop supergroup. He recruited Dan Bejar, the nucleus of indie heroes Destroyer, and Neko Case, who at that time was still transforming from her role as the drummer for Maow into a old-school country diva. "Frankly, I didn't really believe he was ever going to do this," Baker admits. "It just sounded like one of those things that people say."

From their first rehearsal in 1997 to their first gig a year later, the collective gradually grew to include bassist John Collins (Nardwuar and the Evaporators), independent film director Blaine Thurier (*Low Self Esteem Girl*) on keyboards, and drummer Kurt Dahle (Limblifter, Age of Electric). "We created a scene within one band," says Newman. "A scene is too scattered when it's ten different bands. I think it's far more focused if you get all the people you want and stick it in one band and say, 'Here's the Vancouver scene.' And tell everyone in Vancouver to protect The New Pornographers because the scene is lost without them."

After attracting some further interest when the track "Letter From An Occupant" appeared on the Mint compilation *Vancouver Special*, Mint gave the band a deadline to finish a full-length CD. In the fall of 2000, the New Pornographers released the stunning *Mass Romantic*, described by Newman as "a weird combination of pop, glam, new wave and indie rock."

As the side-project band attracted attention, so did the media's interest in the collective nature of the project. Newman says a principal reason for the album's successes was the support within and surrounding the collective. The band Vancouver Nights, led by Sara Lapsley, featured contributions from

Pornographers' Bejar, Newman and Collins on its well-received 2000 debut album. The solo career of Neko Case — an American whose early '90s stint at art school in Vancouver nurtured her musical growth — has drawn from a larger CanRock community to comprise her collaborators and rotating band members, including Newman, Matt Murphy (Super Friendz, Flashing Lights), the Local Rabbits, the Sadies, Don Kerr (Rheostatics), Brian Connelly (Shadowy Men), Carolyn Mark, David Carswell (Smugglers) and Linda McRae (Spirit of the West). Much like the Halifax Pop Explosion in the early '90s, The New Pornographers' collective success was a result a small pool of talent mixed with the efforts of a small team of believers elevating the music to unexpected heights. Newman is a firm believer in the influence of a community.

"There are a lot more good bands here than there ever has been," says Newman of the Vancouver scene in 2000. "There was never a point where I thought anyone was really that good in Vancouver. If no one is really that good, then there's nothing really pushing anyone to be that good. When I heard Destroyer's *Thief*, I thought it was so amazing that I considered it a challenge in that The New Pornographers record can't suck because there's this precedent set. It was the same thing with Neko's *Furnace Room Lullaby*. We had to put out a record of the same calibre. Considering they're both Pornographers, you have to save face somehow."

The response to the album was heartwarming for any independent pop music fan. Along with heaps of critical praise from the Canadian press, the disc found strong reviews in American staple publications — *Rolling Stone*, *Spin* and the *New York Times* — as well as landing some commercial radio play and a Juno award for Best Alternative Album. Even more surprising was their showcase at the 2001 sxsw festival in Austin, Texas, where Ray Davies of the Kinks performed with them.

"I feel vindicated," admits Newman of the New Pornographers' success. "I also feel like I made a record that is better than anything that I've done before. I blame no one but myself for past failures. It is not the audience's duty to love your music, it is your duty to convince them that they love you."

Between the success of *Mass Romantic* and Neko Case's ever-increasing international profile, it was an affirmation for Bill Baker and Randy Iwata and their 10-year-old label that their efforts and accomplishments in CanRock history were not in vain, and that the thaw was over. Baker says, "I can't describe the thrill I get from seeing the name 'Mint' in a record review in *Rolling Stone*, or being able to call a distributor overseas and actually having them know who we are. It's an exciting time again for legitimate reasons, as opposed to the hyper-inflated stock market scenario."

East meets West: Chris Murphy and Neko Case, with
Matt Murphy (Flashing Lights) and Dan Bejar
(New Pornographers) in the background, April 1997
(Photo by Paul Clarke)

In the first five years following the CanRock renaissance, the most unlikely Canadian export success story has been Montreal's cinematic and orchestral Godspeed You Black Emperor! The nine-piece instrumental post-rock collective shun all media interviews and official photographs, their debut album *F#A#* was only available on vinyl for the first year of its release, and very few of their tense and eerie compositions are less than 15 minutes long. In the two years following the international release of their debut on the tiny Chicago indie Kranky, they toured America and Europe constantly — slowly graduating from artists' squats to larger theatres — and their anti-media stance only made the media even more intrigued. Furthermore, the band's Montreal home was perceived as an exotic explanation for the wintry music. Praise for the 2000 double album *Lift Your Skinny Fists Like Antennas to Heaven* was universally ecstatic, and was championed by the equally media-shy Radiohead. Through it all, Godspeed parlayed their perceived eccentricity into a mystique that distanced them from any notion of corporate success.

In an exclusive 2000 interview with *The Wire* magazine, guitarist Efrim reflected on what Godspeed's trendy popularity actually meant to a band comprised of committed outsiders. "It's just like being in high school again," says Efrim, "and everything that's going on all around you is all fuck-wads who think that you're a complete jerk-off, or that you and all your friends are freaks. Why would you worry? Maybe every now and then you'll corner someone like the prom queen when she's drunk and she'll confess some dark secrets to you and you'll think that that makes some kind of sense, but the next day everything's back to normal — it never ends. You never leave high school — we're still there."

Gord Downie, the singer from Canada's most popular band of the CanRock Renaissance, is only two degrees of separation away from the underground heroes of Godspeed You Black Emperor!: both have worked with Dinner is Ruined's Dale Morningstar. Downie's own philosophy isn't that far removed from Godspeed's; he agrees that in order for one's art to progress, an artist cannot depend on popularity contests, trends or resting on laurels. "The time it takes to ponder an accomplishment is time away from doing the next thing," says Downie. "I say that to my shame, because really, you should be able to work towards something and then enjoy it to a certain extent. But I've always been wary, superstitious even, and I don't use phrases like 'winning formula' because I think that's death."

More and more, fans and artists are shunning corporate culture and taking matters into their own hands out of sheer necessity. "We don't have choices anymore," says Yvonne Matsell. "I've stopped listening to the radio. When CFNY was 'on the edge' it was interesting because they'd play stuff nobody else would play, and you'd always have a diverse sense of what was out there. Now it's so formatted, and I think it's just awful. You're not able to hear people like Ron Sexsmith on the radio — it's all word of mouth, and sometimes that takes a lot longer to get places. And by that time, the artist's label has dropped them. Unless they're into a long-term development with an artist, which doesn't really exist, those artists sell a minor amount of records, and do a lot of hard work touring."

For rock bands both over and under mainstream radar, jumping in a van and touring is as crucial as it was in 1985. Prog-punk Victoria veterans NoMeansNo have sustained themselves for over 20 years now by touring Europe and the west coast of the States. Winnipeg's political punk/folk/rock band The Weakerthans sold major-label-numbers of their powerful album *Left and Leaving* within the first six months of its 2000 release on the community-minded co-op indie G7, based solely through print support, word of mouth, campus radio and touring North America and Europe. Sarah Harmer spent over a year on the road across Canada and the U.S. promoting *You Were Here*, at which point she was selling out venues everywhere, including lucrative American markets.

The new wave of Canadian musicians, who look beyond their own borders with greater confidence without diluting their art for the international mainstream, have developed their own niche in the global market. Sarah Harmer muses, "People say after shows, 'What is up with Canada? There are so many great musicians we love down here.' There seems to be some advantage that way already, for some people, especially with live music. But I don't know what impressions people have. I definitely get a lot of references to 'the cold' in the music."

"I don't think anybody [in Europe] cares about us being Canadian," says King Cobb Steelie's Kevin Lynn. "We don't get jokes about the Barenaked Ladies or Céline Dion. They always ask us if we know Godspeed You Black Emperor! because that seems to be the only Canadian band they've heard over there. In that way, this country has more of a hip reputation now. There's a different perception of Canadian bands these days, because a lot more are touring Europe now. It's helps a bit to be Canadian: it's obscure and weird enough and has a good reputation for music these days."

Regardless of the subjective quality of the music, the fact remains that although it's a bit easier to be a Canadian band in the wake of the Renaissance, the odds are still stacked against any Canadian band — even commercial ones that enjoy major label support from day one. "Everyone likes to crap on Our Lady Peace because where did they come from?" asked Rusty's Ken McNeil in a 1996 interview. "[OLP] have been on the road since 1994 in a fuckin' van, they worked their asses off, and then when they come home all people can do is shit on them. I don't love OLP, but I respect how hard they have worked. It's an urban thing too, because if you get outside Toronto, people love OLP, and they are the same kids that like Change of Heart."

Career longevity in Canada is still a fleeting notion, argues songwriter Tom Wilson. "Being an entity in the Canadian culture in any part — whether you're writing books, making music, painting or whatever — no matter what, you all come down to being the captain of the Toronto Maple Leafs: You're worshipped and your ass is licked for four or five seasons and then they ship you right the fuck out. I wish we could all be George Armstrongs and retire in great standing."

Blue Rodeo's Jim Cuddy reflects on the CanRock Renaissance by saying, "The period of time we're talking about is historically significant for Canadian music, and it was such a glorious time to live through. It's created some aesthetics for us that were all about bands taking control and doing things themselves. There was also such a great amount of support from each other, and none of this would have been possible without that."

The artistic course of CanRock has been irreversibly altered, thanks to everyone mentioned in the preceding pages. The next generations now have a truly diverse and proud cultural legacy to maintain, and meanwhile younger genres like hip-hop must now fight many of the same battles CanRock did in 1985. But one can never assume that all these gains can be taken for granted. Cultural imperialism still afflicts Canadians, whether it comes through the media or our own indoctrinated mindsets. Just like it was in 1954, when the Massey Commission sounded warning bells about the fragility of Canadian culture; like it was in 1971 when CanCon rules were initiated; like it was in 1985 when the musicians in this book decided that we have not been the same; like it was in 2001 when author Robert Wright, in a book subtitled *The Greying of Canadian Nationalism*, argued that, "The notion that Canada is a unique sort of place producing a parochial culture is waning. I think The Tragically Hip will be the last 'Canadian band.'"

The years between 1985 and 1995 were incredibly fascinating, but the art created then is merely part of a continuum that must keep growing and finding new audiences, lest it all be in vain. Isn't it amazing what you can accomplish, when you don't let the nation stand in your way?

You hear every day how they're going away
guess they just don't understand
The singer is the voice of the people
And his song is the soul of our land
So singer please stay and don't go away
There's so many words to be said
For a land without song can't stand very long
When the voice of its people is dead

Singer, you must search for your place on the earth
While the same for your nation is true
So lift up the soul of your country
And a place will be found here for you
But don't go and run 'til your song has been sung
And the words of your soul have been said
For a land without song can't stand very long
When the voice of its people is dead

You may pile up your gold but the pride of your soul
Is the small bit of hope you've installed
On the children who'll come this way tomorrow
In search of the right way to go
So singer, sing on like the first ray of dawn
With your promise of day just ahead
For the land without song can't stand very long
When the voice of its people is dead.

— Stompin' Tom Connors, "The Singer
(The Voice of the People)," 1978

Play on, my friends, in this black-walled club on skid row
Full of kids whose heads are turned or held up, bored, by numbing elbows
They are sitting deaf behind the space they've left for you to play for
And they're done with listening to the other band of friends they came for
Strum those chords of glory that you have composed with skill and patience
Even though you play to distant crowds with blank or hidden faces
Sing these songs with all your soul and do not let all these conditions
Drag you down because among the feeble crowd is one who listens

I am hidden in the dark
you can't see me but my heart is lifted up with every note that rings
So please don't let this end and do not give up on this friend

Play on, my friends, in this jam-packed concert hall that
Holds the screaming moshers, clueless watchers, people who will loudly
Call your name out as they've done before at all their favourite concerts
By some bands that they've forgotten now, whose posters they have tossed out
And even though you play to frantic crowds who hear but do not listen
There are ears that listen closely here and eyes with awe that glisten
Sing these songs with all your soul and do not let all these conditions
Drag you down because among this frantic crowd is one who listens

I am hidden in the crowd
you can't see me but the sound that you are sending lifts my spirit up
So please don't let this end and do not give up on this friend.

— Local Rabbits, "Play On," 1998

Selected Cast of Characters

Bruce Allen: highly opinionated Vancouver manager who masterminded many of that city's biggest corporate success stories, including Loverboy and Bryan Adams

Chuck Angus: co-founder of L'Etranger; organizer of Save The Rails tour; Grievous Angels; journalist

Tom Anselmi: singer, Slow, Circle C, Copyright

Neal Arbick: vocalist, A Neon Rome, Jesus and His Mutants, Mahendra

Ric Arboit: president of Nettwerk Records; former studio and live engineer

Peter Arsenault: guitarist/vocalist, Jellyfishbabies; bassist/vocalist, Doughboys, All Systems Go!

Charles Austin: bassist/vocalist, Super Friendz, Neusiland

Bill Baker: co-owner, Mint Records

Brent Bambury: host of *Brave New Waves* 1985–1995; host of *Midday* 1995–2000

Keith Bates: manager, A Neon Rome

Jaymz Bee: bandleader of the Look People, the Bee People, Royal Jelly Orchestra

Mike Belitsky: drummer, The Lone Stars, Jellyfishbabies, Jale, The Vees, The Sadies; singer/songwriter, Cheticamp

Robert Benvie: guitarist/vocalist, Thrush Hermit, Tigre Benvie

Moe Berg: singer/songwriter and guitarist in The Pursuit of Happiness, Modern Minds, Facecrime; solo artist; fiction author

Art Bergmann: The Shmorgs, the K-Tels, Young Canadians, Los Popularos, Poisoned; solo artist

Jello Biafra: singer, Dead Kennedys; owner, Alternative Tentacles label; collaborator, DOA, NoMeansNo; spoken word artist; political activist

Dave Bidini: founding Rheostatics rhythm guitarist/vocalist/songwriter; journalist; author

Ian Blurton: bandleader, guitarist and vocalist with Change of Heart,

Blurtonia; drummer for A Neon Rome and Cowboy Junkies 1985; producer

James Booth: singer, The Ten Commandments; manager, L'Etranger; CFNY staff 1983–1985; MuchMusic producer 1985–1994; producer at CBC's *Radio Sonic*

John Borra: bassist, Change of Heart, A Neon Rome, Ron Sexsmith, The Boneheads; solo artist

Anne Bourne: cellist and keyboardist for Change of Heart, Jane Siberry, Loreena McKennitt, Blue Rodeo, and others; solo artist

Randy Boyd: co-founder of Psyche Industry records; employee, Pipeline Records, Cargo Records

Colleen Britton: drummer, Jellyfishbabies 1985–1987; Cool Blue Halo

Michael Brook: guitarist, the Everglades, Martha and the Muffins; inventor of "infinite guitar"; producer, Mary Margaret O'Hara's *Miss America*

Chris Brown: keyboardist, The Bourbon Tabernacle Choir; Rheostatics session player; Don't Talk Dance; touring keyboardist for Barenaked Ladies and The Tragically Hip; one half of duo with Kate Fenner

"Dove" David M. Brown: bassist, Jr. Gone Wild

Malcolm Burn: singer, Boys Brigade, Pregnant; producer/engineer for Crash Vegas, Blue Rodeo, Daniel Lanois, Neville Brothers, Patti Smith, Lisa Germano, others

Kevan Byrne: guitarist/vocalist with King Cobb Steelie, Heimlich Manouevre

Neko Case: American transplant to early '90s Vancouver scene; drummer in Cub and Maow; bandleader of country project Neko Case & Her Boyfriends; member of New Pornographers

Andrew Cash: singer/songwriter, guitarist, L'Etranger, Ursula, Cash Brothers; solo artist; journalist

John Wesley Chisholm: singer/songwriter/guitarist, Black Pool; guitarist/songwriter, Johnny Favourite Swing Orchestra

Dave Clark: drummer, Rheostatics 1982–1994; Dinner is Ruined 1995 to present; Gordon Downie's Goddammed Band; leader of the Woodchoppers Association

Greg Clark: veteran Halifax club owner, Club Flamingo, Double Deuce, Birdland, The Marquee

Greg Clow: electronic music live events promoter; Toronto DJ; music journalist

Stephen Cooke: bassist, The Deluxe Boys; *Halifax Herald* entertainment writer

Colin Cripps: guitarist/songwriter, Crash Vegas; also the Spoons, Heavenly Brothers, Jim Cuddy Band, Junkhouse; producer

John Critchley: guitarist, singer/songwriter in The Ikons, 13 Engines; solo artist

Kevin Crompton (a.k.a **cEvin Key**): drummer, Images in Vogue 1981–1985; multi-instrumentalist, Skinny Puppy, Download, Doubting Thomas, Tear Garden and various other electronic projects

Jim Cuddy: singer/songwriter, guitarist in The Hi-Fi's, Blue Rodeo; solo artist

Jonathan Cummins: guitarist, the Doughboys 1989–1993; leader of Bionic; Montreal music journalist

Kim Deschamps: pedal steel guitarist, the Cowboy Junkies 1987–1990, Blue Rodeo 1992–1999; solo artist

Tony Dewald: drummer, Deja Voodoo; co-founder, Og Records

Hugh Dillon: singer, The Headstones; actor; CanRock badboy from Kingston, Ontario

Ed Dobek: drummer, Jr. Gone Wild, The Vinaigrettes

Bob Doidge: manager, Grant Ave. studio; early Daniel Lanois collaborator

Julie Doiron: bassist/vocalist, Eric's Trip; solo artist; owner, Sappy Records

Colin Doroschuk: member of Men Without Hats; leader of Centrifugal Force

Ivan Doroschuk: keyboardist Heaven Seventeen; leader of Men Without Hats; solo artist

Stefan Doroschuk: Men Without Hats, The Mackenzie-Parker Gang, Three O'Clock Train

Gord Downie: singer/lyricist, The Tragically Hip; solo artist; poet

Marc Durand: producer, Men Without Hats, the Box; former partner in Alert Records

Brian Eno: innovative British producer who pioneered ambient recording

Sam Feldman: powerful Vancouver booking agent

Kate Fenner: vocalist, Bourbon Tabernacle Choir; touring vocalist with The Tragically Hip; one half of duo with Chris Brown

Jay Ferguson: guitarist/vocalist, Sloan, The Deluxe Boys, Kearney Lake Rd.; co-owner of Murderecords

Tom Ferris: bandleader, Moev; co-founder of Nettwerk Records

Josh Finlayson: guitarist, Skydiggers, West Montrose, Gordon Downie's Goddamed Band

Richard Flohil: Toronto folk music promoter/journalist; Mariposa Festival; Stony Plain Records publicist

Mark Gane: guitarist, Martha and the Muffins, M+M

Mark Gaudet: drummer, Eric's Trip, Elevator

David Geffen: old-school '60s music business mogul; founder, Asylum Records, Geffen Records, the David Geffen Company; co-founder Dreamworks

Jake Gold: co-founder, The Management Trust; manager, The Tragically Hip, The Watchmen, others

Michele Gould: singer/songwriter, Lava Hay, Taste of Joy

Allan Gregg: co-founder, The Management Trust; Decima Research, television host

Handsome Ned a.k.a. **Robin Masyk**: Toronto neo-traditionalist country singer

Sarah Harmer: solo artist; singer/songwriter and guitarist, Weeping Tile

Tom Harrison: Vancouver music journalist; singer for Bruno Gerussi's Medallion

Eve Hartling: guitarist/vocalist, Jale

Ron Hawkins: singer/songwriter, The Lowest of the Low, The Rusty Nails

Kevin Hearn: keyboardist, The Look People, Corky and the Juice Pigs, Rheostatics, Barenaked Ladies; solo artist

Amy Hersenhoren: Toronto concert promoter; former manager, King Cobb Steelie, Change of Heart; employee, Raw Energy Records; co-founder, Lunamoth Records

Chris Hooper: drummer, Grapes of Wrath, Ginger, Gentlemen of Horror, Kill Pigs, Ralph

Tom Hooper: bassist/singer, Grapes of Wrath, Ginger, The Gentlemen of Horror

Chris Houston: bassist in the Forgotten Rebels; One-Eyed Jacks; solo artist; composer, "Surfin' On Heroin"

Mark Howard: producer/engineer at Grant Ave. Studio; Daniel Lanois collaborator

Tracy Howe: member of Rational Youth; former member of Heaven Seventeen

Paul Hyde: singer, Payola$, Rock and Hyde, solo artist

Randy Iwata: co-founder, Mint Records; graphic artist

Jerry Jerry (**Woods**): bandleader of Jerry Jerry and the Sons of Rhythm Orchestra; Edmontonian transplant to Montreal

Martha Johnson: singer, Martha and the Muffins, M+M

Mark Jowett: guitarist, Moev 1981–1986; co-founder/head of A&R Nettwerk Records

Kevin Kane: guitarist, singer/songwriter in the Grapes of Wrath, Empty Set; solo artist; producer

John Kastner: guitarist/singer, Asexuals, Doughboys, All Systems Go!

Greg Keelor: guitarist, singer/songwriter in The Hi-Fi's, Blue Rodeo; solo artist

Joe "Shithead" Keithley: bandleader, DOA; solo artist; founder of Sudden Death Records

Geoffrey Kelly: singer/songwriter, wind instrumentalist in Spirit of the West

Don Kerr: drummer/cellist for Ron Sexsmith, Dinner is Ruined 1989–1993, Rheostatics 1995–2001, Bob Wiseman; producer and engineer, Gas Station studio

Steve Koch: guitarist, The Handsome Neds, the Viletones, the Demics, Running Kind, Crybaby, the Boneheads, John Borra Band

Kevin Komoda: producer and studio engineer; keyboardist, Pest 5000, Rational Youth, Action Man on Assignment, The Blueprints; engineer and staff for *Brave New Waves*

k.d. lang: Edmontonian renegade country-turned-pop vocalist

Michel "Away" Langevin: drummer/lyricist, Voivod; visual artist; member of Men Without Hats on the *Sideways* album

Bob Lanois: Hamilton producer, engineer, photographer

Daniel Lanois: Hamilton-bred producer, U2, Bob Dylan, Peter Gabriel and others; solo artist

Jocelyne Lanois: bassist, Crash Vegas, Martha & the Muffins, Silent Spring

Augusta LaPaix: founding host of *Brave New Waves*

Elliott Lefko: independent '80s Toronto concert promoter, later with MCA/Universal/House of Blues Concerts; founder, Rightside Records

Joyce Linehan: Canadian A&R rep for Sub Pop records in the early '90s

Sebastian Lippa: singer/songwriter, The Hardship Post, Speedo

Suzanne Little: singer/songwriter, Lava Hay; solo artist

Kevin Lynn: bassist, King Cobb Steelie; campus radio veteran; visual/video artist

Colin MacKenzie: indie label impresario, Murder, Perimeter, Cinnamon Toast; manager, Jale

Mack MacKenzie: bandleader, Three O'Clock Train; Mackenzie-Parker Gang; solo artist

Bernard Maiezza: keyboardist, Change of Heart, A Neon Rome, Cookie Duster

Andy Maize: singer, Skydiggers, Direktive 17, West Montrose

John Mann: lead singer/songwriter, guitarist in Spirit of the West

Pierre Marchand: producer and principal Sarah McLachlan collaborator since 1990; also Greg Keelor's *Gone*, Rufus Wainwright

Hugh Marsh: violinist for Bruce Cockburn, Mary Margaret O'Hara, Peter Murphy and others; solo artist

Waye Mason: owner, No Records

Jim Masyk: guitarist, the Sidewinders; brother of Handsome Ned and keeper of his musical estate

Yvonne Matsell: Toronto club booker, Ultrasound and Ted's Wrecking Yard; organizer of the NXNE festival

Michelle McAdorey: singer/songwriter, Crash Vegas, Cold Fish/Corect Spelling; solo artist; collaborator, Greg Keelor, King Cobb Steelie

Terry McBride: co-founder of Nettwerk Productions, head of Nettmanagement

Scott McCullough: guitarist, the Doughboys, Rusty

Bruce McDonald: filmmaker of *Roadkill*, *Highway 61*, *Hard Core Logo*; video director

Mike McDonald: singer/songwiter, guitarist and bandleader of Jr. Gone Wild; solo artist

Brenndan McGuire: producer for Super Friendz, Sloan, Rebecca West, Jale, By Divine Right, Tristan Psionic; live sound engineer for Sloan

Sarah McLachlan: singer/songwriter; anchor of Nettwerk Records' roster; former ticket girl at Club Flamingo; singer, The October Game

James MacLean: Montreal manager of Voivod, All Systems Go!, Ivan, The Nils

Alyson McLeod: drummer/guitarist/singer, Jale, Skreech, Speedo; bassist/vocalist, The New Hardship Post

Lewis Melville: Guelph multi-instrumentalist, producer, engineer, solo artist; co-founder of DROG Records; auxiliary member of the Rheostatics and Skydiggers

Glenn Milchem: drummer, Change of Heart, Andrew Cash, Groovy Religion, the Garbagemen, Plasterscene Replicas, Blue Rodeo 1992 to present; bandleader, The Swallows

Mark Milne: co-founder of Sonic Unyon label; guitarist in Tristan Psionic

Peter Moore: producer/engineer for Cowboy Junkies, Jr. Gone Wild, Handsome Ned, countless other roots and punk bands

Dale Morningstar: bandleader of Dinner is Ruined; producer and engineer at the Gas Station studio, guitarist in Gordon Downie's Goddamed Band; Woodchoppers Association

Chris Murphy: bassist/singer/guitarist/drummer, Spent, Aware, Kearney Lake Rd., Black Pool, Sloan, The Super Friendz; co-owner of Murderecords

Matt Murphy: guitarist/singer, The Super Friendz, Lil' Orton Hoggett, Flashing Lights and many other Halifax bands; no relation to Chris

Ken Myhr: guitarist, Jane Siberry and the Cowboy Junkies; producer; solo artist

Darryl Neudorf: producer/engineer; drummer, 54·40, Empty Set

William New: singer, Groovy Religion; founder, Elvis Mondays; club booker

Mary Margaret O'Hara: Toronto singer/songwriter; Go Deo Chorus; guest vocalist, The Henrys

Dave "Rave" Ogilvie: producer/engineer for Skinny Puppy, Nine Inch Nails, Sloan, etc.

Kevin Ogilvie (a.k.a. **Nivek Ogre**): vocalist, Skinny Puppy, W.E.L.T., Ministry, Revolting Cocks

Mike O'Neill: bassist/singer/songwriter in the Inbreds; solo artist

Neil Osborne: singer/songwriter/guitarist in 54·40

Allison Outhit: singer/guitarist/songwriter, Rebecca West; Bubaiskull, Flags for Everything, Jeffrey's Wake, Staja/tanz and various other Halifax projects

Steven Page: singer, Barenaked Ladies

Patrick Pentland: guitarist/singer, Sloan; co-owner of Murderecords; Happy Co., The Ripping Convulsions

Holger Peterson: founder, Stony Plain Records; host of CBC Radio's *Saturday Night Blues*

Ford Pier: keyboardist, Jr. Gone Wild, Roots Roundup; guitarist, DOA, Veda Hille; solo artist

Jennifer Pierce: singer/guitarist, Jale; singer, No Damn Fears; The Vees

Joel Plaskett: singer/guitarist, Thrush Hermit, Joel Plaskett Emergency

Jonathan Poneman: founder, Sub Pop Records

Don Pyle: drummer, Shadowy Men on a Shadowy Planet, Phono-Comb; programmer, King Cobb Steelie, Greek Buck; producer; journalist

Brock Pytel: drummer/songwriter, the Doughboys; singer/songwriter, solo artist

Daniel Richler: television music journalist on MuchMusic and *The New Music*; host of CBC Newsworld's *Big Life*; editor-in-chief of Book Television

Ed Robertson: guitarist/singer, Barenaked Ladies

Bob Rock: Vancouver punk/hard rock producer, Poisoned, Pointed Sticks, Metallica, The Cult; guitarist, the Payola$, Rock 'N Hyde, Rockhead

Don Rooke: slide guitarist, Mary Margaret O'Hara; bandleader, the Henrys

Peter Rowan: manager for Julie Doiron, early Sloan, Eric's Trip, Hardship Post; former owner of DTK Records

Henri Sangalang: bassist, Kearney Lake Rd, Flashing Lights

Patti Schmidt: host of *Brave New Waves* 1995 to present, singer/bassist in Pest 5000; co-founder of Derivative Records

Andrew Scott: drummer/songwriter, Sloan; visual artist

Joey Serlin: guitarist/songwriter, the Watchmen

Ron Sexsmith: Toronto singer/songwriter

Jane Siberry: Toronto singer/songwriter; founder of Sheeba Records

Gord Sinclair: bassist, The Tragically Hip

Jean Smith: singer/lyricist in Mecca Normal; solo artist; poet; riot grrrl progenitor

Alex Soria: singer/guitarist/songwriter, Nils, Chino

Seymour Stein: founder of Sire Records, best known for signing Madonna, the Ramones, Talking Heads

Cal Stephenson: co-founder of Nettwerk Records, member of Moev

Andy Stochansky: Toronto drummer, Ani DiFranco, Bob Wiseman, Meryn Cadell; singer/songwriter, solo artist

Chip Sutherland: entertainment lawyer; manager of Sloan and various other bands; co-owner of Perimeter Records; musician, Black Pool, Flags of Everything

Kurt Swinghammer: Toronto visual artist; singer/songwriter, guitarist; video director

Rob Taylor: bassist, Change of Heart 1981–1992

Jean-Yves "Blacky" Theriault: bassist/songwriter, Voivod 1983–1991; multi-media designer

Chris Thompson: guitarist, Eric's Trip; singer/songwriter, Moon Socket

Christian Thorvaldson: guitarist, Slow, Circle C, Copyright

Martin Tielli: singer/guitarist in the Rheostatics, Nick Buzz; visual artist

Margo Timmins: singer, Cowboy Junkies

Michael Timmins: guitarist/songwriter, Cowboy Junkies; film composer

Dave Ullrich: drummer, the Inbreds; founder, PF Records

Gerard Van Herk: guitarist/vocalist, Deja Voodoo; co-founder, Og Records; professor of linguistics

Bill Varvaris: founder of *Surfin' Bird* zine; Pipeline Records head; Bonaparte Distribution (later Cargo)

Tim Vesely: bassist/songwriter, Rheostatics; Andrew Cash

Barry Walsh: guitarist/vocalist, The October Game, Jeffrey's Wake, Flags for Everything, Cool Blue Halo, Galore

Larry Wanagas: manager, k.d. lang

Chris Wardman: guitarist, Blue Peter; producer, Art Bergmann, Leslie Spit Tree-o, Watchmen, others

Dan Webster: Montreal concert promoter; former partner in Pysche Industry Records; former manager at Foufounes Electriques

Woody Whalen: founder, Mag Wheel Records

Rick White: singer/guitarist, Eric's Trip, Elevator; visual artist; recording engineer

Tom Wilson: singer/songwriter, guitarist, Junkhouse, Florida Razors, Blackie and the Rodeo Kings; solo artist

David Wisdom: CBC host *Night Lines*, *Radio Sonic*, *Pearls of Wisdom*; keyboardist, U-J3RK5

Bob Wiseman: singer/songwriter; producer; original Blue Rodeo keyboardist 1985–1992

Michael Phillip Wojewoda: producer; drummer, Pigfarm

John Wright: drummer, NoMeansNo, the Hanson Brothers

Rob Wright: bassist and vocalist, NoMeansNo, the Hanson Brothers, Mr. Wrong

Moses Znaimer: media impresario, founder of CITY-TV/MuchMusic/Bravo, etc.

Selected Critical Discographies

Overture: Everybody Knows This Is Nowhere

Bryan Adams. *Reckless* (A&M, 1984) If it wasn't for the CanRock Renaissance, this would have been the single defining Canadian album of the '80s. Whew!

The Band. *Music From Big Pink* (EMI, 1968)

—. *The Band* (EMI, 1969) While there's a strong case to be made for this as one of the greatest Canadian albums of all time, one really does have to wonder why all of Robbie Robertson's narratives were fixated on America.

Leonard Cohen. *I'm Your Man* (Columbia, 1988) Here was another first-wave icon on the comeback trail, inspiring songwriters of the Renaissance. In Cohen's case, this was one of his finest, coolest and most humorous collections of songs ever, rivalling his work in the early '70s.

—. *The Future* (Columbia, 1992)

The Demics. *New York City* (OPM, 1996) Collects the 1979 Ready Records EP, lost sessions and live tracks. Includes a studio and live version of "(I Wanna Go To) New York City."

Fifth Column. *To Sir With Hate* (Hide, 1986) Produced by Michael Phillip Wojewoda.

—. *Work* (Hide cassette, 1988)

—. *All-Time Queen of the World* (Hide, 1990)

—. *36D* (K/Sub Pop, 1994)

Lewis Melville. *Niagara* (DROG, 1995) The ubiquitous sideman of the CanRock Renaissance steps to the forefront with a large cast of friends, including the Skydiggers' Wayne Stokes, Rheostatics' Dave Clark, the Bird Sisters, and the Plasterscene Replicas' reclusive guitarist Charlie Salmon.

—. *Not Really a Bluegrass Album* (DROG, 1997)

The Northern Pikes. *Northern Pikes* (independent, 1984)

—. *Scene In North America* (independent, 1985)

—. *Big Blue Sky* (Virgin, 1987) A strong debut of new wave, country and folk rock. Formed in 1984, this Saskatoon quartet — consisting of bassist/vocalist Jay Semko, guitarists/vocalists Bryan Potvin and Merl Bryck, and drummer Don Schmid — earned the tag 'prairie pop' with their blend of radio-friendly melodies, glossy production and country/folk-rock song struc tures. Their early new wave dabbling made its way into the band's first few releases, and eventually caught the attention of Virgin Records. They broke up in 1993; all but Bryck explored new projects until their reconciliation in 2000.

—. *Secrets Of The Alibi* (Virgin, 1988)

—. *Snow In June* (Virgin, 1990) The band's only consistent album.

—. *Neptune* (Virgin, 1992) Features a duet with Margo Timmins.

—. *Gig* (Virgin, 1993) A fine epitaph of the band's first phase.

—. *Hits And Assorted Secrets 1984–1993* (Virgin, 1999)

—. *Live* (Northern Pike/Outside, 2000)

—. *Truest Inspiration* (Square Dog, 2001)

Oh! What a Feeling (EMI, 1996) An amusing 4-CD retrospective of Canadian pop history, heavy on the schlock rock, fluff pop, and one-hit wonders. Very little Renaissance representation. Includes "Tears Are Not Enough."

Oh! What a Feeling 2 (EMI, 2001) Adds some hip-hop and '90s dance-pop, and a bit more Renaissance.

Rough Trade. *Birds of a Feather: The Best Of* (True North/Sony, 1985) Rough Trade could never sustain interest through an entire album, so it's best to stick with the singles. Sadly, "B-Movie" is missing, but this is some of the most entertaining Canadian pop of the early '80s. There's a whole generation of Canadians weaned on Carole Pope songs and David Cronenberg movies — what does that say about our sexuality?

Rusty. *Fluke* (Handsome Boy, 1995)

—. *Sophomoric* (Handsome Boy, 1997)

—. *Out of Their Heads* (Handsome Boy, 1998)

Stompin' Tom Connors. *Fiddle and Song* (EMI, 1989) His comeback record, featuring the ode to "Lady k.d. lang."

—. *A Proud Canadian* (EMI, 1990) Not an entirely comprehensive compilation, but certainly the most seminal, as this is the one that introduced an entirely new generation to Stompin' Tom. Closes with his finest moment, "The Singer (Voice of the People)."

—. *More of the Stompin' Tom Phenomenon* (EMI, 1991) It says a lot about the diversity of MuchMusic programming at this time that "Margo's Cargo" was a hit video single.

Kurt Swinghammer. *This is Culture* (independent cassette, 1984)

—. *PoMo a Go Go* (Fringe, 1991)

—. *Vostok 6* (Righteous Babe, 1999) An ambient concept record about the first woman in space. "Blue" sounds like 25th century folk music.

Glittering Prizes and Endless Compromises

Cub. *Betti-Cola* (Mint, 1993) Charming amateurism and a natural approach to bubblegum songwriting. Neko Case plays drums on four tracks.

—. *Come Out Come Out* (Mint, 1994) Features their best song, the whimsical "New York City," which deserves a place alongside "New York New York" for timeless romantic songs about the Big Apple.

—. *The Day I Said Goodbye* EP (Lookout!/Mint, 1995)

—. *Box of Hair* (Mint, 1996)

—. *Mauler! A Collection Of Oddities* (Au-go-go, 1996) Australian greatest hits with rare tracks.

Ron Hawkins. *The Secret of My Excess* (Shake, 1995) A disappointing debut that didn't endear him to those still bitter about the Lowest of the Low break-up.

—. *Greasing the Star Machine* (w/ the Rusty Nails) (Outside, 1997)

—. *Crackstatic* (w/ the Rusty Nails) (Outside, 2000) Produced by Ian Blurton, this is Hawkins's finest rock moment in terms of intensity, songwriting, and emotion. The quieter moments are sublime as well.

The Inbreds. *Hilario* (PF/DROG, 1993)

—. *Kombinator* (PF/DROG, 1994; Tag/Atlantic, 1995)

—. *It's Sydney Or the Bush* (Tag/Atlantic, 1996)

—. *Winning Hearts* (Murder, 1998)

It Came From Canada, Volume One (Og, 1985).

It Came From Canada, Volume Two (Og, 1986)

It Came From Canada, Volume Three (Og, 1987)

It Came From Canada, Volume Four (Og, 1988)

It Came From Canada, Volume Five (Og, 1989)

Lowest of the Low. *Shakespeare My Butt* (independent, 1991)

—. *Hallucigenia* (LSD/A&M, 1993) Their live shows had always been electric, but fans didn't seem prepared for this loud rock record. Maybe the band wasn't either; they broke up shortly after. Includes "Life Imitates Art," dedicated to Mr. Bergmann.

Mike O'Neill. *What Happens Now?* (Perimeter/Universal, 2000) Produced by Michael Phillip Wojewoda and featuring Matt Murphy, Don Kerr, and Charles Austin.

On the Road (Raw Energy/A&M, 1993) A definitive compilation of cross-Canada "grunge" bands, for lack of a better term: Dinner is Ruined, Change of Heart, the Imagineers, Deadbeat Backbone, Eric's Trip, King Cobb Steelie and others. It also introduced Jale and The Wooden Stars.

Phono-Comb. (with Jad Fair) *Monsters, Lullabies and Occasional Flying Saucers* (Shake, 1996) Reid Diamond and Don Pyle of Shadowy Men collaborate with Amerindie eccentric Jad Fair for some *Brave New Waves* sessions; one of only two BNW sessions that were released commercially. Phleg Camp is the other.

—. *Fresh Gasoline* (Quarterstick, 1996) Dallas Good, later of the Sadies, and Beverly Breckenridge, formerly of Fifth Column, join the proceedings for a solid Shadowy romp.

Shadowy Men On A Shadowy Planet. *Savvy Show Stoppers* (Jetpac/Cargo, 1990) A collection of singles from the preceding five years, which coalesce into an essential album for any Canadian indie rock house party. Guitarist Brian Connelly, bassist Reid Diamond and drummer Don Pyle all contribute equally to the energy and seemingly effortless composition, with minimal repetition — a rarity in instrumental rock bands.

—. *Dim the Lights Chill the Ham* (Jetpac/Cargo, 1991) The band's true masterpiece of composition, musical skill, and downright dorkiness. Memorable melodies and dancefloor-fillers are littered throughout this classic album.

—. *Sport Fishin'* (Jetpac/Cargo, 1993) Writing 20-second stings in between *Kids in the Hall* skits was beginning to effect their attention span.

Shuffle Demons. *Streetniks* (Stubby, 1986) Catchy songs, crazy costumes, and guerilla busking helped introduce squalling saxophones to people who didn't like jazz, and comedic rap lyrics to people who didn't know what hip-hop was. The raw, streetlevel production still holds up.

—. *Bop Rap* (Stubby/Stony Plain 1988) Features the "Hockey Night In Canada" theme.

Under The Volcano: The Fallout of Vancouver Punk

Art Bergmann. *Crawl With Me* (Duke Street, 1986)

—. *Sexual Roulette* (Duke Street, 1988)

—. *Art Bergmann* (Polygram, 1991)

—. *What Fresh Hell Is This?* (Sony, 1993)

—. *Design Flaw* (OPM, 1998) Tentative return with acoustic run-throughs of best material (with help from Chris Spedding). Genuinely moving, considering the history.

—. *Vultura Freeway* (AudioMonster, 2000) Curious flashback to demos for Poisoned sessions. Contains early versions of later album cuts and some great lost songs. Recorded 1984.

Copyright. *Circle C* (DGC, 1991)

—. *Love Story* (Vik/BMG, 1997)

—. *The Hidden World* (Vik/BMG, 2001)

Dayglo Abortions. *Out Of The Womb* (independent, 1981) Formed in Victoria, B.C., the band deliberately pushed the boundaries of free speech. While this drew the expected hardcore following, their infrequent appearances in mainstream media usually drew the equally expected derision. Few (if any) bands of the era have continually polarized the entire Canadian musical community with their dedication to shock and provoke.

—. *Feed Us A Fetus* (Fringe, 1986)

—. *Here Today, Guano Tomorrow* (Fringe, 1987) This album and *Fetus* prompted the first test of the Canadian criminal code's obscenity provisions since their creation in 1959. The charges came from a Nepean, Ontario police officer whose daughter had bought the albums, leading to the seizure of hundreds of copies from Fringe and its affiliated distributor, Toronto record store The Record Peddler. Although charges against the band were dropped early on, the 1988 trial set a precedent when Fringe was found not guilty of distributing obscene material. If nothing, an interesting example of how Canadian and U.S. civil rights attitudes possibly differ.

—. *Two Dogs Fucking* (GOD, 1991) The band's response to the trial.

—. *Little Man In The Canoe* (GOD, 1995)

—. *Corporate Whores* (GOD, 1996)

—. *Stupid World, Stupid Songs* (GOD, 1998) Compilation.

—. *Death Race 2000* (GOD, 1999)

Deep Six (C/Z, 1986) First significant compilation of Seattle bands. Includes Green River, Soundgarden, Malfunkshun, etc.

DOA. "Royal Police/Woke Up Screaming/Disco Sucks/Nazi Training Camp" 7" (Sudden Death, 1978)

—. *Triumph Of The Ignoroids* EP (Friend's, 1979)

—. *Something Better Change* (Friend's, 1980)

—. *Hardcore '81* (Friend's, 1981)

—. *War On 45* EP (Fringe, 1982)

—. *Bloodied But Unbowed: The Damage To Date '78–'83* (CD Presents, 1983)

—. *Let's Wreck The Party* (Alternative Tentacles, 1985)

—. *True (North) Strong And Free* (Rock Hotel/Profile, 1987)

—. *Murder* (Restless, 1990)

—. *Talk - Action = Zero* (Restless, 1991)

—. *The Dawning Of A New Error* (Alternative Tentacles, 1991)

—. *13 Flavours Of Doom* (Alternative Tentacles, 1993)

—. *Loggerheads* (Alternative Tentacles, 1993)

—. *The Black Spot* (Essential Noise/Virgin, 1993)

—. *Festival Of Atheists* (Sudden Death, 1998)

Green River. *Dry As A Bone* EP (Sub Pop, 1987)

—. *Rehab Doll* EP (Sub Pop, 1988)

The Hanson Brothers. *Gross Misconduct* (Wrong, 1992)

—. *Sudden Death* (Virgin, 1995)

Last Call: Vancouver Independent Music 1977–1988 (Zulu, 1988) Double disc VanPunk compilation featuring most of the major figures and crucial singles. One of the most important CanRock documents.

Los Popularos. *Born Free* EP (Sensible, 1982)

Metallica. *Metallica* (Elektra, 1991) Along with *Nevermind*, probably the most influential rock album of the '90s, courtesy of Bob Rock.

The Modernettes. *Teen City* EP (Quintessence, 1980)

—. *Gone . . . But Not Forgiven* (Challenger Sound, 1981)

—. *View From The Bottom* EP (Vox Desperatum, 1982)

—. *Get It Straight* (Zulu, 1995) Compilation. They would have been great even if punk had not opened the door.

NoMeansNo. *Look, Here Come The Wormies* 7" (Wrong, 1980)

—. *Betrayal, Fear, Anger, Hatred* 7" (Wrong, 1981)

—. *Mama* (Wrong, 1982)

—. *You Kill Me* EP (Undergrowth, 1985) First recordings as a trio.

—. *Sex Mad* (Psyche, 1986; Alternative Tentacles, 1987)

—. *The Day Everything Became Nothing* (Alternative Tentacles, 1988)

—. *Small Parts Isolated And Destroyed* (Alternative Tentacles, 1988)

—. *Wrong* (Wrong/Alternative Tentacles, 1989)

—. *Live & Cuddly* (Wrong/Alternative Tentacles, 1991)

—. *0+2=1* (Alternative Tentacles, 1991)

—. w/Jello Biafra, *The Sky Is Falling And I Want My Mommy* (Alternative Tentacles, 1991)

—. *Why Do They Call Me Mr. Happy?* (Alternative Tentacles, 1993)

—. (As Mr. Right & Mr. Wrong) *One Down And Two To Go* (Wrong, 1994)

—. *The Worldhood Of The World (As Such)* (Alternative Tentacles, 1995)

—. *Dance Of The Headless Bourgeoisie* (Alternative Tentacles, 1997)

—. *One* (Alternative Tentacles, 2000)

The Payolas. "Money For Hype" (NB, 1979)

—. "China Boys" (Slophouse, 1979)

—. *The Payolas* (A&M, 1980)

—. *No Stranger To Danger* (A&M, 1982)

—. *Hammer On A Drum* (A&M, 1983)

—. (as Paul Hyde & The Payolas) *Here's The World For Ya* (A&M, 1985)

Pointed Sticks. "What Do You Want Me To Do/Somebody's Mom" (Quintessence, 1978)

—. "Lies/I'm Numb" (Quintessence, 1979)

—. "The Real Thing/Out Of Luck" (Quintessence, 1979)

—. *Part Of The Noise* (Zulu, 1995) Compilation. Includes aborted sessions for Stiff Records in England.

Poisoned. *Poisoned* EP (Independent, 1986)

Rock 'N Hyde. *Under The Volcano* (Capitol, 1987)

Slow. "I Broke The Circle" (Zulu, 1986)

—. *Against The Glass* EP (Zulu, 1986)

Sons Of Freedom. *Sons Of Freedom* (Slash, 1989) One of the most immediately influential albums of its time, foreshadowing the grunge phenomenon by at least two years. The band built a loyal following through punishingly loud shows and frontman James Newton's penetrating songs. However, this proved to be too much for the mainstream and long gaps between releases and touring resulted in their undoing. Still powerful.

—. *Gump* (Chrysalis, 1991)

—. *Tex* (Divine Industries, 1995)

SNFU. *. . . And No One Else Wanted To Play* (BYO/BYC, 1985)

—. *If You Swear, You'll Catch No Fish* (BYO/BYC, 1986)

—. *Better Than A Stick In The Eye* (Cargo U.S., 1988)

—. *Last Of The Big Time Suspenders* (Cargo U.S., 1991)

—. *Fuck You Up Like A Bad Accident* (Epitaph, 1996)

—. *Let's Get It Right The First Time* (Epitaph, 1998) Originally from Edmonton, grew to share DOA's legendary status in hardcore circles through tireless touring and commitment to fans during punk's fallow years in the late '80s. After a brief layoff, found a younger audience upon signing with trailblazing L.A. label Epitaph (Offspring, Bad Religion). Frontman Kenny Chinn remains one of Canada's most under-appreciated live performers.

Vancouver Complication (Pinned, 1979) Includes The K-Tels' "I Hate Music," DOA's "Kill This Pop" and "I Hate You," and Pointed Sticks' "Marching Song."

Young Canadians. *Automan* EP (Quintessence, 1979)

—. *Hawaii* EP (Quintessence, 1979)

—. *This Is Your Life* EP (Quintessence, 1980)

—. *No Escape* (Zulu, 1995) Compilation.

Folk of the Eighties: Montreal

All Systems Go! (independent 1999; reissued Shock Records, 2000)

Asexuals. *Featuring: Asexuals* 7" (Og, 1983)

—. *Be What You Want* (Psyche Industry, 1984) Poli-teen hardcore.

—. *Contemporary World* (Psyche Industry, 1985) John Kastner's last stand.

—. *Dish* (Cargo, 1988) Rebirth in Replacements clothing.

—. *Exile From Floontown* (Cargo, 1991)

—. *Fitzjoy* (Hypnotic, 1996)

Bionic. *Bionic* (Sound King, 1998) Jonathan Cummins finds his feet again.
Blinker the Star. *Blinker the Star* (Vibrant Cobra, 1994; Treat and Release, 1995)
—. *A Bourgeois Kitten* (A&M, 1996)
—. *August Everywhere* (Dreamworks, 1998)
The Box. *The Box* (Kardiak/Capitol, 1984)
—. *All The Time, All The Time, All The Time* (Kardiak/Capitol, 1985) Like their debut, this CD was guilty of both great songs and complete silliness.
—. *Closer Together* (Alert, 1987) The lyrics are still corny, but these are great sing-a-long pop songs.
—. *The Pleasure and the Pain* (Capitol, 1990)
—. *A Decade of The Box* (Alert, 1993) Greatest hits.
Bran Van 3000. *Glee* (Audioworks/Select, 1997; Capitol, 1998) Irreverent and carefree genre-hopping hip-pop, created by video director Jamie Di Salvio and a loose community of late '90s Montreal scenesters.
—. *Discosis* (Grand Royal/EMI, 2001)
Chino. *Mala Leche* EP (Mag Wheel, 1999)
Condition. *Dirty Business* cassette (Og, 1982)
—. *Mumbo Jumbo* (Psyche, 1985) Evil lounge music that taps Montreal's sexy side.
—. *Red Hot and Blue* EP (Amok, 1986) Anti-purist swampy jazz struts with one of the best covers of Peggy Lee's "Fever."
—. *Swamp Walk* (Amok, 1989)
Ray Condo and His Hardrock Goners. *Crazy Date* (Pipeline, 1986) Condo's finest moment, resurrecting forgotten roots classics and injecting them with electric energy with the help of guitarist Eric Sandmark, fiddler Edgar Bridwell, upright bassist Clive Jackson and drummer Peter Sandmark. "Skala Bop Baby" and the title track are highlights.
Deja Voodoo. *Gumbo* cassette (Og, 1982)
—. *Cemetery* (Og, 1984) Cheese and crackers, anyone?
—. *Too Cool To Live Too Smart To Die* (Midnight, 1985)
—. *Swamp of Love* (Og, 1986)
—. *The Worst Of* (Og, 1987) Collection of 7"s and compilation appearances is the band's definitive moment. Includes "Monsters in My Garage" and the Canadiana classic "Raised by Wolves."
—. *Big Pile of Mud* (Og, 1988)
—. *Live at the Backstage Club, Helsinki Finland* (Og, 1990)
The Dik Van Dykes. *Nobody Likes* (Og, 1987)
—. *Waste Mor Vinyl* (Og, 1989)
Doughboys. *Whatever* (Pipeline, 1987)
—. *Home Again* (Restless, 1989)
—. *Happy Accidents* (Restless, 1990)
—. *When Up Turns To Down* EP (Restless, 1991)
—. *Crush* (A&M, 1993) Soda pop and bleach: Chemistry for the band's biggest moment.
—. *Turn Me On* (A&M, 1996)
The Gruesomes. *Tyrants of Teen Trash* (Og, 1986) What they lack in proficiency they compensate for in snotty good times.
—. *Gruesomania* (Og, 1987) Their calling card.
—. *Hey!* (Og, 1988) The 1.5-minute title track became a fluke MuchMusic hit.
—. *Cave-In* (Tyrant, 2000) A shockingly good comeback album that stands next to *Gruesomania*.
Ivan. *The Spell* (UFOria/Tox, 1997)
Jerry Jerry and the Sons of Rhythm Orchestra. *Fighting Socialism* cassette (Rubber, 1984)
—. *Road Gore: The Band That Drank Too Much* (Og, 1985)
—. *The Battle Hymn of the Apartment* (Pipeline, 1987; Aquarius, 1990) His shining moment, featuring "Runaway Lane" and "Pushin' For Jesus," got lost in legalities and by then it was too late.

—. *Don't Mind If I Do* (Aquarius, 1992) Loungy and surprisingly flat.

—. *The Sound and the Jerry* (solo album) (Aquarius, 1997)

The Kingpins. *The Kingpins* (Stomp, 1996) The Gruesomes' Bobby Beaton plugs into the ska formula with a band that stands above other trend-jumpers.

—. *Let's Go to Work* (Stomp, 1998)

The MacKenzie-Parker Gang. *Ride for Glory* (Cloud Nine, 1999)

Men Without Hats. *Folk of the '80s* EP (Stiff, 1980)

—. *Rhythm of Youth* (Statik/Sire/MCA America, 1982; reissued in 1997 as a 2-for-1 CD with *Folk of the '80s Part III*)

—. *Folk of the '80s Part III* (Statik/Sire/MCA America, 1984)

—. *Freeways* EP (Sire, 1985) Pre-*Rhythm of Youth* material collected.

—. *Pop Goes the World* (Mercury/Polygram, 1987)

—. *The Adventures of Women and Men Without Hate in the 21st Century* (Mercury/Polygram, 1989)

—. *Sideways* (Polygram 1991) A 180 degree turn that ended MWH as they started — with guitars.

—. *Greatest Hats* (Aquarius, 1996) Includes unreleased mixes and a cover of Roxy Music's "Editions of You."

Mitsou. El Mundo (Isba/Tox, 1988) Bubblegum hits like "Bye Bye Mon Cowboy" tagged her the Québécois Madonna.

—. *Terre Des Hommes* (Isba/Tox, 1990) This is a finely crafted dance-pop album that brought the singer an appeal beyond her soft-core videos. Two songs co-written by Ivan.

Nils. *Now* (independent, 1982) Self-released demo tape.

—. *Sell Out Young* EP (Psyche Industry, 1985) The best thing they ever did.

—. *Paisley* EP (Seigfried, 1986)

—. *Nils* (Rock Hotel/Profile, 1986)

—. *Green Fields in Daylight* (Mag Wheel, 1996) Essential listening. Compiles all recorded material except the Profile album.

Pest 5000. *Patti Christ Superstar* Double 7" (Derivative, 1994)

—. *Inter/a/bang* (Derivative, 1996) A finely textured hidden gem from Derivative Records flagship artists. An eclectic quintet that melded the best aspects of the underground: new wave, post-punk, electronic, noise and indie rock.

—. *Palimpsest* (Derivative, 1997) Remixes and 7" compilation.

Primitive Air Raid (Psyche Industry, 1984)

Rational Youth. *Cold War Night Life* (YUL, 1982; reissued 1997, EMI)

—. *Rational Youth* Mini-LP (Capitol, 1983)

—. *Heredity* (Capitol, 1985) A comparatively folkie record, with plenty of acoustic guitars outshining the synths.

—. *To The Goddess Electricity* (October, 1999)

Scratches and Needles: A Tribute to the Nils (Mag Wheel, 1998)

Something to Believe In (BYO, 1983) Compilation album featuring the Nils' classic "Scratches and Needles."

Starbean. *Refuting The Extraterrestrial Hypothesis* (Derivative, 1997) Described by Jonathan Cummins as "low-rent New Order." Former Doughboy and Pest 5000 member Jon Ascenscio makes another surprising musical turn.

Three O'Clock Train. *Wig Wam Beach* EP (Pipeline, 1985)

—. *Muscle In* (Pipeline, 1986)

—. *It Takes A lot to Laugh, It Takes a Train To Laugh* (Justin Time, 1991)

—. *Anthology* (Just A Memory, 1996) Compiles the first two releases.

Time Machine: The History of Canadian '60s Garage Punk and Surf 1985–95 (Stomp, 1996) Stomp Records pays tribute to the Og generation with this compilation including the Gruesomes, Shadowy Men, Ten Commandments, The Mongols, Windsor's Lost Patrol, Calgary's The Vindicators, and the Smugglers.

Voivod. *War and Pain* (Metal Blade, 1984)

—. *RRRÖÖÖAAARRR* (Noise, 1986) Hands down the best title in the book.

—. *Killing Technology* (Noise, 1986)

—. *Dimension Haltross* (Noise, 1988)
—. *Nothingface* (Mechanix/MCA,1989)
—. *Angel Rat* (Mechanix/MCA, 1991) Stoner rock. The band's most accessible moment.
—. *The Outer Limits* (MCA/1993) The psychedelic stroll continues. Snake's last stand.
—. *Negatron* (Hypnotic, 1995) Features "Nanoman" co-written by Ivan.
—. *Phobos* (Hypnotic, 1997)
—. *Kronik* (Hypnotic, 1998)

Yeah, It Matters: Change of Heart and Post-Punk Toronto

A Neon Rome. *New Heroin* (New Rose/Rightside, 1986)
—. *All The Children Are In* (unreleased) Recorded 1988.
Blurtonia. *Adventures In The Kingdom Of Blurtonia* (Web Of Sound, 1999)
—. *Blurtonia* (Web of Sound, 2001)
John Borra. *John Borra* cassette (Jeb, 1997)
—. *Band* (Cousin Jeb, 1999) Picks up where Handsome Ned left off.
Change of Heart. *The Black March* cassette (independent, 1982)
—. *Push* cassette (independent, 1983)
—. *50 Ft. Up* (Primitive, 1986)
—. *Slowdance* (Primitive/Fringe, 1987)
—. *Soapbox* (Cargo, 1990)
—. "Tired Of Waking Up Tired" (Cargo, 1991) Split 7" w/Shadowy Men, each band
    interpreting The Diodes' classic in their own ways.
—. *Smile* (Cargo, 1992)
—. *Tummysuckle* (Lunamoth/Virgin, 1994)
—. w/John Oswald, *Tummysuckle Ruse* 7" (Lunamoth, 1995)
—. *Steel Teeth* (Virgin, 1996)
Groovy Religion. *Thin Gypsy Thief* (Psyche, 1986)
—. *Tom, A Rock Opera* (Handsome Boy, 1990)
—. *Canadabis* (Handsome Boy, 1998)
Jolly Tambourine Man. "Apple Strudle Man/Sweater In Sri Lanka" (independent, 1984)
Max Webster. *Max Webster* (Anthem, 1975)
—. *High Class In Borrowed Shoes* (Anthem, 1976)
—. *Universal Juveniles* (Anthem, 1980)
NoMind. *Tales Of Ordinary Madness* (Lone Wolf, 1988) Flat-out proto-grunge/metal.
Scott B. Sympathy. *Neil Yonge Street* (Smokeshow, 1990)
—. *Drinking With The Poet* (Fringe, 1992)
Tricky Woo. *Sometimes I Cry* (Sonic Unyon, 1999) Produced by Ian Blurton.

Northern Wishes & Visionary Flounders

The Barenaked Ladies. *Barenaked Lunch* cassette (independent, 1990)
—. *Barenaked Ladies* cassette (independent, 1991) aka "The Yellow Tape." Features four
    tracks re-recorded on *Gordon*, as well as their hilarious-yet-questionable cover of
    Public Enemy's "Fight the Power."
—. *Gordon* (Sire/Warner, 1992)
—. *Maybe You Should Drive* (Sire/Warner, 1994) Muzak production by Ben Mink.
—. *Born on a Pirate Ship* (Reprise, 1996) "The Old Apartment" is the lone stand-out.
—. *Rock Spectacle* (Reprise, 1996) The American breakthrough, a live album displaying
    their true strengths. Mixed by Wojewoda.
—. *Stunt* (Reprise, 1998) One novelty hit ("One Week"), one great song ("It's All Been
    Done") and not much else sells millions and leaves America with a bad impression.
—. *Maroon* (Reprise, 2000) Finally fulfils all of their songwriting potential: no gim-
    micks, witty satire, and as usual, the musicianship is impeccable.

Big Sugar. *Big Sugar* (Hypnotic/A&M, 1992) This inauspicious debut shows Gordie Johnson's first dabblings in the wide-ranging influences that will comprise the band's scope. As on all releases, significant songwriting contributions from BTC's Andrew Whiteman and Dave Wall.

—. *El Seven Niteclub* (Hypnotic/A&M, 1993) Live recording from The Rivoli featuring most of the band's circle of Queen Street friends.

—. *Five Hundred Pounds* (Hypnotic/A&M, 1993) For the most part a loud, raw blues-rock record that turned back the clock to the early 1970s. Signature song "Ride Like Hell" co-written with BTC's Andrew Whiteman.

—. *Dear M.F.* EP (Hypnotic/A&M, 1995)

—. *Hemi-Vision* (A&M, 1996) The mainstream hard rock record that was expected, but with strong reggae overtones, courtesy of now-full-time bassist Garry Lowe.

—. *Heated* (A&M, 1998)

—. (as Alkaline) *Extra Long Life* (A&M, 2000) Johnson's dub reggae alter ego.

Bourbon Tabernacle Choir. *A First Taste of Bourbon* cassette (independent, 1987)

—. *If Hell Had a House Band* cassette (independent, 1989)

—. *Sister Anthony* (Applaud The Potato/independent cassette, 1990) A lot of a soul and not much focus, but full of joyous and infectious spirit. "The Little Vagabond" turns the William Blake poem into a saloon singalong.

—. "Put Your Head On/As Right As They Want To Be" (Applaud the Potato cassette single, 1991) Tastefully produced by Bob Wiseman. The a-side was also featured in *Highway 61*, while the flip is one of the band's funkiest moments, featuring an unlikely rap by Wiseman.

—. *Superior Cackling Hen* (Yonder/Sony, 1992)

—. *Shy Folk* (1995, Yonder) Seamless.

—. *1985–1995* (Tycoon/Sony, 2000) A compilation of album tracks and often-superior live versions, as well as a few oddities. A few glaring omissions, however.

Chris Brown and Kate Fenner. *Other People's Heavens* (1997, B-Music/DROG) A tentative debut, recorded with a drum machine. Features a cover of Mary Margaret O'Hara's "Help Me Lift You Up."

—. *Geronimo* (1999, B-Music/DROG) A gorgeous combination of brilliant full-band performances, Fenner's finest vocal moments, and captivating, emotional songwriting. Too many highlights to list.

—. *Great Lakes Bootleg* (B-Music, 2000) Recorded live on tour opening for The Tragically Hip.

—. *O Witness* (B-Music, 2001)

Meryn Cadell. *Angel Food For Thought* (Intrepid, 1991) After years of Elvis Monday appearances and cassettes, Cadell debuted with this astounding album of spoken word and song that immediately established her as a unique voice. Most people picked up on the novelty factor of songs like "The Sweater," which became a fluke hit and landed her an American record deal, but this is a multi-dimensional and serious work that stands the test of time. Different *is* what we're looking for. Features Tim Vesely, Dave Clark, Bob Wiseman and Jim Creeggan in supporting roles.

—. *Bombazine* (Sire, 1993) "Steam Clean Express" is a full-band collaboration with the Rheostatics.

—. *6 Blocks* (Handsome Boy, 1997) Criminally obscure. Cadell has fully transformed into a torch singer extraordinaire, but when she wants to wield her sense of humour ("Slippery") she's still fiercely funny. Chris Wardman's beefy production punches up the rhythm section on the rock numbers, and drenches the sombre, sometimes harrowing slower tracks with lush strings. "Lying" is co-written with and features Martin Tielli, and Mary Margaret O'Hara guests on two tracks.

Holly Cole. *Don't Smoke in Bed* (Alert, 1993) Features Mary Margaret O'Hara's "So and So," as well as Cole's pop breakthrough "I Can See Clearly Now."

—. *Dark Dear Heart* (Alert, 1997) The title track and "Brighter Lonely Day (Run, Run, Run)" are O'Hara compositions.

Holly Cole, Rebecca Jenkins, Mary Margaret O'Hara, Jane Siberry and Victoria

Williams. *Count Your Blessings* (Alert, 1994) A Christmas recording for the CBC, with all five women trading lead vocals and singing harmony, accompanied by Siberry pianist Tim Ray.

Dinner is Ruined. *Burn Yer Dashiki* (Gas Rackett, 1992)

—. *Love Songs from the Lubritorium* (Raw Energy, 1993)

—. *Worm Pickers Brawl* (Gas Rackett, 1994)

—. *Ice Cream, Drugs and Rubber Goods* (Gas Rackett, 1996)

—. *Elevator Music for Non-Claustrophobic People* (Sonic Unyon, 1997)

—. *A Maggot in Their Heads* (Sonic Unyon, 1999) The logical sequel to *Love Songs*, with the new line-up riding every twist and turn. Plenty of freak-outs alongside countrified campfire songs.

—. *A Ray Charles Kind of Party* (Sonic Unyon, 2000) Boogie-rock gets tossed into the mix, along with a Ma Rainey cover and the positively Springsteenian epic "Slumberland."

Don't Talk Dance. *Don't Talk Dance* (WEA, 1995) A side-project for BTC's Chris Brown, Big Sugar's Gordie Johnson and BNL's Tyler Stewart, featuring guests Ed Robertson and Dave Wall; Kate Fenner provides sultry back-ups on a dub reggae version of Stompin' Tom's "The Ketchup Song."

The Henrys. *Puerto Angel* (Trainrec, 1994) The debut by Don Rooke's band casts a captivating, languid spell. Mary Margaret O'Hara's "Dark Dear Heart" is one of her strongest compositions.

—. *Chasing Grace* (Trainrec, 1996) Four songs feature O'Hara.

—. *Desert Cure* (Trainrec, 1998) More perfect rainy day music, with Rooke's intoxicating slide work at the forefront. O'Hara appears on three tracks, experimenting more with vocal sounds rather than conventional melodies.

Veda Hille. *Path of a Body* (independent, 1994) This Vancouver singer/songwriter writes intricate, prog-ish and poetic piano pop, with an admitted Rheostatics influence in the opening track, "Driven."

—. *Spine* (independent, 1996)

—. *Here is a Picture (Songs for E Carr)* (independent, 1997) A perfect companion to the Rheostatics' *Group of Seven* project, and not just because it's just like old times: the Central Canadian boys versus the solo girl on the west coast. Commissioned for a Vancouver dance company and incorporating some of Emily Carr's own poetry, this is a vivid and engaging work that may be Hille's best.

—. *You Do Not Live in This World Alone* (independent, 1999)

Look People. *Stop Making Cheese* (Amok, 1986)

—. *More Songs About Hats and Chickens* (Quantum, 1989)

—. *Small Fish, Big Pond* (Quantum, 1990)

—. *Boogazm* (Hypnotic/A&M, 1991) Features their cover of War's "Low Rider," with Chris Brown on trombone.

—. *Crazy Eggs* (Hypnotic/A&M, 1993)

Scott Merritt. *Serious Interference* (independent, 1983; Duke Street, 1985) This introduced the Brantford, Ontario songwriter as a fiercely talented new voice. His sound straddles rural and urban sensibilities, and his intricate and evocative guitar playing is equal parts African and North American folk laced over reggae rhythms. Recorded at Grant Ave. Studio in 1982, there are some shades of Eno and Lanois, like the use of sampled voices and a dependency on delay pedals. Marketed as a male Jane Siberry and an obvious influence on Martin Tielli. "Transistor" was an underground radio hit. Unfortunately, Merritt's talents soon got dwarfed by '80s technology; here, they shine in all their pure glory.

—. *Gravity is Mutual* (Duke Street, 1986) Featured the minor hit "Overworked and Underprivileged."

—. *Violet and Black* (Duke Street, 1989)

Moose: The Compilation (Polygram, 1991) A worthy document of Toronto's roots scene of the early '90s compiled by Richard Chapman, featuring the previously unreleased Rheostatics track "Woodstuck," a raw hoser rock anti-hippie classic.

Moose Lodge (Polygram, 1992) More of the same, and the fleeting Toronto bass-heavy supergroup Thumposaurus, featuring bassist Alisdair Jones (NoMind), bassist John Borra, cellist Anne Bourne, drummer Glen Milchem and keyboardist Bob Wiseman.

Dale Morningstar. *Dale Morningstar* (DAM, 1988) For a record released in 1988, it sounds remarkably like 1983. "Answers/Upside Down" compares with new-wave pop like "I Melt With You." John Press, aka Dr. Pee, appears on bass and horns.

Nick Buzz. *Nick Buzz* (Dark Light, 1995) Featuring Martin Tielli on vocals, with violinist Hugh Marsh, keyboardist Jonathan Goldsmith, and bassist Rob Piltch, playing operatic avant-garde circus music. Features stunning cover of Joni Mitchell's "River."

Mary Margaret O'Hara. *Miss America* (Virgin, 1988; Koch, 1996)

—. *Christmas* EP (Virgin, 1991)

Rheostatics. "Satellite Dancing" b/w "My Generation" 7" (1981)

—. *Rheostatics and the Trans-Canada Soul Patrol* cassette (1983) Notable only for an early version of "Soul Glue."

—. *Greatest Hits* (X Records, 1987; re-issued on DROG, 1993)

—. *Melville* (Intrepid, 1991; DROG, 1994)

—. *Green Sprouts Meet the King of Thunder Bay* (official bootleg cassette, 1991) With *Brave New Waves* interviews and sessions, unreleased songs, goof-offs, live tracks, and the very early new wave track "Sometimes I Feel Like an Elevator," which is later heard sampled on 1994's "Me and Stupid."

—. *Green Sprouts Meet X-Mas Brown And More* (official bootleg cassette, 1991) With songs recorded live on CIUT, *Whale Music* demos, live tracks and interview segments.

—. *Whale Music* (Intrepid, 1992; on Sire, 1993)

—. *Introducing Happiness* (Sire, 1994)

—. *Whale Music* OST (Sire, 1994)

—. "Fan Letter to Michael Jackson" 7" (Galaxy, 1995)

—. *Music Inspired By the Group of Seven* (DROG, 1996) Kevin Hearn's keyboard work is the driving force on this suitably picturesque, experimental work.

—. *The Blue Hysteria* (Cargo, 1996; re-issued on DROG, 1999) The most inconsistent Rheos record suffered because of great expectations.

—. *Double Live* (DROG, 1997) Accurately captures the beauty and chaos of a Rheostatics live show, complete with highs and lows. This is essential listening not just for the performances and memories, but for odd songs that have been live favourites for years and yet inexplicably left off "real" albums. The perfect auditory companion to Bidini's book *On a Cold Road*.

—. *The Nightlines Sessions* (DROG, 1998) Novelty numbers aside, this lo-fi treat features some of the best non-conceptual original material of the Don Kerr years.

—. *The Story of Harmelodia* (Perimeter, 1999) Their most ambitious project ever, and the most creative fruition of their association with producer Michael Phillip Wojewoda. Only an intrusive narration stops it from achieving true greatness. Contributions from Kevin Hearn, Gord Downie, Sarah Harmer, Kurt Swinghammer, and Dave Merritt.

Jane Siberry. *Jane Siberry* (independent, 1981)

—. *No Borders Here* (Duke Street, 1983)

—. *The Speckless Sky* (Duke Street, 1985)

—. *The Walking* (Duke Street, 1987)

—. *Bound By the Beauty* (Duke Street, 1989)

—. *When I Was a Boy* (Reprise, 1993) Her masterpiece.

—. *A Collection* 1984-1989 (Duke Street, 1994)

—. *Maria* (Warner, 1995) A sidestep into jazz that no doubt confused newcomers taken with *When I Was a Boy*.

—. *Teenager* (Sheeba, 1996) Siberry revisits songs written when she was a teenager — the most appropriate project to launch a vanity label.

—. *A Day in the Life* EP (Sheeba, 1997) A soundscape experiment.

—. *Child* (Sheeba, 1998) The first of three double live albums recorded in New York City; this one is Christmas-themed, and works surprisingly well with the help of an incredible band.

—. *Lips* (Sheeba, 2000)

—. *Trees* (Sheeba, 2000)

—. *Hush* (Sheeba, 2000) A mostly choral work in which Siberry interprets various spiritual songs. Perhaps her lushest production to date.

Sweet Relief II: Gravity of the Situation, The Songs of Vic Chesnutt (Sony, 1997) Mary Margaret O'Hara and Hugh Marsh tackle Chesnutt's tragicomic, suicidal song "Florida."

Dave Wall. *Lozenge* (Hypnotic/A&M, 1993) An acoustic secular gospel soul album by Wall, Gordie Johnson, and Wall's many Bourbon associates, particularly Andrew Whiteman.

The Outsiders: Punk, Politics & Poetry

Moe Berg. *Summer's Over* (Iron, 1998)

Andrew Cash. *Time And Place* (Island, 1988)

—. *Boomtown* (Island, 1989)

—. *Hi* (Sumo/MCA, 1993)

Cash Brothers. *Raceway* (independent, 1999)

—. *Phonebooth Tornado* (Four Chord, 2000)

—. *How Was Tomorrow* (Rounder/Universal, 2001)

Bruce Cockburn. *Humans* (True North, 1980)

—. *Inner City Front* (True North, 1982)

—. *The Trouble With Normal* (True North, 1983)

—. *Stealing Fire* (True North, 1984)

—. *World Of Wonders* (True North, 1985)

—. *Waiting For A Miracle* (True North, 1987) Greatest hits and two new songs, including the title track.

—. *Big Circumstance* (True North, 1988)

Direktive 17. *Direktive 17* EP (Macbeth, 1984) Andy Maize's debut. Could have gone on to bigger things, but thankfully didn't.

Grievous Angels. *Toute La Gang* (independent, 1988)

—. *One Job Town* (Stony Plain, 1990) Featuring vocalist Michelle Rumball and some of Chuck Angus's best Canadiana songwriting.

—. *Watershed* (DROG, 1993)

—. *Waiting For The Cage* (DROG, 1996) A concept record about Northern Ontario mining communities.

—. *22 Trailer Park* (Jimmy Boyle, 1999)

L'Etranger. *Innocent Hands* EP (Sensible, 1982)

—. *Running Out Of Funtown* EP (Sensible, 1983)

—. *Sticks And Stones* EP (independent, 1986, reissued as Andrew Cash, *Sticks And Stones* EP, 1987)

Mecca Normal. *Mecca Normal/The First* LP (Smarten Up!, 1986; K, 1995)

—. *Calico Kills the Cat* (K, 1988)

—. *Water Cuts My Hands* (K/Matador, 1991)

—. *Dovetail* (K, 1992)

—. *Flood Plain* (K, 1993)

—. *Jarred Up* (K, 1993)

—. *Sitting on Snaps* (Matador, 1995)

—. *The Eagle & The Poodle* (Matador, 1996)

The Mods. *Twenty 2 Months* (OPM, 1995) Crucial inspiration for L'Etranger. Recorded 1978-80.

Odds. *Neopolitan* (Zoo/BMG, 1991)

—. *Bedbugs* (Zoo/BMG, 1993)
—. *Good Weird Feeling* (Warner, 1995)
—. *Nest* (Warner, 1996)
—. *Singles Individually Wrapped* (Warner, 2000) After TPOH, the most clever power-pop band of the era. Each album is packed with hits, but best moment is still "Wendy Under The Stars" from Neopolitan. It's what the singer of "I'm An Adult Now" wishes his coming-of-age was like.

The Pursuit Of Happiness. "I'm An Adult Now" (independent, 1986)
—. "Killed By Love" (independent, 1986)
—. *Love Junk* (Chrysalis, 1988)
—. *One-Sided Story* (Chrysalis, 1990)
—. *The Downward Road* (Mercury, 1993)
—. *Where's The Bone* (Iron, 1995)
—. *The Wonderful World Of . . .* (Iron, 1996)
—. *Sex & Food: The Best Of . . .* (Razor & Tie, 2000)

Skydiggers. *Skydiggers* (Enigma, 1990)
—. *Restless* (Fre, 1992)
—. *Just Over This Mountain* (Fre, 1993)
—. *Road Radio* (Warner, 1995)
—. *Desmond's Hip City* (Hip City/DROG, 1997)
—. *Still Restless* (Hip City/DROG, 1999)
—. *There And Back* (Hip City/Outside, 2000) Live.

Spirit of the West. *Spirit of the West* (independent, 1985)
—. *Tripping Up The Stairs* (Stony Plain, 1986)
—. *Labour Day* (Stony Plain, 1988)
—. *Save This House* (Warner, 1989)
—. *Go Figure* (Warner, 1991)
—. *Faithlift* (Warner, 1993)
—. *Two-Headed* (Warner, 1995)
—. *Open-Heart Symphony* (Warner, 1996)
—. *Weights & Measures* (Warner, 1998)

Universal Honey. *Magic Basement* (independent, 1993)
—. *Earth-Moon Transit* (independent, 1996)
—. *Universal Honey* (Oasis/Universal, 1999)

Ursula. *Happy To Be Outraged* (Shy, 1995) Companion piece to Andrew Cash's *Hi*.

Acadian Driftwood: The Creation of the Daniel Lanois Sound

Willie P. Bennett. *Collectibles* (Dark Light, 1991) A CD compilation of tracks mostly from 1977's *Hobo's Taunt* and 1978's *Blackie & The Rodeo King*.
Blackie & The Rodeo Kings. *High Or Hurtin'* (True North, 1996) Tom Wilson, Stephen Fearing and Colin Linden pay tribute to Willie P.
—. *Kings Of Love* (True North, 1999) More of the same but with some fine originals thrown in. Wilson's "Lean On Your Peers" is one of his best.
Boys Brigade. *Boys Brigade* (Anthem, 1983)
Michael Brook. *Hybrid* (Opal, 1985)
Harold Budd/Brian Eno with Daniel Lanois. *The Pearl* (Opal, 1984)
Malcolm Burn. *Redemption* (Anthem, 1988) A dry run for his move into the wider production sphere and light years from Boys Brigade.
Crash Vegas. *Red Earth* (Risque Disque/WEA, 1989)
—. *Stone* (London, 1993)
—. *Aurora* (Sony, 1996)
The Dave Rave Conspiracy. *Three Octave Fantastic Hexagram* (Gritty City, 1993) Dave Rave Des Roches cut his teeth as the singer/guitarist in The Shakers with fellow Steeltown institution Tim Gibbons. After briefly replacing Frankie Venom in

Teenage Head, he relocated to New York City in the early '90s where he formed The Dave Rave Conspiracy with former Washington Squares bassist/vocalist Lauren Agnelli, guitarists/vocalists Coyote Shivers and Gary Pig Gold and former Television drummer Billy Ficca. The line-up would only exist for this excellent album recorded between New York and Grant Ave. Studio, Hamilton, which also features Gibbons, Daniel Lanois, Colin Cripps, and Bob Doidge. One of the strongest songwriters Hamilton ever spawned.

—. (as Lauren Agnelli & Dave Rave) *Cowboy Flowers Sessions* (Mystery Tone/Outside, 1995)

—. *Confetti* (independent, 1997) Compiles various phases of Agnelli and Rave's individual careers.

—. *Heaven & Earth* (independent, 1999)

Bob Dylan. *Oh Mercy* (Columbia, 1989)

—. "Series Of Dreams" (The Bootleg Series, Vol. 1–3, Columbia, 1991) This anthemic outtake clearly would have knocked *Oh Mercy* out of balance. Too bad the rest of the album didn't sound like it. See also "Dignity" on Greatest Hits Vol. 3 (Columbia, 1994)

—. *Time Out Of Mind* (Columbia, 1997)

Brian Eno. *Ambient 4: On Land* (EG, 1982)

—. *Apollo Atmospheres and Soundtracks* (EG, 1984)

Florida Razors. *Beat Music* (independent, 1985)

—. *Half A Rock 'N Roll Record* (independent, 1986) Both are archetypal Steeltown rawk, although Tom Wilson is clearly entrenched in Delta mud. The blueprint for Junkhouse, once the southern sympathy was removed.

Peter Gabriel. *Birdy* Soundtrack (Geffen, 1985)

—. *So* (Geffen, 1986)

—. *Us* (Geffen, 1992)

Joe Hall. *Travelling Without Deodorant: The Best Of Joe Hall (1972–1988)* (Cordova Bay/Ragged Pup, 1998) Tracks from *HJ Boenke* and *On The Avenue* recorded by Bob and Dan in the late '70s.

Emmylou Harris. *Wrecking Ball* (Elektra, 1995) Even more of a collaboration than Lanois's previous productions, with one album he completely redefined Harris's interpretive artistry. His guitar solo on "May This Be Love" is worthy of Hendrix himself.

—. *Spyboy* (Eminent/Stony Plain, 1998) Live, with Buddy Miller stepping in admirably for Lanois on stage. Older material is transformed in Wrecking Ball fashion.

—. *Red Dirt Girl* (Nonesuch, 2000) All originals this time, with Malcolm Burn carrying on production duties.

Jon Hassell. *Fourth World, Vol. 2: Dream Theory* (EG, 1981)

—. *Aka Darbari Java* (EG, 1983)

—. *Power Spot* (ECM, 1986)

—. *Flash Of The Spirit* (ECM, 1988)

Junkhouse. *Strays* (Sony, 1994)

—. *Birthday Boy* (Sony, 1996)

—. *Fuzz* (Sony, 1998)

Daniel Lanois. *Acadie* (Opal, 1989)

—. *For The Beauty Of Wynona* (Warner Bros., 1993) More rough edges, but songs like "The Messenger" and "A Lot Of Love To Give" resonate with the same raw honesty at the heart of Acadie. Both albums are essential as examples of contemporary Canadian folk-rock.

—. *Sling Blade* Soundtrack (Island, 1996) Includes tracks by Tim Gibbons and one-time Junkhouse bassist Russ Wilson.

Luba. *Secrets And Sins* (Capitol, 1984)

Luscious Jackson. *Fever In Fever Out* (Warner Bros., 1996) The sexiest album of its year and proof that Lanois could still produce convincing pop music.

Martha and The Muffins. *This Is The Ice Age* (Virgin, 1981)

—. *Danseparc* (Current, 1982)

—. (as M+M) *Mystery Walk* (Current, 1984) This wouldn't sound out of place alongside Eno's African pop experiments with the Talking Heads.

—. *Then Again: A Retrospective* (EMI, 1998)

Ray Materick. *Best Friend Overnight* (Asylum, 1975)

—. *Fever In Rio* (Casino, 1979) Hard to believe Lanois is even there.

Willie Nelson. *Teatro* (Island, 1998)

Neville Brothers. *Yellow Moon* (Warner Bros., 1989)

—. *Brother's Keeper* (Warner Bros., 1990) Malcolm Burn takes Lanois's place with lesser results.

Parachute Club. *Parachute Club* (Current, 1983)

Pregnant. *After Dinner Mints* (Handsome Boy, 1996) Malcolm Burn's return to performing. Still waiting for more.

The Anthony B. Quarrington Limitation. *Top Ten Written All Over It* (Posterity, 1978) Still a vital force in the Canadian jazz scene.

Quarrington Worthy. *Quarrington Worthy* (Posterity, 1979)

Raffi. *Singable Songs For The Very Young* (Quality, 1976) Unbelievably, the album that put the Lanois brothers on the map. Still selling today.

Robbie Robertson. *Robbie Robertson* (Geffen, 1987)

—. *Storyville* (Geffen, 1991) Robertson reconnects with the New Orleans vibe, but, oddly, not with Lanois.

SIANspheric. *Somnium* (Sonic Unyon, 1995)

—. *There's Always Someplace You'd Rather Be* (Sonic Unyon, 1998)

—. *Else* (Sonic Unyon, 1999) Includes remixes and live tracks; notably, unrecognizable version of Teenage Head's "Shag Shack."

—. *The Sound of the Colour of the Sun* (Sonic Unyon, 2001)

Simply Saucer. *Cyborgs Revisited* (Mole, 1989) The definitive document of Canadian anti-rock, harnessed (partially) by Bob Lanois. Recorded 1974/75.

Sylvia Tyson. *Sugar For Sugar, Salt For Salt* (Salt, 1979) In hindsight it could have been a warm-up for *Wrecking Ball*. If only you could go back in time.

U2. *The Unforgettable Fire* (Island, 1984)

—. *The Joshua Tree* (Island, 1986)

—. *Achtung Baby* (Island, 1991)

—. *All That You Can't Leave Behind* (Island, 2000)

In the Spirit of Crazy Horse

Borrowed Tunes (Sony, 1994) Double disc Young tribute by Canadian artists. Not many surprises apart from Crash Vegas' "Pocahontas," and Bourbon Tabernacle Choir/Rheostatics' exuberant "Everybody Knows This Is Nowhere." Merely confirms the influence.

The Bridge: A Tribute To Neil Young (Caroline, 1989) Features the Pixies, Sonic Youth, Dinosaur Jr., Soul Asylum, etc. One of the few tribute albums of lasting importance.

Crazy Horse. *Crazy Horse* (Reprise, 1971) Poignant display of Danny Whitten's wasted talent. Includes "Come On Baby Let's Go Downtown," "I Don't Want To Talk About It," and Young's "Dance Dance Dance."

—. *Crazy Moon* (Epic, 1979) Mostly forgettable material, but interesting to hear Young as a sideman in the band.

John Critchley. *Crooked Mile* (Sound King, 2000)

Crosby, Stills, Nash & Young. *Déja Vu* (Atlantic, 1970)

—. "Ohio" (Atlantic, 1970)

—. *Four Way Street* (Atlantic, 1971) CD adds Young's "Cowgirl In The Sand/The Loner/Cinnamon Girl" solo medley.

—. *American Dream* (Warner, 1988) Approach with caution.

—. *Looking Forward* (Warner, 1999) Once again it's Young's songs that make this of any interest.

54·40. *Selection* EP (Mo-Da-Mu, 1982)

—. *Set The Fire* (Mo-Da-Mu, 1984)

—. *54·40* (independent, 1985; Warner, 1986) Still their most complete work, before the innocence rubbed off. Shouldn't be overlooked that it also inspired Hootie & The Blowfish.

—. *Show Me* (Warner, 1987)

—. *Fight For Love* (Warner, 1989)

—. *Sweeter Things* (Warner, 1991) Compiles singles from the Warner years.

—. *Dear Dear* (Sony, 1992)

—. *Smilin' Buddah Cabaret* (Sony, 1994) Lethargy creeps in.

—. *Trusted By Millions* (Sony, 1996)

—. *Sound Of Truth* (Sony, 1997) Reissue of Mo-Da-Mu recordings.

—. *Since When* (Sony, 1998) Their most coherent work since Dear Dear. A good lazy summer record.

—. *Heavy Mellow* (Sony, 1999) Live.

—. *Casual Viewin'* (Sony, 2000)

Hayden. *In September* cassette (independent, 1994)

—. *Everything I Long For* (Hardwood/Sonic Unyon, 1995)

—. *Moving Careful* EP (Hardwood/Sonic Unyon, 1996)

—. *The Closer I Get* (Hardwood/Universal, 1998)

Pearl Jam. *Merkinball* (Epic, 1995) CD single of "I Got Id/Long Road," from Mirror Ball sessions, featuring Young on guitar and pump organ.

13 Engines. *Before Our Time* (Nocturnal, 1987)

—. *Byram Lake Blues* (Nocturnal, 1989)

—. *A Blur To Me Now* (Capitol, 1991)

—. *Perpetual Motion Machine* (Capitol, 1993)

—. *Conquistador* (EMI, 1995) Double vinyl includes extra tracks.

—. *Perfect Largeness* (Nocturnal, 1997) Single CD reissue of first two albums.

Treble Charger. *NC-17* (Smokin' Worm/Sonic Unyon, 1994) Includes original (and definitive) version of "Red."

—. *Self=Title* EP (Smokin' Worm/Sonic Unyon, 1996) Their last great moment before succumbing to major label makeovers.

—. *Maybe It's Me* (ViK/BMG, 1997)

—. *American Psycho* (ViK/BMG, 2000)

Weeping Tile. *eePee* (WEA, 1995) Includes "Don't Let It Bring You Down," and original version of "Basement Apt."

—. *Cold Snap* (WEA, 1995)

—. *Valentino* (WEA, 1997) The fact that this raw rock album didn't register with more listeners showed that most people preferred Sarah Harmer as a folkie.

Neil Young. *Neil Young* (Reprise, 1968)

—. *Everybody Knows This Is Nowhere* (Reprise, 1969)

—. *After The Goldrush* (Reprise, 1970)

—. *Harvest* (Reprise, 1972)

—. *Journey Through The Past* (Reprise, 1972)

—. *Time Fades Away* (Reprise, 1973) An under-appreciated Canadian classic containing many of Young's most emotional performances ("Journey Through The Past," "Love In Mind," "Don't Be Denied"). Initially dismissed for its rawness, which turned out to be years ahead of its time.

—. *On The Beach* (Reprise, 1974) Another forgotten classic. Although saturated with a marijuana vibe, side two ("On The Beach," "Motion Pictures," "Ambulance Blues") is Young's longest sustained moment of brilliance on record. Along with *Time*, part of the "Missing Six" not available on CD.

—. *Tonight's The Night* (Reprise, 1975)

—. *Zuma* (Reprise, 1975)
—. *American Stars 'N Bars* (Reprise, 1977)
—. *Decade* (Reprise, 1977)
—. *Comes A Time* (Reprise, 1978)
—. *Rust Never Sleeps* (Reprise, 1979) Crazy Horse assimilates punk, or was it vice versa?
—. *Live Rust* (Reprise, 1979)
—. *Hawks & Doves* (Warner Bros., 1980)
—. *Re-Ac-Tor* (Warner Bros., 1981)
—. *Trans* (Geffen, 1982) The genre-hopping begins. A new wave mess.
—. *Everybody's Rockin'* (Geffen, 1983) Rockabilly fluff, but the videos were great.
—. *Old Ways* (Geffen, 1985) Wears better with age, but at the time was another unwant-
  ed curveball.
—. *Landing On Water* (Geffen, 1986)
—. *Life* (Geffen, 1987) Crazy Horse at their lowest. "Prisoners of Rock 'N Roll" still
  sounds like a distress call.
—. *This Note's For You* (Reprise, 1988)
—. *El Dorado* EP (Reprise, 1989) Only source for the great "Cocaine Eyes."
—. *Freedom* (Reprise, 1989) The restoration begins.
—. *Ragged Glory* (Reprise, 1990) Crazy Horse at their peak.
—. *Arc/Weld* (Reprise, 1991)
—. *Harvest Moon* (Reprise, 1992)
—. *Lucky 13* (Geffen, 1993)
—. *Unplugged* (Reprise, 1993)
—. *Sleeps With Angels* (Reprise, 1994) A chilling record, haunted by Kurt Cobain.
  Echoes Young's mid-'70s period in terms of darkness, but "Change Your Mind" is
  an enduring ray of light. Possibly his best moment of the '90s.
—. *Mirror Ball* (Reprise, 1995) With Pearl Jam.
—. *Rock 'N Roll Cowboy: A Life On The Road 1966–96* (bootleg, 1996) Until Young's
  long-awaited Archives is released, this is the best source to fill in the missing gaps
  of his career. Includes "Ordinary People" among many other unheard master-
  works.
—. *Dead Man* Soundtrack (Vapor, 1996)
—. *Broken Arrow* (Reprise, 1996) Although not as cohesive as Ragged Glory, its best
  moments make the band's interaction sound effortless.
—. *Year Of The Horse* (Reprise, 1997)
—. *Silver And Gold* (Reprise, 2000)
—. *Road Rock, Vol. 1: Friends And Relatives* (Reprise, 2000)

Folk You: Roots Revisited

Jeff Bird. *Jeff Bird* (DROG, 1995)
—. *Everything Has Come Clear and Plain to My Understanding* (DROG, 1997) More focus
  on instrumental pieces, ranging from classical to loping reggae.
John Bottomley. *Songs With the Ornamental Hermits* (Latent/BMG) This gorgeous
  modern folk album was the best non-Junkies release on Latent. Production by T-
  Bone Burnett, John Oliveira, and Joceylne Lanois sounds remarkably cohesive,
  with Bottomley's warm voice weaving it all together.
Cowboy Junkies. *Whites Off Earth Now!* (Latent, 1986; BMG, 1989) Haunting, delicate,
  and occasionally terrifying. Anyone who only knows their glossy pop side would
  do well to go back and listen to this.
—. *The Trinity Session* (Latent, 1987; BMG, 1988)
—. *The Caution Horses* (BMG, 1990)
—. *Black-Eyed Man* (BMG, 1992) Their best stab at mainstream music, with their pretti-
  est pop singles.

—. *Pale Sun Crescent Moon* (BMG, 1994) Ken Myhr's lead guitar playing makes this occasionally more heavy-handed than it has to be, otherwise, a cool desert vibe prevails.

—. *200 More Miles: Live 1985–1994* (BMG, 1995) Double live contract release, ranging from their very first public performance — an extremely thrashy, amateurish take on Carl Perkins's "Bad Boy" — to sold-out shows across North America.

—. *Lay It Down* (Geffen, 1996)

—. *Miles From Our Home* (Geffen, 1998) For the first time, huge production doesn't bury the Junkies. Unfortunately, their record company did.

—. *Rarities, B-Sides and Slow Waltzes* (Latent, 1999)

—. *Waltz Across America* (Latent, 2000) Live.

—. *Open* (Latent, 2001)

Great Speckled Bird. *Great Speckled Bird* (Bearsville, 1969; Stony Plain, 1994) Legendary Canadian country-rock album. Ian and Sylvia Tyson joined guitarist Amos Garrett and a funky backing band to create a sound that easily matches the hybrids of Gram Parsons and the Byrds. Produced by Todd Rundgren.

Greyhound Tragedy. *Demi Dog* (Raging Postman, 1996) Led by ex-Jr. Gone Wild guitarist Steve Loree, this band's blistering live show didn't translate to disc.

Handsome Ned. *The Ballad of Handsome Ned* (Virgin, 1989) Mostly Sidewinders material, as they were the only one of Ned's combos to spend quality time in the studio.

—. *The Name is Ned* (Linkhorn/Northern Heritage/EMI, 2000) The whole story, with live material from the Cameron, unreleased tracks, plenty of covers, red-level radio performances, and appearances from all of his bands. This double disc closes with a version of Merle Haggard's "Tonight the Bottle Let Me Down" with Blue Rodeo, recorded at the end of a boozy night at the Horseshoe.

Jane Hawley. *As We Walk On Thin Ice* (Hawley Records, 1992)

Chris Houston. *Hate-Filled Man* (Caucasion/Zulu, 1986) Packaged with a real Astroturf cover and featuring Greg Keelor on backing vocals, eternal Horseshoe bartender Teddy Fury on drums, Jack DeKeyzer on guitar, and trumpeter Herb Spanier. Og Records' Del Picasso described his music as "seamy-underbelly perverted blues," an entirely apt description. Features the perennial "Surfin' on Heroin."

Jr. Gone Wild. *Less Art More Pop* (BYO, 1986) The American pressing has an early version of "God Is Not My Father."

—. *Folk You* cassette (independent, 1989)

—. *Too Dumb to Quit* (Stony Plain, 1990) Bill Henderson's production streamlines the sound a bit, but the buzzsaw guitars still chime through. With the exception of Dove's "Sleep With a Stranger," the non-McDonald tracks bog down the flow.

—. *Pull the Goalie* (Stony Plain, 1992)

—. *Simple Little Wish* (Stony Plain, 1995)

k.d. lang. "Friday Dance Promenade" b/w "Damned Ol' Dog" 7" (Bumstead, 1983)

—. *A Truly Western Experience* (Bumstead, 1984; Sire, 1985)

—. *Angel With a Lariat* (Sire, 1987)

—. *Shadowland* (Sire, 1988)

—. *Absolute Torch and Twang* (Sire, 1989) All cows, no punks. But "Pullin' Back The Reins" might be her best vocal performance aside from her duet with Roy Orbison.

—. *Ingenue* (Sire, 1992)

—. *Even Cowgirls Get the Blues* (Sire, 1993) lang and Ben Mink run wild and create some of the best music of their partnership.

—. *All You Can Eat* (Sire, 1995) In all her newfound celebrity, she forgot how to write songs.

—. *Drag* (Sire, 1997) A dim attempt to return to the torch of *Shadowland*. Perhaps the concept is to blame: every song is about smoking, including an extremely ill-advised cover of Steve Miller's "The Joker." Features a song commissioned from Jane Siberry, "Hain't It Funny?" Well, no.

—. *Invincible Summer* (Sire, 2000)

Carolyn Mark. *Party Girl* (Mint, 2000) The former Vinaigrettes bandleader and Jr. Gone Wild disciple steps to the front and establishes herself as one of the brightest new Canadian songwriters, if only for "Edmonton." Elsewhere, she balances cleverness with heartbreak like many of her country heroes, and rounds up an all-star Can-Rock cast: Ian Blurton, Brian Connelly, Elevator, Sarah Harmer, Greg Keelor, etc.

The Mike McDonald Band. *Is This Thing On?* (independent, 2000) A slightly confounding record, as McDonald goes for more of a pop approach. Nonetheless, there are still some classic McDonald compositions.

Ford Pier. *Meconium* (Wrong, 1995)

—. *12-Step Plan, 11-Step Pier* (Sudden Death, 2000)

Roots Roundup. *Rootrospective* (Groundup, 1997) This Vancouver party band were road warriors in the early '90s. *Rootrospective* compiles tracks from their four albums, and demonstrates how their reggae, ska and funk grooves - mostly driven by powerhouse bassist Keith Rose - made them such a live attraction. "Roots Rock (Rub a Dub On the Road)" is a shout-out to the Canadian touring circuit. Five tracks feature keyboardist Ford Pier, recorded after his departure from Jr. Gone Wild.

Smash The State: A Compilation of Canadian Punk Rock 1979-81 Volume Two (No Exit, date unknown). Features the *Be My Barbie* 7" single by the Malibu Kens, the teenage band of Jr. Gone Wild's Mike McDonald.

Tamarack. *A Pleasant Gale* (SGB, 1983) Traditional folk trio from Guelph that inspired Jane Siberry, Cowboy Junkies, and many others. The line-up has undergone numerous changes — this album features Jeff Bird and Randy Sutherland — but James Gordon was the anchor until the late '90s. Here, his arrangement of "Mining For Gold" is the one Margo Timmins lifted for *The Trinity Session*.

Viletones. *A Taste of Honey* (OPM, 1994) Seventeen songs recorded in two hours in 1977, including "Screaming Fist." Guess you had to be there; this re-issue only lends credence to Vancouver's claim of punk superiority.

The Vinaigrettes. *Atta Boy Girl* (Vinegarecords, 1994) Led by Carolyn Mark — along with Brigette Wilkins and Kim Stewart — and featuring drummer Ed Dobek (Jr. Gone Wild, Jerry Jerry), these Victoria indie rock wiseacres spun clever tales with a beach party beat. Features Ford Pier and someone named k.d. lang credited as being part of a "chorus of angels."

—. *Gross Negligee* (Vinegarecords, 1996)

The Importance of Being Sloan

Back From The Garden: A Tribute to Joni Mitchell (Intrepid, 1992) Features Sloan's take of "A Case of You" produced by The Cult's Jamie Stewart.

Hear and Now (DTK Records, 1992) Features the original version of "Underwhelmed."

Kearney Lake Rd. Unreleased Recordings (1988-89) Pray that Jay Ferguson, Chris Murphy and Henri Sangalang can one day come to an agreement about releasing some of these recordings. There are some wonderful songs that hardcore Sloan fans would love.

Much @ Edgefest '99 (Universal, 1999) Sloan's rare track "Glad To Be Hear" is fun but typical.

Sloan. *Peppermint* EP (Murder, 1992)

—. *Smeared* (DGC, 1992; Murder 1998)

—. *Underwhelmed* EP (DGC, 1992) Ultra-rare U.K. import sought after for its bonus tracks: the peppy "Amped" and the epic MBV-like dirge "Sleepover."

—. *I Am The Cancer* EP (DGC, 1993) Another U.K. single featuring the best of the early Sloan b-sides: "Ragdoll" and "Laying Blame."

—. Stove/Smother/Laying Blame split single with Eric's Trip (Murder/Cinnamon Toast, 1993) Sloan and Eric's cover each other. Sloan's contribution can be found on *DGC Rarities Volume 1* (1994).

—. *Twice Removed* (DGC, 1994; Murder, 1998)
—. Stood Up/Same Old Flame 7" (Murder, 1995) Foreshadowed the recording aesthetic that would come. A side wins.
—. *One Chord To Another* (Murder, 1996)
—. *One Chord To Another/Live at a Sloan Party* (The Enclave, 1997) Worth buying again for the bonus disc — a homage to the Beach Boys *Live at a Beach Boys Party*, and some entertaining stabs at their influential alphabet: from April Wine to Modern Lovers to Stereolab.
—. Untitled "Rhodes Jam" 7" (Murder, 1997) A limited edition art excursion to warm up an instrument that would be well used by the band between 1998 and 2000.
—. *Navy Blues* (Murder, 1998)
—. *Four Nights at the Palais Royale* (Murder, 1999)
—. *Between the Bridges* (Murder, 1999)
—. *Don't You Believe A Word* EP (Murder, 2000) U.K. single which features two bonus tracks "Summers My Season," and "At The Edge Of The Scene."

Never Mind the Molluscs: The Halifax Underground

Basic English. *Sweet Panic* (Risque Disque, 1990)
Black Pool. *Cemeteries* (independent, 1989)
—. *We The Living* (Justin MCA, 1991) Produced by Terry Brown. A most unlikely major label debut for Chris Murphy.
—. *Seahorse* (Groundswell, 1993)
—. *Scraps from the Table* (Lucky Life/ independent, 1995)
Broken Girl. *Broken Girl* (Sappy Records, 1996) Julie Doiron's first solo outing.
Cod Can't Hear (DTK Records, 1992) Live album compiled from the first Halifax Independent Music Festival.
Cool Blue Halo. Goes Like This 7" (No Records, 1995)
—. *Kangaroo* (No Records, 1996) Barry Walsh's finest pop moment. An album that deserved as much attention as the more 'well-known' releases of the Halifax Pop Explosion, but arrived a little too late.
Julie Doiron. *Loneliest in the Morning* (Sappy Records, 1997)
—. *Will You Still Love Me* EP (Tree Records, 1999)
—. *Julie Doiron and the Wooden Stars* (Sappy Records, 1999)
Elevator to Hell. *Elevator To Hell* (Sub Pop, 1996)
—. *Eerieconsiliation* (Sub Pop, 1997)
—. as Elevator Through. (Murder/Sub Pop, 1998) *The Such: Original Music From The Motion Picture*
—. as Elevator. *Vague Premonition* (Sub Pop, 1999)
Eric's Trip. *Eric's Trip* cassette (independent, 1990)
—. *Caterpillars* EP cassette (independent, 1991)
—. *Drowning* EP cassette (independent, 1991)
—. *Warm Girl* cassette (independent, 1992)
—. *Belong* EP 7" (NIM Records, 1992)
—. *Peter* EP (Murder, 1993) The lo-fi, dark side of the Sloan.
—. *Songs About Chris* EP (Sub Pop, 1993)
—. *Julie And The Porthole To Dimenti´a* 7" (Sappy, 1993)
—. *Love Tara* (Sub Pop, 1993) Largely cited as the definitive Eric's Trip release: excessively lo-fi, and overly intimate.
—. *The Gordon Street Haunting* EP (Sub Pop, 1994)
—. *Forever Again* (Sub Pop, 1994) a.k.a. The Breakup of Rick and Julie.
—. On The Road South 7" (Sub Pop, 1995)
—. *Purple Blue* (Sub Pop, 1996) This is where it all ends. Driving the psychedelic wedge between two camps.
—. *Long Days Ride Until Tomorrow* (Sappy/Sonic Unyon, 1997) Housecleaning the live and unreleased for the fans.

The Flashing Lights. *Where The Change Is* (independent, 1999) Matt Murphy indulges himself with an album full of mod revivalism. It works.
—. *Elevature* EP (independent, 2000)
—. *Sweet Release* (SpinART, 2001)
Hardship Post. *Moodring* cassette (independent, 1993)
—. *Hack* EP (Murder, 1993) Justifiably stamped the "Nirvana" tag on this St. John's trio.
—. *Somebody Spoke* (Sub Pop, 1995) Grunge traded for angular new wave.
Hip Club Groove. *Trailer Park Hip Hop* (Murder, 1994). Indie hip hop from Truro, N.S. Good teen fun. Two-thirds of the band would be drafted into Toronto's Len.
Jale. Aunt Bettie 7" (Cinnamon Toast, 1992)
—. A Sort of Grey 7" (Derivative/Cinnamon Toast, 1993)
—. Gold Leather with Heel Detail 7" (Cinnamon Toast/Genius, 1993)
—. *14 08 93* (Sub Pop, Germany, 1993)
—. *Dreamcake* (Sub Pop, 1994)
—. *Closed* EP (Murder, 1995) Alyson McLeod's last dance.
—. *So Wound* (Sub Pop, 1996)
—. *Hey Hey* EP (Sub Pop U.K., 1996) Rare U.K. import with bonus tracks.
—. *True What You Say* 7" (Sealed Fate, 1997)
Jellyfishbabies. *Jellyfishbabies* (Plot, 1986)
—. *The Unkind Truth About Rome* (Lone Wolf, 1990)
Never Mind the Molluscs (Sub Pop, 1993) Sub Pop's east coast territorial pissings in the model of the *Deep Six* compilation.
Out of the Fog: The Halifax Underground 1986 (Flamingo Records, 1986) Ground zero for the Halifax underground's recorded history. A collector's item for Sarah McLachlan's first appearance on the October Game track "Grind."
Joel Plaskett. *In Need Of Medical Emergency* (No Alternative, 1999)
—. (as The Joel Plaskett Emergency) *Down At The Khyber* (Brobdingnagian, 2001)
Plumtree. *Mass Teen Fainting* (Cinnamon Toast, 1995)
—. *Predicts the Future* (Cinnamon Toast, 1997)
—. *This Day Won't Last At All* (Cinnamon Toast/Endearing, 2000)
Rebecca West. *Burners On* (Cinnamon Toast, 1995) Highly recommended.
—. *Six More Weeks of Winter* EP (Cinnamon Toast, 1997)
The Super Friendz. *Sticktoitiveness* cassette (independent, 1994) The band would later resurrect this title for their 1996 American re-release of *Mock Up Scale Down*
—. *By Request* 7" (Murder, 1994)
—. *Mock Up Scale Down* (Murder, 1995) Catchy as hell.
—. *Play The Game, Not Games* 10″ (Murder, 1996)
—. *Slide Show* (Murder, 1996) A varied, but quality album that shows three songwriters each in their own creative corner of the band's triangle.
Thrush Hermit. *Nobody Famous* cassette (independent, 1992)
—. *John Boomer* cassette (independent cassette, 1993)
—. *Ammo* 7" (Cinnamon Toast, 1993)
—. *Marya* 7" (Genius, 1993)
—. *Smart Bomb* EP (Murder, 1994) Earned this quartet the cruel nickname "Clone", but still an enjoyable septet.
—. French Inhale 7" (Genius, 1994)
—. *The Great Pacific Ocean* EP (Murder, 1995) Produced by Steve Albini.
—. *Take Another Drag* 7" (Bong´load, 1995)
—. *Rock and Roll Detective* EP (Elektra, 1997)
—. *Sweet Homewrecker* (Elektra, 1997) The first full-length boasts some of the Hermit's killer moments, but this album could have benefited with some heavy editing.
—. *Giddy With The Drugs* 7" (Murder, 1997)
—. *Clayton Park* (Sonic Unyon, 1998) Ending an admirable career on the highest note. The swan song in the Halifax Pop Explosion.
Tigre Benvie. *Year Of The Mutt* (independent, 2000)
Trim Crusts Where Desired: Cinnamon Toast Records Compilation (Cinnamon Toast,

1994) The 7" label in town compiles their catalogue. Wonderful moments from the familiar (Jale, Rebecca West) and the unknown (Les Gluetones).

Al Tuck. *Arhoolie* cassette (Murder, 1994)

—. *Brave Last Days* EP (Murder, 1994) Never fit into the "Pop Explosion" category, but was championed as a Halifax treasure by many in that scene (Sloan helped release his first two LPs, Jale brought him on tour, members of Thrush Hermit still cite him as an important local influence). The Dylan comparisons are justified.

—. *The New High Road of Song* (Brobdingnagian, 2000)

The Vees. *The Vees* EP (Murder, 1997) The remaining members of Jale do what they do best one more time.

The Path of Thorns: Nettwerk Records

By Divine Right. *All Hail Discordia* (Nettwerk, 1997)

—. *Bless This Mess* (Nettwerk, 1999) Although it was a Hip-endorsed, stadium-ready, summer-friendly rock pop gem but Nettwerk didn't have the patience to see it through.

—. *Good Morning Beautiful* (Linus, 2001)

Decadence (Nettwerk, 1995) Box set compiling ten years of an independent force in Canada matched by none other. Does a great job of outlining the label's history throughout its first decade - aurally and visually — through some impressive multimedia. Minor complaint: Where are the Grapes of Wrath?

Delirium. *Semantic Spaces* (Nettwerk, 1994)

—. *Karma* (Nettwerk, 1997) Inoffensive electronica lite with a revolving roster of vocalists from former Skinny Puppy/Front Line Assembly member Bill Leeb (Wilhelm Schroeder). Features the megahits "Firefly" and "Silence" (with Sarah McLachlan).

—. *Poem* (Nettwerk, 2000)

Download. *The Eyes of Stanley Pain* (Nettwerk, 1996)

—. *III* (Nettwerk, 1997)

—. *Effector* (Nettwerk, 2000)

Ginger. *Ginger* EP (Nettwerk, 1993)

—. *Far Out* (Nettwerk,1994)

—. *Suddenly I Came to My Senses* (Capitol, 1996)

The Grapes of Wrath. *The Grapes of Wrath* EP (Nettwerk, 1984)

—. *September Bowl of Green* (Nettwerk, 1985; reissued Capitol, 1986) Acoustic new wave.

—. *Treehouse* (Capitol, 1987)

—. *Now and Again* (Capitol, 1989)

—. *These Days* (Capitol, 1991) The swan song of Grapes Part One.

—. *Seems Like Fate: 1984–1992* (Capitol, 1995) Anthology compiling the first chapter of this band. Includes rare tracks such as the excellent cover of Pink Floyd's "See Emily Play."

—. *Field Trip* (Song Corp, 2000) The Limited Edition version of the CD includes a bonus disc with significantly reworked classics and covers.

Joni Mitchell. *Ladies of the Canyon* (Elektra, 1970)

—. *Blue* (Elektra, 1971)

—. *Court and Spark* (Elektra, 1973) These three albums represent the essential Mitchell. Though Lilith Fair would make the female singer/songwriter a hot commodity, few have matched the level of songwriting that exists here.

Kevin Kane. *Neighbourhood Watch* (On/Off/Cargo, 1995) Excellent porch music that never left the basement.

Lava Hay. *Lava Hay* (Nettwerk/Polygram, 1990)

—. *With a Picture in Mind* (Nettwerk, 1992)

Suzanne Little. *Be Here Now* (Nettwerk, 1995)

Sarah McLachlan. *Touch* (Nettwerk, 1988; reissued in the U.S. by Arista, 1989) Despite rocketing McLachlan's career and acting as the focal point to a costly authorship trial, this album has not aged well.

—. *Solace* (Nettwerk, 1991)

—. *Live* (Nettwerk, 1992). Limited release live disc from Solace Tour.

—. *Fumbling Towards Ecstasy* (Nettwerk, 1993)

—. *The Freedom Sessions* (Nettwerk, 1994) Includes a multimedia component.

—. *Rarities, B-Sides, And Other Stuff* (Nettwerk, 1996) Definitely for the fans. Includes a multimedia component.

—. *Surfacing* (Nettwerk, 1997) The Top 40 Trojan Horse of Lilith Fair.

—. *Mirrorball* (Nettwerk, 1999) This greatest hits live record showcases McLachlan's exceptionally professional band. Other than crowd noise and a few digressions, the performances are spot-on to their studio counterparts.

Moev. *Cracked Mirror* EP (Noetix, 1981)

—. *Rotting Geraniums* EP (Go, 1982)

—. *Zimmerkamph* EP (Go, 1982)

—. *Toulyev* EP (Nettwerk, 1984)

—. *Alibis* EP (Nettwerk, 1984)

—. *Dusk to Desire* (Nettwerk, 1986)

—. *Yeah, Whatever* (Nettwerk, 1988)

—. *Head Down* (Nettwerk, 1990)

—. *Obituary Column, Ha!* (Nettwerk, 1991) Greatest hits compilation compiling singles and 12" remixes.

—. *Suffer* EP (independent, 1999)

Mystery Machine. *Glazed* (Nettwerk, 1995)

—. *10 Speed* (Nettwerk, 1995)

—. *Headfirst into Everything* (Nettwerk, 1996)

Rose Chronicles. *Dead and Gone to Heaven* EP (Nettwerk, 1993)

—. *Shiver* (Nettwerk, 1994) Nettwerk exposes their 4AD longings through this ethereal pop signing. Musically and lyrically drenched in effects, yet it's a Venus Fly Trap for any Anglophile.

—. *Happily Ever After* (Nettwerk, 1996) Less pop, more texture — but the lyrics are still sub-gothic diary entries. For such a promising talent, this was a sad epilogue indeed.

Skinny Puppy. *Back and Forth* cassette (independent, 1983)

—. *Remission* (Nettwerk, 1984)

—. *Bites* (Nettwerk, 1985) "Death Disco" features their first 'hit' "Smothered Hope."

—. *Mind: The Perpetual Intercourse* (Nettwerk, 1986)

—. *Cleanse, Fold and Manipulate* (Nettwerk, 1987)

—. *VIVIsectVI* (Nettwerk, 1988)

—. *Rabies* (Nettwerk, 1989)

—. *12 Inch Anthology* (Nettwerk, 1990)

—. *Too Dark Park* (Nettwerk, 1990) This environmental thematic-heavy recording moves the group into artier territory.

—. *Ain't It Dead Yet?* (Nettwerk, 1991) The audio version of Puppy's 1987 Toronto Concert Hall concert film from the video released in 1987.

—. *Last Rights* (Nettwerk, 1992)

—. *Back and Forth Series Two* (Nettwerk, 1992)

—. *The Process* (American, 1996) Piecing together the final years of Puppy.

—. *Brap* (Nettwerk, 1996)

—. *ReMix Dys Temper* (Nettwerk, 1998)

—. *The Singles Collect* (Nettwerk, 1999)

—. *B-Sides Collect* (Nettwerk, 1999)

Taste of Joy. *Trigger Fables* (Nettwerk, 1995)

Wild Strawberries. *Carving Wooden Spectacles* cassette (independent, 1990)

—. *Grace* (independent, 1991)

—. *Bet You Think I'm Lonely* (Strawberry/A&M, 1994; reissued by Nettwerk, 1995) One of the smartest collections of actual and would-be AM radio hits. Their best moment.

—. *Heroine* (Nettwerk, 1995)

—. *Quiver* (Nettwerk, 1998) Trading the pop for the production.

—. *Twist* (Universal, 2000)

Trust Yourself: Blue Rodeo

Blue Rodeo. *Outskirts* (Risque Disque/WEA, 1987)

—. *Diamond Mine* (Risque Disque/WEA, 1989)

—. *Casino* (WEA, 1990)

—. *Lost Together* (Warner, 1992)

—. *Five Days in July* (Warner, 1993)

—. *Nowhere to Here* (Warner, 1995)

—. *Tremolo* (Warner, 1997) Blue Rodeo took themselves for granted on this one, and so did their audience. Notable for the punk rock "Graveyard" and the Keelor/Cuddy collaboration with Crash Vegas' McAdorey/Cripps on the fiery rocker "No Miracle No Dazzle," originally demo-ed as a country number for *Five Days*.

—. *Just Like a Vacation* (Warner, 1999) Double live from the *Tremolo* tour, with inspired reworkings of "Trust Yourself," "Better Off As We Are," and a drunken Saskatoon lounge take on "Florida."

—. *The Days in Between* (Warner, 2000) Another polished pop bid, but engineer Trina Shoemaker takes a far less streamlined approach than *Casino*. "Sad Nights" is Cuddy's best ballad since "Bad Timing," and "Rage" is a touching Keelor tribute to his late friend Keith Whittaker of the Demics.

Jim Cuddy. *All in Time* (Warner, 1998)

Kim Deschamps. *Take Me Away* (independent, 1998) Deschamps displays surprisingly strong tenor vocal chops. The songwriting is incidental, but this is primarily an instrumentalists' album, and a good one at that. Produced by Scott Merritt.

Greg Keelor. *Gone* (Warner, 1997)

Bruce McCulloch. *Shame-Based Man* (Atlantic, 1995) Perhaps Bob Wiseman's most interesting production challenge, he dressed up McCulloch's skits with the help of Shadowy Man Brian Connelly and Wiseman's rhythm section at the time, Don Kerr and Hugh Phillips. Stands up to many repeat listens.

Pine Ridge: An Open Letter to Allan Rock/Songs For Leonard Peltier (Warner, 1996) Keelor organized this benefit album for the Leonard Peltier Defense Committee featuring Sarah McLachlan, The Tragically Hip, Skydiggers, Change of Heart, John Borra, Michelle McAdorey, Jane Siberry, Michael Ondaatje, and solo efforts from both Keelor and Cuddy.

Razorbacks. *Go To Town* (OPM/Warner, 1987) Rockabilly contemporaries of Blue Rodeo and Handsome Ned, and often seen busking on Queen St. in their early days.

—. *Live a Little* (OPM/Warner, 1989)

The Sadies. *Precious Moments* (Bloodshot, 1998) A raucous collection of don't-blink-or-you'll-miss-'em instrumentals and twangy traditionals from second-generation shitkickers Dallas and Travis Good. Carrying on the tradition of bluegrass brother duos for a post-punk world.

—. *Pure Diamond Gold* (Bloodshot, 1999) Causes Keelor to dub the Sadies "the best rock-'n'-roll band on the planet." One half of this album recorded at his farm with Shadowy Man Don Pyle; the other half is produced by Steve Albini.

—. *Tremendous Efforts* (Bloodshot, 2001) Keelor and Albini join forces, with Keelor contributing raucous lead vocals to "Loved On Look." Elevator's Rick White produces two tracks.

Bob Snider. *You* cassette (Amatish, 1993) The songwriting is equally funny and heartwrenching, drenched with dorky double-entendres, and brought to vivid life by an all-star Queen St. cast and Wiseman's production. Unsurprisingly, Snider soon was hailed as an heir to Stompin' Tom. Sadly unavailable beyond its initial cassette run.

—. *Caterwaul & Doggerel* (EMI, 1995) Snider is left a bit too bare on his major label debut, produced by Don Kerr.

—. *Words and Pictures* (EMI, 1997) Producer David Baxter provides a slightly Parisian band for Snider's heartfelt tales, including James Gray, Anne Bourne and Ron Sexsmith. Fewer novelty songs.

The Swallows. *Turning Blue* (Magnetic Angel, 1999) Glenn Milchem steps out from behind the kit to play practically everything on his second solo release; a mid-'80s indie cassette was his first foray.

Bob Wiseman. *Sings Wrench Tuttle: In Her Dream* (Risque Disque/WEA, 1989)

—. *Hits of the '60s and '70s* cassette (independent, 1991)

—. *Presented by Lake Michigan Soda* (Warner, 1992)

—. *City of Wood* (Warner, 1993)

—. *Beware of Bob* (Sabre Toque, 1994)

—. *Accidentally Acquired Beliefs* (Warner, 1995) Overproduced and clunky, stripped of the charm of the earlier albums. "Stay Untraceable" one of the few redeeming features; also features a cover of Neil Young's "Love is a Rose."

—. *More Work Songs From the Planet of the Apes* (GFC, 1998) One of his best before Wiseman began composing television music to pay his bills. Maybe someday he'll release the CBC session he recorded in Kingston with Gord Downie, Sarah Harmer, Mike O'Neill, 13 Engines' Grant Ethier, and himself.

Two Solitudes: The Tragically Hip

A Tribute To Hard Core Logo (BMG, 1996) Various bands "interpret" the music of this fictional Canadian punk band. Includes Headstones, TPOH, Doughboys, cub, Odds, Super Friendz among others.

Gordon Downie. *Coke Machine Glow* (Universal, 2001) Far removed from Downie's rock-'n'-roll day job, and subtly rewarding on an entirely different level.

Hard Core Logo Soundtrack (BMG, 1996) Classics like "Rock 'N Roll Is Fat And Ugly" and "Edmonton Block Heater" performed by Hugh Dillon and Swamp Baby. Also includes tracks by Teenage Head, The Ramones and Chris Spedding.

Headstones. *Picture Of Health* (MCA, 1993)

—. *Teeth & Tissue* (MCA, 1995)

—. *Smile & Wave* (Universal, 1996)

—. *Nickels For Your Nightmares* (Universal, 2000)

The Mahones. *Draggin' The Days* (Kinetic, 1994)

—. *Rise Again* (Everything Must Go, 1996)

—. *The Hellfire Club Sessions* (True North, 1999) Produced by The Hip's Johnny Fay.

Plasterscene Replicas. *Plasterscene Replicas* EP (independent, 1985)

—. *Glow* (Raining, 1988)

Teenage Head. *Teenage Head* (Epic, 1980) The first mainstream punk success story in Canada, which sounds like simply a great rock record today. The Hip and The Headstones would not have existed without The Head.

—. *Frantic City* (Attic, 1980) Contains most of their best moments, from "Wild One" to "Disgusteen."

—. *Some Kinda Fun* (Attic, 1982) The decline begins, but they do not go quietly.

The Tragically Hip. *The Tragically Hip* EP (Rock/RCA, 1988; MCA, 1989) CD adds "All-Canadian Surf Club." Original vinyl copies rapidly increasing in value.

—. *Up To Here* (MCA, 1989) CanRock for the masses, when it was so badly needed.

—. "Live At The Misty Moon, Halifax" (MuchMusic Big Ticket, 1990) Significant for rare public airings of unreleased "Crack My Spine Like A Whip," "Get Back Again," and "It's Just As Well."

—. *Road Apples* (MCA, 1991)

—. *Fully Completely* (MCA, 1992)

—. "Courage" CD single (MCA, 1992) Includes live tracks.

—. "Locked In The Trunk Of A Car" CD single (MCA, 1992) Includes live tracks.

—. *Live At The Roxy* (bootleg, 1992) Source of the radio-only "Highway Girl," with "Double Suicide" monologue.

—. "Land" (Cargo, 1993) Single recorded with Another Roadside Attraction line-up to benefit Clayoquot Sound protests.

—. *Day For Night* (MCA, 1994) Their masterpiece. Limited U.S. version on Atlantic includes live tracks; notably, riveting "New Orleans Is Sinking" incorporating "Fire In The Hole" and "Nautical Disaster."

—. *Trouble At The Henhouse* (MCA, 1996)

—. *Live Between Us* (Universal, 1997) A curious release considering the wealth of live material they have on hand. A definitive live set needs to be assembled.

—. *Phantom Power* (Universal, 1998) Confident return after inconsistent *Henhouse*.

—. *Music@Work* (Universal, 2000) Aside from the title track, their most challenging album to date, proven by the response from even longtime fans.

UIC. *Our Garage* (Fringe, 1986) Formed in rural southwestern Ontario, this powerful quintet could have matched The Hip album for album if they had received similar breaks.

—. *Like Ninety* (Og, 1989) Blistering live album recorded at Lee's Palace.

The Watchmen. *McLaren Furnace Room* (Sumo/MCA, 1992)

—. *In The Trees* (MCA, 1994)

—. *Brand New Day* (MCA, 1996)

—. *Silent Radar* (EMI, 1998)

Epilogue: Where the Change Is

Neko Case & Her Boyfriends. *The Virginian* (Mint, 1997) This album, an unexpected success for all involved, proved Case the gutsiest belter western Canada had seen since the 1984 arrival of k.d. lang. Six of the twelve tracks are originals, and Matt Murphy (Flashing Lights, Super Friendz) contributes "Honky Tonk Hiccups."

—. *Furnace Room Lullaby* (Mint/Bloodshot, 2000) All originals this time out, some co-penned with Ron Sexsmith and the Local Rabbits, and Case sinks her teeth into them with an emotional weight not yet present on *The Virginian*. Like Levon Helm 40 years earlier, this American brought out the best in her Canadian bandmates to create true country soul, and the world couldn't help but take notice.

Destroyer. *Thief* (Catsup Plate, 1999) This is a prime example of one of the most astounding new Canadian songwriters dwelling in obscurity, although perhaps future New Pornographer Dan Bejar likes it that way: on the opening track he sings about the "joy in being from the temple."

—. *Streethawk: A Seduction* (Misra, 2001) With beefed-up production following his Pornographic experience, Bejar returned with an even more captivating collection of songs that had lucky listeners across the land analysing his lyrical verse and singing along to his dangerously improving songcraft.

Godspeed You Black Emperor!. *F#A#* (Constellation, 1997; Kranky, 1998) The aural equivalent of an apocalyptic late night drive through desolate urban and spooky rural landscapes, with stray radio signals drifting in and out of consciousness. It's easy to see how the band's singular sound, along with their mystique, captured the world's attention.

—. *Slow Riot For a New Kanada* EP (Constellation/Kranky, 1999)

—. *Lift Your Skinny Fists Like Antennas to Heaven* (Constellation/Kranky, 2000) A double CD that benefits from Godspeed's various side projects (Fly Pan Am, A Silver Mt. Zion, One-Speed Bike) and intense tour schedule, which bring a more expansive and comprehensive focus to the material.

Guelph Happens (DROG, 1994) Features two tracks from King Cobb Steelie's sessions with Steve Albini, "Slump" and "Italian Ufology Today," both of which were re-done by Laswell on *Project Twinkle*. These versions are better.

Sarah Harmer. *Songs For Clem* (with Jason Euringer) (Cold Snap, 1999) Recorded on her back porch, Harmer unintentionally launched her solo career with this acoustic collection of standards. Her voice sounds like it could easily be found on a dusty old '78, and her take on Nancy Griffiths's "Trouble in the Fields" is a guaranteed tear-jerker.

—. *You Were Here* (Cold Snap/Universal, 2000) By refurbishing her "Basement Apt." with a drum machine, Harmer had her first huge hit, but this album was no sell-out.

Kyp Harness. *Nobody's Fool* (Amatish cassette, 1991)

—. *God's Footstool* (Amatish, 1992) Song for song, Harness's greatest achievement. He finds a more comfortable rap cadence for his wordier songs, and emerges as a full-blown romantic. Don Kerr's kitchen-sink production is complementary and charming. Players include Blurton, Borra, Wiseman, Morningstar, and Sexsmith.

—. *Welcome to the Revolution* (Amatish, 1994)

—. *Houdini in Reverse* (independent, 1998) Almost matches the greatness of *God's Footstool*. "You're the One" is one of the best love songs ever composed in this country, and deserves to played at every wedding of socially conscious lovers.

—. *All Her Love* (independent, 2001)

Heimlich Maneuver. *Heimlich Maneuver* cassette (independent, 1988) Kevan Byrne of King Cobb Steelie's '80s hardcore band.

King Cobb Steelie. *King Cobb Steelie* (Raw Energy/A&M, 1993) A powerful record that quickly made KCS the talk of the Canadian underground. A fan favourite because it's the first and only time the band put their punk rock roots at the front of the mix.

—. *You Said a Mouthful* EP (Raw Energy/A&M, 1993) Remixes by Steve Clarkson, aka The Invisible Lobe, the band's live sound engineer and on-stage programmer.

—. *Project Twinkle* (Lunamoth/EMI, 1994) Recorded in a rush when the band had the opportunity to work with Bill Laswell, the attempts at conventional rock are embarrassing. But when they let their hair down ("Technique," "80% Knockout") the results are magical and unlike anything else near the CanRock mainstream at the time.

—. *Junior Relaxer* (EMI, 1997) Their most comprehensive album, touching upon all the band's strengths.

—. *Mayday* (Rykodisc, 2000) Shrunk to the core trio of Byrne, Lynn and Armstrong, featuring Michelle McAdorey, Tamara Williamson and Spookey Reuben. A dense delight.

Local Rabbits. *The Super Duper* EP (En Guard, 1993)

—. *You Can't Touch This* (Murder, 1996) A rock-o-ramic tour de force, touching on country, blues, disco, and soul — all with wide-eyed enthusiasm that at times borders on the absurd.

—. *Basic Concept* (Murder, 1998) Some attempts at maturity are more successful than others, but "Play On" alone redeems the album.

Ashley MacIsaac. *Hi, How Are You Today?* (A&M, 1995)

—. *Helter's Celtic* (Loggerhead, 2000) Proof that when left to his own devices and creative approach to deadlines, MacIsaac is a complete mess. After this, he focussed exclusively on traditional, gimmick-free material.

The New Pornographers. *Mass Romantic* (Mint, 2000) Every song has at least three surefire pop hooks. A dense, overwhelming sugar rush.

Ron Sexsmith. *There's a Way* cassette (independent, 1987) Produced by Kurt Swinghammer.

—. *Grand Opera Lane* cassette (Amatish, 1991; independent, 2000) Produced by Bob Wiseman. This will sound quite surprising for fans of Sexsmith's best-known work, as it displays more of a horn-driven soul influence than simply a balladeer, as on

"Spending Money." Greg Keelor attempts some fast-pickin' rockabilly on "Gonna Get What's Mine." Listening to this, Sexsmith's early '90s anonymity is all the more incredulous.

—. *Ron Sexsmith* (Interscope, 1995) Introduced him to the world as a balladeer par excellence. Produced by Mitchell Froom, with one track from the aborted Lanois sessions.

—. *Other Songs* (Interscope, 1997) Some weak and obvious material dilutes this album's strengths; the throwaway title seems apt.

—. *Whereabouts* (Interscope, 1999) His most fully realized work with Froom, and a flawless collection of songs.

—. *Blue Boy* (Linus, 2001) Produced by Steve Earle, and featuring a cover of Kyp Harness's "Thumbelina Farewell."

The Smugglers. *At Marineland* (Nardwuar the Human Serviette Records, 1991) Features the civic anthem "Vancouver B.C.," the hilarious video for which still gets airplay.

—. *Atlanta Whiskey Flats* (PopLlama, 1992)

—. *In the Hall of Fame* (Pop Llama, 1993) Collects the first two albums and 7" singles.

—. *Selling the Sizzle!* (Mint, 1996)

—. *Buddy Holly Convention* EP (Mint, 1997)

—. *Growing Up Smuggler* (Mint, 1998) A live recording from Spain celebrating the band's tenth anniversary. Features detailed and highly entertaining liner notes, which are more memorable than the actual performance.

—. *Rosie* (Mint, 2000)

Superconductor. *Heavy With Puppy* (Boner/Tupelo, 1992)

—. *Hit Songs For Girls* (Boner/Tupelo, 1993)

—. *Bastardsong* (Boner, 1996)

Vancouver Special (Mint, 2000) Featuring exclusively Vancouver acts, this was the first exciting indie rock comp in years, perhaps since Raw Energy's *On the Road*. It kicks off with an inevitable appearance by Nardwuar the Human Serviette, and features the New Pornographers, Pepper Sands, Destroyer, Vancouver Nights, and the Riff Randells covering the Pointed Sticks' "Somebody's Mom," from the VanPunk class of '78.

Weakerthans. *Fallow* (G7 Welcoming Committee, 1997) After resigning as bassist in Winnipeg political punk band Propagandhi, John K. Samson formed the Weakerthans with other hardcore refugees. The music is anthemic three-chord power punk with folkie interludes, like the jaw-dropping simplicity of "None of the Above."

—. *Left and Leaving* (G7 Welcoming Committee, 2000) Produced by Ian Blurton, the punk songs have more crunch and the folk songs are more shimmering. Samson's prose-like lyrics were the most literate in CanRock of the day — even Gord Downie admitted he was taking notes.

Zumpano. *Look What the Rookie Did* (Sub Pop, 1995) Echoing Bacharach/David and Brian Wilson, Carl Newman's pop talent reaches a new level.

—. *Goin' Through Changes* (Sub Pop, 1996) A far superior follow-up, a beautiful pop album that peaked at merely being a critical favourite.

—. *The Only Reason Under The Sun* (Murder 7", 1996) Features a cover of the Beatles' "The Long and Winding Road."

Sources

Interviews

The majority of these interviews were conducted for the specific purposes of this book. Some were conducted for or may have been excerpted in *Id* magazine, *Exclaim!*, *eye Weekly*, the *Silhouette*, or the *Kitchener–Waterloo Record*. All interviews were conducted individually or by a combination of Michael Barclay, Ian A.D. Jack, and Jason Schneider. (month/day/year).

Kris Abbott: 4/18/97
Chuck Angus: 11/11/98
Tom Anselmi: 2/26/98
Ric Arboit: 4/3/98
Charles Austin: 3/5/97, 4/4/97
Bill Baker: 6/12/97, 2/27/01
Brent Bambury: 3/11/95
Brad Barker: 4/18/97
Bobby Beaton: 5/18/00
Jaymz Bee: 8/21/00
Mike Belitsky: 2/14/98, 8/20/00
Willie P. Bennett: 5/9/01
Robert Benvie: 3/23/97, 9/6/00
Moe Berg: 4/18/97, 2/16/01
Art Bergmann: 5/7/97
Dave Bidini: 10/24/96, 11/23/96, 7/6/97
Jeff Bird: 8/11/97
Ian Blurton: February 1997, 8/20/97
James Booth: 9/18/00
Laura Borealis: 4/5/97
John Borra: 7/23/97
Scott Bradshaw: 9/27/00
Colleen Britton: 10/16/00
Chris Brown: 11/16/97
Dove Brown: 11/14/00

Warren Campbell: 8/26/00
Cameron Carpenter: 2/16/98
Andrew Cash: 1/27/98, 4/20/00
John Chisholm: 8/28/00
Dave Clark: 5/5/00
Greg Clark: 10/15/97, 8/27/97
Greg Clow: 10/3/00
Holly Cole: March 1997
Stephen Cooke: 8/29/00
Colin Cripps: 8/14/97
John Critchley: 6/5/00
Jim Cuddy: 9/9/98, 6/27/99, 12/12/00
Jonathan Cummins: 7/10/97
Kim Deschamps: 5/7/98
Tony Dewald: 5/10/00
Hugh Dillon: 10/22/97
Bob Doidge: 3/27/00
Julie Doiron: 6/19/97
Colin Doroschuk: 6/15/97
Ivan Doroschuk: 5/14/97, 10/24/00
Stefan Doroschuk: 9/21/00
Gord Downie: 10/3/00
Howard Druckman: 7/30/97
Marc Durand: 4/3/97
Steve Earle: 1/16/01
Angie Fenwick: 6/12/97

Jeff Rogers: 02/16/98
Don Rooke: 9/7/00
Peter Rowan: 7/10/97
Andrew Scott: 6/01/97, 8/15/00
Joey Serlin: 1/28/98
Ron Sexsmith: April 1997, 11/8/00
Jane Siberry: 9/12/00
Gord Sinclair: 10/3/00
Alex Soria: 9/20/00, 9/4/00
Laura Stein: 2/14/98
Catherine Stockhausen: 11/15/97
Chip Sutherland: 2/9/98
Kurt Swinghammer: 5/25/00
William "Skinny" Tenn: 4/23/01
Jean-Yves Theriault: 11/30/00

Chris Thompson: 7/3/97
Martin Tielli: 1997
Margo Timmins: 6/29/98, 11/7/00
Michael Timmins: 4/26/00
Gerard Van Herk: 5/3/00
Tim Vesely: 9/25/00
Barry Walsh: 8/26/00, 2/9/01
Dan Webster: 11/15/00
Woody R. Whalen: 8/22/00
Rick White: 7/2/97
Tom Wilson: 8/14/97
David Wisdom: 8/30/00
Michael Phillip Wojewoda: 4/8/00
Drew Yamada: 4/4/97

Overture: Everybody Knows This Is Nowhere

"If I could describe cool to you": Del Picasso, from the liner notes to *It Came From Canada Vol. 1*, Og Records, 1985.

"At some point during the decisive decade 1985–1995": Peter C. Newman, *The Canadian Revolution 1985–1995: From Deference to Defiance.* (Toronto: Viking, 1995), xvi.

"If you only read the work of dead foreigners": Margaret Atwood, *Survival: A Thematic Guide to Canadian Literature.* (Toronto: House of Anansi Press, 1972), 15–16.

"I grew up thinking everything had already happened.": Gina Arnold, *Route 666: On the Road to Nirvana.* (New York: St. Martin's Press, 1993), 3.

"Back in 1985, Canadians seemed so diffident": Newman, xii.

"It took nearly a decade of living in America": Barney Hoskyns, *Across the Great Divide: The Band and America.* (New York: Viking, 1993), 1.

"What an impossible situation we leave": Stompin' Tom Connors, *Stompin' Tom and the Connors Tone: The Legend Continues.* (New York: Viking, 2000), 405.

"Tom's voice drew me back across the ocean": Dave Bidini, *On a Cold Road: Tales of Adventure in Canadian Rock.* (Toronto: McClelland and Stewart, 1998), 191.

"At one point in the evening": Connors, 445.

"That's my style, man": Wilder Penfield III and Bob Thompson, from "Northern Lights: The $10 million national daydream," *Graffiti*, April, 1985.

"It is our belief": Nicholas Jennings, *Before the Gold Rush: Flashbacks to the Dawn of the Canadian Sound.* (New York: Viking, 1997), 230.

"Any broadcaster who played 'Yummy Yummy Yummy'": Jennings, 231.

"The prophets of doom": Jennings, 232.

"I think it's a hugely mediocre system": Mary Dickie, "The Strife of Bryan," *Impact*, January 1994.

"No one ever really asked me much": Andrew Flynn, "The Canadian Infiltration: How the World Was Rocked," Canadian Press, 22 December 1999.

Also referenced:
Bidini, Dave. "Stompin' Tom: Man of Mystery, Man of Song." *Nerve*, October, 1986.

Did You Get My Message on the People's Radio?

All Augusta LaPaix quotes are from a transcript of *Brave New Waves*'s 15th anniversary broadcast, 4 February 1999, as are the following quotes from Brent Bambury and Patti Schmidt:

"John Cage represents *Brave New Waves*": *Brave New Waves*, 4 February 1999.
"In the early days, we'd have these": *Brave New Waves*, 4 February 1999.
"We had punk rock bands": *Brave New Waves*, 4 February 1999.
"We interviewed her and she sounded rational": *Brave New Waves*, 4 February 1999.
"I left the show with": *Brave New Waves*, 4 February 1999.
"I think it's the most brilliant privilege": *Brave New Waves*, 4 February 1999.
"Much Music is obliged to play 10 per cent": Alan Neister, "Rock Around the Clock," *Graffiti*, November 1984.
"It drives people crazy": Bill Reynolds, "The Maturing of the Canadian Music Industry." *Canadian Musician*, April 1989.

Also referenced:
Galloway, Matt. "*Brave New Waves* Toasts 15 Weird Years." *Now*, 4 February 1999.
Rayner, Ben. "Making Waves." *Toronto Star*, 7 February 1999.

Glittering Prizes and Endless Compromises

"I don't expect or want": Kim Hughes, "Combo Sparkles with Satirical Nuance." *Now* 9 August 1991.
"I don't like to blow my own horn": Mary Dickie, untitled article. *Music Express*, November 1992.

Also referenced:
Druckman, Howard. "Demons Exorcise Jazz Spirits," *Metropolis*, July 26, 1990.

Under the Volcano: The Fallout of Vancouver Punk

"If DOA has really broken up": Alex Varty, "DOA Alive Or Dead?" *Georgia Straight*. December 14–20, 1979.
"'lead' guitarists": John Armstrong, liner notes to Young Canadians *No Escape* (Zulu 1995).
"They said, 'Nah, you go and have fun'": Armstrong, *No Escape* (Zulu 1995).
"Despite the general hostility": Joe Carducci, *Rock and the Pop Narcotic*. (Chicago: Redoubt Press, 1990), 18.
"I think what really makes us": Anthony Hempell, interview with Rob Wright, *Discorder* September 1993.
"I'm allergic to cool": Hempell, *Discorder* September, 1993.
"People were interested": Dario Adamic, interview with John Wright, *Zips & Chains* #10, January, 1997.
"We were different": Hempell, *Discorder* September, 1993.
"We've always considered": Adamic, *Zips & Chains* #10.
"We've always tried": Adamic, *Zips & Chains* #10.
"We were doing four-track recordings": G. Bone/Chris Gonzalez, interview with Rob Wright, *Monkey Mag* #4.

"Andy didn't really want to join": Adamic, *Zips & Chains* #10.

"He had a much better idea": Stuart Green, "Timeline: NoMeansNo." *Exclaim!*, September 2000.

"The purpose of music": Hempell, *Discorder*, September 1993.

"Around 1985, there was a 'punk club'": Jonathan Cummins, "NoMeansNo, Sex Mad" *Chart*, March 1996.

"I was raised a Methodist": Sarah Frances, interview with Rob Wright, *Small Parts*, January 1998.

"DOA did their first tour of Europe": Adamic, *Zips & Chains* #10.

"Suddenly there was a lot of money": Green, *Exclaim!*, September 2000.

"He just got sick of touring": Hempell, *Discorder*, September 1993.

"NoMeansNo has taken on its own life": Richard Moule and Gord Westmacott, interview with Rob Wright, *Id*, 5 October 1995.

Also referenced:

Bateman, Jeff. "The Music Industry in Greater Vancouver." *Greater Vancouver Book*. (Vancouver: The Linkman Press, 1999).

Harrison, Tom. "Between a Rock and a Hyde Place," *Canadian Musician*, June 1987.

McDonagh, Grant. Liner notes to *Last Call: Vancouver Independent Music 1977–1988* (Zulu, 1988).

Folk of the Eighties: Montreal

"Pierre Trudeau's dream come true": Benjamin Russell, "Breaking Out In Montreal." *Canadian Musician*, August 1988.

"The synthesizer is the folk instrument of the '80s": Peter L. Noble, *Future pop: Music for the Eighties*. (Toronto: Musson, 1983), 126.

"Bands like the Fuzztones": Patrick Lejtenyi, "Back from the Grave," *Exclaim!*, June 2000.

"We started when we were kids": Jenny Ross, "Letter From Montreal: Breaking Nils, Fighting Skins, Etc.." *Graffiti*, February 1987.

Also Referenced:

Collie, Ashley. "The Box." *Canadian Musician*, May 1985.

Collie, Ashley. "Men Without Hats." *Canadian Musician*, May/June 1984.

Collie, Ashley, "Men Without Hats: Le Renouveau: Pop Go The Charts." *Canadian Musician*, February 1988.

Dannen, Fredric. *Hit Men*. (New York: Vintage, 1991).

Gareau, Dave. "Tackling Values Without A Hat." *Smash*, 30 November 1989.

Littlejohn, Maureen. "Man Without Hate." *Network*, February/March 1990.

Russell, Benjamin. "Breaking Out In Montreal." *Canadian Musician*, August 1988.

Sutherland, Alastair. "Men Without Hats: Going Sideways." *Music Express*, June 1991.

Yeah, It Matters: Change of Heart and Post-Punk Toronto

"If you can't say": Philip Martin, "Neon Rome: Human First." *Graffiti*, July 1987

"I believe the sound": Dave Rave, review of Change of Heart *Slowdance*, *Nerve*, June 1987.

all Bernard Maiezza quotes taken from "Neal Arbick: From A Neon Rome To Mahendra." *Exclaim!*, September 1993.

"At the end of the night": Bruce Lam, "Elvis Has Left The Buildings" *eye*, date unknown
"Neon Rome is a comedy act": Jack Slack, *Nerve*, January 1987.
"I went through so much pain": Maiezza, *Exclaim!*, September 1993.
"We rehearsed at Spartan Studios": Glenn Milchem, "Thanks For The Change Of Head." *Exclaim!*, April 1992.
"Michael arrived feeling": Milchem, *Exclaim!*, April 1992.

Northern Wishes & Visionary Flounders

"There was a play written": Chris Burns, *Graffiti*, March, 1988.
"They've got that high lonesome sound": David Wisdom, liner notes to the Rheostatics's *The Nightlines Session*, DROG, 1998.
"A voice baked in the kiln": Tim Peacock, live review of Manchester International performance, *Sounds*, 18 November 1989.
"The most cathartic female presence": *Time Out* review of Miss America, referenced in article by Jon Wilde, "Xmas Crackers," 14 December 1991.
"They got talking": Michael Hollett, "Go Deo Chorus Makes their Forever Sound." *Now*, 24 March 1983.
"The first night": Hollett.
"Rusty and Hendriik's singing": Hollett.
"Belonged in a padded cell": Chris Roberts, "A Bridge To O'Hara." *Melody Maker*, 26 November 1988.
"Initially, we didn't like": Hollett.
"Sometimes I can speak better": Hollett.
"Somewhat unique long-term": Hollett.
"Personally, I don't mind": Hollett.
"We've tried recording": Hollett.
"When Virgin came along": Kate Lazier, "In a Room of Her Own." *Canadian Composer*, February 1989.
"He had very strong ideas": Lazier.
"I don't think Virgin knew": Kim Hughes, "O'Hara Tells Tales on Miss America," *Now*, 10 November 1988.
"[Virgin] listened to it": Lazier.
"When I think of compromise": Lazier.
"When I didn't get this record out": Hughes.
"Certain things are always alive": Wilde.
"You always think that if": Hughes.
"Slightly distracted by the possibilities of life": Roberts.
"I think a lot of people they say are": Roberts.
"One of the most important": Marion Finlay, "London Critics Crazy for Mary Margaret." *Toronto Star*, 8 March 1989.
"A voice that appears to be": Peter Kane, review of O'Hara's Duke of York performance, *Sounds*, 18 March 1989.
"Epileptic Edith Piaf": Terry Staunton, review of O'Hara's Duke of York performance, *New Musical Express*, 18 March 1989.
"I don't think it was my dancing": Wilde.
"That song you did": relayed by Don Rooke during author interview
"O'Hara is that rare talent" Chris Dafoe, "In That Strange Way, Mary's Marvellous," *Toronto Star*, 14 February 1991.
"I have to trust": Hollett.

"When I look back": Wilde.

"The biggest problem": Wilde.

"This sounds like weird advice": Perry Stern, "Jane Siberry Reaches the Snapping Point," Network, April/May 1993.

"Really, Brian's most important contribution": Author unknown, "The Divine Miss S." New Zealand Herald, 11 February 1994.

"This record is more whole": Carl Arrington, Rolling Stone, 21 April 1994.

"I was dumbstruck": Stern, Network, April/May, 1993.

Also referenced:

Bidini, Dave. "Rheostatics' Irish Tour October '88," Canadian Musician, April 1989.

Druckman, Howard. Jane Siberry article (title unknown), Canadian Musician, December 1985.

Druckman, Howard. "Jane Siberry: The Bottom Line." Graffiti, December 1987.

Druckman, Howard. "Jane Siberry: This is My Voice." Canadian Musician, February 1990.

Kenny, Glenn. Review of O'Hara performance at St. Ann's Church in Brooklyn, Hollywood Reporter, 18 December 1998.

No Borders Here, Jane Siberry fan website www.smoe.org/nbh

O'Hara fan site: www.westnet.com/consumable/1996/10.01/revohara.html

Potter, Mitch. "O'Hara Shines in Debut," Toronto Star, 10 February 1989.

Punter, Jennie. Jane Siberry article (title unknown), Impact, September 1993.

Rave, Dave. Record review of Rheostatics' Greatest Hits, Nerve, December 1987. ("What a relief! A local album that doesn't instantly sink in its own amateurism.")

Taubin, Amy. "High-Wire Act," Village Voice, 28 October 1998.

The Outsiders: Punk, Politics & Poetry

"Lying is not only saying": Albert Camus, The Outsider. (London: Penguin, 1990), 118.

"My baby boomer background": Eunice Amarantides, "Singing In A Dangerous Time." The Other Side, January/February 1985.

"Canadians love to flirt with anti-Americanism": Amarantides, The Other Side, January/February 1985.

"I don't see the idea": Mitch Potter, "Cockburn Thinks About Eternity . . . And Laughs." Toronto Star, 19 April 1997.

"I realized as soon as it's an image": Potter, Toronto Star, 19 April 1997.

"Every artist has the responsibility": Amarantides, The Other Side, January/February 1985.

"When I hear about people": Barney Hoskyns, "Todd Rundgren: Go Ahead, Ignore Me." Mojo, February 1998.

"In rock and roll": Anne Dawson, "Rock Lures Kids To Butts: Singer." Toronto Sun, 3 April 1997.

Also referenced:

Cantin, Paul. "Skydiggers: But not THAT hip. . . ." No Depression, May/June 1998.

Krewen, Nick. "Punk Lives Once More On Local Label." Toronto Star, 27 February 2000.

Acadian Driftwood: The Creation of the Daniel Lanois Sound

"When it comes to making music": Brian Wilson, *Inside Tracks: A First-Hand History of Popular Music from the World's Greatest Record Producers and Engineers*. ed. Richard Buskin. (New York: Spike 1998), ii.

"the tobacco belt sound": *Mariposa: Under A Stormy Sky* (Lyric Film and Video Productions, 1991).

"doing research": Lester Bangs, "The Ambient Mr. Eno." *Musician*, November 1979.

"[These groups] used traditional line-ups": Joe Carducci, *Rock and the Pop Narcotic*. (Chicago: Redoubt Press, 1990), 222.

"get people prepared for death": Bangs, *Musician*, November 1979.

"I see myself maneuvering": Bangs, *Musician*, November 1979.

"Jon Hassell had a": Andy Gill, "To Infinity And Beyond." *Mojo*, June 1998.

"I was a little disappointed": Larry LeBlanc, "Daniel Lanois," *Network*, January/February 1988.

"With Brian, we would start": LeBlanc, *Network*, January/February 1988.

"Eno was a definite influence": Martha Johnson, "A Brief History Of Times With Martha & The Muffins," Muffin Music, 1995.

"an attempt to create something": Gill, *Mojo*, June 1998.

"My best memory of that tour": Michael Brook biography, *Breakdown* http://fringedigital.com/brook.

"I discovered that the astronauts": Gill, *Mojo*, June 1998.

"Harold Budd's intention": Gill, *Mojo*, June 1998.

"Chris Blackwell thought": Robert Sandall, *Q*, November 1990.

"He said, 'There's a guy'": *Rocky World: Zen And The Art Of Music Making* (Warner Music Vision, 1993).

"It was not a simple record": LeBlanc, *Network*, January/February 1988.

"All the tracks were laid down": LeBlanc, *Network*, January/February 1988.

"It was meant to be a joke": Spencer Bright, *Peter Gabriel: An Authorized Biography*. London: Pan, 1999, p. 265.

"There was a certain confidence": LeBlanc, *Network*, January/February 1988.

"I think we allowed": LeBlanc, *Network*, January/February 1988.

"A lot of those songs": LeBlanc, *Network*, Januray/February 1988.

"He was thrilled": LeBlanc, *Network*, January/February 1988.

"I had plenty of room": Bill Dillon, "Hamilton's Bill Dillon's Guitar Wizardry," *Canadian Musician*, April 1988.

"I couldn't lift equipment": Bruce Mowat, "Westdale to the West Coast: A Life In Rock." *Hamilton Spectator*, 16 December 1998.

"He'd get around": Mowat, *Hamilton Spectator*, 16 December 1998.

"My Canadian roots": Kerry Doole, "Double Exposure." *Canadian Composer*, Spring 1993.

"From someone who has an ear": Stuart Bailie, "He Is Risen," *Q Bob Dylan Collector's Edition*, October 2000.

"It was a strange situation": Anil Prasad, "Crash Vegas: Bringing It All Back Home." *Innerviews*, 19 December 1989.

"Greg and I": Prasad, *Innerviews*, 19 December 1989.

"I'm a huge Neil Young fan": Prasad, *Innerviews*, 19 December 1989.

"It was not an easy thing": Dan Hughes, "Crash Vegas Leaves No Stone Unturned." *Network*, April/May, 1993.

"I guess my sense of commitment": *Rocky World* (Warner Music Vision, 1993).

Also referenced:

Krewen, Nick. "Daniel Lanois On Recording." *Canadian Musician*, October 1997

Mowat, Bruce. Liner notes to Simply Saucer, *Cyborgs Revisited* (Mole Records, 1989).

Nott, Glen. "Sound Advice." *Hamilton Spectator,* 10 November 1999.

Wodskou, Chris. "SIANspheric Stereophonic Blitzkrieg." *Exclaim!,* July 1998.

In The Spirit Of Crazy Horse

"All you have to do now": "History Of The Band." *Year Of The Horse* press kit, October Films, 1997.

"[Young's] songs": Kit Rachlis, "Decade." *Stranded*, ed. Greil Marcus. (New York: Da Capo, 1996), 173.

"Their sullen and brooding approach": Chris Varady, liner notes to 13 Engines *Perfect Largeness* (Nocturnal, 1996).

"We're not a noise band": Howard Druckman, "Touring Fires Up New 13 Engines LP." *Metropolis* 22 December 1988.

"We wanted a plain sound": Steve Cribar, "13 Engines," *The Cutting Edge* Vol. 2, 1991.

"Does Toronto really need": editorial, *The Magazine*, November 1990.

"'One Day In Your Life' is about": Neil Osborne, "54·40 Shows Us." *Graffiti*, August 1987.

"It's my version": Osborne, *Graffiti* August, 1987.

"Our philosophy": Nancy Lanthier, "Platinum Is The Best Revenge." *Canadian Composer*, Summer 1993.

"Dear Dear was a record": Denise Sheppard, "A Strange Kind Of Karma." *Impact*, August 1994.

"It's not intentional patriotism": Amber Meredith, "Weeping Tile." *Chart*, January 1996.

"I think you have to examine": Meredith, *Chart,* January, 1996.

"I never realized": Billy Talbot, interview on MuchMusic, August 1996.

Also referenced:

Harrison, Tom. "54·40: Without A Fight," *Canadian Musician,* August, 1986

Kent, Nick. "Neil Young and the Haphazard Highway That Leads to Unconditional Love," *The Dark Stuff: The Best Of Nick Kent.* London: Penguin, 1994.

Williams, Paul. *Neil Young: Love To Burn, Thirty Years Of Speaking Out, 1966–1996.* London: Omnibus Press, 1997.

Young, Scott. *Neil And Me.* Toronto: McClelland & Stewart, 1997.

Folk You: Roots Revisited

"No matter how many times Ned's done a song": Tim Powis, live review of Handsome Ned, *Nerve*, February 1986.

"I would like to be global": Leslie Bennetts, "k.d. lang cuts it close." *Vanity Fair*, August 1993.

"I think being alternative": Jay Scott, "Yippee-I-O k.d.!" *Chatelaine*, January 1988.

"I had started playing guitar": Phil Sutcliffe, "k.d.'s country epiphany." *Mojo*, September 2000.

"While she claims": Liam Lacey, "k.d. lang is Alberta's oddball gift to music." *Globe and Mail*, 1 November 1984.

"I dedicated myself to country": Howard Druckman, "k.d. lang," *Network*,
    July/August/September 1988.
"I look goony in long hair": Brendan Lemon, "Virgin Territory." *Advocate*, June
    1992.
"I would hope I can attract both men and women": Lemon.
"I'm a very androgynous-looking woman": Scott.
"I don't think people could take the passion in my singing": Lacey.
"I thought she was talented": Les Wiseman, "Country Punk." *Vancouver Sun*, 15
    March 1986.
"Sure it's corny": Lacey.
"I don't need them to see": Lacey.
"At a showcase at New York's": Wiseman.
"You're what country music": Victoria Starr, *k.d. lang: All You Get Is Me*. (Toronto:
    Random House, 1994), 58.
"I promise to deserve this award": Perry Stern, "Sustaining the Edge." *Canadian
    Musician*, April 1987.
"I like that record now": Mim Udovitch, "How Did a Lesbian, Feminist, Vegetarian
    Canadian Win a Grammy and the Hearts of America?" *Rolling Stone*, 5 August
    1993.
"Call me torch'n'twang": Mitch Potter, "k.d. lang." magazine unknown, February
    1987.
"k.d. became an affront to everything": Dave Bidini, record review of *Angel With a
    Lariat*, *Nerve*, March 1986.
"You're lucky if you find someone": Starr, 100.
"The end of a dream": Burt Kearns, "Canadian Cowpie." *Spin*, September 1988.
"Politically, this album is very correct": Kearns.
"At it's worst, Nashville is an inbred family": Scott.
"They're threatened by what they don't understand": Udovitch.
"It's because she really loves the music": Scott.
"We all love animals" Starr, 142.
"We got well over 1,000 letters" Bennetts.
"The time has come for me to let go. . . ." Starr, 135.
"Now you know all the rumours": Starr, 221.
"She says that the two things": Udovitch.
"Even though I was never accepted on country radio": Lemon.

Also referenced:
Masyk, Jim. Liner notes to *The Name is Ned*, Linkhorn/EMI, 2000.
www.cowboyjunkies.com
k.d. moonglow website: home.macau.ctm.net/~tina71/index.htm
The History of Jr. Gone Wild website: www.well.com/user/sjroby/indexh.html

The Importance of Being Sloan

Also Referenced:
Arsenault, Tim. "Sloan: Canada's Grunge Rockers Get Smeared." *Canadian
    Musician*, December 1992.
Bliss, Karen. "Sloan: Can't Stop Pop." *Canadian Musician*, September/October 1996.
Brophy, Aaron (editor). "The Top 50 Canadian Albums And Singles Of All Time."
    Chart, July/August 2000.
Dickie, Mary. "Everything They've Done Right." *Impact*, July 1996.
Galloway, Matt. "Experimentation Fuels Sloan's Return." *Now*, 19 September 1996.

Ladouceur, Liisa. "Sloan: Alive and Kicking." *Chart*, July 1996.
Ladouceur, Liisa and Meredith, Amber (editors). "The Top 50 Canadian Albums and Singles Of All Time." *Chart*, March 1996.
Punter, Jennie. "Pop Division," *Impact*, November 1994.
Rocchi, James. "Don't Call It A Comeback." *Id*, 25 July 1996.
Waters, Christopher. "Sloan: Retro Renegades Pair Past with Present and Come Up Twice Removed." *Network*, September/October 1994.
www.sloanmusic.com
www.sloan-a-d-n.com

Never Mind the Molluscs: The Halifax Underground

"You won't see these bands": "*Out of the Fog*: Guiding Light of the Underground Scene." *Halifax Herald*, 1986.
"*Out of the Fog: The Halifax Underground*": Bull, Philip. "Out of the Fog." *Nerve*, January 1987.
"As a child, I was never": Timothy White, "Sarah McLachlan: Irony & Ecstasy." *Billboard*, 8 January 1994.
"The music my parents brought": Liisa Ladouceur, "Sarah McLachlan." *Pulse*, July 1997.
"The Murderecords mafia": "The 25 Most Important People In New Music." *Shift*, March 1998.

Also Referenced:
Covey, James. "Next Exit: Halifax, Nova Scotia." *Alternative Press*, February 1995.
Gooch, Brad. "Sleepless in Halifax." *Harper's Bazaar*, September 1993.
LeBlanc, Larry. "New and Traditional Mix in Canadian Maritimes." *Billboard*, 28 August 1993.
McNeil, Legs and McCain, Gillian. *Please Kill Me: The Uncensored Oral History of Punk*. New York: Penguin, 1997.
Punter, Jennie. "Jale: Trascending and Evolving." *Impact*, June 1996.
Punter, Jennie. "The Super Friendz: Murder In The First." *Impact*, October 1995.
Robbins, Ira A. (editor). *The Trouser Press Guide to '90s Rock*. New York: Fireside, 1997.
Sharp, Keith. "Eric's Trip: Word Is Out." *SoundCan*, May 1993.
Shaw, Kyle. "Hardship Post: Satori, but No Nirvana." *Chart*, June 1995.
Shaw, Kyle. "But Where Is Eric Going?" *Impact*, April 1996.
Waters, Christopher. "Rebecca West." *Exclaim!*, June 1995.
Waters, Christopher, "Two Tales of a City (Thrush Hermit/Super Friendz)." *Exclaim!*, February 1997.
Zeitoun, Mary-Lou. "Jale: Stubbornly Casual." *Impact*, November 1994.
www.tranquileye.com/fog/

The Path of Thorns: Nettwerk Records

"The idea was to have Sarah": Ian Bailey, "Suing Songwriter Pictured as Creative Force in McLachlan Album." Canadian Press, 5 November 1998.
"I think a lot of people are looking at me": Karen Bliss, "Darryl Neudorff Busy Despite McLachlan Trial." *Jam! Music* 17 December 1998.
"They persisted with very serious allegations": Dene Moore, "Another Legal Victory for McLachlan." Canadian Press, 28 August 2000.
"I guess I had some kind of belief": Ian Clayton, "McLachlan Wins Another Court

Victory," *Vancouver Sun*, 28 August 2000.

"Images in Vogue was really an idea": Greg Clow, "cEvin Key." *Chart*, February 1996.

"Life through a dog's eyes": Michael Nigro, "Skinny Puppy: 24 Hours in Vancouver," *Alternative Press*, February 1991.

"He was looking for something to break out of": Liisa Ladouceur, "Nivek Ogre." *Chart*, February 1996.

"We did an assassination": Chris Twomey, "Taming Skinny Puppy." *Nerve*, December 1985.

"Remember the eerie feeling": Perry Stern, "Animal Rights Rule!" *Graffiti*, November 1988.

"What we're presenting": Perry Stern, "Canine Caterwauling." *Graffiti*, September 1986.

"the Bruce Springsteen mentality": Stern, September 1986.

"My friend was the first to spot one": Stern, *Graffiti*, November 1988.

"I find it paradoxical": "Capitol's Skinny Puppy arrested in an alleged vivisection mishap." Capitol Press Release, October 1987.

"I personally felt I flopped": Michael Nigro, "Skinny Puppy: 24 Hours In Vancouver." *Alternative Press*, February 1991.

"I understand why Ogre was doing it": Nigro.

"With *Touch* I didn't have anything": Nancy Lanthier, "Into The Deep End." *Impact* December 1993.

"I didn't know what image was": Liam Lacey, "In Person." *Globe and Mail*, 15 June 1991.

"I was kind of showing off on *Touch*": Lanthier.

The mourning of lost innocence": Kurt B. Reighley, "Sarah McLachlan." *Paper Magazine*, March 1994.

"We'd send them stuff": Chris Mundy, "Flower Child With A Filthy Mind." *Rolling Stone*, 30 April 1998.

"It's unfortunate whenever past business dealings": Adam Drake, "Successful Settlement Reached in Former Nettwerk Partnership Claim." Nettwerk Press Release, 4 June 1998.

"There's always a new beginning after something dies": "Last Rights." Nettwerk Press Release, 1992.

Key had informed *High Times*: Missy Hendrix, "Barking Up The Right Tree." *High Times*, January 1993.

"At the beginning the band was fuelled by": Clow, *Chart*, February 1996.

"To them there was always a problem": Clow, *Chart*, February 1996.

"It's a fitting final record": Liisa Ladouceur, "Nivek Ogre." *Chart*, February 1996.

"I do believe *Fumbling Towards Ecstasy*": Paul Tingen, "Pierre Marchand: Producing Sarah McLachlan, on Land and on Sea." *Mix Magazine*, June 2000.

"I look at music as a bit of a diary": Megan Olden, "The Art of Contradiction." *Mondo*, Spring 1997.

"This person wasn't the only guy": Kathy Silberger, "Sarah McLachlan." *Rolling Stone*, 25 December 1997.

Also Referenced:

Bateman, Jeff. "The Grapes of Wrath." *Network*, June–August 1990.

Farley, Christopher. "Galapalooza!," *Time*, 21 July 1997.

Fitzgerald, Judith. *Building a Mystery: The Story of Sarah McLachlan and Lilith Fair*. (Kingston: Quarry Press, 1997).

Harrison, Tom. "Nettwerk's Blueprint for Success." *Canadian Musician*, October 1985.

MacIntosh, Dave. "The Post-Apocalyptic Opera of Skinny Puppy." *Nerve*, October 1986.

Pittaway, Kim. "Tumbling Towards Ecstasy." *Chatelaine*, November 1996.

Schulte, Frank. "Grapes of Wrath: Aged To Perfection." *Canadian Musician*, December 1991.

Sheppard, Denise. "Ginger: Onwards and Upwards . . . and Upwards." *Impact*, November 1994.

Stern, Perry. "Colourful Moev Paints Dark, Brooding Images," *Metropolis*, February 1989.

"The Sea of Waking Dreams: A Sarah McLachlan fansite": www.aquezada.com/sarah/

www.netweb.com

www.lastsigh.com

Decadence (Nettwerk, 1995) 5-CD retrospective box set with multimedia component

Trust Yourself: Blue Rodeo

"Robbie played my guitar!" "Isn't rock'n'roll pathetic?": Howard Druckman, "So Long to Saloonland." *HMV Magazine*, April 1991.

"My whole thing now is": Bruce Headlam, "Bad Attitude." *Saturday Night*, July/August 1991.

"I felt that the songs were well crafted": Letter to Blue Rodeo from Bob Roper dated October 29, 1984, reprinted in the liner notes to *Just Like a Vacation*, Warner 1999.

"If you've dropped acid": Warner bio, 1999.

"I walked into the rehearsal space": Warner bio, 1999.

"Call it Western Pop": Perry Stern, *Metropolis*, 30 March 1989

"That song is about an infamous gig": Warner bio, 1990

"I've always known": Daryl Richel, Q&A with Bob Wiseman, published at www.moregoatthanthegoose.com/interviews/bobwiseman.htm August, 1999.

"It was a waste of time": Richel, August, 1999

Also referenced:

"Bobby Wiseman's Dream Comes True" by Bill Reynolds, *Metropolis*, October 5, 1989.

Two Solitudes: The Tragically Hip

"So MuchMedia": Barclay, review of Gordon Downie *Coke Machine Glow*, *eye*, 29 March 2001.

"It was really, really rough": Lynn Messerschmidt, "Tory Pollster Picks Kingston Rock Group: 'Raw And Dynamic.'" *Kingston Whig-Standard*, 28 January 1988.

"the honor and glory": Greg Burliuk, "Hip Recognized As 'True Kingstonians,'" *Kingston Whig-Standard*, August 30, 1991.

Also referenced:

Batten, Jack. *The Leafs: An Anecdotal History of the Toronto Maple Leafs*. (Toronto: Key Porter, 1994).

Bouw, Brenda. "Ole Brown Eyes Is Back." *National Post Business*, May 2000.

Burliuk, Greg. "They're Chips Off The Old Block." *Kingston Whig-Standard*, 8 April 1991.

Epilogue: Where the Change Is

"One of the best songwriters": Kieran Grant, *Toronto Sun*, 26 July 2000.

"It's just like being in high school again" David Keenan, "Life Stinks." *The Wire*, May 2000.

"Everyone likes to crap on Our Lady Peace" Robin Dickie, *Impact*, March 1996.

"The notion that Canada is a unique sort of place" Michael Dojc, "Slick Sexy and Stupid." *Now*, 25 January 2001.

Index

(photos are indicated by italics)

Date Due

AUG 1 5 2005			
NOV 1 7 2006			
NOV 1 2 2006			
DEC - 5 2006			
DEC 0 2 2006			